The Road to the SUNDANCE

MY JOURNEY

INTO

NATIVE SPIRITUALITY

The Road
to the
SUNDANCE

Manny Twofeathers

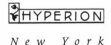

New York

Library of Congress Cataloging-in-Publication Data

Twofeathers, Manny.
      The road to the sundance : my journey into Native spirituality / Manny Twofeathers. — 1st ed.
          p.   cm.
      Originally published: My road to the sundance. Phoenix, Ariz. : Wo-Pila Pub., c1994.
      ISBN 0-7868-6215-7
      1. Twofeathers, Manny.   2. Sun dance.
    3. Spiritual formation.   4. Indians of North America—Biography.   I. Title.
    [E90.T88A3   1996]
    299'.7'092—dc20
    [B]   95-50732
              CIP

FIRST EDITION

10   9   8   7   6   5   4   3   2   1

Book design by Deborah Kerner

This book is dedicated to all the Sundancers,
no matter where they dance . . .
All men, women, and children who have gone
to the Sacred Tree to pray.

I wrote this to honor them and in
respect for our Sundance.

This book is in
honor of my mother

HELEN T. RENDON

and in
memory of my father

MANUEL M. RENDON
(to whom I dedicated my Sundance in 1994)

A c k n o w l e d g m e n t s

I want to show my respect by honoring the Spirits of all the Sacred Directions. They brought me all I needed, to find my way to the Sundance.

I would like to thank all the people I have met in this new direction in my life, each and every one. You know who you are, so many of you are mentioned. "*Wo-Pila*"—I am deeply grateful.

Also a special thank you to Linda Goytia, who took the picture of me on the cover of this book—who promised she would send it and did.

Many thanks to my agent B. J. Robbins, whose belief in this book has taken it places I had only dreamed of. To our first editor at Hyperion, Lauren Marino, for giving up her comforts of home to come to the Sundance and camp, to experience everything first-hand, to help in the editing—now you're family! And thanks so much to Laurie Abkemeier, my second editor at Hyperion, for her thoroughness and remarkable editing of my book—for doing an incredible job while maintaining the integrity of my words.

A very special *Wo-Pila* to Jodi Olson from Las Vegas. Many things in our lives were made better because of your help. Your selflessness warms my heart and is very much appreciated.

Thanks also to everyone in my family, especially Rockie, Stormy, Mary, Becky, Dory, and Oriona, who gave me so much confidence and support while I was writing this book. A big thank you to my mother-in-law, Lynne Babuin, for her much-appreciated help. Our dear friend Sharon Passero, who was always there when we needed her and has always encouraged me, also deserves my deepest gratitude.

Finally, I want to honor my wife, Melody (formerly Betty Hutton), for her excellent memory; for her expertise at the computer and for spending endless hours at it; and for her love, devotion, and patience with me.

The Seven Sacred Directions

The seven directions are a gift from the Great Spirit. They all form a perfect balance for us to live in comfort as humans. Without any one of the directions our Spirits would be just a few wisps of energy drifting without aim in the vast expanse of the universe.

The East Direction is where the sun rises every morning, bringing the whole world new life and us our daily blessings.

The South Direction is where the warm winds come from to bring an end to the coldness of winter and new life to all.

The West Direction is where the sun brings a balance to our days. The sun goes down to allow us to sleep and nourish our minds and bodies.

The North Direction is where the cold winds come from. They bring us relief from the hot summer and balance to the warmth.

The Above Direction is the home of the Creator and where the Eagle flies. From above comes our spiritual energy and above is where our prayers are answered.

The Below Direction is our Mother the Earth. It is the celestial body that is our home. The one that needs our love, respect, and protection; without her there is no life, for she gives us everything we need to live.

The Inner Direction is where our spiritual energy lives and learns. Our bodies should also have our love and respect, for it is a gift and a home for our spirits while they learn humbleness and to suffer.

Introduction

The Sundance is a way of sacrificing for the privilege of having a direct connection with the Creator. It is one of the seven special ceremonies brought to the Plains Tribes by the White Buffalo Calf Woman to allow a way to give thanks and show gratitude. It is a way to humble ourselves, pray for the healing of others, and ask for a better way of life for everyone.

It is a spiritual awakening for some, and a spiritual commitment for others. I had attended a few Sundances over several years, but never as a participant. Whenever I heard that one was taking place, I felt compelled to go and be around the energy, like a moth to a light. I never understood my attraction to it. I would stand for hours where I could see the dancers and wonder, "Why do they do this?" Whenever I left, I felt sad and empty although I never understood why.

The first Sundance I ever saw was being held in Fort Duchesne, Utah. I asked for and received permission to sell my crafts, but after the first day I realized my heart wasn't in selling. In the distance I could hear the singers, the drum, and the eagle whistles, and they seemed to be calling me to the Sundance Arbor.

The Ute people hold what is called a "Thirst" Sundance. They undergo four full days of hard dancing and praying without anything to drink or eat the entire time. It is extremely difficult just to complete the ceremony. The dancers blow constantly on an eagle-bone whistle, which dehydrates them very quickly, making the four days almost intolerable. But

Sundancers continue the ritual because they believe the Creator gave man the eagle whistle to call the eagle spirit. (An eagle flies the highest of all the birds, so that spirit is the one that carries prayers to the Creator.)

The eagle whistle is made from one of the wing bones, and tied to the front of the whistle is an eagle plume, which is an inside feather almost like the down of the eagle's breast. We use this feather because it comes from a place close to the eagle's heart and so carries with it the power of the eagle's heart and is very strong. When we blow on an eagle whistle, our breath moves the plume up and down, and this becomes part of our prayers. If you're open to spirituality, the sound made by the eagle-bone whistle will leave a permanent imprint on your heart and soul. The haunting cry stays with you, no matter where you go or what you do.

The Arbor is where the dancing takes place. It represents the Circle of Life and is divided into four sections symbolizing the four stages of life: infancy, adolescence, adulthood, and elderly. The Arbor also has four different gates to honor the four main directions. It is most of all the house of our prayers and where many different, but very important, ceremonies are performed. Of all the ceremonies, the Sundance is the main or final ceremony of the year, excluding the Sweat Lodge ceremony, which is performed all year—although not in the Arbor.

The Sacred Tree is a crucial part of the Sundance ceremony. It represents the Creator, but only after it has been cut and placed in the center of the Arbor. We attach our prayer ties (small pieces of cloth, tied with tobacco and prayers) to the tree, and it becomes our God in physical form during our Sundance.

A live tree is not used because the Plains people were always on the move; they had a different location every year when they held the ceremonies. Nowadays the Sundance Chief chooses a tree a year in advance. It is always a cottonwood, and he blesses it four times over the course of the year.

At that first Sundance in Utah, I stood for two days simply watching the dancers and praying, thinking how great it was for me, just being there. My spirit felt light; I wanted to fly. Then reality set in: I had to earn a living, so I left.

A few weeks later I found myself back in Fort Duchesne, long after the Sundance was over. Driving through the town, I had a strong urge to go to the Sundance Arbor, so I followed that impulse. With butterflies in my stomach I turned off the main highway. I didn't know why I was going there; I knew no one would be there. Maybe the Spirits wanted me to go by myself and feel the Sundance energy, to experience it alone. The closer I got to the Arbor, the more nervous I became. I kept questioning myself, wondering what I was doing there.

When I reached the road leading into the Sundance grounds, I was elated to see the tree was still there. All the offering flags were waving happily, and it stood proudly. I don't know why, but I had the distinct impression that the tree was happy to see me; that it was lonely and needed my company.

To respect its sacred space, I parked my van away from the tree, got out, and walked toward it. It was good to be alone with it and to have this moment of privacy. The closer I got, the stronger the tree's energy became. I started feeling the sorrow, the tears, and the pain from the Sundancers who had prayed here. I had to touch it.

As I touched the tree, I looked up and saw all the prayer flags and offerings, waving gently. When I did, I was overwhelmed. All the emotions and energies from the previous Sundancers, combined with the tree's healing energy, overcame me. I started to cry. Tears formed and spilled out of my eyes. It was as though the tree needed my emotions. I gave the tree what it wanted, willingly, without shame, as I prayed.

To this day, I don't know how long I was there, but when it was over I felt an enormous relief. I didn't realize that I had been kneeling, and as I stood up, I realized that I had also been under a lot of stress from my responsibilities. The Sacred Tree had paid me back for visiting it. It had given me relief from all the pressure and anxiety I had been experiencing. As I backed away, I felt humbled.

Getting closer to the van, I saw another car. It was a tribal policeman. He asked me what I was doing there, and I explained that I had just come to the tree to pray. I'm sure he could see the traces of emotion left on my face. Understanding, he quietly told me it was okay. He asked if I was a Sundancer, and I said no. He said he understood my wanting to pray, because he was a Sundancer and knew the power of the tree. We talked for a little while longer. He wished me well, and then I left.

Driving away, I was filled with happiness. I wanted to shout out my experience and let the world know my joy.

EAST — YELLOW

"New Beginnings"

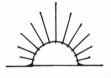

R I S I N G

S U N

1985: SACRAMENTO, CALIFORNIA . . .

It all started at about 6:30 on a Sunday morning. It was pleasant and cool, and I felt great. For two days I had been displaying my silver and turquoise jewelry at a Native American conference in Sacramento, and at the end of the day, I was going home. A couple of my good friends in Sacramento had asked me to stay with them (a common native custom), and this gave me a chance to visit and to save some money.

I woke up early that Sunday morning, quietly took a

shower, got dressed, and eased myself out of the house. I figured I'd go to a nearby restaurant and have a great big breakfast. After that, I'd get my jewelry ready and set up early.

I had been away for several days and was beginning to miss my kids. I'm never cheerful that early in the morning, especially when I haven't had my coffee, but on this particular morning I was feeling extraordinarily happy. I felt a little strange and almost light-headed. A couple of times I tried to analyze my feelings, but I just felt too good to worry about them. Deep inside, I had a strange sensation that this was going to be a very special day somehow. I had a good feeling of anticipation, but didn't know what it was I was anticipating.

As you can imagine, on an early Sunday morning there wasn't much traffic anywhere. I had been moving down the freeway at a pretty good clip when my exit came up. I slowed quickly and eased my old van off the freeway. When I came to the first intersection, the light had just turned red, so I stopped and waited for the light to change back to green.

I waited and waited and must have looked at my watch three or four times in just as many seconds. As I sat there, I got a faint whiff of hot oil from the engine. I thought to myself, "I'd better watch how fast I drive this old van or I'll find myself walking."

When the oil smell disappeared, so did thoughts of the van's condition. My mind drifted; I wondered if sales were going to be better than the day before. Again I noticed that the engine sounded pretty good. It was idling really smooth and easy.

My mind returned to the present. Starting to get a little irritated, I thought, "When is this @#$%^&* light going to change?" I looked around, then glanced into my rear-view mirror, thinking, "If there are no cops around I'm going to cross." Then I thought, "The light must be stuck or something. It's probably broken." I was thinking very seriously of

6

running it and started dreaming up excuses I could tell the cop if I got caught. A hundred thoughts raced through my mind as I sat there getting more and more irritated at the dumb light that wouldn't change.

I was hungry. I hadn't had my first cup of coffee yet, and that made my cigarettes taste terrible. Lights or whatever shouldn't keep a guy from the little things in life that mean so much! I'm sure you've heard about the old bear coming out of hibernation? Well, that is exactly how I was starting to feel.

We all act a bit childish when things don't go our way. I was approaching that state and didn't want my good mood ruined by anything—especially by a traffic light.

Then I thought, "Ha! Ha! I'll bet there's a cop somewhere pushing the buttons that make the lights change just waiting for me to screw up so he can bust me. No sir, you're not going to get me that easily. I'll wait you out."

About this time, through my irritated and aggravated state, I started to hear something. At first it was very, very soft, almost like a whisper at the back of my mind. Though I didn't know what it was, I thought I recognized it, and I started getting chills. It's very hard to write a sound, but I'll try. It started softly, a shrill whisper—"Sherii—Sherii—Sherii—Sherii." As it went on, it got louder and louder.

I knew I had heard that sound before and tried to figure out where and when. So familiar, yet its origin eluded me. It almost became painful trying to recall such a beautiful and haunting sound.

Since I had an older van, I thought, maybe it was developing a new crippling syndrome. God, I prayed it wasn't. The old van was already worth $30,000, just from repairs.

The "Sherii—Sherii—Sherii—Sherii" sound kept getting louder and kept going on and on.

I cocked my head, turning it slowly, trying to find where

the sound was coming from. It wasn't the engine. I thought it might be the radio, so I reached over and tried to turn it off, but it was already off. Perhaps something in the back was making the sound because of vibrations from the engine?

I turned completely around in the seat. Carefully I looked at everything back there. There was nothing. As I straightened out and sat back in the seat, the light was still red, and I sat, a little shaken, and listened to that musical, eerie sound.

As I listened, I felt goose bumps all over my body. I was having trouble swallowing, as if something had gripped me by the throat. My heart was having trouble deciding whether to stop beating or jump out of my chest. Although I was afraid, I knew deep inside my soul that a very special message was coming to me.

It was then that I finally recognized the sound. I felt covered by a warm, quiet mixture of sound and peaceful energy, and a great sigh escaped from my long-held breath. I knew without any doubt what I was hearing. It was not one but several eagle wing-bone whistles. Exactly like the ones I had heard at the Sundances.

I broke into a sweat as I fully realized what was happening to me.

In my mind I was swiftly transported to that sacred Sundance tree far away—to that lonely tree in Fort Duchesne where I had prayed and felt so much emotion. Again I was kneeling at its base with my hands on its rough bark. I could hear it talking to me.

I distinctly heard the words meant for me: "You have searched long enough. It is time that you look to us for your destiny and direction. There is much to do." I didn't think about where I was or what I was doing. My thoughts were of how soft the voice was, and I wondered what it meant. I couldn't quite understand what was happening to me.

Realizing I was back in my van at the traffic light, I felt my mind fill with questions. I sat there for a minute, confused and a little scared. Looking down at my hands, although I couldn't see anything, I swore I could still feel the tree's rough bark. Had I really been there or had my thoughts been so real I could feel reality with my mind?

I believe that all of us have experienced those little shivers of unexplainable feelings. That's what was happening to me that morning. The eagle whistle and thoughts of the Sundance were now freshly burned into my brain. The soft voice that had spoken to me, had left me badly shaken. For a moment I had been at the Sundance tree in person.

Coming out of this experience as if from a dream, I shook my head. Unknown to me, a car had pulled up behind me and softly honked its horn. I looked up. The light had changed to green. Putting the van in gear, I slowly crossed the street and continued to the restaurant.

I didn't understand what had happened in those few moments at the light. I did know that something very important had happened to me. Somehow I knew that it was going to change my life in a big way.

The different emotions I experienced in that moment are difficult to explain, yet very real to native people. Though many of us get away from our ancient beliefs, I suppose we never really lose them. They are deeply ingrained in our genes. And though many of us have become urbanized and walk through life going through the motions of living, eventually there comes a time when we realize that what we have spiritually is not ours.

What *is* ours is the deep spirituality passed on to us by the Spirits. When we realize that, most of us return to the Sweat Lodge and other ceremonies. We return to try to learn, and to once again belong to, something so natively ours. I have come to realize that this was my first vision, and it came to me because I was at a point in my life when I needed it. The Spirits were telling me it was time to return to my native spirituality. They were showing me the way, and it was my choice whether or not to follow.

After the show ended that Sunday evening, I drove back home to the Mi-wok Rancheria near Tuolumne, California. Driving through Oakdale was a breeze. I think I hit one red light and was through before I knew it. I headed east into the foothills of the Sierras. It was late when I reached the town of Sonora.

It had been raining a little in the foothills earlier. The road was still wet, and the tires sounded like they were singing as I drove along. I left Sonora behind me and realized that I was almost home. Where did the time go? My mind wandered, thinking about my vision. I hardly felt the trip. My mind was still full of the sounds of eagle whistles.

Arriving home, I found my wife, Vivian, waiting up for me. She had hot coffee ready. As she poured me a cup, she asked me how the weekend had gone. It didn't take me long to tell her that I'd had a good weekend, but I wanted to tell her about my experience. I tried to explain what had happened. I suppose she understood, but I could see that she didn't fully appreciate the importance of the occurrence. She took it very lightly.

I attempted to explain how I had felt receiving this spiritual visit, and tried to convey the confusion, fear, apprehension, and joy that I felt. Somehow I couldn't make myself understood.

After that, I became very inquisitive and aggressive, trying to find out about the Sundance, because at that point I knew absolutely nothing. In my anxiety to find out, I must have approached people the wrong way. I found myself unable to get answers from anyone.

It may be hard to believe, but some native people are

Christians through and through. They are brainwashed into believing that the Sundance is the work of the devil. How wrong they are.

There I was: a naive person just awakening to something new that felt so good. I stupidly thought that all native people believed this way. So when I asked the wrong people, they moved away from me as if I were a leper!

Oddly enough, though I had been to several Sundances, I never made any close friendships with anyone there. Perhaps this was because I was so out of touch with my own spirituality. I was lost and had left religion and spiritual life behind.

I was born and reared a Catholic, through no choice of mine and through no fault of my parents. They taught me what they thought was the best for me. By the time of their birth into this world, native spirituality had been suppressed by the Spanish Catholic religion for four hundred years and had been all but forgotten. Even today all my relations still practice Catholicism. I was the first to break from that mind prison.

Going into the church was always a little scary to me. I could never talk aloud; we felt that we had to talk in a whisper. The teachers who taught us made us feel important. They were getting us ready to do the church's bidding as we grew older. They were teachers during the week, and on weekends they would be partying and drinking.

My parents had a restaurant in Ajo, Arizona, for many years. The "after the bar closed" crowd would always go there to eat. I saw many of the same people—my teachers and other pillars of the community—drunk, fighting, staggering, and falling.

When I was ten years old, I decided to become an altar boy, helping the priest at Mass services. I did this for several months. I would get up early in the morning, ride my bike to town about three miles away, and sell newspapers to men on their way to work. I'd make two cents off each paper I sold for ten cents!

With that job finished, I would go to the church and get my black-and-white altar-boy gown on. Then I'd light candles and perform all my other tasks to get ready for the 7:30 a.m. Mass.

It always seemed majestic in the church. It was so quiet and peaceful, yet scary, in there. I never liked the smell of candles. It reminded me of funerals. I was always curious to see what the priest was doing behind the great big altar. That was where we got ready before Mass.

I watched as the priest performed his daily ritual. At the time it seemed like quite a ceremony to get his habit on. Wide-eyed, I would stand there watching, not wanting to move a muscle.

After Mass, I would head for school.

The altar boys met once a week. At one of the meetings, we got a new young priest. I was sick and couldn't make it to the meeting or even to church the following Sunday.

When the next week's meeting came around, I was there, but the new priest wasn't. I still hadn't met him by the next Sunday morning. After selling my papers, I went dutifully to church.

When I got there, I found the priest standing in front of the church. He appeared worried as he looked up and down the street, trying to control his irritation.

When I walked up, I said good morning. He answered kind of gruffly. I asked what was wrong. He replied that the altar boys had not shown up, and he needed to start Mass immediately. We took turns helping the priests, and that Sunday was not my turn, but naturally I offered to help him.

He turned angrily toward me and between clenched teeth said, "What the hell do you know about being an altar boy?"

He didn't even wait to hear my answer, just turned and walked back into the church. I stood there dumbfounded. All I could think was, this is the man who was above reproach? This is the man I'm supposed to respect and follow? Everything I had learned since childhood evaporated in a matter of seconds that morning in front of the church.

I stood there for a moment, torn between the truth just revealed to me and the fear of the punishment I was going to get if I didn't go to church. The truth won out. This single event made me wonder, even with my young mind, how much was truth and how much was not. I said a prayer to the Gods, or whoever was in charge, not to hold it against me and walked away from the Catholic church, returning only once for my father's funeral.

When I lost my dad recently, the funeral services were held at the same church I had attended in my childhood. The service started well enough, I suppose, with the priest discussing my father's good points—the usual litany about how much he would be missed. Then he turned my father's service into a recruiting exercise by telling us that it was too bad we had to come back to church under these circumstances. He went on to say that at least we were back in the church, and that we should continue to come to Mass. He carried on and on in the same recruiting mode for several minutes. He turned my father's funeral mass, which was a chance for me and my family to mourn and think of him, into an opportunity to guilt-trip us into coming back to the church! I was angry and disgusted by it all.

After leaving Catholicism, I looked into the Baptist Christian faith as a teenager. But I was only there to meet girls. It was fun for a few months, until I realized that I was still not satisfied spiritually. Disappointed in Christianity, I became a guy looking for thrills and good times. I made friends with a couple of guys, and we ended up in Seattle, Washington.

A few months after moving there, I was walking home from work when two people stopped to talk to me. They were both Japanese. One was an older man and the other a middle-aged woman. They smiled very politely, bowed, and greeted me.

I was a little apprehensive because in big cities when people smile at you they usually want something. So, with a bit of hesitation I said hello. They handed me a pamphlet and asked if I had ever been to a Buddhist meeting.

I said, "No, I don't even know what you mean."

It was a little hard to understand what they were trying to tell me, but I was ripe for the picking. Disenchanted by Christianity, I was open to anything else that might come along.

The Japanese couple realized I was interested, so they really poured it on and I attended some of their meetings. I found Buddhism very interesting and different, and tried to be serious and faithful to this new belief.

Through meditation you were supposed to get whatever you wanted by focusing on it while you chanted a very old chant, "*Nam-yo-ho-ran-ge-kyo.*" The sound emitted when you said the chant made a vibration. This vibration enabled you to connect with the universe and receive anything you desired. I was always chanting for women, booze, and parties.

Boy, did it work! For a long time after leaving Seattle, I was burned out on booze and parties, though I never got tired of girls. I was also burned out on Buddhism. I realized that I had used it in a selfish way, perhaps because I didn't fully understand it. While I still respected Buddhist beliefs, I decided not to use any faith in that manner, so I stopped going to the meetings.

When the eagle whistles sounded for me that Sunday morning in Sacramento, I had been living on the Tuolumne Miwok Rancheria, a small reservation not far from Sonora, California. My wife and I had four children—Rockie, Stormy (Elena), and twin girls, Mary and Becky. Shortly after that, the lease on our rental house ran out, and we decided to move.

We ended up in Blackfoot, Idaho. There are many native people there who bead, and some of the best beadwork in the country still comes from that area. I had been making native crafts for several years but not in a very serious way, at least not to earn a living at it. When I married Vivian, we got more and more into making leather crafts. She was white and Blackfoot, and enjoyed making a living this way.

Our life in Blackfoot, Idaho, wasn't much different from anywhere else. We made crafts, cut beads, and I went on the road to sell them. Several years earlier, I had noticed that no one in the country made faceted hand-cut beads, so I decided to try to figure out how to do it. After many tries and fine-tuning I succeeded. We were the only people in the country who knew how to cut beads at the time, so we had a good market.

My little Dorina was born that June in Pocatello, Idaho. Her birth occurred just when I began my Sundance journey. It was an event that told me that I was on the right path.

That month I went to a Sundance at Fort Washakie, Wyoming, on the Wind River Reservation, where they were allowing crafts people to set up. We could sell in an area that was quite a distance from the Sundance Arbor. After deciding to go to Fort Washakie, I suddenly started feeling a funny little sensation in the pit of my stomach. I didn't know what was wrong with me, but I almost lost the desire to go there because of my fear and apprehension. It was as though I knew that by going there, my spiritual quest would become clear—a new path. Maybe I feared what I might find and didn't feel I was ready to do what was being asked of me.

I left Blackfoot early in the morning and stopped in Idaho Falls to buy groceries for my few days in Fort Washakie. Later I ate lunch in Jackson Hole, Wyoming, then passed by the Grand Tetons and the southern tip of Yellowstone Park. Between there and Dubois, Wyoming, is some of the most beautiful scenery in the world. Apparently, the Creator was either in a very good mood when He made that area or He had time on His hands and was feeling creative. He did a great job.

The afternoon that I drove in to the Arapaho Sundance, the weather was hot and sticky. When I stopped the van, it felt as if the heat consisted of tiny hammers, trying to beat me down.

I got out of the van. I stretched and felt the full force of the sun. Then I thought of the men and women who were going in to Sundance and how hot it was going to be. I felt sorry for them.

I went over to check on the setup. The guy in charge was not very friendly, and they wanted a large fee for a space. I decided to get a tribal permit instead for twenty dollars that was good for a year. Then I could set up anywhere on the reservation.

I set up at an intersection away from the Sundance. That's where I met Allen Enos. Allen was a young man in his mid-thirties, slender, about six-feet-one, with a light complexion and a soft voice. He always had a smile ready! He became my "Grandfather," the one who introduced me to the Sundance. (The term "Grandfather" is used as a form of respect by most traditional people. It is a word to refer to "God" or to someone we respect very much, or to a person who sponsors or introduces another person into the Sundance. Some use their tribal language words for its equivalent, and others use the word "Uncle" as the term of respect. That is why I refer to so many young men who came to Sundance as my "nephews.")

I had my cut beads laid out. There had always been just two places to get cut beads, in Czechoslovakia or Japan. So when my wife and I started cutting beads some people just couldn't believe that we knew how. We hadn't been cutting beads very long so we were very proud of them. When Allen walked up, he was surprised at how many I had.

He remarked, "Boy, the Japanese are sure cutting a lot of beads, and all sizes, too."

Japanese cuts are considered inferior to the Czech cuts. His tone of voice was almost sarcastic, and I was very offended by his insult.

"I beg your pardon," I said indignantly. "*We* cut these beads."

Allen looked a little surprised by my aggressive reply, but he did have the presence of mind to calm himself. He started to make another comment, but stopped. This took a great deal of self-control because he's a pretty tough character. I was happy he had calmed down because I know a warrior when I see one, and he was right in front of me. In my eyes, a warrior is someone who not only stands up for his or her rights with whatever it takes but is also a good provider who doesn't mind helping others, has compassion, and is very spiritual. And I didn't want to get into a fight with this warrior.

He said, "Sorry, I didn't mean to offend you!"

That set me back a little, and I apologized for the outburst. I explained how I'd heard that remark in the past, and it upset me quite a bit if someone compared our cuts to Japanese cuts.

Though we had started off on the wrong foot, I found out Allen was not a bad sort. We visited awhile, talking about mutual interests. I told him about my family, he told me about his, then he left.

The following afternoon, Allen came back to see me and I asked him if he knew where I could get eagle feathers. At the time I really didn't know why I was searching for them. I just wanted to have some in my possession because I had never had one.

He said that he had some and brought me a large paper sack from his car. As he handed it to me, I felt good receiving those feathers and asked him what I could give him in return, or what I owed him.

"Nothing at all. I don't sell eagle feathers," he replied.

During this period of my life, I knew nothing about traditions, and so I didn't realize the importance and significance of eagle feathers to our people. Here I was completely ignorant, offering to pay for something sacred. To traditional people, having an eagle feather means that that person has earned it. But a lot of others just have them because they are a native thing, without having earned them. Now I realize that the feathers of an eagle are sacred and are not to be hung on the rear-view mirror of a car or placed on a cowboy hat as a decoration. They are for us to use only in ceremonies.

Now it was my turn to apologize to him.

"It's okay," he said. "You didn't know, and it's a gift from me to you."

"So I can give you a gift if I want to?" I asked. Now I was being more careful about how I said things.

"I didn't do that so I could get something in return," he answered.

"Well, I want you to take these to your wife," I said, and gave him cut beads of each color that I had, which was quite a few. That exchange of gifts helped to start a friendship that has lasted for years.

Before Allen left, I asked him why he had decided to give me those feathers. He replied that he didn't know. He just had a feeling that I was going to need them pretty soon. Then I remembered my quest, or desire, to learn about the Sundance, so I asked him if he knew any Sundancers or anyone connected to the Sundance.

"Why do you ask?"

"I was told that I had to Sundance," I replied.

"By whom? Who told you, you had to Sundance?"

"Man, I really don't know," I said, and went on to tell him of my vision in California.

"You're right, it sounds like you were being told to do a Sundance," he replied after much thought. "So what are you going to do about it?"

"Well, I want to go into a Sundance, but everyone I ask refuses to talk to me about it."

"How serious are you about dancing?" Allen asked me.

"Well, I don't know. The Spirits said I had to do it. I guess if I can find someone to help me or teach me, I'll do it."

He said, "I'm a Sundancer, and if you're serious about this, be here by the last Sunday in July."

"What do I have to bring?"

"Nothing, just bring yourself. I'll call you the week before to see if you've changed your mind or if you still want to go."

It was getting late, and I started packing up my things. Allen helped me. We said our goodbyes, and I left Fort Washakie.

I was very excited because I had finally found someone to help me. The meeting reminded me of the old proverb,

"When the student is ready, the teacher will appear." Now I had found a Sundance and a Sundancer.

I returned to Blackfoot and continued working. There wasn't a day that went by that I didn't think about the upcoming ceremony. Most times while driving to and from powwows or a show, I would get so scared that I'd start praying. I still didn't know what I was getting into, only that I had made a very important commitment and was terrified that I would fail. I was too ignorant to be afraid of anything else.

I'm glad I didn't know about the thirst.

I'm glad I didn't know of the hunger and the long, hot hours spent under the blazing sun.

I'm also glad I didn't know that when you dance once, you commit yourself for four years! If I had known all these things, then I might not have had the courage, the will-power, and the strength to go through with it all.

At the time, I wanted to Sundance no matter what.

Good to his word, a week before the Sundance, Allen called. I told him we were leaving that day to come to Fort Washakie.

My family and I pulled in later that night and stayed at Rocky Acres campground, between Fort Washakie and Landers, Wyoming. The next day Allen came after us and led us to the Sundance grounds. It took us two days to set up camp. We had to go long distances to cut a certain type of bush used for walls and shade around the camp. This is a tradition for both the Shoshoni and the Arapaho, the two tribes that live on the Fort Washakie Reservation.

After making camp, we started gathering wood for the Sweat Lodge ceremony. Although people go into it to sweat, the main purpose of the Sweat Lodge is to purify.

Purification in the Sweat Lodge is a total body, mind, and spiritual cleansing in preparation for performing any of our sacred ceremonies, especially the Sundance. Once the ceremony starts, the people going through it must remain celibate. They can't even touch anyone who hasn't gone through the Sweat Lodge ceremony. Most lodges last about a half hour per round, each round lasting approximately twenty to thirty minutes.

At the beginning of each round more red-hot rocks were put into the lodge, keeping it good, hot, and interesting. The first three days of purification were spent praying: going into the lodge and concentrating on our reasons for Sundancing. We were getting ourselves mentally and physically prepared because of the difficulties we would face in the ceremony. We would have a four-round sweat at least once a day. They were good, hot sweats.

The Shoshoni people perform the Sweat Lodge ceremony differently from other tribes. We had four days of purification and prayer before the dancing began.

The lodge was right next to a cold, clear, fast-running river. It came in pretty handy because in the Shoshoni Sweat Lodge ceremony, the people could come out of the lodge between rounds and go into the river. Or they could just stand around, smoke, and visit.

During the dance many men can be driven to the brink of insanity. Some can't tolerate the thirst and hunger, even though it is part of the sacrifice to get your prayers answered. Some get so thirsty and hungry that their commitments cease to mean anything to them. They will go to any lengths to satisfy their desires, if allowed.

People ask me, "Why do you Sundance?" I always say, "So my prayers can be answered!" To some people it may seem quite an elaborate ceremony for just praying. Anyone can get down on their knees and say a little prayer. It takes a special person to willingly put themselves through this kind of sacrifice. Putting your ego and personal comfort aside for a few days takes someone strong in spirit. However, it is a lot more than that. To Sundance means something different to everyone.

Most of us pray only when we need it and only when we're in trouble. I'm as guilty as anyone in doing this. In the Sundance you learn the meaning of being selfless. It humbles you. The first obligation, or rule, if you will, is that you never pray for yourself. You let others pray for you.

When we dance, we are not just praying for now or for today, but for the whole year and the whole world. We are praying for all of humanity. We also pray for others in our family, for a sick relative or loved one. We are pleading for our brothers in the rain forests who are losing their land, as we once lost ours. We also pray for the starving people of the world, and for abused men, women, and children.

This is our way to humble ourselves to the Creator. We beg that He intervene on our behalf and help us strengthen our lives so that we may live better. We also give thanks for all the good things that Grandfather (God) has given us up to this point in our lives.

We are willing to sacrifice ourselves so that all goes well on our Mother Earth. Wasn't Jesus Christ also a Sundancer? He was willing to sacrifice himself so the world could evolve into a better place through spirituality and showing us the way. Not that I would compare myself and other Sundancers to Jesus Christ, but his sacrifice for others did help to change the world. In his time, he was a man with a prayer and a message—just like we are. Perhaps our sacrifice can help make a difference, too.

We spent four days relaxing, getting our eagle whistles ready—making sure they worked properly and were easy to get sound from. That's when I started needing the feathers that Allen had given me weeks before. As we were sitting there working on our traditional regalia, Allen smiled and looked up at me. "See Manny, I told you that you were going to need those feathers soon."

The regalia for each warrior dancer is a shawl, which is normally worn by women over their shoulders. Men wear it around their waists like a skirt and don't wear any shirts. Around our necks we wear our traditional ermine skin necklace and our eagle whistle.

In the bag Allen gave me I also found some good, long, fluffy plume feathers, which were perfect for my eagle whistle. I used what I needed. As other men came by, I gave the remaining feathers away, as needed.

Everybody was drinking large quantities of water. Some were drinking sports drinks. Finally I got curious enough to ask why everyone was drinking so much. They all turned and looked at me as if finally realizing that not everyone there knew all the rules. One guy said, "You'd better drink all you can. It'll be a long time before we drink again."

There was very little conversation all that afternoon. I could feel an uneasy or nervous energy radiating off everyone. This was a serious event, and they all knew how hard it was going to be. The days had been really hot. In the afternoon the ground was hot enough to burn our feet. I thought I was the only one there who was completely ignorant. I found out later, there were quite a few people going in for the first time. I was the oldest—in my forties—and pushing my years pretty hard.

Another thing we did that afternoon was eat a venison stew. Allen's wife, Zedora, fixed a large pot of it, and it was delicious. It had lots of vegetables in it, but not one grain of salt. They said that if we ate salt, it would cause us to dehydrate faster.

The first day of the Sundance finally arrived. This was the day that would change the rest of my life, though I didn't know it at the time. It was the day I had been excitedly expecting, yet dreading.

The night before, the sun finally dropped below the horizon. A frenzy of quiet activity started. Everyone was quietly making last-minute touches on themselves and their Sundance outfits. The smell of the dust in the air was suddenly very prominent. Dust stirred up by bare and moccasinned feet became part of the energy and part of the special moment.

The smell of the burning wood also invaded my nostrils and became part of my memories, as did the smell of the bubbling venison stew mingled with the different smells of wood smoke, dust, and sage. People all over were smudging themselves with the smoke of our medicine sage. The smell of humans was everywhere. Perspiration, nervousness, apprehension, and even joy have a distinct smell. They were all there. They were all creating a beautiful memory for my first Sundance.

Everybody was within themselves praying to Grandfather in their own way. The energy was charged up. There was electricity in the air surrounding us, the excitement was contagious. Everyone could feel the enormous energy. It was a wonderful feeling that I can still feel when I sit down and remember that evening.

When it was completely dark, Allen came up to me and said, "Well, Manny, here we are. How do you feel?"

Shaking my head, I replied, "Man, I can't explain it, but I feel like I'm floating!"

"That, my friend, is the Sundance energy," he smiled.

Suddenly from off in the distance where the Arbor was, we heard the drum. A beautiful sound mellowed by distance. Then one helper yelled, "Sundancers, let's go! Come on, it's time to line up!"

We walked from our camp to the Arbor, a bunch of

unidentified figures wrapped in colorful Pendleton blankets. As we walked, some of us were barefooted, and some of us were wearing moccasins.

The Sundance grounds we walked to that night were new. For years the Sundance was always held right in the middle of Fort Washakie. Then the government started building houses pretty close to the grounds. As the Sundance Chief once said, "One important thing about the Sundance is that every morning we must greet the sun as it rises. With all the houses, we can't see the sun as it comes up." Although that was the main reason for changing the location for the Sundance, there was another reason. In the center of Fort Washakie, there were also drunks who came around to taunt and yell obscenities at the Sundancers. They would call us devils and idiots for sacrificing the way we were. They called themselves "good Christians."

I felt good about the change because I was new and it was my first Sundance. This was a new place, and it was the first Sundance at this location.

Walking toward the Arbor, I stepped very gingerly. Not only were there many small, sharp rocks, there were cactus needles, which were tough on my bare feet.

After assembling behind the Arbor on the west side, everybody stood in two lines. I was sticking as close as I could to Allen.

I found out later that Allen always picked the spot in line that would place him in the Arbor on the north side. It's the hottest and hardest place to be in the Arbor for most of the day. Lots of Sundancers avoid that spot because whoever ends up there suffers the most. Allen and I were on that spot for three full days.

The Sundance sure makes you appreciate a lukewarm drink of water. It really makes you appreciate a small spot of shade or a little breeze on a hot summer day. When you get down to basics, it's surprising at how little it really takes to make you happy or at least satisfied.

We started walking, each line going around opposite sides of the Arbor. One line is led by the Sundance Chief, the other by one of his helpers. As we rounded the Arbor, we met the other line moving in the opposite direction. We were blowing our eagle whistles as we walked around and around. It was so dark there was no way of recognizing anyone.

It was an eerie feeling to be involved in something so strange to me. I felt that I had gone back one hundred years in time. I could see many people standing quietly, watching us prepare ourselves to enter the Arbor.

The smell of dust and sage was strong, yet comforting. It felt like a friend, something familiar. We continued our walk until we had circled four times. Then the Sundance Chief led us into the Arbor. We did not leave the Arbor from Friday night just after dark until Monday afternoon. In retrospect, it doesn't seem like a very long time. When you're in there, however, every hour seems like an eternity.

The Arbor, the resting place for the dancers, is not only to rest the physical bodies. It's also a place to meditate, to concentrate and pray for the things that you need, to think about the prayers you need answered. Some people who are new to the Sundance think the Arbor is a place where the Sundancers relax and have their cigarettes. This is wrong— there is nothing to drink, nothing to eat, and in many Sundances they even ask you to give up your cigarettes.

Eventually, I did find an escape from the suffering. It didn't happen for a couple of days, and when I did finally discover it, it was as if the tree, the Sacred Tree, had talked to me. It taught me to pray, pray, and pray hard. My prayers could be answered, and I could endure what I was going through. My prayers were my escape.

You know something? I had found what I was looking for, and felt such joy and peace with everything and everyone that I didn't have time to think of my suffering. I found out that things only bother you when you pay attention to them. So, if you ignore the suffering and focus on the beauty that you wish, it changes everything.

For three days, I went through many things, and I really don't know what to call the experiences. Can I call them better changes? Can I call them sufferings or spiritual awakenings? I do know one thing to be a fact: The Sundance changed my life like nothing else could have. I know, without any doubt, I'm a much better man. At least, I feel that I am and so does my family.

I was honored that the Shoshoni allowed me to participate in their most sacred ceremony with them. I can only return their respect and honor by not writing about what occurred during this Sundance ceremony. If it is ever to be told, I'll leave that to be told by a Shoshoni elder.

So we danced and danced.

And prayed and prayed.

I thought the first day was not very difficult. But everyone is different, and I could see other dancers were already suffering. As time went on, it was more noticeable. We danced late that first night.

The following morning we were up early. We greeted the sun, then had a little time to prepare ourselves for the day. Sometime in mid-morning we started dancing again. The sun got hot early. As the day progressed, it got hotter and hotter as we danced to and from the Sacred Tree.

When we danced back to our place, our feet would be burning. Sore feet from the heat or hot ground are one thing. But the bruises from the sharp rocks and cactus stickers impaling your feet make the suffering more intense. Add to that the number of times we danced back and forth.

Now I knew why Allen had asked me how serious I was about dancing. He later told me that many people say they want to Sundance, but when it gets right down to it, they find all kinds of excuses why they just can't make it "this time." It's very, very hard. The person who goes through the Sundance ceremony must have an important reason.

Personally I respect all Sundancers. Sundancers are a special breed of person. Every one of them has gone to suffer and pray willingly. I believe that no matter where the Sundance is or who is running it, they are all done for the right reason. They are all special. There is no easy Sundance. You go there to pray, and to suffer, and you should. You should sacrifice yourself so your prayers can be heard and answered.

As one Sundance Chief told me, "If you want to go on a picnic, take your whole family and go to the river. This is *your* Sundance. It's only for three days. Make the most of it. Pray and dance hard." He said this because late in the afternoon when it was the hottest, some Sundancers would sit out a few songs. There is no written rule that says a Sundancer has to dance every song. It is an individual choice.

By Sunday afternoon, everyone was getting very dry. I would try to spit, and my saliva was so dry it was like rubber strings. Some of us were having trouble talking. It was so hot. The constant blowing on our eagle whistles dried us out even faster. Swallowing was completely out of the question; by that time there is nothing to swallow anyway.

We always looked for a dancer who looked ready to collapse from heat exhaustion, hunger, and dehydration. We believe that this is when a Sundancer is truly close to the Creator and is very powerful spiritually. He is pulling the "Sun Power" down on himself and the whole Sundance. It is the ultimate in power and energy a person can receive during a Sundance, even if it's just for a few seconds. We strongly believe that when the body grows weaker, the spirit grows stronger.

This is what every Sundancer is striving for.

This is when a person receives his vision.

This is when we receive direction from the Creator.

The more people this happens to in the Sundance, the more power we all receive to get our wishes and prayers fulfilled. It is a great honor to have this happen to an individual. When a dancer is showing signs of exhaustion, he receives encouragement to keep on dancing. The drummers will pick up the beat and keep on singing and drumming. When that special dancer dances back to his spot, the other dancers push him back out.

It is a wonderful feeling and yet a pitiful sight to see. The person it's happening to receives respect from everyone. If the dancer falls, many dancers who are close, rush out to touch and share his energy and power. To show our respect for what he has just been through, we pick him up gently and carry him back to his spot. If he has a little shade, we lay him down so he can rest.

The Sundance goes on.

Sometimes we have two or three different groups who drum and sing for us. So we go on and on and on. The sun beats down on us for hours.

After two days of almost unbearable heat, the Sunday sun reached the end of its long, hot journey across the Wyoming sky. It finally decided to give us some rest from its fiery bright energy. Though dry, hungry, and tired, we felt our spirits rise with joy. We felt the ever-present evening breezes and the coolness provided by the evening shadows.

Late in the night, the dancers stopped and tiredly lay down on their sleeping rolls. The drummers also showed signs of fatigue. The songs got slower and further apart.

Finally, when there were only a few dancers left, the singers finished their last song. They got up, stretched, and by one's and two's left the Arbor.

The dance was over for the day. Here and there I saw dancers wrap themselves up in sheets and head for the out-house. As I lay down, thinking and praying for my children, my parents, and everyone else, I looked at the beautiful stars lighting up the sky.

I thought, "Thank you, God, for all the blessings you've given me throughout my life. For my beautiful children, my brother and sisters, and my wonderful parents, who have always been there for me. Most of all, thank you for bring-ing me to this Sundance. I finally have a way to thank you for all you have given me." As I lay there giving thanks, I drifted off to sleep.

Morning arrived quietly. I heard someone cough and I awoke. Where I lay, I could see through the leaves of the Arbor wall. Although they were different constellations, the stars were still shining brightly. They had a cool, regal, almost aloof look to them. They looked different to me. I was not used to seeing this group of stars, and not used to wak-ing up at this time of the morning.

I felt an urgency to get up. Mother Nature was calling. I had to answer the call of nature the first two days of the Sundance, but I figured that was normal. As I left my warm blankets and felt the cool air hit me, I had to move.

Getting up quickly, I went to the outhouse. It amazed me how much liquid I still had to get rid of. It had been three days since I had had anything to drink. Well, like one dancer said, "Just because you quit drinking, doesn't mean that your kidneys stop working!"

When I returned, everyone was in high spirits and putting on their finest regalia. I also pulled out my best shawl. It was bright red and had an eagle sewn on the front. I was very proud of it because Allen and his wife, Zedora, gave it to me. We wrapped them around ourselves like skirts.

The rumor started going around that we weren't going to get out until late that night. You can't believe how tough that is to hear after three days without food or water. Allen pulled me to the side and told me that the rumor always started for the discomfort of the first-time Sundancers. They do go late sometimes, but this doesn't happen too often.

We had to watch the flagpole in front of the camp of the Sundance Chief, who was away from the Arbor. If the flag was all the way to the top of the pole, we would be staying late. If it was at half-mast we would get out around twelve or one o'clock in the afternoon.

This was the last day.

As we danced and blew on our eagle whistles, I could hear dancers gagging because of the lack of moisture in their mouths. I was feeling pretty bad myself. Once, I started retching and couldn't stop. When I finally did, I was pretty weak and shaken, but continued dancing.

The reason we go without food or water and blow on our eagle whistles is to help us focus and to reach an open and accepting state of heart and mind. This brings us insight and helps us become open to receiving our visions. It says something about the way we live today that such drastic measures are needed.

Many spectators came into the Arbor for blessings. Some dancers brought in their families and others to be blessed. It was a little beyond my understanding, but Christian ministers were coming into the Sundance Arbor and asking the Sundance Chief to give them blessings. In turn, they asked if they could bless other people from their congregation in the Sundance Arbor. It was beautiful to see the mixing of beliefs the way it happened there. At least I'm glad that these people have the intelligence to recognize the Arbor as a sacred place, as sacred as any church anywhere.

The morning went slowly and seemed to stretch until the next weekend. The sun decided to take it easy on us poor Sundancers. Maybe it thought we had suffered enough. The morning couldn't have been better. It was the most pleasant of the whole time. It eased our suffering a little.

Suddenly, Allen grabbed my arm. When I looked at him, he pointed with his chin, directing me to look at the flag, now flying at half-mast.

"Thank you, Grandfather," I said to myself.

Suddenly the people were no longer coming into the Arbor. The blessings were over. The energy within the circle felt charged and exciting. Even the spectators could feel it. People were starting to smile and laugh. Some were holding their fists up to the dancers. A sign of victory, as if saying, "Good man, we are proud of you."

Then the Sundance Chief tied up his sheet.

Everybody started following his example. The sheets we had used to cover ourselves at times during the Sundance now concealed us from the spectators' eyes. At first I didn't understand why. Then it was explained to me. We were about to have our first drink of water in three days. This is sacred water, to be received with humbleness and respect. It was too personal to be seen by anyone else, other than your Sundance brothers and God.

They brought two large, old, metal milk cans, each filled with fresh spring water. After bringing the water in, the helpers placed it before the Sundance Chief. He prayed over the water, gave thanks for it, then with his blessing he poured it into buckets. His helpers brought it to us.

One by one, they let each dancer drink his fill. It was a quiet time, filled with reverence. It felt like his own personal ceremony was taking place, as each Sundancer took his first drink.

As the helpers stopped in front of me, one of them took a large dipper full of cool, sweet, well water out of the bucket. He raised it high enough to clear the edge of the bucket. Water splashed and dripped off the sides of it. It looked fantastically delicious. The helper was not moving fast enough. The whole process seemed to be in slow motion.

I was sitting on the ground watching as all this was happening. My throat felt stretched tight as my head tilted back. I tried to swallow as I looked at that beautiful water, but all I could do was croak. The feeling was so intense that I couldn't have talked even if I had wanted to. He slowly lowered the dipper to me. By then I wanted the water so bad that I was ready to stand up and reach for it, yet I held myself down on the ground waiting for the water to come to me. I felt I had earned the right for the water to come to where I was sitting.

At long last the dipper was in my hands. Wanting to just guzzle it down and get some more, I stopped myself and thought of the last three days. Then I thought of the flag. What if it had been all the way to the top? I still wouldn't be drinking. I thought of the Spirits that had helped me so much.

I raised the dipper in gratitude and respect, and to honor Grandfather and the Spirits. Slowly I tipped the dipper, letting a small amount of water drip out and splash on Mother Earth to honor her. Now I felt that it was my turn. With shaking hands, I raised the dipper to my mouth. That first sip was like nothing I had ever experienced. It was heaven. I could feel that wonderful, wet trickle, slowly working its way down my dry throat. It was like putting water on a sponge. I continued to take small sips.

After the first taste that didn't do much, I was finally

starting to make a little saliva in my mouth. Each time I took a sip, my lips trembled. Little drops escaped my lips. They would race down my chin, then drop off, landing in my lap. At long last I was feeling halfway human again. Reluctantly I surrendered the dipper. It passed on and on to the other Sundancers until the helpers reached the end of the line. Everyone had water, and we started taking our sheets down.

Earlier that morning we had given our sleeping rolls and anything else we didn't need to relatives, so we didn't have much to carry out. Finally, we lined up and the Sundance Chief held his hand up for us to follow him.

It was finally over.

As we filed out of the Arbor, the spectators lined up on each side of the entrance. As we walked between them, the people reached out to touch us. They thanked us for our prayers. Everyone was smiling, laughing, and shaking our hands. It was a wonderful feeling. I got very emotional and shed a few tears of thanks and gratefulness.

The people who had prayed and stood by us until the last drumbeat had suffered almost as much as we had. I found out later that many people had fasted with us. They went without water for three days and in a way it's harder than what we had done. They had water, food, and other cold drinks right in front of them and still went without drinking. It's harder to resist if what you want is right there in front of you. You have no one to stop you except yourself.

Lots of people wanted our sun energy, the energy that for three days we had pulled down onto ourselves. That energy is powerful, it's clean, it heals and cures.

As I was walking, I felt exhilarated, I felt so good it was like walking on feathered ground. Now I didn't feel the small, sharp rocks that had made my life so interesting for the last three days. I was no longer worried about the small cactus stickers that had attacked my feet at every opportunity.

Now that the time for eating was close, I didn't feel any hunger. At the end of the line, I could see a large crowd ahead of me. Sundancers wrapped in white sheets dispersed and headed in different directions to wherever their camps were. I could see them all clutching something in their arms.

Suddenly it was my turn. A Sundance Chief's helper stood on the ground right behind a pickup truck. He was handing each Sundancer an unexpected surprise: a large, striped watermelon. I thought I didn't have any liquids left in my body, but the sight of the big, beautiful watermelon made saliva slowly moisten the whole inside of my mouth.

Again, I had received another surprise. It's amazing how little things have so much meaning. When a person has suffered and has had to do without the basic things in life, little things mean a lot. A chair to sit on, a drink of water, a small meal, becomes all that is important in life. Even a small piece of bread becomes something to think and dream about when you are in that state.

My wife and family were all there waiting for me. My children looked like they had also been in the Sundance— tired and drained—especially my twin girls. I believe that in their innocence, and because of their love for me, they tried to take the pain, hunger, and thirst from me. Since then I have found out that in their own way they are very powerful individuals, especially Becky, who has always been the runt of the family. Her energy is so strong, only my influence as her father can keep her on the right track. I realize that someday I'm going to let her go, to do the things she needs to do for the Creator. She has strong leadership qualities and has had this energy since childhood.

When I saw them and felt their anxiety for me, my emotions welled up. My heart felt as though it was convulsing. "My God," I thought, "these babies have been suffering for me as much as I have."

The enormous swelling I felt in my chest rose into my throat and brought tears to my eyes. Right then, I felt so much love for them and the whole world that I knew this was the reason I Sundanced.

We walked back to camp. It was a quiet and slow process. I set the slow pace and everyone stayed next to me. The children wanted to touch and hug me as we all walked along, which made the progress even slower. Despite my intense joy at seeing my children, the main reason I was dragging my feet was that I felt an unexplainable sense of loss. I felt an emptiness inside as if I were leaving a part of myself behind.

The only comparison I can come up with for this feeling is when a woman gives birth. After giving birth, she goes through a feeling of loss or emptiness. The Sundance is a trial and test of your spirit. It's exhilarating, yet incredibly difficult, like childbirth. Although I will never go through childbirth, I did share and witness the birth of my youngest daughter, and I have my wife's testimonial to what she felt.

What I saw and experienced at that first Sundance is as close to going to the other side without making the permanent transition. During this experience, I gained strength, appreciation for the basics in life, and respect for all humanity.

I learned how to cope with pain, hunger, and all other things that make life unpleasant. I learned that we must consider others before we act. If we hurt others, even unintentionally, we hurt ourselves.

As native people, we don't always have specific words for everything. We do believe that if we do wrong to someone else, it comes back to us. Some people call this Karma.

Our connection with nature, our Mother Earth, and

with the heavens, allows us to know and feel things that others overlook. It's not because of any other reason except that we have developed a sensitivity to the earth. The elements and human connections have never been lost.

I believe that every living thing on this earth is born with that special sensitivity, but, through no fault of our own, we learn to overlook many laws of nature. For our convenience and progress, our environment suffers. Believe this, when nature decides, she's going to put things back where she wants them. We are not going to change nature. We have to respect nature and try to live with her, which is something we forget. Native people have learned that trying to force nature—or as we call her, Grandmother (the earth)—to bend our way, is to look for disaster.

What I mean to say is that instead of trying to be so logical, we should use a little of the common sense God gave us. Have we become so intellectual that we can't believe in the simple things? It's almost as if we follow down a road of destruction because we learn to believe only what we can see . . . and see only what we want.

When the Creator formed the earth, He had us in mind and made everything perfect and balanced. When all was running smoothly, He created humans and set up the food chain for the vegetables and animal world. *So why did He create us?*

The answer is hard to find, but very simple in content. We native people believe that when the earth was brought to life, the Creator had to think of everything.

Even before He created the animals to walk the earth, He knew that He was going to create humans, and spirituality would be needed. So He had to supply a means for them to protect themselves spiritually as they were learning.

The best thing He brought us was the "mother plant." This very first plant He created was called "sage," or "*Pejuta Wakan*," as the Lakota people call it. It is sacred to all traditional native people. We believe that the Creator gave it to native people to use in whatever way we need. It was not to be sold in every store and by everyone. What many people don't understand is that this medicine sage is not the same thing that grows in Europe, and it's not cooking sage. It's a special sage that has always grown in this hemisphere and has always been used by spiritual people for spiritual reasons. For our peoples, raping the land of sage for profit is equal to prostituting your sister or mother.

The Creator knew that we would need the smoke from the sage to cleanse our bodies and our spirits. Therefore He made different sage plants so the sage could survive at different altitudes and in different areas. He wanted His children to have sage available to them everywhere.

After Grandfather made sure we had what we needed for our spirituality, He created humans. He made each of us different. He knew that we had to be different because He was going to give us distinguishing features from the other animals.

We have free will, creativity, intelligence, courage, integrity, resourcefulness, pride, and, best of all, the ability to love. However, the Creator also gave us the ability to overemphasize our own worth in the form of the ego. We must all learn to have respect for each other and all other living things on this earth. We also need to learn to stop being judgmental of others. No matter how we feel, we all share this earth mother together. Whether we like it or not, we are all brothers and sisters.

When we learn these simple things, we have taken the first step to becoming a useful part of this earth, instead of a detriment.

When we finally arrived back at camp, the women had laid out a feast on a long table. I was only the third Sundancer to arrive back. The others were standing around just waiting. My reserves and control started collapsing when I saw all that beautiful food! They had prepared steaks, stew, fry bread, cold chokecherry juice, chokecherry pudding, coolers full of cold soda pop, cold watermelon, and boiling-hot coffee. There were so many wonderful things to eat. I looked around and realized everyone was as hungry as I.

We waited for one of the Sundancers to do a blessing and give thanks for a good Sundance. With that done, everybody started digging in. I didn't know what to eat first, so I had a small piece of meat wrapped in a tortilla, burrito style. Then I had a piece of watermelon. Then I asked for a cup of coffee. I never realized how good food tasted. The food mixed with the smell of burning wood made me realize how much there is to appreciate in this short life of ours.

I found out later that I had lost twenty-five pounds in those three days. Unfortunately, it doesn't stay off. Dehydration causes the weight loss, so once you replace the fluids in your body, you are right back where you began.

After everyone had relaxed and eaten, and the sun started to go down, one by one, each Sundancer began relating what had happened to him—what he had felt, seen, or experienced. It was beautiful to sit, listen, and wonder where all this energy had come from, and listen to stories and the crackling of the burning wood in the campfires. The small children scooted off to bed, and the older people just kept on talking and visiting. It felt good to not be dancing on those sharp little stones. I was glad to be smoking a cigarette, having a cup of coffee, and just relaxing.

If you have ever sat around a campfire as the earth quiets down after a long day, you'll know that it's a unique experience to feel our Mother Earth relax after watching over her children all day long.

As it got later, the adults started drifting to wherever

they were staying for the night. Not everyone was camping with us. As they left, they bid us farewell because some were pulling out early. Lots of dancers and people who helped us had to get back to work. Some had traveled long distances and had gone to great expense to attend or help at the Sundance.

As I've said, nobody is told they have to come to or be at the Sundance. Dancers, helpers, and everyone else are there because they want to be—which impressed me. Invariably the last thing everyone says is, "See you next year!" And even though you're still in a semi-shocked state, you are already looking forward to the next time.

That night, I lay there under the stars trying to go to sleep, but I couldn't. I kept reliving the Sundance. I was still high from what I had received—that huge spiritual uplifting and happiness at having found the Sundance. Most importantly, I was struck with wonder at the new world that was open to me now, and I knew I would never be the same.

I lay there so at peace with myself and my newfound world that I felt as if I never closed my eyes. Before I knew it, the sun was coming up.

In the distance I heard a couple of cars start and quietly drive away. The drivers seemed reluctant to leave and break the peaceful spell of that sacred place. The departure of those first two cars was like a signal. From all around the Sundance grounds, I could hear people starting to talk. Car doors slammed, babies cried, and more cars left the camp. Someone in our camp put kindling on the hot coals left over from the night before.

After everyone had gotten up and eaten, we started to break camp. It took several hours to accomplish. With all that done, our footprints and tire tracks in the dirt were all the marks that remained. Even the holes where our shade poles had been were refilled. There wasn't one tiny piece of trash, paper, or anything, anywhere. Everyone left their camps clean.

Not long after that first Sundance I went to Oklahoma on a selling trip. The native people of that state are the finest you can meet anywhere. They made me feel so welcome, and I fell in love with the countryside around Tulsa. I set up at a large native arts and crafts show in Tahlequah and met quite a few wonderful Cherokee people. Tahlequah is considered the capital of the Cherokee nation. It is where all the people searching for their Cherokee roots go to find out about their heritage.

I was so taken by the people and area that when I returned to Idaho, I talked Vivian into moving there.

The year went by so quickly, that before I knew it, it was time to return to Wyoming for another Sundance.

S O U T H — W H I T E

"Warm Winds"

R A I N

We left Oklahoma about two weeks before the Sundance was to begin because I wanted to arrive at Fort Washakie with plenty of time to help with the camp and Arbor.

We got our camp set up early, but I was not allowed to help with the Arbor. It's never set up by the dancers; it's always done by the helpers. In fact, I have never had the occasion to see it being put up, since I was always dancing.

The erecting of the Arbor can be complicated and diffi-cult. It takes many men a long time to put it up, and sometimes it feels as though it's not going to be done in time for the dance.

At one Sundance, I really got worried because it was late afternoon, and there wasn't anyone around the Arbor. I mentioned it to Allen. He just shrugged a shoulder and told me not to worry. The next time I thought about it, I looked again. Like magic, the Arbor was complete.

This day there was still no one around that I could see, but I stopped worrying about it. That was someone else's job. Our job was to pray and to dance.

We had plenty of time to cut brush for our camp and dig the holes for the frame. The frame consists of whatever materials are available, usually two-by-fours, four-by-fours, tepee poles, or whatever is on hand. Since it's not a permanent structure, we don't feel that what we use to make it is important—only that it serves the purpose. You know what they say, as long as the shell covers the nut . . .

As the days went on, more Sundancers arrived. Some would come by and stop at our camp. We were happy to re-establish old acquaintances from the year before. A Sundancer, Benny, grinned when he saw me and asked, "Hey, Manny, come back for seconds?" This being my second time made me an old-timer. I felt welcome and proud of myself.

Some guys only come to the Sundance once and never return because of the suffering they experience. Others will do anything to get there.

We heard of one guy who was riding his motorcycle to the Sundance from western Montana. Because he thought he was going to be late, he was speeding and got stopped. Fortunately, there was a Native American police officer at the station where they took the man, so when the Sundancer explained why he was speeding, the officer understood and spoke on the Sundancer's behalf. They released him so he could get to the Sundance. He was lucky that he had found someone who respected the Sundance and the people who take part in it.

I guess that even if it's not supposed to be a macho thing, people still reserve judgment on how a man can act under extreme conditions. Those people, the Shoshoni, and I guess all native people, place a great deal of importance on bravery. Bravery has always been and continues to be a large and very important part of our warrior societies and our way of life.

In the Shoshoni Sundance, women don't enter the Arbor. If they want to Sundance they must have a male member of their family inside the Arbor, and then they are only allowed to remain outside the brush wall of the Arbor next to their relatives. They are on their own about whether they drink or eat during the Sundance; no one watches them or forces them not to.

In the old days, the people judged you on how you endured hardships. People wanted to know if you would and could persevere in times of trouble. Could you be dependable and trustworthy? Many people believe that the Sundance is a test of these characteristics, so this time several Sundancers were a little bit nicer greeting me than they had been my first year.

Now that I knew what was happening, things were a little easier. However, there were some things they had forgotten to tell me: for example, when you dance once, you have made a commitment to Sundance for four years, and once you're in the Arbor, you can't leave for *any* reason.

The reason it becomes impossible to leave is that once all the Sundancers have come together, we become one entity. We become a solid force, and, as one, our power is tremendous. All our prayers will be answered. If even one person leaves the circle of a Sundance, it can cause a weakness in the rest of us. It weakens us not only as individuals, but it also harms our ability to function as one. It's like when a person loses an arm, a leg, or another part of the body. The body is still alive, but its abilities become limited. This is the reason you should know what you're getting into from the very beginning—before you start—because once you're in, there is no going back. If necessary, you would be kept there by force to keep from breaking the Sacred Circle.

My second Sundance happened much like the first. I was feeling pretty confident. I thought that my first one had been fairly easy. In a year you forget many things: the aches, pains, thirst, and hunger.

One elder I told about my feelings looked at me for a long time. Then he said, "Don't be so cocky about it, and show more respect. The Spirits are there to help you, but if you take it lightly, they have ways of humbling you and making you show respect. They can make the Sundance very hard on you."

He was absolutely right.

We had gone in on a Friday just like before, and the first night was quickly over. The drum started early the next morning and then they started singing. The songs were beautiful, and the energy was good. Everyone was happy and excited, and dancing strong and hard.

We would rush at the tree and, after touching it for power and energy, dance back to our spots. We were blowing furiously on our eagle whistles the entire time. I danced without regard for my physical condition. I danced without regard for the future of my next three days. Most dancers would pace themselves so they could last the entire dance. They advised me to do the same, but I didn't. My energy was so high that I just couldn't help myself.

I wanted to dance. I wanted that Sun Power on me. I wanted to feel the total glory of the Sundance. I had fallen in love with the Sundance and its beliefs. I knew that I had found the very best for myself. I didn't understand it all, and I knew I never would. Some Sundancers dance all their lives and learn more every time they dance. It's very much like an ongoing lesson in life.

I heard that some people, for whatever reasons, will call down the Sun Power on other dancers. The object is to elevate those dancers with so much power and energy that their dancing creates a pull of energy, causing them to have a vision right there in the Sundance. I also heard some dancers do the same thing with malice in their hearts—calling down the Sun Power on one dancer, causing him to dance until he drops from exhaustion. Once a dancer has reached that point of dehydration, he suffers immensely through the remainder of the Sundance. Though it's a very hard thing to do, that's what every Sundancer is there to experience, a vision and connection with the Creator.

I don't know if that's what happened to me, but I was badly dehydrated by Saturday evening. This was only the first day, and I was starting to have hallucinations as it grew later. The evening saved me.

I don't believe anyone knew what I was going through. The only one who could have known how I felt was Allen, and he only made a slight, passing remark about how tired I looked.

Sunday morning, after greeting the sun, everyone got ready to start dancing. Although there was only room for one drum at a time, when one group of singers tired, another group took its place. There must have been five or six groups of singers, and they were eager to be singing. They started singing all those beautiful Sundance songs, one after another. Such beautiful songs, every one of them. (They stay in your mind, and long after a Sundance, you find yourself singing them over and over in your head for months.) They didn't give us much time to rest.

This new day was the same as the previous morning, it got hot very early. There wasn't even the slightest breeze stirring, and I was incredibly thirsty.

By the middle of the afternoon I started retching because my mouth was so dry from dehydration. There wasn't saliva in my mouth, instead there was a gummy substance that made me sick to my stomach. I was starting to feel the effects of the previous day. After another night without water, it became hard to pray as my thirst took over my concentration.

In the next few hours I suffered like I never had in all my life. I had gone without water for long periods before, but never like this. I can't tell you how I looked, but I can tell you how I felt.

By now hunger had ceased being a big problem. The thirst and deep, dry feeling now dominated my thoughts. It started behind my eyes, reached into my mouth, down my throat, and engulfed my entire body. Although the thirst centered in my mouth and throat, my arms and legs felt detached from the rest of me. It felt as if my head were floating high above me.

The feeling was almost beyond words. Mostly it was a beautiful, glorious feeling because I knew why it was all happening to me. Yet, a small part of my brain questioned my sanity: Why am I doing this to myself? Is it worth it?

Then thoughts of my children invaded my brain, and my friends who needed prayers all reminded me of why I had made my commitment. I realized that in spite of the fatigue and fuzziness, it was worth everything I was going through.

We are all guilty of getting ourselves into situations in which we question our actions and priorities. And we also have a tendency to be selfish. We ask ourselves, "What am I getting out of this?" But why must we always think of ourselves first? The Sundance is about thinking of others before yourself. When you sacrifice yourself, you are showing God and the whole world that you are willing to give of yourself so that others may live better.

The drumming and singing continued. The hot sun was blazing down on us as if trying to give us as much of its heat and energy as we could take.

By now, many of us were really suffering and some dancers were staggering, which automatically makes the drummers sing faster and harder. It also makes the songs longer. They are trying to see if any of us are on the verge of collapsing, and, if we are, they will keep on singing until someone does fall. It is a great honor to fall with exhaustion during the dance. It brings great honor to the Sundance, the Chief, and all the dancers. The more dancers who go into this state, the greater the honor.

As I rushed at the tree I was praying hard for my father and my mother. Each time I danced back from the tree I blew hard on my eagle whistle. I was asking God to please answer my prayers. I had so many people to pray for, each time I danced back and forth I focused on another person.

When I first made the commitment to Sundance, I was afraid to face the unknown because of my lack of knowledge. In one of my prayers before the Sundance, I asked the Creator to help me. I asked Him to give me the courage to go through the Sundance and the strength to complete it. If He did, I would let my hair grow long in His honor. I also promised Him that I would let it grow until my commitment was over. Long hair has always been a possession of pride for the native warrior as well as a challenge to a warrior's enemy. Traditionally, by wearing your hair long you are taunting your enemy and asking if he is man enough to take it.

After I completed my first Sundance I started to grow

my hair and told my parents about my choice. "Well," my Victorian father said, "no man with long hair can come into my house." I felt rejected and hurt by my father's reactions to my choices, but I didn't blame him for acting the way he did. My parents brought us up to be humble, keep a steady job, and wear our hair short. That's what the Christian society demanded of us, so in a way I understood. My dad just didn't know any other way. I tried to tell him why I had to let it grow, but he would not listen to reason. So I explained to my mother about the Sundance and the significance of growing my hair. Although she understood, she had to stick by my dad, right or wrong. Because of my commitment, I didn't see my parents for five years.

Although I was hurt by their rejection, I also understand why my parents never claimed their native heritage. In the 1940s, the prejudice against "Indians" was rampant. It was better to be a Mexican than an Indian. In the summer there was a community pool in Ajo, and swimming privileges were segregated by race. Fridays through Sundays were for the white kids only. On Mondays and Tuesdays the Mexican kids got to swim. On Wednesdays they let the black and Indian, or Indio, kids swim. And on Thursdays the pool was disinfected and refilled with clean water.

I grew up as a Mexican, although my ancestry was mixed with native blood, and so I didn't understand the discrimination. The irony behind all this is that many young Mexicans today are claiming their "Indian" heritage and searching spiritually for their roots—like I did. Today, there is a new sense of pride in being Native American, and things aren't as bad as when I grew up.

Over the next several years, I kept praying at every Sundance that my father would accept me the way I was. I was praying hard for him this time when I backed away from the tree, staggered, and fell down hard. I felt my breath leave me. My head was reeling, and I went into an almost hypnotic state. I could see everything going on around me, and I could hear those beautiful Sundance songs, but I couldn't control my arms and legs. My legs were twitching, trying to cramp. I wanted to get up and dance some more, but I couldn't will my legs to move. It was a frightening feeling. I had my bedding rolled up in my spot just behind me. As I tried to get up, my legs just stretched out in front of me.

Allen had gone out to the Sacred Tree, and as he danced back I saw him stagger. When he was back all the way, he stopped and looked at me with a question on his face. He didn't say anything. He just looked and understood that now I was going through a very personal experience.

I didn't know it myself, but I was going through a very real vision. The hunger, the thirst, and the heat were combining their energies to put me in contact with the Great Spirit. Now I knew He was giving me his undivided attention. In essence, He was letting me know that moment was mine. He had listened to my prayers. Since I was willing to sacrifice, He was now willing to answer my prayers, and He was also going to let me know about my future through a vision that would later be interpreted by an elder. This was the moment when I was going to receive direction for my life.

My world, my eyesight, everything as I knew it went blank. Just as suddenly, everything came into focus, but seemed so unreal. I could see the green leaves of the Arbor brush—so bright, so green, they almost glowed. The sky was an intense blue. Everything I looked at was vibrant and in clear, sharp detail.

The sun was extremely bright, but it no longer felt hot. It didn't bother me in any way. It felt so pleasant, I just wanted to sleep. I was the only one in the Arbor. All the other dancers seemed to disappear. There was no more drumming or singing. It was absolutely still. I was lying just north of the Sacred Tree with my feet pointing toward it. My eyes were closed, yet I could see all those things.

Suddenly, I heard a loud, flapping noise. I opened my eyes and there between the poles in the roof of the Arbor, I saw a huge spotted eagle descending into the Arbor. He was so big I knew he couldn't possibly fly between the rafters. But they were invisible to the eagle. He flew right through them as though they didn't exist, soared to where I was lying, and landed lightly on my chest.

I couldn't move. My body was rigid with fright. I felt the pressure of his weight on my chest. I could smell his feathers, hot from the sun. I could feel the warmth of his body.

As the eagle stood on my chest, in slow motion he looked into my eyes. I could see very clearly the golden flakes in the iris of his eyes. I tried to read a message or figure out what he wanted me to do. I couldn't, but I got the distinct feeling that I didn't have to be afraid.

I felt myself relax, and as I did, each of his talons slowly gripped my chest. Slowly, one by one, the talons pierced my skin and dug into my flesh. I flinched, expecting pain, but, surprisingly, felt only the popping sensation as each talon broke through my skin. As I lay there, the eagle continued to look right into my eyes.

His look said, "I told you that if you overcame your fear, it would not hurt."

So I lay there, held my breath, and waited to see what was going to happen.

The eagle slowly spread its magnificent wings, and ever so slowly, started flapping them. I could smell and taste the dust disturbed by its wings. In two or three huge flaps, we were off the Arbor floor. As we lifted off, the eagle seemed slow because of my weight.

About this time I felt my soul separate from my vision. It was as though I were leaving my vision to become an observer. The eagle had told me that he was going to take me up to show me where I could help others.

The eagle spirit and I soared high above the ground, so high I could see the curvature of our Mother Earth. He was showing me that I would be helping people in all directions, and that I would be ready when the time was right. A medicine man would tell me and show me the way to help people.

I could see my vision below me—the eagle with my body, flapping between the ground and the rafters. I realized that I had split into three separate entities of myself: my physical body on the ground, my spirit being pulled by the eagle's talons, and my soul watching the entire scene from above.

As we soared higher, I felt fear, but only because I had nothing to hold on to. My spirit seemed suspended next to the eagle spirit as he spoke to me in thoughts. Suddenly, I was back in my vision. Again I could feel the wind stirred up by the eagle's wings. We moved past the rafters, and the realization hit me: I was being taken from the Sundance! My thoughts screamed, "I don't want to leave this Arbor. I'm not done with my Sundance!"

Boldly, I grabbed for the rafters and yelled at the eagle to let me down, that I didn't want to break the circle. I reached out with both arms. When I grabbed the rafter, I felt the pain in my chest where the eagle's talons had pierced my flesh. The spotted eagle kept flapping his wings hard, then harder and stronger. It was as if he were trying to break my grip from the rafter. Desperately, I hung on. His huge wings were so powerful for a moment I felt like letting go. Then I felt the power of our Sundance and the importance of not breaking the Sacred Circle, so I hung on.

Suddenly, one then another of his talons started ripping out of my chest.

I felt the pain then. It was a good pain because I knew that I was not to leave the Sundance. I was not going to break the Sacred Circle.

As the last talon ripped out of my flesh, my grip on the rafter finally broke. I landed softly on the floor of the Arbor.

As I woke from my vision, I was still next to my bedroll. I opened my eyes and looked around. Everything was the same as before. The drummers were still singing; the Sundancers were still dancing and going to the Sacred Tree.

Had it only been a dream?

Had it only been thoughts going through my mind? Or hallucinations?

I really wasn't sure what had happened. All I knew was that it seemed real, very real. So real that I still felt pain on both sides of my chest above my breast. I felt as if the eagle's talons had virtually torn out my flesh. It felt so real, I looked down and touched my chest to see if I was bleeding.

I staggered. I had to get on my knees and stand up. I stood swaying and wondering if I would fall. I felt confused as I stood there looking around. Everything was back to normal. Nobody seemed to have noticed a thing that had happened to me.

It had been so real for me that I just knew everyone else must have seen and felt what I did. It took me a few minutes standing there to clear my mind and come back to reality.

As I stood there shaking my head, I looked at the tree. I could feel an intense energy coming to me from it. It was almost like magic. The tree was helping me and giving me strength to continue.

There were also two small trees, freshly cut and placed between each dancer. I got up and felt a coolness come to me from those trees with their bark removed. They were moist and damp.

By now we were all dry, so we accepted gratefully the feel of moisture from those beautiful trees. It was so wonderful to feel dampness on our parched skin.

The singers were still drumming and singing.

I put my eagle whistle in my mouth and rushed at the tree. When I got to it, I embraced it and asked Grandfather to give me strength and direction. I thanked Him for what He had given me and for what He had chosen to let me see. I still didn't realize that it was a vision.

I danced back to my spot and blew furiously on my eagle whistle. I couldn't believe it. I felt like I was getting drops of moisture back into my mouth from my eagle whistle. It was wetting the inside of my mouth at first, then I felt my throat moisten. I was getting help from the Creator and the strength and courage needed to survive this very hard Sundance.

The elder had warned me to be careful, that some dances were more difficult than others, and this one was proving to be just that. It was overwhelming, almost more than I could take, but I feel it was also a test by the Creator. As though He were telling me, "You had an easy one. Now try a hard one."

Suddenly, I felt so good with that little bit of moisture in my mouth and my throat. I felt happy. I started looking around at my brother Sundancers and thinking, "I'm going to make it. This is it. I have had the sign that tells me I am going to finish the Sundance."

I looked at everyone and noticed they were going through difficulties. They were dehydrated and suffering. I started praying for them, saying, "Grandfather, help my brothers," and the answer I got for my prayers was almost like electricity. Slowly the whole Sundance seemed to start picking up and getting more life into it. Even the singers and the drummers perked up. The energy had changed. It was so beautiful that everyone felt happy. The dancers looked better, and it was getting toward evening and was becoming cooler.

The dance continued, and I had no problems after that. Late that evening, as everything finished, the drummers went back to camp. We were finished for the day.

Tired from the long, hot day, the Sundancers lay down and rested. This was Sunday night. We knew that the hardest, longest part of the Sundance was over. We knew the next day would be the last. Everything was right.

I lay there thinking, thanking the Creator for helping me as he did in that one special moment. I got up from my bedroll and walked to where the Sundance Chief was sitting on the west side of the Arbor. As is tradition when seeking counsel, I brought him some tobacco.

I shook his hand, sat down, and said, "I want to share something with you. I need some guidance from you."

He asked, "What do you need?"

He didn't even know my name because so many Sundancers come and go every year that he can't keep track of everyone.

I told him what had happened to me that day, how I had suffered. I told him how, in a way, I wish it had happened in the middle of the Arbor so everybody would have known about it.

He said, "That's okay, it was only supposed to happen to you. It's your vision. My interpretation is that there are other Sundances. The Lakota people pierce their chest. I think the spirits were telling you that you have to do that some day. Also that you are to help heal others, no matter who they are. But not yet, not until you are ready."

I asked, "Why do they bring the vision to me here?"

He explained, "Because that was one time that your mind, body, and spirit were ready and open to receive this message. So it came to you in a very sacred place. Then you would know that it was real and not just your imagination. It wasn't just a dream or just a thought. This did happen to you. This is how we get our visions."

He answered my questions, and it scared me to death. Just the thought of piercing made me ache all over. I thought, "My God, I can't do that." However, that was his answer.

I asked him one final thing, "When do I have to do this?"

He said, "When you are at the Sundance the first time, you make a four-year commitment. The reason the Spirits demand this is so that they can see that you are sincere in following the Sundance spirituality and traditions. You must go to the Lakota Sundance and pierce as your vision told you, but first you must finish your four years with the Shoshoni people."

After receiving the interpretation of my vision, I returned to my bedroll and lay down. Everybody was starting to get into their blankets because the air was starting to get a little chilly.

I lay quiet for a while, just listening to the sounds. By the center of the Arbor the guards started their fire and kept it going all night. As I drifted off to sleep, my mind was full of wonder at what had happened. I couldn't believe my mouth had saliva. It was no longer dry like it had been for two days. The last thing I recall was looking through the branches of the Arbor leaves, at the stars.

I woke about one or two o'clock in the morning. It was cold, and the wind was blowing very hard. We got hit by a big storm that night. It was almost like an answer to all of our prayers. We couldn't touch or allow any water to touch our lips or go into our mouths, but we could feel the humidity in the air. When you're parched the way we were, moisture can be absorbed through the skin.

At the Sundance, many people said not to let water touch you in any way—even on the arms, the hands, or the face—when it rains. It just makes your body cry out for more moisture, and when it doesn't get it, the suffering is twice as hard as it was before.

It was cold, windy, and stormy all night. We had quite a bit of rain, but by morning it was clear. It was Monday, so we all got up and put on the best shawl skirt that we had. We put on our finery because we wanted to look good. We wanted to show that, although it was hard on us, we were proud of what we had done and of the suffering we had endured. Proud to be allowed the privilege to pray for other people.

The Creator had seen fit to let us survive, to live and talk about what we had experienced. We knew we had done our small part. Everybody got ready and greeted the sun. We always get up before the sun rises, to greet it and allow its warmth into our hearts.

The dancing went on for the remainder of the morning. Finally we concluded the Sundance that Monday afternoon at about one o'clock. Leaving the Arbor was the same as before: we got our watermelon, and people thanked and greeted us. It was such a joyous occasion. It felt as if every breath we took, every second of thirst we suffered, was all worthwhile simply because of the gratitude shown by the people who waited for us to leave the Arbor.

In preparing the Arbor, some people endure much hardship and strenuous work. They keep us going with their support. They cook for and feed the drummers and singers. There is so much to do, it's almost easier to be inside the Arbor dancing than to be outside.

It is toughest on the Sundance Chief. Four days before the Sundance, during the purification days, the Sundance Chief has one full week of fasting. He allows himself only a very small amount of liquids, such as coffee or tea, but never water in its pure state. For a full week, the Sundance Chief already suffers. Then he suffers, fasts, and is without water with us for three and four days during the Sundance. Finally, for four days after the Sundance, he prays and gives thanks for all we received.

Tuesday morning I got up and went outside. I saw the Chief's lonely figure standing there in the middle of the desert. He raised his pipe and arms to the Great Spirit, the east, and the rising sun.

When a man is chosen by the Spirits to be a spiritual leader, he must be willing to lead by example. He can't ask others to do things he hasn't done himself. That's the reason he starts his ceremonies and suffering long before the dancers have arrived.

It is such a beautiful ceremony, but it is not for the weakhearted nor the timid. It takes great courage to be a Sundance Chief, to commit yourself to that sacrifice. It's not easy. Anybody who sacrifices for another should be respected and helped in any way possible.

My family and I returned to Oklahoma and continued our daily quest for our livelihood.

Early the next summer, we left Oklahoma so that we could attend powwows before the Sundance. The powwows we go to are gatherings of people where natives from many different tribes dance for competition, and where local people get the opportunity to buy arts and crafts from the people who make them. We attended a couple of small powwows in Colorado and then went to Taos to see some acquaintances.

We had been there a few days when Carpio, a friend we were staying with, asked me to drive his car down to Santa Fe. They were having auditions for extras for the miniseries, *Gambler III*, with Kenny Rogers. To make a long story short, although reluctant at first, my whole family ended up as extras on the set. I played a Sioux chief.

Before the shooting of the film started, I asked Kenny Rogers' brother Leland if they wanted to have a Sweat Lodge with us. After agreeing to it, we built it right on the movie grounds. There were several of us, including Kenny Rogers; his brother Leland; the producer, Ken Kragen; and the director, Dick Lowry. It was a good sweat. Kenny was surprised at how long we were in the lodge.

It was fun being with people who were new to the Sweat Lodge ceremony; they were great. It was here I met Larry Sellers, a Sundancer from Rosebud, South Dakota. Immediately after they filmed my segment, we left for the Sundance.

We went through the usual ritual, preparing our eagle whistles and getting our ceremonial outfits ready. Of course, it was always good to see the people at the Sundance. They became very important friends to us.

The Sundancers greeted me more enthusiastically than they had my first and second years. They made me feel like I was one of them now. The days passed as the Sundance came and went. It wasn't quite as hard as my second one, but it was still tough. Everyone suffered quite a bit. Thirst was again a major factor in my suffering.

I always prayed for my family, my wife, and my children. I especially prayed for my father and mother, that their health would last and they would be well. Also that my father would come to accept me with my long hair.

On Sunday I saw something that almost caused me to have a nervous breakdown.

It all began when the drummers were taking their noon break, and we had only one group singing for us. Most of us were just resting. Some guys were asleep. I was lying on my bedroll. The man next to me was one whom I had looked up to and respected since I had met him. Though he was younger than I, he had been around the Sundance all his life, so in my book, that made him pretty special. At the time, he hadn't been married long, but he and his Cheyenne wife had a small baby.

Right outside the Arbor, she was sitting with the baby. In the guise of showing him the baby underneath the baby's blanket, I saw the woman hand him the baby's bottle full of water. And I saw him put the nipple of the bottle in his mouth and start sucking on it.

I was shocked. I turned and looked at my wife, sitting in her chair just beyond me. She also had a surprised look on her face. I asked her, "Did you just see what I saw?" She nodded her head. She couldn't say anything. I then asked him, "What in the world are you doing, man?" Although I tried, I couldn't quite keep the anger out of my voice.

He tried to be casual about it and said, "Oh, it's okay, I'm just rinsing my mouth out."

Angrily I retorted, "If it's all right, why don't they let all of us do that?"

"It's okay, it's okay, Manny," he said, trying to calm me. He didn't want anyone else to know what I had seen.

It devastated me. All I could think of was, once again I'm being let down hard. Maybe I just demand too much from others. Maybe I expect too much. I'm not very tolerant when a word is given. I'm not one to forgive going back on a man's word.

He immediately returned the bottle to his wife. My wife was livid, as she also took the Sundance very seriously. She told his wife to take the baby back to camp and not bring water to the Arbor ever again. His wife got up and almost ran from the Arbor. She knew they had done something profoundly wrong. They also knew that it wasn't a secret any longer. Someone had seen what they had done. I turned my back to him and didn't even want to see his face. I was deeply hurt by what he had done.

Now thinking back, I wonder if I had judged him too harshly. Did I have the right to judge him at all? He didn't hurt me, he only hurt himself. Then again, everything that occurs within the Sundance circle does affect everyone in it. Did he in fact weaken our spiritual strength? Were all of our prayers answered? Or were some left unanswered because of his actions?

I think most of my anger was because he used an innocent child to cheat. The breakdown didn't happen until the next day, when I had had all night to think about it. After the sun-greeting ceremony, I called Allen aside and told him what I had seen. He couldn't believe it either.

During the telling, a combination of hunger, thirst, fatigue, and emotion surged through me. The result was devastating. I was distraught and heavily disappointed. I even tried to give away my pipe. It's hard to write what I felt, how hopeless everything looked because of one man's actions. I was crying in front of my brother Allen and couldn't seem to control myself.

This is when I believe I had my spiritual breakdown. He understood and waited patiently until my grief had expended itself. For days afterwards, I felt empty and cheated.

In retrospect I believe it was indeed a spiritual breakdown. Since then, I've given the experience a tremendous amount of thought and have realized that I learned two important lessons. First, the experience showed me that no matter how deeply embedded in spirituality anyone is, the fact remains that we are still scared, lonely, and weak human beings. Second, I learned that no man should be put up on a pedestal; no one human being is above reproach. If you put someone up on a pedestal, they will surely fall some day. This has been demonstrated repeatedly with religious and spiritual leaders. Perhaps the Creator is showing us to rely on ourselves and Him only.

At the end of the Sundance, something else dramatic happened to me. As I was coming out, we were all happy, tired, and hungry. We were very thirsty, and the people were standing outside, greeting us and shaking our hands. While walking up, I looked to my right. Just beyond the people sitting in front was an older woman. Our eyes made contact. I just smiled, nodded my head, and went on. When I got to the end of the line, they handed me a watermelon. I turned left, and a young man came and touched my right shoulder. He said, "Excuse me, sir. Would you pray for my mom?"

I couldn't hear him too well because he had mumbled the request and there was so much noise. People were talking to each other and laughing and congratulating the Sundancers. I wasn't feeling normal yet. I frowned and looked at him. I said, "I am sorry, what did you say? My throat is very dry." I could hardly speak.

Again, he repeated, "My mom wants to know if you will pray for her."

It took a second for me to comprehend this. I asked, "Why me?"

"She wants you to pray for her. No one else."

"I'm just a Sundancer, I'm not a medicine man," I said lightly.

"That's okay," he went on. "She wants you, no one else, to pray for her."

"I would be honored, if she thinks I'm the right person."

"Yes, you are the one she wants."

I turned around, handed my wife the watermelon, and said, "I will be right back."

I went with him to his mother, who was sitting down. She had the most beautiful face, a wise-looking face. She had long gray hair, and was so regal, so elegant, you would have sworn she came from the ancient courts of Europe.

To be so honored in this way, to pray for one of our elders, is an honor beyond description. I was close to tears. I knelt down before her and looked in her eyes. I asked quietly, "Grandmother, am I the one you called for? I'm not a medicine man. I'm just a Sundancer."

"Yes, I want you to pray for me, son. I feel that you can do something to help me."

"Please tell me how can I help you?"

She explained, "I have arthritis throughout my body so bad I can hardly walk. I can't walk without a cane or someone helping me. If you could just bring me a little relief from the pain I would be grateful."

So, I put my hand on her right knee, grabbed hold of both her hands with my left hand, and started praying. I don't recall what I said, but I know that I was praying so hard that tears came to my eyes. I tried with all my energies within me. I don't know what to call it, it could have been a personal contact with God, maybe. She might have thought that I was able to do more than just a prayer.

I guess I prayed for two or three minutes. As I stood up, I said, "Grandmother, I feel very inadequate in doing what you ask of me. I have done the best I can. I know it wasn't very long, but I'm tired and very thirsty."

With relief on her face, she said, "That is all I wanted, for you to touch me and say a little prayer."

"Before I leave," I told her, "I want you to understand one thing. Although this prayer was short, I am not through praying for you. For the next four days no matter where

I am, I will be praying for you. I will pray that you receive help."

"That's all I want," she said gratefully. "Thank you."

As I turned to leave, I touched her shoulder and walked to where my family was waiting. While walking away, I turned to look back at the woman and her son, but they had vanished. On our way back to camp, my wife asked me, "What did she want?"

I said, "Just a prayer. That's all she wanted was a prayer and a little relief from her pain."

I felt very humbled by the experience. She had chosen me out of seventy-five other Sundancers. To me that was a great honor. Had this been a reward for my faith? Was what I had seen the other Sundancer do a test of my beliefs, a test of my faith in the Spirits and the Sundance? Had the Spirits seen in me a man who believes in them so much that they granted me the ability to help others with prayer?

That night I went out by myself away from all the other people camped there and prayed for her.

I never knew her name, that beautiful lady. I've never forgotten her or her energy. I wish now I had asked her name, or to know her children, her grandchildren. I went and prayed, and for some reason it was so intense that I cried for her again.

Now I stop and look back at that experience and realize it was a test for me. Perhaps she was sent to help me learn a lesson. We believe that sometimes the Creator sends a helper to teach us. If she was a helper, I think her mission was to show me I was now ready to help people. In helping her, it gave me confidence in my ability to help others. I believe that through her, Grandfather was showing me how close I was to my vision coming true.

Though I was tired, thirsty, and wanting to eat the watermelon in my hand, would I give that pleasure up to help someone unknown to me? If it was a test, I suppose I passed it.

The following morning we left and traveled toward South Dakota. I'm not sure why we headed in that direction, we were just going. I kept listening to the radio for information about tornadoes: where they were going, and how far away from us they were. One crossed in front of us, and one crossed behind. We came to a little town called Valentine, Nebraska, and camped at a trailer park. That night, I went out.

While I was praying for her, a big thunderstorm came. For some reason, when I prayed for her I became emotional again, maybe because I was still fresh from the Sundance. There was thunder, lightning, and hail, so I had to cut the prayer short, but that didn't take away any of its power.

We left there the next morning and passed through Mission, South Dakota, and the Rosebud Reservation. At the time, I never knew what my connection might be to that area, or what pulled me there. We drove through the village of Parmalee, South Dakota, and stopped at a small store, way out of the way. I don't know why I asked the owner, "Are there any Sundances going on around here?"

He said, "Yes, there is one going on." Then he gave me directions.

However, my wife said she wasn't ready for another Sundance so soon after the last one, so I let her talk me out of it. I'm not going to put the blame on her. I was also tired, and the Sundance had worn me out. That summer before we left for the Sundance, we had looked around and found a house in southwestern Colorado. We put a down payment on it and told them we'd return after the Sundance, so we headed back in that direction.

Not long after that, I made a sales trip up around

Jackson Hole, Wyoming, and up through Fort Washakie, where the Sundance took place. I made a swing back toward Denver, Colorado, but before getting to Denver, I got very sick. I was out of energy and had trouble holding my head up.

I got to the convention center, where they were having a native arts and crafts show. While there I got a booth and set up my arts and crafts to do some retailing, but during the show, I almost fell down twice. I didn't know what was going on. At first I thought maybe I was just hungry, but I had eaten plenty, so I knew it couldn't be that.

The second time it happened, I almost fell out of the chair. Some concerned friends took me to a male nurse on the grounds. The nurse asked, "What's the problem?"

I said, "I think I've had a heart attack."

The guy went haywire. He was in worse shape than I was. He started to shake and say, "Ah, ah, ah, ah . . . I better call 911 . . . uh . . . the ambulance." He looked around frantically. He couldn't find the phone, and all the time it was sitting right next to him.

As sick as I felt, it was still comical watching his reaction to the situation. He finally got an ambulance for me. When they got me in it, they checked me out, put me on an IV, and sped me to the hospital. They were still checking me out as the ambulance raced through the traffic. At the hospital, they put me on a cardiovascular receiver and discovered that I'd had two minor strokes within an hour. I didn't even know what was going on. I thought it was just bad dizzy spells. Then they told me that when I got back home I should check with my doctor to see what was wrong.

At the time, I didn't even have a family doctor, so I just found one in Durango, Colorado, who told me my biggest problem was that I had serious high blood pressure. Apparently, it affects some people more at high altitudes. And we had just bought a house two or three months before that sits over eight thousand feet high! There I was staggering around. I couldn't do anything. I was almost totally unable to function at home.

I told my wife and kids I couldn't handle it. I had to move to a lower altitude, so we moved back to Oklahoma.

We returned to the town of Inola and found a house to rent. The following summer I got sick, and my blood pressure was up again, so I couldn't make it to the Sundance. Allen called me and said they had moved the Sundance grounds from up on the mesa, where I had been Sundancing for three years, back to downtown Fort Washakie. He continued, "I'm not going to the Sundance this year. I don't like that place. Too many drunks come around yelling obscenities at us and stuff. It's not a good place for a Sundance. So I won't be going."

Throughout the sickness, with everything I had gone through, I felt empty—as though a big piece of my life had been cut out by not going to the Sundance. Yet I knew that healthwise I wasn't ready, and the location wasn't good for me. So, I thought, this is the way it's supposed to be.

That year would have been my fourth year.

In my mind I couldn't picture myself going back to the Sundance if I had to sit and listen to drunks and other people who didn't believe our way. By now I figured that I wasn't going back to the Shoshoni Sundance. I asked Larry, the Sundancer from Rosebud, if I could finish my fourth Sundance there.

He said, "Of course you can, Manny. You're more than welcome to come with us. We'll help you any way that we can."

Three weeks before the Shoshoni Sundance the phone rang, and it was Allen.

"What's going on?" I asked.

He said, "The Sundance is back on, Bud. It's back on the mesa where you danced your first three years." He was very enthusiastic and happy. "You're going to love it. It's really going to be a good one this year."

I groaned, "Oh my God, I already committed this summer to the Rosebud Sundance with Larry." I explained everything to Allen. He seemed crestfallen, but told me to do what I had to do.

Now I was sick to my stomach. I really didn't know what to do. The Shoshoni people honored me by allowing me to dance with them. I couldn't let them down. So I told Allen, "I'll be there."

He said, "Okay."

When I told my wife that it was back on in Wyoming, she said, "What are you going to do about South Dakota?"

I said, "Well, we'll go to the Shoshoni, and I'll dance there. Then we'll go to South Dakota and tell Larry that I've already finished my four years."

So, that year we went. We prepared just like the other three years.

Incidentally, when you make a commitment for four years, nothing says you have to do them consecutively. The agreement with the Creator is to dance four years. If it takes you six years to finish four years, that's fine, just as long as you finish them.

We went there, we prepared, I Sundanced, and it was a very hard one. I want to point out that I hardly ever mention hunger because hunger is not a factor. When you get so dry, you forget everything else. What really becomes prominent is your thirst. The hunger you can live with. You can go several days without eating. Although the first twenty-four hours without food can be hard, after that it gets easier. So, we went through the Sundance. Other than its difficulty, and losing another twenty-five pounds from lack of moisture, it was a good Sundance, and a beautiful one.

There's nothing common about any Sundance, they are all difficult and have special things that happen when you're there. Although it would be hard to top my second and third Sundances, because of my vision and somebody asking me to pray for them, it was still special.

We finished with the Sundance and said our farewells to all our friends. Before the Sundance was over, I had brought my gifts for the giveaway and honored the drum by giving gifts to the drummers. It is our way of thanking the spirit of the drum. It doesn't matter that it was not the same drum I had been dancing with the previous years. I was giving thanks. That was my giveaway; I had to have a giveaway because it was my fourth Sundance and I was finishing my commitment.

I honored many of my friends whom I had danced with for four years, who had encouraged me and had given me strength or energy to get through rough spots. I honored Allen, Benny, Edgar—the Sundance Chief—and most of all I thanked and honored the Creator. I asked Him to look after my family, I was deeply grateful to Him for helping me these four years.

After it was over, we drove north to Rapid City. When we were looking for Larry, we visited another Sundance because we heard he might be there. When we stopped, we saw men dancing and piercing, which frightened my wife. She wouldn't even get out of the van. Although she wouldn't admit it, she was deathly afraid of the piercing ceremony, even just seeing it through the bushes that lined the camp. This was also the first time I had seen it from the outside, and I realized I was glad I'd finished my four years. Frankly, the whole scene scared me, too.

We ended up in Mission, South Dakota. We got a few groceries there and tried to find Larry. I already had directions. We went to where his stepmother lived and found him.

Grinning, he said, "You're sure here early. The Sundance isn't until this coming weekend."

I explained cautiously, "Larry, we just came by to tell you that I can't do the Sundance. I have already finished my four years. They called me and told me that the Shoshoni Sundance was on again. That's where we are coming from."

"That's okay, Manny. I appreciate you coming by and letting me know, instead of just not showing up. No, you've got no obligation except to yourself. If that satisfies you, it should be good enough for everybody else."

I didn't know what he meant at the time, although I would find out later.

W E S T — B L A C K

"S e t t i n g   S u n"

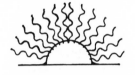

D A Y ' S   E N D

After we left Larry's house, there was an eerie silence in the van. When I told Larry that I wasn't going to be dancing with them, I felt an emptiness inside that I couldn't explain. Then I got to thinking about what he had said to me about my being satisfied with fulfilling my commitment.

What he didn't say was that I had made that commitment not only to myself but to the Creator as well. I realized that my commitment had been made for me by my vision. I kept remembering my vision and thinking about what it meant for me. It had been so vivid, I couldn't just forget it.

We headed back to Oklahoma, and when we arrived home Sunday evening, I knew it was when the Rosebud Sundancers were going through the purification ceremony. The actual Sundance wouldn't start until the following Thursday.

Monday I worked in our shop all day. But no matter how hard I worked, I couldn't tear the thought from my mind that I was abandoning the Creator by not completing my commitment. Although my promise was made under unusual circumstances, that is what Larry had meant. I said I'd be there, and the Creator wasn't going to let me forget it easily. He was going to make me uncomfortable.

Tuesday morning I got up and worked again all day, making crafts—lances, war clubs, and war shields—trying to get the thought of the Sundance out of my mind. Most of my time at the shop was spent alone. My kids were in school and my wife was at home.

By Wednesday morning I couldn't handle it anymore. I was watching CNN to see what had happened during the night while I was asleep, when my wife walked in and said good morning.

I said, "I'm going to the Sundance."

"I knew it, I could feel it," she said. "I'm surprised you waited until Wednesday, I thought you were leaving Monday morning. I've got your suitcase all packed. I fixed you some sandwiches after you went to bed, so you are all ready to go."

"I am really sorry I am spending this time and money going."

She said, "You know you have to go."

She knew about my commitment, she just didn't want any part of it because, unlike the Shoshoni Sundance, the Lakota Sundance involves the piercing and ripping of flesh. I can't blame her for fearing it either, because it is something alien to many people. They find it hard to accept seeing other human beings suffer, but that's all part of our prayers.

I drove all day and all night. When I arrived the next morning, they were already in the Sundance. Heartbroken because I had tried so hard to make it, I found Larry. Everyone greeted me and made me feel welcome. My friend Steve's sister, Chrys, and I walked to the Arbor. I saw Larry and Steve, and they were happy to see me.

Larry said, "You came back, did you?"

"I had to, Larry."

With a knowing smile on his face, he nodded his head. As though he knew that I would be there, but also that I had to find out myself.

He said, "Look Manny, get yourself together, get some rest today because it isn't easy. It's really hard. You can come in tomorrow morning."

"I could use some rest," I said gratefully.

When I got back to camp, the women there to support Sundancers told me what I needed: a head crown of sage wrapped in cloth, ankle and wrist bands in the same material, and a skirt. They got some long stems of sage for me and helped me put everything together.

The next morning I lay there for the longest time, wide awake, anxious to get going into this new Sundance the Creator was showing me. I felt excited and nervous. I don't know how much I slept that night, but it couldn't have been long.

When it was time to get up my stomach lurched. This was it. I jumped up and went over to Steve's tent and called him. He got up, and we put our towels around us and walked barefoot to the sweat lodges. It is an exhilarating feeling to be up that early for such a special occasion.

But this Sundance was a lot different from the others. They had four sweat lodges behind the Arbor, and the fire pit was burning. The flames were high. Several people started to gather.

The morning air was cool. As we walked up to the sweat lodges, I had a little tingling sensation at the pit of my stomach. I felt apprehensive, somewhat nervous, and a little scared, and so many things were going through my mind. I kept thinking of the vision that I had had two or three years before.

The first thing I felt was the heat from the big fire. It was warm and friendly and seemed to wash my apprehension from me. Not only did the fire have a calming, soothing effect on me, it also seemed to relax everyone else. There is something very special about the fires that are heating up the Stone People (we show the stones respect because they are so important in that ceremony) for the sweat lodges, getting them ready to bring us their breath. We would have our bodies, minds, spirits, and energies purified by them.

As we walked away from the sweat lodges, we heard someone call. The faint and muffled voice from the sweat lodge said, "Come on in, we've got room for two more." Made of slim branches, the sweat lodges are small enclosures built low to the ground and covered with blankets to help keep in the steam. So we got down on our hands and knees, and crawled into the sweat lodge.

When entering any Lakota sweat lodge, a person always says the words *"Mitakuye Oyasin,"* which mean "all my relations." A very loose interpretation is that you're asking the spirits to cover all the people of the world in your prayers. We believe we are all related, which is why the Sundance colors are red, yellow, white, and black: the four races. We are all one people.

When we got in the sweat lodge, the leader called out, "All right, bring me seven rocks, seven Grandfather rocks." By that, he meant he wanted some rocks about the size of a head. The fire keeper walked over to the fire pit with a pitch-fork and got the first rock. As he brought it into the lodge, the leader guided it into a special spot and placed it in the small hole in the center of the lodge. They repeated the process six more times.

As each rock was brought in, one Sundancer sprinkled a few pieces of cedar on top of the hot rocks. Right away they started popping and sending out a beautiful, rich scent of cedar into the sweat lodge. All of us were sitting there, waiting solemnly.

The Sweat Lodge is a very important ceremony in our culture. Anyone who has been in one knows how close you are to the other people. Almost immediately after the first stone was set in the hole, the sweat started beading up on my forehead. It trickled down my neck and back. It was so pleasant after coming in from the cool air outside.

When the seventh stone was in place, they brought a bucket of water. We asked a blessing for it from the Grandfather rocks, then closed the door flap, plunging our-selves into total darkness.

Once we leave the sweat lodge, there is never a discus-sion about what we heard or talked about while inside. If someone discusses anything heard in the sweat lodge when they go outside, we believe the problem returns to the person talking about it. The whole purpose of the Sweat Lodge ceremony is to leave all your problems inside, and to ask for blessings on all of our relatives. We also give thanks that we are all at the Sundance, and we ask for strength and the courage to go through it.

All I could think of was the sensation I had had during my vision, and my chest, after three years, began to itch again. I admit that I felt a little bit of dread and hoped that I wouldn't fail.

It was a quick, one-round sweat, which is traditional in

the Lakota Sundance, because we purify each morning before entering the Sacred Arbor and every night after leaving. Sometimes the lodges can get pretty hot. Most of the time the Sundance leaders are the ones that run the *Inipi*, or Sweat Lodge ceremony. They are pretty considerate of the dancers and don't want to dehydrate them or cause us to have a harder time within the Sundance.

We came out of the Sweat Lodge and shook hands with the others, people I had never met in my life. Coming out of the Sweat Lodge is like being born again. Going in there and leaving behind all our aches, pains, and troubles feels like starting life all over, without any human or spiritual problems.

In essence, we are all coming from our Mother Earth's womb, the Sweat Lodge. Some believe that because we sweat together, we become brothers and sisters—even though there is a separate Sweat Lodge for the women. This time there were many female Sundancers. As givers of life, the women brought a very powerful, beautiful, and special energy into the Sundance.

The leaders allowed us each to take one blanket and put it under the Arbor. Between songs we could rest and pray. I was very nervous and scared, especially since I had seen others get their chests pierced. I prayed. I asked Grandfather to please help me, to give me the courage to do it well, like a warrior, like a man. Like a person who believes, truly believes, in our spirituality. Many others were also praying. I know now there were quite a few new people, just like myself, going in for their first time, although I was one of the older ones.

We started lining up on the west side of the Arbor. It was nice and cool. I thought, "I should have kept my blanket with me." But we couldn't, so we stood there, waiting. I had goosebumps all over my body. There was a beautiful, quiet hush. I could hear the murmur of the people who were still around the fire pit and other Sundancers' voices as they talked quietly.

From way over on the other side of the Arbor we heard one man hit the drum. It seemed to startle everyone, though we had been waiting for it. It took my breath away. Everything stopped, even the murmurs. Now we were all waiting for the first eagle whistle to be blown. The drum sounded again.

That Sacred Drum. The heartbeat of our people sounded to call all the Sundancers, to let them know it was time to come and get into line. It was time to see the sun, greet it, and welcome it into our Sundance, time to sacrifice ourselves for others.

The Sundance Chief blew his eagle whistle loudly, three or four times, and started moving forward. When they saw him move, the drummers started drumming. The slow and measured beat of the drum escorted us into the Sundance Arbor.

Then the song started. Oh, what a beautiful song it was. I had never heard this song in my life until then. It gave me goose bumps all up and down my body. I was choked with pride. These songs have been handed down to younger singers for hundreds of years, and every tribe that has the Sundance ceremony has its own songs in its own language. I was humbled by the knowledge that I was listening to the same songs that Crazy Horse, Sitting Bull, and all the other Sundancers before me had heard.

I felt grateful and honored to be in the lineup with the Lakota warriors and warriors from other tribes. We started blowing on our eagle whistles, first one, then another, and we kept blowing on them. I felt the lurch in my stomach again. The time was drawing near. I was starting my first Lakota Sundance. Overwhelmed, I started blowing my eagle whistle to keep my emotions in check.

People from all the different camps had come out to watch us. They came to see their loved ones, brothers, cousins, and uncles, going into the Sundance. To pray and to support them.

I prayed, "Grandfather, give me strength and courage to do this with honor."

They were drumming and singing the "Going In" song. We believe that good Spirits live in each of the four main directions—east, south, west, and north—so we stopped to honor the four directions, four times, then we entered the Arbor. When I walked in, I became emotional, yet happy. I was finally at the Sundance that I had had a vision about so many years before. Tears filled my eyes. It may not be manly to do this, but I didn't feel bad because I was in the presence of the Creator.

I didn't go to the Sundance for my ego. I went there, humbled, and I wanted my prayers answered. I wanted my family taken care of. As we went in, we made a complete circle inside the Arbor. They went into another song, and the beat picked up, lifting everyone's spirits. It was so good to be alive and in the Arbor.

As the sun rose higher and the sky got brighter, I was overwhelmed at the sight of so many dancers. Men and women, all beautifully dressed, all there together to pray. There were about a hundred of us in there. All the colors the Sundancers wore were bright and beautiful. The traditional Sundance colors—red, yellow, white, black, for the four directions—were visible, as were blue for the sky above, green for the earth below, and purple for the inner spirit.

We danced and danced. I was finally getting over being cold; dancing was warming up my body. I was carrying my own sacred, ceremonial pipe on my left arm, and my eagle-wing fan in my right hand. The bowls of the Sacred Pipes are made from pipestone. There's only one good place that stone is found, in Pipestone, Minnesota. It's believed that the reason it's red is that the stone was colored by the blood that native peoples have shed from war and from suffering. As custom dictates, my pipe was given to me by a friend. A person must never buy his own pipe. We believe that when you need it, it will come to you. As we danced around the Arbor, I felt great and very proud. I had come so far, and I was finally here.

As the day progressed, we went through all the ceremonies. We greeted the sun, and each placed his pipe, or *Chanupa*, down on the altar. We had been dancing about an hour and a half by the time we finished the "Pipe" song, so we took a rest under the Arbor. Right away I saw other people getting marks on their chests and backs, then walking out to the tree to release their ropes. This is part of the preparation for the piercing ceremony. Knowing I would be one of them soon, I felt my stomach lurch as I watched them. My time for being pierced was entirely up to me. It would be done when I asked for it.

That was another thing that made my stomach reel. How long would it take me to decide? Would I have the courage to walk up to a Sundance leader and say, "I am ready to pierce"? Just the thought made me dizzy and swallow hard. As the realization hit me, that I was here to go through with it, I felt alone. My family was not with me. Steve and the others were only acquaintances so far. I had come alone, and I had to stand alone.

There were a couple of Sundancers inside the Arbor who had been pierced the day before. We rested a few minutes, got our blankets situated, and introduced ourselves. I found out that these Sundancers were to stay pierced three or four days. As is customary, they wouldn't break loose until the last day. It impressed me, their tolerance of suffering, their ability to cope with the pain and to withstand all that tugging and pulling on their flesh for four days. It also humbled me.

Suddenly a Sundance leader stood up and said, "*Ho-ka-hey*, come on, let's go, it's time to dance."

Everybody got up, and being the new one, I followed what everybody else did. I was fortunate to have a few friends to explain things to me before they happened. We formed the circle, and the singers started another song. At the time, I didn't know it was a piercing song. We danced and danced, and I noticed a Sundance leader dancing toward another Sundancer, his feet in perfect rhythm with the beat of the drum. The rhythm of his body movements as he danced and moved around portrayed his confidence and pride. His hair, long and flowing, gave him a regal, almost saintly look.

When the Sundance leader reached the man who was being pierced, it was clear that the man was waiting for him. The Sundance leader grabbed his wrist bracelet, and they moved out of the circle, dancing around the Arbor, then to the Sacred Tree.

You can't believe or understand how I felt inside. The dread that was in me was immense. I thought, "What am I doing here? Why did I make this commitment?" With my next breath, I assured myself, "It's okay, this is your vision. You must be here."

So I started praying, "Grandfather, when I go to pierce, please give me the energy and the courage to finish. To do it like a man, a warrior, a spiritual person. Please don't allow me to do anything to dishonor my people and the other Sundancers."

I kept on and danced hard. Maybe I was being a little selfish; some of my prayers were for myself to have the courage to do it right. It's a very hard decision to make, to go there willingly and get pierced. You do it without any anesthetic or any of the modern conveniences to take away the pain. Just to let somebody else cut your flesh takes trust and faith in the Creator. I couldn't believe I was even considering it, but I was.

I spoke to other Sundancers about it, and they told me, "It's a commitment between you and Grandfather. You don't have to do it."

As is human nature, I welcomed a way out, or a way to justify not going through with it. For a few minutes, I thought about not going through with the piercing, but then I realized I didn't come all this way from Oklahoma just to back down. Fear is a small thing to overcome when the rewards are so huge. Making that contact with the Creator, having your prayers answered, means so much more than just a little bit of fear or pain. I realized when the other Sundancers told me I didn't have to pierce, the Spirits had been testing my sincerity and my decision to be there.

We had more pipe songs; during them no one was pierced. Then we had more piercing songs; during these, sometimes as many as six or eight men were pierced.

Many women were dancing and a few were also getting pierced. They would pierce on their arms or wrists. I'm sure it was just as painful as it was for the men.

We then had a piercing song, during which several men were being pierced on their backs. They were tied to several buffalo skulls—each weighing between twenty and thirty pounds—bound together in a row. Depending on the dancer, they would tie three or more skulls together for him to drag.

By dragging the skulls, we honor the buffalo by giving back all that he has given to us. He gave us his blood, flesh, pain, and life, so we could have nourishment to survive. He gave us abundance in all ways. This was our way to show respect and gratitude for *Tatanka*, our buffalo brother, and the sacred tradition. Also, we respect the buffalo because we believe that he is the bearer of courage and strength both physical and spiritual.

We danced for three hours. It was really hot. I was still tired from the Sundance in Wyoming just two weeks before because I hadn't had enough time to recuperate.

As has happened on occasion, sometimes we are short on drummers. Often there will be powwows going on in the immediate area, and many drummers would rather go to the powwows instead of the Sundances. At the Sundances it's all voluntary. Unlike at powwows, no money changes hands. The drummers are fed and given all they want to drink. They are drumming for a spiritual ceremony. So sometimes we are unable to get enough drums, and we have only one or two drum groups to sing. This makes it harder on them, so they have to rest quite a bit. Since all liquids and foods are forbidden around the Arbor, they have to go to our camp or somebody else's camp to eat. Without drummers and singers we can't dance, so we must rest until they come back.

However, this time we had it pretty good. We had three different drum groups, and they kept us busy dancing. We danced and finished out the day.

They allowed us to return to camp on an honor system. Nobody holds an axe over your head and says you can't do this or that. You made the commitment with the Creator. Nobody watches you. If anyone does anything wrong, he or she must answer to the Creator.

This is one of the things I learned. In the Sundance, don't try to be judgmental of everything and everyone. Let people do their own thing, as you do yours. Each of us has a mind of our own, and what is right for one person may be wrong for another. That doesn't mean that it is wrong for both. It only means that we think differently, and we should try to honor and respect other people's ways of thinking.

As my first day ended, I felt energized and knew that

the Spirits had been with me and that my guides had led me to the right place. The other things I had gone through were almost like stepping stones to get me to where I was now. If I felt that I had fallen in love with my first Sundance with the Shoshoni people, I felt even more so that way with the Lakota people. I felt I was home.

I woke up early the next morning because of my anticipation of the day ahead. I've never been one to need an alarm clock. At 3:45 a.m., I was awake. By 4:30 they started calling us.

Steve was already up, and as we headed for the sweat lodges, I knew something was different about my energy. I felt light-headed. I believe I was also feeling the Sundance energy. It's a very tangible thing when you're willing to receive it. For the first time, since taking the Sundance path, I felt strangely at peace with myself and completely unafraid. It wasn't resignation, it was a calm acceptance of whatever the Creator was bringing me. I felt so light on my feet, as if I were gliding instead of walking to the sweat lodges. For a moment I thought maybe my blood pressure was high, but everything was wonderful.

Since developing high blood pressure, I sometimes find it difficult to breathe in the sweat lodge and my blood pressure will rise. I'm not even supposed to go into sweat lodges, according to my doctor, but I do it anyway. I walked up to the fire pit area where they had the fires going to keep the rocks hot. I saw this other man there, who was a Sundance leader.

He looked at me and said, "Come on." He waved at me with his hand. "Join me in the sweat."

I followed right behind him. The sweat lodge filled quickly until there were about thirteen men inside. They brought the rocks in. We sprinkled them with cedar and thanked the Creator for the past two days.

We thanked Him for allowing us to Sundance on this third day, and the Sundance leader started singing the "Four Directions" song in Lakota. I offer the words in English.

> To the West the Sacred Stone Nation
> To the North the Sacred Stone Nation
> To the East the Sacred Stone Nation
> To the South the Sacred Stone Nation
> To the Heavens, Great Spirit, take pity on me
> The People to the Heavens
> Grandfather, take pity on me the family.

I had never been able to sing in the sweat lodge before because the heat was so intense that I was unable to catch my breath. But this time, I found myself clearheaded, and my throat was so clear that I felt a big bubble of joy just burst inside me. I started singing, and sang the whole song with the leader.

I said to myself, "Today I pierce. I pierce first round, first song."

Once I made that commitment, I felt elated. I couldn't believe that I was making a commitment to let someone cut into my chest so my prayers would be heard. I felt very, very humble, as if I were finally *there*.

Each time you learn something more about the Sundance and experience something new, you feel as if you've reached a higher plateau of spiritual understanding. As if you arrived at another place. It's like adding pebbles to the entire pile that is you. You add those small stones one at a time and each of them brings a bit more knowledge.

No matter who we are or how knowledgeable we are, we never stop learning. We never know it all. The Creator is so infinite that He is always feeding little tidbits of information and knowledge so we can become better persons. I cherish every piece of information, every little stone that I can add to that pile. I'm grateful that with all this, the Creator also gives us choices and free will.

Coming out of the sweat lodge, I headed back to camp and never said anything to anybody. I went through the motions of getting ready as if I were in a dream. Everything was close by me. I dressed and was ready in three minutes. When I got to the Arbor, the first person I saw was the Sundance leader who had brought me into the sweat lodge.

"Brother," I said and shook his right hand with both of my hands, "thank you, thank you very much for a wonderful sweat this morning."

He gave me a puzzled look, so I explained about my trouble breathing in the sweat lodge.

"It was the first time I have been able to sing this song all the way through. I feel that it was you who inspired me to sing the way I did."

"I am happy that you sang it with us. Manny, thank you for showing gratitude and respect like this. Not too many people think about it anymore. Though we are spiritual, we forget to give credit where it's due. Thank you for that."

Then I told him, "When we go in, I'm piercing first round."

"*Ho*! I'm glad to hear that," he said smiling.

He knew I was a new man. He knew I had only danced yesterday, but my spiritual energy was so high that he also knew it was time for me to pierce. He asked, "When did you decide? When did you know?"

"When we were singing the 'Four Directions' song, I knew it was time for me to go."

He said, "Okay, it'll be done just the way you want it."
Then I realized that the "Four Directions" song had taken me

back to my vision—to when the spotted eagle and I had soared high in the heavens, when he had shown me where I was to help people, in the four directions.

Now, mentally and emotionally I was ready. Physically, I hoped I was, too. I didn't know what my tolerance for pain was. I'd smashed my fingers and stubbed my toes a few times. I'd even cut myself accidentally in my life. I'd had toothaches and headaches, but could I cope with this? Did I have strength and courage to go through with this ceremony? After thanking the Sundance leader, I went and sat by myself in the Arbor on my blanket.

I felt so alone. I guess that's the way life is when a person faces a challenge. He might have support from friends or relatives, but ultimately we must face pain, heartbreak, and personal trials alone.

I prayed for guidance. I prayed for direction.

All the spirits were coming to me and saying, "This is the time. You are at the right place. It is your turn to offer your flesh, blood, pain, and suffering for the people you want healed. Don't worry. You are ready."

It was a fresh morning in South Dakota. The fire pit, the sweat lodge, Grandfather's breath, the steam coming off the stones, all made memories for me. It stayed burned in my mind, the memory of my first piercing Sundance, my first Lakota Sundance.

Now being a bit wiser, I was committing myself to another four years. I did it without any remorse or hesitation, and without expectations except to ask for blessings from the Creator.

We lined up again. The Sundance Chief started blowing his eagle whistle, so we moved forward. I waited for the dread and fear to start in the pit of my stomach, but my wait was in vain. They never arrived. As we entered the Arbor from the east side, I felt myself calmed by the sound of the drums.

We greeted the sun, prayed, and danced for over an hour and a half. It was a beautiful first song. We placed our pipes, *Chanupas*, at the altar and went to our blankets to rest.

The Sundance leader walked up to me and asked, "Is this it?"

I looked at him, eye to eye, and replied "This is it, Brother."

"Okay, where do you want to be pierced?"

I pointed to the places on my chest.

He asked, "Once or twice?"

"Let's go for both sides. I came from too far away to get pierced on only one side."

He took the time to explain to me, "Manny, this is your first time, are you sure you want both sides? Most new guys and first-timers will only pierce once to make sure they can endure the pain."

"I'm sure. I want both sides done. I can do it. The Spirits came to me this morning and told me that I was ready."

He says, "That's fine. It's all up to you." So he marked both sides of my chest. When my friends saw that my chest was marked, they came and shook my hand. They told me to be strong, to have courage.

One Sundance leader, Lessert, said, "Manny, it's painful, but you're a warrior. Don't worry."

"Lessert, I want you and Norbert to do the piercing for me. Will you?"

Laughingly, he replied, "You bet we will. How many you want?"

I asked Steve if I could use his rope, so we left the Arbor, untied the rope, and laid it out. By now I had time to think again. My stomach and brain were turning. I was getting very nervous. My heart was beating faster and faster. I kept telling myself this was my decision. This is where I should be. This is where the Creator wanted me to be.

The next song started, and Lessert yelled, *"Ho-ka-hey."* We all got in line in our appropriate places and danced out. Every time we danced, we ended up in the same spot. I felt good.

From then on it was almost like a whirlwind of action. Henry, an art professor at the University of Maryland, who would become a very dear friend of mine, knew I was going to pierce because of the marks on my chest. He grabbed my wrist and gently pushed me forward out of my spot. This way the Sundance leaders knew I was piercing.

The Sundance leader danced up to me. He grabbed my sage wrist bracelet and took me around the Arbor, always going clockwise until we got to the west side.

He took me to the tree and said, "Brother, you are going to experience something very, very sacred. You are going to be very close to God, to the Creator. Make the most of this time because you will be one on one with Him right now."

He continued, "This tree is a sacred tree. It'll give you confidence and courage. It represents God. Ask it for whatever you want. Give it your prayers, respect, honor, and it will do as you wish. This is the place where many good men, good warriors, come to pray."

Then he left me, and I stood there for a few minutes. I prayed. I felt reluctant to leave the tree when another Sundance leader came and asked, "Are you ready?"

It seemed everything started to move in slow motion, perhaps because I was anticipating the event, but it didn't seem to be happening quickly enough.

With a nervous smile, I nodded *yes*.

They laid me down on a buffalo robe.

I handed them my scalpel.

They took the crown off my head.

They said to put it in my mouth.

They told me to bite down on my crown, because the piercing is very painful.

Lessert said, "If you will pray, and pray hard to the Creator it won't hurt because He'll be answering your prayers."

I lay there on the ground, looking up into the sky. Then I handed Lessert my piercing bones. He got down on his knees next to me, and his father knelt by my left side.

I felt both of them grab my chest and rub it with some dirt, because I was sweaty and slippery. This way their thumbs and fingers wouldn't slip.

They pinched up my skin, and I felt as the knife went into my flesh.

I felt a sharp, intense pain in my chest, as if somebody had put a red-hot iron on my flesh.

I lost all sense of time.

I couldn't hear any sounds.

I didn't feel the heat of the sun.

I tried to grit my teeth, but I couldn't—my crown was in my mouth.

I prayed to the Creator to give me strength, to give me courage. I was doing it for my children. I begged that the Creator look after my children, their health and happiness. That all their needs be taken care of.

Then I felt them do something else.

They were putting my piercing bone through the wound.

As Lessert was tying it up, I felt something on the left side of my chest. I was concentrating so much on my prayers that to me it felt like somebody tugging on my arm. I barely noticed. When Les got through tying my rope around my piercing bone, he and his father grabbed my arms. Les said, "Come on, get up. You're done."

I said, "Wait a minute, Lessert. I want both sides pierced."

He said, "They are."

I looked down, and you know what?—I was pierced on the left side, too. Yet I had felt absolutely nothing. I felt nothing because my prayers to the Creator gave me courage and strength to endure.

When I stood up, I did feel pain. I felt pain, but I also felt that closeness with the Creator. I felt like crying for all the people who needed my prayers. I prayed they could get enough to eat. I prayed for all the people who are sick in the world. It brought tears to my eyes. It shamed me to have tears appear, because I thought if the other dancers saw them, they might think I was crying because of the pain. But the pain did not compare to what I was receiving from this sacred experience. The rope at my end was tied to the two piercing bones in my chest. The other end was tied to the Sacred Tree about twenty feet from the bottom. I was tied to the tree with that rope as securely as a child is tied to its mother by the umbilical cord. The only way off that cord was by ripping myself off.

Lessert told me to go ahead and get into place, wherever I wanted to dance. I pulled my rope and danced out. I was dancing because they were still drumming and singing. It was still going on. I will never forget those songs. They are so beautiful, so calming. I went out as far as my rope would reach. I leaned back and the flesh on my chest pulled out tight. As I was praying to the tree, I could feel the pain in my chest. All my friends had come around to stand behind me and give me support, to receive that energy from me. All that energy I was going to pull down from the sun to help us, to help answer our prayers.

Running through my mind were thoughts of disbelief that I was actually doing this. Every time I leaned back on my rope, I felt intense pain in my chest. It became a raw ache that reached all the way down to my toes. Every time I looked at my piercing bones, I saw the faces of my children. I knew this was for their protection and my way of giving my pain for them. This was why Grandfather had brought me here.

It felt glorious and explosive. The energy was high and brilliant. I danced and then Lessert waved at me with his fan. He said, *"Ho-ka!"* as he pointed at the tree. "Go to the tree and pray."

I got to the tree, knelt beside it, and put my arms around it. I thought of my mother and father. I asked *Tunkashila*, Grandfather, to watch over them, then danced back to my spot and pulled back on the rope again.

One dancer next to me whispered, "Pull back, pull it tight. Stretch your flesh. It will break easier when you're ready to break loose."

Looking into my eyes, Steve danced in front of me with his eagle fan; he started tapping and hitting on my rope in a downward motion. He was trying to help me stretch the flesh.

I smiled at him and said, *"Wo-Pila.* Thank you, Steve."

Again, Les waved his eagle fan and yelled, *"Ho-ka-hey."*

Then I went back to the tree and prayed the second time. Embracing the tree, I could smell the warm cloth wrapped around it. The tree felt soft because there was so much cloth from the many people who had tied on their prayer ties. They wanted their prayers answered. I danced back to my spot.

Les yelled, *"Ho-ka,"* a third time.

I went to the tree and prayed. I prayed for everyone that I could think of. I prayed for people I didn't know, I prayed for all those I might meet during the coming year. There is so much to pray about. So many people that need prayers. It boggles the mind to remember people by name, or try to remember those who need your prayers to heal them.

Finally he said, "*Ho-ka,*" for the fourth and final time.

I danced back to the Sacred Tree. Again, I embraced it. I knew that when I left here I would be breaking free from it. It would be like separating myself from my mother, like breaking the umbilical cord. I would be free. I prayed for the courage to break loose on my first attempt.

Lessert walked up to me and said, "When you go this time, go fast, go hard. You have to break loose. The only way you can get off this rope is to break away and tear the flesh out. So run backwards fast. Don't worry, those guys will catch you."

I prayed to Grandfather: "This is it. You brought me this far, please don't fail me now. Give me the courage to finish this piercing ceremony like a man, like a warrior."

As I finished my prayer, I started running.

I went back, back. I looked at the tree and said silently, "Grandfather, please give me strength."

I ran faster and faster and faster.

I hit the end of the line.

I heard my flesh tear, rip, and pop.

I saw the rope bouncing way up into the tree.

It dangled there for a second, then dropped.

While this was going on, I fell backwards.

I had broken loose.

It was surprising how strong the flesh was. It didn't tear easily. It took all my strength and weight to break loose. Steve and a couple of the other Sundancers caught me when I fell.

I was so happy, I let out a big yell. I jumped up and down. I had finally done what I had envisioned at that Shoshoni Sundance, so long ago. I was at the top of my spiritual being then. My energy was flashing. The energy around me was sparking many people. They gained a lot, I feel, because my energy was so hot. I brought that Sun Power down on myself and all the people who came to support me.

Steve grabbed my arm bracelet and took me around the Arbor to the spot where I had started. As I ran by the other Sundancers, they were all patting me on the shoulder. Most of them were men who had been pierced in the past, who knew about the pain, the happiness, the jubilation. All or most would be pierced before the weekend was over.

I felt high, like I had reached that ultimate plateau of human spirituality. But eventually I found out that I was wrong. There was more to follow.

After several more Sundances, I realized that this was not the ultimate. There are other plateaus to experience. New heights of awareness to achieve in the Sundance circle, and other circles as well. This was just the beginning of my journey.

We finished that Saturday evening. After leaving, I walked around visiting other people and other camps, wearing my scars like badges of honor. Although it isn't seen as showing off, it is viewed as an honorable thing we have done. The piercing of the body, the giving of our pain, blood, and flesh so others may live well.

Saturday evening, I thanked Norbert Running, the Sundance Chief, and told him that I'd like to stay, but I had to get back to Oklahoma. I had left my family unattended and without money, and it would take me all of Sunday to get back.

He said, "You came, you danced, you pierced, you have to go. Everybody understands, including the Creator. The commitment you made was to Him and not to me."

On Sunday evening, when I arrived home, my wife was a little upset because I had pierced. I knew it bothered her, but she didn't make it a big issue, and I was grateful. She knew that I had done something that was important to me and that I had done it to try to help others. I had so many people who needed prayers—my parents, my sisters, and brother. It appeared the Creator had chosen me, from my family, to be the Sundancer. I felt honored. This is why I felt that I had to be there, and my wife seemed to understand.

NORTH — RED

"Cold Winds"

S N O W

In January I left Oklahoma to do a show in Santa Monica, California. I met some Sundancers and ended up spending a lot of time there selling crafts because we needed the money. And during the winter, California was the only good place to sell my native crafts.

My wife was making crafts at home, while I made them in California. With the crafts she sent me, I was doing well and always sending money home. By mid-May, my wife decided she had had enough of that kind of life.

Once I was talking to her, chatting about what was

going on. Our conversation was a little tense, but nothing special, I thought. She wanted us to invest in a trailer, and I said no. So she said, "I guess that's all I have to say. I'll talk to you later. I love you."

I didn't answer her. I just hung up.

The next morning, I received an overnight letter from my wife. She told me not to bother coming back; she didn't want to hurt me anymore. She wrote: "This life is over. I am tired of being a telephone wife."

I went into a state of shock. I couldn't believe what I was reading. After fifteen years of marriage, I never expected to hear this. Other than our talk the day before, everything seemed fine.

What hurt the most was the thought of being left out of my children's lives.

I couldn't blame her, though. After being away from her and the kids for so long, I had gotten to a point where I didn't miss them as much as before. That frightened me. It was almost as if they ceased to mean anything to me.

I started praying to Grandfather. I said, "Grandfather, what's happening to me? I'd hoped for a better life. This is why I Sundanced."

The realization of what was happening hit me hard. I blamed myself, then I became consumed with anger toward my wife. Then I blamed myself some more. My mental state began to deteriorate. Filled with grief, remorse, even bitterness, I felt abandoned.

In my attempts to pray, I felt even Grandfather had left me behind. When you're beating yourself up, you don't think you're worthy of Grandfather's help. Then I rationalized in my head for a while that this may be a good thing. Maybe I was supposed to be free again. When this happened, I started drinking. I drank to dull the pain.

When I ran out of booze, I would feel the pain over the loss of my children. Deeply hurt, I drank for about a month. I felt a rage against this woman who had done this to me. I had trusted her completely and had never questioned anything she did. Yet, suddenly, she told me not to come home.

All this time, I was wandering aimlessly from place to place, from powwow to powwow. Once at a powwow in Cupertino, California, I was dancing in a competition in the arena, but my mind wasn't on dancing, because of my emotional state. The song was a "Sneak Up," a special dance for hunters or warriors.

I didn't realize I was dancing the wrong way for that song until one dancer casually danced near and informed me it was a "Sneak Up." Embarrassed, I just turned and walked out of the arena.

Tom, the emcee, and my friend, made an excuse for me. He said, "Sometimes us old-timers go to so many powwows that we forget one song from the other." He knew what I was going through. Everyone did, and they tried to help me through it.

I went outside and looked off into the distance. I didn't know that someone was taking a picture of me. (It's the one on the cover of this book.) The woman who took it wanted to try to capture the moment. She told me about it later and asked my permission. At the time, I was angry that she had invaded my privacy. When I look at it now, and the expression on my face, the picture seems to say everything. Right then, my mind was on my loss. The Creator had decided to take away all that I held dear to me: my family.

The feelings of grief and devastation were hard to take, and I realized then that all I had now was the Sundance. The Creator was teaching me to depend on my spirituality for strength. The pain would pass in time, but the Sundance, my spiritual foundation, would be forever.

After that, I was still wondering, what had I done? Why did this happen? I blamed myself during the entire month while I was drinking.

Then suddenly, one morning, I woke up. I was in Monterey at a campground. I rolled over, sat up in bed, grabbed a bottle of beer, and took a drink. I stopped and looked at the bottle and at the mess I called a bed. I looked at the overflowing bag of dirty clothes. I looked at myself and what I had become in just one month. I didn't like what I saw.

Then I asked myself, "What in the world are you doing? You are having a beer for breakfast. This is absurd. You've never had a drink this early in your life. Why now?"

I checked my pockets and found only three dollars. Then I checked the crafts box. It was empty. Well, there I was, almost flat broke, no food, no crafts, and no prospects. Again I thought to myself, my God, what am I doing to myself?

I got up, took a shower, and shaved. I felt better than I had in weeks. I headed out and stopped at a big hardware and crafts store.

The only way I could get a fresh start was to steal materials I couldn't afford. I walked around, debating whether to do it. It bothered me to consider stealing what I needed to make some money. Ironically, the items I needed were to make one of our spiritual symbols, the Medicine Wheel.

I took a deep breath, and decided that above all I had to survive. This was the only way that I knew how. I asked forgiveness. Then I went and found the largest chamois cloth they had. It was smooth, soft, pliable leather. I walked around the store for a long time until, finally, I slipped it into my shirt. I paid for the other items that were under a dollar, and I walked out.

I don't do this kind of thing. I got scared, scared that I might be stopped, that I could be caught and thrown in jail for that little piece of chamois cloth. But I needed that leather to make the Medicine Wheels. I needed something to sell, to make, to buy myself some food and some gas, at least to get myself going again.

I was at rock bottom.

I didn't know what I was going to do. I didn't even have enough money left to pay for another night at the campground. I stopped my van in a parking lot. It wasn't too far from where I had taken, or should I say stolen, that piece of chamois cloth.

I cut up the leather into strips and wrapped the wooden hoops I used to make Medicine Wheels. The spirits were with me. The Creator was also close to me in my time of need.

Everything went so smoothly, so fast, and the wheels turned out beautifully. I finished them in record time. I knew of a store, in Pacific Grove, so I went there and showed the owner what I had. The woman said, "Oh my God, you've got Medicine Wheels? I have had more calls for these in the last couple of weeks. I'll take all six of them. I'll need more. How many can you make me?"

I said, "As many as you want."

She said, "Make me another thirty, then I'll have thirty-six. Then I'll have three dozen, and that'll hold me for a good part of the summer."

I asked, "Would it be possible to get a little advance on the order? I need to buy leather and stuff to make them with."

She said, "Sure, I'll give you half the cost of my order. Okay?"

I figured the money for the six Medicine Wheels plus the deposit on the other thirty put me in good shape. Good, I was happy. Now things were starting to look much better.

I ate a good breakfast, then returned to the same store where I had stolen the leather. I was afraid to go to the manager and admit what I had done because I felt terrible and so guilty. I also thought that maybe they could still throw me in jail.

Instead of confessing, I walked in and bought all the supplies I needed. I wanted to compensate them or apologize in some way for what I'd done, so I bought more than enough to make the other Medicine Wheels. I felt a little better, but to this day I still feel bad, and I've never forgotten about it. I have been into that store on two other occasions since then, and I've always bought more than I needed. In the end, that piece of chamois has cost me quite a bit because of my guilty feelings.

The Creator must have forgiven me because my life has returned to normal. I never blamed anyone for my actions or for the situation I found myself in.

I finished the order, and that gave me plenty of money. I filled up the gas tank in my van, bought more supplies (leather, beads, feathers) and returned to the campground. I made shields, Medicine Wheels, and leather necklaces. Within a couple of weeks I was back on my feet. I was forgetting the pain too, or at least it had diminished. I was feeling a lot better about myself. I could take the heartache a little bit better.

So I headed south toward Los Angeles. I drove on to Torrance to see my native brother, Wolfhawk, and while we were eating dinner, the subject turned to the recent changes in my life.

I said, "Wolfhawk, I don't know what I did wrong. I don't know where I messed up, where I screwed up."

He said, "Manny, let me tell you something. I've seen you work and work many hours, putting the welfare of your family first above your own comforts. I've watched you send money, and more money, home."

He continued, "You didn't screw up, she did. It's not your fault, man. I wondered how long it would take you to realize it. Apparently you haven't let yourself see it, yet. So it's my job to tell you, to let you know, that it was not you who screwed up. It was her."

He said, "Let it go. Send money to the kids. Tell them that you love them every chance you get. Write to them on their birthdays, on Christmas, on Easter. Send them a card, send them twenty dollars, thirty dollars, a hundred dollars when you can. Remember always to tell them that you love them so they won't forget you."

I took his advice.

I learned how to make an old/new article called a "Dream Catcher." (By "old/new" I mean that it's an old belief or tradition that, after many years of being forgotten, is once more becoming very popular.) Many people are familiar with how Dream Catchers help people overcome nightmares and bad dreams.

Long ago, they were only made by the medicine man in the tribe. He would be called on if someone was having difficulty sleeping, or having nightmares. The medicine man would consult the spirits, then make a Dream Catcher for that individual. He went through many prayers and a sacred ceremony while making each Dream Catcher, and it was considered bad medicine for anyone else to create one for any other reason or by any other method.

It all started when I decided to teach myself how to make them. When I made the first one, several of my friends saw it and laughed. They said, "That one is for nightmares, not for dreams."

I thought it was pretty good, but I wasn't quite getting the stitch right. I racked my brain trying to figure it out.

When I was at a powwow in Fresno, California, I ran into a good friend of mine from Bakersfield. A wonderful little lady, her name is *Wia Chanupa*, meaning "Pipe Woman." She took one look at my Dream Catcher and said, "God, Manny, that looks awful. I wouldn't show that to anybody!"

Wia showed me that I was missing just one little step and after she showed me how to fix it, I got busy making more Dream Catchers.

I never did fix that first one I made, but apparently it didn't matter. I was at a powwow when a woman from across the arena saw it and came running. She said, "I'll take that Dream Catcher."

"Well, it's sixty dollars."

"It's okay, I'll take it."

After paying me, she said, "If it was a hundred fifty dollars, I would still have bought it."

"Well you know, I want you to be happy," I grinned.

"Oh, no, that's okay. Sixty is fine."

At times, I would sit in my van, right on the beach for a week, and make Dream Catchers. It was very hard to sit there alone hour after hour, working. It gave me time to think. Sometimes I felt like my chest was going to burst; I missed my kids so much.

When the thinking became too painful, I would get out of the van and ride my bike up and down the Strand at Redondo Beach—just to be around other people—until I was too tired to think any more.

It wasn't long after that I saw four friends of mine, Jesse, Sonny, Lonnie, and Marty, up in San Juan Bautista. They were going to their first Sundance.

I told them, "Look, guys, it's pretty tough there, and I'm an old hand at it now. I've been to one Lakota Sundance, and I have four under my belt at the other place, so I'm an old-timer to the Sundance circle. I'll be there the day before to support you when you go in the Arbor, and Wednesday night to help you and give you any advice that I can."

They thanked me unanimously, and said they hoped I could make it.

I headed to South Dakota and arrived the day they were going into the Lakota Sundance. I pulled in at about seven o'clock in the evening. The boys were sitting in the tepee, and they were very happy to see me. They were as anxious and as frightened as I had been my first time.

I sat and talked with them until long past midnight. Finally, it was time to go to sleep, so I left them alone and went to bed.

In the morning when they went in, I was encouraging and wished them luck. It was important to me to be there when they went in because I had been alone for my first piercing Sundance. I was glad they had each other for company. I felt that I had done my job by keeping my word that I would be there, and I was proud of all of them. They all danced, and three of them pierced that first day.

Marty did not pierce because he had not made that commitment to Grandfather. Personally, I think if he never pierces it might be better. He is a Vietnam veteran (173rd Airborne) and was badly wounded in action. I feel he has given enough pain, flesh, and blood for all of us. He is a good warrior and "nephew."

Shortly after the piercing ceremony, I said goodbye and left.

I had another Sundance brother, Lionel, who was going into his first Sundance over in Porcupine, South

Dakota, on the Pineridge Reservation. I had told him I would help him prepare for his *Hanblecheya* vision quest and his Sundance.

When I arrived, the weather was hot and muggy. Lionel and I shook hands and hugged. He motioned for me to sit and asked if I wanted something to drink. He had his tent pitched right under a nice, shady tree and had been there a few days already, getting the Arbor prepared for the Sundance.

I stood for a second to stretch my legs and look around. I caught my breath as I looked east. The land and high, white sandstone cliffs were magnificent. The cliffs were outlined with the green of the grass. Mingled with the glorious, deep, green grass were soft, dusty, grayish blue stalks of medicine sage. The colors made the place seem mystical and beautiful.

The Sundance Arbor was in a nice secluded area that was mowed and raked every year so that it would be a decent campground for people who come to the Sundance. With no electricity or running water, the only conveniences were those you brought with you.

I noticed that Lionel was a bit nervous and apprehensive. This was his first time to dance, so he was happy to see me. I was a familiar, friendly face from home.

We spent the afternoon visiting, drinking coffee, and talking about mutual friends. I told him about Sonny, Jesse, Lonnie, and Marty. They were also friends of his. It comforted him to know some of his friends had just gone through their first piercing ceremony.

After eating, I helped him put together his crown and his ankle and wrist bracelets. We also made some tobacco ties to put on the Sacred Tree. I helped him prepare his flags and the altar for his Chanupa, his pipe.

We had coffee late that night. By this time most of our

visiting was done. We sat there for long moments in silence, feeding small sticks into the campfire. From time to time, others would stop and visit, then leave. It was so pleasant to sit and relax after so much driving.

Following tradition, I went to look for David, the Sundance Chief, to give him some tobacco. I found him sitting behind Lionel's tent drinking a cup of coffee and talking with Al and Bernice, two of the elders who were also husband and wife. When he knew that what I had to discuss was important to me, he stood up, and we started walking away from the others. I told him what had happened to me with my family, how I was hurting and missing my kids.

He gave me a great deal of advice. What he said made me realize there may be a good reason it happened, though I won't go into the details. I respected what he told me, and I accepted it.

Then he said, "The only thing you can do now is pray for your children. Pray that maybe someday they will return to you. When they grow up, they will want their dad. They'll want to know where you are. They'll want to be with you. Meanwhile, pray for them, and pray hard. The biggest thing is to pray for forgiveness for your wife."

He continued, "I don't believe it was her fault. Circumstances pushed you two apart, and maybe through prayer she'll reconsider."

"No," I replied, "I have too much pride. It is over."

There was a long pause. We had both stopped walking. He stood for a long, quiet moment. I stood waiting. Finally, as if he had received confirmation from the Spirits, he nodded his head.

As we started walking back to camp, he said, "Well, if it is over, just be strong, and take the best road open to you, the Sundance. Did you come to dance?"

"I came to visit and help support Lionel."

"*Washtelo*, good," he answered. "Please make yourself at home. You're always welcome here."

His energy was quiet and unassuming, yet so powerful. I quickly came to respect this man, and he's the one I now follow in the Sundance. He has got the energy that others are seeking. He comes by his spirituality quite naturally, from a people whose very existence depends on their deep, spiritual beliefs.

After our talk, we returned to camp for more coffee and met with three other young men who impressed me: Bo, Marvin, and Tony. Bo was one of David Swallow's Sundance leaders. He was also the son of Pansy, the women's Sundance leader. Marvin and Tony were married to Al and Bernice's two daughters. They were Sundancers, drummers, and singers, and respectful young men.

I spent seven wonderful days there. I volunteered to go to Rapid City, and returned with the things we needed, and some things we didn't. The time passed, sometimes slow, sometimes fast, but always hot. Every evening was a blessed relief, because it always cooled off.

David took Lionel up to the mountain on his vision quest—one way to seek guidance for your spiritual life. This was four days before the Sundance began.

Before he left, I said, "Brother, if you need anything spiritually, please let me know. I'll be in tune with your energy. Send a message if you need help, and I'll be with you."

About two o'clock in the morning I felt something hit the side of my van. It startled me, and I woke up instantly. Then there was another, louder thump, farther away from me, toward the front. And then there were three small bangs on the front bumper. The sound worked its way around to the driver's side, and when it got even with me, it stopped. I jumped up and looked around.

I thought maybe someone I just met was trying to scare me or pull a joke on me. I looked and no one was there. It was dark, but I could see well enough in the moonlight, and I couldn't spot anybody.

It got me thinking, "What is this?" Then I swallowed hard and realized, "My God, my brother Lionel is in trouble. He's asking for my help."

So I found my smudging shell and grabbed a big piece of medicine sage. After finding my lighter, I lit the sage, got out of my van and started praying. "Grandfather, please help those three."

There had been three who went up the mountain, so I asked help for all three of them in case it was one of the others asking for help. I forget exactly what I said, but I know I prayed hard for them to have the courage and strength to do their "*Hanblecheya*," which is the Lakota word for vision quest.

"Help those warriors make it through the night. Help them find their direction and advice," I asked Grandfather. I knew that one of them was in trouble, and was worried it was my brother Lionel.

Suddenly, off in the east, I heard David start drumming and singing. Apparently he also knew that someone needed help. His voice and the drum were hauntingly beautiful. Muted by distance, the sound seemed to come from somewhere out of the past.

Two days later, when they came down from their vision quest, we learned who it was.

I had just finished eating, and I was enjoying a cup of coffee. David was leaving to get the three men from their vision quest. They had been up there for two days and two nights. Besides Lionel, there were two others that went up; one was a white man, Thomas, from Nebraska, the other was Lakota from Pineridge. He was the one who had the problems. He got scared and began hallucinating. He thought everybody had forgotten about him, and so he walked back down.

He asked me where everybody was, and I told him that David had gone up the mountain to get him. Embarrassed, he was nervously trying to explain why he had come down. I didn't realize it at the time, but even I wasn't supposed to acknowledge his presence because doing so breaks the spiritual energy from the *Hanblecheya*.

The experience humbled me. *Hanblecheya* is a hard thing to do, and still many people would judge him harshly. I think it made me realize how serious all this is. It's very sacred: the *Hanblecheya*, the *Inipi*, the Sundance. Everything is important to us, and no part of it should ever be taken lightly by anyone.

If a person walks away from the *Hanblecheya* sight by himself, he has committed a terrible sacrilege. When one who is seeking a vision leaves without the spiritual people who took him up there, it is considered bad medicine for him and his family. It is disrespectful of the Great Spirit and of the ceremony. Not only that, it is very embarrassing for the relatives or anyone associated with the person.

No one should insult or show disrespect toward anything related to the Sundance or native spirituality. Amazingly enough, there are so many people who go to one *Hanblecheya* and suddenly feel they are experts. They see one Sundance, and they are experts at the Sundance. By invitation, they see and participate in a Sweat Lodge, and the next week they are at home, calling themselves shamans and building a sweat lodge, usually improperly.

Most people don't even know the meaning of the word "shaman." According to the 1994 Grolier Encyclopedia, the word comes from tribal groups in Siberia, where a shamanistic religion dominates the tribe. It has nothing to do with, and should not be used in connection with, Native American culture or spirituality.

These people who call themselves shamans are running their own Sweat Lodges and charging money for it. This is wrong and only brings bad medicine to those who participate. Our spirituality is not for sale to anyone at any price. That people would even consider profiting from our ceremonies makes us angry, and some of our people who find out about it will attempt to put a stop to these practices.

I don't want to pass judgment; the Creator will take care of that. Often people act out of ignorance, or their intentions are good. This we realize. However, it's time people were made aware of what they are doing to our spirituality.

People should understand that when they do a vision quest, or a Sweat Lodge, they are opening themselves up to the spirit world. We also believe strongly that there are good spirits and bad spirits. We might call them spirits or call them medicine. There are bad energies out there, and people have to understand that they leave themselves wide open to this. They shouldn't be interfering with things they don't understand. Besides that, it is sacrilegious to prostitute another man's spiritual beliefs. We don't appreciate it, yet so many people are doing it for sheer profit.

After meddling in this way, some people call me to help them out of whatever they have brought on themselves. Some say that they feel snakes in their heads. Others say that they can't sleep because spirits are hitting them and keeping them awake for days at a time. One person told me someone's spirit guide took her spirit guide to another planet! When we try to give these people advice, they either don't want to hear it or never believe it.

Experiences with such people made me realize that I

had stepped into a spiritual world that is there to benefit and help to the fullest. There is no limit. I can be helped, I just have to believe, show respect, and pray. The rest will come naturally. As the old saying goes, *"Action is the fruit of thought."* So when you think of something, it will come true if you pray for it. A prayer is no more than a thought going from you to the universe or to the Creator.

The problem of the young man coming off the hill was straightened out when David returned. He counseled the young man. He didn't condemn him or hold against him what he had done. He just told him he shouldn't have done it.

I always say the Creator is not there to hurt us. He's only here to hold us to our word and serve as a spiritual foundation for us.

Wednesday afternoon we went to get the Sacred Tree for the Sundance. When David told everyone that we were leaving for the tree, people pulled up their cars to get in line for the procession. As we pulled out, there were a dozen cars lined up. We drove an hour to the turnoff, then five miles off the highway along a rough, dirt road to where the cotton-wood tree was that would become the Sacred Tree.

After cutting it down, we carried it on our shoulders to the flatbed trailer and tied it down. People were sitting all over and around the tree, holding on to it. Protecting it from any harm. It was so beautiful.

A mile and a half from where we had cut the tree down, we saw a friend of ours. His name is American Eagle. He and another gentleman were walking ahead of us. Suddenly a great, big bull stood in front of them. It was a Hereford bull, and he stood looking at the procession of cars and the pick-up with the tree, then pawing the ground and looking at us.

I could almost read his thoughts, "What in the world are they doing on my turf?"

American Eagle and the other man walked toward the bull. American Eagle was carrying his medicine staff. He shook it at the bull. The bull was irritated and started pawing the ground faster as though preparing to charge. Luckily we were close enough to the two men so that David could yell at him, "Hey, American Eagle! You better leave that bull alone. He doesn't know you're carrying your medicine stick with you. You'd better get back in the pickup before he hurts you!"

It was fortunate that we got there when we did. The two men got in the pickup. The bull—intimidated by all the cars, the tree, the truck, and the noise—trotted off. He certainly hadn't been afraid of two old-timers getting closer and closer to him, almost threatening him. We all had a good laugh, but it wouldn't have been funny if something had happened.

The drive back was beautiful, because as we drove down the highway with the tree on the trailer, people would pull off to the side of the road. They stopped their cars to allow the tree to go through because it was a sacred tree. This didn't happen just once. We passed many pickups, cars, and vans. Everybody slowed and stopped on the side of the highway.

We got the tree within a couple hundred yards from the Arbor and stopped the trailer. Everyone gathered around the tree. As one, we picked it up and put it on our shoulders. The tree measured about fourteen inches in diameter at the base. It was green and very heavy. Slowly we started moving. The walk was dignified. Although many of us were struggling, we were all quiet. As we carried the tree, we had to make the traditional four stops before we got it into the Arbor.

After moving the tree into the Arbor, we finally were able to lay it down. The ground inside the Arbor is sacred. It is the only place the tree can touch the ground. Anywhere else, and the tree loses its purity and cannot be used for the Sundance. Long ago, if the Sacred Tree touched the ground, the Sundance would be cancelled.

While the tree was lying there in the Arbor, many prayers were offered to it. We thanked it for giving its life so that we might have our Sundance, and we let it know it was going to become a sacred symbol for us.

Everybody who was going to dance and pierce had to tie on their ropes. They stretched their ropes out to different areas of the Sundance Arbor. When everything was ready, we started pulling the tree up with all the ropes. Once we hoisted it up, we formed a circle around the tree to keep it standing straight. A hole had been dug in the center of the Arbor. It was deep enough to support the tree. A crew of men started burying the base of the tree. They tamped the dirt down so that even a strong wind couldn't blow it over.

When it was finally standing proudly, it was late in the evening. It had all sorts of flags and colors, including offering flags made by many different people. Everybody had their ties up and ropes on the tree. They were ready for the next day.

The tree ceremony was over.

It looked like everybody was happy and ready. You could sense an intangible feeling of joy in the air. It was dark when we were through, and slowly everybody started disbursing back to their own camps. Everyone knew that morning would come very, very early.

I returned to the camp with Lionel. David, Bernice, and Al were sitting around drinking coffee and having supper, and we joined them. After everyone was through eating, we sat around the campfire, visiting. Tired and ready to hit the sack by this time, I decided to go to bed.

The next morning, as I put my clothes and shoes on, I heard somebody yelling, "Ho! Sundancers, let's go. It's 4:30, its time to get up. The sun is almost up."

Even though the sun was still two hours off, the Sundancers have to get up that early so they can go and do a Sweat Lodge purification, then come back to camp and get dressed.

I still got up even though I wasn't going to Sundance with them. I had my own Sundance to go to and was just there to help Lionel, which I had done. I didn't want to sweat that morning because I had to leave soon and wasn't sure if it would be that day or the following day.

I went over to the Sweat Lodge area to see if anything was needed, found out nothing was, so I returned to camp. I still hadn't had my first cup of coffee, and they had a fresh pot on, so I followed my nose to it.

After my coffee, I returned to the sweat lodges again, to see if I could help. They had already designated men to pass the hot stones into the sweat lodges. I felt sort of lost and left out. It was strange not to be in the Sundance. I kept asking if anyone needed my help. One guy asked me to help him with his eagle whistle, so I helped him get it going again. Another guy asked me to help him finish his ankle and wrist bracelets. I was glad to be of assistance. It is an honor and privilege to be accepted by everyone because I am an elder, and I'm there to help a brother.

Everybody was happy to be there, in such a friendly atmosphere. Everybody was feeling energetic, although a little cold since it was so early in the morning. On the first day of the Sundance even the smells were invigorating. The smell of burning wood, sage, and cedar filled the air. It was burning in the sweat lodges. You could even get faint whiffs of the hot steam coming out of the sweat lodges.

As things progressed, I saw the men leave the sweat lodges and return to their camps to get ready. Everyone was ready with their beautiful colored regalia on and skirts made out of shawls. I watched in awe and thought, "Next week I've got to go through this at my Sundance."

Slowly, they got in line. They looked for friends they wanted to be next to during their four days of suffering. By being together they gained support and magnified the energy that comes to every Sundancer.

Finally, I heard the Sundance Chief. *Sheriiii-Sheriiii* . . . He blew on his eagle-bone whistle and told everybody, "Get ready, men. Get ready. We are going in to pray." The line started moving forward as the drums started, slowly at first. Gradually, the beat picked up and they played the "Going In" song. You could hear it playing across the Arbor over on the south side.

As they moved around the Arbor, they made the traditional four stops to honor the four directions. A couple of Sundancers held cans that had hot coals burning inside. They kept putting cedar boughs in the cans. The leaves smoldered and smoked. It was a purification smoke, and it smelled wonderful.

They followed each other around to the left, dancing. Everybody who was dancing was supported by brothers, cousins, aunts, and uncles. Many campers gathered around the Arbor to see the procession of dancers and people who had made the commitment.

After everyone was in place, the "Going In" song turned into the "*Chanupa*" song. The dancers all walked back under the Arbor, single file, as the song finished. Ten to fifteen minutes later the drummers and singers started singing again. A

Sundance leader stood up and said, "*Ho-ka-hey* . . . let's go. One more round, let's go."

They started the second song. I sat in the background under the Arbor. I was there to offer my support. I kept looking at all my brothers and sisters who were out there, suffering. They were going through a lot, and I was thinking, "At least I'm standing on the outside. I can keep my shoes and shirt on."

As the day grew older, the sun started getting hotter and hotter. I thought to myself, "My God, how could they be taking it out there?" I looked at one after another to see how they were holding up. No one was complaining or saying it was too hot. Humbled by the experience, everybody seemed to be honored for the opportunity to dance and pray for others. It was such an incredible feeling, standing there, watching them suffer without thinking of themselves. My chest swelled with pride to be a witness to this sacrifice and to know I was one of them. This Sundance belonged to everyone there.

The day passed slowly. I could see the dancers starting to tire a little bit at a time as the heat reached its peak. Then the sun slowly started sliding downhill to the other end of the horizon.

David Swallow Jr., being a good leader, had seen the condition of the dancers and let everyone know that it was their last song.

Before they could come out of the Arbor, they had to do one more thing. The "Pipe" song. They picked up their pipes, then danced out of the Arbor. The pipes were placed in a sacred lodge, where all the pipes are kept during the night. There was always a guard placed in front of the door so no one could enter the lodge and disturb the pipes.

From their first Sundance until the fourth, almost all

Sundancers have pipes, but they have not yet earned the right to perform the ceremonies with them. The pipes are theirs, but they are only in their care until they have finished their first commitments. After four years, they become pipe carriers. Only at that time are they believed to be responsible and knowledgeable enough to heal and to offer blessings, all in the name of the Creator.

It was about six o'clock when they came in from the last round. Everybody started going into one of the three sweat lodges. As they got ready, they dropped to their knees and quickly crawled in.

Everyone was happy as the day ended. Everybody had danced and prayed, and now it was time to relax for the night.

At the time, David didn't have any tepees set up, which would have given the people who wanted to remain in the area around the Arbor a place to sleep. So he allowed everybody to return to their camps.

My camp was simply my van. I parked right next to Lionel's tent, so I was close to everyone else. When I got there, they already had coffee and a pot of stew cooking. Getting some of both, I savored the first bite, rolling it around in my mouth. After going all day without food, I was hungry. I took my time.

Al and Bernice were about my age and had been dancing all day. Tired, sitting quietly, they talked and sipped their coffee. Elders are allowed to return to camp at night to eat and drink a little for health reasons. I sat close to them after helping myself to another cup of coffee. There were quite a few people there—their daughters, sons, Richard, Lionel, and other people I didn't know.

Bernice said softly, "Manny, you would honor us if you would dance with us tomorrow, just for one day."

I didn't know what to say. Then I replied, "Bernice, I

have my own Sundance to go to. I am honored you are asking me to dance, but I have another commitment already."

"We know, we just want you to honor us and dance with us one day. I've got to tell you something, Manny. This afternoon tired me out. The sun was really hot. But every time I looked and saw you dancing, it didn't matter that it was hot." She stopped, took a sip of coffee, and continued, "Just the way you were dancing—your motions, your sincerity—helped me. The look on your face really inspired me and kept me going when I felt the most tired."

Al looked up and nodded his head quietly. He says, "Me too, Manny. We would like you to dance with us."

Their son Richard added, "Yeah, Bro', come on, man, dance with us one day. Dance and suffer with us for one day."

When people offer you that much respect, you can hardly refuse such a humble request. At some point you have to consider their feelings above your own. I had no choice, really, but to say I would.

So, once again I forgot tradition. I forgot it in the spirit of the moment. When you make a commitment to Sundance, it's never for just one. It's a four-year commitment. When they talked me into it, they talked me into dancing with them for four years.

That wasn't their intention, I'm sure. It really doesn't matter because I'm committed to the Sundance for the rest of my life, as long as my health holds out. If I'm financially able, and it won't jeopardize my family, I'll Sundance from now on. It isn't as though I got talked into it with my eyes closed; my eyes have been wide open every time I have made a commitment.

I felt wonderful that they should honor me in such a way. After agreeing to dance with them, I saw Bernice get up and walk away. A few minutes later she returned.

She said, "Manny, since you agreed to dance with us, I want to honor you with one of our shawls. This will be your skirt. Honor us by wearing our family colors. Everyone who sees you in the Sundance will know that you are dancing with us and for us . . . for the Tail family."

It was such an honor, I got all choked up and thanked her. I told her, "You don't have to do this. I've got my own shawl."

She said, "Take it, it's okay. You are going to honor us by wearing it."

Bowing my head respectfully, I accepted the shawl. There was a chorus of glad voices. Everybody was saying, "All right, Manny, all right." Everybody was happy, laughing, and smiling, shaking my hand and slapping my back.

"I have to get a crown and ankle and wrist bracelets made," I said.

Everybody jumped in to help, and in five minutes they had them ready for me. They tied a couple of small eagle feathers on my crown. Suddenly, there I was, all ready to go into another Sundance that I had never thought of doing.

All I had come to do was help my brother Lionel through his *Hanblecheya*, his vision quest, and the Sundance. This was his first Sundance, and I wanted to see him off on the right foot. Now these beautiful people honored me.

I went to my van after everybody left and headed for their own blankets. I slept well, considering I was a little nervous about the next day. Only I knew what I had to do in this Sundance, too.

Next morning I was up early and did my traditional morning sweat. Afterwards, I headed back to my van and got all dressed up.

I was back at the Arbor when David arrived. He knew from the night before that I was going in, and was glad to see me join the circle. We talked and waited for the other guys.

One at a time, everyone arrived from their camps ready to dance. We started lining up. Everyone was in the same order they had been in the previous day. I got to fudge between two other guys who had been in the day before. Usually when you come in late, you always go to the end of the line, but it was a small Sundance.

I could feel the little pins and needles from the mown-down bushes. The ground was cool under the soles of my feet. It was such a good feeling to be there. The Sundance Chief started to blow his eagle whistle, letting everyone know it was time to dance and pray.

Somebody yelled, "*Hoka-hoka-hey*, time to go."

The drums started, and again I relive that incredible feeling of entering the Arbor, into that all-healing Sacred Circle.

We went through the first dance and greeted the sun, prayed at the tree and put our pipes on the altar so they faced the east. Then we rested.

While we were resting, I went to the Sundance Chief and said, "David, I want to pierce first round."

An incredulous look came over his face. He said, "Manny, you don't have to pierce."

Al heard me and also said, "No, no, Manny, you don't have to pierce."

Turning to face both of them, I said, "Al, David . . . you honored me by asking me to dance with you. Where I come from there are no free rides."

Al looked down at the ground almost as if he were sorry for what he had asked me to do. They never thought for a moment that I might pierce for them.

I grabbed Al's hand, and I shook it. "Don't feel sad. It is my honor to do this for you. I am happy that I can pierce for you and your family. Look at me and smile with me, brother. Laugh with me because this is what it is all about. It is about praying for each other, helping each other and knowing that you have somebody who is willing to suffer for you."

Al looked in my eyes and smiled. He shook my hand and said, "*Ho . . . Washtelo . . . Wo-Pila.*"

David, sitting in his chair, stood up and shook my hand. The man told me that if this is what I wished, it was a commitment between me and the Creator. "We will do as you ask."

They hadn't even prepared the paint to mark the chests with yet. It's not typical paint. It's a mixture of red dirt, clay, and water. A Sundance leader came over, and they told him to wet the paint. "Manny's going to pierce on this first round."

When they painted my chest, the look on Bernice's face was filled with emotion. She said, "Manny, you don't have to do this." She hadn't heard the previous conversation.

"Bernice, I have to."

She looked at me and said, "You are my brother, and I have to honor and respect what you want to do."

When the next song began, right away they started singing the "*Chanupa*" song. David went over and said something to them. They changed it from the "Pipe" song into the "Piercing" song. As we were going out, I stood right at the entrance of the Arbor where we do the dancing and praying.

It was as though a signal went out. When the "Piercing" song could be heard throughout the camp, people started coming to see who was getting pierced. The shade around the Arbor started filling up. Everybody went by, shook my hand, and thanked me. I was thanking them, though not as individuals. In my heart I was thanking them for this day.

When they were finally all in, Richard, a Sundance leader, came and took me right to the tree. After praying for a couple of minutes at the tree, I walked around and handed David one of my throwaway scalpels.

I looked at David and said, "*Ho-Wana*," meaning "I'm ready."

I called Lionel to come in and be with me while I was pierced. I lay down, and they pierced me on both sides. I remember looking at Lionel's face. He had a look of pain and anguish. The people around me went through so many strange feelings and sensations. When I looked at them, I saw that they were praying for me, and hurting for me. They cared about my pain, about my blood and my flesh that I was giving up. I saw it in their faces, I saw it in their eyes.

After being pierced, I stood up and I moved back away from the tree. I started dancing. Almost everyone standing under the shade was now behind me, supporting me on that first dance. I danced and danced. Four times I went to the tree. On the fourth time after going to the tree, I prayed and I asked for strength and courage. I wanted to do this right for my new Lakota brothers and sisters.

I gathered up my rope as if I were going to lasso something in front of me. As I started moving backwards, I let go one coil of rope at a time, I was going back faster and faster. Finally, as I dropped the last coil, it never made it to the ground. I hit the end of the rope. For that one split second of time, I felt like something had reached from the heavens and touched my chest, my face, my head, and my heart.

The next second, I jumped up and yelled. I was happy to have honored these people. I was happy that I had done it with bravery, that I had succeeded.

That was the turning point of the day. The day ended as beautiful rays lit the Sundance Arbor from over the mountain tops. Everybody was happy and jubilant. After the sweat, everyone shook my hand and thanked me for the dance. We spent the rest of the evening just visiting.

I told them, "Tomorrow I have to leave, but I'll be here in spirit with you. I will be dancing with you every day."

Lionel smiled, "Will we see you next year?"

Smiling back, I replied, "You bet!"

I got up early the next morning to watch them go in to the Arbor. After they were inside, I said my goodbyes and left, heading south and east toward the Rosebud Reservation.

A mile before I got to the mass grave at Wounded Knee, I could feel the restless spirits from that horrible time, asking me for my prayers. Just as I do every time I pass the spot, I stopped and paid tribute to all the men, women, and children who had their lives taken so suddenly, and so tragically. I stopped, prayed, burned sage, and cried for their pain and the injustice of it all.

While I was driving, my mind wandered. I felt lost because I had left Lionel behind. We were very close spiritually, and I considered him a true brother. I was feeling lonesome because I had no one to talk to or share my thoughts with. Maybe this was why I kept going from place to place: to have a cup of coffee and someone to share conversation with.

My thoughts traveled from one friend to another. Where could I go next? Who could I visit after the Sundance? I was always careful I didn't overstay my welcome, even if I was lonely. I feared rejection if I stayed too long.

The loss of my family had subconsciously taken its toll on me. My self-confidence had been dealt a terrible blow. I began thinking of my children again. To see them and talk to them would be the answer to all my prayers. One thought that occupied my mind was, "When am I going to see them again?" I ached for the arms of my children around my neck.

When I got to Rosebud, I went straight to the grocery store in the town of Mission. I replaced bread and canned goods that I had used at the Sundance and purchased anything else I might need for the next four or five days. I bought ice for my cooler and a couple of gallons of water.

Then I headed over to Rosebud Village. As I drove through town, I started seeing people I knew, people I had Sundanced with.

Our Sundance was on top of a hill and was appropriately called Ironwood Hilltop Sundance. Already, people were starting to set up the camps where they had stayed for years.

I drove around and saw two native men, Emmanuel and Thomas, from California. This was their first Sundance, and I was their "Grandfather." I knew they would make me proud.

There was one area, sticking out from the hill, south of the Arbor. We called it "California Ridge" because so many people from California came and camped there at the Sundance. I went there first. Setting up camp for me was just a matter of stopping my van, and I was home.

I spent Wednesday morning getting myself ready and putting the final touches on my regalia.

In the afternoon, we headed out to get the Sacred Tree. This was a much larger Sundance than the previous one. There must have been twenty or thirty cars following the truck with the trailer to go get the tree.

Traditionally, while everyone is cutting down the tree, the Sundance Chief selects another one for the following year. He takes tobacco to it, prays to it, and lets it know that it will be our Sacred Tree soon. There is more said to the tree, but only a Sundance Chief knows what is said.

When we went to cut down our tree, we realized that it was right in the middle of a poison-oak patch. There must have been more than one hundred people, and every one of us trampled through it. We had to push the poison oak out of the way with our feet and hands to get to the tree.

Two children who are pure of heart, spirit, soul, and body are supposed to strike the first blows. So we had a little girl take the first axe strike to the tree, and then a little boy. Then they let the older guys, like myself, take a few swings. It was quite an honor to be selected.

After the old warriors took their swings, they let the young warriors chop it down really quickly. When the tree was close to coming down, they pushed it, and all the young warriors got under it. Slowly, slowly they took one whack at a time, until it was resting firmly where it couldn't fall and touch the ground because it was supported by all the men. When it was cut loose, we trampled back out.

Even with all that poison oak, to the best of my knowledge not one person involved in the ceremony got a rash or anything from it. Now that's unheard of. You can imagine two or three or maybe ten people being immune, but for everyone to be like that? This is powerful medicine.

We were there for a sacred purpose. We were there to get that Sacred Tree, the tree of life that meant so much to us.

We carried it up and put it on the trailer. Again as we traveled down the highway, people pulled over and stopped. Those who lived in the area knew the sacredness of the tree. They would stop as a sign of respect.

We must have traveled about ten miles, then we took it off the trailer. This time it was a larger tree, but there were more people to carry it, so it wasn't quite as difficult.

We made our four stops before we got to the Arbor, then inside the Arbor near the center, laid down the tree. This time I was there in time to tie my own rope on it.

When I was in Porcupine, I went to David with a problem and asked him what to do. I told him that the Spirits had entered my mind in a dream I had during the summer while sleeping in my van in California. The Spirits gave me a message: I had to pierce every day of my Sundance. It would be for my children. I should pierce once on each side, every day for the full four days. The dream scared me to death.

When David consulted with the Spirits and asked them if they truly wanted me to do this, the Spirits answered yes. That's what I must do so my children would be protected. The only way to guarantee that they would never be abused or mistreated was to pierce every day during the Sundance.

After settling down, I looked for a Sundance leader. I told him what had happened. We went into the Sweat Lodge together. He asked the spirits to bring him some kind of sign or word about what to do. Again the Spirits came and said, yes, that is the way they wanted me to go if I wanted my children protected.

Normally, the Sundance Chiefs don't allow people to do more than one set of piercing. If someone wants to do two, it should be two in front and two on their back, while dragging buffalo skulls. If they feel they must drag buffalo skulls, or if they have made that commitment, then it's okay. Doing more than that in one Sundance is frowned on, or it isn't allowed at all.

The leader told me, "You know, the Spirits are telling you to do this. We should still go and talk to Norbert and make sure that it's okay with him. He runs this Sundance."

The Sundance Chiefs are trying to keep glory-hunting people out of there. If someone is looking for glory, we let them know this is not the place to build their ego. So we went to Norbert, and we told him what had happened, word for word.

Norbert said, "Well if you made that commitment, and they told you that, that's the only way to do it. You've got my blessing."

He went on, "I know that this will be a hard and painful

Sundance for you. Not only are you going to feel the pain of those piercing wounds, but you are also going to feel the heat of the sun, thirst, and hunger. Another pain that you are going to feel is the pain of your limbs. Your arms are going to hurt, and your legs will ache. You will pay a heavy price for what you're asking. But you have the strength and the courage to do it."

So with that done, I started praying heavily. I prayed for the courage and the strength to accomplish what I had to do. Since I had already completed one piercing, I told them that was the first one of my four days.

When we went in Thursday, I didn't pierce. I danced. And then Friday morning I was the first one to pierce. I can't begin to relay to you how hard it is to go through that much hunger, pain, and thirst. Even though I had Sundanced many times, each time was just as difficult as if it were the first time. It took all the energy I could muster to keep myself on my feet.

The tiny veins on the tops of my feet started bursting. The tops of my feet turned black and blue, like a big bruised club at the end of each leg. All those vessels bursting, along with all of the hours dancing in the hot sun, increased my suffering. Pierced and pulling back on the tree, I smiled at Harold, a new Sundance brother I had met, who was from Pennsylvania. He was fast becoming a close friend. I had met him and his wife, Carlotta, the year before, when we both pierced simultaneously.

I pierced Friday, Saturday, and again Sunday. By Sunday, my entire chest was inflamed, one whole mass of pain. Piercing ripped my flesh open every day. It was gratifying for me because I knew that every time I ripped my flesh out of my chest, my children were being protected.

No single piercing was for any particular child; each piercing was for all of my children. I prayed that my children would come back to me someday and be kept from harm. I prayed hard for this.

I finished that Sundance, my third Lakota Sundance and my seventh Sundance overall. What a wonderful relief to complete it, and what a beautiful feeling. I know I've said it before, but I had found something that I really felt strongly about and truly loved.

The Sundance will always sustain you. All you are expected to offer is belief, respect, and prayers.

A B O V E — B L U E

"Star Path"

O R I O N ' S
L I G H T S

While I was at the Lakota Sundance, I knew something dramatic was going on in my life, but I couldn't quite put my finger on it. I was soon to learn that my wife was, at that very time, processing divorce papers.

When I left South Dakota, I returned to California only to find a letter from the courts of Oklahoma informing me that on July 31, there was going to be a divorce hearing. If I didn't appear in court, they would take it as an indication that I wouldn't contest any of the court rules or terms they laid out. They would go ahead and grant her a divorce under those conditions. I am almost positive that she knew I wouldn't be there to receive the letter. She knew I'd be at the Sundance.

Of course, when I received the letter, it was a month-and-a-half old, so there was no way I could have made it on time or contested it. Now it was final. It was hard to believe, it had all happened so fast. I didn't fight for my children, because the very best I could ever be was a poor mother. I figured I would send them money and learn to live with the situation. My ex-wife was a good mother to them.

Soon after, friends from Oklahoma kept giving me reports that she was not treating our kids well. Their welfare concerned me, and that was why I was praying so hard that Grandfather would take care of them and that no abuse would befall any of them. I was willing to give my blood, my flesh, and my pain to have my prayers answered.

It really hurt when I found out the divorce was final. Not that it hurt to be divorced. What hurt was to lose my children. I didn't know what I was going to do without them. So much of my life focused around them, and suddenly they were gone from my life. I wondered what they were thinking of all this, and of me. I wondered what their mother had told them and if they blamed me. I certainly couldn't go to Oklahoma. Not yet. I didn't know what I would do when I saw her and felt it was better to stay away. I was still angry.

After that Sundance, I traveled up into northern California. Life was treating me really well. Everything I made I sold. It started to get late in the fall, and I began to feel human again. I was sending the kids some money every week—always money orders in their names, so they would know their dad was trying to take care of them and was thinking of them. Much later, my son told me, "Mom said you sent us money in our names because you thought she couldn't cash it. She cashed every one of them and would give us five dollars of it, then use the rest for herself or the house."

No matter what she did, she was a good mother and a good wife to me for fifteen years. I hold nothing against her.

I headed to Quartzsite, Arizona, and sat in the desert for two weeks making Dream Catchers. At the time there weren't too many people making them. Those of us who were had found it hard keeping enough made for the people who wanted them. After the two weeks, I walked into one store, and they didn't even ask me the price.

The owner said, "Manny, you've got Dream Catchers?"

"Yes, I've got a bunch."

"We'll take them all," he said.

It didn't surprise me. They were very, very popular. Naturally, I was happy and grateful that the Creator had given me such a great way to make money. It was especially good for me because of my high blood pressure; the work was quite relaxing and not too stressful.

Heading back to California, I parked my van at the house of a friend, Wolfhawk, who lived in Torrance. I put myself on a minimum of at least ten Dream Catchers a day. It didn't matter what size or what color. I made them all sizes—from five-inch wooden rings to eighteen-inch rings. At the end of every week, I had seventy Dream Catchers made. Not bad for a guy living in his van without too much overhead. Things were going well for me.

Winter came and went in Torrance. I told my friends I wanted to head back to Tucson, Arizona, because in February, there would be a big gem and mineral show—the largest in the world. Every hotel and motel room in town would be full. Many motel rooms would be turned into retail and wholesale stores for the exhibitors, who would fly in from all over the world. It was a great place for me to wholesale my crafts.

My only concern was sending money home occasionally and trying to make sure my kids lived well. Of course, I didn't want to send too much because from what I had heard, not all the money was spent on them. Apparently some of it was going to support my ex-wife's new drinking habit.

I headed down to Julian, California, to see my buddy Emmanuel. I had brought Emmanuel into the Sundance. He was a good friend. When I got there, he was happy to see me and asked how I was doing.

"I'm doing great. I'm just kicking back, making Dream Catchers."

"Well, look," he said, "I just moved into another house. This cabin is just sitting here empty." He continued, "If you want, you are welcome to stay there. The rent is paid for another month. There's a bed, color TV, a VCR, refrigerator, and a shower. You can stay there and make your crafts. You don't need to go anywhere. Get out of the van for a few days and stretch. If you want to stay longer than a month, I'll pay for another month. No problem."

Emmanuel has a heart of gold. He's always willing to help anyone who needs it. I thanked him and took him up on his generous offer. Right across the street from the house was a working-man's restaurant. Across the street from the restaurant was a video store with more than five thousand movies. What more could I want?

Every morning, I would get up early, walk across the street, and have breakfast. Then I would walk back to the cabin and work, making five to ten Dream Catchers. Go have lunch, come back, make a few more, and then have dinner. Usually by then Emmanuel was around, and we would go have dinner at a good restaurant in the area. At night I would watch videos. I was really enjoying myself. Local people would come over and say they had heard I was making Dream Catchers. I would show them what I had and sell one or two a day.

Twenty, thirty, or forty bucks was pretty good, when you didn't have any overhead. I was making money, making Dream Catchers, and it wasn't costing me any rent. I was a little lonely, but overall I was living pretty well.

However, one Sunday morning I got up and had a strong, strong urge that I had to get to Tucson. I have always been one to follow my intuition and to rely a lot on my senses and my prayers.

In a matter of minutes, everything changed. One moment I was almost completely at ease with myself and with my place in life. And then suddenly, the energy changed completely. Within twenty minutes I was ready to go.

Just as I was finished loading everything into the van, Emmanuel drove up and said, "Manny, what's going on? What are you doing?"

"I've got to get to Tucson."

"But, you're all loaded up," he noticed. "You don't have to pay any rent here. You don't have to take off."

"Oh, I wasn't going to leave until I saw you," I said, "I just want to get there."

"What's the urgency?" he asked.

"I don't know really, I just have to go . . . now."

When he understood I was serious, he shook my hand, and we gave each other a big hug. I told him I'd see him later. A few minutes after that I was in my van and heading down the road. About four hours later I arrived at my parents' house.

Things had improved with my parents. I had been in touch with my mom before Christmas, and she asked me to come home so I wouldn't spend the holiday alone. I told her that my hair was still long. My dad was on the extension, and she said, "Did you hear that?"

My dad said, "I don't care if your hair is down to the floor. Come home, Son."

Finally, my prayers were answered.

When I arrived at my parents' house on Christmas Day, my dad came out to greet me. My mom was crying with happiness that after five years her wayward son was finally home again. My dad was happy to see me. It was the first time he'd seen me with long hair, but he didn't make one comment about it. Later we visited my sister Norma, and as we left her home I heard my dad whisper to my mom, "He doesn't look half-bad with long hair, does he?"

My mom turned and gave him a shocked look, not believing what she was hearing.

They understood now that I was a Sundancer and what that meant. My dad seemed to have a new respect for me. He had heard from other people about the Sundance, and how hard and admirable it was to be a Sundancer. At some point, he mentioned what I was doing to one of his friends who knew about the Sundance from reading about it. He looked surprised and asked, "Manny is a Sundancer?" When my dad confirmed that I had danced several times, his friend explained that he knew about it and that it was a very difficult thing to do, that it was painful, and only very committed people follow that spirituality.

I believe the conversation had a lot to do with changing my dad's mind.

I spent another day with my parents. The next morning, I got up early, and Mom wanted to fix me breakfast. I declined. She asked me if I'd stay a few more days.

I said, "Thanks, Mom, but I can't stay. I've got to get to Tucson."

She said, "Why do you have to get? I've never seen you have to get anywhere."

"Mom, something is urging me to get there right away. I don't know what it is."

I reached Tucson at about noon that day and went to see my friend Anna, who is a promoter. She promoted a big show in Tucson and had a tent set up with booths inside and out. We walked around talking for a little while, but she was busy, so I left her alone and went my own way.

Little did I know that the next day I would find out why I was compelled to come to Tucson. It would prove to be a major turning point in my life.

Early the next morning, I woke up, had my breakfast, then headed back to Anna's tent. As I walked around outside I ran into Nan and Dave, a couple of people I knew, who were set up selling crafts. We talked for about an hour. I told them I was making Dream Catchers.

Nan pulled me aside and said secretively, "Hey, come here. Everybody's trying to make it on the native thing and trying to cash in on the Dream Catcher deal."

I asked her, "What do you mean?"

"Come here, I want to show you something."

So she led me inside and brought me to a table full of crudely made Dream Catchers! A short, little white woman was behind the table. Nan turned around and left, but I stayed there. I started scowling at the woman, and she looked at me with her innocent, hazel eyes and said, "Hi, can I help you with anything?"

I asked her, "Who made these Dream Catchers?"

She said, "A Choctaw lady from Arkansas."

"Well, true, authentic Dream Catchers are made by medicine people," I said angrily.

Taken aback by my aggressive tone, I could tell she felt

uncomfortable. She said she didn't mean to offend anyone, and asked me if I knew about them.

"Of course, I know about them. I make them. Did you know that . . . " And I proceeded to lecture her on how it had been a tradition from ancient people, and how only elders made them for people who had problems sleeping. I was really upset that a white woman, from God knows where, was trying to sell in my territory!

She said, "You make them yourself?"

"Yeah."

"I'd like to see them."

This had turned from a lecture to a possible business deal, and since business is business, I turned to her and said, "Well, I'll go get some."

"I can follow you out to your car," she said, "My girl-friend will watch the booth."

We walked out there, and, by now, I was trying to show off. I showed her all of my Dream Catchers, in all sizes and colors.

"Oh my God, you made these?" She asked.

"Hey, I make all of them, and I don't need anybody's help."

"I'll tell you what, if you make them for me, I can sell them by the truckload!"

I looked at her, incredulously, but trying not to show it, "You can?"

She replied, "I've got connections in Canada like you can't believe!"

She was telling me that she was going to buy Dream Catchers by the truckload from me. However, I found out later she really was quite a nervy young lady. She would commit herself to things financially, without a cane to hang on, all the while trying to think positively. As it turned out she didn't have *any* money to *buy* a truckload! Regardless, I had to admire her for her courageous and entrepreneurial nature. It was wonderful.

We walked back into the tent, talking and making plans. My mind was in a whirl. I was calculating how much money I would make and thinking that I'd have to hire people to help me.

We finally introduced ourselves to one another. Her name was Melody. We both felt pretty good about meeting. I told her that I was going to see some friends of mine but that I'd be back later.

So, I took off and found Thelma and her husband. They have stores in New York and Long Island and they did quite a bit of buying from me. In fact, they bought me out. Thelma asked me to make more Dream Catchers before the show finished. They wanted to have some to take home. When we finished business, Thelma said, "Manny, we're having supper at Carlos Murphy's. You want to join us?"

I said, "I would love to join you, but I just met this young lady. I was going to ask her if she wanted . . . "

"Heck," Thelma said, "Bring her with you."

"You sure you don't mind?"

"Not one bit, we can just write it off as a business expense."

I said, "Great! Oh, but Thelma, I don't even know if she wants to go or not. I'll ask her and see what she says."

I felt pretty good. I had an invitation for dinner, I had met a nice young lady, and my pocket was full from the sale. By now I had spent most of the day with Melody and discovered that I really enjoyed her company.

I went back to where Melody was and told her that I had to go to the post office to mail my son some money. It was his thirteenth birthday that day, and I always sent a bit extra on the kids' birthdays. Then I had to try to find a motel room to take a shower.

She offered, "If all you need is a shower, you can go over to my motel room. There's nobody there. Here's the key. Just bring it back when you're done. It's too hard to find a motel room in Tucson at this time."

Well, I was a perfect stranger, but I guess she felt she could trust me. I found the motel room where she was staying, and I went in and took a shower. It took me quite a long time to get ready, so when I got back to her booth, it was almost time for her to close.

Although she never said it, I think she was a little bit worried that she had given her room key to a person she didn't know. She must have questioned herself for being so trusting, because when I came in, I noticed a look of relief on her face.

Then I asked her, "Well, look, I've been invited to this dinner tonight over at Carlos Murphy's. Do you have any plans? Are you going out with Darren and Sheila?" By now I had met her friends she was with.

She said, "Well, no. They have plans, but I didn't want to go with them anyway. I'd love to go with you."

Thelma and her husband were already there when we arrived. While we had dinner we visited and talked shop. We had a good old time and ate some fine food.

Afterward, we drove back to her motel room, and, after parking our vans, we took a walk. We walked up the street to a fast-food place. As we sat there, we started holding hands and talking about Canada and the places I had been. I felt stupid. There I was, a fifty-two-year-old man, holding hands like a teenager. I felt ridiculous, but it didn't feel wrong. Though we had originally met to discuss business, our being together created a new chemistry.

I ended up helping her at the show. Then we left Tucson together and went north to Flagstaff. We traveled together for a couple of weeks, selling and making crafts. After a while Melody said she really had to get back to Canada.

By then, I was thinking, I really love this woman, and I enjoy her company. I really hated to let her go, so I thought, "Well, maybe I'll go with her to Canada. If things work out, I'll stay. If not, I can always come back." I talked to her about it, and she was delighted that I wanted to come.

It was quite an adventure going up there. We ended up at a New Age show there, which was quite interesting. It opened my eyes to many things that I hadn't encountered before. That show was my first introduction to a new way of life and a new circle of friends.

Once the summer was in full swing, Melody and I returned to the states to attend the Sundance.

This was the first Sundance Melody had ever seen. Just as her world had opened my eyes to many things, my world that is the Sundance opened her eyes to many different things. She saw how people prayed and suffered for their beliefs. It made her a believer. Since then she has accepted the native way and knows that it is a good way to follow spiritually.

Before she met me, Melody's own spiritual background was quite varied. She had had a lot of exposure to Catholicism as a child, evangelism as a teenager, then was lost for a few years in early adulthood. It wasn't until she was in her mid-twenties that she discovered esoteric teachings and beliefs. She had the right ideas; being kind to others, trying to heal the planet, thinking positively. When I met her, she had her own metaphysical crystal business called "CrystalEyes," which exposed her to many new philosophies and beliefs. She ended up with a mishmash of beliefs, and she danced to her own drum. She believed in one God and prayed to God regularly in her own way.

Ironically, a few months before we met, she had mentioned to a friend that she wondered why she was carrying so many native-oriented products. Now we know why: it led up to our meeting.

Melody's first Sundance was very special and inspiring for her. It was on the Rosebud Reservation, and she was quite overwhelmed and moved by the things she saw there. It was a very intense ceremony, but it had been especially tough on her because she was now five months pregnant. On top of that, we had just learned from the doctor that we were expecting twins! Melody was finally able to meet many of the friends I had been Sundancing with for a couple of years.

And two of Melody's friends, Joe and Mieke, made a fifteen-hundred-mile pilgrimage from Ontario, Canada, just to pray and to support us. They gave up their time, effort, and sleep to help any way they could. Mieke gave free psychic readings to everyone who wanted them. Many native people took advantage of her generosity. Joe was busy in the cook shack, helping out, washing pots and pans, and watching the front gate as security. It was a big comfort for Melody, having friends from home who could hold her hand while she watched me in the Sundance.

This Sundance began like all the others. The Sundance Chief followed tradition: we had sweats, did our prayers, and danced hard. But this was a special ceremony for several reasons.

The year before, I had wanted to pierce my back and drag buffalo skulls. I had wanted to do it for my children.

We strongly believe the buffalo brings us an abundance of spiritual energy, so that we can cope with everyday life and the realities of our world. This is the reason we pierce our backs and drag as many buffalo skulls as we can bear. The more there are, the more power we receive from the buffalo.

142

However, I didn't do it that year, because I had no one to help dress and take care of the wounds afterwards. This year, though, I had Melody with me. She told me she would care for my wounds.

On Saturday morning, they marked my chest and back to indicate where I was going to be pierced. Melody stood in the shade around the Arbor watching the dance. When she realized that I had marks on the front and back, she knew something was up. She was crying, and holding Mieke's hand. I hadn't explained anything to her about dragging skulls, and no one else had dragged skulls yet, so she didn't know what the marks on my back meant.

I knew if I told Melody what I was going to do ahead of time, she would get upset, and in her condition, I didn't want her to worry.

When I went to the tree to pray, I untied my rope and stretched it out to the northwest side of the Arbor. All my friends knew that was where I danced and prayed while attached to the tree, so everyone moved to stand near Melody. That Saturday morning, I was the first to pierce.

After my chest had been pierced, I was standing in my spot, dancing and praying. I looked across and saw my friend Harold. He had been pierced right after me. We danced back and forth to the tree, the traditional four times. On the last time, as I ran backwards, I saw Harold break loose one split second before I did. When I broke loose, a Sundance leader took my wrist bracelet and ran with me around the Arbor to the west side.

They had four buffalo skulls tied together waiting for me. The anticipation of feeling the weight and pain that come from dragging buffalo skulls actually becomes something good and joyous, rather than something to fear. At the same time, it is a way for us to give thanks in a special and sacred way.

This is also the reason I make my piercing bones out of buffalo leg bone. It seems as though every year this leg bone comes to me. I cut a section out of the middle of it. Then I split it lengthwise. I file and sand down the pieces of bone to the size of ballpoint pens. Then I sharpen the ends into points to make them easier to use during the piercing ceremony. I always give them away to people significant to me, whom I love.

They pierced my back and attached the four skulls. Using the sacred staff (our spiritual flag or symbol), I started slowly moving forward. The pain on my back was immense. I gritted my teeth and started praying hard, asking for courage and strength. Stopping to honor each direction as I reached it, I made one complete circle of the Arbor. On my second round, just past the north direction, the left piercing broke loose. I stopped, not realizing what had happened. I had felt a hard jerk on my back and some pain. But the pain seemed to center itself more on the right side now, and I didn't know why.

My Sundance brother Henry danced next to me. He leaned over and told me, "Keep going, Manny. One side broke loose."

I leaned into the other side, thinking it might break loose, too. Being out of balance like that made it much more difficult to pull the skulls.

I got them moving again and continued around the Arbor until I had gone four complete rounds. The right-side piercing had held the whole time. Finally, it was time to break loose. I backed up to the skulls. A few of my Sundance brothers sat on the skulls, and I took off running. I hit the end of the rope and broke easily enough. Though still in pain, I was thankful it was over. Melody had tears streaming down her face, and I could tell it had been difficult for her to watch. I had asked her before we started

Sundancing to be strong for me, and, all things considered, she was very brave.

Sunday morning, I didn't dance because the two piercings had taken a lot out of me, and I felt I'd fulfilled my commitment. Midday, I went to the Arbor, carrying my old pipe and another beautiful pipe I had just received from Todd, a pipe maker from Pipestone. The sacred pipe that I had had for five years was magnificent. It was fully covered with cut beads and the designs were geometric. My ex-wife had made it for me, and I didn't feel the same way about it anymore. It couldn't bring on the special feelings it used to. It was time to pass it on. I prayed the previous night and asked the spirits what I should do. The message came to me through thoughts.

When I got behind the Arbor, while the other Sundancers were resting between rounds, I called for Harold and Henry.

They were both happy to see me. As they walked up, they were smiling and laughing. Harold asked me, "What happened Manny, you feeling lazy today?"

I replied, "Come here, I've got something for you."

When they were standing in front of me, I presented my old pipe with the beading on it to Harold.

He gave me a puzzled look, as though asking me, "Why are you giving me this?" He couldn't speak. He didn't know what to say to this gesture.

"Harold, do you remember saying to me that if I ever wanted to get rid of this pipe, I should give it to you? Well, Brother, here it is. It's yours."

Henry was getting upset, and asked, "What's wrong? Why are you doing this?"

Turning, I held up the other pipe to him and said, "Henry, it's time for you to have a new *Chanupa*. Please take this, it's my gift to you."

I could tell by their faces that they thought I was leaving the Sundance for some reason. They had tears in their eyes and they shook their heads as if to say, "No, Manny, you can't do this."

Then I explained to them that it was time that I had a new pipe to go with my new life. I wasn't leaving the Sundance, I only wanted to honor my two Sundance brothers. Both looked at me and, not knowing what else to do, embraced me. All three of us shared tears together. It was a special moment for all of us.

Melody and I left the Sundance Monday morning and drove to Rapid City for a couple of days' rest and much-needed showers.

After we recuperated, we left Rapid City and drove south through the South Dakota Badlands on the road that goes straight to David Swallow Jr.'s Sundance in Porcupine. I had another three years with David and his people.

We were well received upon our arrival to the Sundance grounds. The people made everyone there feel welcome. I introduced Melody to everyone, and she made a lot of friends.

It wasn't long after arriving that we had to go cut down the Sacred Tree. Melody stayed behind at camp and prepared dinner. It was getting hard for her to move around, and it was extremely hot.

Everybody gathered behind David's pickup to follow him to the Sacred Tree. The convoy continued until we pulled off the main highway. David pulled the pickup close to the edge of a river and stopped.

Opening the door, he said, "This is it, boys!"

I saw him pointing across the river. I asked David, "Can't we get any closer than this? How are we going to get the tree here?"

He replied, "This is as close as we can get . . . and we're bringing it back on our shoulders!"

I said, "Oh."

I looked back and saw people getting out of their cars. David removed his boots before getting into the water. As I entered the water in my bare feet, I felt my connection with Mother Earth. Suddenly a common occurrence became a very special moment in my life.

Something triggered my sensitivity, something happened to my soul. A soft, intense feeling of peace and contentment came over me. I felt the warm water around my feet. I felt the cool, soft mud squish up between my toes. Both seemed to massage my feet.

It was as though Mother Earth was telling me that the next four days were going to be hard on my feet, and she wanted to show me that she could also be gentle on them. The river was about a foot deep, but it was very wide and had a slippery, muddy bottom. After crossing, we gathered around the Sacred Tree.

Once we cut down the tree, we placed it on our shoulders and began walking across the river. Fortunately, it wasn't very big. Everything went well, until we started slipping on the mud. Then it became very difficult to carry it without touching the ground or water. Slowly we made it across and started up the steep embankment on the other side. I slipped and fell, more than once, trying to get up the side. It was very difficult. Once when I fell, I used my body to keep the tree from falling on the ground. Finally, with strenuous effort, we got it on the trailer.

Two hundred yards from the Sundance grounds, we took the tree off and carried it toward the east entrance of the Arbor. By now everyone was hot and tired, and it was getting to be early evening. When we gently laid it down inside the Arbor, the base was lying right at the edge of the center hole. Melody was waiting along with many others. They had the prayer ties and flags that we were going to hang on the limbs at the top of the tree. It was such a beautiful sight: all those people walking up, saying prayers, and tying flags on the tree.

The Sundance Chief tied the traditional silhouette of a buffalo, a man, and an eagle wing to the branches. He did that so the Creator would recognize the men who were praying. The buffalo was on the tree because of its sacredness to us; the eagle wing represented the eagle that would take our prayers to the Creator. The man represented all humanity.

Sundancers started coming from all over to tie their ropes to the tree. Things got quieter around the tree. As each person finished, he or she would stand in a circle away from the tree so that other people would have better access to it.

Finally, the Sundance Chief announced, "Grab hold of your ropes, we're going to stand it up."

We started pulling, then some men got underneath the tree, pushing it up higher and higher until it was standing straight. Once the leaves were free of the ground, people remained still, waiting for the tree to stand erect before moving. The only movement was the vibration from the men who were struggling to stand the tree up. When the tree was straight, it was like a tension was broken. All the leaves started flickering and waving. There was a slight breeze that just made them dance. It was so beautiful and majestic.

The base of the tree sat in a deep, four-foot hole. After centering it in the hole, we had two or three men start shoveling in the dirt and tamping it down. The only thing holding the tree up was the ropes. They looked like spiderwebs branching away from the tree. Eventually the tree was standing alone in all its glory.

As each man walked up to it, he found his rope and tied

it down around the tree. By securing the ropes to the tree, they wouldn't be flopping around when we danced the next day.

Once the tree was up, there was a pause as though everyone was holding his breath for a minute. It was so impressive and awesome to see this magnificent tree and to watch it come alive. Now it stood alone like it did before it was cut down.

Melody and I returned to the van. We had a light supper, then I took off my muddy, dirty clothes next to our van and crawled in. The blankets were a welcome relief. I must have been tired because morning arrived quickly.

The next morning we did our traditional sweats and danced into the Arbor. It got hot very early that morning, but it was beautiful. Everyone was in great spirits. This was Melody's second Sundance in two weeks.

After we greeted the sun and placed our Sacred Pipes on the altar, we retired to the dancers' resting place. We were all sitting around visiting and introducing ourselves to dancers we didn't know. It was a good time to meet new brothers. It was a good time to encourage all the new Sundancers, to help them overcome their nervousness. We joked around, to alleviate the fears of the new dancers, because for some this is a scary thing.

Before the Sundance, Al managed to get a buffalo. It was bought from the tribal herd on the reservation. He had it butchered, and he had the skull lying back behind the Arbor.

Al asked, "Lionel, do you want that buffalo skull?"

Lionel looked surprised. "Really?" he said. "Yeah, I really like it, and it would look good in my living room. Sure, I'll take it."

I looked at Al and then at Lionel. I said, "Al, you're giving Lionel that buffalo skull?"

"Yeah." He was wondering what I was getting at.

I said, "And you accepted it, right, Lionel?"

"Yes, I am very grateful. I was secretly hoping this would happen."

"Well, Al, you realize what you have just committed Lionel to, don't you?"

A look of surprise and confusion crossed their faces. Then Al began to understand what I was talking about.

"That's right, Al," I said, "you gave it to him. He's accepted it. Now he's got to pierce his back and drag that skull."

Al explained, "I knew all this, but when I gave it to him, that is not the way I meant it."

I went on, "I know, and I realize you didn't do this to hurt him. I don't want to see him go through any pain, but that's the traditional way. He's got to earn the right to have that buffalo skull in his home."

Al looked at Lionel and said, "It's true, Lionel. I'm sorry, I forgot."

Lionel said, "Oh, man. Things are really serious around here!" Then he laughed, "If I had known, I could have picked one up for fifty dollars at the trading post!"

Everybody burst out laughing.

An old-timer listening to all this said, "Hey, Lionel, I'll drag it for you for fifty dollars! I'll pierce and drag it for you. You give me fifty bucks, and you can take the skull home!"

Then another guy jumped up and said, "I'll do it for forty!"

Then I chimed in, "Well, I'll do it for twenty-five. I don't mind getting pierced."

Everybody was laughing and making a big joke out of it because it had been so very serious at first. Then Lionel quietly asked, "Do I hear twenty?!"

Another round of laughter started.

150

Finally, after the laughter had died down, Lionel said, "Well, Al," as he shook his hand, "I accepted the skull. If I have to pierce for it and drag it, I'll do that."

Al said, "You think he should do it now?"

"It doesn't matter when, Al, as long as he drags it. You gave it to him, so it's up to you when."

Reluctantly, Al said, "What I mean is, it's really getting to smell bad. It's been dead for three days, and it still has the hide and everything on the skull. It hasn't been boiled or anything."

"Actually, it might be better this way," I said. "It's green and heavy. If the Creator wants him to drag it around all four times, Lionel will remember it well. If the Creator doesn't, he'll break loose before dragging it too far."

But in the end, they decided to wait until the following year for Lionel to drag the skull. He wanted to drag a skull that didn't smell so bad.

The dance continued all day. Later that afternoon Lionel came to me with tobacco while we were taking a break. He said, "Brother, I would be proud if you would do the piercing for me."

This was quite an honor, particularly since I had never pierced anyone before. His asking made me feel emotional. I took the tobacco and said, "Yeah, I'll do it for you. I'd be honored, Brother."

When you go to an elder to ask for advice or a favor, the traditional way is to go to them with a tobacco offering. Sometimes, when you don't have a bag of tobacco, you can use a cigarette. If the elder isn't committed to something else, he almost can't refuse to do the bidding.

So I explained to Lionel, "Whenever you take tobacco to an elder, first tell him what you want him to do. Before you give him the tobacco, give him the opportunity to refuse. If it's something he can't or doesn't want to do, that gives the elder the option of backing out if he wants." Lionel, like everyone else, including myself, was still learning.

The piercing song began. We placed Lionel where everybody could shake his hand as they went out of the rest area into the Arbor. I took him to the center tree and said, "Lionel, it's going to be a good one. It'll be okay. Don't worry, little brother."

He smiled nervously, "I'm not worried."

I let him pray for a while. I went to David and explained that I might have to put my glasses on. In recent years my eyes had been getting worse, and I needed reading glasses for anything up close. He told me to tie some sage on them, so the Spirits would accept them. When I brought Lionel to the buffalo hide and laid him down, he handed me his scalpel to pierce him. I closed my eyes as I put my hands on the tree. I asked, "*Tunkashila*" (Lakota for "the Creator") to give me compassion and to guide my hands. I asked for better vision, so I could see what I was doing.

When I opened my eyes, my eyesight was better than ever before, as though the brightness of the sun had increased tenfold. The whole world brightened up for me.

When I knelt down next to Lionel, I was on his left and David was on his right. David did the first piercing. I held the flesh while he did it, and then inserted the cherrywood piercing stick through Lionel's flesh. While David was tying the rope on, I grabbed and pinched the flesh together. David reached across to help me hold the flesh up. I took the knife and slowly slid it into his flesh. I felt a slight little pop as the sharp pointed scalpel broke through the flesh and then another pop as it went through. I didn't want to hurt my brother Lionel any more than I had to.

Slowly, slowly, I sawed and pulled the blade to my left to widen the hole that I had made. Blood sprang up immediately through the wound. It was hard to see what I was doing. David took Lionel's piercing stick and put it through the wound. Immediately we knew the wound wasn't big enough. Shaking his head, David indicated that I should cut some more. It would tear out if we tried to push it through his flesh. David pulled the piercing stick out, and I inserted the knife in and cut a bit more. Slowly, ever so slowly, I cut down until the opening was about a half-inch in length. Then David grabbed the piercing stick and pushed it through the cut, through the wound that I had inflicted on my brother's chest. This time it slid through easily.

I looked at his face, and it was expressionless, just a little pale. I knew the pain he was going through. I had felt it many times in the past. But I also knew that he was a warrior. When I tied his rope on, I made a figure eight around the wooden stick. Finished with our work, we picked him up.

I shook his hand and said, "Brother, you're on."

I could tell by the dazed look in his eyes that he was in pain and shock, so I kept him moving and talking. After a few minutes I could see that he was feeling better.

Many people can't take the pain and the shock that accompany the piercing ceremony, just as many people have trouble accepting an injection at the doctor's office. Piercing is done under the harshest conditions possible, as tradition dictates. It may seem crude to other people, but to us we are doing the very best for that person, the best we know how. We do it with the Creator's blessing and with as much compassion as possible.

I helped Lionel with his rope. I was trying to take it easy on my brother. I knew that he was in pain and hurting, but I also knew he was there by choice. Nobody ever told him he had to be there. I also realized he had found his spirituality, his road, and he was quite happy and content with it. That is what makes the Sundance so wonderful, the choice to be there is your own.

As Lionel backed up, his rope was tight. I told him to breathe deeply and pray hard—the harder he prayed, the less pain there would be. I kept telling him gently, "Pull back and stretch that flesh. The more you stretch it now, the easier it will break when the time comes. It hurts, I know, Brother, it hurts. Pull it back."

He pulled back until the rope was taut. It was bouncing then stretched tight. His chest was way out of proportion. I said, "*Ho ka*! Come on, go to the tree, and pray, Brother."

He danced toward the tree, then knelt on the ground and prayed to our God that we can touch, pray to, and cry with. He got up.

Lionel pulled back, stretching and stretching. The pierce on the right side suddenly popped off. He looked at me with surprise.

He said, "It fell off. It broke loose!"

"Hey, that's good, Brother. Now you only have one to break loose. The Spirits are smiling on you. Be grateful, be grateful that they are smiling on you. They are trying to make it easier for you. That's good."

He smiled at me. He was stepping lighter now, and with more vigor.

By now he had been to the tree three times. I told him, "This time when you go to the tree, run hard on your way back. Don't worry, I'll be here to catch you."

As the Sundance Chief, David controls when people go to and from the tree to pray when they are piercing. He waved Lionel on to the center. We went with him to the tree.

"You are ready to break loose. You only have one side to break," David softly spoke to him, giving him words of encouragement for the last round before breaking loose.

I saw David wave his fan at Lionel, telling him to break loose. I couldn't believe that little guy could run as fast as he could. He turned around and was running really fast from the tree. As he hit the end of the rope, he started to fall, and I caught him under the arms and picked him up. "All right, Brother, you're loose."

He was so happy. "Manny, I did it!"

"You bet, Brother, it's done."

I led him around the Arbor back to his place, and everybody was touching him. Everyone wanted to feel his energy, that tremendous energy given to a Sundancer when he pierces that is so beautiful and contagious. It was good to watch him slowly, softly descend from his spiritual high.

Meanwhile, Melody was very tired and decided to lie down in the van to rest awhile. She had burned herself out from so many days of dancing, first over at Rosebud and then at Porcupine. Slowly, she climbed into the van. Leaving the doors open to catch any faint breeze that might happen by, she stretched out to rest, and, though uncomfortably hot, she dozed off.

After sleeping awhile, she woke up and could hear the drums. Suddenly, she felt something move. It was her babies, moving inside her for the first time. Then she felt them again. She got up and couldn't believe it. It was the thrill of her life. She was so excited she couldn't restrain herself and started to cry, wishing she had someone there to share her miracle. She got up, came over to the Arbor, and asked me to come over to where she could talk to me. "What's wrong?" I asked. I was confused because she was crying, but she was also smiling.

She said, "The babies moved for the first time. They were listening to the Sundance drums and started moving." Then she continued, "I've felt them move a couple of times already. It almost feels like they start dancing every time they hear the Sundance drums."

Naturally, I was thrilled. It was such a beautiful thing and even more special because it happened at the Sundance.

I believe that where children are when they hear their first sounds is important. I can't think of anything more wonderful that could happen to a person, to have the first sound one hears and responds to be the sound of Sundance drums beating.

BELOW — GREEN

"Mother Earth"

GIVER
OF LIFE

After the Sundance was over Melody and I headed back to Buffalo, New York, and Niagara Falls, where we had a storage shed. We had just started renting a three-bedroom house in the town of Richmond Hill, just north of Toronto. We continued exhibiting at shows and selling our crafts all over Canada. As life went on, things got a bit easier for both of us.

One morning we were preparing for one of the biggest New Age psychic fairs in Canada, if not North America, when the phone rang. It was an old friend of mine from Oklahoma.

I asked him, "How did you get my phone number, Bob?"

"It wasn't easy, I called all over California. My friend, are you sitting?"

"What do you mean?"

He says, "It's about your ex-wife. She got killed in a traffic accident last night."

We had been separated and divorced for a while now, so it really didn't bother me emotionally. I felt absolutely nothing toward her. My first thought was how the kids were, and I asked Bob about them.

"They are fine, just fine. They're here at my house. What do you want to do about them?"

Still in shock, I tried to gather my thoughts and said, "Look, I don't have any money right now. I have a four-day show starting tomorrow. If you could watch them, I'll pick them up after the show."

He said, "Okay, wire me permission to accept responsibility for these kids or the welfare department is going to come in and take them. If they do that, you will have a really difficult time trying to get them back when you get here. By then, they will have them placed in foster homes."

I pleaded with him, "Don't let anyone touch my kids, Bob. Please, keep them together for me. I appreciate your concern and your friendship. I'll call you when I get ready to go."

You really learn a lot about your friends in times like these. I thanked God for Bob's intervention and prayed I would have a good show so I could afford to get my children.

The world that Melody had introduced me to showed me things I didn't know existed. The first show she took me to, she was selling her crystals and gemstones, and I tried to act as though I saw that sort of crowd all the time. Melody just laughed at me. She knew I was uncomfortable around some of the people. We saw some rather odd individuals, including UFO abductees, palm readers, astrologists, and hypnotists. The show really opened my eyes to things that I was familiar with in some way, but not in the way I was seeing them there.

After that introduction I told Melody about how, for thousands of years, our people had been consulting the Spirits for guidance. Some older medicine people used different methods to help people. There were those who used feathers, sticks, small bones, and even stones. Others would use the "hands on" way of healing and helping. Much of it was done by drumming and singing while they contacted the Spirits for advice.

So this was not a strange world for some of us First People. We just don't have a name for it, that I know of. A good native friend of mine, Ted Silverhand, calls himself a seer and does "readings" for people. I heard he's very good at what he does.

For myself, it's something I've had all my life. I always had people asking me for advice and telling me their problems. It seemed I always had words of comfort for them and knew what to tell them in their times of need. I helped a few couples resolve their problems when they were at the point of breaking up.

It was so much a part of me I didn't realize that I had a gift. I'm very grateful for it. I never realized anyone would be willing to pay me for the advice I had to offer. I was so wrong. People pay counselors and consultants for advice everyday.

The Creator brought me a way to help people and feed my family. It's a fair and good exchange. That's what Melody showed me. I now know that I am a seer, interpreter, adviser, and counselor, and very good at it. I have a great deal of experience and have received testimonials of my ability to predict people's futures and advise them how best to use that information. I'm proud to be a part of this old and honorable practice.

So now that my children were alone, I would be faced with a major expense just to go get them. Out of the blue, our friends Barry and Carol called and asked if they could give us some money. Another friend, Georgina, offered a financial gift. Ted Silverhand gave us money to help. Then Carl, Shawna, and Melva offered their financial help. This generosity from everyone really choked me up. There weren't words to thank them. I was very grateful and thanked the Creator for bringing me such special people in my time of need.

It is hard to give everybody credit who deserves it, because so many people do. People I didn't even know came from everywhere to help us. Everyone who gave money gave it unconditionally, without strings or a time limit to pay it back. Without their help, I don't know how we would have done it. It was a lot easier to get my kids.

Right after the show, Melody saw me off at the airport in Toronto. After everyone's help and what we had earned, I had three thousand dollars to take with me. By evening I was in Tulsa, and my friend Bob met me and took me to his house.

When I got to Bob's house, my four daughters and one son were there waiting. My twin girls, Mary and Becky, had just had their tenth birthday. The accident had happened right before their birthday. Some friends of the family, Barbara, Mildred, and Sherry, bought them a couple of presents. I was very grateful.

Seeing my kids for the first time in two years was an emotional event for everyone. I had missed them immensely and done many prayers for them. I pierced for their protection and safety. I prayed to get them back someday, but I sure didn't expect it to happen this way.

That was why the Spirits told me at the Sundance the year before that I had to dance and pierce every day for my children. They were trying to see if I was worthy or willing to sacrifice for my children. My red chest was swollen, inflamed with pain, and it burned from so many piercings. God now knew that if they were with me, I would make sure they were protected in all ways.

I strongly believe the Creator warned my ex-wife to stop neglecting our kids, as I understand she did for quite a while, leaving them alone for long periods of time at the condemned house they lived in. Perhaps, the Creator warned her that if she didn't stop, drastic steps would be taken to protect those children.

Although the kids didn't like being so overprotected from the curious neighbors, I hoped that one day they would understand that Bob and Dee Dee had done them and me a big favor by picking them up at school before the news of their mom's accident spread throughout town. That protected them from the so-called friends and neighbors—from the gossip and stares, and from pointing fingers—until I got there.

I picked up my children and took them away from all that. All of my ex's friends had gone through the house like tornadoes. They had taken my guns, silversmithing tools, clothes, chainsaws—everything my ex-wife and I had together, even the kids' clothing. Luckily, some friends who used to work for us had been able to save a few of the really personal items that belonged to my wife, things she wanted to leave the kids. That was good, and I appreciated it.

All this time I had a sick feeling in my stomach, wondering how I was going to deal with having my kids back in my life. Though Melody said to bring them up and we'd manage, how would it be when reality set in? Melody had no experience with children at all; she'd been an only child. How was she going to handle all the kids, especially when she was pregnant for the first time?

I knew it would be difficult for all of us and would change our lives, but my heart ached for my children every time I thought about how their whole world had been turned upside down, overnight. I wondered how they felt to be suddenly in the care of a father they hadn't seen in two years—to find themselves with no home, no mother, no clothes, and no creature comforts. The only thing they had to hang on to was faith in their dad. I felt so sorry for them, for their losses and confusion. They were all clinging to me, their only hope for protection from the storm in their lives.

Bob took me to the town of Claremore, and we bought a station wagon just the way it was sitting in the car lot. I didn't even know if it was in good or bad shape. In my state of mind, the only thing I could do was depend on *Tunkashila*, God, to help me. So, I bought the station wagon, put the kids in it, and left for Canada. I hadn't even been in Oklahoma for twenty-four hours.

On the drive home, all five kids wanted to sit by me in the front seat. It was as if the backseat was too far from me. I was all they had now. The first stop we made was in Joplin, Missouri. We stopped at a motel room, and all the kids took showers. We stopped at a store, and I bought them each two new sets of clothes. After everyone had dressed and cleaned up, I took them out to dinner. They couldn't eat enough! They looked so thin and undernourished. I wondered what life had been like for them while I was gone. It broke my heart just to think about it.

We worked our way slowly, steadily all the way north to Canada. When we reached home, naturally Melody had embraced the change in her life. She had taken our house and turned it into a home for the new arrivals. She found bunk beds, mattresses, sheets, pillows, and pillowcases for the kids. It was quite a job for a woman who was seven months pregnant, and it was a big job for anybody to go from an only-child family atmosphere to caring for five children she had never met before. I was very proud of her and always thanked God and the Spirits who brought her to me. It was all in preparation for this. Melody had prayed for someone to share her life with, and her strong prayers called me from California to Tucson. The call was powerful. God knew that eight months later, I was going to need her and so would my children.

When the kids arrived, friends from everywhere came to help Melody get ready. Bags and bags of supplies arrived everyday—clothes, shoes, toys, books, everything they could possibly need. The generosity of people overwhelmed me. News traveled fast about what had happened to the children, and everyone was supportive and helpful.

Shortly after the children arrived, Melody and I got married. Although she was seven months pregnant, I wanted Melody to be married and have everything legal when she gave birth. My son Rockie gave her away at a civil ceremony, and all my daughters stood up with us. They were just beautiful. They had accepted Melody and her love from the first moment they walked in the door. I was very happy about it.

Perhaps planning for the wedding and adjusting to Canada helped the kids keep their minds off the trauma they had gone through. I think it made them feel more secure in their new home and environment.

We had a wonderful reception at the house of Melody's mother, Lynne. There were many tears of joy and laughter.

A couple of months after the wedding, in late December, Melody started to experience some pain one night after dinner. We called the hospital, and they suggested a warm bath and a beer, to make her relax, which she did. However, the pain was getting worse, so we called the hospital again. Now Melody was lying down and the nurse asked me to put her on the line. When Melody described the pain she was having, the nurse told us to bring her in, she was in labor! They said they'd be ready for her.

There were about six inches of fresh snow on the ground and our driveway had a slight incline. I shoveled and cleared it as best I could while my daughter Stormy helped Melody get ready. It was hard for her to walk, but we got her in the car. I still had trouble backing out and worried that we might get stuck in our own driveway. Again, Grandfather was watching over us.

We headed to the hospital, and by now it was snowing heavily. The flakes were large and wet. The wipers were having trouble keeping the windshield clear. York-Central Hospital was only eight miles from where we lived, but because of the snow it took about half an hour to get there.

At the hospital, the nurses took Melody directly into the labor room. Stormy and I went in and stayed with her through her seven hours of labor. We heard that wasn't very much for a first birth, but to me it felt like days. It hurt me to see Melody in so much pain. I wished there were some way I could take it from her. Stormy, who was only thirteen, was helping Melody breathe and holding her hand through it all. She had attended a couple of prenatal care classes with Melody. Being the oldest daughter, Stormy had been responsible for all the kids when her mother was gone, so she was mature beyond her years.

We had found out a couple of months before that there was really only one baby, not two as we had thought. The delivery was completely natural. No drugs, no cut, the baby just arrived. Melody gave birth so fast that Stormy ended up holding one leg while I held the other. Of all the children I have fathered in my life, this was the first one I ever saw being born. What an amazing sight it was.

At the Sundance the previous summer, I had prayed for a healthy baby, and she turned out beautiful and perfect in every way. I made a commitment to Grandfather to pierce my back and drag buffalo skulls, to thank him for bringing her to us in good health and complete.

We named her Oriona (Or-ee-on-ah) after the constellation Orion. Her middle name is Estrella, which is Spanish for "star."

After the birth, they took Melody and the baby upstairs to a room, so Stormy and I left. It was about six o'clock in the morning. As Stormy and I walked out, the first thing I saw on the ground were three small snow sparrows, pecking away at some crumbs on the hospital steps. The Spirits had brought me a native name for my little daughter, Little Snow Sparrow.

After Melody and the baby got home we all settled into a routine controlled, of course, by the whims and temperament of the baby. It took that little baby's energy to unite us as a family, and the kids instantly fell in love with their new little sister.

Spring was upon us before we knew it, and we started thinking about the Sundance. It was getting to be time for me to go and give thanks, to show my appreciation for all we had received in the past year.

The Sundance season arrived and we got ready. Money

just appeared, it seemed, when we needed it. We bought a pop-up trailer that could sleep eight, we loaded up the car we had from Oklahoma (which was miraculously still running), and headed toward South Dakota, camping out along the way.

This particular trip was really special to me. Although my children attended all four Shoshoni Sundances in Wyoming with me, this would be their first Lakota Sundance. They were finally going to see the piercing that terrified their mother.

We traveled along, and stopped in Pipestone, Minnesota, where I buy my pipes to take to the Sundance. We met with some of our other friends who were coming to the Sundance from Maryland. We went down to the quarries and saw Todd, Ray, and other guys I knew who were carvers.

Commercially, there are many versions of "peace pipes" sold throughout the country. However, a pipe from Pipestone has a card stating its authenticity, and the pipes are made only by native people. Sometimes I buy several pipes and give them to the Sundance Chief, so he can give pipes to those Sundancers he deems worthy.

The giving of a pipe is very important, and something to be thought about carefully. When the Sundance Chief gives a pipe and makes someone a pipe carrier, the Sundance Chief becomes responsible for whoever carries and whatever happens with that pipe. Traditionally, you can't buy yourself a pipe, it must be given to you. To be a pipe carrier is a sacred responsibility, and not to be taken lightly.

I don't believe a pipe should be considered a sacred object until it has been in a Sweat Lodge and has had a medicine person breathe life into it. When it is given the breath of life, the power to cure, then I believe it is sacrilegious to buy or sell that *Chanupa*. It becomes a living entity, and you don't sell living beings. This is why I will not buy or sell any part of the eagle and will not sell a Sacred Pipe. There is quite a bit of dissention about what's right and what's wrong. I personally believe a pipe is just an object, just like anything else, until it goes through the ceremony. Many tourists buy pipes at the center at Pipestone.

I believe that the natives who have been there for gen-erations quarrying the pipestone are the only ones who should be able to sell those pipes. It's a gift given to them by the Creator. This is the way they feed their families. In the old days, although they didn't sell them, they used to trade them for ponies. They traded for pemmican or dried buffalo jerky. They traded for deer skins or beads. Everything that was tradable. So, if anybody should be able to sell the pipes, I think it should be those people. They are the only people from whom I will buy a pipe. I will trade for a pipe, if the occasion arises and the trade is fair. As far as I am concerned, that is acceptable and makes me happy.

After meeting the other Sundancers in Pipestone, we head-ed toward South Dakota. Before we arrived, something remarkable happened. One of my girls, Rebecca, who was ten years old at the time, told me, "Daddy, I want to Sundance. I want to be in there with you and share. I want to experience it."

I sat and had long talks with her. My son Rockie, who was fifteen, also said he would like to be in the Sundance with me. It humbled me, my two children honoring me like this. That they should choose to follow me in the Sundance and the way of the *Chanupa*, and the Red Road. We sat and talked and I asked them questions—why they wanted to dance, what the Sacred Pipe meant to them, and so on—to understand why they wanted to do it. I felt their answers were appropriate, so I allowed them to dance with me. I also explained that they had to dance four years before they really made up their minds about piercing or not piercing. I think my son was glad of that. He felt he wasn't ready for piercing yet. He just wanted to be with me in the Sundance.

We reached the Sundance, and there was quite a controversy because Ironwood Hilltop Sundance had broken apart. A family argument about whose property the Arbor was on had been the reason. Our Sundance grounds had moved to Hollow Horn Bear. The Sundance Chief from Hollow Horn Bear had given permission to us to Sundance on their grounds until we found a permanent place.

The year before, I had asked the Creator to give me a healthy, normal baby. If my prayer was answered, I would commit myself to honor the Creator and my baby by piercing my back and dragging buffalo skulls. The Creator had answered my prayers, and now was the time to fulfill my commitment. The Arbor in a Lakota Sundance circle is not big, but it feels that way if you are dragging buffalo skulls. Melody told me later that when people around the Arbor realized I was going to pierce, at least fifty of them ran to stand behind me and my family. It was as though everyone knew something special was about to happen and wanted to be a part of it and support me.

First I was pierced in the front, once on each side. When I broke loose and danced around the Arbor, I immediately returned to the Sundance leaders and asked that they pierce me on my back. When I was getting pierced, I asked Lessert to make this a special piercing. I did not want to break loose until I had done my four turns around the Arbor.

He said, "Okay, it's up to you." When he finished, he leaned close to me and whispered in my ear, "Manny, that's guaranteed to hold till Christmas!" He had made the piercing deep.

Sometimes they don't want to hurt you, so they don't pierce too deep. But because of the weight of the skulls, men break loose before they have finished what they came there to do. I wanted to make sure they pierced me deep enough so the flesh wouldn't break before I was finished.

While standing there being pierced, my mental state was high. It felt good to be giving back something for all the Creator had given me. Henry came and stood in front of me to give his personal energy and support. He looked right into my eyes and held both of my biceps with his hands as the blade cut me. He watched to see if I was all right and had the courage to see this through.

After Lessert pierced me, he said, *"Ho-ka."* He smiled at me, "Okay, Manny, you're all right."

They tied me to the buffalo skulls. I was fortunate, I believe, because there were only four skulls, and they only weighed twenty to thirty pounds each.

I asked for my baby daughter to be brought to me. I told them, "I'm going to carry her around with me."

They brought Oriona, my Little Snow Sparrow, to me and I held her in my arms. It was quite a sight to see: me, an older, tanned native man; and my daughter, a blonde wistful baby, a blonde dressed in a white outfit for the ceremony. (At times I called her my Little Jellyfish.) It felt so wonderful, the experience of carrying my child, whom God had given to me with all her limbs and as normal as any child could be.

Afterwards Melody explained to me, as best she could, what was going on while I carried the baby around. There wasn't a dry eye anywhere. Men, women, and even some Sundancers were crying. My girls, Stormy, Dory, and Mary, were crying and holding on to each other. It must have touched people's hearts to see a man suffering for his daughter. Maybe they felt I was carrying a part of them. As though the baby represented every person who witnessed the special ceremony.

True to my request, and true to the friend who pierced me, both places where I had been pierced hung on as I danced around the circle. I could feel the gravel under my feet. I could feel gentle breezes. I could smell sage. I started slowly from the west, stopped first to the north to hold my baby high to the Spirits of the north for their blessings, and then continued.

With the skulls dragging behind me, I had to lean forward, sometimes almost parallel to the ground. As the skulls tumbled around, they landed on their foreheads and teeth. When the teeth hit the ground, they dug down and yanked me backward. The pain was excruciating.

I danced on. I offered my baby to the east, and when I got to the south I offered her to the south. Each time I stopped and offered her to a direction for blessings, it was difficult to get started again. Usually, when dragging skulls, you are given a sacred staff for each hand to help pull you along. However, when I took the baby and was offered the staff, the Sundance leader said, "You're not gonna need this." He took it out of my hands as though he knew I would have the strength to pull without it. Finally, I went around and stopped, and I offered my baby to the west. Now I had to do my four rounds.

I was yanked back and forth, back and forth. I started moving forward and then I started going a little faster. I felt so good, but I was tiring out quickly. My mouth and my throat were so dry, yet I still felt full of energy. I felt as though I were pulling the whole world behind me, yet I had the energy of everyone in the Arbor helping me.

The baby was quiet, looking around. She played with the feathers on my eagle-wing fan. My blood from the two piercings on my chest had stained the white outfit she wore. Melody would later decide to keep the outfit so that one day she could explain to the baby what it was all about.

I went around my second time, trying to catch my breath. I started going around the third time, and I suddenly felt stronger. I believed the baby gave me energy. The support of everyone watching and praying for me gave me strength. The courage from the Creator helped me to keep going.

Everyone was feeling my pain. As I reached the west side of the Arbor, they stopped me. I thought I had another round to go, but they said, "That's it, Manny. You have gone around four times."

I stopped. I was feeling very exhausted, and my heart was pounding. I wasn't perspiring because I was so dry.

Someone took the baby from me, and then Henry said, "Okay, Manny, it's time to break loose. Its time for you to break from the skulls."

A big friend of mine from Olympia, Washington, a red-headed, freckle-faced Sundancer named Don said, "Manny, I'm with you, Brother. What do you need me to do?"

I asked him to sit on the first skull. Smiling at him, I said, "Hang on, Don, I'm going to take you for a ride." Smiling in return, he turned and walked toward the skulls.

Then my children Rockie and Becky sat on the second and third skulls, anchoring them so that I could break loose. After everyone was in place and ready, I stood as close as I could to the skulls. Another Sundancer was waiting to catch me.

I took off running at a full gallop. I was running fast and low. I wanted to make sure that I broke the first time. If a person doesn't break the first time, he has to try again and again until he succeeds.

At the last instant, right before I broke loose, I looked

over at Lessert, who had pierced my back. He was standing there looking, but not at my face. He looked at my back, and as I broke loose, I saw a look of disbelief on his face. He was surprised that I broke loose as easily as I did.

I had fulfilled my commitment to Grandfather. I had carried my baby around four times, as I had asked the Creator to help me do.

My job was done, and I had done it with honor, respect, and many prayers. The Great Spirit saw no reason for me to be hooked up to those skulls any longer, so he allowed me to break out on the first try.

We finished out the day with much joy and good wishes from other people. That day was a long and hot one, but a good one. It had been hard on me.

At this Sundance we were allowed to return to our camps. When I got back to mine, it was not quite dark. Many people were visiting each other, talking about the day. I sat by our camp in the shade.

Another Sundance Chief had come to support me. He sat down, and my girls brought him a cup of coffee and a sweet roll. "Manny, when are you coming to my Sundance?" he asked quietly.

"I'm doing this Sundance, then I have to go to the other one that asked for my help."

Disappointed, he said, "You could do the same with me. You could come help us. I would really like to have you there. You've got powerful medicine."

I started to feel swayed, because he was the man I had felt so good with the first time I did my piercing. He was persuading me to go with him. Then I thought of the controversies that surround the Sundances. And this Sundance Chief runs one of them. He doesn't want anyone but Lakota people or Native Americans to Sundance with him.

There are mixed feelings, egos, and politics involved in

certain Sundances, because they are becoming accepted by people from all over the world, people with different cultures and beliefs. Among the native people, there are arguments about whether to accept these outsiders or not. In some Sundance circles, the native people want to keep the Sundance exclusively a Native American ceremony. It depends on the Sundance Chief.

Although I'm not a Sundance Chief, I do have my own opinions, and I've been to the Sacred Tree enough times to feel that I can express them. Some Chiefs allow outsiders into their Sundance, to dance and worship with us. Yet others don't want anyone except Native or First Americans in their Sundance. Then there are some Sundance leaders who don't want anyone except Lakota (Sioux) dancing in theirs. I've heard some say, "We don't want any white people," or, "We don't want any Mexicans here." I'd like to ask them, "What is a Mexican? Isn't it a mixture of European and native? What is the blood line of the so-called full-bloods?" I'm sure that if there are any pure-bloods left, there are very few. Most people are of mixed heritage, whether we accept it or not. That doesn't make us love *Tunkashila* and the Sundance any less than the so-called full-bloods.

Then there is the matter of money. Who has the money to give us so that we can have a Sundance? The white people do. We native people certainly do not. The white people are the ones willing to help us, and all they ask in return is to be allowed to pray with us. Granted, there are people that use our way to profit and abuse our spirituality. But Grandfather can handle them. We can't blame all white people for the acts of a few. They don't like to be categorized any more than we do.

One Sundance Chief, Norbert, expressed it well when he said, "The Sundance flag has four colors in it. It doesn't belong just to us, it belongs to everyone who is willing to honor, respect, and sacrifice for our beliefs. If anyone is willing to learn, we should be willing to teach and not to judge other people by their color."

During my talk with the Sundance Chief, I explained that I felt I had committed myself enough for the year. Possibly in the future, I would Sundance with him.

He gave me a message that the Spirits told him to bring me. They told him that because of the way that I Sundance, and how often I've been pierced, that I was now ready to help people. I would be given two special stones as a way to help people. They would not be crystals, just ordinary stones, special healing stones with powerful medicine in them.

This was ironic to me because, unknown to him, I made a good part of my living making "Stone People Medicine." The process of creating these small stones was also brought to me in an unusual way, and now I was selling them all over the world. What he was telling me seemed quite a coincidence.

He told me I would know when they came to me, it would be under such unusual circumstances that I would know. "Manny, I don't know why I am saying this to you or doing this. I was told to do it, so there it is."

I replied, "I don't know anything about healing. I wouldn't know what to do or say."

He said, "No, none of us do. We all have to learn. When it comes to you, you will know and you will be shown the way. The same way you were told to come to the Sundance and pierce. You will know what to say, what to do. It's going to be very good for you. Remember, it's not you doing it, it's the Spirits helping you do it. With the stones, you will help people."

Here was the message that the spotted eagle had given me in the Shoshoni Sundance: that I will be shown how and when to help people. Just as the eagle had given me the message, now it was brought to me again by a medicine man. This message could not have come from a stronger source. I had to believe this Sundance Chief's message was from the spirit of the spotted eagle.

I have always had problems with words like "healer," "healing," and things related. There are too many people claiming they can heal, sometimes with profit being the only intention, so I use these words carefully. This message telling me I was to heal people was told to me by a Sundance Chief who had received the message from the Spirits, and so I believed it wholeheartedly. Neither of us had anything to gain from this, because there is never any charge for spiritual healing of this kind. I never hold out my hand for money for what I do.

It is also known that once you have suffered at the Sundance for four years, you have earned the privilege and the right to give blessings to people in the name of the Creator. To cleanse houses, cleanse people, give names, whatever people ask for you to do, you can do. You have earned the privilege and the right.

We left the Sundance. My brother Henry from Maryland was having a Sundance two weeks after that, and I told him that I couldn't make it. He asked me, "Come over. I really need you."

I said, "Henry if I can, I will, and if I don't, it's because I'm not supposed to be there."

We headed south to Oklahoma, so my kids could see some of their old friends. From there we went to Arkansas to see some of Melody's friends, and then on to Memphis, where we stopped to have breakfast with some dear, old friends, John and Betty.

Something very interesting occurred after breakfast. Taking me aside, John told me he had something for me. It was my first sign since my conversation with the Sundance

Chief. John honored me with a beautiful, smooth stone and explained that he knew I needed it for something—he wasn't sure what. It was quite an honor and exciting to receive this gift so soon after being told it would come to me. I hadn't seen John in years. He knew nothing about what the Sundance Chief had told me, yet here he was giving me a stone. After he had given it to me, I told him everything. He just gave me a knowing smile.

Then we headed north toward a powwow in Ohio. I was honored when they asked me to do the blessing of the grounds. I did it in an unusual way: I used four veterans because we as natives have always respected and honored the warriors. I put one in each direction to guard that entrance. When the prayer was over, I brought them back in. It was a beautiful ceremony and a fantastic powwow. We were there for three days.

During the powwow, another interesting event happened to me. A non-native woman set up next to us and approached me with a gift: a stone. She explained that she'd been carrying it for about two months and didn't really know why. She had picked it up at a Sundance in Northern Ontario, near Manitoulin Island. Her son had been in the Sundance, and while there she was told by the Spirits to bring this stone with her to Ohio. She had no idea whom it was for or why she was bringing it, but she was told it was for someone.

When she presented it to me, she felt good and became very emotional. She knew that it belonged to someone else, that it wasn't hers. Her only job was to carry it to the person it belonged to, and she realized who that person was the minute she saw me. When she gave me the stone, I knew instinctively that this was the second of the two stones I had been waiting for.

That's the way things happen when you are in this spiritual world or are communicating with the Spirits. The Spirits create a drama, so you remember that it is not you, but they, who are doing the healing. They teach you how to use the signs they send in the right way. It might seem unusual, but it is very real.

Right after the powwow we stopped at a campground. We checked our messages from home and found out that one of our customers from Baltimore had called and said she needed a large shipment of our crafts. When Melody returned the call, she took the order, and it was quite substantial—enough for us to drive there to deliver it. We still had a couple of weeks before the kids had to return to school.

We would also be able to visit my Sundance brother Henry and some of our friends who lived in the area. Melody was happy to go there because she knew that Henry's Sundance had been the weekend before, so I wouldn't be tempted to participate.

When we got to Baltimore, it was hot and humid. We paid for a motel room and just kicked back for the rest of that day. The next morning we went to our customer's store. During our conversation, she mentioned, "There's a woman I know who always dances at Henry's Sundances. She told me that they're getting ready. In fact, they start today."

It was Thursday. Henry's Sundance must have been rescheduled. I looked at my wife.

Melody said, "I can't believe this. It was supposed to have been last weekend."

The store owner said, "It was. They changed the date for some reason or other. I don't know why."

Melody did not want me to Sundance again because of my sunburn and because it would be my second Sundance in a couple of weeks. It was getting a bit hard for this old man. We called on another customer, then headed out to Henry's place, where the Sundance was.

When we arrived, there was already quite a crowd singing and dancing. They'd gone in that morning.

When Henry and Harold saw me, they were very happy. We all got emotional. Here I was, needed, and I didn't know it. The Spirits had again manipulated my life to take me where I was needed, and where I had to be. After their greeting, I told them, "Look, I've got my trailer over at a campground. We'll get here early, and I'll dance with you tomorrow."

Everybody was really happy, except Melody. She was a bit upset because she knew it had been Henry's prayers that had brought us here. She was worried about my health after the previous Sundance.

That evening, while we were having dinner together, Melody dropped a bomb. "I'm going in to Sundance with you tomorrow. I want to be there with you and for you," she said.

We both started to cry. I felt like the whole dining room had gone quiet. It was the last thing I expected to hear from Melody. Once, shortly after meeting in Tucson, Melody said that if there was ever a time I couldn't Sundance for health reasons, she'd go in my place. It humbled me that she would consider going through it, especially now. My daughter Becky also wanted to go in.

The next day, we brought our trailer and set it up at Henry's. Becky, Melody, and I went into the Sundance later that morning. My son Rockie didn't go in. He wasn't ready for another one so soon.

They took us to a sweat lodge, then we entered the Arbor from the east and started Sundancing. It was wonderful to have Melody there, and to have Becky with me again. This was a small Sundance, but a good one, a powerful one.

The day before, we saw a young native man named Jim

lying on the ground. Since the morning before he'd been suffering with a severe migraine headache. Melody had asked me to try to help him.

I said, "No, it's not time. He's paying some kind of Karma, or he's suffering for a reason. It's not time. If he's like that tomorrow, I'll help him."

The next day, I saw Jim again, still very sick. I went right to him and told him, "Come on, get up."

He said, "No, I can't. I'm too sick. My head hurts bad."

I asked him to come into the Sweat Lodge with me. I called some others, to make four warriors. I felt I needed them to form my healing circle: one warrior for each direction. We took him inside for about half an hour. (What the spirits bring to a person in this ceremony is not for public knowledge, so I cannot divulge it here.) Coming out, we took Jim and laid him back down where he was before. He lay there for a while. During a break, I went over and visited with some friends. Not long after, Jim came up to me. His eyes were as clear as could be where they had been full of pain and anguish before.

With a big smile, he said, "Manny, I want to thank you for doing whatever it was you did. I don't know what kind of medicine you have, but it is good. You're gonna help a lot of people."

He shook my hand and went back to his spot under the Arbor. He was really grateful, and I was surprised that I had done something so positive. The Spirits brought Jim to me to help me see how this healing worked.

After that, I found out that I was there for several reasons. First was because Henry wanted to be the first to be pierced at his own Sundance. He had never been pierced because there had never been anybody qualified to do it. He asked me if I would, and of course, I couldn't refuse him. We danced the next day, and I pierced him.

That morning, Melody and I rested on separate blankets between rounds. When I got up to put my sage crown on, my piercing bones fell out. I had inserted them in the side of my crown, so they'd be handy. Melody looked at me, but I didn't say anything. She knew that I felt they fell out because I should use them again. She had a sick look on her face.

The next day, I told Henry I wanted to be pierced, last piercing round. During the break, Harold came up to me and said, "Manny, I want to pierce for you in your place. You've done enough for us already."

Very moved by the gesture, I said, "Harold, you don't have to do that for me. It's my obligation."

"Manny, please, let me have this privilege."

I looked at him for a long, long time, thinking and asking myself if this was something that could be passed to someone else. Harold wouldn't give me a chance to think it over any more. He asked me for my piercing bones.

By this time, Melody was crying and thanking Harold. She was really worried about my health. Melody honored Harold with a special gift, to give thanks. She gave him something that meant a great deal to her. It was a large obsidian arrowhead necklace that I had made for her when we first met.

My brother Harold's gesture moved me deeply. It created a stronger bond between us. Strangely enough, when Harold was pierced, halfway through the song the piercings on both sides suddenly fell off. It was amazing. Neither Harold nor I could believe it, but both of us were happy.

That Sundance was beautiful. Many people came and honored me, and brought my family many things. I was humbled by the experience. It was my second Sundance in one year and I thought, "I may be getting a bit too old for this. Past the half-century mark and still dancing like that?"

My wife said that it served as an inspiration to the younger people coming up. Seeing a guy like me who's diabetic and has high blood pressure, dancing and suffering, encouraged them to go on.

We finished our commitment to Henry's Sundance, packed up our trailer, and headed back to Canada.

INNER — PURPLE

"Spirit Within"

SPIRITUALLY FULFILLED

Life in Canada was beautiful. When we arrived, though it was early in September, a blanket of autumn was already starting to cover the landscape of rolling hills. The trees looked happy to be shedding their green leaves of summer. They seemed to be dancing with joy as they displayed their new fall dresses of golden and crimson leaves.

Later that same year, we had another tragedy strike our family. While coming back from a show in Montreal, I was beginning to have severe pain in my abdomen. I kept passing it off as indigestion, but it grew progressively worse. On the drive back, I was complaining about my weight and said to Melody, "Wouldn't it be nice if I could just go to a hospital somewhere and lose weight!" That taught me to be careful what I ask for.

After four days of constant pain, I felt I couldn't handle it anymore. I was hesitant to go to the hospital because I didn't have any medical insurance. In Canada, every resident has free medical coverage, but I did not have access to it because I was an American.

One evening, I was lying down and didn't want to get up. Melody and the kids were worried. While I was lying there, it occurred to me that I should try to heal myself using the stones I was given. I started praying with them. I asked God, if they really worked, to heal me—not just for my own purposes, but also for my family. Shortly after that, the pain forced me to give in to Melody's wishes and go to York-Central Hospital.

When we arrived at the emergency room, the doctor told me that I was a very sick man and would not be able to leave. When they told me how much it would cost per day, I started to get up to leave. The doctor told me to wait, that something could be worked out financially. He also secretly told me that I could not be refused medical attention and surgery if needed.

After being admitted, I remained there for ten days. During that time I contracted pneumonia, and the infection meant they couldn't remove the gallstones they had found in my gall bladder. I was on intravenous fluids and antibiotics my entire stay in the hospital. No food or water. I lost twenty-five pounds.

The pneumonia was so persistent, they decided to release me for a couple of weeks until the infection cleared up and they could operate to remove the gallstones. The last day before I left, they put me through several more tests.

When the doctor in charge of my case came in with the X rays, he had an astonished look on his face. He couldn't believe what he saw. The gallstones had dissolved. They simply weren't there anymore, but they knew I hadn't passed them. He said that in all his years as a doctor, he had never seen anything like it. I tried to explain to him about the healing I had given myself, but he seemed to dismiss it entirely.

Maybe this form of medicine is just too intimidating in this day of advanced technology? Perhaps it is lack of belief? Personally, I knew it was the healing I did on myself that dissolved the gallstones. It didn't really matter whether he believed it or not; I knew my medicine had helped me cure myself. It's like the old expression "Physician, heal thyself," meaning, the true doctor or man of medicine should be able to heal himself in order to offer methods of healing to others. I felt the Creator brought me a way to heal myself, to make me realize that I also could help others. It helped me to build confidence in the new way of healing I had received.

I went home to recuperate. The entire ordeal put a tremendous strain on my family and our finances. We mulled over what to do for most of the month.

That winter the Canadian economy started a slow downward slide. Our customers were wary of buying more stock because of the way things were going. Our business was in trouble. Sales were way down. Everywhere we went the story was the same. "Your things are beautiful, but we're not buying now." This worried me. No sales and the price of food inched higher and higher every day. It was a sickening feeling to go out day after day and come home with little or no money.

I started praying hard to Grandfather and asked him to bring me direction, to show me a way to get my family into a better situation. As if by a miracle, I started receiving in my thoughts an answer to my prayers. At first I didn't want to say anything to anyone. I didn't want to build their hopes up if I couldn't fulfill what I was thinking. My thoughts kept saying, move back to the States.

On the afternoon of November 30, when I finally mentioned it to Melody, a look of delight came over her face.

"If only we could," she cried. "It could be the answer to all my prayers."

The next day was a Friday, and we were going to go out again to try to sell. We were facing a pretty slim weekend if we didn't sell anything. We made several calls without success. In desperation, I thought about a store that had called me the year before. At the time, the owner had asked me to stop by with my crafts. I don't know why, but I never went to see him. Now I was desperate and searching for an angel.

We pulled into Upper Canada mall parking lot in Newmarket where his store, "Nature's Yard," was and called him from the car phone. Michael came on the line and was really glad to hear from us. He asked us where we were calling from, and when we said from the parking lot, he told us to come right up.

Taking one look at all the crafts we had, he paused for a minute. Then he took everything we were holding, put it to the side, and said, "I'll take all this, and triple it for my other two stores as soon as possible." He asked us to balance it out so there would be an equal amount for each store.

My head was spinning. We started taking inventory of what we had on hand. It was quite a substantial amount. Tripling it answered our prayers for a way to move to the States. Melody was amazed!

After that day, we gave notice to our landlord, and an interesting thing started to happen. People came out of the woodwork to buy our crafts. Everything fell into place for us to go. That is usually how you can tell if you're on the right track about something. If you find most things keep going wrong, and there are obstacles everywhere you turn, rethink what you're doing and try something else. You'll know it's right if everything goes your way. When you're on the right path, obstacles disappear. We knew all this money coming in wasn't to keep us there. It was Grandfather's way to get us going.

On December 19, exactly twenty days after deciding to move, we were on the road to Arizona. In that short time, we had packed, sold all our furniture, closed our lives in Canada, and headed out. It was an emotional time for Melody. She had always wanted to move to the States, and now it was happening. She was leaving her friends and family behind to make a fresh start.

On Christmas day, we arrived at my mom's house in Ajo, Arizona. It was a wonderful Christmas. Most of my children had never met or known their grandparents. After losing their mother, it was good for them to have a sense of family. My sisters and brother all made them feel welcome and loved. It was also the first time Melody met my mom and dad. After visiting for a couple of days, we headed for Phoenix to find our new home.

It took us about a year to get situated and get our business off the ground. Unfortunately, when Sundance season came about that summer we didn't have the money to go. Perhaps Grandfather was keeping us from going, for whatever reason. This really depressed me. It was the first year I would miss the Lakota Sundance since I had started. It was a difficult thing for me to face.

The remainder of the year was spent growing our business and expanding our product line. I found myself on the road a lot. Phoenix couldn't support us the way Toronto had, so Melody had to hold the fort by herself often. We were careful not to be separated for longer than three weeks in a row. We didn't want what had happened in my previous marriage to happen to us.

That February while set up in Tucson at the gem and mineral show, we received word of my dad's passing. We immediately packed up and prepared for the funeral.

By the spring of 1994, I had made the commitment to go to the Sundance no matter what the expense. Even if I had to go by myself, I was not going to miss another one.

As an elder, it was my responsibility to help organize things, so on the first weekend in July, I had an orientation meeting at Marge and Mario's house in Altadena, California, for anyone who wanted to attend. At the meeting, we found out there would be another Sundance in Colorado, being put on by the same Sundance Chief, David Swallow. The South Dakota Sundance was scheduled for the middle of August, but the one in Colorado was slated for the middle of July. This made it a better time for us to attend, and financially easier, so we decided to go to Colorado.

We had two weeks to prepare. In order to raise some cash for the Sundance I had to make a quick sales trip to northern California. The trip was tough. Everywhere I went, people said they were worried about the economy and didn't have any money. I found it very hard to make a sale, but I was determined to go to the Sundance. Slowly, from a small sale here and another one there, I gathered and saved the money we needed.

On the day we left Phoenix, the temperature was 115 degrees. We took two vans and pulled our pop-up trailer. My son stayed home, and our five girls came along. What an adventure! Their energies and temperaments are so different from each other, it made for an interesting and challenging trip—to say the least. I had to handle the reins of that team with one iron fist and one kid glove.

We stopped in Albuquerque to pick up Rose Marie, who wanted to attend the Sundance with us. She was a healer I had met at a Whole Life expo in Albuquerque (it's a combination psychic fair and alternative-healing exhibition), and it was her dream to go to a Sundance. So she came with us and helped with the driving.

We arrived at the Sundance grounds, near the town of Buffalo Creek, the next evening well before dark. The natural beauty of the camping grounds around the Arbor was absolutely breathtaking. Yet it appeared that Mother Nature had manicured the area just for our benefit. The Arbor was big and had fresh-cut evergreen boughs lying over it, offering a wonderful shade. With the Rocky Mountains surrounding us, it was an ideal camping spot.

The Sundance Chief, David Swallow, was very happy to see me with my family. He asked me to set up in a spot next to his camp. There was a clear brook running nearby, lots of trees, and a beautiful landscape. Nature had been busy, making the meeting place for the Spirits and the humans a place to remember.

Sunday was tree day. Rose Marie and Melody had driven into town for supplies and groceries. When it came time to get the tree, excitedly the people in our camp got ready to go. There were a couple of my adopted nephews from California. They had come to pray and offer their support to all the other dancers. There was Big Jon from Los Angeles, Little John from Benecia, and Mario, who had come to dance and pierce from Pomona with his girlfriend, Taran. (Another nephew, Paul from Cerritos, didn't arrive until the following day.)

By this time a large crowd was gathering. I called my girls and started following the others. I felt something in my stomach. Some people call it "butterflies." To me it was more like a restless spirit within me. A spirit that wanted to be noticed, not just with indifference, but with emotion.

Of all the tree ceremonies I have mentioned so far, this one touched me the most, and I don't know if it was because of the loss of my dad, or if it was the pain that I felt for my mother. I hadn't shed any tears since my father's passing, but now I cried for my mother's pain and anguish. They had just celebrated their sixty-first wedding anniversary before he died.

Somehow the words David said at this tree moved me as no others had. Somehow I related the tree giving its life so we could Sundance, to my father giving life to four other siblings and me. Suddenly, I felt as if the spirit of my father was within the tree, talking to me. As the first axe strike hit the tree, I felt a profound sorrow for that tree. Perhaps I felt that it was passing on to another life just as my dad had done recently. I know deep inside there was a relationship between the two events.

For the first time since his passing, tears came to my eyes that were just for him. A part of my sorrow had to do with unresolved differences between us. There would be no other opportunity to talk things over. There had been so many feelings, thoughts, and experiences I wanted to share with him. Now that wasn't possible. Through the years it seemed that every time I went home, things would be fine for a couple of days, then our relationship would begin to feel strained. I truly would have loved to find out what it was about me that made him react the way he did. Regrettably, we never had that opportunity. The chance for resolution was no longer there, and for that reason I was mourning. In my mind and heart, I dedicated this Sundance to my dad's memory.

The tree went up as beautiful and as proud as all the others. Many people tied their ropes and prayer ties on it.

There were many things being asked of the tree. The energy was high around the Arbor. We all returned to our camps to prepare for the next day. We left the Sacred Tree alone at last as if to give it the respect and time it needed to prepare itself for us and the next four days.

Monday morning, Grandfather blessed us with a warm and cloudy day. Long before sunrise, Sundancers from all over gathered around the fire pit, getting ready to go into the sweat lodges. Melody and I got up, grabbed our towels, and headed down to the same place.

The smell of dust was already starting to make its presence known. It mingled with the wood smoke rising from the fire pit. I could see a few Grandfather rocks poking their red-hot faces through the mounds of hot coals. The coals and ashes also were giving us their pleasant and distant smell.

Crawling in on my hands and knees, I felt something almost like an embrace from the sweat lodge. What a comforting feeling. As we sat there quietly, waiting for the Sweat Lodge ceremony to begin. I felt a tremendous sense of relief as one of the dancers started softly singing the "Four Directions" song.

I ran into an old Sundance brother and leader, Bo from South Dakota. Everyone was in a jovial mood. When enough guys were ready to fill the sweat lodge, we started the first sweat. It was good and hot.

Returning to camp, I started getting ready. When Melody returned she got all her things, including her bedding, and moved to the woman's tepee. She was going to be dancing for four days and couldn't return to camp for any reason. There was a pain in my chest for her because I knew the ache of hunger and the deep knife thrust of thirst that she would soon be enduring.

My heart went out to her, but she wanted to pray and was determined to do it. All I could do was be there, be strong for her, and help her pray. She was praying for me—that was important to her—and in turn, I would pray for her. There was nothing personally to gain from being there. Only others to whom the prayers are directed would gain anything.

As I look back on it, day one passed rather swiftly, but at the time it seemed long and slow. It's amazing how quickly we forget the pain and the thirst. Several people pierced that day, and we all danced hard.

The second day I received word that my good friend Dick Smith, his wife Connie, and her father had arrived from Burbank, California, to support me. This day was harder—everyone was thirstier and hungry. I had a commitment to drag buffalo skulls and was going to do it on the last day. However, when I thought more about it, I decided that I should do it on the second day, while I still had the strength.

That morning, I picked up my baby girl, Oriona, and she nuzzled me with her nose and gave me a kiss on the cheek. "Daddy, can I dance with you today?" she asked.

I'm not sure if she remembered the time I carried her in the Sundance two years before, but it was almost as if she knew I was going to be dragging skulls. It really touched me. As I embraced her I said to her, "Sure you can, Honey. You're gonna dance with Daddy."

So after going in, we put our pipes on the altar and the dancing started in earnest. The very first piercing round was the round for me to drag the skulls. Right away I got my back marked to show where I wanted to be pierced. I told David and Bo that I wanted to stay pierced and drag the skulls. They needed to pierce me deeply, so I could try to drag the skulls all four rounds. There were eight, fairly large skulls.

They took me to the tree to pray. After a couple of minutes, a Sundance leader asked me if I was ready. I nodded yes. I walked over and stood on the buffalo hide. With David on one side and Bo on the other, I handed them my piercing bones. I felt David grab the flesh on my back. I felt the knife cut into my back, but my prayers were so deep and intense there was very little pain. By the time it was Bo's turn to pierce my right side, my prayers for strength had been answered—I didn't feel a thing.

Suddenly, as if awakening, I felt both of them grab my arms and lead me toward the west side of the Arbor. Melody handed me Oriona. She was smiling and looking around at everyone with curiosity on her face rather than fright.

There were eight warriors carrying the eight skulls behind me. David believes that each man dragging skulls should at least make one complete circle with the skulls attached to his back. Therefore he had the skulls carried by the warriors one full circle around the Arbor. While we were dancing, I heard someone say, "*Wamblee*, eagle!" I raised my head and saw two beautiful spotted eagles circling the Arbor directly above us. Since I was dancing, I couldn't keep looking at them, but I was told that they disappeared into the sun. I was really honored to have their presence while I danced and pierced. It meant that all my prayers would be answered and anyone praying with me would have their prayers answered.

Getting back around to the west side, the warriors put down the skulls. It was my time to move them by myself. As I started leaning into the rope, at first I felt like I was trying to pull the world. Ever so slightly I felt the skulls start to move. Then suddenly the left side broke loose. My thoughts were that I didn't want to break yet. I wanted to drag the skulls, so as carefully as I could, I continued pulling with my other side. The weight was too much, my right side broke loose as the skulls started to move again. I suppose Grandfather didn't want me to go through the pain and suffering required to move that kind of weight.

When I broke loose, I yelled with joy and ran around

the Arbor, holding the baby. This was my third time dragging skulls, and I was happy to have made it through again.

I returned Oriona to my wife and went to the center of the Arbor, the Sacred Tree. After praying and giving thanks at the tree, David and Bo were waiting for me to finish my prayers. When I was through, they turned me around. The pieces of flesh that were hanging off my back were cut off and placed in small pieces of red cloth. They were my flesh offerings and were tied to the tree.

Many people ask me, "Why do you pierce? Why do you mutilate your body like this?"

It's not mutilation or self-torture. It is our way, our very sacred way of giving a small piece of the only thing we truly own, our bodies. We feel that anything other than the body is something material that we can live without. Flesh, blood, and pain is all we truly own. It is the flesh of the body that houses our spirit and soul. Piercing is a way to give our living flesh to the spirit world, so the Spirits will listen to our prayers and pleas.

More men pierced and prayed and broke loose. It was a beautiful Sundance. The singers' voices were still strong, and we had two drums singing all the sacred songs for us. Again we were blessed with a partly cloudy sky. When the sun was out and hot, Grandfather would always bring us a cloud to cool us off a bit.

I had been on blood pressure pills for several years and diabetes medication since 1991. My wife was very concerned about this because we had accidentally forgotten the high-blood-pressure pills. At high altitudes my blood pressure would rise, my head would start buzzing, and I'd get very sick.

When we were dancing, Melody and several others were praying I could overcome this illness. All their prayers for me have been answered. Since that Sundance, I haven't had to take any blood pressure pills, and I am down to one diabetes pill a day (quite a drop from the three I was tak-ing before.)

On the third day, one of my twin daughters, Becky, joined us in the Sundance Arbor. She had wanted to dance all four days. As an old experienced Sundancer, I knew how hard this was, so I convinced her to dance only the last two days.

The third day was the healing ceremony. It seemed like all the people who were there to support us gathered around the Arbor for healing from the Sundancers. We believe that within the Sacred Circle, every Sundancer who willingly goes in to suffer and give of himself or of herself has the right to be a healing tool. That Sundancer earns the right, during that special day, to offer healing with the Creator's blessing. Every dancer slowly proceeded around the Arbor, doing their best to help the people who were lined up. The cere-mony lasted about four hours, and many people cried when the Sundancers prayed for them.

When we were getting our pipes from the altar, Melody looked up and saw a cloud. It was in the exact shape of a buffalo skull. When she pointed it out, several other dancers also saw it. It was clear; there was no doubting that it was a buffalo skull. It was a good medicine sign that meant strength and abundance for everyone. The day was longer than usual. We didn't get out of the Arbor until long after dark.

Day three was over, and everyone was tired. I could tell the thirst was taking its toll on all of us. I could see Melody suffering quite a bit. Incidentally, it was Melody's birthday, and she was happy to be helping others and to be at the Sundance on her special day. Becky was having a very hard time; she hadn't realized how hard David's Sundance would be. By the end of the first day, she was glad she had com-mitted to only two days.

The final day arrived, and it was the hottest day since

the Sundance had begun. The morning was beautiful, bright, and sunny. We were told the day would be shorter than the others. Everyone was happy. They had all undergone a very challenging trial and had made it. Many others who had only made a one-day commitment joined on the last day to dance.

The Sundance leaders and helpers (including me) had to be pierced on the last piercing round. When the time came, we all gathered in the center. One by one, all the Sundance leaders were pierced.

I wanted Melody to be with me when I was pierced, so I asked the women's Sundance Leader, Pansy, to bring Melody to the tree. She brought Melody a couple of minutes early and told Melody to get on her knees. When Melody knelt down, her knees landed on the small, hot pebbles. Her knees blistered and burned.

When they pierced me, we all moved to the southwest side of the Arbor. I was happy to see Rose Marie; my daughters Stormy, Mary, Dory, and Oriona; my nephews, John, Jon, and Paul. They were all there supporting me. We danced until it was time to break loose. There were four of us piercing this last round. We all broke loose. Al and Bernice's son, Richard, was called in to do the piercing on David. He danced strong and hard while dragging the skulls. It's very difficult to drag skulls far when they are so heavy and there are so many.

During the last couple of rounds, your mind races frantically. Who still needed prayers, or whom may I have missed? You realize that the time to Sundance is ending until next year. Although you can pray to the Creator anytime, it's as though your prayers are stronger during this sacred ceremony. I'm sure everyone goes through this experience before the four days are over.

Since it was David's last time to Sundance in the Arbor

in Colorado, it was a very special year for him. You could see he was leaving a part of himself behind, as others had before him. The people had lost their previous Sundance Chief to the Creator and had asked David to run the Sundance. It was his fourth and last year. His commitment to the Denver people was complete. They would have to choose another Sundance Chief.

We left Buffalo Creek the next morning and stayed around the Boulder, Colorado, area for the next couple of weeks. We were recuperating, making crafts at the campsite, and wholesaling to native craft shops.

The remainder of 1994 was spent selling our crafts and getting ready for the next Sundance. As 1995 began, some changes occurred. My son Rockie turned eighteen and decided to move out, to test his wings and perhaps grow up a bit. That made it a lot easier on Melody. Now all she had were the girls to take care of.

Our business was growing and getting better all the time. We were very fortunate to have become so successful with our spiritual crafts—the Stone People Medicine, Medicine Circles (Wheels), Spirit Crystals, Dream Keepers, and Dream Catchers.

It seems the spirits were pleased with my willingness to give of myself. They rewarded me with a way to make a living that not only helps people, but helps me feed my family. With my health affecting my work, I was grateful to have a creative method to make a living that didn't take its toll on me physically. Everything is created in an assembly-line fashion at home. All the girls, including Oriona, help out in some way. Everyone has a job. It teaches the girls a way to make a living and helps develop their creativity.

Our Stone People Medicine has become incredibly popular, and we now have customers in Israel, Japan, Europe, New Zealand, and the U.K. We have so many letters from people thanking us for our Dream Catchers, Medicine Wheels, and Stone People Medicine. They are testimonials that we are doing the right thing.

On several occasions, people have approached me and pointed at the Dream Catchers, and said they don't work. They said that their child's sleep was more disturbed and that the child was not sleeping well at all. The Dream Catchers do work, but what most people don't know is that only the ones made by medicine people will work. Dream Catchers made by others, people who don't know their significance, are just decorations. They have no spiritual medicine to work the way they are supposed to.

If you're thinking of buying one, find out who made it and what kind of person they are. Ask about their spirituality. Ask if they have earned the right to make spiritual items like that. Yours or your child's well-being is at stake. Be sure the person you get one from is someone you're comfortable with. Every Dream Catcher we make has a card on it saying the following:

THE DREAM CATCHER

A very old native belief, that as you sleep and dream, the dreams good or bad, leave you to come true. They are attracted to the Dream Catcher's web by the Dream Spirits. The web permits the good dreams to escape through the round hole in the web and become reality. The bad dreams get stuck in the web and vanish with the first rays of the new sunlight.

The dates for the 1995 Sundance were August 9th for tree day, with the actual dance occurring from the 10th through the 13th.

There were several people who had told me they wanted to go to the Sundance to either support or dance. This amazed me because it was such a distance to journey. Most people only have to travel within their own city to pray, and now these people were willing to travel great distances to join us in our prayers.

We were glad to be going to South Dakota, where the Sundance in Porcupine is very traditional. I hadn't seen Al, Bernice, and Richard Tail since 1991, so I was happy to be going there again. A lot had happened in four years.

As the time grew closer, we had decided to make some changes in our lives. I went east for a month to set up at four native arts and craft shows. While I was gone, Melody and the girls got ready for us to move. They had yard sales every weekend and sold all our furniture and other things. We decided to move into a trailer for a few months. This was a fairly last-minute decision, sparked mostly by the high cost of living where we were. Melody also decided to home-school the girls because she was unhappy with what public schools offered. This also allowed us to be mobile and spend more time together as a family. The way things were, I had to do a lot of traveling alone.

Melody managed to fly up to Chicago to do the last show with me at Notre Dame University campus. It was very successful, but the whirlwind of activity really started when we got back to Phoenix. We had to rent a storage space, sell the rest of our things, pack what was left, and get ready to move. We bought another comfortable travel trailer (after selling the pop-up) that slept eight.

During our yard sales, the heat was unbearable. It was as though the Spirits were angry with Phoenix. It seemed the very ground itself groaned with the blistering waves of heat. It was miserable.

The day to leave the house had finally arrived, and it

was the hottest day of the year. Phoenix was having record-high temperatures, and the peak that day was 125 degrees. We left that home for the last time at around 3:30 in the afternoon. Melody didn't have air conditioning in her van, and I couldn't use the a/c in mine because I was pulling the trailer. So we were hot and anxious to get going. Then disaster hit.

Melody had gone on to check the mail and would meet me at the gas station. I was about six blocks from our house when suddenly the radiator hose blew, and I had to stop. I managed to pull into the parking lot of a gas station. After all that we had been through, this single obstacle almost made me have a nervous breakdown. It was rush hour, and road service couldn't get to me for at least two hours, since there were so many cars breaking down because of the heat. We still had to drive about three hours to my mother's house in Ajo, and we were stopped short.

Both Melody and I believe that everything happens for a reason, and as hard as that philosophy is to take sometimes, it was all we had right then. Gratefully, I called my sister Virgie's husband, Jerry, for help. I was thankful that he was there to help us. He helps everyone in the family with their vehicles, and he got there in about an hour. After much running around to get the right part, we were finally on the road again around eight o'clock. Everyone was exhausted, hungry, and ready for bed, so we decided to stay in Phoenix that night and leave the next morning. No one really noticed Melody's face.

The next day, we had some more running around to do, and we were on the road by noon. The heat was up to 115, and it was getting worse. None of us realized that with the windows open, driving in the heat was similar to putting your face in front of an oven for a couple of hours. By the time we got to Ajo, Melody's face was bright red and very badly burned from the heat. She also had sun stroke and was pretty sick. Her face had actually blistered from the heat and wind burn.

We decided to spend a couple of days in Ajo at my mom's, before setting out for South Dakota. It was just the medicine we all needed. My mom's house is the only place on earth where I feel I can truly relax and rest.

On Sunday I discovered that my piercing bones had been left in storage in Phoenix. As much as I hated to go back, once I'd started out on a trip I had no choice. My piercing bones were too important to be left behind. I suppose I could have made other ones, but these were special, and I had worked long and hard getting them ready for the ceremony.

Early Monday morning, we headed for South Dakota. Our first night on the road was spent in Truth or Consequences, New Mexico. Melody's face was a swollen mess. She was in agony, and I didn't know how to help her except to treat it as a severe sunburn. We were putting sunburn lotion and spraying cool water on her face. The burn was so deep that it remained hot. The only thing we could do was keep it cool.

When we reached Albuquerque, Melody went to a pharmacy and was very relieved to find a cream that completely eased her pain. Within hours she felt and looked a lot better. She was sensing that maybe the Creator didn't want her to Sundance, and she didn't want to meet all the people coming to the Sundance looking like a creature from *Star Trek*.

We arrived in Rapid City on Friday and set up at the KOA Campground. It was the same weekend as the motorcycle rally in Sturgis, South Dakota, that turned South Dakota into Motorcycle State. There were bikers from all over the United States and Canada. I was a little nervous about my girls going anywhere alone, but we made it to

Sunday without incident. All of the bikers we encountered acted respectful. Many were family men, and some had their ladies with them.

While there, we shopped for our giveaways. It was Becky's fourth Sundance, and my fourth with David Swallow Jr. We wanted to honor the Sundance and all those people we Sundanced with. It was also Lionel's giveaway, so he met us in Rapid City and bought the things he needed as well. The people who danced with me—drummers, singers, the Sundance Chief, the Sundance leaders—all had to be honored. We wanted to give some of the Sundancers' families things they may not have otherwise been able to get.

The people on the Pineridge reservation have the highest unemployment rate in North America, and life is very difficult for them. The government supplies them only with starchy foods and commodity cheese. Unlike so many other underprivileged cultures, the Native American people by nature are not complainers. They have a lot of pride. It's like the old adage, "The squeaky wheel gets the grease." Perhaps if they complained and lamented more about their plight, like so many other cultures, there would be more help available. What a tragedy that in such a rich and diverse country as the United States a lifestyle of poverty and deprivation has been left to the original people of this land.

The winter months are especially hard. It's hard to imagine what these people do when they run out of propane or need warm clothes. They are always getting hand-me-downs or, worse, nothing at all.

It was important to Melody that they receive some new things, so we did what we could. We also arranged for watermelons to be picked up on the last day of the Sundance. We wanted to get at least fifty watermelons—covered with ice and ready to be eaten—for the hungry and thirsty Sundancers when they came out on the last day.

Driving on to the reservation Sunday afternoon, I had a mixture of anticipation, nervousness, and relief. We had made it again. It was my time to give thanks to the Creator, and I was grateful that the Creator allowed me to come again to pray.

The Badlands were spectacular in their beauty and colors, but unyielding and harsh in the heat. The glorious sunsets and sunrises reminded us of the work of the Great Spirit. Yet Sundancing on this land was excruciating when it was hot and the ground was full of stickers.

At times I envy the quiet relatives who live on this wonderful land. They seem to absorb the quietness of the land into their souls. Then I think about the hard life they endure day after day, and I realize I'm glad that I am where I am. Still my heart aches for them. I wish I could have them all with me always.

Arriving on the Sundance grounds, several people who had come on my invitation were already there. Snowy and Conrado from San Diego had arrived a few days before to help any way they could, and Billy from Texas was there to do the same.

We set up camp, then Melody and I walked around to see who was there. The grounds were so quiet. Everyone seemed to be in their own separate worlds preparing for the days ahead. There was a lot that needed to be done before the Sundance started, and David Swallow Jr. had not arrived yet.

Bernice and Al Tail were welcome sights. They were the first people we saw as we started visiting.

Soon others I had invited arrived: Jon and Jodi from Las Vegas; Phil from Hemet, California; Mario from Pomona, California; Arthur from Searchlight, Nevada, with his nephew Mike; Bert (an herbalist and natural healer) and Big Jon from Los Angeles; Dale and Terry from Ontario, Canada;

Suzanne from Woodland Hills and Judy from Santa Maria, California; Karen from Missouri; Jason from Landers, California; Gil from Riverside, California; his sister Thelma and her husband, Raul, from Silver City, New Mexico; Rose Marie and her husband, Marshall, from Rio Rancho, New Mexico; and Lauren (the first editor of this book) from New York City. They all honored me by coming to help or to Sundance. All of them arrived at our sacred ground as though pulled by invisible strings tied to their hearts and souls. It was touching that the Creator had given me the gift of knowing to invite all these beautiful people. To see this group of selfless individuals make this incredible journey to suffer and pray truly warmed my heart.

It is important for me to mention these people, especially because they all traveled a long journey at great personal expense. They became relatives and part of my spiritual journey just by offering to pray and suffer with me and all the rest of the people on that sacred ground. Also, their contribution made my thirteenth Sundance the most memorable and interesting of all my Sundances.

The tree from the year before was still standing with all the prayer ties and flags on it. For some reason, Sunday night before David arrived, the tree was taken down and cut up for firewood. In all my years Sundancing, I had never seen this happen. Several Sundancers were very upset about this, including me. To my knowledge, the tree was to be taken down in ceremony during the day with the Sundance Chief present, and it was never to be cut up for firewood. Perhaps this was a sign of things to come.

On Monday, with Snowy's encouragement, Conrado approached me with sincerity to ask if he could Sundance for his father. He wanted to fulfill a promise he'd made some time ago: that if his father's health improved, one day he would Sundance for him. His sincerity and concern for his father brought tears to our eyes. I told him I would ask David. This was the first time Conrado had been to a Sundance, and he needed to be made aware how serious this commitment was.

Also, Arthur said he wanted to Sundance for his father, who had a tumor in his head. Then Suzanne told me that she had to Sundance, Jason wanted to dance, and Gil asked if he could dance! Even Rose Marie asked if she could dance. I had never been asked by so many people before. I sat with each one individually and had long talks. I wanted them to understand the seriousness of what they had asked me to help them start. It was a wonderful feeling to introduce them to such an incredible journey.

This was when I truly realized that my job wasn't to be a Sundance Chief, but to introduce individuals to the Sundance and set them on their journey. Often I had wondered what the Creator wanted of me, and it had now become very clear. Perhaps with my experience and with David Swallow Jr.'s leadership and spiritual guidance, many others could benefit from the spirituality and selflessness the Sundance offers.

That Monday afternoon, Melody and I went to the community center to pick up a package. We had asked a friend of mine, Neill, to send us some flat boughs of cedar from Washington State, and he had shipped me a forty-pound box of flat cedar clippings. They were clean and freshly picked. He had included a note and artwork engraved on a hand-split cedar board. It was addressed to me and to the people of Porcupine. I was very moved by his gesture, and we were all very grateful to have them.

On Tuesday, while we were in Rapid City getting more supplies and water, Sean and Jim arrived from Ohio. Jim was so anxious to Sundance that he didn't wait until I got back to approach David and ask his permission to Sundance.

He'd been a firekeeper and doing Sweat Lodge ceremonies for six years, and now felt he was ready to Sundance.

Sean and Jim had driven from Toledo, Ohio, and I suppose when they got there Jim wanted to find out right away if he would be allowed to dance. So without me there to take him, he went straight to David and was met with a disappointing answer. David told him he must help with the fire, security, or whatever is needed at the Sundance for four years before dancing. Jim was devastated, and his friend Sean was sad for him. He knew why Jim wanted to Sundance and how much it meant to him.

Melody and I came back from Rapid City and heard the news. I had a long talk with Jim. I told him I didn't understand why, but it wasn't my place to question David. I also told him that now he had found out not everyone is allowed to Sundance. Apparently, David had seen something in Jim that made him refuse the way he did. I don't know what it might have been.

The rest of the day and on Wednesday, Jim walked around helping, but he seemed lost. He helped others make their piercing bones and helped them get ready to Sundance. At about noon, Jim came to me with tobacco and asked if I would please talk to David again on his behalf. I explained that I would do it, but if David refused him again, he would have to carry out David's wishes.

I called the people who had come with me and wanted to Sundance. There were seven of them. They each needed to learn how to put tobacco in their pipes, as it is done in ceremony every time they fill them. At this time I also told them that mine was not the final word on whether they would be allowed to dance. David had the ultimate say. If he refused any of them entry into the Sundance, they must give him their pipe, to be used by someone else who needed it to go into the Sundance. The reason, I told them, was because

David can sometimes feel when people are not sincere or not ready to do what they're asking to do.

After everyone had their pipes ready, we walked to David's camp. David and Gerald Ice, one of David's Sundance leaders, were waiting for us. Everyone who wanted to dance sat on the ground in a semicircle facing David. I sat on his right side, and we placed a chair in front of him. Leaning close to David, I said, "This young man, Jim, who I'm bringing up here, told me that he's already been to see you, and you refused him to Sundance this year. He's asked me to speak to you on his behalf, and if you could please reconsider his request. Yours is the last word, and I've explained to each of them that if you refuse any of them, they must 'gift' their pipe to you so you can use it."

David nodded his head and said, "Okay, Manny, bring him up."

I motioned for Jim to come and sit on the chair. For a long moment, David sat there looking at Jim, as though receiving his guidance from the Spirits. Then David said, "Usually when I say something like this, I have a very good reason, and I don't change my mind. Usually, people don't come back to ask the second time. You're a smart man. You came back a second time, and you brought one of my Sundance leaders with you. You are sincere, and your heart is good."

As he leaned forward to take Jim's pipe from him, he asked, "How many days are you going to dance?" Nervously, Jim also leaned forward—not knowing whether to give him his pipe, shake his hand, or what—and almost fell out of his chair. David and I had to suppress a laugh, so as not to take away from the seriousness of the situation.

Everyone else was also accepted into the Sundance. Relieved that they didn't have to give up their pipes, they headed back to their camps.

Melody and Jodi had gone into Rapid City while all this was going on. They got back just in time to go to get the tree with everyone else. There were nearly thirty cars and vans lined up on the highway, heading out to get our Sacred Tree. It was about 5:30 in the evening. By the time everything was finished it would be dark. It would be hard to put the tree up in the dark, but that is the way things were going.

We drove about thirty minutes and pulled off the main highway onto the land where the river was. Everyone had to climb down a steep bank and cross the river to get to the tree. The river had only about a foot of water in it. Melody, Stormy, and Lauren stayed on the side where the trailer was because they didn't have shawls, and all the women attending had to wear a shawl over their shoulders. That was the traditional way to show respect to the tree and the Sundance Chief.

David said some prayers, then asked a young girl to come and swing the first chop at the tree. A native girl around four years old assisted in taking the first swing, then a small boy took his turn. Next, an elder was asked to take a swing.

Finally, all the Sundancers were cutting the tree down. Maybe it was my imagination, but it seemed that everyone was chopping at the tree too fast, and too aggressively. Maybe because it was getting late, but it seemed that all the men were almost angry while cutting it down. It was different from any other time I'd witnessed the tree-cutting ceremony, and I was a little uncomfortable. I wondered if anyone else noticed. It was time for the tree to drop and for us to catch it. Then something terrible happened. The tree started to fall and broke in half! Many people openly wept. Everyone was shocked. Everyone looked at everyone else, wondering what was going to happen.

David said to all who could hear, "Traditionally, when something like this happens, the Sundance is over. However,

I know that many of you have traveled long distances to Sundance, so we are going to try again. Everyone will suffer for this tree, and I will have to drag buffalo skulls for this tree," he continued. "If this second tree breaks or even touches the ground, that will be it. The Sundance will be over for this year."

My emotions were running high. How could this happen, I wondered. Why did it happen? Right then I decided I would do everything physically possible to keep the second tree from hitting the ground. Even if it meant I had to put myself under it, I wasn't going to allow this one to hit the ground. Apparently others had the same thoughts as I did. Maybe we were all being tested; every Sundance seemed to have some special lesson involved. This was just the beginning, I thought, and wondered how it would affect the rest of the Sundance.

The second tree received the same ceremony David had given the first tree. Soon it was time for it to come down. This time everyone was on their guard so that the tree was caught and didn't touch the ground. The tree was about fifty feet high and perhaps two feet in diameter. It was a big tree, and it took everyone's strength to keep it off the ground. Slowly it was carried across the river and up the muddy banks to the trailer that was waiting to carry it. For the first time since I'd begun Sundancing, all I offered in help was encouragement to the younger people.

By now the sun was slipping behind the western skyline. What a magnificent sunset. Remarkably, in the eastern skyline sat the moon, just as full as could be.

With tremendous effort and struggle, they managed to get the tree on the trailer and secure it with ropes to ensure it didn't fall off. Everyone else who had been watching was getting ready to drive out and follow behind the trailer.

Silhouetted against the western sky, with the oranges,

yellows, and reds mixed together, were the black figures of Sundancers standing guard over their Sacred Tree. The tree's branches looked black against the brilliant colors of the August sunset. I couldn't help but hold my breath for a moment at the sight of it, knowing that the next time we saw the sun, we would be in the Arbor, praying.

By the time we got back to the Sundance grounds, it was pitch black. Many vehicles drove up to the Arbor and put their headlights on so the Sundance Chief and the Sundancers could see. Carefully the tree was lifted off the trailer and carried into the Arbor through the east gate. There was a hole prepared and ready so the tree could be put up. The Sundancers placed the tree on the sacred ground with the base close to the hole.

David said some prayers and everyone was asked to attach their prayer ties and flags. Then the Sundancers tied their piercing ropes to the tree and pulled the rope to pre-pare to raise the tree.

With tremendous strength, the Sundancers and other men there helping out pushed the tree toward the hole and started pushing it up. All the Sundancers who had their ropes extended were moving around the Arbor to balance the tree, while others filled the hole with earth. Soon, the tree was in place and swaying in the darkness.

The full moon behind the tree gave it an eerie look. Lights from the cars reflected the glorious colors of the flags and prayer ties. Silently the tree stood, regally waiting to ful-fill its destiny. The leaves shimmered in the light, as though shivering, anticipating the next day, when the tree would become the Creator.

Exhausted and spent, I headed back to camp with Melody. She had to get her things together now because she needed to spend the next four nights in the women's tepee, close to the Arbor. It worried me because she had just recovered from the severe burns on her face. I wished she would dance only two days, but she was determined to go the distance, and I couldn't stop her.

It was almost 11:00 p.m. when I finally got to bed. My mind had a hard time shutting down for sleep after all that had happened.

My internal clock woke me up at 5:00 a.m., and I jumped up and got ready to go to the first sweat. I woke up Lionel, then headed for the sweat lodge. I was the first of the men to arrive, so I started yelling, calling all the Sundancers to get up, to come to the sweat lodges. Someone always has to do that. It seems even though the Sundancers know they have to get up, they want someone to tell them when to do it. I was surprised to see Melody was already up and waiting by the women's sweat lodge. (She has a really hard time waking up in the morning.)

Before I knew it, we were lined up for the Going In ceremony. The sun came up over the sandstone cliffs, east of the Arbor. Because of my diabetes, I was wearing moccasins and couldn't feel the ground under my feet. But the air was warm and beautiful. The low murmurs of the Sundancers standing around talking and the smell of burning cedar were calming. I'm sure it made wonderful memories for a lot of people that morning.

As with all my other Sundances I felt a tremendous sense of pride as we lined up to enter the Sacred Circle. I felt an exhilaration course through my body and goose bumps popped up all over as I heard the drum and the first high notes of the singers' voices.

Once inside the Arbor, the time for self-sacrifice was once again before us. I couldn't help but think about how grateful I was to be there to give thanks. We had had a very good year and had many things to be thankful for.

Melody hadn't noticed that I'd had the clay marks put

on my back. I was planning to drag buffalo skulls the first piercing round. My health problems dictated that I should do it right away. It was important for me to make sure I was strong enough to drag the skulls before I got too weak to do a good job at it. This would be my fourth and last time to drag skulls.

My piercing round finally arrived. Lionel took me into the center, and Melody stood near me while they pierced my back. I wanted her to know that it was okay. The only thing I could do was smile at her. I knew it was hard for Melody to watch me. She had tears streaming down her cheeks. She knew I had asked them to pierce deeply, so I could drag the six skulls all four rounds.

The sun was getting hotter, and it was still mid-morning. They tied the skulls to my back, and six Sundancers carried the skulls to the west gate of the Arbor. My right piercing broke as soon as we moved. This meant I would be dragging the skulls on one piercing.

Melody handed Oriona to me. She was wearing a special outfit that she had picked out herself for the occasion. Oriona asked Melody why she was crying and told her to be happy for her daddy. She showed a lot of wisdom for a three-year-old.

Once more I was carrying Oriona. She would give me strength while I danced around the Arbor. After honoring the four directions on our journey around the Sacred Circle, we reached the west gate. The dancers set the skulls on the ground while David prayed with me.

All the people from my camp, and those who had come on my invitation, fell in behind me while I pulled the skulls. Many of the men and women around the Arbor were weeping for me and at the sight of carrying Oriona.

Grasping Oriona tightly to me, I leaned forward. The weight of the six skulls stopped me in my tracks. Slowly, ever so slowly I started leaning and pushing forward. I was scared that my other piercing would break and that I wouldn't be able to drag the skulls. I wanted to have the chance to suffer and pray. I had waited all year for this and wanted to go through with it. Slowly the buffalo skulls started moving for me. As we were moving, I felt overwhelming gratitude to the Spirits for allowing me to drag the skulls. First I prayed that I wouldn't break loose and would have the strength to do this. Then I prayed for all my relations and the tree that we had lost. By the beginning of my fourth long trip around the Sacred Circle, my mouth was very dry. My energy was almost gone. I had been carrying around Oriona the first three rounds, and I couldn't carry her anymore. Putting her down, I asked her, "Honey, can you dance with Daddy?" Bo, the Sundance leader fanning me with his fan, whispered in my ear one word, "Run."

"Run?" I thought to myself. "I'm having trouble walking!" Bending over, I spoke to my little girl and said, "Honey, Daddy needs your strength. Daddy needs your help. Daddy needs to run."

Looking up at me and smiling, Oriona said, "Okay, Daddy." And she started moving forward pulling on my fingers as if wanting to run. I started moving faster. I ran about five feet and suddenly the other side broke loose. What a wonderful feeling: that my prayers would be heard and answered. I had completed my four years of dragging skulls. I felt a sense of pride, a sense of spiritual accomplishment at having completed my commitment.

The rest of that day went by slowly and was extremely difficult for everyone, it seemed. It was hard to believe that so many would be so exhausted and drained when it was only the first day. Rumor had it that several women were around the Arbor on their moon time. If that were true, it would explain why so many Sundancers were so weak.

The rumors were justified. A couple of the women went around asking the women near the Arbor that very personal question. Several women answered that yes, in fact, they were on their moon. They were firmly asked to leave the Sundance Arbor area. Most were good about leaving after learning what it does to the Sundancers in their weakened condition. All Sundancers, including the women, suffer from the high energy that women on their moon put out. It has a dramatic effect on Sundancers because of their weakened condition.

The next morning was much like the first. Mario joined us this morning and committed to three days. Then one at a time, Jason (who is sixteen years old), Arthur, Conrado, and Mario came to me to tell me they wanted to pierce that day. Then one by one as the day progressed they fulfilled their commitment to the Creator. What a beautiful sight it was to see those young warriors giving of themselves for all their relations.

I don't remember what round it was when Mario wanted to pierce, but we took him to the tree, and, after he was pierced, we carried the skulls for him one round. When he started the second round, he broke easily; the Spirits were smiling on him. When he returned to the sacred tree, one of the Sundance leaders reached for the eagle staff and Mario, thinking he had a hold of it, let the staff go. It fell to the ground. I never saw it happen, but David told me about it and told me that because Mario was my nephew, he had to drag the buffalo skulls again for having dropped the staff. After that round was over, I told Mario about it. I explained that if he didn't want to do it, I would drag the skulls for him because he was my nephew and I had introduced him to the Sundance circle. As I finished saying that, Bo walked up and said he would drag them if Mario didn't want to because it was his eagle staff that Mario had dropped. Mario, surprised that two men were willing to drag the skulls for him, said he would drag them and couldn't leave that responsibility to anyone else. He agreed to drag the skulls the next day, but he wouldn't get the chance until the last day.

David decided to have the healing round halfway through the second day. Melody told me she was glad to have the healing round then. She was having trouble coping with the heat and had been resting when the Sundancers were called to the healing round. She told me she was grateful to be thinking of helping others when she was immersed in her own exhaustion. The healing round actually made her feel better, thinking of the others who needed healing. It was a good round.

Shortly after the healing round, without telling me, Melody left the Sundance. She had started her moon time, and to show respect for the other dancers, she left the Sundance grounds right away.

On the third day, Gil from Riverside joined us. He works for the California prison systems, and for years he has been helping inmates. Both native and non-native men and women have the Sweat Lodge available to them with Gil's help. It was Gil's turn to dance and pierce. He did it with pride and courage.

A very good friend of mine, Bert from Marina Del Rey, California, was a very much appreciated member of our camp. Being of traditional Filipino descent, a lot of his ancestors' medicine ways are the same as ours: they sweat, they pray, and they heal. Bert is a very experienced healer who uses acupuncture and herbs. He danced and prayed with us and beaded medicine bags for people. He used herbal medicine to heal many of the Sundancers right after they had been pierced. Both Sundancers and supporters expressed their gratitude for his being there. Every year, Bert makes a pilgrimage to South Dakota and attends

Sundances to help any way he can, using his special medicine and experience.

That evening, Lionel and I went back to camp. And as we got there, Melody and Jodi left. They didn't want their moon to affect us.

Later, Melody told me about the conversation that took place between Jodi, Judy (a Lakota woman from California), and her. They were discussing various cases of severe child abuse in each of their lives, from personal and other people's experiences. There was a great deal of healing going on during the conversation. Melody, Jodi, and Judy shed some tears for all the children who had been abused.

They didn't solve all the problems of the world, but some powerful issues were being brought to the surface, not only right then but throughout the Sundance. We heard about many people going through serious personal issues. It was as though the Spirits were there to help us heal ourselves from things in our present and our past. Many people were moved to tears by this spiritual energy.

On Sunday, everybody looked better and stepped lighter. It was the last day. Even Bob, a man who had been pierced every day since the first day of the Sundance, started lifting his feet higher.

Phil and another Sundancer, Rose Marie, joined us. She had made a commitment to pierce once on the last day, and she was there to fulfill her commitment. The whole day was hectic because many dancers had waited to pierce on the last day. We encouraged people to pierce on other days, but when they'd had a vision it was hard to make them change their minds. On the last day, all the helpers and Sundance leaders also had to pierce for the privilege of having helped.

Now it's time to mention the last person who danced with us. Though she didn't pierce, I want the world to know that Suzanne, a nurse from California, proved to me and everyone else that she was one of the strongest dancers out there. She danced strong and hard for four days, never for an instant losing sight of her purpose for being there and her commitment.

That afternoon a cold wind had moved in from the north, so the hungry and thirsty Sundancers weren't too interested in cold watermelons. We almost had to beg people to take them.

The Sundance ended late that night. I was honored and privileged to have danced with so many strong and dedicated people. I am proud and honored to know each and every one of them.

Well, one more year and another Sundance is over. Sometimes I wish they would last more than four days. Then again, I'm glad they don't. I don't think I could take more than four days of it in any one year. Though the Sundance is over, the memories, the smells, and above all the new acquaintances that are found will live on in my heart until the next time we find ourselves together at a Sundance. I'm glad to have been chosen by them to show their road to the Sundance.

Native spirituality is not a matter of taking, and then taking some more. Always when we take, we give, and every time we give, we take. Balance is always practiced by the native people. When you see bumper stickers and T-shirts that say, "Walk in balance in this life," we don't mean to walk in balance like walking on a tightrope. We mean walking in balance with nature and with each other. It means respect for everything: plants, all animals, our Mother Earth, ourselves, and above all, respect for the Spirits. If you take the life of a tree, plant two more, because then you are giving one of them a chance of survival: if one of them should die, there is still one to replace the one that you took.

People come from all over the world to attend the Sundance, from the mountains of Peru, from Europe and Tibet. There have been Aztecs, Navajos, Danes, Tohono O'Odhams, Apaches, Canadians, Germans, Afro-Americans, Japanese, and even a Buddhist monk. There are no racial or religious barriers for people who come to share the Sundance with us as long as they come in a good way and with respect for our ways. There are representatives from all four races at the different Sundances. It is something we share with our brothers and sisters. It doesn't matter what color their skin is. We are one, together on this planet. We should pray, dance, and give thanks to the Creator together. That's what makes the Sundance so beautiful, so pure, and so powerful.

We, the Native American People, the Indigenous People, are the keepers of the Sundance beliefs. We are the teachers of the Sundance beliefs. It is our job to show others the way to our spirituality. What we learn from our visions, we must share with others.

Having now survived thirteen Sundances in ten years and having been pierced many times, I am grateful. Grateful for the opportunity and proud to Sundance with the Shoshoni, Lakota, and members of all the other tribes I have danced with.

The Sundance was God sent to me. The Creator gave me something that would please me and fulfill my spiritual cravings. Every day I thank the Creator for bringing me the Sundance and the Ceremonial Pipe. I found what had always been there for me. All I had to do was look and ask. After searching all over and in other beliefs, I had overlooked what was natively mine. It seems so simple now.

I had finally found a spiritual awareness within myself

and was content with what I had found. I also felt a great weight lifted from my spirit. Although the spirit itself has no substance or physical restraints, I believe that when our spirits are without direction or focus, there is a great, almost physical stress put on our lives until we find our individual spirituality.

That spiritual stress then invades our physical body, creating an uneasy restlessness. We find ourselves always looking for relief. We find ourselves searching until we get something we are content with. Some people choose Buddhism, Judaism, or Christianity, and some feel comfortable with Hinduism. There is something for everyone. It's just a matter of feeling good about what you find.

I've committed myself to the *Chanupa*. I have committed myself to Sundancing every year as long as I live. Unfortunately, I cannot follow the Sundancing year-round; it's very hard because of our lifestyles.

Many of us tend to forget our spirituality until we are in need of help, but the Sundance is never forgotten in my home. At every meal we give thanks. Sometimes we hold hands and form a prayer circle. Sometimes we don't. At every meal I give thanks to the Creator for having given the Sundance to me. Every time I wake up, I give thanks that I am here for my children one more day. I don't ever know what that day is going to bring, but I hope that it will always bring tranquillity to the world and peace to my family.

I always pray that people stop and realize what we are doing to our Mother Earth. Many don't seem to care about anything, except what is important to them. We should stop and realize that this is the only world we've got. This planet we are standing on is like our heart. This planet that we abuse daily, it's our heart. Without it we don't have a life. We don't survive. We don't exist.

Again and for the last time I want to ask you that same question I have asked. Why did God or the Creator decide to create us humans?

Here is my answer to that question.

I believe that God, the Creator, needs us to worship Him. Without us, He doesn't exist. No God is a God if He has no one to acknowledge Him. I believe that since He needs us to recognize Him as a god, it's His obligation to take care of us. In this way, He pays us back for our worship by answering our prayers. We can demand His help, and He has an obligation to give it to us. Our obligation is to worship and show respect.

I wonder sometimes why it took me so long to find the Sundance. It seems there were so many times in my life when I would have been a better person had I been Sundancing. As one Sundance Chief told me, it's very possible that I was just not ready, and the Spirits wanted me to wait until I was.

Now that you have finished reading this, you have knowledge that places you on a higher spiritual plateau. Make a commitment to yourself, always walk in balance and do not judge others. Be grateful for the things you receive and always remember to give in return.

This journey has been a long and hard one for me, but in a good way. You have witnessed my hopes, fears, desires, feelings, and the baring of my soul. All this was necessary, as it led me to the road to the Sundance.

Afterword

My first experience with the Sundance happened many years ago. It awakened me spiritually and caused many changes in my life. It also brought about the events that left me feeling compelled to write this book and to pass on my message.

At the end of March of 1994, Melody and I had gone to New Mexico on a selling trip. Our route took us in and around Albuquerque. Between sales we visited some very good friends of ours, Arnie and Norma Jean Sidman, who have a nice print shop on Lomas Boulevard. Arnie has often printed things for me and other native people, always declining payment, always remaining a friend.

Our trip took us up through Santa Fe, then up to Taos, New Mexico. After we saw our good friends Lyn and Michael in Taos, we reluctantly headed back down the hill to Albuquerque. The trip back seemed to go by quickly although the road is slow and curvy. Melody seemed preoccupied and was quiet most of the trip. I thought that the trip had been too short and felt uneasy, as though something had been left behind or left unsaid. I felt that way because something that needed to be resolved while in Taos had not even been addressed. What was so funny was that I didn't even know what I needed answers to. I just knew that I felt an emptiness that caused me to feel all these emotions. Perhaps the Spirits were preparing me for all the things from my past—for soon I would be reliving the past, however painful it might be. I know that during the days before, while I was being led in this direction, I made life really miserable for my wife and those around me.

Pulling into Albuquerque, we were treated to a beautiful picture that can only be seen in the West, a spectacular sunset. We thought of driving on to Arizona, but decided against it, since we were both tired. We found a motel, got something to eat, and went to bed early.

The next morning I was up early. Melody was having trouble detaching herself from the blankets. After I had my shower and while she had hers, I just kicked back and watched the news.

When she was done, she sat on the bed across from me. Suddenly an intense pain knifed through my head. "Oh my God," I thought, "I'm having a stroke."

I had never experienced anything like it and it really scared me. Melody saw me sitting there holding my head with both hands and knew I was in pain. She asked me if I was okay. I couldn't answer. I just kept holding my head and moaning from the pain. I tried to keep from making any sound but the pain was just too intense. Another moan escaped my lips.

By now Melody was really worried. She said, "Honey, are you all right?" Then she asked the same question again, but this time with a hint of panic in her voice. Then, "You want me to call a doctor?"

I shook my head and held my hand up to her to stop. In my head I was hearing voices. Though the pain was slowly subsiding, it was sharp enough that I was still conscious. Then I heard a voice say, "Don't worry, you're not sick. You're not having a stroke. You are fine."

Imagine that! My own mind was telling me not to worry, that I wasn't having a stroke. I felt I was losing my mind. My thought conversation continued. "Don't worry, you're fine. We have a message for you, and we wanted to get your attention."

"Who is 'we'?" I wondered

Clearly, I received the answer, "We are the Spirits."

I asked, "What Spirits?"

"Just listen to what we have to tell you. You must write a book about your spiritual life. You must share all you have experienced with others. You must tell everything since the day we brought you the eagle whistles, that morning so long ago."

Through all these exchanges of thoughts in my head, all I was aware of was the presence of my wife and her concern for me. I had no thoughts of where I was or anything else. It happened so fast that I didn't have time to reflect on other things.

"How do I do that?" I asked in my thoughts.

"You already have in your mind what you have lived through and suffered. You will know what to say. Say only the truth. But we will help you when you need it."

By now the pain in my head was gone, but I still felt drained and dazed. Apparently I didn't look very good, because my wife was still looking at me strangely, and she asked me again if I was all right. I told her that I felt better, and that I had been visited by the Spirits.

I sat thinking of what had occurred and shook my head in disbelief. I was telling myself that it hadn't really happened, that it was only thoughts running wildly through my head. But what about the pain? Had I actually had a stroke? I was still in a daze and not thinking straight.

Finally, Melody couldn't take my silence any longer: "What in the world happened to you, Honey? You looked awful! Please tell me what the Spirits told you."

"They said they had a message for me, and the pain was just to get my attention. They told me to write a book about my spiritual life since the beginning, when they brought me the sound of the eagle whistle. I guess they mean when I heard them in Sacramento."

And so this book began. For a few weeks I ignored the call. I didn't want to write this book, and I didn't know why I had been told to share my experiences. So much of what I've seen and done is personal. I didn't want to share my visions with everyone. Only the Spirits and I should know about them. Yet there was a voice inside me telling me to share what I know and what I've learned. I felt as though the Spirits would intervene and rearrange my thought patterns to include what they wanted me to do.

It was very frustrating. It was as though I was in a constant thought battle against myself. One second I would think of something to write in the book, then I would reject it for one reason or another. Then again I would hear words in my mind that I had to write down. My mind was on the verge of bursting with ideas and refusals.

Suddenly one day I just couldn't keep it under restraint any longer. The Spirits just would not be denied. The battle was over. I was overcome with undeniable determination to start writing.

From what I have learned, the Spirits that the Creator designated to help us include a Human kind; the Animal Spirits; and the Black, or Bad, Spirits. I'll briefly try to explain how I believe they work. (I won't elaborate because that's a complete book of its own.)

The Human Spirits are the old people who have lived in the past. Though they are gone from this life, they continue to integrate with those of us on the earth to guide us on different paths in this life, but only if we are willing to accept these responsibilities. They can only guide us by bringing us thoughts, ideas, encouragement, and the ambition to do what they ask. Sometimes they make their presence known; most times they don't. Sometimes they say who they are and their names; then again, at times, they don't. They come to us in different ways, but always when they do, it's very dramatic, so there's no doubt in your mind about what's going on.

Many people confuse random thoughts with visions. If every thought crossing our minds was a vision, we would be constantly confused. Our minds would tend to wander all over the universe, and our path and decisions would be constantly changing with our thoughts. There are ways of telling the difference.

The Animal Spirits are mostly to help us with both physical and material things; then there are the Black, or Bad, spirits. There are people who feel more comfortable receiving their guidance from a Black, or Bad, Spirit. But the Black Spirit's most important function is to form that very important element for our world called balance.

When I conceded to the Spirits, they took over my life and my family's life. I would write and write, all of it in longhand. Throughout the writing of this book and the editing of it, I always felt as though the Spirits never left my side. Anytime I got sidetracked or was getting lazy, they'd step in and inject me with enthusiasm to keep going, to keep writing.

One night after the book was finished, they came to me again in a dream. They told me the reason I had been picked to write this book was that I had shown my willingness to suffer for the people I was praying for. Also, although there were others with more knowledge of the Sundance, I was the Spirits' choice to put *my* experiences on paper.

The Spirits are concerned with the lack of interest shown by the younger people in all areas of spirituality. They are worried that the long-standing native tradition of the Sundance will be lost by the newer generation.

No one really knows how old the Sundance is or how long it has been around. We do know that for us there are no other ways to worship.

At every Sweat Lodge ceremony someone always seems to remember to give thanks to our elders: those who had the courage and this spirituality so deeply rooted that they went into hiding when the government tried to take it from our people in the late 1800s. I equate the suppression of our spiritual beliefs by the government and by the established churches with the suppression of Jews and their beliefs by the Nazis during World War II, and black people brought to America as slaves. I just can't understand why people tried to force us to worship something other than what we wanted. All this without even trying to understand us and our beliefs.

The Sundance is a gathering of people assembled to pray only for others, to show their love for others, and to love, honor, and show respect for the world. Like the Jews, we were persecuted for not believing or even knowing about Jesus Christ. Yet all along we had the same God. Thanks to that God, the Sundance has survived. Perhaps this book will do what the Spirits intended it to do—bring more people to the Sundance or, if nothing else, arouse people's curiosity about it and make them want to know more.

This is how I was compelled by the Spirits to do some of their work for them. To them I give my most profound thanks and gratitude for having selected me for this. They also know that if I'm called again to serve them in other ways, I will. For I have proven that to them many times over at the Sacred Tree, in our sacred Sundance.

Praise for *Darling* by Richard Rodriguez

"[Rodriguez's] charming, associative prose is reminiscent of James Baldwin. . . . *Darling* is a revelation."   —*Financial Times*

"Richard Rodriguez may be the most empathic essayist in America. . . . His sentences are reliable joys: liquid and casual, they slip in and out of philosophy and anecdote noiselessly, like people padding through an empty chapel, expecting to hear nothing more than the sound of their own passage."   —Sasha Frere-Jones, *The New Yorker*

"An eccentric mélange of a book . . . Under Rodriguez's guidance . . . all the pieces are connected slowly until the project as a whole reveals itself. It's as if you've been wandering for miles in a desert and, suddenly, your salvation appears."   —NPR.org

"The ten essays of this 'spiritual autobiography' are beautiful examples of thinking something through with not just intelligence and verve but wholeheartedness and compassion. . . . [Rodriguez] is among the very best essayists of his generation. . . . These magnificent 'personal-classical' essays will be read and enjoyed for many decades to come, darling."   —*The Washington Post*

"[Richard Rodriguez's] doubt-seasoned Catholic belief reveals the time he inhabits as out of joint, freeing him from what Chesterton called 'the degrading slavery of being a child of his age.' He's as free as a suicide bomber, this master of the literary essay." —*Commonweal*

"It would not be a stretch to call Rodriguez our greatest living essayist. . . . He is an inward writer who is always looking out toward issues of race, spirituality, sexuality, and heritage."

—David Gessner, *Ecotone*

"With compassion and profundity of vision, Rodriguez offers a compelling view of modern spirituality that is as multifaceted as it is provocative."   —*Kirkus Reviews* (starred review)

"Engaging and readable, this highly personal and candid discovery . . . will delight Rodriguez's fans."

—*Library Journal* (starred review)

"*Darling* is a remarkable collection, one that will no doubt strengthen Rodriguez's reputation as being one of America's finest essayists."

—*El Paso Times*

"*Darling* is . . . the biography of many intersecting ideas: the relationship between gay rights and women's rights; the relationship between unforgiving landscapes and enduring faith; between cities and their scribes; between a homosexual man and his church."

—Leslie Jamison, *New York Times Book Review*

"For some readers, 'delighting with complexity' may seem a conundrum. It can be a valid experience as anyone familiar with Rodriguez's lucid writing will attest. Further, analyzing complexity—as a topic from a literary perspective—does not mean writing to confuse; it means opening up a complicated issue with clarity."

—*The Buffalo News*

PENGUIN BOOKS

DARLING

Richard Rodriguez is the author of *Hunger of Memory, Brown*, and *Days of Obligation*. He is a fellow of New America Media. He was a longtime contributor for *PBS NewsHour* and continues to write for *Harper's Magazine*. He lives in San Francisco.

© DOMINIC MARTELLO

Darling

a spiritual autobiography

RICHARD RODRIGUEZ

penguin books

PENGUIN BOOKS
Published by the Penguin Group
Penguin Group (USA) LLC
375 Hudson Street
New York, New York 10014

USA | Canada | UK | Ireland | Australia | New Zealand | India | South Africa | China
penguin.com
A Penguin Random House Company

First published in the United States of America by Viking Penguin,
a member of Penguin Group (USA) LLC, 2013
Published in Penguin Books 2014

Acknowledgments to publishers of previously published chapters appear on page xi.

Grateful acknowledgment is made for permission to reprint excerpts from the following copy-
righted works:

Hell by Kathryn Davis. Copyright © 2003 by Kathryn Davis. Used by permission of The Wylie
    Agency LLC.
"The Crack-Up" from *The Crack-Up* by F. Scott Fitzgerald. Copyright © 1945 by New Directions
    Publishing Corp. Reprinted by permission of New Directions Publishing Corp.
"The Enchanted" from *Four Plays* by Jean Giraudoux. Copyright © 1948, 1950 by Maurice Valency.
    Reprinted by permission of Hill and Wang, a division of Farrar, Straus and Giroux, LLC.
The Daring Young Man on the Flying Trapeze by William Saroyan. By permission of The Stanford
    University Libraries.
The Stone Diaries by Carol Shields. Copyright © Carol Shields, 1993. Published by Viking, a mem-
    ber of Penguin Group (USA) LLC.

THE LIBRARY OF CONGRESS HAS CATALOGED THE HARDCOVER EDITION AS FOLLOWS:
Rodriguez, Richard.
Darling : a spiritual autobiography / Richard Rodriguez.
pages cm
ISBN 978-0-670-02530-5 (hc.)
ISBN 978-0-14-312588-4 (pbk.)
1. Rodriguez, Richard, 1944–   2. Catholic Church—United States—Biography.
3. Christian pilgrims and pilgrimages—Israel.   4. United States—Religion.   I. Title.
BX4705.R6375A3 2013
282.092—dc23
[B]   2013017046

Printed in the United States of America
10 9 8 7 6 5 4 3 2

Set in Palatino   Designed by Carla Bolte

Penguin is committed to publishing works of quality and integrity. In that spirit, we are proud
to offer this book to our readers; however, the story, the experiences, and the words are the
author's alone.

For the Sisters of Mercy of the Americas

A Note to the Reader

All the chapters within were written in the years after September 11, 2001—years of religious extremism throughout the world, years of rising public atheism, years of digital distraction. I write as a Christian, a Roman Catholic. My faith in the desert God makes me kin to the Jew and the Muslim.

Throughout, and especially in the chapter "Darling," I have altered many names and fictionalized some events and locations.

Hugo House, a writers' workshop in Seattle, solicited the chapter called "Tour de France"; it was reprinted in the *Kenyon Review*. The *Wilson Quarterly* published the chapter on Cesar Chavez, "Saint Cesar of Delano." *California*, the alumni magazine of the University of California, Berkeley, first published "Disappointment." "Final Edition" appeared in *Harper's Magazine*. *Harper's* also published an earlier version of the chapter that appears here as "Jerusalem and the Desert." A two-page sketch of the final chapter, "The Three Ecologies of the Holy Desert," was first printed in *Image*.

Contents

Darling

one

Ojalá

One summer evening in London, many years ago, I was walking
through green twilight in Hyde Park when I attracted the gaze of
a large woman who was wearing several coats; she was tending to
two children, a girl and a boy—her grandchildren, I surmised. As
I passed, the woman posted a radiant, recognizing smile. "Ara-
bie?" she asked.

I smiled, too. I shook my head, as though sadly. *No.*

Now I am not so sure.

In the predawn dark, a young man is bobbing up and down behind the pillar of an airport lounge a few yards from my departure gate. I watch from behind my newspaper. The man turns in a
circle before the floor-to-ceiling window, beyond which an air-
liner lumbers upward like a blue whale to regain the suspended
sea. The young man cups his hands behind his ears, then falls out
of sight.

One other passenger sees what I see. "Someone should call the
police," the woman says out loud, not to me, not to anyone—a
thought balloon.

To say what? A Muslim is praying at Gate 58.

In the final months of my parents' lives—months of wheelchairs
heaved into the trunks of cars, months of desperate clutchings at

handrails and car doors—I often drove them to the five-thirty Mass on Saturday evenings.

One Saturday in mid-September 2001—a day without fog, a warm evening sky—I steered my mother's wheelchair out of the church, careful of the radius of the thing, careful of her toes. All of us at Mass felt a need for congregation that evening. In the interval between last Saturday and this, we had learned something terrible about the nature of religion.

Several women of the parish leaned over my mother's wheelchair, as they often did. A few months hence, when my mother could no longer leave the house, these same women would ring the doorbell of my parents' house to bring Holy Communion to my mother.

Terrible times, the women murmured among themselves, all of them in tropically colored blouses. *Terrible, terrible times!*

Something had happened in the sky. In a way it was more extraordinary than a mystic's vision—the vision, for example, of Caryll Houselander, the English artist, writer, bohemian. London, 1918: Houselander, a young woman of sixteen, was on her way to buy potatoes for her family's dinner. She knew she must not tarry on the way home. Suddenly, above her, as she recounts, "wiping out not only the grey street and sky but the whole world," was an icon of Christ the King crucified. Houselander goes on to explain, as all mystics must but never can explain, that she saw with her mind's eye.

We of the congregation had not seen with our minds' eyes, but through our television screens. We saw people—they were so far away but we knew they were people, they were not cinders or the leaves of calendars; we saw people who had no alternative but to consign their bodies—their bodies, I say, but I mean their lives—

to the air, people who are loved, I believe, by God, even as I believe their murderers are loved by God. Falling.

A friend of mine, a Jew, called at about that time to ask if there was ever a time when I did not believe in God. My answer was no. Her answer was no also.

It was in the weeks following the terrorist attacks of September 11 that I came to the realization that the God I worship is a desert God. It was to the same desert God the terrorists prayed.

The cockpit terrorists believed, furthermore, that God is honored by violent death, by the violent deaths of the hapless people who worked in those towering buildings, or who were visiting there, or delivering something on that particular day, at that particular hour.

I do not believe what the destroyers believed—that God is honored by a human oath to take lives. I do not believe God can be dishonored. The action of the terrorists was a human action, conceived in error—a benighted act. And yet I worship the same God as they, so I stand in some relation to those men.

I long have assumed, as a Christian, a Roman Catholic (by the favor of colonial Mexico), that I am a younger brother to the Jew, because the Jew and I worship the same God, and the Hebrew Bible is mine also, though less mine—*cf.* Jesus Christ: *Salvation is from the Jews.* For most of my life, though, I have scarcely regarded the Muslim—despite centuries of Muslim rule of Spain, a country to which (by the favor of colonial Mexico) I am related; and despite the fact that Brother Dennis, classroom 119, Christian Brothers High School, Sacramento, 1962, famously opined that Islam is, indeed, "a true religion"; and despite the fact that the Muslim claims Abraham as father, as does the Jew, as do I.

As increasing numbers of Muslims declare war in their hearts against "Crusaders and Zionists," I endeavor to put away my ignorance about Muslims. War is one of the most intimate human behaviors. Soldiers know it. Boxers know it. Schoolchildren know it. Adversaries grow as preoccupied with one another as do young lovers. The general must try to imagine the battlefield the other way around, like a hairdresser working in a mirror. Thus am I drawn to the customs and thoughts of the one who threatens me. I strain to hear what he is saying about me among his confreres.

The first Arabic word I learned in the aftermath of September 11 was *jihad*.

Despite the suspicion with which Americans regarded Jewish and Catholic immigrants in the nineteenth century, despite the persecution of Mormons, Americans are unaccustomed to thinking of a religious war as having anything at all to do with us. Religious wars happen elsewhere. Religious wars happened long ago. Saracens and so forth. Albigensians. And yet the legend of our nation's founding concerns Puritans seeking refuge from religious persecution in England and finding that refuge on the shore of the North American continent.

At the dawn of a worldwide religious war that Americans prefer to name a war against terror, I feel myself drawn to Islam, drawn to read the Koran, even to kiss the Koran—melodramatically, but sincerely—as I did one evening recently in front of a university audience. I meant to honor Islam. I meant to convey that, as a Christian, I consider myself a loving brother to the Muslim, as I am to the Jew, by the favor of Father Abraham.

In the months after September 11, at various international airports, I found myself facing security officers in glass booths who fastidiously turned the pages of my passport, as though they were reading. But they were not reading. Their eyes did not leave my face.

Don't look evasive don't look steely don't look sly.

The inked tongue of the stamp machine was held suspended over my passport all the while, but then it was put aside. I was directed to accompany another officer to a no-man's-room for a second scrutiny.

I am looking at a photograph of members of the bin Laden family of Saudi Arabia. They are on holiday in Sweden. It is 1971—nearly ten years after Brother Dennis's ratification of Islam—a bland, sunny day. The young men and women in the photograph are smiling; they pose in front of a pink Cadillac limousine; they are dressed in the mode of Carnaby Street. These young bin Ladens are, for the moment, at ease in a jolly old world.

But one among the bin Laden heirs is missing from the photograph; one has a spirit that wants to concentrate, to contract, rather than to absorb.

Thirty years after the Sweden photograph, the face of Osama bin Laden appears on every television news show, every magazine cover, every newspaper, in the world. Bin Laden smiles benignly. His brown eyes observe the mechanics of my nightmare from the obverse, as a choragus would. He sees all the props. He sees bindles of hundred-dollar bills; he sees passports, airline tickets, box cutters. He watches as Internet commands burn through fiber-optic cables; he sees a peerless blue sky. He foresees his own smile, holy jubilation, dancing brothers, brothers dancing. He anticipates the pleasure of Allah.

The young terrorists whom Osama bin Laden dispatched into

the twenty-first century had some acquaintance with the West. They knew several languages, foremost among them the language of technology. At some point in their lives, they had discovered a wish or an imperative to separate themselves from their own human desires. They were trained to move between the snares of the devil and to maintain their resolve to kill the people they passed among. (*Look them in the eye. Do not look sly. Smile.*)

Hi.

September 10, 2001. Imagine the heartsickness of these young men, imagine the leaky bowels, the frequent swallowings, the swollen tongues, the reflexive yawns. Imagine the bathroom of a Days Inn as your chapel of vigil, where you sanctify yourself through the "Last Night." Imagine the sickening ablutions you are instructed by your captain to make: the shaving of hair from your body, the cloying scent of cologne, the prayers whispered into the palms of your hands and then applied to your secret body, like the blessings your mother long ago placed on you. Imagine the wish to flee.

When you emerge from your hotel room at dawn, you will be a crusader, impersonating a Crusader. Become what you hunt.

I send for a language course in Arabic because I want to hear what they are saying. I want to hear their quarrel with me. I want to taste their curses on my tongue; I want to imitate the posture of their prayers. I yearn to hear the strange heckling voice of God. Anyway, the software is incompatible with my computer. I call the number for technical support. I am connected to an aural hive that sounds like a train station in Delhi. I talk to a succession of optimistic young men in a room full of optimistic young men, all named Sayyid, all schooled in patience.

I realize I am unable to learn Arabic because I am unable to learn computer-ese. The power the young have over the old is the spirit of an age. In our age, technology is optimism. Technology is a new kind of democracy, supplanting borders. Nothing to memorize, only connect. I doubt if Sayyid would be able to afford the complicated computer system my computer quack has set up for me. But Sayyid understands it, which I never will.

Because I am unable to follow the simplest instructions over the phone, Sayyid asks permission to "enter" my computer. "I will set up a chat line so you can ask me questions while I work."

I do not avail myself of the chat line. Files appear. Bars race across the screen like bullet trains. Files topple into the trash. *Ding.* A message from Sayyid:

THERE YOU GO.

WHAT DO I DO?

CLICK THE ICON AND GO TO LESSON ONE.

Lesson One: Bintoon. A girl. Waladoon. A boy.

The power the old exert over the young is the power to send the young to war—flesh in its perfection dropped into a hellish maze of stimulus and response in order to defend an old man's phrase. A phrase! What? The American way of life? Yes. It galls me to say it, but yes. This paragraph costs me nothing. And yet I know it cost the life of a boy or a girl with a ready body and a mind not ripe. No one will come to question me this evening.

Often young American soldiers from Kansas or Arizona, upon being dispatched to the desert, speak of entering into the Bible. The terrain they mean. The tribal dress. Away in a manger.

We six-o'clock newsers have become accustomed to hearing the distant voices calling to us from the craters of bombed cities— *Allah akbar,* the voices cry. We understand what they are saying, young men writhing on gurneys. They are saying: *Mama! Help me! Save me! Kill them! God have mercy!*

In the no-man's-room at the Toronto airport, an old man—probably younger than I am—murmured *Salam Ahlaykom* when I sat beside him on a yellow plastic chair facing a blinded window.

I suppose I do look Arabic. No, you know what? I don't look Arabic—not if you know what you're looking at. In the eyes of border guards, my features are kind of floaty. Indeterminacy is possible grievance in the eyes of border guards.

The Muslim terrorist with his backpack slung on one shoulder arrives at the gate at Logan International Airport. He is an American college student en route to California, where, perhaps, it will be sunny and warm later today.

Hi.

During America's notorious sixties, I remember hearing some young Mexican Americans righteously foretell the Mexican *reconquista* of the southwestern United States. It was only a matter of time, these young people said, and sincerely believed, before history would bite its own tail; before ascending birthrates in Phoenix or Dallas would herald a just conclusion to the Mexican-American War.

Such a prediction was soon trampled by increasing numbers of immigrants arriving in the American Southwest, fleeing the civic failure of Mexico, certainly not seeking to perpetuate Mexico's influence in time or territory.

The dream of *reconquista* assumes that history revolves, that historical patterns are circles, even that a certain narrative point can be applied to history, like poetic justice, karma, Pyrrhic victory, irony. I think the circular clock face encourages us to think roundly—a finite numerology (Roman numerals, Arabic numerals) of 12 or 24; the tilt of Earth, the revolving seasons, the orderly succession of the sky. In the Digital Age, the age we have entered, time is no longer counted as recurrence but is cast forward to the unmaking of glaciers, the starvation of continents, the extinction of species.

I was sitting—beneath a clock, as a matter of fact; an old-fashioned pendulum clock with Roman numerals—in a student café near the Universidad Complutense de Madrid. I listened as a North African student predicted to me the Muslim reconquest of Europe. And his prediction, too, seemed a kind of circularity. He cited ascending birthrates of Muslim immigrants and declining birthrates of native Europeans. Europe is disappearing, he said. He foresaw a Muslim Paris, a Muslim Vienna, a Muslim Madrid—Muslims sleeping in the cradles, Muslims warming themselves at the firesides, Muslims filling the boulevards of a faithless, child-less Europe. The earnest young man imagined the interrupted era of Muslim influence in Europe, a medieval golden age of tolerance and algebra and clock making, would be restored by the will of Allah. The young man's Spanish was better than mine.

My skepticism concerning all notions of *reconquista* is skepti-cism toward the view that history is restorative. I get older but I do not grow wiser. It is only by shedding skin, by turning pages, by ordering stronger spectacles, by having my hair cut, that I seem to be restoring myself to a circular pattern, that I seem to progress toward youth and capability, though my progress is ac-tually a decline.

I seem to be forgetting something as my eyes weaken and my patience sharpens into a desperate, childish hunger: I am forget-ting that one must become as a little child. (To reach the kingdom of Heaven, in Jesus's formulation. Or to apprehend an intuition of that kingdom—surely that is to believe in circularity?)

I seem to be missing rooms and days, days so tall I could not see an end to them. I miss persons who no longer exist.

———

Oh, c'mon, Frank, at least leave it up till New Year's Day.

What miracle of neuron and synapse allows one to laugh out loud in remembrance of a moment so long past? I see Frank (with my mind's eye); I hear Frank's sugar-cured voice. Frank is my landlord. How he amuses me! I watch Frank pluck a red bow and a pert artificial bird from an evergreen wreath and then dump the wreath into a trash bag.

I'll tell you something, Richard: There's nothing so over as Christmas. (December 26, perhaps 1985.)

Twenty-five years later, this same Frank woke to see his adored older brother, Cassius, standing in the doorway of the hospital room where Frank was taken after his last bedroom fall. Cassius was in his air force uniform, looking exactly as he had that summer morning in Birmingham, sixty years earlier, when Cassius paused in Frank's bedroom doorway before he turned and left for the war. *Cassius? Are you here or am I there?* But Cassius could not see Frank, or, if he could, he could not speak.

On a television documentary I watched last night, a Chilean astronomer said that the calcium in our bones is made of stardust. He was not speaking metaphorically.

Those who are old claim the advantage of far sight. The older you get, the more you remember; the more you forget, the more you regret. The more you sift. There remains the problem of reliability. My friend Florence: Florence is ninety-two. She cannot remember what she had for lunch or even . . . she looks at her watch . . . she supposes she must have had lunch by this time. Yet her mind can recall a day in 1925, a spring day: the back door is standing open because the kitchen is too warm. She can see a quarter moon with a pointed chin on the page of the calendar as she opens the back door for her mother, who is too warm; her mother preparing the Sabbath meal. The meal is going to be spoiled because her father and her eldest brother will quarrel; their father will leave the table. Florence shrugs. She forgets what point she was illustrating with the calendar, the too-warm kitchen, the anger of men.

I catch a glimpse of my mother through the doorway of our kitchen. I am just about to leave for school; it must be cold—I am zipping up my jacket, my binder between my knees. "See you later, Mama."

Ojalá, my mother calls.

My mother appended *ojalá* to every private leave-taking; my father never did. I heard the Spanish expression pristinely—I had heard it all my life. *Ojalá* meant *ojalá*. If I'd had the best friend I dreamed about, someone who would follow me about, who would want to know what everything meant, I would have told him *ojalá* means something like *I pray it may be so*—an exclamation and a petition.

Growing up, I thought the American expression *God willing and the creek don't rise* to be a variant of my mother's *ojalá*, which it is. I learned only this year, however, that the expression refers to Creek Indians, rather than to a swollen waterway.

In fact, the name of Allah was enshrined in the second and third syllables of my mother's *ojalá*. I doubt my mother knew that, though maybe she did. I didn't. The expression is a Spanish borrowing from the Arabic commonplace prayer *Insha'Allah*—God willing.

The nun stands apart as the women coalesce about my mother's wheelchair after Mass; she waits for the miasma of parrot-colored blouses to clear before she approaches. The nun's job is to minister to the elderly of the parish. She knows every old person by name;

she knows their children's names. She knows my name. I remember to ask after the health of her brother, who is ill in a town in southern Italy.

Not so good. I hope to visit him this winter.

Four months later, at the hospital where my father lay sunk in a coma, the Italian nun, whose brother had somewhat improved, stood at the foot of the bed, next to where my mother was seated. "We remain optimistic," my mother implored the nun. My desperate mother.

Leo is dying, Victoria, the nun said.

My mother tried to remove her hand from the nun's hand. The nun would not release her.

We need to pray for Leo, the nun said.

Oh, my poor mother. Proud as a mare, fiery as a mare, and now as frightened as a mare, my mother relinquished her spirit to the nun's calm instruction; she bowed her head and prayed like a schoolgirl for the old man who had been her husband for seventy years.

A year later, my mother died.

As many as four thousand Spanish words derive from Arabic. In 1492, when Columbus sailed the blue, when the Moor and the Jew were, by order of the Crown, expelled from Spain, Barbary already peppered the tongues of Spaniards.

Spaniards took Arabic words, or variants of remembered Arabic words, to the New World and salted the raw backs of Indians with them or whispered them in lust. So that, five centuries later, my Mexican mother, as a sort of reflex, would call upon Allah to keep the expected structure of her world intact. *Ojalá, Mama.* If the department store sale is still on. If the fog lifts. If it doesn't rain. If the results are negative. If we are all here next Christmas.

A characterization I have heard in recent years, at academic conferences on the Middle East, is that Christianity is a religion of guilt; Islam is a religion of grievance. Difference among the desert religions, rather than commonality, is the point drawn.

The argument proceeds: The theoretical Christian is weighed down by the knowledge of Original Sin. (If I were a young man, I would swear to you that I have never met a Christian who is weighed down by the knowledge of Original Sin. At my present age, I will tell you I have never met any human being who is not weighed down by the knowledge that men and women must fail.) The theoretical Christian inclines toward self-recrimination, which is reckoned a good thing, because self-recrimination is a corrective to anger. The theoretical Muslim knows no such fetters in his theology. The Prophet Muhammad rejected the notion of Original Sin. In the version of Islam that Western academics dispense at conferences, *jihad* is holy in the Koran and grievance can be expiated only by retribution.

Political theorists at secular academic conferences largely refrain (in my experience) from characterizing Judaism, though both Islam and Christianity are fractures of Judaism, glosses on Judaism, branches of Judaism—Judaism the root.

I must tell you: As a Christian, I am not flattered to hear academics describe the readiness of Christians to accept their guilt as a superior asset for living among people of disparate beliefs. It seems to me that Christians have inclined often enough, in our history, to harbor grievance. But it makes me uneasy to hear any academic assessment that implies that Christians are better equipped to live in a secular society than Muslims. As an American, I have never found an easy rhyme between my religion and my patriotism. Indeed, my religious life—born Mexican Catholic and raised Irish Catholic—has often been at odds with my

American faith in new beginnings. Even that wonderful phrase, "new beginnings," seems to me less a redundancy than a kind of tonic baptism, like Coca-Cola.

New beginnings: Grandma Moses said that if she ever got so down on her luck she couldn't make ends meet, why, then, she'd rent a church hall on credit and make pancakes. Maybe charge fifty cents. I don't know what it is about pancakes, she said, but if you make them, people will always come.

America is a faith, perhaps pancakes its sacrament. Opportunity comes to those who put away the disadvantages of family or circumstance and entrust themselves to the future. The point of the American story is simple enough for a child, particularly an immigrant child, to grasp: The past holds no sway in America.

Complicating my American faith, however, was the circumstance that Catholics—like high-church Protestants and like many Jews—describe themselves religiously by reference to the past and to the Old World. Regardless of any national variant of Catholicism (like Irish or Mexican), we are universal in faith— *Roman* Catholics, my Church taught me to say.

Don't you think it curious that so many Americans characterize their religious lives with reference to foreign allegiances? We are Dutch Reform; we are the Russian or the Greek Orthodox, or the Armenian or Syrian; we are the Russian, or the Galician, or the German, Jews; we are German Lutherans; we are Anglo Catholics; we belong to the Church of England! Even those Puritans of old who so famously sailed away from the intolerable Church of England ended up on the windy shore of Massachusetts, clutching their cloaks about them, gazing forlornly from history books that name them "English Puritans."

Richard Rodriguez wanted no accent in his voice, no ethnic shadow to his progress. Nevertheless, his Church educated Richard to imagine himself connected to a past much older than American optimism.

The odd thing is how well I remember my Roman youth, how well I remember the first of my Popes in the 1940s and '50s. That would be the forbidding Pope, Pius XII, with the beautifully molded head, the hook nose, the spectacles, the pewter complexion—all the more forbidding when he was laid out dead in the pages of *Life* magazine. He was a historical enigma, my first Pope. After more than fifty years, I am filled with the same dread looking at those photographs of him, and with a kind of heartsickness, for I think I really did love that dark man.

Pius XII, John XXIII, Paul VI—the roster unrolls with the century. My American childhood passed from Harry Truman to Dwight D. Eisenhower to John F. Kennedy. Castel Gandolfo was as much a part of my imagination as Camp David.

Americans experience time in two distinct ways—as religious people and as people of no religion. Just so, we experience ourselves as a historical people and as people who are not implicated by history.

Being an American and being religious did not, early on, seem a conflict to me; these were two distinct ways of being, like school and summer. I read fewer lives of the saints than I read books about American heroes—inventors, presidents, explorers. I read the life of Saint Thérèse of Lisieux as well as the life of Louis Pasteur, her contemporary, her countryman. I assumed pasteurized milk was a boon to humankind. I assumed Saint Thérèse was praying for us, as she promised she would: *I will spend my heaven in doing good upon earth.*

With Mark Twain, I wondered at the incomprehensible ways of foreigners—myself an altar boy, a familiar of Latin prayers and incense and candles and images. I was still a number of years away from the more complicated versions of American innocence to be found in the fiction of Henry James, whose American heroine in Europe "blushed neither when she looked . . . nor when she felt that people were looking at her."

On my first day at college, a sophisticated young man, a Belgian, wandered into my dormitory room like a prince in a play, noticed the crucifix my mother had pinned to the lining of the suitcase I was unpacking, said: *I suppose you are a Roman.*

I was going to say my parents came from Mexico, but then I saw what he meant. Yes, I said, a Roman. And I realized it was true—that I had had an ulterior life for as long as I could remember.

I grew up during the changeover to Technicolor. Behind *Auntie Mame* and *Three Coins in the Fountain,* behind the draperies of scarlet and gold of the Second Vatican Council, lay the deserts of the Nuclear Age—the Holocaust, Hiroshima, the Soviet Gulag.

The recesses of my late-adolescent mind were black-and-white deserts—foreign films—for I grew up in the aftermath of the war, the Age of Pasolini, Bergman, and Fellini. The human face—Humanity—was a projection on a screen. Utterances from the face were sometimes inane, wreathed with smoke, discontinuous, lapsed (in foreign films continuity was not always an important consideration). The voice confounded the movement of the lips; the translator confounded the voice. After two wars, humanity was desperate to account for its survival.

I reached my majority in the Age of Freud, Joyce, Beckett, Auden, Eliot, Nabokov. The "New Criticism" was taught in colleges—the technique of approaching a work of literature as though literature exists in its own sphere, removed from history, biography, jealousy, the smell of the river. I prized artificiality over life—I had a great hunger to experience the portrayal of life, in books, in theater.

I grew up in the Age of Existentialism, whereby Man, capital *M*, is alone and free but without recourse to a crucifix that fills the sky. And yet all this café seriousness—you will have noticed—came from the Catholic world, from Europe. I was raïsed without much sense of trespass. Saint Thérèse easily coexisted with Samuel Beckett. Both spoke French. Both were harrowed by a world empty of God. One reinvented drama to accommodate an absence of meaning. One waited patiently as, in her own simile, a sparrow in a hedge waits for the fog to clear, for the sun to be revealed.

Pius XII, John XXIII, Paul VI, John Paul I . . . it became the habit of John Paul II to address the history of the Roman Catholic Church with contrition. The old man issued over ninety formal apologies—virtually a chronicle of Western civilization. He apologized for the Church's persecution of Galileo. He apologized for the Spanish Inquisition, for the persecution of Jews, for the mistreatment of Martin Luther, for the denigration of women; he apologized for the colonial mistreatment of Native peoples in the Americas; he apologized for violence against Orthodox Christians. John Paul II apologized to the Muslim world for the sacking of Constantinople by the Crusaders in 1204.

The Pope's penitential impulse coincided with a time in the history of the Church when fewer Roman Catholics, particularly in Europe and North America, were availing themselves of the sacrament of Penance. Penance is a sacrament out of line with the postmodern sensibility, for it seeks to alleviate sin—a word we no longer employ. In secular America, the holistic mode of self-forgiveness, self-dispensed, prevails. The pop-psych revivalism of afternoon television involves "owning" one's destructive behaviors; one embarks on a "healing path"; there follows a pledge, many tears, a commercial break. We are a Bathetic Age.

The U.S. government has apologized lately for a number of historical offenses—from slavery to the incarceration of American citizens of Japanese ancestry during World War II. But the truth is that we Americans are too individualistic to huddle together under a collective apology or a collective guilt. We don't understand what it means to apologize for the sins of a past generation. The American disclaimer: *I wasn't even born yet!*

As a Roman Catholic, I am prepared to say I am sorry for the Crusades. As an American, I hear some *Jihadist* curse American Crusaders—in English—as he passes in front of a BBC camera, and I am astonished because he implicates me.

As a Roman Catholic, I confess a past I had no part in, a past to which I adhere, a past that is shameful. But as soon as the old man sitting in the yellow plastic chair in the no-man's-room at the airport in Toronto starts going on about Crusader dogs, I think to myself: *Get over it, old man; you weren't even born yet!*

The two temples of my youth—of Rome, of America—were not unrelated. The first was my parish church—Sacred Heart Catholic Church, at 39th and J streets, in Sacramento. Sacred Heart Church remains one of the few figments of my dream life that survives and that I am able to revisit without disappointment. Within and without, the architecture is Romanesque—a Roman arch set with mosaic rises above the altar. The Harry Clarke Studio of Dublin City, Ireland, glazed the colored windows in the late 1920s.

My last year of grammar school coincided with the opening (again in the pages of *Life* magazine) of the Second Vatican Council and the desire of the "universal" Church to become, in the Pentecost metaphor of that era, "a Pilgrim Church on earth." The Church would henceforth speak in all the languages of the earth. My life became less Roman, thereby. The grandeur of the Latin

Mass was lost to me; my rhetorical exception from the naive American novel dissolved. At an early age, therefore, I experienced nostalgia. Nostalgia remains specific in my imagination: the Latin mass, the windows painted by the Harry Clarke Studio in Dublin, the German music favored by Anton Dorndorf, the parish's choir director. My nostalgia was for Europe.

It never occurred to me with any intellectual or emotional force until 2001—odd, because I had seen every Bible movie released between 1951 and 1964—that Christianity, like Judaism, like Islam, is a desert religion, an oriental religion, a Semitic religion, born of sinus-clearing glottal consonants, spit, dust, blinding light.

The Christian calendar has two "deserts"—Advent and Lent—two penitential preludes to the great feasts of Christmas and Easter. Though Christianity has sojourned so long in Europe that the penitential seasons are now imagined as seasons of gaunt—winters of the soul, rather than deserts. These expanses of cold time are symbolized by an ecclesiastical weather of purple cloth.

Which brings me to the second temple of my youth. The Alhambra Theatre in Sacramento was constructed in 1927 to resemble a tall white Muslim fortress. The Alhambra belonged to the generation of exotically themed movie houses that rivaled the fantasies people gathered to enjoy in them. In midsize towns and county seats across America, alongside the five-and-dimes and the Greco-Roman banks and the two-story department stores, there were neon-lit palaces, many with romantic themes derived from Spanish Arabia—the Alcazar, El Capitan, the Valencia, the Granada. Such palaces featured velvet proscenium curtains, wrought-iron balustrades, frescoes, starlit skies.

Roman days. We entered the Alhambra through a shaded garden. We walked among palms, alongside a reflecting pool, to reach the box office. On the screen, we saw sandal-shod feet, greaves laced to the bulging calves of Roman soldiers, raised standards of the legions of Caesar. A soundtrack of French horns and kettledrums bellowed like a herd of bullocks as marching troops kicked up the dust of some god-forsaken outback of empire. The camera found the eyes of Consul Stephen Boyd. We were relieved to be provided, at last, with a point of view. Stephen Boyd surveyed the desolation, raised his eyes to the balcony where I sat portioning a small box of Milk Duds to last through a crucifixion. A legend appeared in the center of the screen:

ANNO DOMINI

XXVI

I became a Christian at the Alhambra Theatre. I suppose I became a Crusader as well. On the screen of the Alhambra Theatre we watched Otto Preminger's *Exodus*, starring Paul Newman; we watched the blue eyes of Paul Newman survey the Mediterranean, espy the approach of the Promised Land, rising and falling, from the prow of the ship. It did not occur to me to imagine another point of view. I saw Palestine from the sea. I became a Zionist at the Alhambra Theatre.

The distance of Arabs from the American imagination made the ornate folly of the Alhambra Theatre possible. Before I was born, Rudolf Valentino caused a sensation playing the Sheik. Valentino was America's first exotic movie idol, though he was neither an Arab nor a Muslim. He was born Roman Catholic, of a French mother and an Italian father. But genealogy was not the point, nor was religion. The point was a dusky seducer of powder-white women. The point was a silken tent under the stars. The point was a theme for the junior prom. Like the Alhambra Theatre's architecture, Rudolf Valentino referred the American imagination to an indistinct kingdom somewhere between *A Thousand and One Nights* and the Old Testament.

For many older Americans, until 2001, Baghdad was a thought inseparable from Douglas Fairbanks.

In the big Bible movies, Arabs were supernumeraries, not yet Muslims. Arabs were sellers at the bazaars, tuggers of camels, blind beggars. Arabs were like the desert—shifty, enduring. Jews and Christians were the main players—buff, brown-nippled visionaries (Victor Mature) who suffered the twisted attentions of stuffed-togas (Peter Ustinov) or gold-sandaled sinners (Virginia Mayo).

Islam had no comparable fraudulent reality for me, not until *Lawrence of Arabia;* not until screenwriter Robert Bolt's desert princes (Omar Sharif, Alec Guinness) stung their camels' necks with batons, uttering exit lines such as "So it is written!" The princes were fatalistic foils to Peter O'Toole's blue-eyed "Nothing is written."

As an adolescent, I read Sir Richard Burton, the nineteenth-century English explorer, because he was there—a maroon half-leather volume on my favorite shelf at the public library ("Travels in Ancient Lands"). Burton smuggled me into Mecca beneath a filthy cloak—Mecca was forbidden to infidels—and he nearly got us killed by standing to urinate, something only an infidel would do. Burton said he knew that but thought no one was watching.

About the time of my hajj with Sir Richard Burton, two examples of Islam in America became apparent to me. When trickster-poet heavyweight champ Cassius Clay espoused the Nation of Islam, renaming himself Muhammad Ali, his conversion immediately drew the world's attention.

In parts of American cities, like Harlem, the South Side of Chicago, and East Oakland, the Nation of Islam was gaining notoriety as a Northern, an ultra-unorthodox, chapter of the Negro civil rights movement. Black Muslims dressed modestly—like Sunday school teachers, like Mormons, like nuns—but they preached what America feared more than integration: They preached separatism, puritanism, anti-Semitism, racial supremacy, a faith against other faiths, a faith against the United States. The Nation of Islam's claim on orthodox Islam was tenuous.

Muhammad Ali was a winner, the heavyweight boxing champion of the world, and, in his own words, a pretty man—a combination of attributes about as choice as anyone can claim in public America. Ali had more attributes still. A sly wit belied his ferocity in the ring. In his run-in with his draft board, Ali spoke with disarming moral authority. Many Americans, especially men of draft age, admired his refusal to fight in Vietnam. We saw in Ali not only a hero of physical culture, but an upstanding man— thoroughly, never obsequiously, an American. (*"I ain't got no quarrel with them Viet Cong."*)

Like many of my generation, I became interested in another Black Muslim. There were no "Sweet-By-and-By" refrains in the testimony of Malcolm X. His voice was the puritan voice of the American North. Malcolm X had a strong story to tell of white racism and of his own degradation, but also of spiritual struggle and change.

I realize now there was always within my mother's *ojalá* the recognition that human lives are doomed to surprise. In 1973 I was a student living in London, a student walking through Hyde Park on a summer evening. My mother wrote in her weekly letter of a neighbor, whose fondest wish was to bring her grandchildren to Sacramento for the state fair, and whose leitmotif in my mother's correspondence was of perpetual reticence—to buy a cake or to play bingo or to go see *The Sound of Music*—because she was saving all her nickels and dimes to treat her grandchildren, etcetera. . . . Well, our friend did manage to bring most of her grandchildren into single file outside the turnstile one blistering August afternoon. As she waved the children forward with her fistful of tokens, she suddenly clutched at her bosom and fell down dead.

In 1964 Malcolm X separated himself from the Nation of Islam to become a Sunni Muslim. This was already a journey away from American provincialism. He traveled to the holy city of Mecca as a requirement of his faith, and he was astonished to meet all the tribes and kinds of people of the earth gathered there. It was in Mecca that Malcolm X found his spiritual inheritance—a vision larger than grievance, larger than America; a vision of belonging to the world and in the world.

Malcolm X was murdered in New York in 1965 as an apostate Black Muslim.

In the same letter, the fairground letter, as an aside, my mother mentioned that the Alhambra Theatre had closed. The property had been sold to Safeway.

At that time, Americans were daily reading about the Viet Cong and Ho Chi Minh in Hanoi and the labyrinthine Mekong Delta. We were abandoning the old downtowns of Amercian cities and their grandiose movie palaces. The theaters were boarded up or partitioned into two or three screens. In 1975 the last American helicopter lifted off from the besieged U.S. embassy in Saigon. Southeast Asian refugees began to arrive in California. By the time I returned to Sacramento, the Safeway Corporation had pulled down Samson's pillars. All that remained of the Alhambra Theatre was a tiled wall on the edge of a parking lot.

The new American movie theater, in the suburban mall, was a box, or several boxes, joined by a lobby of no romantic implication. Mall theaters did have the advantages of gigantic screens, rocking seats, free parking, and elaborate sound systems that could portray explosions and epic destructions with what we supposed was astonishing verisimilitude.

Among the many things we learned on the morning of September 11 was that epic destruction does not necessarily carry a sound in our memory or in our mind's eye.

two

Jerusalem and the Desert

On the flight from London I sit opposite a rumble seat where the stewardess places herself during takeoff. The stewardess is an Asian woman with a faraway look. I ask how often she makes this flight. Once or twice a month. Does she enjoy Israel? Not much. She stays in a hotel in Tel Aviv. She goes to the beach. She flies back. What about Jerusalem? She has not been there. What is in Jerusalem?

The illustrated guidebook shows a medieval map of the world. The map is round. The sun has a beard of fire. All the rivers of the world spew from the mouth of the moon. At the center of the world is Jerusalem.

Just inside the main doors of the Church of the Holy Sepulcher, tourists seem unsure how to respond to a rectangular slab of marble resting upon the floor. Lamps and censors and trinkets hang suspended above the stone. We watch as an old woman approaches. With some effort, she gets down on her knees. I flip through my book: *This marble represents the Stone of Unction where Jesus's body was anointed. This is not original; this stone dates from 1810.* The old woman bends forward to kiss the pale stone.

I have come to the Holy Land because the God of the Jews, the God of the Christians, the God of the Muslims—a common God— revealed Himself in this desert. My curiosity about an ecology that joins three religions dates from September 11, 2001, from prayers enunciated in the sky over America on that day.

Most occidental Christians are unmindful of the orientalism of Christianity. Over two millennia, the locus of Christianity shifted westward—to Antioch, to Rome, to Geneva, to the pale foreheads of Thomistic philosophers, to Renaissance paintings, to glitter among the frosts of English Christmas cards. Islam, too, in the middle centuries, swept into Europe with the Ottoman carpet, but then receded. (On September 11, 1683, the King of Poland halted the Muslim advance on Europe at the Gates of Vienna.) Only to reflux. Amsterdam, Paris are becoming Islamic cities.

After centuries of Diaspora, after the calamity of the Holocaust in Europe, Jews turned once more toward the desert. Zionists did not romanticize the desolate landscape. Rather, they defined nationhood as an act of planting. The impulse of the kibbutz movement remains the boast of urban Israel: to make the desert bloom.

The theme of Jerusalem is division. Friday. Saturday. Sunday. The city has been conquered, destroyed, rebuilt, garrisoned, halved, quartered, martyred, and exalted—always the object of spiritual desire, always the prize, always the corrupt model of the eventual city of God. The government of Ariel Sharon constructed a wall that separates Jerusalem from the desert, Jerusalem from Bethlehem, Easter from Christmas.

Jerusalem was the spiritual center of the Judean wilderness. It was Jerusalem the desert thought about. It was Jerusalem the prophets addressed. Jerusalem was where Solomon built a temple for the Lord and where God promised to dwell with His people. Jerusalem was where Jesus died and was resurrected. It was from Jerusalem that Muhammad ascended to heaven during his night journey.

My first impression of the city is my own loneliness—oil stains on the road, rubble from broken traffic barriers, exhaust from buses, the drift of cellophane bags. At the Damascus Gate an old woman sits on the pavement, sorting grape leaves into piles—or some kind of leaves. It is hot. Already it is hot. Late spring. It is early morning. There is a stench of uncollected garbage, and the cats, light and limp as empty purses, slink along the blackened stone walls. Shopkeepers are unrolling their shops.

I turn into the courtyard of the Church of the Holy Sepulcher, the site of Christ's burial and resurrection. A few paces away, within the church, is Golgotha, where Jesus was crucified. Golgotha, the Place of the Skull, is also, according to Jerusalem tradition, the grave of Adam. Jerusalem is as condensed, as self-referential, as Rubik's Cube.

I wait in line to enter the sepulcher, a freestanding chapel in the rotunda of the basilica. A mountain was chipped away from the burial cave, leaving only the cave. Later the cave was destroyed. What remains is the interior of the cave, which is nothing. The line advances slowly until, after two thousand years, it is my turn. I must lower my shoulders and bend my head; I must almost crawl to pass under the low opening.

I am inside the idea of the tomb of Christ.

I will return many times to the Church of the Holy Sepulcher during my stay and form in my mind an accommodation to its clamorous hush, to the musk of male asceticism—indeed, I will form a love for it that was not my first feeling. Though my first impression remains my last: emptiness.

I wait for Haim Berger in the lobby of a hotel in Ein Bokek, one among an oasis of resorts near the Dead Sea. The lobby is a desert of sand-colored marble. The lobby's temperature is oppressively beige; it would be impossible to cool this useless atrium. My cell phone rings. It is Maya, the director of the travel agency attached to my hotel in Jerusalem. Haim will be late one hour. Look for him at ten o'clock.

I watch a parade of elderly men and women crossing the lobby in bathing suits to catch a shuttle to the sulfur baths. They are so unself-conscious about their bodies they seem to walk in paradise.

I imagine I am waiting for someone in shorts and boots and aviator glasses, driving a Jeep. A Volkswagen pulls up and parks haphazardly.

A man bolts from the car. He is willowy of figure, dressed all in white, sandals, dark curly hair. He disappears into the hotel, reemerges. We wait side by side.

I cannot go to the desert alone. I am unfit for it. The desert requires a Jeep. It requires a hat and sunglasses and plastic liters of warm water it is no pleasure to drink. It requires a guide. It requires a cell phone.

Just now the man dressed in white begins patting his pockets, searching for his chiming cell. "*Ken . . . shalom*, Maya," I hear him say. Then, turning toward me, "Ah."

Haim Berger is full of apology. He has taken his wife to an emergency room. Yes, everything is all right. Just a precaution. There is an Evian bottle for me in the car. We will switch to the Jeep later.

Within ten minutes I am standing with Haim on the side of the highway. We look out over a plain, over what once was Sodom and Gomorrah. Haim asks if I know the story. Of course I know the story. Which, nevertheless, does not stop him from telling it. We might be standing near where Abraham stood when "Abraham saw dense smoke over the land, rising like fumes from a furnace."

I ask Haim if he is religious. He is not.

———

All three desert religions claim Abraham as father. A recurrent question in my mind concerns the desert: Did Abraham happen upon God or did God happen upon Abraham? The same question: Which is the desert, or who? I came upon a passage in 2 Maccabees. The passage pertains to the holiness of Jerusalem: *The Lord, however, had not chosen the people for the sake of the Place, but the Place for the sake of the people.* So, God happened upon Abraham. Abraham is the desert.

An old man sits at the door of his tent in the heat of the day.

Between that sentence and this—within the drum of the hare's heart, within the dilation of the lizard's eye—God enters his creation. The old man, who is Abraham, becomes aware of three strangers standing nearby. They arrive without the preamble of distance. The nominative grammar of Genesis surpasses itself to reveal that one of these travelers is God or perhaps all three are God, like a song in three octaves. Abraham invites the Three to rest and to refresh themselves. In return, God promises that in a year's time Abraham's wife, who is long past childbearing, will hold in her arms a son.

Abraham's wife, Sarah, in the recesses of the tent, snorts upon hearing the prognostication; says, not quite to herself: Oh, sure!

God immediately turns to Abraham: *Why does Sarah laugh? Is anything too marvelous for God?*

Sarah says: I am not laughing.

God says: *Yes, you are.*

In 1947 a Bedouin goatherd lost a goat and climbed the side of a mountain to look for it. The boy entered a cave—today the cave is known worldwide among archaeologists as Qumran Cave 1. What the boy found in the cave—probably stumbled upon in the dark—were broken clay jars that contained five sheepskin scrolls.

Four of the scrolls were written in Hebrew, one in Aramaic. More scrolls were subsequently found by other Bedouin and by scholars in adjacent caves. The discovered scrolls—including a complete copy of the Book of Isaiah—are the oldest-known manuscript copies of books of the Bible.

The scrolls date to the second century BC. Scholars believe the Jewish sect of Essenes, of the proto-monastic community of Qumran, hid the texts we now know as the Dead Sea Scrolls. No one remembers whether the goatherd found his goat.

Haim is not religious but he offers to tell me a curious story: Last year he took a group of students into a mountainous part of the desert. He had been there many times. He had previously discovered markings on rocks that seemed to indicate religious observance; he believes the markings are ancient.

On the particular day he describes—it was the winter solstice— as the group approached a mountain, they saw what appeared to be a semicircle of flame emanating from the rock face, rather like the flame from a hoop in the circus. Haim knew it was a trick of the light, or perhaps gases escaping from a fissure in the rock. He walked before the mountain in an arc to observe the phenomenon from every angle. He repeats: He was not alone. They all saw it. He has photographs. He will show me the photographs.

Haim's love for the desert dates from his military service. His Jeep broke down one day. He cursed the engine. He slammed the hood. He took a memorable regard of the distance. Since that day, he has become intimate with the distance; he has come to see the desert as a comprehensible ecosystem that can be protective of humans.

Haim has tied a white kerchief over his hair.

Haim says: "Bedouin know a lot. Bedouin have lived in the

desert thousands of years." Haim says: "If you are ever stranded in the desert—*Are you listening to me? This may save your life!*—in the early morning, you must look to see in which direction the birds are flying. They will lead you to water."

Haim stops to speak with admiration of a bush with dry, gray-green leaves. "These leaves are edible." (Now I must sample them.) "They are salty, like potato chips." (They are salty.)

Of another bush: "These have water. If you crush them, you will get water. These could save your life." He crushes a fistful of leaves and tears spill from his hand.

The child of Abraham and Sarah is named Isaac, which means "He Laughs." Sarah proclaims an earthy Magnificat: *God has made laughter for me, and all who hear of it will laugh for me.* From the loins of these two deserts—Abraham, Sarah—God yanks a wet, an iridescent, caul: a people as numerous as the stars. From the line of Sarah, royal David. From King David's line will come Jesus.

One's sense of elision begins with the map. Many tourist maps include the perimeters of the city at the time of Herod's temple, the time of Christ. *This once was . . . Built over the site . . . All that remains . . . This site resembles . . .*

This is not the room of the Last Supper; this is a Crusader structure built over the room, later converted to a mosque—note the mihrab, the niche in the wall.

The empty room is white—not white, golden. *Is the air really golden?* As a child in Omaha, my friend Ahuva was ravished by the thought—told her by an old man in a black hat—that the light of Jerusalem is golden. An ultra-Orthodox boy wanders into the room (a few paces from this room is the Tomb of King David, the anteroom to which is dense with the smell of men at prayer;

upstairs is a minaret); the boy is eating something, some kind of bun. He appears transfixed by a small group of evangelical Christian pilgrims who have begun to sing a song, what in America we would call an old song.

I am alone in the early morning at St. Anne's, a Romanesque church built in the twelfth century. The original church was damaged by the Persians; restored in the time of Charlemagne; destroyed, probably by the Caliph al-Hakim, in 1010. The present church was built by the Crusaders. Sultan Salah ad-Din captured the city in 1192 and converted the church to a madrassa. The Ottoman Turks neglected the structure; it fell to ruin. The Turks offered the church to France. The French order of White Fathers now administers St. Anne's. Desert sun pours through a window over the altar.

Not only is the light golden, Ahuva, but I must mention a specific grace. Around four o'clock, the most delightful breeze comes upon Jerusalem, I suppose from the Mediterranean, miles away. It begins at the tops of the tallest trees, the date palm trees; shakes them like feather dusters; rides under the bellies of the lazy red hawks; snaps the flags on the consulate roofs; lifts the curtains of the tall windows of my room at the hotel—sheer curtains embroidered with an arabesque design—lifts them until they are suspended perpendicularly in midair like the veil of a bride tormented by a playful page, who then lets them fall. And then lifts. And then again.

I walk around the wall of the city to the Mount of Olives, to a Christian sensibility the most evocative remnant of Jerusalem, for it matches—even including the garbage—one's imagination of Christ's regard for the city he approached from Bethany, which was from the desert. The desert begins immediately to the east of Jerusalem.

All the empty spaces of the Holy City—all courts, Tabernacles, tombs, and reliquaries—are resemblances and references to the emptiness of the desert. All the silences of women and men who proclaim the desert God throughout the world, throughout the ages, are references and resemblances to this—to the Holy City, to the hope of a Holy City. Jerusalem is the Bride of the Desert.

The desert prowls like a lion. I am fatigued from the heat, and I look about for some shade and a bottle of water. Having procured both at an outdoor stand (from a young man whose father kneels in prayer), I grow curious about an entrance I can see from the courtyard where I rest. Perhaps it is a chapel. An old man is sitting on the steps near the entrance. I approach him. What is this place?

"The Tomb of Mary," he answers.

Inside the door I perceive there are steps from wall to wall, leading downward. I can discern only the flickering of red lamps below, as if at the bottom of a well. When I reach the level of the tomb, an Orthodox priest throws a switch and the tomb is illuminated. It is a shelf of rock. The legend of the Dormition of Mary and the Catholic doctrine of the Assumption—neither of which I understand very well—lead me to wonder whether this is a spurious site. I decide I will accept all sites in this junk room of faith as true sites. I kneel.

A few years ago the bone box of James, the brother of Jesus, was raised from the shady world of the antiquities market. I believe the box has been discredited (dust not of the proper age within the incising of the letters). Authenticity is not my point. The stone box is my point. For it creates emptiness. Jerusalem is just such a box—within its anachronistic walls—a city of ossuaries, buried, reburied, hallowed, smashed, reconstructed, then called spurious or probable in guidebooks.

I have brought five guidebooks to Jerusalem: The Archeological. The Historical. The Illustrated. The Practical. The Self-Absorbed. Each afternoon, when I return to my hotel, I convene a colloquy among them—the chatter of guidebooks. I read one and then another.

The closed nature of the city frustrates my interest. My mind is oppressed by the inaccessibility of the hive of empty chambers, empty churches, empty tombs. The city that exists is superimposed in some meaty way over the bone city I long to enter. The streets are choked and impassible with life, the air stifling, the merchandise appalling. I feel feverish, but I think it is only the heat. I make the rounds of all the gates to the Temple Mount until at last I find the entrance that Israeli security will let me through—the passageway for infidels.

The sun is blazing on the courtyard. Even the faithful have gone away. Elsewhere the city is vertiginously sunken—resentments and miracles parfaited. Here there is a horizontal prospect.

The Al-Aqsa Mosque and the Dome of the Rock have been closed to non-Muslims since my last visit. I stand outside the shrine and try to reconstruct the interior from memory—the pillars, tiles, meadows of carpet. The vast Muslim space is what I remember. Islamic architecture attempts the sublime feat of emptiness. It is the sense of emptiness enclosed that is marvelous. The dome is the sky that is made. The sky is nothing—the real sky—and beggars have more of it than others.

Muslims own Jerusalem sky. This gold-leafed dome identifies Jerusalem on any postcard, the conspicuous jewel. Jews own the ground. The enshrined rock was the foundation for the Holy of Holies of Solomon's temple, the room that enclosed the Ark of the Covenant. The rock is also the traditional site of the near sacrifice of Isaac by Abraham. God commanded Moses to commission

Bezalel the artisan to make the ark. The Book of Exodus describes two golden cherubim whose wings were to form above the ark a Seat of Mercy—a space reserved for the presence of the Lord. The architecture for the presence of G-D has been conceptualized ever after as emptiness.

The paradox of monotheism is that the desert God, refuting all other gods, demands acknowledgment within emptiness. The paradox of monotheism is that there is no paradox—only unfathomable singularity.

May I explain to you some features of the shrine?

A man has approached as I stand gazing toward the dome. He looks to be in his sixties; he is neatly dressed in a worn suit. The formality of syntax extends to his demeanor. Obviously he is one of the hundreds of men, conversant in three faiths, who haunt the shrines of Jerusalem, hoping to earn something as informal guides.

No thank you.

This is the Dome of the Rock, he continues.

No thank you.

Why are you so afraid to speak to a guide? (The perfected, implicating question.)

I am not afraid. I don't have much time.

He lowers his eyes. *Perhaps another time.* He withdraws.

My diffidence is purely reflexive. One cannot pause for a moment on one's path through any of the crowded streets or souks without a young man—the son, the nephew, the son-in-law of some shopkeeper—asking, often with the courtliness of a prince, often with the stridency of a suitor: *May I show you my shop?*

Emptiness clings to these young men as well—the mermen of green-lit grottoes piled with cheap treasure—men with nothing to do but fiddle with their cell phones or yawn in their unconscious beauty and only occasionally swim up to someone caught in the unending tide of humanity that passes before them.

May I show you my shop?

No thank you.

To speak of the desert God is to risk blasphemy, because the God of the Jews and the Christians and the Muslims is unbounded by time or space, is everywhere present—exists as much in a high mountain village in sixteenth-century Mexico as in tomorrow's Jakarta, where Islam thrives as a tropical religion. Yet it was within the ecology of the Middle Eastern desert that the mystery of monotheism blazed. And it is the faith of the Abrahamic religions that the desert God penetrated time and revealed Himself first—thus condescending to sequence—to the Jews.

Behind the wall of my hotel in East Jerusalem are a gasoline station and a small mosque. The tower of the mosque—it is barely a tower—is outfitted with tubes of green neon. Five times in twenty-four hours the tubes of neon flicker and sizzle; the muezzin begins his cry. Our crier has the voice of an old man, a voice that gnaws on its beard. I ask everyone I meet if the voice is recorded or live. Some say recorded and some say real.

I believe God is great. I believe God is greatest.

The God of the Jews penetrated time. The Christian and the Muslim celebrated that fact ever after with noise. In the medieval town, Christian bells sounded the hours. Bells called the dawn and the noon and the coming night.

In the secular West, church bells have been stilled by discretion and by ordinance. In my neighborhood of San Francisco, the announcement of dawn comes from the groaning belly of a garbage truck.

No one at the hotel seems to pay the voice any mind. The waiters serve. Cocktails are shaken and poured. People in the court-yard and in the restaurant continue their conversations. The proprietress of the place turns a page of the book she is reading.

At four o'clock in the morning, the swimming pool is black. The hotel is asleep and dreaming. The neon ignites. The old man picks up his microphone to rend our dream asunder.

It is better to pray than to sleep.

The voice is not hectoring; it is simply oblivious. It is not like one's father, up early and dressing in the dark; it is like a selfish old man who can't sleep. The voice takes its permission from the desert—from the distance—but it is the modern city it wakes with enforced intimacy.

The old man's chant follows a tune; it is always the same tune, like a path worn through a carpet. And each day the old man be-comes confused by the ornamental line—his voice is not agile enough to assay it. His voice turns ruminative, then puzzled. Fi-nally, a nasal moan:

Muhammad is the prophet of Allah.

River Jordan water runs between my toes—a breathtakingly com-fortable sensation. I have taken a bus tour of Galilee; the bus has stopped at the Yardenit Baptismal Site, which resembles a state picnic grounds. I watch a procession of Protestant pilgrims in rented white smocks descend some steps into the comfortable brown water.

Protestantism is the least oriental of the desert faiths. Protes-tants own little real estate within the walls of Jerusalem. They own nothing of ancient squabbles between the Holy Roman Em-pire, the Byzantine Empire, the Ottoman Empire. Protestants are free to memorialize sacred events without any compulsion to stand guard over mythic ground.

For example, the traditionally venerated site of Christ's baptism is near Jericho. After the Six-Day War in 1967, that location was declared off-limits to tourists. And so this place—Yardenit—of no historical or religious significance, was developed as a place to which Christians might come for baptism ceremonies. The faith of evangelical pilgrims at Yardenit overrides the commercialism that attaches to the enterprise (*Your Baptism videotaped by a professional*). One bank or the other, it is the same river, and pilgrims at Yardenit step confidently into the Bible.

Distance enters Abraham's seed with God's intimacy. A birth precedes the birth of Isaac. There is domestic strife of God's manufacture. For God also arranges that Sarah's Egyptian servant, Hagar, will bear Abraham a son. That son is Ishmael; the name means "He Listens." Sarah soon demands that Abraham send Hagar and her son away. *I cannot abide that woman. She mocks me.*

So Hagar and Ishmael are cast into the desert of Beersheba as Abraham and Sarah and the camels and tents and servants and flocks flow slowly away from them like a receding lake of dust.

Abruptly Haim tells me to stop. "Listen! The desert has a silence like no other," he says. "Do you hear a ringing in your ear? It is the bell of existence."

Not far from here, in Gaza, missiles are pitched through a blue sky. People who will be identified in news reports this evening as terrorists will shortly be killed or the innocent will be killed, people who even now are stirring pots with favored spoons or folding the last page of the morning paper to line the bird's cage.

I hear. What do I hear? I hear a truck shifting gears on a highway, miles away.

God hears the cry of Ishmael: God finds Hagar in the desert

and rescues her dying child by tapping a spring of water—a green silk scarf pulled from a snake hole. God promises Hagar that Ishmael, too, will be a nation. From Ishmael's line will come the Arab tribes, and from the Arab tribes, the Prophet Muhammad.

Mahdi, my Palestinian guide, pulls off the main road so I can see the Monastery of the Temptation in the distance. (Mahdi has been telling me about the years he lived in Riverside, California.) The monastery was built upon the mountain where Christ was tempted by Satan to consider the Kingdoms of the World. And here are we, tourists from the Kingdoms of the World, two thousand years later, regarding the mountain.

A figure approaches from the distance, surrounded by a nimbus of moisture. The figure is a Bedouin on foot. A young man but not a boy, as I first thought. He is very handsome, very thin, very small, utterly humorless. He extends, with his two hands, a skein of perhaps twenty-five bead necklaces. He speaks English—a few words like beads. "Camel," he says. "For your wife, your girlfriend."

"This is camel," he says again, fingering some elongated beads. I ask him who made the necklaces. His mother.

There is no sentimentality to this encounter. Sentimentality is an expenditure of moisture. The Bedouin's beseeching eyes are dry; they are the practice of centuries. He sits down a short distance away from us while we contemplate the monastery. He looks into the distance, and, as he does so, he becomes the desert.

Moses, Jesus, Muhammad—each ran afoul of cities: Moses of the court of Egypt, Jesus of Jerusalem, Muhammad of Mecca. The desert hid them, emptied them, came to represent a period of trial before they emerged as vessels of revelation. Did they, any of them, experience the desert as habitable—I mean, in the manner of Haim, in the manner of the Bedouin?

After he fled Egypt, Moses took a wife; he took the nomadic life of his wife's people as a disguise. Moses led his father-in-law's flock across the desert to Mount Horeb, where God waited for him.

As a boy, Muhammad crossed the desert in Meccan caravans with his uncle Abu Talib. Muhammad acquired the language of the Bedouin and Bedouin ways. As a middle-aged man, Muhammad was accustomed to retire with his family to a cave in the desert to meditate. During one such retreat Muhammad was addressed by God.

The Jews became a people by the will of God, for He drove them through the desert for forty years. God fed the people Israel with manna. Ravens fed Elijah during his forty days in the desert. After his ordeal of forty days, Jesus accepted the ministrations of angels. Such supernatural nourishments of the body suggest a reliance on God rather than an embrace of the desert.

In *The Desert Fathers*, Helen Waddell writes that the early Christian monks of the desert gave a single intellectual concept to Europe—eternity. The desert monks saw the life of the body as "most brief and poor." But the life of the spirit lies beyond the light of day. The light of day conceals "a starlit darkness into which a man steps and becomes suddenly aware of a whole universe, except that part of it which is beneath his feet."

There are people in every age who come early or late to a sense of the futility of the world. Some people, such as the monks of the desert, flee the entanglements of the world to rush toward eternity. But even for those who remain in the world, the approach of eternity is implacable. "The glacier knocks in the cupboard, / The desert sighs in the bed," was W. H. Auden's mock-prophetic forecast. He meant the desert is incipient in the human condition. Time melts away from us. Even in luxuriant weather, even in luxuriant wealth, even in luxuriant youth, we know our bodies will fail; our buildings will fall to ruin.

If the desert beckons the solitary, it also, inevitably, gives birth to the tribe. The ecology of the desert requires that humans form communities for mutual protection from extreme weathers, from bandits, from rival chieftains. Warfare among Arab tribes impinged often upon the life of the Prophet Muhammad. In response to the tyranny of kinship, Muhammad preached a spiritual brotherhood—discipleship under Allah—that was as binding as blood, as expansive as sky.

The Christian monastic movement in the Judaean wilderness reached its peak in the sixth century, by which time there were so many monks, so many monasteries in the desert (as many as eight hundred monks in some of the larger communities), that it became a commonplace of monastic chronicles, a monkish conceit, to describe the desert as a city.

I am driving with Mahdi through Bethlehem, then several Bedouin settlements to the east, leading into the desert. The road narrows, climbs, eventually runs out at the gates of Mar Saba, a Greek Orthodox monastery.

A monk opens the gate. Mahdi asks in Arabic if we may see the monastery. The monk asks where we are from. The monk then takes up a metal bar, which he clangs within a cast-iron triangle.

Waiting in the courtyard below is another monk. He greets us in English. Obviously four bangs, or however many, on the contraption upstairs summons English. The monk's accent is American. He, too, asks where I am from. He is from St. Louis.

We are first shown the main church. The church is dark, complexly vaulted, vividly painted. We are told something of the life of Saint Saba, or Sabas, the founder of the monastery. Saba died in AD 532. "He is here," the monk then says, ushering us to a glass case in a dark alcove, where the saint lies in repose. "The remains are uncorrupted."

The monk carries a pocket flashlight that he shines on the corpse of the saint. The thin beam of light travels up and down the body; the movement of the light suggests sanctification by censing. The figure is small, leathern, clothed in vestments. This showing takes place slowly, silently—as someone would show you something of great importance in a dream.

We ask about another case, the one filled with skulls. They are the skulls of monks killed by Persians in AD 614. One has the impression the young monk considers himself to be brother to these skulls, that they remain a part of the community of Mar Saba, though no longer in the flesh. One has the impression grievance endures.

The monk next leads us to the visitors' parlor. No women are allowed in the monastery. In this room the masculine sensibility of the place has unconsciously re-created a mother's kitchen. The monk disappears into a galley; he returns with a repast that might have been dreamed up by ravens: tall glasses of lemonade, small glasses of ouzo, a plate of chocolates. The lemonade is very cool, and we ask how this can be without electricity. Butane, the monk answers. For cooking and refrigeration.

The monk's patience is for the time when we will leave. Until this: "What has brought you to the Holy Land?"

I have come to write about the desert religions, I reply. I am interested in the fact that three great monotheistic religions were experienced within this ecology.

"Desert religions, desert religions," the monk repeats. Then he says: "You must be very careful when you use such an expression. It seems to equate these religions."

I do mean to imply a common link through the desert.

"Islam is a perversion," he says.

A few minutes later, the monk once more escorts us through the courtyard to the stone steps. He shakes my hand and says what I remember as conciliatory, though it may not have been: "The desert creates warriors."

Haim makes his living conducting tours of the desert. He is, as well, a student and an instructor at Ben-Gurion University of the Negev, where we stop briefly to exchange vehicles.

Haim invites me into his house; he must get some things. Haim's wife is also a graduate student at the university. There are some pleasant drawings of dancers on the walls. The curtains are closed against the desert. Mrs. Berger returns while I am waiting. She is attractive, blond, pregnant, calm. "You turned on the air-conditioning," she says to Haim—not accusatorily but as a statement of (I assume unusual) fact. "I have to gather some things," he replies. I ask if I may see the photograph of the mountain.

"Ah, Haim's mountain." Mrs. Berger conveys affection, indulgence.

Haim goes to his computer, pulls up the images: the mountain from the distance. Closer. Closer. The suggestion of a rectangular shape. I hesitate to say the shape of tablets; nevertheless, that is how it appears. It is difficult to ascertain the scale. Yes, I can see— along the top and side of the rectangular shape there are what appear to be flames.

Haim carries several filled grocery bags out to the Jeep. We leave Mrs. Berger standing in the dark kitchen. *Goodbye.*

Stephen Pfann looks to be in his forties. His hair is white; he wears a beard. He has large pale eyes of the sort one sees in Victorian photographs. It is because of his resemblance, in my imagination, to a Victorian photograph that I attribute to him the broad spirit of Victorian inquiry. Stephen's discourse has a dense thread count, weaving archaeology, geology, history, theology, also botany and biology. Stephen's teenage children seem adept at reining him in when he is kiting too high. He and his wife, Claire, administer the University of the Holy Land, a postgraduate biblical institute in Jerusalem. Stephen says he would be willing to take me to Qumran. He suggests an early morning expedition and promises, as well, an Essene liturgy at sunrise.

My imagination runs away: prayers within a cave. Clay lamps, shadows. Some esotericism in the liturgy and a sun like the sound of a gong.

On the appointed morning, Stephen picks me up at my hotel. As it is already bone-light, I presume we have missed the sunrise. But, in fact, we are reciting psalms on a level plain beneath Cave 1 as the sun comes up over Arabia, over Jordan, over the Dead Sea. The light is diffuse, though golden enough. The texts remark the immensity of creation. (I am thinking about a movie I saw. An old man—Omar Sharif—whispers as he dies: "I am going to join . . . the immensity.")

We have been joined here by several others, two Pfann children and a forensic pathologist connected with the University of the Holy Land.

Stephen mentions "the umbilicus," by which term he means the concentration of God's intention on this patch of earth. Underfoot is a large anthill—a megalopolis—then a satellite colony, then another, then another, the pattern extending across the desert floor.

The old woman bends forward to kiss the pale stone.

We begin our climb to Cave 1. The air has warmed. Stephen Pfann, in his stride, points at minute flora; his daughter nods and photographs them. He and his children are as nimble as goats. "Is everyone all right?" Pfann calls downward.

I am not all right. I am relegated at several junctures to using both hands and feet. The good-natured pathologist climbing ahead of me is watchful and discreet with his helping hand, all the while recounting the religious conversion that brought him to the Holy Land.

The cave is not cool, by the way. A smell of bat dung. I hear Stephen saying something about the rapidity of the transfer of heat molecules from one substance to another. (The dryness of the cave preserved the scrolls.) I am perspiring. I am making toe marks in the dust.

Hundreds of thousands of years ago, water receded from this cave. Two thousand years ago, an Essene—probably an Essene— filled a basket with grating clay jars and climbed to this cave to hide the holy scrolls against some intimation of destruction. Sixty years ago, a Bedouin goatherd, muttering goat curses—an old man now if he survives—came upon five clay vats spilling revelation.

The community of Qumran was destroyed by Roman legions in AD 68.

Dogma strives to resemble the desert: It is dry; it is immovable. Truth does not change. Is there something in the revelation of God that retains—because it has passed through—properties of desert or maleness or Semitic tongue? Does the desert, in short, make warriors? That is the question I bring to the desert from the twenty-first century.

The Semitic God is the God who enters history. Humans

examine every event that pertains to us for meaning. The motive of God who has penetrated time tempts us to imperfect conjecture. When armies are victorious, when armies are trodden in the dust, when crops fail, when volcanoes erupt, when seas drink multitudes, it must mean God intends it so. What did we do to deserve this? King David psalmed for the vanquishing of his enemies, did he not? There is something in the leveling jealousy of the desert God that summons a possessive response in us. *We are His people* becomes *He is our God.* The blasphemy that attaches to monotheism is the blasphemy of certainty. If God is on our side, we must be right. We are right because we believe in God. We must defend God against the godless. Certitude clears a way for violence. And so the monk's dictum—the desert creates warriors—can represent centuries of holy war and sordid prayer and an umbilicus that whips like a whirlwind.

In Afghanistan's central plateau there were two mountain-high Buddhas. For centuries, caravans traveling the Silk Route would mark them from miles away. The Bamiyan Buddhas were destroyed by the Taliban in 2001; their faces are now anvils, erasures. An inscription from the Koran was painted beside the alcove of the larger Buddha: *The just replaces the unjust.* Just so do men destroy what belief has built, and they do it in the name of God, the God who revealed Himself in the desert, the desert that cherishes no monuments, wants none. *There is no God but God.*

On July 16, 1945, the first nuclear weapon was tested in the American desert. The ape in our hearts stood still. Wow.

The desert creates warriors, by which construction Saint Sabas meant (for it was his construction) that the monk discerns his true nature in the desert—his true nature in relation to God—and the discernment entails learning to confront and to overcome the temptations of human nature. In that sense, a warrior.

The desert creates lovers. Saint Sabas desired the taste of an apple. The craving was sweeter to him than the thought of God. From that moment Sabas foreswore apples. The desire for apples was the taste of God.

Desert is the fossil of water. (Haim has been at great pains to point this out—striations in mesas and the caverns water has bored through mountains of salt, and salt is itself a memory of water.) Is dogma a fossil of the living God—the shell of God's passage—but God is otherwise or opposite? Perhaps it is that the Semitic tongues are themselves deserts—dry records of some ancient fluency, of something feminine that has withdrawn. The Semitic tongues descend from Shem, son of Noah, survivor of the Flood. Abraham was of Shem's line. Perhaps the Semitic tongues, inflected in the throat, recall water.

I have often heard it observed by critics of the desert religions that monotheism would have encouraged in humankind a more tender relationship to nature if the Abrahamic God had revealed Himself from within a cloak of green. The desert encourages a sense of rebuff and contest with the natural world. Jesus cursed the recalcitrant fig tree right down to firewood.

The desert's uninhabitability convinces Jew and Christian and Muslim that we are meant for another place. Within the deserts of the Bible and the Koran, descriptions of Eden, descriptions of the Promised Land, resemble oases. For Jews, Eden was predesert. For Christians and Muslims, paradise—reconciliation with God—is post-desert.

In the Koran, paradise is likened to gardens underneath which rivers flow. For Christians, paradise is an urban idea, a communion, the city of God. The commendation of the body in the ancient rite of Christian burial prays that angels may come to lead the soul of the departed to the gates of the holy city Jerusalem.

I purchase for five shekels a postcard scene of Jerusalem in the snow—black-and-white—the sky is dark but Jerusalem shines swan, a royal city. I will show you the photograph.

I follow Haim a quarter of a mile to a grove of untrimmed date palm trees. I have seen their like only in ancient mosaics, the muted colors, the golden dust. In their undressed exuberance these palms resemble fountains. But they are dry; they prick and rattle as we thread our way among them. We could just as easily have walked around, couldn't we? I suspect Haim of concocting an oasis experience. But his glance is upward, into the branches of some taller trees. Haim is hoping for what he calls a lucky day. If it is Haim's lucky day, we will see a leopard. Recently, a leopard entered the town of Beersheba. Haim suspects the creature may be lurking here.

But it is not Haim's lucky day. We continue up an incline, alongside a muddy riverbed. Winged insects bedevil my ears. We walk around a screen of acacia trees, at which Haim steps aside to reveal . . . a waterfall, a crater filled with green water! There are several Israeli teenagers swimming, screaming with delight as they splash one another. A tall African youth stands poised at the edge of the pool.

This Ethiopian Jew (we later learn) has come to this desert from another. He has come because the Abrahamic faith traveled like particles of desert over mountains and seas, blew under the gates of ancient cities, and caught in the leaves of books. Laughter, as spontaneous as that of his ancestress Sarah, echoes through the canyon as the boy plunges into the stone bowl of water. Displaced water leaps like a javelin.

I am standing in the Negev desert. I am wet.

John the Baptist wrapped himself in camel hide. He wandered the desert and ate the desert—honey and locusts and Haim's gray leaves. John preached hellfire and he performed dunking ceremonies in the river Jordan. People came from far and wide to be addressed by the interesting wild man as "Brood of Vipers." When watery Jesus approached flaming John and asked for baptism, John recognized Jesus as greater than he. It was as though the desert bowed to the sea. But, in fact, their meeting was an inversion of elements. John said: *I baptize only with water. The one who comes after me will baptize with Spirit and fire.*

Desert is, literally, emptiness—its synonyms "desolation," "wasteland." To travel to the desert "in order to see it," in order to experience it, is paradoxical. The desert remains an absence. The desert is this empty place I stand multiplied by infinite numbers—

not this place particularly. So I come away each night convinced I have been to the holy desert (and have been humiliated by it) and that I have not been to the desert at all.

Just beyond the ravine is a kibbutz, a banana plantation, a university, a nuclear power plant. But, you see, I wouldn't know that. The lonely paths Haim knows are not roads. They are scrapings of the earth. Perhaps they are tracks that Abraham knew, or Jesus. Some boulders have been removed and laid aside. From the air-conditioned van or from the tossing Jeep or through binoculars, I see the desert in every direction. The colors of the desert are white, fawn, tawny gold, rust, rust-red, blue. When the ignition is turned off and the Jeep rolls to a stop, I pull the cord that replaces the door handle; the furnace opens; my foot finds the desert floor. But the desert is distance. Nothing touches me.

Yet many nights I return to my hotel with the desert on my shoes. There is a burnt, mineral scent in my clothing. The scent is difficult to wash out in the bathroom basin, as is the stain of the desert, an umber stain.

Standing, scrubbing my T-shirt, is the closest I get to the desert. The water turns yellow.

I tell myself I am not looking for God. I am looking for an elision that is, nevertheless, a contour. The last great emptiness in Jerusalem is the first. What remains to be venerated is the Western Wall, the ancient restraining wall of the destroyed Second Temple.

After the Six-Day War, the Israeli government bulldozed an Arab neighborhood to create Western Wall Plaza, an emptiness to facilitate devotion within emptiness—a desert that is also a well.

I stand at the edge of the plaza with Magen Broshi, a distinguished archaeologist. Magen is a man made entirely of Jerusalem. You can't tell him anything. Last night at dinner in the hotel garden, I tried out a few assertions I thought dazzling, only to be met with Magen's peremptory *Of course.*

Piety, ache, jubilation, many, many classes of ardor pass us by. Magen says he is not a believer. I tell Magen about my recent cancer. If I asked him, would he pray for me here, even though he does not believe? *Of course.*

Western Wall Plaza levels sorrow, ecstasy, cancer, belief. Here emptiness rises to proclaim its unlikeness to God, who allows for no comparison. Emptiness does not resemble. It is all that remains.

"No writing! You cannot write here." A woman standing nearby has noticed I carry a notebook. I have a pen in my hand. The woman means on the Sabbath, I think. Or can one never write here? It is the Sabbath.

"He is not writing anything," Magen mutters irritably, waving the woman away.

three

The True Cross

A little water and the desert breaks into flower, bowers of cool shade spring up in the midst of dust and glare, radiant stretches of soft colour gleam in that grey expanse. Your heart leaps as you pass through the gateway in the mud wall; so sharp is the contrast, that you may stand with one foot in an arid wilderness and the other in a shadowy, flowery paradise.

—Gertrude Bell, *Persian Pictures*

A sixty-nine-year-old body is still beautiful. It refuses any covering. A nurse is standing by the bed when we walk in. The nurse attempts to drape the genitals of the man on the bed with the edge of the sheet. But the hand of the man on the bed plucks the sheet away.

I'm afraid modesty is out the window, the nurse says.

There are two large windows.

There are three chairs for visitors, comfortable chairs; there is a foldout sofa for a spouse—that would be Peter, Luther's partner of thirty years, more than thirty years. Peter called two days ago. He said it was time.

So Jimmy and I drove to Las Vegas on Holy Thursday. Luther has been Jimmy's friend for more than forty years. They met when they were both shoe-leather messengers at a law firm in San Francisco; that was before FedEx, before fax, before e-mail. In those days the windows of the nineteenth floor of the Standard Oil Building could be opened to the hum of traffic below; "Proud

Mary," KFRC-AM Top Forty toiled through the speaker of a transistor radio on the windowsill behind the dispatcher's desk.

Peter hasn't slept properly for weeks. He tells me he shoves the couch against the bed at night so he can hold on to Luther's hand.

One time, when Luther had to go home to South Carolina on family business, Jimmy went with him. They walked through the woods behind the house where Luther had grown up. Luther pointed to a branch distended over a brown creek. *The old people used to tell us Jesus's cross was made of yonder tree. Every Easter, the tree puts out white blossoms by way of apology.*

The body on the bed slowly turns. Bares its teeth. Luther is smiling. Luther wants to tell Jimmy something right away. He motions with his hand: *Mama came to me a few days ago. She said it wasn't time yet.*

One time, Luther's Mama woke up in the middle of the night and there was this old man sitting on her bed. You go away, she said to the old man.

Weren't you scared, Mama?

No, not especially, but I didn't like it.

Maybe you were asleep.

No, sir, I wasn't.

Well, what'd he do?

He just sat there staring at the floor like he was waiting for further instructions. You go away right now, I told him; I clapped my hands at him like I was a cross little schoolteacher, and I pulled the covers up over my head and said my prayers.

Who was it, Mama?

I don't know who it was; I pulled up the covers and said my prayers. He went away and he never came back.

Mama died more than ten years ago.

The desk clerk at the Bellagio upgrades us to a suite—large, but not as commodious as Luther's room at the Nathan Adelson Hospice on North Buffalo Drive. The view from Luther's room is of the parking lot of a small business park. A placard on the wall next to the window cautions hospice visitors to park only in designated slots.

At the Bellagio, our room overlooks the hotel's six-acre lake, an allusion to Lago di Como. The Bellagio's lake has an advantage over its inspiration: At fifteen-minute intervals, jets of water are witched up into the air by a Frank Sinatra–Billy May rendition of Frank Loesser's "Luck Be a Lady." The jets shimmy, they fan, they collapse with a splat when the hydraulic pressure deserts them. Beyond Lago di Como, we can just see the tip of the Eiffel Tower.

In 1955 the management of Wilbur Clark's Desert Inn invited Nöel Coward, the British playwright and composer, to perform a cabaret act in Las Vegas.

Coward rather imagined he might end up tap-dancing to tommy-gun fire, so prevalent was the Vegas association with gangland. But he was agog at the money offered—thirty grand a week—at a time when his career was in a slump. (Coward had been superseded on the London stage by a new generation of playwrights; there wasn't much call in the West End or on Broadway for brittle drollery.) But then, Nöel Coward was a legend, and Las Vegas, because it was on the make, preferred legends.

Stars who might be on the downward slope of Hollywood or New York can achieve tenure in Las Vegas if they deliver what is remembered. Coward fit the bill. Frank Sinatra, Wayne Newton, Liberace, Cher, Debbie Reynolds, Tom Jones, Charo, Mitzi Gaynor,

Céline Dion, Bette Midler, Patti Page—the golden legends of the Strip are as odd as you please, but Las Vegas audiences (as used to be the case in London and Paris, and perhaps still is) have long, fond memories.

Upon his arrival, Coward wrote colleagues in London: "The gangsters who run the places are all urbane and charming." During the course of Coward's run, *Life* magazine photographer Loomis Dean rented a Cadillac limousine, stocked it with ice and liquor, and drove Coward fifteen miles into the desert to photograph him taking a cup of tea in the wilderness, attired in what Coward described as "deep evening dress." The photographer used the desert as the geographical equivalent of a straight man. The famous photographs perfectly captured the incongruous equipoise that describes the Vegas aesthetic.

Forty years ago, more than forty years, my friend Marilyn announced she was going to Las Vegas to see Elvis Presley. "Come," she said. "You have to see Las Vegas at least once before you die," she said.

We drove through a summer night. Sheet lightning blinked in the eastern sky. I listened as Marilyn described her father's gambling addiction—how he never lost a gentleman's amiability at the gaming table, how he had squandered most of his mother's fortune.

The Las Vegas hospitality industry is understandably respectful of losers. Marilyn's father never paid for a hotel room in Las Vegas, or for a meal or a drink. The city's generosity extended to the good loser's next of kin. All Marilyn needed to do was to phone her father, who, in turn, phoned the general manager of the Flamingo Hotel. The Flamingo comped us in what I guess you would call the wink of an eye.

In the morning, Marilyn passed her name to the Flamingo concierge, declaring we had come to see Elvis at the International. Elvis at the International was sold-out for the entire run. The concierge picked up the phone, called a uniformed officer of comparable rank at the International. And it was done. The only question that devolved to Marilyn and me was how much to tip the headwaiter at the International.

Elvis Presley first came to Las Vegas in 1956, when he was twenty-one years old. Middle-aged audiences in Las Vegas heard him with interested puzzlement at that time. Elvis was fresh—he was certainly famous—but he displayed none of that finger-snapping, syringe-in-the-toilet, up-tempo flash that Vegas found so inebriating. In 1969, on his return, Presley was nearer in age to the women in the audience, and he had learned the Vegas sell.

The messenger room at the law firm in San Francisco was like a prison movie—time measured in poker games, crossword puzzles, knives, novels. A never-neatened splatter of *Playboy* magazines on a junked conference table. Perpetual "Proud Mary." One corner of the room supported a mountain of legal briefcases. Another corner was a parking lot for dollies. There were fifteen messengers who sat on fifteen oaken office chairs facing the dispatcher, as in a minstrel show. When a messenger returned from a hike, his name was added to the bottom of the list; he sat down. (Messengers must be male. No experience necessary.) When a messenger took a hike, his name was crossed off the top of the list.

Luther got into the habit of stopping by a senior partner's office every afternoon for a chat, as if they were two free citizens of Athens. Luther found the Old Man interesting—his stories of growing up in turn-of-the-century California, of riding his pony over golden hills, of boarding a train that took him away to Har-

THE TRUE CROSS   57

vard College, of homesickness, of scarlet fever. "Well, that's how I learned self-reliance," the Old Man said.

The Old Man was interested in Luther, too. Luther had gumption. Luther had learned self-reliance from his mother, who worked in a chicken-processing plant, who raised ten children, whose husband left.

Where's Luther? The dispatcher ran his finger down the list of scratched-out names. Proud Mary, *unh, unh*. Luther was in the Old Man's office, everyone knew.

One day, after Luther had been working for the law firm for a year, he told the Old Man he figured it was about time he tried something else.

Like what?

Like working for the phone company. The Old Man grabbed up his telephone and barked "TelCo" to his secretary, which was short for: Please get me the president of the telephone company.

Once the president of the telephone company had been procured for him (the firm represented every major California utility), the Old Man hollered into the receiver, as if from the bridge of his yacht: "Look, F., I have a young man here desirous of a career change. I'm going to send him over. Whom should he ask for? Sears as in catalog? Good-o! Love to Dotty."

Luther went for his appointment at the phone company. He wore the black suit that he and Andrew and Jimmy shared. The suit belonged to Luther, but they all wore it—Andrew to be a pallbearer, Jimmy to be best man, Andrew to the opera, Luther to apply for a job at the phone company.

Right off, the employment manager offered Luther a job as a messenger. Luther pivoted on his heel, walked back to the law firm, elevator to the nineteenth, straight into the Old Man's office. Messengers didn't have to knock. Luther stood facing the Old

Man. With a shamed and thumping heart, Luther said: *If I wanted to be a messenger, I could have stayed right here.*

The Old Man didn't get it right away, that Luther had been of-fered the job he already had. Once he did understand, the Old Man seized the phone with relish, catching the scent of hare. "Now look here," the Old Man's voice rolled like thunder over Mr. Sears's salutation. "I meant for the kid I sent to get a leg up. He's already a messenger. Why would you offer him a job as a messen-ger? I'm going to send him back, and I expect you to offer him a decent job."

The Old Man slammed down the telephone and winked at Lu-ther: "Off you go, kid."

The following week, Luther began training in the switch room of the telephone company. Over the years, he worked himself into the highest classification of every job he was assigned; he moved from switchman to trunk man to optical-fiber cable work. (The Old Man died.) To something so specialized he was one of only two or three technicians who knew how to do whatever it was he did.

The joke among the three friends was: Who gets to be buried in the black suit? And what will the mourners wear?

We establish a little routine. Twice a day I commute between the hospice on North Buffalo and the Bellagio on Las Vegas Boule-vard South. Drop Jimmy off in the morning, spend a couple of hours at the hospice, pick Jimmy up in the late afternoon. In be-tween, I look around. There is a street in town named Virgil. The famous hotels on the Strip are not actually located in Las Vegas, but in an unincorporated entity called Paradise.

In the nineteenth century, Rafael Rivera, a Spanish scout—a teenager—joined a trading exploration party out of New Mexico that sought to establish a new trail to Los Angeles. Their hope was to find fresh water along the way. The party left Abiquiú in November of 1829. Rivera separated from the group at the Colorado River junction. He was, as far as anyone knows, the first European to enter the valley, to find the two lucky springs there, or, at any rate, to infer water from the vegetation of the valley. Rivera named the oasis Las Vegas—"the Meadows."

The main street downtown is named for John Charles Frémont. In 1844 Frémont led a surveying expedition that followed the San Joaquin River south, through the long Central Valley of California. At the Mojave River, Frémont's party veered eastward, crossed the Sierra, then followed the Old Spanish Trail for a time. Las Vegas was already a place of refreshment along the Spanish Trail, a trail that had been blazed more than a decade earlier by Rafael Rivera. Frémont recorded two streams of clear water: "The taste of the water is good, but rather warm to be agreeable." The streams, however, "afforded a delightful bathing place."

John Frémont died of peritonitis in a boardinghouse in New York City on July 13, 1890. No one I talk to can tell me what happened to Rafael Rivera; whether he returned to New Mexico or Old Mexico or Spain; whether he married; where he lies buried.

Recently, a complex of hotels and condos and offices in a sober international style has opened on the Strip under the mundane designation CityCenter. Its owners obviously intend a kind of restraint Las Vegas normally does not engage—gray exteriors, dark atriums. The visitor could be in São Paulo or Seoul or wherever the money flies. A cab driver tells me the new complex will not draw because there is no craziness to it. Here, you gotta be crazy, he says. Togas. Tigers. Tits.

In the lobby of the Aria hotel, part of the CityCenter complex, an eighty-four-foot-long sculpture, *Silver River*, by Maya Lin, is suspended behind the registration desk like a bough. Credit cards click across the marble counter as hotel guests check in or out. Maya Lin's sculpture is a trace-image of the Colorado River; it was cast from thirty-seven hundred pounds of "reclaimed" silver—sauceboats and Saint Christopher medals. The sculpture resembles artery, lightning, umbilicus, statistical graph.

During the week we are in town, there is a competition in Las Vegas among investors who are interested in developing a gangland museum. (And, two years later—Valentine's Day, 2012—the $42 million Mob Museum has opened.)

Other American cities might prefer to forget a criminal past. Las Vegas foresees profit in promoting its dark legend as an invitation to middle-class visitors to risk a little carelessness—to gamble more than they should, to tip the topless waitress more than necessary. Compared with Berlin in the thirties, compared with Ciudad Juárez today, compared with nineteenth-century America of the robber barons, compared with Chicago of the twenties, compared with Wall Street, "Sin City" must seem a wader's pool of wickedness. The sin on show is not what would be unimaginable in Indianapolis. Rather, it is precisely what Indianapolis would come up with if Indianapolis were charged with imagining Sin City.

On the grounds of the Flamingo Hotel, over by the wedding chapel, stands a monument to the mobster Benjamin "Bugsy" Siegel. Hollywood mythmakers credit Siegel with the idea of Las Vegas. Siegel's idea of Las Vegas was the idea of luxury and chance in a landscape where there was no chance of luxury.

Benjamin Siegel was born in 1906 to Russian immigrant parents in the Williamsburg section of Brooklyn, New York. He constructed his sense of glamour—of class, I think he would have said—against the meanness of the streets of his childhood and the distant Manhattan skyline. According to *Bugsy,* the 1991 Barry Levinson movie, Las Vegas was a sandlot prior to Siegel's coming. In truth, by the time Siegel conceived the potential for money in Las Vegas, there were already hotels and gambling parlors downtown, along Fremont Street. And the El Rancho Vegas had opened in 1941 on the two-lane highway that would later become the Strip—six years before Siegel's Flamingo.

What Siegel conceived was an aesthetic, and a pretty good one: He intended to build a resort in a desert-moderne style— something along the lines of Frank Lloyd Wright, something along the lines of Palm Springs—a lure for the best class of people, by which Siegel meant Hollywood. L.A. likes to think of Las Vegas as the populuxe mirage of Hollywood, a place where middle-class tourists look like movie stars but aren't, spend like millionaires but aren't.

Siegel went overbudget constructing his dream and the fancy people didn't show. Mobsters were looking at a loss. Benjamin Siegel was shot in the head in Beverly Hills, California, on June 20, 1947. He is buried in the Hollywood Forever Cemetery, Hollywood, California.

No sooner had Peter left to make some phone calls and to try to take a nap than Luther turned his head toward Jimmy: *Bathroom.*

I'll tell the nurse, said Jimmy.

Hurry, Luther said.

Jimmy hurried. The nurse was at her station. Mr. Thomas needs to make a bowel movement, Jimmy reported. The nurse turned from her computer, paused, as if she were about to say something wonderfully unhelpful. Instead, she said: OK, I'll talk to him.

Mr. Thomas, the nurse said, coming into his room.

Bathroom, said Luther. (Bambi.)

You are too weak to get to the bathroom, Mr. Thomas. There is a plastic towel underneath you—she gave the towel a tug. You can have a bowel movement right where you are. Press the buzzer if you need me. The nurse placed another half-plastic, half-paper sheet over Luther's midriff. She glanced at the thermostat. She left the room.

Luther turned toward Jimmy, removed the sheet, smiled. *Bandage*, said Luther.

There is no way Jimmy is afraid of Luther—Morphine Luther, Luther Demented, Luther with one foot in the grave. But this, Jimmy saw, was play.

Bandage? Jimmy said.

Luther grabbed the aluminum bed gate and rolled himself onto his right shoulder. Now Jimmy could see Luther's backside was papered over with a disc of green latex.

Off, said Luther.

Jimmy examined the bandage. (Probably a bedsore.) What's that for?

Off, said Luther. (The Red Queen.) Luther came late to the literature of childhood. In his thirties he read nursery classics. He loved them. The Alice books. *The Rescuers. Winnie-the-Pooh*.

I'll ask the nurse, said Jimmy.

Excuse me, he said. Again. I'm sorry but Mr. Thomas cannot have a bowel movement because there is a bandage covering his bottom, Jimmy reported to the nurse at her station.

If you press the button, someone will come, said the nurse at her station. The bandage will not hinder Mr. Thomas, she added.

Jimmy returned to the room to tell Luther he could have a bowel movement with a green latex waffle pasted to his behind. The game had progressed in his absence.

Chair, smiled Luther, his purse-arm extended vaguely. (Mrs. Miniver.)

You want to sit for a while?

Down. Luther indicated the bed gate. Jimmy crouched to examine the lever of the bed gate, then finally succeeded in lowering it.

Pull, Luther said; he proffered his hand.

Jimmy pulled Luther to a sitting position; he put his arm around Luther's shoulder to support him. Luther was already fishing for the floor with one bare foot.

Let me pull the chair up to the bed. I'll have to lay you back down for just a minute, Jimmy said.

Pull! (Red Queen.)

Jimmy pressed the button.

Within seconds, the nurse.

He wants to sit in the chair, Jimmy importuned.

Who turned off the air-conditioning?

I don't know, Jimmy said. (He had watched Peter turn off the air-conditioning before he left. Luther gets too cold, Peter said.)

The nurse switched the air-conditioning on. It's easier for him to breathe if the room is cool, the nurse said. To Luther: When the aides have finished what they're doing, we'll put you in the chair.

I think I can manage it, Jimmy said.

It takes three people, the nurse said; it won't be long. She raised the bed gate and covered Luther with a sheet. Luther smiled. (Harpo Marx.) The nurse left. Luther plucked the sheet away, grasped the bed gate.

Down.

Well, let's just wait. . . .

Down, said Luther. (Red Queen.) Jimmy put down the gate and sat on the edge of the bed; he put his arm around Luther's waist to prevent Luther from slipping to the floor. Luther did not acknowledge the counterforce; he grunted forward in medicated slow motion; he now had both feet on the floor.

Peter walked in.

He wants to sit in the chair, Jimmy said helplessly.

Peter snapped off the air-conditioning. He loves that chair, Peter said. All right, come on old man, Peter said. He easily transferred Luther into the recliner. Has he eaten? To Luther: Have you eaten?

Luther shook his head slowly. Smiled.

All on a summer's day.

Though I found no school in town or library or government building named in his honor, my vote for the founding father of today's Las Vegas would go to Herbert Clark Hoover, the thirty-first president of the United States. Hoover signed the bill funding the construction of the great dam that today bears his name.

In 1928 Hoover won the presidential election by a wide margin. A year later, the stock market crashed, leading to the Great Depression. Americans blamed Hoover for a financial collapse he did not cause but could not cure. Thus did Hoover, a superabundantly competent man, become a byword for incompetence. "Hoovervilles"—encampments of destitute Americans—sprang up across the country.

After President Hoover authorized the construction of the dam at Black Canyon, the state of Nevada revoked its ban on gambling. Las Vegas did not feel the brunt of the Depression, in part because as many as five thousand men found work, albeit dangerous work, building the dam. Las Vegas conspired with human nature to provide the laborers with weekend entertainments that would separate them from their pay.

In the winter of 1933, President Hoover was obliged to travel from the White House to the Capitol in the backseat of an open limousine alongside Franklin D. Roosevelt, the patrician president-elect. In a flickering news clip, we see the two men exchanging a few words as the car moves up Pennsylvania Avenue. Roosevelt spontaneously raises his hat to the crowd. Hoover's face is constrained with discomfort; he resembles W. C. Fields, the comic tragedian.

Two years later, in 1935, President Roosevelt passed through Las Vegas on his way to dedicate the new dam; he called it Boulder Dam, as did other members of his administration, and so it was called for fourteen years. Only a motion by a later Republican Congress would cement Hoover's name to the project that changed the West.

By whichever name, Hoover Dam was evidence that Nature could be harnessed: that the unruly Colorado River could be made to water the dry land of several western states, that the power generated from the controlled flow of water could light up the night.

Good Friday. Yellow tulips, closed and as thumpable as drumsticks, are massed at the entrance of the coffee shop at the Bellagio. They remind me of those phalanxes of acid-yellow flowers from behind which desert tyrants address the world with *frown, and wrinkled lip, and sneer of cold command.*

In Percy Bysshe Shelley's burlesque of royal pride, "Ozymandias," a desert traveler comes upon *two vast and trunkless legs of stone,* beside which, half buried in the sand, lies a toppled royal visage. Some long-dead artisan has incised on the monument's pedestal a deathless boast:

"My name is Ozymandias, king of kings:
Look on my works, ye Mighty, and despair!"

Over millennia, rulers of desert kingdoms, and not only rulers but prophets, and not only prophets but shepherds, but slaves, but women, have brooded on impermanence. There is not another ecology that so bewilders human vanity. Thus must palace engineers and the slaves from foreign lands be pressed into raising Pharaoh's pyramid over and against all, withstanding dynasties of sand and wind. It is a testament to the leveling humor of Las Vegas that Pharaoh's dream of eternity is mocked by the pyramid of the Luxor Hotel. The Luxor's pyramid is not made of limestone blocks but of rectangles of smoked glass that reflect and appear to change density according to the constant fluctuations of the desert sky.

In 1972 Robert Venturi, Denise Scott Brown, and Steven Izenour published an architectural monograph, *Learning from Las Vegas,* in which they celebrated the disregard for history, for propriety, for landscape in the architecture of suburban sprawl—Wienerschnitzel Chalets, Roundtable Castles, Golden Arches—an attitude best exemplified, they wrote, by the Las Vegas Strip. Their homage came at a time when East Coast architectural schools were in thrall to postwar European brutalism and city planners disregarded any necessity for delight.

In the years following the sensational Venturi–Scott Brown–Izenour essay, "old" low-rise casinos along the Strip were replaced, one by one, by grandiose hotel towers that, nevertheless, at ground level, invited tourists to inhabit cinemascopic fantasies: Rome. Egypt. Venice. Las Vegas was constructing an elaborate jest against the instinctive human fear of impermanence. Las Vegas cajoled its visitors to be amused at what the Romantic poet and the ancient prophet regard as the desert's morbid conclusion. The Eiffel Tower, the Empire State Building, Caesars Palace—

nothing in the world is rooted, nothing is permanent, nothing sacred, nothing authentic; architectural conceits are merely that.

Herbert Hoover died of a massive hemorrhage on October 20, 1964, in Suite 31-A at the Waldorf Towers in New York City. He is buried at the Herbert Hoover Library in West Branch, Iowa—the town where he was born.

No truer daughter does Las Vegas have than Dubai on the Persian Gulf, with its penthouse views of the void, its racetrack, its randy princes, its underwater hotel. Dubai and the oil-rich Arab kingdoms have purchased an architecture of mirage that is incongruous, and, therefore, defiant of the desert. Dubai has water slides, an ice palace, an archipelago of artificial islands in the shape of palm trees. The geometry that springs from the desert's plane is an assertion of human inanity in the face of natural monotony.

Even the sacred city of Mecca has taken some calibration from Las Vegas. Within the precincts of the Grand Mosque in Mecca stands the holiest site in Islam—a stone building without windows that was built in ancient days by Abraham and Ishmael. The Gate of Heaven is located directly above the cubical structure called the Kaaba. The Kaaba, covered with black silk draperies, represents the fixed point where the eternal and the temporal intersect, and around which the tide of living humanity circumambulates, counterclockwise.

For the infidel—for me—the Kaaba represents what is ancient beyond recall, but for the faithful, the Kaaba is a touchstone: affixed to a corner of the Kaaba is the Black Stone of Heaven, a stone given to Abraham by the Angel Gabriel.

Today looming over the tiny black cube is the Makkah Clock

Royal Tower, a tower reminiscent of Big Ben—a much bigger Ben—taller than the World Trade Center, with a golden crescent as its finial. Within the Makkah Clock Royal Tower is the eight-hundred-room Fairmont hotel. At its base there is a mall with four thousand shops. The Bin Laden Group, the engineering firm founded by the father of Osama bin Laden, is responsible for the overscale buildings set down upon Mecca.

Percy Bysshe Shelley died by drowning at the age of twenty-nine on July 8, 1822, when a small schooner was lost in a storm off the coast of Italy. Shelley's body was recovered from the sea and burned in a funeral pyre on the beach, after the ancient Greek fashion. Shelley's heart was not consumed by the flames and was buried under a motto devised by his friend Leigh Hunt—*Cor Cordium* ("Heart of Hearts")—in the Protestant Cemetery in Rome.

The Bellagio Conservatory and Botanical Gardens occupies a volume of cubic space reminiscent of a nineteenth-century train station. People come and go. There are hundreds of tulips and bluebells and daffodils, foxgloves, hollyhocks; there is a dense, loamy smell. There are false flora and fauna among the real—bees, ants, ladybugs, butterflies, giant poppies, toadstools. Georgic implements of gigantic scale (flowerpots, watering cans, hoes) are strewn among the flora as if abandoned by a race of giants. Most wonderful are leaping, flashing jets of water that materialize and disappear in midair. These I watch for many minutes, knowing the water or fluid must be encased in a translucent conduit, like Luther's oxygen tube, but I cannot see the tubes, cannot detect how it is done.

The Bellagio's floral exposition is a celebration of spring and does not attach itself semantically or symbolically to Easter.

On Good Friday afternoon I am stalled on Interstate 95; I am on my way to the hospice. The commuters surrounding me are headed out of town for the weekend or into town for the weekend, so there is that much of pending Easter, but nothing of Good Friday, beyond my own lonely sense of appropriate Good Friday weather (overcast, as in the Sacramento Valley of my childhood). The van ahead of me has a sign in Spanish on its bumper: ONLY GOD KNOWS IF YOU WILL RETURN. I try to recollect the Russian novel or memoir; I think it is one of the childhood reminiscences of Gorky, but the scene memory serves is too dimly lit for me to recognize the woman who stands at the window in pale, pinkish light. In fact, I do recognize her, but she is the wrong woman at the wrong window, the wrong light and season; she is a woman from a Pre-Raphaelite painting—*Mariana* by Millais—whose back is fatigued. Everything in the provincial Russian room behind the wrong woman is in readiness—the spoons, the linen, the breakfast breads, the samovar; she has stayed behind; the others have gone to midnight Mass, miles away. It is the dawn of Easter. The woman imagines the vibration of cathedral bells through the frozen air and the cracking of ice beneath the blades of the sled. Only God knows if they will return.

Luther is in bed; the head of the bed is raised. Jimmy is sitting in a chair beside the bed. Peter has gone to the airport to pick up Andrew and John. The oxygen prong is out of Luther's nose; the tube snakes under the pillow. Do you want the oxygen tube? Jimmy asks.

Luther nods.

What difference does it make? OK, something to do, I think to myself as Jimmy hooks the loop behind Luther's ears. Within two minutes Luther has torn the prong away. His breath is clotted with phlegm, like Maya Lin's *Silver River*.

Luther's eyes slide toward Jimmy on a slow tide of conscious-ness. *Light,* he says. You want the light on? Jimmy asks. *Light,* Lu-ther says again, flicking his hand slightly. Then, summoning all his power: *You are in the light.* Oh, sorry, says Jimmy; he moves his chair toward the foot of the bed. Luther flicks his hand again: *More.* Jimmy moves farther away. Luther seems momentarily de-lighted by the power of his wrist. I don't know if he means he can't see Jimmy because Jimmy is sitting in front of the window or if Jimmy is blocking light that is precious. After Jimmy makes one further move, Luther nods, smiles, sleeps. Either way.

Entr'acte

On YouTube: The lights dim. A kettledrum rumbles through the pit as the silver limousine drives forward onto the stage's reflect-ing surface. Light pours from the proscenium like rainbow melt. The chauffeur hops to; he crosses in front of the limousine to stand at attention, his hand poised on the handle of the down-stage door. The strafing beams fuse into a single column of preter-naturally white light as the chauffeur opens the door.

Liberace emerges; Liberace unfolds; Liberace pops; his arms open wide—O glory! He wears a sequined Prince Regent suit and a white fur coat with silver lamé lining and a Queen Isabella collar as high as a wingback chair. The chauffeur kneels—knighthood is in flower—and adjusts his Master's train, twenty paces of fur car-pet. Somehow Liberace now holds a microphone (diamonds on his fingers); the chauffeur must have passed it to him when we were looking elsewhere.

Liberace questions the audience: "Do you know what kind of car this is?"

Golly.

"It is a silver Rolls-Royce. I bought it in England and brought it back here."

We bid farewell to the chauffeur. We give him a hand. His name is Thorn. Or Thor; we didn't quite . . . "We'll see more of Thor later," Liberace promises with lupine relish. Thor drives the limousine off, stage left. Another round of applause for Thor. For Rolls-Royce. For England!

Liberace addresses us as the Big Bad Wolf might address an infant or a canary or a little lamb lost—a petting voice, not unkind. Necessarily, he supplies all the answers to his petit catechism. It is exactly the cadence and the Socratic method of Mister Rogers. He tugs the tonnage of his train along the lip of the stage. To some women seated in the first row: "Yes, you can feel it. Do you want to feel it? It's nice, isn't it? Do you know what it is?"

Golly.

"It is virgin fox! I had this made for a command performance I gave for Her Majesty, the Queen of England."

Press PAUSE.

Regard the rapacious eye the Wolf casts over his audience; he wets his lips as the women in the first row reach forth gingerly to pat his plush. An invitation to pull the fox's tail is an example of Las Vegas's complicated negotiation with the middle class. The middle-class tourist is invited to approach luxury on a budget, as long as she loses money. Your AARP membership card will get you an upgrade; hotcakes come with the room; parking is free. On his side of the footlights, Liberace is permitted to play the last sissy in America as long as the women in the front row agree to pretend to believe that Liberace is a great friend of the Queen of England; that Liberace is a sleeping prince who just hasn't found the right woman; that Thor has a chauffeur's license.

Liberace died on February 4, 1987, in Palm Springs, California. He is entombed in Forest Lawn Memorial Park (Hollywood Hills), Los Angeles.

The only time I hear Peter—or any of the staff at the hospice—refer to the Strip hotels, it is with reference to parking. Peter likes to park at the Flamingo; he says the exits are easy and some of the hotel's vintage modernist fixtures interest him. An aide at the hospice asks me where I am staying. "I used to park at the Bellagio," she says, "but now I park at the Renaissance." (As far as I can tell from my precious few conversations with the citizens of the real Las Vegas, the Strip is a free parking lot.)

The last time I was in Las Vegas it was to give a speech on public education. An emissary of the association I was to address picked me up at a small hotel I can't remember and drove me to a vast Greco-Gonzo extravaganza along the Strip I can't remember.

The next morning, the same emissary took me on a tour of the city before my plane departed. The Angel Moroni blew a summons eastward atop the Mormon Cathedral. Many miles of stucco; miles and miles of sky. At a café, I expressed surprise at the façade normalcy of domestic Las Vegas.

"But that's just what Las Vegas is," my companion replied. "The real Las Vegas is normal. An air force town, a university town. We are forming a symphony orchestra."

A normal American city does not have hundreds of hotels whose headliners are stitched-up gods and goddesses, whose entertainments are plumed masques, parodies of human sacrifice.

All week I have been puzzling how a city as defiant of death as Las Vegas can provide a hospice on North Buffalo Drive that is as morally and functionally serious as the one that harbors Luther.

Solo Dios sabe si volverá. Henry David Thoreau schoolmarmed his nineteenth-century countrymen with the assertion that one could not be a true traveler unless one left one's gate with no certainty of return. The art of walking involves an ability to saunter—the word derives from a French expression for people who have no homeland (*sans terre*), or from the French word for Holy Land—*Sainte Terre*—which became the noun used to identify religious pilgrims, *sainte-terres*. They have no particular home, Thoreau writes, but they are "equally at home everywhere."

Family trips of my childhood always began with a prayer. I suppose when one goes on vacation, one is courting death in some fashion, tying the morgue tags onto one's suitcase. But then, too, vacations are respites from death, from thoughts of death. I have sometimes wondered why friends under medical death sentences have undertaken arduous trips or undertaken arduous labors. To put some distance between themselves and death—the obvious answer.

Once, at Westminster Abbey, I paused to read the epitaph of Edmund Spencer:

HEARE LYES (EXPECTING THE SECOND
COMMINGE OF OVR SAVIOVR CHRIST
IESVS) THE BODY OF EDMOND SPENCER,
THE PRINCE OF POETS IN HIS TYME
WHOSE DIVINE SPIRRIT NEEDS NOE
OTHIR WITNESSE THEN THE WORKS
WHICH HE LEFT BEHINDE HIM.
HE WAS BORNE IN LONDON IN
THE YEARE 1553 AND
DIED IN THE YEARE
1598.

The expressed hope of dust, pronounced in a present tense, dizzied me. Westminster Abbey might crumble—must crumble—Spencer's vigil will continue until the end of time. I was leaving London that afternoon. A storm was forecast. I imagined an airplane spiraling upward into a black sky.

One can become overwhelmed on vacation—I have become so—by thinking thoughts that are too large. There is a condition identified in psychology textbooks as the Stendhal syndrome, also called, or related to, the Jerusalem syndrome, that describes a tourist's overwhelmed response to great works of art or to a sudden apprehension of scale, antiquity, multitude, death—the accompanying fear is of one's insignificance, but also of squandered opportunity.

Of course, a vacation city must be defiant of death, a desert city like Las Vegas doubly so, for it is a city built on a desolate landscape. My predicament is that I am here for death and the city of distraction is in my way.

Never had I seen blacker hair or whiter skin or a being more made for limelight. Elvis Presley appeared within a ten-thousand-watt corolla—The Messiah of Memphis. He was romantic, agile, potent. He wore a chest-baring Prince Charming jumpsuit—the "Burning Flame of Love" costume, designed by Bill Belew. Presley was already, that night in 1969, playing to the midnight sun—both feet planted in the Liberace–Peggy Lee weird. He stood very still. His nostrils dilated as though he smelled the crowd in a feral way.

I grew up in an America that shared certain narratives. It is not the same now. Everyone had seen Elvis on *The Ed Sullivan Show;* everyone had seen the photographs in the pages of *Life* magazine—photographs of Tupelo, Mississippi, where he grew up, an only child; of the haircut, when he was inducted into the army; of the sleeping private through the train window; of his parents, Vernon and Gladys—of Gladys, his mother, with such dark eyes; of his leave to visit his mother's bedside; of his mother's grave.

The platter spun at 45 rpm. The aural helix opened like a can of white-meat Apollo: an engorged voice; a slurred diction; a humpy, syrupy croon. Elvis wasn't black. He wasn't white. He wasn't masculine. He wasn't feminine. He wasn't inimitable. He was a liberator.

The theme of Elvis's show that night was the theme of Las Vegas (the gambler's prayer)—resurrection. During an interlude, between sets, the voice of a woman called through the dark in a calm voice: "Elvis, I am your mother." Immediately, several security men were weaving among the tables. Elvis did not look in the direction of the voice. He raised a bottle of Gatorade to his lips as all eyes watched the security men escort a woman in a two-piece suit through a door in the wall that closed silently behind them.

After the Elvis show, Marilyn and I went to another hotel, to a lounge that seated no more than fifty people, to watch the "Ike and Tina Turner Revue." Tina Turner whipped the Ikettes through an aggressive choreography of stiletto heels, swinging wigs; wheels of sweat spraying from the stage. The Turners were already reprising their hits from the fifties; to that extent they were furiously treading fame, sinking. (Las Vegas lounge acts are a sink.) This was two years before every Top Forty radio station in America was pumping "Proud Mary."

Elvis Presley's final performance at the Hilton Hotel was in December of 1976. He was scheduled to return the following winter. He died at Graceland, his home in Memphis, in August of 1977 at the age of forty-two. He is buried at Graceland.

Peter has gone home to change clothes. The nurse has given Luther two shots. Luther alternates between sleep (a boiling gurgle in his chest) and high-pitched, teakettle trills (bird-like, hymn-like), or he perseverates, with every exhalation, *Mama Mama Mama Mama*.

Peter returns. Luther is aware of Peter's presence; he begins to coo plaintively. I know, says Peter, I know I know I know I know. Peter massages Luther's chest. It seems to me Peter is massaging too hard, as if he would press every last drop of noxious humor from Luther's body. Luther visibly relaxes. Peter's voice, Peter's hands are the only comforts on earth.

Nomadic people of the desert have, for centuries, woven carpets that are floral meadows or geometric pleasances. Desert carpets refresh those for whom the desert is transient, repetitive. The desert is the day between the nights, the dry between the wetness of the stars. Carpets are portable gardens of repose.

At twilight, Las Vegas signs, visible from miles away, are like carpets flung up into the sky. Pulses of light chase one another about a grid of lapidary. Las Vegas signs are not so much calling the traveler to rest as calling the dead to life. Calling the loser to luck. To change. To chance.

Late in the evening we return to the hotel coffee shop and once again we pass through the Bellagio Conservatory and Botanical Gardens. Mr. McGregor's Good Earth is no longer lit from the skylight but by saturated theatrical lighting. Now I can see all the gigantic miniatures—pots and shards and all—are painted with phosphorescent colors: an installation reminiscent of Claes Oldenburg. All is hushed and holy in some trashy way, and disarmingly innocent.

All the hotels around here cast spells of one kind or another to lure you in—gondolas, snow leopards. One feels flattered. In every other city of the world, the impulse of a luxury hotel is to exclude, isolate, intimidate. Elsewhere in the world, or even a mile out of town, a looming desert or an empty sky is bent on reminding you of your insignificance—lessons of mortality, lessons of austerity, lessons of depletion. The lesson of Las Vegas is *Hey, no problemo*.

Which does not mean that Las Vegas cannot be unsettled. There was the fire of 1980 that killed eighty-five people at the MGM Grand Hotel. There was the night in October of 2003 at the theater of the Mirage Hotel: During the Siegfried and Roy show, a 380-pound tiger became distracted by someone or something in the audience. The tiger slowly turned its attention toward the auditorium and began to move downstage, unfettered. Roy Horn interposed himself between the tiger and the audience. The tiger took Horn's neck in its mouth and dragged him offstage. Some in the audience applauded.

Early in 1951, the federal government began testing atomic weapons at a site in the desert, sixty miles north of Las Vegas. At the first detonation, the roulette wheel maintained its orbit; dealers' hands did not pause. Chips rattled. Ice rattled. Customers rattled. Las Vegas resorted to its renowned humor. A bartender at one of the Strip hotels came up with an Atomic Cocktail; a beauty shop downtown advertised the Atomic Bouffant.

In 1993 Steve Wynn, at once the sultan of Las Vegas and its Tiresias (Mr. Wynn is afflicted with retinitis pigmentosa), envisioned a thirty-story luxury hotel—the world will never have seen its like—rising from the ashes of the once-fabulous Dunes.

On a calm October evening, therefore, two hundred thousand spectators lined Las Vegas Boulevard South. Heralded by cannonade from the pirate ship harbored in the lagoon of the Treasure Island Hotel (another of Wynn's visions), the south wing of the Dunes Hotel—not yet forty years old—was dynamite-imploded. The crowds cheered.

Back in the sixties, when the "old" Dunes was running at full-tilt, a thirty-five-foot fiberglass sculpture of a raffish sultan stood over the entrance to the hotel, as upon a parapet, to welcome travelers to his desert kingdom. Tastes change. The kitsch idol was eventually removed to the hotel's golf course as a relict of the age of personified brands. One day an electrical short in some chamber of the sultan's heart caused him to melt to the ground. The city of antique lands was amused by the tragic kismet.

Luther and Peter moved to Las Vegas because their apartment building in Berkeley was converting to condominiums. For what it would cost to buy their two-bedroom apartment, they could get a new house in Las Vegas. Peter was enthusiastic; Luther was iffy, but if that was what Peter wanted.

Initially, we heard excitement about their house. Luther's medications, though, were not controlling his condition as effectively as they once had. He was tired all the time; there was nowhere to walk; you had to get in the car and drive to a mall if you wanted to take a walk. Luther couldn't drive because he couldn't see; he had various cancers—of the eye, of the jaw. Whenever Jimmy called, Luther was just watching TV, watching Miss Oprah.

But then Luther found a new doctor, someone efficacious. New meds! Turns out, the drugs should have been changed years ago. Luther began to feel well and he began to feel better about Las Vegas. He liked the extremes of it—the heat, the cold, the flats, the mountains. He liked being a house owner in the desert—the strangeness of it! He said he felt like a pioneer. He talked about special window treatments, solar screens—unknown in Northern California. Barack Obama ran for president and Luther's HIV was undetectable.

Now that Luther lies dying three miles away, we finally visit his house. I am in the backyard with Peter. Peter has observed that some neighbors persist in planting grass. The summer burns it all away. Come September, the lawns need to be reseeded. When Peter and Luther wanted to plant some trees, they had to call out a contractor with machines of the sort that are used in mines. Look, Peter says, attempting to dig with his heel in the backyard dirt. The desert refuses his heel.

I ask Peter if he and Luther ever go down to the Strip to see the shows. Only when friends come to town, he says. People in town rarely go. Though there are special rates for townies. The musicians that interest Luther—singles and groups from the sixties—often play the lounges at smaller hotels, and they sometimes go to those.

The Moulin Rouge hotel and casino opened on the west side of town in 1955 and catered to a black clientele. Nat King Cole, Louis Armstrong, Lena Horne, Pearl Bailey, and many other stars performed there. The Original Sin of Sin City had nothing to do with the sexual gaming Las Vegas now advertises. Las Vegas—the western town, the Mormon town, the mobster town, the stardust town—was a Jim Crow town well into the 1960s. Las Vegas granted dispensations to excess only within limits—white limits.

Black entertainers could perform at the Strip casinos, but they could not eat or drink or gamble or take rooms in them. This story may be as apocryphal as the rest of Las Vegas: One evening, exiting the stage door of a famous hotel and crossing the pool area, Dorothy Dandridge slipped off one of her pumps to cool her foot in the pool. Someone observed Miss Dandridge—an employee or a guest. The management of the hotel had the pool drained and scoured.

Holy Saturday afternoon. Luther seemed more heavily sedated than on Friday. The bed was level; the air-conditioner was off.

A young man's head appeared from around the door. Glasses. Balding. Do you know . . . ? His entire body slid into the room, leaving the door as it was. Does Mister . . . Do you know if Mr. Thomas has any religious affiliation?

Baptist, said Jimmy, standing up. Raised Baptist; he went to several churches along the way, but.

I'm not a Baptist minister, said the young man. In fact, I'm not a minister; I'm studying to become a chaplain. Don Jensen. Hi. Do you think Mr. Thomas would object to a prayer?

No, I'm sure not, said Jimmy. (Later, when recounting the chaplain's visit to Peter, Jimmy learned that Luther had been confirmed as a Lutheran in Berkeley.)

Mr. Jensen had sweat rings under his arms. Jimmy indicated Mr. Jensen should take the chair near the bed. Mr. Jensen leaned forward to speak directly into Luther's ear. Mr. Jensen did not raise his voice. Luther did not stir.

Honestly, you never know who will attend your last hours. When my friend Marty's mother was dying, they called the rectory for a priest. There was no priest available. Really? No priest? Not a one, said a woman at the answering service. The hospice had a rabbi on call. How about a rabbi? In the end, Marty's mother liked the rabbi so well she canceled her order for a priest.

You are a lucky man, Mr. Thomas. Mr. Jensen spoke calmly into Luther's ear. It is a great blessing to die on Easter Sunday. Our Lord rose from the dead and tore off his shroud and tossed it in a corner like so much dirty laundry. Then he walked out into the first light of sunrise and the gates of his kingdom were opened forevermore. You will enter into that kingdom this very day. Jimmy looked to the palm tree in the parking lot, then back to the face of the man speaking calmly into Luther's ear. If there is anything that is holding you back, any misgiving, let us resolve it now in the love of God. Believe God loves you, Mr. Thomas. I am going to say the words our Savior taught us. You follow along as best you can: Our Father, Who art in heaven, hallowed be Thy name. Thy kingdom come, Thy will be done, on earth as it is in heaven. Give us this day our daily bread and forgive us our trespasses as we forgive those who trespass against us, and lead us not into temptation but deliver us from evil. For thine is the kingdom and the power and the glory for ever and ever. Amen.

Mr. Jensen stood; he traced a cross upon Luther's forehead with his thumb; he nodded to Jimmy; he left the room.

If he couldn't make it home for Easter, Luther would always send his mother a check so she could buy herself a new Easter outfit, a dress and a hat—a great big old Pizarro hat, as he called the wide brims and short crowns she favored.

One day, when Luther was four or five, he looked up and saw a tiny silver plane crossing the sky. *Look, Mama,* he said. His mother was pinning clothes on the line. *When I grow up I am going to ride through the sky like that.* His mother looked up where he pointed, then bent once more to her basket. *Mama, you're sad because you think I never will, but I will.*

"Class," Bugsy Siegel remarked, "that's the only thing that counts in life. Class. Without class and style a man's a bum; he might as well be dead."

Holy Saturday. It is the last hour of Sabbath for the Jews—the setting of the sun. Cher's face, bedizened with jewels, floats over the Strip like a Byzantine icon. A large crowd of pedestrians makes an aimless *paseo* among the hotels.

I am making my way up Las Vegas Boulevard to the Easter Vigil Mass at Guardian Angel Cathedral, just beyond the Wynn. At intersections, escalators transport pedestrians to crossways over the streets. Along both sides of the overpass corridor are Mexican families selling bottled water from ice chests. The prices are better than in the hotel shops and people do buy. There are long lines of touts—young Mexican men who snap advertisement cards together, as one might oppose two playing cards to make a clicking sound like the stops on a wheel of fortune. I accept a few cards to see what they are. One is for a bar called the Library. The others entitle the bearer to a dollar off a drink or a ten percent discount or some similar enticement to seek out one among the hundreds of lounges and casinos in the hotels along the Strip and downtown.

To get to the overpass, the pedestrian must thread his way through a cul-de-sac of shops—like Paris, I hear one tourist say; like Jerusalem, I think to myself. There is no other way to cross the street. The crowd is aimless, the crowd is distracted, the crowd is expectant, the crowd feels lucky. The Strip is actually rigidly controlled. Taxis cannot pick up or leave off passengers on the street, but only at hotels. There are entertainments that are free—the dancing waters, the pirate ship, the Roman gods with animated eyes—but these are hotel inducements. I don't notice any buskers on the streets; they would interfere with the flow; the flow is everything; a great deal of money depends on the flow.

I had taken a walk earlier Saturday morning to locate the cathedral and to learn the hour of the Easter Vigil Mass. I passed the pirate ship on my way and I studied it for a time. The crow's nest was shrouded in drab velvet—obviously the stage for some eventual derring-do. Riggings and ladders would be climbed; the mast would be descended. The pirate ship looked down at heel as, I suppose, a pirate ship ought. At that hour of a Saturday morning, the pirates were still in their beds, somewhere in the real Las Vegas.

But now I pass the ship in twilight. The velvet curtain is thrown open (and as red as one could wish it under theatrical lighting). The pirate captain brandishes his sword (white-hot as a laser) to signal the cannonade; the ship is enveloped in fogs of colored smoke. (Tolstoy's description of the Battle of Borodino: colored smokes, fairyland.)

One's purpose is buffeted by the confusion of entertainments and architectures. There are loudspeakers in every palisade, under every hedge, overhead in every arcade. Huge digital screens on the sides of hotels project *David Copperfield Live!* One's thoughts are not one's own. This is some other syndrome. The Happy Hour syndrome. The Happiest Place on Earth syndrome. This must be how non-Christians feel at Christmastime (the Jewish antiquaire, played by Erland Josephson, making his way through the darkening streets of Stockholm in Ingmar Bergman's *Fanny and Alexander*).

By the time I pass the Wynn, the crowds thin and the Strip recedes. I see a Thai restaurant and the cathedral behind it. The main doors of the church are locked. I am late. I enter through a side door. The place is packed; an usher directs me into the choir loft where there are some families with children but the majority are solitary latecomers like me. I take a pew behind a woman whose posture I read as burdened.

The Cathedral of the Guardian Angel belongs to the modest Las Vegas of the fifties and sixties—of low-rise hotels and casinos. Moe Dalitz, a reputed mobster in Cleveland and a revered philanthropist in Las Vegas, donated the land for the construction of the church and selected the architect, Paul R. Williams, an African American, who had designed Frank Sinatra's house and other celebrity homes in Palm Springs. Two marble angels flank the altar—the sort of angels one might see in any nineteenth-century cemetery. Behind the altar is a large mosaic mural of the softest modernist declension—intersecting mandala (free form rather than cubist), and within the mandala are several emergent figures; foremost is Jesus. The figures free themselves of shroud-like encumbrances. It is Resurrection as the Ballet Russe de Monte Carlo or the Ice Follies might conceive of Resurrection. The mural is poor religious art but it is profoundly in period—a period after World War II; a spirit of resurrection exemplified by Coventry Cathedral, the United Nations, the founding of Israel, the Salk vaccine, the Second Vatican Council. As its period coincides with the period of my poor soul's formation, I am forgiving of the mural's ecstatic silliness, its inchoate hope.

In the balcony of the cathedral, I find myself aligned with banks of loudspeakers suspended stage left of the nave.

The Epistle is performed theatrically. A man wearing a gray turtleneck rises from the congregation—he is miked; he is Saint Paul—to address us intimately, urgently, from the first century. In fact, I have always wanted to see this done, and it is done very well. But it does not please me for being so thoroughly done. There is no pleasing me tonight.

The bishop sits on his throne like Old King Cole, his head resting on his hand. The Mass proceeds as a series of divertissements, in the manner of the Royal Ballet—attempts to rouse the bishop from his unaccountable melancholy. The master of ceremonies tries everything—baptisms, confirmations, fiddlers three. Nothing seems to work.

Peter returned to the hospice with Andrew and John. Luther seemed to know his friends were there. He struggled to open his eyes and he finally succeeded, his eyes sliding beneath their sliced lids. Did he see? Yes, we thought he did.

Then the nurse came in and she said they were going to bathe Luther and make him more comfortable. She asked us to wait outside. While we waited in the corridor, three women—the nurse and two aides—filed past us with armfuls of folded sheets and towels.

The three women were not solemn. We heard their light, cheerful voices through the door, as if they were dressing a bride. Then we heard a heart-rending aw-w-w-w—the sound women make when an infant does something adorable. Did Luther say something? Or make a gesture of some kind? Then we heard an outburst of laughter that as quickly became consolation: Oh, honey, it's alright, it's alright. (Was Luther weeping?)

By and by, the door opened; the women left, their eyes downcast. We filed back into the room. They had turned Luther three-quarters on his side. He was leaning upon a bank of several pillows, as Christ leans upon a rock in paintings of Gethsemane. They had arranged him for his Passion. He was gasping. His teeth were bared. My heart involuntarily pronounced aw-w-w aw-w-w-w aw-w-w-w.

After a scintillating "Alleluia"—the loudspeakers buzzing with cymbal sizzle—all in the congregation stand as the Easter Gospel is proclaimed in the cathedral. When the Sabbath was over, Mary of Magdala, Mary the mother of James, and Salome, bought spices with which to go and anoint him. And very early in the morning on the first day of the week they went to the tomb when the sun had risen.

It was called the Dogwood tree.

I leave immediately after Communion. Outside, a black desert wind. (The forecast for Easter morning is for showers and dust storms. Aren't those antithetical?) Though he risks a fine for doing so, a cabbie—Pakistani or Indian—picks me up on the sidewalk along Las Vegas Boulevard South. Business has been lousy, he shrugs; he took a chance. He asks why I am in town. I tell him about Luther. He tells me about a cousin of his who is dying of cancer.

All along the bright holiday boulevard, he describes a woman dying alone on the other side of the world, under tomorrow's sun. He drops me off on the shore of Lago di Como, on the Eiffel Tower side.

Luther Thomas died Easter Sunday, April 4, 2010.

four

Tour de France

A knucklehead fell out of a tree.

The judge had promised us, the twelve of us, a trial lasting no more than two days. It was not until the fifth day that the plaintiff (a flat-voiced teenaged boy) took the stand to explain why he had climbed a tree in Golden Gate Park in the first place, how he ended up on the ground with a broken arm.

Just foolin' around.

The boy's parents' lawyer claimed the park maintenance crew of the city and county of San Francisco should have cut the dead wood out of the tree.

Personal injury. The phrase summons scars more recently sustained, and another summer, when I was lying on a bed in St. Mary's hospital in San Francisco, thinking about Aix-en-Provence.

My thorax had been unpacked and repacked like one of those fire-hose boxes you see in old buildings. A foot or so of O-gauge track burned down my belly whenever I raised myself, whenever I twisted to answer the phone.

On a television set hanging from the ceiling, Lance Armstrong, cancer survivor extraordinaire, was making a triumphal progress up the lime-leafed Champs-Élysées. I forget which among his victories this was.

Whatever else cancer is, cancer is a story that leads away from home. Even the luckiest stories involve harrowing prompts and trials. Lance Armstrong endured trials so dire I have seen him weep in the recounting of them on TV.

My cancer story began in Paris, also on a bed, where I was watching the aftermath of the Madrid train bombings on television. I had been troubled for several weeks by night sweats. I was due to travel to Spain in two days. The doctors were not initially concerned. Some low-grade infection, perhaps to do with prostate.

No doctor I consulted subsequently ever uttered the word "cancer." The oncologist told me the X-rays showed a growth two inches long. "Growth" is a word I had previously associated with maturation, even wisdom. The unaccountable burst of inches after a childhood summer. Or the daffodils in Hyde Park after that first lonely winter of graduate school. The oncologist's growth was some kind of ghostly scallop, a story-eater.

My first impulse was responsible and mundane. Update my will. Get my tax returns in order. Ask a thoroughly unsentimental friend to serve as my medical executor.

My next impulse was to visit a Dominican priest. At this juncture, I entered a second euphemism.

I am a Roman Catholic old enough to have grown up calling the seventh sacrament of the church *Extreme Unction*. There was no mistaking a sacrament with such a name. One summoned a priest to the bedside of a relative to anoint the care-worn forehead with holy oil. The ceremony was so wedded to death in the Catholic imagination that the concern of irresolute relatives was always that poor old Nonno would wake up to see a priest fussing about him and die of fright.

So as not to frighten Nonno, therefore, the Catholic Church

has jettisoned the term and now refers to the "Anointing of the Sick."

That is what I got. I got oil on my forehead and hands. And then I asked the Dominican priest, who is a friend of mine, to hear my confession.

I had not been to confession for several decades—a sin in itself. You might imagine I left many trash bags full of sins in the priest's office that afternoon.

Bless me father, for I have sinned. This is my first confession in thirty-two years. . . .

The substance of my confession is the conclusion of the story. I will return to the parish rectory and what I discovered in preparing to confess three decades of my life. But, first, I need to explain why it was that, even as Lance Armstrong rode, like ancient Paris, past cheering crowds, I was thinking about Aix-en-Provence while recuperating at St. Mary's.

I have never been to Aix-en-Provence. My best friend in college, Ted Mayhew—of course, that is not Ted's real name—had passed a defining summer there. I was forever pestering Ted about places in the world he had seen and I had not. My curiosity on the subject of Aix elicited from Ted only disparagement of his parents, particularly his mother, with whom he was perpetually annoyed.

When he was sixteen years old, Ted stayed two months with friends of his parents in Aix. He spent that summer drawing and painting. Ted's ambition was to be an artist. I hadn't known that. He returned home to New York with three water-plumped sketchbooks. He put the sketchbooks away on a shelf in his bedroom before he returned to his New England prep school in September.

In November, when he came home for Thanksgiving, Ted noticed his sketchbooks were out on the dining room table. He took them back to his room.

On the Friday after Thanksgiving, his mother summoned Ted to the living room for a grown-up chat. She had taken the liberty of showing Ted's sketchbooks and watercolors to an elderly and well-known society painter. The old man had looked over Ted's work and opined the boy would not amount to more than an amateur. His talent was not large enough.

Ted's mother had several voices. When she portrayed pragmatism, she had recourse to New England. It was his mother's bad Katharine Hepburn that killed Ted: *Knot. Lodge. Nuff.*

Ted never picked up a paintbrush again.

In the years since that summer morning at St. Mary's hospital, I have sat among bald women in doctors' offices. We all read—and reread by mistake—the well-worn issues of *People* magazine. Thus have I attended the idylls of Brad and Angelina and all the remote bright stars.

From those same issues of *People* magazine I have come to learn the sequence of women in Lance Armstrong's life—from wife Kristin to Sheryl Crow to someone named Tory, and a much younger Ashley. Most recently, there was an "amicable separation" from Kate Hudson.

I seem to remember it was Sheryl Crow who was waiting for Lance Armstrong on that summer day in Paris. He wore the yellow jersey that represented laurel.

One day, while visiting the Mayhews' Manhattan apartment, I admired Ted's watercolor of a rose-covered wall in Aix-en-Provence. His mother had given it a prominent place in the room, surely denoting some pride, I ventured. *Only because it matches her peach-colored walls,* Ted replied in Brunswick blue.

The Filipina nursing assistant (half my age, with sorrowing eyes) stood beside my bed, adeptly silencing the alarm of the drip monitor.

Beautiful flowers, she said. She meant on the windowsill.

Take them, I said.

Really, you don't want them?

I want you to have them, I said. Left unsaid: On so many mornings, dear Filipina-stranger-checking-my-vitals, you have bathed my torso and legs and back. You have brought what clutter and cheer you could to this sterile room. You deserve the flowers on the windowsill, for you are like spring.

Though what I have learned from being around the sick and the dying is that it is one thing to clean a stranger, quite another thing to wipe your father or your mother. Intimacy changes everything.

I would extend this generalization to cover the matter of personal injury. It is one thing to suffer hurt from a tree in Golden Gate Park, but quite another to suffer an injury from a parent, a lover, a best friend, a teacher whose favorite you thought yourself to be.

Strangers drop hydrogen bombs on strangers. But when you were in fourth grade, your best friend blabbed your secret to a cafeteria table of boys. Your best friend did this only to get a laugh.

Though it was Sunday my oncologist came into the hospital room just as Lance Armstrong ascended the dais. The oncologist was leaving the next day on vacation. A doctor with a Polish surname would take over on Monday.

The oncologist pulled back the sheet. Over his shoulder, Lance Armstrong kissed the several hired Graces whose fate it was to bestow his prize. The doctor unbuttoned my hospital tunic. The crowd cheered. "Healing nicely," he said, admiring the gathering of my flesh. I did not look.

Will it go away? The scar, I meant.

"Nope, sorry," the doctor said. "But it is my impression that women like men with scars."

Bulls like men with scars. Mine reminds me of Andy Warhol's scar after a madwoman shot him in the stomach. Even that is to beg some heroic cast. My scar looks like the seam up the front of a Teddy Bear.

Bless me, father, for I have sinned.

After three unshriven decades, what I discovered, in rehearsing my failures as a human being, was not how many sins I had committed, but how small they were.

Bless me, father, I have lived my life in lowercase.

No Joycean blasphemy. No Miltonic grandeur. Only so many homely cruelties, inflicted without much thought or care.

To summarize: I was the boy in fourth grade who told my best friend's secret, to get a laugh. I do not even remember what the secret was.

Do you suppose he does? Even small wounds have long consequences. After three unshriven decades, what frightened me most during my *examen* was the realization that I had nurtured so many small wounds inflicted on *me*.

That was what I was thinking about as cancer survivor extraordinaire, Mr. Lance Armstrong, coasted up the Avenue des Champs-Élysées. The boy crashing out of the tree like a lumpen sloth. My best friend in fourth grade scalded by laughter. The sensible Park Avenue matron killing her artistic son as blithely as she would twist a bright bow.

Sheryl Crow bit her lip, turned away as though the sun were in her eyes. Brilliant Lance Armstrong raised thin arms over his head in triumph.

I seem to remember it was Sheryl Crow who was waiting that summer day. Perhaps I misremember. Perhaps it was Tory. Or Helen of Troy.

five

Darling

1. *Theatricals*

You never met Helen, did you? My younger sister. Helen and I used to pretend. I was Murray Perahia and she was the Duchess of Alba, stepping up to the maître d', beads of sweat dripping from our credit cards onto the carpets of London, of Paris. People did turn. I was Al Pacino and she was the Duchess of Zuiderzee-sur-Mer and Swansdown. We avoided their stares. I was that Indian tennis star—I've forgotten his name. We requested a table in a quiet corner. Helen sold off her duchy; she was Tina Chow or somebody like that; Marguerite Gautier. She was the Countess de Gooch ("Fabulous wealth, the de Gooches!"). Helen spent her youth memorizing *Auntie Mame* and the Marx Brothers. ("Is my aunt Minnie in here?") Our desperate drollery snagged on table linens, waggled the ice buckets as we were forward-marched to our table. Not a bad table, either, considering.

I was the lonely gay brother with a fellowship abroad who lived in a bed-sit in Chelsea; who kept a stack of coins on the mantel to feed into a slot in the gas heater; who brought Indian take-out back to my room on Sundays; who read John Milton and *Harpers & Queen* beneath the lowest cone of a tricolor pole lamp (turquoise, chartreuse, orange) that blinked whenever Mr. Okeke charged across my ceiling.

Helen was my hardheaded disciple, my treasurer, my Galatea.

Now that she was grown and had a job working for a bank in California, she thought she might as well drop by London for Easter, pokey little London, she said, whereas the flowers were already out in Paris.

Darling, I would say, as waiters circled us in magic, will you have a sweet? No inflection was too outlandish for Helen; no serve went unreturned: "Why do we leave brown coffee-burble stains on our cups and nobody else does?" Tina Chow looked bemusedly across the dining room; she studied the chaste coffee cups she saw other diners lower from their lips. "I'll have the Indian pudding, please."

"Darling" is a voluble endearment exchanged between lovers on stage and screen. The noun is overblown, dirigible; strikes the American ear as insincere. Nevertheless, "darling" became a staple of married life on American television in the fifties: Good morning, darling. Remember, darling, the Bradshaws are coming for dinner tonight. What's wrong, darling?

"Darling" was a most common salutation in letters between soldiers and their wives or girlfriends during World War II. Lovers surprised themselves in the act of portraying themselves with a heightened diction—in that way attempting to convey an awareness that their lives were drawn by Tolstoyan engines of history.

One night in Boston I went out to dinner with my editor and his wife—this was my first editor, the beloved editor, and I was in awe of him; I still am in awe of him. The editor kissed me on the cheek as we parted and called me his "darling boy," as if thereby investing me with the Order of Letters Genteel. It was among the happiest nights of my life; I was filled with sadness as I watched the two of them, the editor and his wife, walk away.

In Neo-classical and Romantic poetry, "darling" is an adjective bestowed upon innocence: darling curls, darling buds. Darling boys.

In stage-Irish, "darling" is ironic, yet still a sentiment bestowed: Sure and you're a darling man altogether, Jack Boyle!

But then the post-lapsarian actress Tallulah Bankhead blared "darling" like a foghorn—fair warning to anyone of sincerity or true affection. By democratizing the endearment, by addressing everyone as "darling"—intimate or stranger, friend or foe—she produced a brilliant comic effect.

You never met Nell, did you? No, you wouldn't have. Nell never liked L.A. Back then, when Nell and I were Beatrice and Benedick of the graduate division, we were more than a bit much. We were alert to the slightest vibration of irony in one another, of pointed glance or quiver of lip or inflection—those stiff twin compasses had nothing on us. Nell! And she looked the very Hogarth of a Nell, a wine-red laugh and green eyes, curly hair and rollicking shoes—any "darling" I sent Nell's way was a struck match to an arsenal of pent theatricality: tosses of mane, wreaths of smoke, crossings of leg. At a bacon-and-eggs café on Telegraph Avenue we favored with our presence, we carried on like the Lunts.

"Look, darling, someone's drunk up all my wine."

Have some of mine.

"But yours is gone, too."

And we can't afford any more.

"Sad. And the sun's gone down."

And the Master's not home.

Just so was "darling" a prop for Cary Grant—as careless a conveyance of cooled emotion as a cigarette case or a fountain pen—an advertisement of his acquaintanceship with ease, ease with life, ease with women, whether he was playing the thief or the playboy or the soldier. The Cary Grant performance was in homage to an-other lower-middle-class Englishman, Nöel Coward. Growing up in Teddington, Coward imagined a leisured class of world-weary sophisticates whose conversations were rank with "darlings." "Darlings" didn't mean anything. "Darlings" were objective-nominative vagaries, starlings in a summer sky. "Darlings" were sequined grace notes flying by at the famous Coward clip—Coward designed his lines to be spoken rapidly and unemphatically.

Something about this personal-classical, asexual, theatrical form of address interested me, pleased me. I studied how to use it.

2. *The Garden of Eden*

Helen and Nell saw the fun of it immediately. You, on the other hand, were my first unwilling darling. L.A. is a city so full of dar-lings, I couldn't understand your resistance at first.

The day your divorce was finalized, we drove up the coast to the Garden of Eden. A right turn off the Coast Highway at the bait-and-tackle shop and halfway up a hill. No view at all. The air was fresh. There was nothing camp about the Garden of Eden but the sign—a neon palm tree bedizened with a hot pink snake. It was a hotel with cabins from the thirties that had been refur-bished to sea drift–moderne. The building was badly damaged by a mudslide in the nineties and is no more. But on a weekday after-noon, in 1982, it was the perfect respite from L.A.

On second thought, Darling, I said, surveying the restaurant through the side window, let's not eat in the dining room; let's go through to the bar and order club sandwiches.

Fine.

Fine as volcanic ash is fine? Fine as an anvil dropped from the Empire State Building is fine? We were great chums a moment ago. What's up? You prefer the dining room?

The bar is fine . . . DARLING.

Broken yolk. Call 911. I steered you, as I would have steered a fizzing depth charger, through the placid mirrors of the Garden of Eden, into the bar. Two clubs, please. They made them with chopped olives, remember? Two clubs and one beer. And one coffee. Black. Black as pork blood. Black as shark bile. Black as . . .

I will have the Syrah, please.

Sorry. One beer, one Syrah. Skip the coffee.

Ex was on your mind, I knew that. You were on edge. I was never the Other Man, careful on that score. I made you laugh, though. Ex was grateful. OK, it was "darling" that pissed you off.

One redhead. Chin resting on hand. The snake's neon tongue flicked long, short, long, short.

One pretender.

3. *Habeebee*

"Darling," Andrew says, with a good-humored sigh. He writes the Arabic word on his napkin with a fountain pen; the ink bleeds away from the word.

"Come weez me to zee casbah," American children learned to say from cartoons without the least idea what a casbah might be. Some kind of nightclub, I imagined, for Shriners. In the course of writing this chapter, I ask Andrew who lives in Cairo to explain to me—not a parlor game, not quite; I am truly interested—how it is possible, in what way is it possible, I mean, for an Arab to address a man, another man, affectionately, as "darling." Still imagining the casbah.

The feminine noun, pronounced *habib-tea,* might be spoken to a wife, to a family member, to a child, to Mata Hari, to Hedy Lamarr.

The masculine noun is pronounced *habeebee.* While it is not advisable to address one's employer or a policeman with such a noun, my friend instructs, one might, in a playful manner—with irony, I assume—address a waiter or a cab driver as "darling." You might be surprised, too, he says, when a man you met for the first time only a few hours earlier phones you at your hotel and opens with a Tallulah, as in: *Habeebee*, why have I not heard from you?

The admirable intimacy and the demonstrative physicality of Arab men among themselves seem to depend on the separation of men from women before marriage, and a curatorial regard of women after marriage, and the consequent mystery and the consequent male anxiety about women—their scarves and blooded rags and watchful eyes—from birth to death. In a region of mind without coed irony, where women are draped like Ash Wednesday statues (as too hot to handle) and stoned to death on an accusation of adultery (as too insignificant to cry over), men, among themselves, have achieved an elegant ease of confraternity and sentimentality.

Do you remember, Darling, we were sitting in the ICU waiting room at UCLA Medical Center when two Arab men, thirties, handsome—one the father, one the uncle, we supposed—entered with two children, two boys? The boys played; the men talked. A tall woman wearing a black veil entered. Her face was exposed. Her complexion was ashen; there were dark circles under her eyes; she was preoccupied, talking into a cell phone. Her burning eyes strafed the room. The men leaned away from each other, stopped talking. The children got up from the floor and took seats. She briefly spoke to the men then left the room, still talking into the cell phone.

The children returned to the floor. The men recommenced their conversation; they spoke Arabic to each other but English to the children. By and by, one of the men, the uncle, lifted one of the boys to his knee. "So, my darling," he said, "do you want to go to Mecca with them? Or will you come to Medina with me?" At which he kissed the boy's forehead so juicily that we immediately turned to each other to mouth: Medina!

A teacher invited me to my niece's prep school classroom to give a talk, and I entered the classroom at 9:05 a.m., how-do-you-do, etcetera. There was my niece in the first row. "Hello, darling"—I addressed her in the familial vernacular in front of ALL her friends. My sister reported to me later that my niece had wanted to DIE. At fifteen, I guess she was a year or two shy of being able to relish a gay uncle in public.

She didn't die. She grew up to be an absolute darling. And a player.

When I was fifteen, I attended a Catholic boys' high school. I prospered well enough. In an all-boys school, as in a patriarchal theocracy, sexual roles are distributed widely. The absent feminine must still be accounted for, as in an all-boys' production of *Julius Caesar*. Roles of pathos were available to boys at my high school, but I eschewed them in favor of a role more akin to Prosecutor, Ironist. I advanced by questions. In some more perfect world, like *American Bandstand*, I suppose I would have been happier in a sexually integrated high school. I knew how to talk to girls. I had two sisters. And I loved to talk. But early nonsexual female companionship would have come at a price. "Sissy" is the chrysalis of "darling."

As a boy, I resisted the aunts' encouragement to go outside with my cousins or to join the group of men standing around the gaping hood of a car, silently regarding an exposed horsepower. I preferred to linger with the women, to listen to gossip, to hear irony concerning the projects of men—irony I was fully capable of sharing.

During my high school years, a boy from my neighborhood named Malcolm chose me to be his friend for a season. His elbow nudged my book in the public library one Saturday afternoon as he sprawled forward across the table feigning some condition— boredom, I suppose. His voice was like shadow—as whispery and as indistinct as shadow, due to an adolescent change. "Do you want to wrestle?" he asked.

I have never met anyone since who speaks as Malcolm spoke: He daydreamed; he pronounced strategies out loud (as I raked elm leaves from our lawn and piled them in the curb)—about how he would befriend this boy or that boy, never anyone I knew; Malcolm went to a different high school. "First," he said, "I will tease him about his freckles. Then I will tease him about his laugh—how his laugh sounds a little like a whinny sometimes. I won't go too far. You should see how his wrist pivots as he drib- bles down the court.

"He's got these little curls above his sideburns. I wish I had those." (He would catch me up on the way to the library.) "What are you reading? We read that last year. Not really a war story, though, is it? Want to go eat French toast?"

Malcolm had a car and an after-school grocery-delivery route and a criminal penchant. I knew, because he told me, he'd been caught breaking into empty houses.

He walked like an illustration from *Huckleberry Finn*—arms akimbo, fingers spread, picking up his knees as though he were stepping over creaking floorboards. He had dark eyes, very white skin, and an expression of condescending pity like that of a raptor bird, if raptor birds had eyes that dark. He said he was part Chickasaw.

What is a season in the life of a high school boy? Four months or so. Malcolm's next season was girls. Basketball and girls.

On summer nights, my mother and Helen and I stayed up late watching old movies. At some point in the movie the women would retire from the table and leave the men to their brandy and cigars. I preferred movies that followed the women upstairs to a region of knowing. . . .

The doorbell rang at eleven thirty.

My mother went to the upstairs front window. I went down to answer the bell. It was Malcolm.

"Come out for a minute," Malcolm whispered.

I closed the door behind me.

"Smell this," he said, thrusting his index finger under my nose.

I did not understand.

He named a girl I did not know. He was ecstatic. He leaned backward on his legs and silently crowed. He jumped from the top porch step down to the sidewalk. He ran away, down the street. I never heard that audacious male voice again. Unfleshed echoes in *Les Liaisons dangereuses*, perhaps, or the memoirs of Casanova, but never again the naked envy of the seducer.

4. Picasso

Because I had arrived early for my nephew's wedding in Golden Gate Park, I decided to walk over to the de Young Museum to look at an exhibition from the Musée Picasso in Paris. Many of the paintings displayed Picasso's naked infatuation with female-ism, with convexity, concavity, bifurcation. The female face, too, was divided into competing arrondissements—one tearful, one tyrannical—like the faces of playing-card Queens.

Concurrent with the Picasso there was an exhibit at the museum of the fashion of Cristóbal Balenciaga, another Spaniard, Picasso's contemporary. But whereas the sexed, sublime painter undressed women as unashamedly as if he had created them, the modernist couturier made formidable casings for women, unassailable pods, chitins, scapulars, shields—made saints of women, made queens, bullfighters, pagodas, nurses, priests, Jeannes d'Arc—conventuals of the Order of Fashion who, thus armed, might one day slay the grizzled minotaur of the maze-like gallery upstairs.

I was the one who insisted it was time for you to lose the jeans and the sweatshirts, Darling. I sat through a rainy Saturday afternoon on a fake Louis Quinze chair in a salon at the Beverly Hills I. Magnin as the Delphic vendeuse consulted her clattering racks to bring forward a succession of looks for you to try. Patience, Darling, I cautioned—I could tell you were about to bolt. The stockroom door opened one more time, and the priestess stepped forward, bearing in her arms a red Chanel cocktail dress that betokened revenge on a shallow, faithless husband.

A middle-aged woman in a brown wool suit tapped my shoulder after Mass. She knew my name. She said she had read an interview I gave to an online magazine on the gay marriage controversy in California. At that time, a Catholic archbishop colluded with officials from the Church of Jesus Christ of Latter-day Saints in a campaign to protect the sacred institution of marriage from any enlarging definition (including civil marriage, which the Catholic Church does not recognize as sacramentally valid). Campaign checks to be made payable to the Knights of Columbus.

The Knights of Columbus is a lay fraternal organization sanctioned by the Catholic Church. The Knights are an admirable bunch of guys—I believe "guys" is the right word—who spend many hours performing works of charity. On festival days, the Knights get themselves up with capes and swords and plumed hats like a comic-opera militia.

The woman in the brown suit did not say she agreed with my comments in the article; she did not say she disagreed. She said: "I am a Dominican nun; some days I cannot remember why."

I will stay in the Church as long as you do, I said.

Chummy though my reply was, it represented my abrogation of responsibility to both the Church and the nun.

A gay man easily sees himself as expendable in the eyes of the Church hierarchy because that is how he imagines the Church hierarchy sees him. The Church cannot afford to expel women. Women are obviously central to the large procreative scheme of the Church. Women have sustained the Church for centuries by their faith and their birthrates. Following the sexual scandals involving priests and children, women may or may not consent to present a new generation of babies for baptism. Somewhere in its canny old mind, the Church knows this. Every bishop has a mother.

It is because the Church needs women that I depend upon women to protect the Church from its impulse to cleanse itself of me.

I shook hands with the Dominican nun and we parted.

But even as I type these words, the Vatican has initiated a campaign against American nuns who (according to the Congregation for the Doctrine for the Faith) promote "radical feminist themes" and who remain silent regarding their Excellencies' positions on women's reproductive rights and homosexuality. A nun's silence is interpreted as dissent in this instance.

The Church—I say the Church but I mean the male church—is

rather shy in the presence of women, even as the God of scripture is rather shy of women. God will make a bond of friendship with a hairy patriarch. God interferes with Sarah through her husband. God courts Mary by an angel.

And yet the God of intention entered history through a woman's body (reversing the eye of the needle). The Church, as she exists, is a feminine act, intuition, and pronoun: The Christian Church is the sentimental branch of human theology. (I mean that as praise.) The Church watches the progress of Jesus with the same sense of his heartbreaking failure as did the mother who bore him. In John's account of the wedding at Cana, Mary might be played with maximum flibberty-jibbertry by Maggie Smith. Jesus struggles to extricate his legs from the banquet table in the courtyard; his companions can't help sniggering a bit. The first showing of Jesus's power over Nature, the changing of water into wine, makes no clear theological sense. But as the first Comic Mystery, the scene makes perfect domestic sense. Jesus is instructed by his mother.

5. The Sisters of Mercy

I would never in a million years have thought of lobbing a "darling" Franz Schurmann's way, though Franz and I had lunch almost every week for twenty years. Now I wish I had, for Franz would have sluiced the noun through the brines of several tongues, finally cracking its nacreous shell. He would have told me something interesting. Or he would have spit the noun onto his bone plate as something the Chinese have no word for, no use for. (The Chinese tongue had become Franz's point of view.)

Not that Franz was unsophisticated or unacquainted with theatricality. As a young man at Harvard, Franz was the best friend of Bertolt Brecht's son. Franz spent several summers living among the colony of European expatriots in Santa Monica, with Brecht and Weigel and Mann and Isherwood.

After Harvard, Franz embarked on a Pashto-idyll, playing the scholar-gypsy to the hilt: two years on horseback through the Khyber Pass on an anthropological search for some remnant of a lost tribe of blue eyes.

When Franz passed through the molars and incisors of remote mountain villages, he was often invited to share a meal with the bearded men who squatted near a fire. The women who had prepared the meal stood several yards away, watching and waiting for the men to finish, for the men to pluck the remnants of food from their beards.

Franz caught a young woman's eye. She held his glance for only a moment before she spat on the ground and looked away, over her shoulder.

The women who educated me—Catholic nuns belonging to the Irish order of the Sisters of Mercy—looked very much like Franz's Afghan village women. They wore veils, long skirts, long sleeves, laced black shoes—Balenciagas all.

Of the many orders of Catholic nuns founded in nineteenth-century Europe, the majority were not cloistered orders but missionary orders—nursing and teaching orders. Often the founders of such congregations came from upper-middle-class families, but most of the women who swelled the ranks of missionary orders had left peat-fumed, sour-stomached, skinny-cat childhoods behind. They became the least-sequestered women imaginable.

It was in the nineteenth century, too, that secular women in Europe and North America formed suffrage movements, following in the footsteps of missionary nuns and Protestant missionary women. Curiously, it was the burqa-like habits nuns wore—proclaiming their vows of celibacy—that lent them protection in the roustabout world, also a bit of a romantic air.

When seven Irish Sisters of Mercy (the oldest twenty-five) disembarked in San Francisco in December of 1854, they found a city filled with dispirited young men and women who had followed the legend of gold. The Sisters of Mercy spent their first night in California huddled together in St. Patrick's Church on Mission Street; they had no other accommodation. In the morning, and for months afterward, the sisters searched among the wharves and alleys of San Francisco, ministering to men, women, and children they found sleeping in doorways.

The *Christian Advocate,* an anti-Catholic newspaper, published calumny about the nuns; the paper declared them to be women of low repute and opined they should move on—nobody wanted them in San Francisco.

In 1855 the Sisters of Mercy nursed San Franciscans through a cholera outbreak. In 1868 the nuns cared for the victims of a smallpox epidemic. In 1906, after the great earthquake and fire, the Sisters of Mercy set up a tent hospital in the Presidio; they evacuated hundreds of the sick and elderly to Oakland across the Bay. City officials in the nineteenth century invited all religious orders to ride San Francisco's trolleys and cable cars free of charge because of the city's gratitude to the Sisters of Mercy.

As they had done in Ireland, the Sisters of Mercy opened orphanages, schools, and hospitals in California and throughout the United States. By the time our American mothers caught up with the nuns in the 1960s—with the possibility of women living fulfilling lives, independent of family or marriage—the nuns had discarded their black robes in favor of sober pedestrian attire. Vocation has nothing to do with dress-up.

Veiled women were seldom thereafter seen on the streets of America or in European cities, not until the influx of immigrant Muslim women from North Africa and the Middle East in the 1980s.

A shadow of scandal now attaches in Ireland to the founding order of the Sisters of Mercy. An Irish government report released in 2009 documents decades of cruelty perpetrated particularly upon children of the working class in orphanages and homes for unwed mothers run by the Sisters of Mercy. One cannot doubt or excuse the record. The record stands.

The Sisters of Mercy of the Americas—the women I revere—are fewer and older. The great years of the order seem to have passed, but the Sisters continue their ministry to the elderly, to immigrants, to the poor. The Sisters are preparing for a future the rest of us have not yet fully comprehended—a world of increasing poverty and misery—even as they prepare for their absence from the close of the twenty-first century.

Nuns will not entirely disappear from San Francisco as long as we may occasionally glimpse a black mustache beneath a fluttering veil. The Sisters of Perpetual Indulgence is an order of gay drag nuns whose vocation is dress-up.

Like the Sisters of Mercy in early California, the Sisters of Perpetual Indulgence took up their mission in bad repute. Unlike the Sisters of Mercy, the Sisters of P.I. have done everything in their power to maintain a bad repute.

They have their detractors. I was one. I wrote against them because I saw them as mocking heroic lives. Thirty years ago I had lunch with Jack Fertig, aka Sister Boom Boom, in a taqueria on Mission Street. He arrived wearing jeans and a T-shirt. On the wall at the rear of the restaurant was a crucifix—not, I assumed, ironic. The nun in mufti approached the crucifix and fell to his knees. He blessed himself; he bowed his head. Whether this was done for my benefit I don't know. There was no follow-up, no smirk, no sheepishness, no further demonstration of piety. I did not question him about it; I was astonished. But, as I say, I wasn't taken in.

Before he died, Jack Fertig converted to Islam.

A few years ago, I stood on a street corner in the Castro District; I watched as two or three Sisters of P.I. collected money in a coffee can for one of their charities. Their regalia looked haphazard on that day—jeans and tennis shoes beneath their skirts, like altar boys. I couldn't help but admire how the louche nuns encouraged and cajoled the young men and women who approached. The Sisters' catechism involved sexual precaution, drug safety, with plenty of trash repartee so as not to spook their lambs: "Do you have a boyfriend, honey? Are you getting enough to eat? Where do you sleep? Are you compliant with your meds?"

I experienced something like a conversion: Those men are ministering on a street corner to homeless teenagers, and they are pretty good at it. No sooner had I applied the word "good" than I knew it was the right word. Those men are good.

The Sisters of Perpetual Indulgence do what nuns have always done: They heal; they protect; they campaign for social justice; they perform works of charity. The Sisters of Perpetual Indulgence have an additional mission: They scandalize.

For example, on Easter Sundays, the Sisters host the "Hunky Jesus Contest" in Dolores Park. The Sisters and their congregation seem only to be interested in satirizing the trappings of S&M already available in Roman Catholic iconography. (One cannot mock a crucifixion; crucifixion is itself mockery.)

I do not believe the Sisters of Perpetual Indulgence are enemies of the Church; I believe they are a renegade church of true vocation. They are scourges; they are jesters. Their enemy is hypocrisy. In a way, they are as dependent upon the Church as I am. They are as dependent on the nun in a brown wool suit as I am. Without the Church, without the nun, they would make no sense at all.

6. The Gray Cat

My father grew up an orphan. The extent of his patriarchy was his sense of responsibility to our family. He otherwise observed no particular rules or rites of masculinity beyond self-possession, and he imposed none beyond respect for our mother. My father was mild and bemused, never touching but lightly, as a child will pet a cat. While our two older siblings had proper names at home, I was "boy" in direct address by my father and "the boy" when I attracted some notice in the third person. Helen was "the girl." Our home was entrusted (in the prayers of our parents) to the care of the Virgin of Guadalupe, and we all rather liked it that way.

Outside the Rodriguez home, God made covenants with men. Covenants were cut out of the male organ. A miasma of psychological fear—fear of smite, fear of flinty tools, fear of lightning—crackled in God's wake. Scripture began to smell of anger—a civet smell. Scripture began to taste of blood—of iron, of salt. I associated heavy, dangerous elements with fathers, with men, but not with my own father.

When I was a child we had a cat. The cat had kittens. She hid them in the shed. The Father Cat, as we called an indolent wild gray, searched for and found the kittens; he smelled them, I guess, or he heard them mewing. He entered the shed. He carried the kittens away in his mouth, one by one, to kill them. I saw the Father Cat flee the shed with a kitten in his soft mouth. I yelled Stop!

I threw a clod of dirt at him. He would not stop, could not; he looked confused, utterly overruled by his natural compulsion. His eyes were terrible; they were not his normal eyes. They were fixed in jealousy—pulled back, as if by some invisible hand at the nape of his neck. That was the name the child's imagination branded him with: The Jealous Cat. He came again. Even after my mother came out to shoo him away with a broom, he loitered at the edge of the yard, biding his time, withstanding the barrage of clods exploding on the wooden fence.

I see dependable Everett Fox (*The Five Books of Moses*) has wondered before me, as thousands before him have wondered, about a "bizarre episode" in *Exodus:* Yahweh divulges to Moses the mission Yahweh has chosen him for. Moses is to return to Egypt and, once in the presence of Pharaoh, is to demand the release of the Israelites in Yahweh's name. Moses accepts Yahweh's command with great trepidation and every excuse in the book—but accepts. So Moses with his wife and sons begins his journey to Egypt. In the desert, at night, Yahweh finds Moses in his tent and seeks to kill him! Moses's wife takes up a flint and cuts off her son's foreskin; she touches the foreskin to Moses's legs and says: "Indeed, a bridegroom of blood are you to me!" Whereupon Yahweh releases Moses.

Everett Fox cites the great rabbi, Martin Buber, who explains this passage (in Fox's capitulation) as "an event that sometimes occurs in hero stories: The deity appears as divine demon and threatens the hero's life. Perhaps this underlines the dangerous side of contact between the human and the divine." Fox explicates the passage further as a prefiguring of the blood smeared on the door lintels of the Israelites during the tenth Egyptian plague.

I can only think of the hormonally conflicted gray cat.

I read an article recently about a medical study that traced a decline in levels of testosterone among new fathers, if those fathers were intimately involved in their infants' care—feeding, holding, changing. Thus does Nurture attempt to vanquish the gray cat.

In Hebrew scripture there is no more valuable signifier than male seed. It is the mucilage of Yahweh's blessing. It is the particulate matter of immeasurable proportion, of metaphor: *as many as, as numerous as* . . . It is the promise of the future. You will hold the desert land by your seed. Multiply, be fruitful, is the overarching instruction. Important kings and prophets come of very bad conceptions. Seed is God's intention, however scattered.

But now it is the twenty-first century and the mitered, bearded, fringed holy men have cast women as gray cats. Destroyers of seed.

7. Daddy and Papa

"He" is the default setting in scripture—Jewish, Christian, Islamic. The perception, the preference, the scriptural signifier, the awe of the desert religions, is of a male God. Father. Abba. Lord. Jesus refers to God always as Father, though he insists that God is spirit. Yahweh is unnameable but for the name He (as I was going to write) gives Himself: *I Am*. There is no "He" in *I Am*. The theologian John L. McKenzie proposes (*The Two-Edged Sword*) that a more accurate translation of the holy name might be: "He brings into being." Bringing into being was a potency that the prophets, the evangelists, the compilers of scripture, conceived anthropomorphically as male.

In the desert cultures of the Middle East, religious communities regard homosexual acts as abominations—unnatural, illegal, unclean. But homosexual behavior does not preclude marriage or fatherhood. The notion of a homosexual identity is a comic impossibility. What alone confers an appropriate sexual identity on the male is fatherhood.

Two young men fussing over a baby girl in a stroller. You were not charmed. You said no straight man would make that kind of fuss.

No straight woman, either, Darling.

The new gay stereotype is domestic, childrearing—homosexuals willing to marry at a time when the heterosexual inclination is to dispense with marriage.

Divorce rates in the United States and Europe suggest that women are not happy with the relationships they have with men, and vice versa. And whatever that unhappiness is, I really don't think gay people are the cause. On the other hand, whatever is wrong with heterosexual marriage does have some implication for homosexuals.

The majority of American women are living without spouses. My optimism regarding that tabulation is that a majority of boys in America will grow up assuming that women are strong. My worry is that as so many men absent themselves from the lives of the children they father, boys and girls will grow up without a sense of the tenderness of men.

The prospect of a generation of American children being raised by women in homes without fathers is challenging for religious institutions whose central conception of deity is father, whose central conception of church is family, whose only conception of family is heterosexual. A woman who can do without a husband can do without any patriarchal authority. The oblique remedy some religious institutions propose for the breakdown of heterosexual relationships is a legal objection to homosexual marriages by defining marriage as between one man and one woman.

The gay counteroffensive to the religious argument is (the

American impulse) to seek an African American analogy to homosexual persecution, to claim some historical equivalence to the government-sanctioned persecution of African Americans over centuries. Many African American churches take offense to that particular tack. From the pulpit, the argument sounds something like: We didn't choose our race; homosexuals choose their lifestyle.

I believe there is a valid analogy to be drawn between the legal persecution of homosexuality and the legal persecution of miscegenation—both "crimes against Nature." But the course more comparable to the gay rights movement is the feminist movement, dating to the nineteenth century.

Suffragettes withstood condemnation from every institution of their lives, condemnation that employed the adjectives of unnatural aspiration, adjectives such as "thwarted," "hysterical," "strident," "shrill." Still, it was the brave suffragette (and not the tragic peacock Oscar Wilde) who rescued my sexuality.

In the twentieth century, gays emerging from the closet were beneficiaries of the desire of women to define themselves outside the familial structure. The feminist movement became inclusive not only of wives, mothers, and unmarried women but also of lesbians, and thus, by extension of nonfamilial sisterhood, of homosexual men, of the transgendered, of the eight-legged acronym, LGBT.

A generation ago feminists came up with "Ms." as a titular designation of gender not based upon marital status or age. Ms. was no sooner on offer than most women I know and most institutions gratefully adopted it. Ms. transported the woman signified out the door and into public life, independent of cultural surmise.

Using the homeliest of metaphors—coming out of the kitchen;

coming out of the closet—heterosexual women and homosexuals announced, just by being themselves without apology, the necessity of a reordered civil society. We are—women and homosexuals are— for however long I don't know, dispensed (by constitutional laws, state laws) from having to fit into heterosexual roles and heterosexual social patterns that have been upheld for so long by reference to "the natural law." Natural law, as cited against sodomy, against abortion, against birth control, against miscegenation, is neither exactly the "natural moral law," which is a philosophical construct—the understanding placed in us by God at the creation— nor exactly the law of Nature; that is, how Nature works. Rather, it is a value placed upon behavior by someone or some agency, most often with reference to some divinely inspired statutory text, that denounces or declares illegal or punishable any deviation from what the authority or the text declares to be natural human behavior. Boys will be boys and girls like glitter.

I know there are some homosexuals who see the gay couples in line for marriage licenses, or filling out forms for adoption, or posing for wedding announcements in the *New York Times*, as antithetical to an ancient culture of refusal that made the best of a short story—of youth and chance and public toilets and then the long half-life of irony and discretion.

There certainly are homosexuals of my generation who never dared hope for a novel of marriage but only one of renunciation. E. M. Forster imagined a marriage novel, but then stipulated it not be published during his lifetime. The Church regards homosexual marriage as a travesty that will promote the undoing of marriage. But I propose the single mother is a greater threat to the patriarchal determination of what constitutes a natural order.

I am thinking of David Grossman, the Israeli novelist, who, in a profile in the *New Yorker,* said: "If God came to Sarah and told her, 'Give me your son, your only one, your beloved, Isaac,' she will tell him, 'Give me a break,' not to say 'Fuck off.'"

I am thinking of the Mormon mother who told me on Temple Square in Salt Lake City: "The Church teaches us that family is everything. And then the Church tells me that I should abandon my homosexual son. I will not do it!"

It is clear to me that civic attitudes toward homosexuality and gay marriage are changing. In countries we loosely describe as Western, opinion polls and secular courts are deciding in favor of the legalization of gay marriage. Nevertheless, the desert religions will stand opposed to homosexuality, to homosexual acts, unless the desert religions turn to regard the authority of women. And that will not happen until the desert religions reevaluate the meaning of women. And that will not happen until the desert religions see "bringing into being" is not a power we should call male only. And that will not happen until the desert religions see the woman as father, the father as woman, indistinguishable in authority and creative potence.

My place in the Church depends upon you, Darling.

8. The Sultan's Wives

But you're right, of course.

"Darling" is a feeble impulse to cover some essential embarrassment in my situation. In my life, I should say. Will I be bringing a spouse, for example. Well, that depends, doesn't it?

It is the queer lexicon that is behind the times now. Is my partner a husband? Is my husband a partner? We are not a law firm. Is my partner my "friend," a wreath of quotation marks orbiting his head? Lover sounds sly. Boyfriend sounds fleeting. Husband sounds wistful.

This might amuse you, Darling, now that you are dead. It wouldn't have . . . well, maybe it would have. In the dawn of a warm spring morning, the road to Jerusalem was shrouded in fog. Jimmy and I arrived at the American Colony Hotel. The Palestinian clerk looked at me, looked at Jimmy. The clerk said there was a problem with our reservation. The problem was that the suite we had reserved—all the suites, in fact—had only one bed.

That's no problem, I said. (I was annoyed with myself; I had asked friends who know Jerusalem well if there would be a problem about our sharing a room. And I had been assured there would not be a problem.)

For the desk clerk, there was a problem.

In a previous life, this wonderful hotel had been the palace of an Ottoman sultan whose several wives were salted away in various rooms that still surround the courtyard; Begum Monday next door to Begum Tuesday, and so on. Now suites.

Ah! The reservation clerk seized upon a solution; he even dinged his little bell.

Please, if we would care to take a little breakfast on the patio, he would see to our room.

After we had finished with breakfast, the clerk led us up a staircase to our room, and voilà: A cot was unfolded and was being made up as a daybed by a middle-aged Palestinian man whose sensibility we were conspiring to protect. The Palestinian man finished smoothing the coverlet then he stood back from the cot. He turned to us, where we stood in the doorway. He smiled. He winked!

Q: Why do I stay in the Catholic Church?
A: I stay in the Church because the Church is more than its

ignorance; the Church gives me more than it denies me. I
stay in the Church because it is mine.

I meant what I said to the nun: I will stay as long as she does. I
may even stay longer. The Church and I have the same dilemma,
really. To wit: "Tradition has always declared that 'homosexual
acts are intrinsically disordered.' [CDF, *Persona humana* 8.] They
are contrary to the natural law. They close the sexual act to the
gift of life. They do not proceed from a genuine affective and
sexual complementarity. Under no circumstances can they be
approved." (*Catechism of the Catholic Church*, second edition, copyright 2001. United States Conference of Catholic Bishops. Libreria
Editrice Vaticana.)

I can walk away from the bishops' formulation of my "intrin-
sic" disorder, but the Church cannot walk away from the bish-
ops' formulation, even though some within the Church may be
sympathetic toward homosexuals. I know this is supremely
boring to non-queers and non-Catholics and readers of Faulkner,
but stay a moment and then we will go to Costco. Sexual
complementarity is not, obviously, insurmountable, or there
would be no problem. I will object with my last breath, however, to anyone denying "genuine affective complementarity" to
queers. I would not deny "genuine affective complementarity"
to a dog. Or a cat. Or a parakeet. (My aunt had a parakeet
named Sanchez. They were devoted to each other.) Or to an
apostle.

At the time I write this, the only institution on earth that recognizes my ability to love is Costco. On the Costco registry, I have a
spouse.

What I will not countenance is that the Church denies me the
ability to love. That is what "affective complementarity" is: It is

love. If that is the Church's position, the Church is in error. Keep the word "marriage." Let marriage mean one man and one woman. (Sanchez died a week after my aunt died.) But I want a word. How about "love"?

We are gathered here, in the sight of the security cameras at Costco, to witness . . .

What are you smiling at, Darling?

9. An Angel Hovers over the Garden of Eden

Can we do something on Sunday? A movie? A walk?

If not each other's walkers, we were certainly each other's talkers. A professor of mine remarked a good many years ago that the vocal cords are the most reliable, longest-enduring sexual organs. It was the exercise of vocal cords that led us to step over the bodies of our sleeping lovers to drive twenty miles north, to slide into the banquette of the Garden of Eden. A brilliant February morning. A foggy July evening. Your skirt hiked up for driving; your yearly new car.

And you were right, Darling. Going through to the bar was a betrayal, a sudden disinclination for intimacy; boredom with your melancholy; the hope of an early evening. Let's make this an early evening. Darling. Because all of a sudden you were going to say—you did say—that I was pretending to be someone I am not. In fact, Darling, I was pretending to be someone I am. Despite my many sins and shortcuts, I have always been a player—on my mother's side.

A player recognizes other players. I once met a German shepherd who was a player. And so was his dog. Oh, come on, what's wrong now? What should I call you, then? Sweetie? Dulcinea?

I had studied so diligently to become a serious man. I stood in awe of serious, competent men—scholars, janitors, fathers.

But I had as well, at the time of the Garden of Eden, an adolescent anxiety about Chekhovian Sunday evenings, about melancholy, about sex. I had endeavored to suggest to you, Darling, without resorting to scarves or cigarette holders—you just never cared to notice—that I had some interest in the casbah, in people you wouldn't approve of. Obviously I had a fear of the casbah, as well. One foot in. "Darling" seemed to fit the bill.

Exhibit A: I wore a suit and tie; Helen carried a purse—teenage brother and sister standing on the sidewalk in front of the Curran Theatre in San Francisco. We had lunched at Normandy Lane in the basement of the City of Paris. We had used the restrooms at the St. Francis. The future was years ahead of us. We were still an hour early for the Saturday matinee. We looked at the photographs of the cast. A Yellow Cab pulled up to the curb. The back door opened. Cary Grant got out of the cab. I nudged Helen. Cary Grant extended his arm into the cab and handed out Dyan Cannon, whose portrait we had just examined. (Dyan Cannon was playing the female lead in the national company of *How to Succeed in Business Without Really Trying*.) Cary Grant drew Dyan Cannon into an embrace. Dyan Cannon melted somewhat. Cary Grant kissed Dyan Cannon on her lips. We watched. Cary Grant got back into the cab; he rolled down the window. "Bye-bye, darling," he called as the cab sped away.

I have found that "darling" serves as a signal to women that one's relationship to them is going to be a comic pas, an operetta, a tease. (If that's the signal you caught, Darling, you were not wrong.)

If a woman returns the serve—if she is a willing player—then you've got her where you want her; "darling" is understood: One is not a sexual player. One is Cary Grant. One has Randolph Scott sewing curtains back at the ranch. "Darling" is the net, not the birdie.

You were not going to join my menagerie of darlings, though, were you, Darling? Just trying you out. Sorry.

Elizabeth Taylor, toward the end of her life, when she could (I imagine) have summoned anyone in the world to dine, spent many evenings at a gay club in West Hollywood, just to be a darling among darlings. She was too fond of life, too fond of people, too shrewd to be shrewd, to retire into mystery.

A favorite darling-ist of mine is Harold Bloom. He's not gay, is he? And yet he darlings like a champ.

But the all-time was Bunny Breckinridge. "Hell-o, darling," Bunny would purr, straightening the lapels of his silk suit, composing his hands (diamond ring) as if he were leaning forward upon a walking stick—a top-hatted chorister's stance, a top-hatted chorister's patience. Bunny could sit without moving for long periods of time, like someone on stage, which, of course, he had been—he had been on the stage. Every thirty minutes he would sigh a two-tone sigh like an ormolu clock to let you know that he was still there, that he would wait you out. Bunny's mannerisms were as those described in some bad translation of a Russian masterpiece. He giggled suggestively. He squeaked with pleasure. He winked salaciously. Face powder dusted his collar; his rinsed white hair was swept back to a meringue peak at the North Pole, like the hair of one of those puff-cheeked Aeolian figures in the corners of antique maps.

And Bunny could soliloquize. Picture Edith Evans, seated on a stone bench in a painted garden in some Restoration comedy. Dirtier, of course. He once recounted, for reasons that had to do with a diamond cross he wore at his throat, the Passion and Death of Our Lord Jesus Christ. At the completion of the narrative, huge tears, clotted with powder, rolled down his cheeks. Bunny is the only human being I have ever met for whom the death of Christ had the immediacy of personal tragedy. "He died for our sins, darling," Bunny confided piteously.

> Then you said: *Why are you telling me all this? If men would only listen to themselves sometimes.*
>
> I said: Men? I'm demonstrating the rhetorical uses of "darling"—as if you were my Orals Examiner.
>
> You: *Then as your Orals Examiner, Darling, I feel I should tell you something important. "Darling" should be intimate; "darling" should be understood, not flung about the room like a stripper's garter. If you feel you really must darling someone in public, and karaoke is not readily available, scribble your sonnet on a napkin and pass it under the table when no one is looking. Don't toss "darlings" around like you are feeding the seals. It is no way to treat a woman.* (Tears.)

Later that same evening . . .

> You: *Should we get a room?*
>
> I: What? (Punctuation cannot convey.)
>
> You: *It's late. We could watch a movie.*
>
> I: I think I've seen this movie.
>
> You: *. . . ?* (Judy Garland.)
>
> I: . . . ? (Houdini.)
>
> You: *You're not interested in women. Say it.*
>
> Zorba the Greek: "God has a very big heart, but there is one sin He will not forgive. If a woman calls a man to her bed and he will not go."

I: I am not interested in sleeping with a woman, if that's what
    you mean. Isn't it odd we say "sleep" when what we
    mean . . .

You: *Thank you. That is what I mean. Was that so hard?*

I: Yes.

So, just like that, we were over the rainbow. You would continue to explore the pleasures of the natural law. There was a
young one, a rich one, a dumb one, a tan—probably gay, we both
agreed. And I was free to darling up a storm—a neutered noun
twirling about a neon palm tree.

When the time came, I wasn't sure how I should introduce
you. . . .

Darling, this is Jimmy, I said.

(Your braceleted arm extended.)

Over time, you stopped making faces; over time, my theatrical af-
fectation became the emblem of our true affection.

You even returned the herring in kind. In a small white bed, in
a curtained cubicle, the prongs of the slipped oxygen tube hissing
about your throat, you endeavored to show you understood who
was holding your hand. With your eyes closed, you raised one
finger and whispered: *Darling.*

10. The Maternity Ward

The maternity wards of Tel Aviv are in a contest with the maternity wards of Ramallah. Might the future depend—as in the Old
Testament—on the number of children your tribe produces? If
Ramallah wins, there will be a Palestinian state. Babies are a political force in the world.

For several years, we, in the West, have talked about the future as a "clash of civilizations," by which we meant primarily a clash between fundamentalists and secular society. The attacks of September 11 seemed to many Americans to join that clash.

September 11 has prompted me to consider the future in terms of a growing, worldwide female argument with the "natural" male doctorate of the beard—a coming battle between men and women.

In China, men outnumber women. That might be the statistic to think about. One outcome of the one-child policy was that many couples contrived to make their one child a son. The result of the policy—the contrivance, the forced abortions, etcetera—is that China prepares for economic, technological, and military preeminence in the twenty-first century, the rare-earth century, the expanding desert century, the starving century, while sustaining a fundamental biological imbalance: There are too few women.

Such an imbalance might seem to favor a patriarchal order by force of number. But because reproduction is such a profound human balance, the rare-woman century may give humans of female gender the opportunity to control, to seize control of, reproduction. If the female gender were ever to control reproduction, then the female gender would control what?

Point of view.

If menses were the parable, not seed—if sea, not ships; if sky, not missiles? If protective imagination were the parable, not domination, not conflict, then . . . ?

If *Silent Night* were the prologue, and not *Sing, Goddess, the anger of Peleus's son.*

Then?

I asked the question of a priest-scholar: If women were to control reproduction, what would women control? The priest paused for a moment before answering efficiently: "Evolution. Who controls the zygote controls the zeitgeist."

It is only after shopping my question around the boys' club that I bring it at last to the banquette of the Garden of Eden.

Here is my question, Darling: Say there is a battle forming between men and women. I do not mean for equality, but for primacy—for who will ultimately control reproduction . . . What are you doing?

Looking for my pills.

What's wrong?

Nothing's wrong. I'm looking for my pills.

So here's my question. What would a woman control if a woman controlled . . . ?

A schoolboy's question. Why must it be a question of "control"?

You haven't even heard the question.

I heard the frame. It's a riddle, isn't it? No doubt there is a correct answer. Tickle me. Amuse me.

I asked Father Rafferty the same question. If women control reproduction, what will women control? You know what his answer was?

I cannot imagine.

No. His answer was evolution. That's good, isn't it?

Are there bones in skate?

So . . . ?

Look, Richard, a woman . . . No I can't speak for Women. I cannot consider your question abstractly. Your question presses against me like an exploded safety bag. Back up! Or should I say pull out? (Once more to the handbag.) *There you are!* (She aligns the arrows on the safety cap.) *Pregnancy is never a hypothetical for a woman. Never. Not even for me. Not even at my age. Cheers.* (Prednisone.) *It is a condition of our existence.*

Your answer is you cannot conceive the question?

No, my dear. My observation is that you cannot conceive! That freedom alone allows you to conceive of conception as a power. Whereas a woman might argue that a refusal to conceive is the only power.

Are you sure you're not just pulling a hetero on me?

Women and men will never be equal. Women will always be superior in knowledge and irony because men will never have a clue what it feels like to have the entire dangerous future of the planet crammed up their twats. I'm not pulling a hetero. I'm pulling a utero.

You are so pleased with your funny that I am rewarded with your laughter, which is like a percolating calliope. Everyone in the Garden of Eden must turn to see what sort of creature could produce such a ridiculous, infectious sound.

11. Three Women

A woman:

Andy Warhol made a tracing of Leonardo's *Annunciation*. Leonardo's painting is venerably burnished—browns, golds, Venetian red. On the left side of Leonardo's canvas is an angel, of idealized profile—one dead eye and two partially aroused pinions. The angel kneels in the manner of a mezzo-soprano cavalier and raises its right hand in benediction; its left hand supports the stalk of a lily.

Mary sits at a reading carrel; her right hand worries the pages of an open Psalter. In the background are some odd topiary—cypress, perhaps—and a garden in which lilies bloom. The vanishing point is a mountain in the far distance. Mary's lap is shelf-like—knees apart, feet braced, as is characteristic of many Annunciation paintings—but not yet receptive to the implication of the angel's presence.

Warhol's silk-screen rendition, a kind of explication, uses three colors—gray, salmon, white (in the version I prefer; Warhol printed several variations)—and crops the scene to a close-up, isolating three elements: On the left, the blessing hand of the angel (the Question, the Proposal). On the right, Mary's hand, restive on the Psalter (the incipient reply, not yet an assent). In the center is the white alp, like a dish of ice cream in a comic book (the Suitor, the Unknowable, the Impossible).

The alp has sent its mouthpiece to ask if it may enter the foreground, overshadow the maiden. Gabriel kneels to proclaim: Hail, Darling, full of grace. The Lord is with thee. Blessed art thou amongst women. And blessed is the fruit of thy womb, Jesus.

"It is *a* woman I want rather than any particular one," the young Victorian novelist, William Makepeace Thackeray, wrote to his mother in frustration.

A woman:

I was crossing Broadway on my way to a theater—a warm spring evening, around seven o'clock, still light. Within the crosswalk, a woman walked alongside me. "Are you visiting New York?" she asked very pleasantly. She was dressed in a creamish, knittish, knockoff Chanel with gold buttons. Forty. Thirty-five, forty. Nice-looking. Not much makeup. Umbrella, just in case. You could tell she was a nice woman, even without the umbrella. "Where are you going in such a hurry?" she asked, trying to keep pace. I'm on my way to the theater, I said. "Would you like some company?" This last she said with desperation; she was cognizant of the absurdity of her question, posed in a crosswalk on Times Square. Oh, no thank you, I said, cognizant of the Greer Garson blitheness of my reply. I'm meeting some friends at the theater. At which her (gloved) hand moved to cover her mouth, stifling a vowel that was sick and sorrowful—humiliation, I thought, at having, on what must surely have been her maiden voyage as a hooker, or nearly, tried it out on a gay man who probably looked as benign to her (my blue suit, perhaps) as she looked to me, and probably I was one of the very few solitary male pedestrians on Broadway who was more interested in seeing a play than in sex with a woman who held an umbrella. I wished her a good evening. Her face crumpled in tears as she turned away to her fate.

You see, I badly needed a "darling" at that moment—to make her smile, even if ruefully; to make it seem we were two adults who knew the score, which we weren't, which we didn't, neither of us.

When William Thackeray died at age fifty-two, a famous author, the most famous English author of his time after Dickens, he left two young daughters and a wife in a sanitarium who suffered from what we would now call postpartum depression. Mrs. Thackeray never recovered but lived a very long time in perplexity, seated in a lawn chair. William Thackeray was buried at Kensal Green Cemetery, London. Several figures in black, famous figures—Penguin paperbacks—accompanied the Thackeray daughters to their father's grave.

But what was that unseemly caterwauling?

Black-clothed figures turned from the open grave to watch the advance of a carriageful of whooping and gesticulating Mayfair tarts in parrot's plumage. The women choired lusty benedictions as their carriage drove round and round the grave: Goodbye Willie, they cried. Toodaloo, Dearie. We had a few laughs, though, didn't we, Darlin'!

A woman:

Jesus of Nazareth is not known for sparing anyone embarrassment, least of all his family, but in his meeting with the Samaritan woman, he displays evidence of knowing the score. As does she. And, as you say, "darling" is understood:

At Jacob's Well. Noon. Jesus rests from a long journey on foot. His friends have gone into town to look for something to eat. A woman approaches the well. She carries a clay jar. Jesus says to the woman, Will you give me something to drink?

Wait, a Jew is asking a Samaritan for a drink?

If you only knew what God was giving you right this minute . . .

I don't see your water-skin, love.

. . . you'd be the one asking for a drink.

You can't drink from mine, though, can you? Defile your inner temple, outer temple, which is it? And the well is deep, trust me. How do you propose to draw water without a skin?

Whoever drinks your water will soon be thirsty again.

If you're afraid of the trots, you should stick to your own well.

No one who drinks the water I give will ever be thirsty again. The water I pour out will become a spring of life.

Oh, well then. In that case (as she lowers her leather bag into the well)—*a skin of my donkey-swill for a drop of your kosher magic.* (She extends the dripping water bag to Jesus.)

Call your husband.

What's that got to do . . . hey! (Snatching back the water bag, splashing them both.) *I don't have a husband.*

You got that one right (Darling); you've had four husbands and counting. But the one you've got now isn't your husband.

Oh, a prophet, too! Should've known from the toenails. My ancestors worshipped on this mountain a long time before you people showed up.

The hour is coming when you will worship the Father neither on this mountain nor in Jerusalem.

Oh, Jerusalem. I was forgetting: True worship only happens in Jerusalem.

You worship what you don't know. We worship what we know; salvation comes from the Jews. But the hour is coming—it is already here—when true worshippers will worship the Father in spirit and truth. That is the worship the Father wants.

Well (Darling), *when the Messiah comes, I'm sure he will explain everything to everyone. Even hillbillies like me.*

You're talking to him.

12. *Mystery*

You were raised Catholic. You said you didn't believe. Much anyway. How one lives one's life is what one believes, you said. You admitted to downright needing Christmas.

And music. Twice you said you didn't know if you assented to the notion of God.

Notion? Existence then. You said you believed in mystery. Mystery? You said religion—any religion you knew about—was a cult of patriarchy. Men in the Bible were better fathers than husbands, you noticed.

A friend who sat with you through the night, one of the worst nights, very near the end, recounted to me how troubled you seemed. *What a bad person I've been,* you said to the friend, to the shadows, to the statues huddled in the shadows (*Wait, are those statues?*), turning your face away. *What a poor mother, what a poor daughter.*

No, no, the friend reassured: Come on, you are a very good mother, your children are wonderful. They adore you. Everyone adores you.

I am thinking of your two-hour theorem, Darling. It is the most fortifying advice I have ever received. You said: I find I can stand anything for two hours. Fly through a thunderstorm. Drive through a desert. Visit a kid in prison. Root canal. Cocktail party in Brentwood. Birth. Financial report. Roast turkey. Just do it and don't fret! Think about getting home. Think about pulling into the driveway. Think about cereal and bananas.

In the morning, your friend said, you opened your eyes, though no one could enter them; you spoke as if from a trance. *How wonderful God is,* you said. *How beautiful it is!*

I mean, who doesn't love the breast, the throat, the hands, the rings, the laughter? Who doesn't love the economy of her ways? Her sudden abandonment to joy? The way she can arrange a bed, a sheet, a blanket, a pillow. The way she can leave everything better than when she entered.

I know plenty of men who can arrange a room. But I am not talking about "taste," I am talking about . . . Partly, it is the patience for folding material—the patience of square corners. But partly it is the carelessness of allowable drift. Of opening a window and closing a curtain and letting the curtain blow as it will.

During World War II, the U.S. military, in an attempt to make men more uniform, studied the art of the hospital, the convent, the feminine. Men were trained to make up their cots in an efficient, spotless, feminine way. Selfless, in other words—literally selfless, as a grave is selfless. One bed must be exactly like the next. Inspecting officers tended to make a metrical fetish of a made bed, a punishment of what should promise ease.

Darling, you couldn't wrap a package to save your soul. I watched as you taped together some wrinkled, flowered, saved remnant of Mother's Day. Then you tied on a wide plaid ribbon. The result was not perfection. It was pretty. Same with your flower arrangements—plunking a fistful of cut flowers into a vase, any vase, any flowers. One would need to study for years to achieve the carelessness of your impulse. An unkempt, Pre-Raphaelite prettiness followed you wherever you went, and I don't understand at all how you came by it. I don't even understand what it was.

Who doesn't love her stockings?

You were dead, so you missed the plump-jowled televangelist Jerry Falwell confiding to the gaunt-jowled televangelist Pat Robertson that the Islamist attack on America was the result not of religious extremism but of divine displeasure with a morally decadent United States of America: *"I really believe that the pagans, and the abortionists, and the feminists, and the gays and the lesbians who are actively trying to make that an alternative lifestyle, the ACLU, the People For the American Way, all of them who have tried to secularize America. I point the finger in their face and say, 'You helped this happen.'"*

He means us, Darling. You and me in the bar of the Garden of Eden, passing those long-past afternoons.

I cannot imagine my freedom as a homosexual man without women in veils. Women in red Chanel. Women in flannel nightgowns. Women in their mirrors. Women saying, Honey-bunny. Women saying, We'll see. Women saying, If you lay one hand on that child, I swear to God I will kill you. Women in curlers. Women in high heels. Younger sisters, older sisters; women and girls. Without women.

Without you.

six

Saint Cesar of Delano

The funeral for Cesar Chavez took place in an open field near Delano, a small agricultural town at the southern end of California's Central Valley. I remember an amiable Mexican disorder, the crowd listening and not listening to speeches and prayers delivered from a raised platform beneath a canvas tent. I do not remember a crowd numbering thirty thousand or fifty thousand, as some estimates have it—but then I do not remember. Perhaps a cool, perhaps a warm, spring sun. Men in white shirts carried forward a pine box. The ease of their movement suggested the lightness of their burden.

When Cesar Chavez died in his sleep in 1993, not yet a very old man at sixty-six, he died—as he had so often portrayed himself in life—as a loser. The United Farm Workers (UFW) union he had cofounded was in decline; the union had five thousand members, equivalent to the population of one small Central Valley town. The labor in California's agricultural fields was largely taken up by Mexican migrant workers—the very workers Chavez had been unable to reconcile to his American union; the workers he had branded as "scabs."

I went to the funeral because I was writing a piece on Chavez for the *Los Angeles Times*. It occurs to me now that I was present at a number of events involving Cesar Chavez. I was at the edge of the crowd in 1966, when Chavez led UFW marchers to the steps of the capitol in Sacramento to rally support for a strike against grape growers. I went to hear Chavez speak at Stanford University. I can recall everything about the occasion except why I was there. I stood at the back. I remember a light of late afternoon among the oaks beyond the plate-glass windows of Tresidder Union; I remember the Reverend Robert McAfee Brown introducing Cesar Chavez. Something about Chavez embarrassed me— embarrassed me in the way I would be embarrassed if someone from my family had turned up at Stanford in a dream to lecture undergraduates on the hardness of a Mexican's life. I did not join in the standing ovation. Well, I was already standing. I wouldn't give him anything. And yet, of course, there was something compelling about his homeliness.

In her thoroughly researched and thoroughly unsentimental book *The Union of Their Dreams: Power, Hope, and Struggle in Cesar Chavez's Farm Worker Movement*, journalist Miriam Pawel chronicles the lives of a collection of people—farm workers, idealistic college students, young lawyers from the East Coast, a Presbyterian minister, and others—who gave years of their lives at subsistence pay to work for the UFW. Every person Pawel profiles has left the union—has been fired or has quit in disgust or frustration. Nevertheless, it is not beside the point to notice that Cesar Chavez inspired such a disparate, devoted company.

We forget that the era we call the sixties was not only a time of vast civic disaffection; it was also a time of religious idealism. At the forefront of what amounted to the religious revival of America in those years were the black Protestant ministers of the civil rights movement, ministers who insisted upon a moral dimension to the rituals of everyday American life—eating at a lunch counter, riding a bus, going to school.

Cesar Chavez similarly cast his campaign for better wages and living conditions for farm workers as a religious movement. He became for many Americans, especially Mexican Americans (my parents among them), a figure of spiritual authority. I remember a small brown man with an Indian aspect leading labor protests that were also medieval religious processions of women, children, nuns, students, burnt old men, under the banner of Our Lady of Guadalupe.

By the time Chavez had become the most famous Mexican American anyone could name—his face on the cover of *Time*—the majority of Mexican Americans lived in cities, far from the tragic fields of California's Central Valley that John Steinbeck had made famous a generation earlier. Mexican Americans were more likely to work in construction or in service-sector jobs than in the fields.

Cesar Chavez was born in Yuma, Arizona, in 1927. During the years of his hardscrabble youth, he put away his ambitions for college. He gave his body to the fields in order to keep his mother from having to work in the fields. The young farm worker accumulated an autodidact's library—books on economics, philosophy, history. (Years later, Chavez was apt to quote Winston Churchill at UFW staff meetings.) He studied the black civil rights movement, particularly the writings of Martin Luther King Jr. He studied most intently the lives and precepts of Saint Francis of Assisi and Mohandas Gandhi.

It is heartening to learn about private acts of goodness in notorious lives. It is discouraging to learn of the moral failures of famously good people. The former console. But to learn that the Reverend Martin Luther King Jr. was a womanizer is to be confronted with the knowledge that flesh is a complicated medium for grace. To learn that there were flaws in the character of Cesar Chavez is again to wonder at the meaning of a good life. During his lifetime, Chavez was considered by many to be a saint. Pawel is writing outside the hagiography, but while reading her book I could not avoid thinking about the nature of sanctity.

Saints? Holiness? I apologize for introducing radiant nouns.

Cesar Chavez modeled his life on the lives of the saints—an uncommon ambition in a celebrated American life. In America, influence is the point of prominence; power over history is the point. I think Cesar Chavez would have said striving to lead a holy life is the point—a life lived in imitation of Jesus Christ, the most famous loser on a planet spilling over with losers. The question is whether the Mexican saint survives the tale of the compromised American hero.

The first portrait in *The Union of Their Dreams* is of Eliseo Medina. At the advent of the UFW, Eliseo was a shy teenager, educated only through the eighth grade. Though he was not confident in English, Medina loved to read *El Malcriado*, the feisty bilingual weekly published by the UFW. Eliseo Medina remembered how his life changed on a Thursday evening when he went to hear Chavez in the social hall of Our Lady of Guadalupe Church in Delano. Medina was initially "disappointed by the leader's unimpressive appearance." But by the end of the meeting, he had determined to join the union.

No Chavez speech I have read or heard approaches the rhetorical brilliance of the Protestant ministers of the black civil rights movement. Chavez was, however, brilliantly theatrical. He seemed to understand, the way Charlie Chaplin understood, how to make an embarrassment of himself—his mulishness, his silence, his witness. His presence at the edge of a field was a blight of beatitude.

Chavez studied the power of abstinence. He internalized his resistance to injustice by refusing to eat. What else can a poor man do? Though Chavez had little success encouraging UFW volunteers to follow the example of his abstinence, he was able to convince millions of Americans (as many as twenty million by some estimates) not to buy grapes or lettuce.

Farmers in the Central Valley were bewildered to find themselves roped into a religious parable. Indeed, Valley growers, many of them Catholics, were dismayed when their children came home from parochial schools and reported that Chavez was upheld as a moral exemplum in religion class.

At a time in the history of American business when Avis saw the advantage of advertising itself as "Number Two" and Volkswagen sold itself as "the Bug," Chavez made the smallness of his union, even the haphazardness of it, a kind of boast. In 1968, during his most publicized fast to support the strike of grape pickers, Chavez issued this statement (he was too weak to read aloud): "Those who oppose our cause are rich and powerful and they have many allies in high places. We are poor. Our allies are few."

Chavez broke his 1968 fast with a public relations tableau that was rich with symbol and irony. Physically diminished (in photographs his body looks to be incapable of sustaining an erect, seated position), Chavez was handed bread (sacramental ministration after his trial in the desert) by Chris Hartmire, the Presbyterian minister who gave so much of his life to serving Chavez and his union. Alongside Chavez sat Robert F. Kennedy, then a U.S. senator from New York. The poor and the meek also have allies in high places.

Here began a conflict between deprivation and success that would bedevil Chavez through three decades. In a way, this was a struggle between the Mexican Cesar Chavez and the American Cesar Chavez. For it was Mexico that taught Chavez to value a life of suffering. It was America that taught him to fight the causes of suffering.

The speech Chavez wrote during his hunger strike of 1968 (wherein he likened the UFW to David fighting the Goliath of agribusiness) announced the Mexican theme: "I am convinced that the truest act of courage, the strongest act of manliness is to sacrifice ourselves for others in a totally non-violent struggle for justice. To be a man is to suffer for others. God help us to be men." (Nearly three decades later, in the program for Chavez's funeral, the wording of his psalm would be revised—"humanity" substituted for "manliness": *To be human is to suffer for others. God help me to be human.*)

Nothing else Chavez wrote during his life had such haunting power for me as that public prayer for a life of suffering; no utterance sounded so Mexican. Other cultures in the world assume the reality of suffering as something to be overcome. Mexico assumes the inevitability of suffering. That knowledge informs the folk music of Mexico, the bitter humor of Mexican proverb. To be a man is to suffer for others—you're going to suffer anyway. The code of *machismo* (which American English has translated too crudely as sexual bravado) in Mexico derives from a medieval chivalry whereby a man uses his strength or his resolve or even his foolishness (as did Don Quixote) to protect those less powerful. God help us to be men.

Mexicans believe that in 1531 the Virgin Mary appeared in brown skin, in royal Aztec raiment, to a converted Indian peasant named Juan Diego. The Virgin asked that a church be erected on the site of her four apparitions in order that Mexican Indians could come to her and tell her of their suffering. The image of Our Lady of Guadalupe was an aspect of witness at every UFW demonstration.

Though he grew up during the American Depression, Cesar Chavez breathed American optimism and American activism. In the early 1950s, while still a farm worker, he met Fred Ross of the Community Service Organization, a group inspired by the principles of the radical organizer Saul Alinsky. Chavez later became an official in the CSO, and eventually its president. He persuaded notoriously apathetic Mexican Americans to register to vote by encouraging them to believe they could change their lives in America.

If you would understand the tension between Mexico and the United States that is playing out along our mutual border, you must understand the psychic tension between Mexican stoicism—if that is a rich enough word for it—and American optimism. On the one side, the Mexican side, Mexican peasants are tantalized by the American possibility of change. On the other side, the American side, the tyranny of American optimism has driven Americans to neurosis and depression, when the dream is elusive or less meaningful than the myth promised. This constitutes the great irony of the Mexican-American border: American sadness has transformed the drug lords of Mexico into billionaires, even as the peasants of Mexico scramble through the darkness to find the American dream.

By the late 1960s, as the first UFW contracts were being signed, Chavez began to brood. Had he spent his poor life only to create a middle class? Lionel Steinberg, the first grape grower to sign with the UFW, was drawn by Chavez's charisma but chagrined at the union's disordered operations. Steinberg wondered: "Is it a social movement or a trade union?" He urged Chavez to use experienced negotiators from the AFL-CIO.

Chavez paid himself an annual wage of $5,000. "You can't change anything if you want to hold on to a good job, a good way of life, and avoid suffering." The world-famous labor leader would regularly complain to his poorly paid staff about the phone bills they ran up and about what he saw as the misuse of a fleet of secondhand UFW cars. He held the union hostage to the purity of his intent. Eliseo Medina, who had become one of the union's most effective organizers, could barely support his young family; he asked Chavez about setting up a trust fund for his infant son. Chavez promised to get back to him but never did. Eventually, thoroughly discouraged by the mismanagement of the union, Medina resigned.

In 1975 Chavez helped to initiate legislation that prohibited the use of the short-handled hoe in the fields—its two-foot-long haft forced farm workers to stoop all day. That achievement would outlast the decline of his union. By the early 1970s, California vegetable growers began signing sweetheart contracts with the rival Teamsters Union. The UFW became mired in scraps with unfriendly politicians in Sacramento. Chavez's attention wandered. He imagined a "Poor Peoples Union" that would reach out to senior citizens and people on welfare. He contacted church officials within the Vatican about the possibility of establishing a lay religious society devoted to service to the poor. Chavez became interested in the Hutterite communities of North America and the Israeli kibbutzim as possible models for such a society.

Chavez visited Synanon, the drug-rehabilitation commune headed by Charles Dederich, shortly before some Synanon members were implicated in a series of sexual scandals and criminal assaults. Chavez borrowed from Synanon a version of a disciplinary practice called the Game, whereby UFW staff members were obliged to stand in the middle of a circle of peers and submit to fierce criticism. Someone sympathetic to Chavez might argue that the Game was an inversion of an ancient monastic discipline meant to teach humility. Someone less sympathetic might conclude that Chavez was turning into a petty tyrant. I think both estimations are true.

From his reading, Chavez would have known that Saint Francis of Assisi desired to imitate the life of Jesus. The followers of Francis desired to imitate the life of Francis. Within ten years of undertaking his mendicant life, Francis had more than one thousand followers. Francis realized he could not administer a growing religious order by personal example. He relinquished the administration of the Franciscans to men who had some talent for organization. Cesar Chavez never gave up his position as head of the UFW.

In 1977 Chavez traveled to Manila as a guest of President Ferdinand Marcos. He ended up praising the old dictator. There were darker problems within the UFW. There were rumors that some within the inner circle were responsible for a car crash that left Cleofas Guzman, an apostate union member, with permanent brain damage.

Chavez spent his last years protesting the use of pesticides in the fields. In April of 1993 he died.

The year after his death, Chavez was awarded the National Medal of Freedom by President Bill Clinton. In 2002 the U.S. Postal Service unveiled a thirty-seven-cent stamp bearing the image of Cesar Chavez. Politicians throughout the West and the Southwest attached Chavez's name to parks and schools and streets and civic buildings of every sort. And there began an effort of mixed success to declare March 31, his birthday, a legal holiday. During the presidential campaign of 2012, President Barack Obama designated the home and burial place of Cesar Chavez in Keene, California, a national monument within the National Park System.

The American hero was also a Mexican saint. In 1997 American painter Robert Lentz, a Franciscan brother, painted an icon, *César Chávez de California*. Chavez is depicted with a golden halo. He holds in his hand a scrolled broadsheet of the U.S. Constitution. He wears a pink sweatshirt bearing the UFW insignia.

That same year, executives at the advertising agency TBWA\Chiat\Day came up with a campaign for Apple computers that featured images of some famous dead—John Lennon, Albert Einstein, Frank Sinatra—alongside a grammar-crunching motto: *Think different*.

I remember sitting in bad traffic on the San Diego freeway one day and looking up to see a photograph of Cesar Chavez on a billboard. His eyes were downcast. He balanced a rake and a shovel on his right shoulder. In the upper-left-hand corner of the billboard was the corporate logo of a bitten apple.

seven

Disappointment

Though California has not inspired the finest American novelists, John Steinbeck's *The Grapes of Wrath* remains one of America's great novels. The native son imagined California from the outside, as a foreigner might; imagined wanting California desperately; imagined California as a remedy for the trial of the nation.

Otherwise, I might think of John Milton when I think of California and the writer's task. Milton devised that, after the Fall, the temperature in San Diego would remain at seventy-five degrees, but Adam and Eve's relationship to a perfect winter day would be changed to one of goose bumps.

The traditional task of the writer in California has been to write about what it means to be human in a place advertised as paradise. Not the Buckeye or the Empire, not the Can-Do or the Show-Me, California is the Post-Lapsarian state. Disappointment has long been the theme of California.

For example, my own:

I cannot afford to live here. I mean I do live here. I rent two large rooms. My light comes from the south. But if I had to move, I could not afford to live here anymore.

In San Francisco, small Victorians, small rooms, steep stairs, are selling for three or four million and are repainted to resemble

Bavarian cuckoo clocks—browns and creams and the mute greens tending to blue. That is my mood. If I owned one of the Victorians, I would, no doubt, choose another comparison. It is like living on a street of cuckoo clocks—and all the cuckoos are on cell phones—I won't say striking thirteen; nevertheless, a version of postmodernity I had not anticipated. Only well-to-do futurists and stuffed T-shirts can afford to live in this nineteenth-century neighborhood.

My complaint with my city is that I am old.

The sidewalks in my neighborhood are uncannily empty save for Mexican laborers and Mexican nannies and Mexican caregivers, and women wearing baseball hats who walk with the exaggerated vigor of a wounded pride (as do I). The streets are in disrepair; the city has no money; really, the streets have never been worse.

Can you imagine Adam and Eve grousing about run-down Eden?

California has been the occasion for disappointment since the 1850s, since men wrote home from the gold fields, from Auburn, from Tulare or Sonora, from tree stumps and tent hotels.

I have no doubt I will prevail here, but you may not think my thicker skin is the proper reformation of an Ohio son. The men here are rough; they grunt and growl and guard their plates with their arms. Now I reach past my neighbor, and grunt, too, and shove, too, and I would cuss just for the pleasure of saying something out loud. I don't believe I have said more than ten words since I came to this place. I realize any oath I might devise would pale next to the colorful flannel they run up here. . . .

And yet the streets are clogged with pickups and delivery vans, cable vans, and the vans of construction workers—certain evidence of prosperity. Crews of men, recently from old countries, work to reconstruct the houses of futurists—houses that were re-constructed not two years ago. One cannot drive down any street without having to go around the pickups and the vans, without muttering under one's breath at the temporary No Parking signs that paper every street, because everyone knows the only reason for the No Parking permits is to enable construction workers to drive to work.

Men from every corner of the world converged on the gold fields in the 1850s, prompting Karl Marx to proclaim the creation of a global society in California, a society unprecedented in the world up to that time. The gold parliament was an achievement of necessity as much as of greed.

Kevin Starr, the preeminent historian of California from the 1850s to the end of the twentieth century, has described California as a chronology of proper names: Stanford. Atherton. Giannini. Disney.

Disappointment came with arrival. Letters went out to the world, diaries, newspaper reports, warnings, laments, together with personal effects—eyeglasses, pen nibs, broken-backed bibles, Spanish Julia's beads—wrapped in soiled canvas. The sto-len claim. Or the fortune squandered. (*Lottie, dear, I have wasted our dream . . .*) The trusting disposition. The false friend. The fog-shrouded wharf. The Spaniard Marquis, etcetera. The ring, the brooch, the opium den, etcetera.

Narratives of disappointment flowed eastward, like an augur-ing smoke, or bumped back over rutted trails, as coffins bump on buckboards, to meet the stories of the desolations of the prairie life, rolled over those, flowed back to the Atlantic shore, where the raw line separating the North and South was beginning to fester.

Nineteenth-century California rewarded only a few of its brotherhood, but it rewarded them as deliriously as an ancient king in an ancient myth would reward. The dream of a lucky chance encouraged a mass migration, toward *"el norte,"* or "gold mountain," or from across the plains of America.

For, as much as California's story was a story of proper names or of luck or election, California was also a story of mass— migrations, unmarked graves, missing persons, accidents. By the time he reaches the 1990s in his great work, Kevin Starr seems to sense an influential shift: The list of singular makers of California gives way to forces of unmaking—to gangs, earthquakes, riots, floods, ballot propositions, stalled traffic.

Disappointment is a fine literary theme—"universal"—as the young high school English teacher, himself disappointed, was fond to say, and it wears like leather.

Disappointment continued to be mined in California's literature throughout the twentieth century. Joan Didion gave us domestic broken-dreamers, not so much driven as driving. In the great Didion essays of the sixties, the mother abandons her daughter on the median of the San Bernardino freeway; dirty dishes pile up in the sink; the hot wind blows from the desert.

The Marxist historian Mike Davis gave us the California Club version of the broken dream—evidence on paper that a deal was cut. The water, the electricity, the coastline—everything can be bought or sold in the Promised Land, and has been.

California's most influential prose has turned out to be that of mystery writers, more in line with John Milton, who regard Eden as only an occasion for temptation and fall. For example, the eighteen-year-old cheerleader from Sioux City returns her engagement ring, a poor-grade sapphire she got from a boy named Herbert (not after the president); cashes in her scholarship to the Teachers College; buys a ticket to L.A., enjoins herself to become the new, the next—*Whaddaya think?*—Jean Harlow. (Ty Burr in *Gods Like Us* remembers so many young women came to California, dreaming of stardom, that Hollywood denominated them as "extra girls.") But the cheerleader ends up a manicurist in Van Nuys; she ends up the blue, blond Jane Doe of the Month in the Hollywood morgue. It requires a private investigator who is broke, dyspeptic, alcoholic, but also something of a Puritan, to want to incriminate California. The golden.

When she retired from the movies in 1933, Clara Bow told reporters: "It wasn't ever like I thought it was going to be. It was always a disappointment."

California's greatest disappointment essay is F. Scott Fitzgerald's *The Crack-Up*—an incautious memoir, meticulous, snide.

What an unenviable prospect, though, to be forced to listen to the same lament—the Hollywood screenwriter's lament—at one o'clock in the morning in the Polo Lounge. I once suffered a very long evening thus, listening to a young man complain, in breath that smelled of boiled eggs for lunch, about the difficulty of being a "serious" writer in a town that idolized Spielberg. It was Spielberg that year; I imagine it still is Spielberg.

Francis Scott Fitzgerald at one o'clock in the morning:

> *I saw that the novel, which at my maturity was the strongest and supplest medium for conveying thought and emotion from one human being to another, was becoming subordinated to a mechanical and communal art that, whether in the hands of Hollywood merchants or Russian idealists, was capable of reflecting only the tritest thought, the most obvious emotion.*

Many decades after Fitzgerald cracked up, I saw with my own eyes a still orbiting fragment of his legend. I saw Sheilah Graham, a tarnished blonde in a black cocktail dress; she floated from table to table at Mr. Chow's restaurant, myopic, bending at the waist to kiss the air behind the ears of revelers. As a public sinner, she was something of a disappointment.

What Fitzgerald was too aureate to imagine was that unfastidious merchants of Hollywood—the ham-fisted, the thick-fingered, the steak-minded—nevertheless could pay somebody (scale) to develop the screenwriter's complaint into a script, into a picture about a pretty-boy screenwriter who ends up floating facedown in a swimming pool on Sunset Boulevard.

The question is: Does California have anything left to say to America, or to the world, or even to itself, beyond disappointment?

True, a vast literature is forming upon the Dewey-decimal Coast. Vietnamese-Californian, Japanese-Californian, Pakistani-Californian, Hispanics, all sorts, including my own. The question many people legitimately ask about this literature is whether our voices describe more than a hyphenated state.

My first literary recognition of California came from reading William Saroyan because Saroyan described the world I recognized. It was as simple as that. Armenian Fresno was related to my Sacramento. It was as simple as that—the extreme Valley heat (outlanders swore they never could stand it; or the flatness, either; or the alfalfa green); also the taste of water from a garden hose—the realization that California, that any life, that my life, therefore, was potentially the stuff of literature.

Here is the quote from Saroyan that I typed and pasted on the inside of my bedroom door, a manifesto:

Try to learn to breathe deeply, really to taste food when you eat, and when you sleep, really to sleep. Try as much as possible to be wholly alive, with all your might, and when you laugh, laugh like hell, and when you get angry, get good and angry. Try to be alive. You will be dead soon enough.

That was Saroyan's "advice to a young writer." I took the advice at a time when I had no expectation of being a writer or any desire or sense of obligation. It comes to me only now, as I type this, that Saroyan's advice has nothing to do with writing; it is advice for any mortal, sentient being.

It would be another two decades before I came upon the words that made me think I had a story to tell—the opening words of Maxine Hong Kingston's *The Woman Warrior:*

"You must not tell anyone," my mother said, "what I am about to tell you."

The immigrant mother's prohibition to her daughter reminded me of my own mother's warning about spreading "family secrets." In the face of California's fame for blatancy—in the face of pervasive light, ingenuousness, glass-and-aluminum housing, bikinis, billboards—Mrs. Hong recommended concealment. Her shrine is a published book.

About this time, Aram Saroyan, William Saroyan's son, published a bitter memoir of his father's last years.

William Saroyan was not on any syllabus I ever saw at Stanford or Berkeley, nor, incidentally, was Steinbeck. Stanford, Berkeley—these were schools established in the nineteenth century by professors from the Ivy League who had come west, like Peace

Corps volunteers, to evangelize California for the Atlantic Enlightenment. So perhaps it was not surprising that, even in the
1960s and '70s, very little attention was paid to California in any
university course, despite the fact that California was in those
years at the center of the national imagination. The only California novel assigned in any course I took, either in college or in
graduate school, was Nathanael West's *The Day of the Locust*, probably because it fulfilled some East Coast expectation that California would come to doom.

And speaking of doom, the editor from *Time* magazine wanted
an essay on California because it was a season (this was fifteen
years ago) when the national newsweeklies were hitting the
stands with titles like "Is the Golden State Tarnished?"

The *Time* editor wanted 750 words' worth of tarnish: "It would
be nice if you could give us a Joan Didion essay."

"What do you mean?" I said.

"You know," she said. "Sardonic."

I unfold and refold that fraying *Time* story whenever I go to
lunch with a California writer, handy to pull out if the conversation turns to New York. When the conversation inevitably turns
to New York.

Anyway, California is getting too old to play the unhappy
child or even the sardonic—too rich, too glued, too Angelica Hus-
ton walking substantially down some steps into the garden—to
play the exuberant, the naïf. And California has grown children
of her own. Two of the most interesting cities in North America
are California daughters: Las Vegas, the open-throttled city, mim-
ics California's youth, when land was cheap and cities were built
in opposition to nature. Tijuana wants so little; she terrifies us for
needing so much.

And: New York, truly, I am sorry to say, is not New York any-

more. I say this having once been the boy who strained—the an-
tenna on our roof raking through the starlight—to catch any
shred of conversation from New York. I watched James Baldwin
interviewed by David Susskind. I watched Norman Mailer chaf-
ing at America on *The Dick Cavett Show*. New York was a conversation. I guess I am stuck there. Buckley and Galbraith, Yale and
Harvard, W. H. Auden and Hermione Gingold.

Unread copies of the *New Yorker* slip and slide on the opposite
end of my couch—damn slippery things. Still, every once in a
while an essential article. When I was in graduate school, and
for many years after, the *New York Review of Books* fed my raven-
ous appetite for Oxbridge-Manhattan conversation. But then . . .
what? I got too old; the conversation got too old. And surely
the world must be larger than New York and London. Even now,
I can pick up right where I left off: *SWM seeks SWF, for argument's sake.*

On an April day in 1970, I saw Dwight Macdonald. We both
were stranded on a concrete island in the middle of Broadway. He
was an old man in a raincoat in the rain. I was a graduate student.
The rain was glorious, tall, immoderate. Everything was glorious.
Broadway. No, I did not dare congratulate Macdonald for his
bravery as a public intellectual, the best of his kind, and for whom
the rain, that day, at least from the look of him, was just one more
goddamned thing. Then the light changed.

Because Irving Kristol correctly predicted the light would
change; that the intellectual center of America would shift from
the shores of the Hudson to the Potomac.

For the writer, the problem of the absence of New York is the
problem of the absence of a critical center, where opinion can be
trusted to support talent or call down the falsely reasoned text.
Washington think tanks are too far gone in the thrall to political

power to provide that center. In the absence of critical structures, where does the young writer from California, or any writer, present herself for review; to what city does she apply for notice and contest? Nowadays, it is not Norman Mailer or James Baldwin who converse on television, it is Mitch McConnell or Harry Reid, and it is poor.

I was once interviewed on C-SPAN during the *Los Angeles Times* Book Festival. Five minutes max, the producer promised. Put this in your ear. Look over there. Five . . . four . . . three . . . two . . . I was standing on a crowded plaza at UCLA between two stalls, one for African American books, another for Latino books. I said to my interviewer, who was in Washington, DC, or a Virginia suburb, which was inside an electronic button, which was inside my ear, that I regretted these two neighboring book booths represented so little understanding of what California is becoming.

The earphone remained as neutral as a can opener.

. . . *I mean California's destiny is marriage. All the races of the world . . .*

Two-second delay. Obviously I have wasted . . . the earphone asked if I was going to attend the Great Debate.

I'm sorry?

"Our viewers are going to watch a debate between California and New York," the earphone enthused (a brightening of tone).

(California would be "represented" by Ms. Arianna Huffington; New York, by Mr. Pete Hamill.)

You'd do better to stage a conversation between Duluth and El Paso.

The earphone paused for an awful moment (*cf.* Bishop Proudie's wife, *Barchester Towers* "suspecting sarcasm") before leaping from my ear.

Americans have been promised—by God, by the Constitution of the United States, by Edna Ferber—that we shall enjoy liberty to pursue happiness. The pursuit constitutes what we have come to call the American Dream.

Americans feel disappointment so keenly because our optimism is so large and is so often insisted upon by historians. And so often justified by history. The stock market measures optimism. If you don't feel optimistic, there must be something wrong with you. There are pills for disappointment.

The California Dream was a codicil to the American Dream, an opening. Internal immigrants sought from California at least a softer winter, a wider sky; at least a thousand miles' distance between themselves and whatever dissatisfaction they felt with "home."

Midwestern California, the California of internal immigrants, was everywhere apparent when I was growing up—in the nervous impulse to build and to live in a house that had never been lived in or died in; where the old lady never spilled milk, the dog never died, the bully never lurked behind the elm tree; where widows and discomfited children never stared at the moon through runny glass, or listened to the wind at night. This California was created by newcomers from Illinois and Nebraska, and it shaped my life. This was California as America's America.

Simultaneous with Midwestern California was the California of Maxine Hong Kingston and William Saroyan, and of my Mexican mother and father and my uncle from India; a California of family secrets, yes, unorthodox ingredients—turmeric, cilantro, curry, *Santa Maria Purisima*—but also some surpassing relief at having found in California a blind from tragedy. The relief California offered immigrants from other countries was comparable to the imagined restoration of the Joads. Though we lived next door to it, to the California of Nebraska and Illinois, ours was a California far removed from the drama of Midwestern disappointment, from the all-new-and-why-am-I-not-happy?

Thus, in my lifetime, I experienced two Californias concurrently. I discovered (because I was attuned to) a sort of hybrid of these two Californias in the writings of John Muir. Muir was born in Scotland; he moved with his family to Wisconsin when he was eleven. Muir saw California with a Midwesterner's delight in the refulgence of it—he called California "the grand side of the mountain." Yet I recognized in John Muir as well the quiet, grateful voice of the immigrant from overseas. Muir sailed into California. He first saw the coastline, as if through Pacific eyes; he saw immediately the implication of the coastline: California (and America) is finite.

When I grew up in the 1950s, freeways offered freedom from implication. California was neurotically rebuilding itself as an ever-rangier house in a further-flung subdivision. As a loyal son of California, I believed in all this, in the "new" and the other "E-Z" adjectives real estate agents employed to lure Midwesterners. And though the advertisement the real estate developer placed in the Midwestern newspaper was not a bluff, too many people believed, too many people came. The traffic on the freeway slowed from Jetsons to "Now what?" to Sig-alert.

What is obsolete now in California is the future. For a century and a half, Americans spoke of California as the future when they wanted to escape inevitability. Now the future attaches consequences and promises constriction. Technocrats in Sacramento warn of a future that is overwhelmed by students, pollution, immigrants, cars, fluorocarbons, old people. Or the future is diminished—water quality, soil quality, air quality, education quality, highway quality, life quality. There are not enough doctors for the state's emergency rooms; not enough blue parking spaces outside; not enough oil, not enough electricity. More blackouts, more brownouts; too many air conditioners, too few houses; frogs on the verge of extinction, a fugitive middle class. To the rest of the nation, California now represents what the nation fears to become. A state without a white center.

The brilliance of Midwestern California, the California that is founded upon discontent, and the reason why so much technological innovation springs from the West Coast, is that having confronted the finitude of the coastline, technologists in Silicon Valley have shrunk the needed commodity—the future (thousands of miles of Zen pathway)—to the size of a fleck of gold dust, to a microchip.

A few months ago, I went to have dinner in Menlo Park, where I met a young man who wore a linen jacket of the very blackest label and the scent of the winner's circle. He owns, very firmly owns, I imagine, on sheaves of legal-sized hard copy, electronic portals (virtual) through which the most ephemeral chatter and the finest thoughts of humankind pass as undifferentiated "content." I imagine Ensor's painting of *Christ's Entry into Brussels* at the Getty.

When I answered the young man's uninterested inquiry by identifying myself as a writer, his only response was to recommend I consign every published sentence I now guard with copyright onto the Web and give it away. *No one owns an idea in this age,* was his advice (and all of a sudden he sounded like someone one would have met on a riverboat). Except his idea, of course.

The young man's fortune comes not from the "content" his technology conveys, or conveys a quester toward, but rather from the means of conveyance—or, no, not even that. He will make more money by, at intervals, changing some aspect of conveyance or by padlocking the old portal (I imagine the Suez Canal) so that people have to pay to modify their means of access. He is set on weaning the minds of youth from the snares of merchandisers ("middlemen" he quaintly calls them). Young people are conveyed to the belief they should obtain intellectual property without paying for it, and without packaging. Packaging is sentimentality.

The young man is content to disassemble, by making "free," all intellectual property and factories of intellectual properties (recording studios, for example, or publishing houses), and all clearinghouses of intellectual properties (such as New York, such as Los Angeles, such as Harvard, such as the Library of Congress), in order that he can charge advertisers more for his arch or his gondola or his Victorian bathing machine.

The technologist now publishes to the world that place is over. California used to be the summation of the expansionist dream; now we foretell constriction. The future has been condensed to the head of a pin. Not Go West, not even Go Home. Rather, stay at home. Run in place. You are still connected, whether you are in the air or on a train or never leave Wisconsin. The great invention—rather, the refinement—of Silicon Valley is iPortability.

For a long season, California was the most important purveyor of narrative to the world. Hollywood was filled with stories in the last century, stories bought and sold, more stories than anyone could listen to or use. When other lures to California were exhausted or quieted down, Hollywood became its own narrative, became the golden dream; people wanted, literally, "to get into the pictures."

But in a California where place is irrelevant, narrative is finished. California is finished. (Narrative "takes place.") And whereas narrative used to take precedence, the argument in Hollywood now is not about the truth of a narrative, or even the salability of a narrative, but about which product format is going to pay off.

Toward the end of dinner, the optimistic young man from Silicon Valley, having imbibed a liter or so of Napa Valley pish-posh '69, got around to his detestation of the congestion of California. In the end, it would appear, he has to live in a real body, in real space, and in real time, and buckled into his hundred-thousand-dollar funk: "Traffic is a bitch every fucking morning."

. . . When you get angry, get good and angry. Try to be alive. You will be dead soon enough.

I, too, was an optimist. Well, I took Saroyan's pronouncement for optimism. Like many children of immigrant parents, Saroyan and I grew up among shadows, grotesque shadows thrown from a grandmother's stories, stories that might show us up as foreigners if they ever saw the light of day. How could the Saroyan boy in Fresno not be beguiled in the direction of games and sunlight? And then limelight? And then Paris?

I saw him once, in Tillman Place Bookshop in San Francisco, a bookstore made of wood, now long gone. He dressed like a stage bohemian; he wore a walrus mustache, and a fedora hat, and his cashmere coat rested upon his shoulders. He threw back his head to bellow, by which gesture he represented mirth. He was entirely admirable and theatrical. Saroyan's literary persona remained that of a carefree bon vivant, at ease with the world and delighted by it, tasting, breathing, laughing like hell. He'd never be a Princeton man—so what?

The legend: William Saroyan, the old man of Fresno, California, and Paris, France, was haunted by the early promise of himself. Critics had withheld from the middle-aged man the praise they once lavished on the youth. He was the same man. What gives? He became dark-minded and spiteful and stingy and mistrustful of friends and family and agents and stockbrokers and the IRS. The world smelled spoiled to him. He felt passed over by the world that mattered, the small, glittering, passing world.

The last time I was in Fresno, about a year ago, I gave a luncheon address at the African American Historical and Cultural Museum to a roomful of journalists from ethnic newspapers and radio and television stations. (The Pakistani radio station in San Diego. The Iranian television station in L.A. The *Oaxacan*. The *Mandarin*.) Everyone in the room spoke interestedly of a California that was crowded with voices, most of which they could not translate but they knew implicated them. No one knew what I was asking when I asked where Saroyan had lived.

The question for the night is the question of content, I think, not conveyance. A new generation of writers in California will not speak of separate neighborhoods, certainly not of brown hills and dairy cows, or of the taste of water from a hose, or of the sound of train whistles at night. Nor will they dote on New York, as I doted on New York. Oh, maybe they will, why deny them that? Perhaps New York will be Shanghai.

In the time of your life, live, was Saroyan's advice. I believe the difference between the literature of California's past and the literature to come will be the difference of expectation. There are children growing up in California today who take it as a given that the 101 North, the 405 South, and the 10 East are unavailable after two in the afternoon.

eight

Final Edition

A scholar I know, a woman who is ninety-six years old, grew up in a tar-paper shack on the American prairie, near the Canadian border. She learned to read from the pages of the *Chicago Tribune* in a one-room schoolhouse. Her teacher, who had no more than an eighth-grade education, had once been to Chicago—had been to the opera! Women in Chicago went to the opera with bare shoulders and wore long gloves, the teacher imparted to her pupils. Because the teacher had once been to Chicago, she subscribed to the Sunday edition of the *Chicago Tribune* that came on the train by Tuesday, Wednesday at the latest.

Several generations of children learned to read from that text. The schoolroom had a wind-up phonograph, its bell shaped like a morning glory, and one record, from which a distant female voice sang "Ah, Sweet Mystery of Life."

Is it better to have or to want? My friend says that her teacher knew one great thing: There was something out there. She told her class she did not expect to see even a fraction of what the world had to offer. But she hoped they might.

I became a reader of the *San Francisco Chronicle* when I was in high school and lived ninety miles inland, in Sacramento. On my way home from school, twenty-five cents bought me a connection with a gray maritime city at odds with the postwar California suburbs. Herb Caen, whose column I read immediately—second section, corner left—invited me into the provincial cosmopolitanism that characterized the city's outward regard: "Isn't it nice that people who prefer Los Angeles to San Francisco live there?"

Newspapers have become deadweight commodities linked to other media commodities in chains that are coupled or uncoupled by accountants and lawyers and executive vice presidents and boards of directors in offices thousands of miles from where the man bit the dog and drew ink. The *San Francisco Chronicle* is owned by the Hearst Corporation, once the *Chronicle*'s archrival. The Hearst Corporation has its headquarters in New York City. According to Hearst, the *Chronicle* has been losing a million dollars a week. In San Francisco there have been buyouts and firings of truck drivers, printers, reporters, artists, editors, critics. With a certain élan, the *San Francisco Chronicle* has taken to publishing letters from readers who remark the diminishing pleasure or usefulness of the *San Francisco Chronicle*.

When a newspaper dies in America, it is not simply that a commercial enterprise has failed; a sense of place has failed. If the *San Francisco Chronicle* is near death—and why else would the editors celebrate its 144th anniversary, and why else would the editors devote a week to feature articles on fog?—it is because San Francisco's sense of itself as a city is perishing.

Most newspapers that are dying today were born in the nineteenth century. The *Seattle Post-Intelligencer* died 2009, born 1863. The *Rocky Mountain News* died 2009, born 1859. The *Ann Arbor News* died 2009, born 1835. It was the pride and the function of the American newspaper in the nineteenth century to declare the forming congregation of buildings and services a city—a place busy enough or populated enough to have news. Frontier American journalism preserved a vestige of the low-church impulse toward universal literacy whereby the new country imagined it could read and write itself into existence. We were the Gutenberg Nation.

Nineteenth-century newspapers draped bunting about their mastheads and brandished an inflated diction and a Gothic type to name themselves the *Herald,* the *Eagle,* the *Tribune,* the *Mercury,* the *Globe,* the *Sun.* With the passage of time, the name of the city was commonly attached to the name of the newspaper, not only to distinguish the *Alexandria Gazette* from the *New York Gazette,* but because the paper described the city and the city described the paper.

The *Daily Dramatic Chronicle,* precursor to the *San Francisco Chronicle,* was founded in 1865 by two teenaged brothers on a borrowed twenty-dollar gold piece. Charles and Michael de Young (a third brother, Gustavus, was initially a partner in the publishing venture) had come west from St. Louis with their widowed mother. In California, the brothers invented themselves as descendants of French aristocracy. They were adolescents of extraordinary gumption at a time when San Francisco was a city of gumption and of stranded young men.

Karl Marx wrote that Gold Rush California was "thickly populated by men of all races, from the Yankee to the Chinese, from the Negro to the Indian and Malay, from the Creole and Mestizo to the European." Oscar Wilde seconded Karl Marx: "It's an odd thing, but everyone who disappears is said to be in San Francisco." What must Gold Rush San Francisco have been like? Melville's Nantucket? Burning Man? An arms bazaar in Yemen? There were Russians, Chileans, Frenchmen, Welshmen, and Mexicans. There were Australian toughs, the worst of the lot by most accounts— "Sydney Ducks"—prowling the waterfront. There were Chinese opium dens beneath the streets and Chinese Opera Houses above them. Historians relish the old young city's foggy wharves and alleyways, its frigates, fleas, mud, and hazard. Two words attached to the lawless city the de Young brothers moved about in. One was "vigilante," from the Spanish. The other was "hoodlum"—a word coined in San Francisco to name the young men loitering about corners, threatening especially to the Chinese—the most exotic foreigners in a city of foreigners.

The de Young brothers named their newspaper the *Daily Dramatic Chronicle* because stranded young men seek entertainment. The city very early developed a taste for limelight that was as urgent as its taste for red light. In 1865 there were competing opera houses in the city; there were six or seven or twelve theaters. The *Daily Dramatic Chronicle* was a theatrical sheet delivered free of charge to the city's saloons and cafés and reading rooms. San Francisco desperately appreciated minstrel shows and circuses and melodeons and Shakespeare. Stages were set up in gambling halls and saloons where Shakespearian actors, their velvets much the worse for wear, pointed to a ghost rising at the back of the house: *Peace, break thee off. Look where it comes again.*

I know an Italian who came to San Francisco to study medicine in 2003. He swears he saw the ghost of a forty-niner, in early light, when he woke in an old house out by the ocean. The forty-niner was very young, my friend said, with a power of sadness about him. He did not speak. He had red hair and wore a dark shirt.

We can imagine marooned opera singers, not of the second, perhaps not even of the third, rank, enunciating elaborate prayers and curses from the Italian repertoire as they stumbled among the pebbles and stones of cold running creeks on their way to perform in Gold Rush towns along the American River. It was as though the grandiose nineteenth-century musical form sought its natural echo in the canyons of the Sierra Nevada. The miners loved opera. (Puccini reversed the circuit and took David Belasco's melodrama of the Gold Rush back to Europe as *La Fanciulla del West*.)

In 1860 San Francisco had a population of 57,000. By 1870 the population had almost tripled to 149,000. Within three years of its founding, by 1868, the *Daily Dramatic Chronicle* would evolve with its hormonal city to become the *Daily Morning Chronicle*. The de Young brothers were in their early twenties. Along with theatrical and operatic listings, the *Chronicle* then published news of ships sailing into and out of the bay and the dollar equivalents of treasure in their holds, and bank robberies, and saloon shootings, and gold strikes, and drownings, an extraordinary number of suicides, likewise fires, for San Francisco was a wooden city, as it still is in many of its districts.

It is still possible, very occasionally, to visit the Gold Rush city when one attends a crowded theater. Audiences here, more than in any city I know, possess a wit in common and can react as one—in pleasure, but also in derision. I often think our impulse toward hoot and holler might be related to our founding sense of isolation, to our being "an oasis of civilization in the California desert," in the phrase of Addison DeWitt (in *All About Eve*) who, though a Hollywood figment, is about as good a rendition as I can summon of the sensibility ("New York critics") we have courted here for 150 years. And deplored.

The nineteenth-century city felt itself surrounded by vacancy— to the west, the gray court of the Pacific; to the east, the Livermore Valley, the San Joaquin Valley, the Sierra Nevada range. Shipping and mining were crucial to the wealth of the city, but they were never the consolations the city sought. The city looked, rather, to Addison DeWitt—to the eastern United States, to Europe—for approbation. If there was a pathetic sense of insecurity in living at the edge of the continent—San Francisco proclaiming itself "The Paris of the Pacific"!—the city also raised men of visionary self-interest who squinted into the distance and conceived of opening trade to Asia or cutting down redwood forests or laying track across a sea of yellow grass.

Readers in other parts of the country were fascinated by any scrap of detail about the Gold Rush city. Here is a fragment (July 9, 1866) from Bret Harte's dispatch to readers of the *Springfield Republican* (from a collection of such dispatches edited by Gary Scharnhorst). The description remains accurate:

> Midsummer! . . . To dwellers in Atlantic cities, what visions of heated pavements, of staring bricks, of grateful shade trees, of straw hats and white muslin, are conjured up in this word . . . In San Francisco it means equal proportions of fog and wind. On the evening of the Fourth of July it was a pleasant and instructive sight to observe the population, in great-coats and thick shawls, warming themselves by bonfires, watching the sky-rockets lose themselves in the thick fog, and returning soberly home to their firesides and warm blankets.

From its inception, the *San Francisco Chronicle* borrowed a tone of merriment and swagger from the city it daily invented—on one occasion with fatal consequences: In 1879 the *Chronicle* ran an exposé of the Reverend Isaac Smith Kalloch, a recent arrival to the city ("driven forth from Boston like an Unclean Leper") who had put himself up as a candidate for mayor. The *Chronicle* recounted Kalloch's trial for adultery in Massachusetts ("his escapade with one of the Tremont Temple choristers"). Kalloch responded by denouncing the "bawdy house breeding" of the de Young boys, implying that Charles and Michael's mother kept a whorehouse in St. Louis. Charles rose immediately to his mother's defense; he shot Kalloch, who recovered and won City Hall. De Young never served jail time. A year later, in 1880, Kalloch's son shot and killed Charles de Young in the offices of the *Chronicle*.

"Hatred of de Young is the first and best test of a gentleman," Ambrose Bierce later remarked of Michael, the surviving brother. However just or unjust Bierce's estimation, the de Young brothers lived and died according to their notion of a newspaper's purpose—that it should entertain and incite the population.

In 1884 Michael was shot by Adolph Spreckels, the brother of a rival newspaper publisher and the son of the sugar magnate Claus Spreckels, after the *Chronicle* accused the Spreckels Sugar Company of labor practices in Hawaii amounting to slavery. De Young was not mortally wounded, and Spreckels was acquitted on a claim of reasonable cause.

When he died in 1925, Michael de Young bequeathed the ownership of the *Chronicle* to his four daughters with the stipulation that it could not be sold out of the family until the death of the last surviving daughter.

San Francisco gentility has roots as shallow and as belligerent as those of the Australian blue gum trees that were planted heedlessly throughout the city and now configure and scent our Sunday walks. In 1961 *Holiday* magazine came to town to devote an entire issue to San Francisco. The three living daughters of Michael de Young were photographed seated on an antique highbacked causeuse in the gallery of the old M. H. de Young Memorial Museum their father had donated to the city to house his collection of paintings and curiosities (including a scabrous old mummy beloved of generations of schoolchildren—now considered too gauche to be displayed). For the same issue, Alma de

Bretteville Spreckels, widow of Adolph, was photographed taking tea in her Pacific Heights mansion in what looks to be a fur-trimmed, floor-length velvet gown. The Spreckels family donated to the city a replica of the Palais de la Légion d'Honneur in Paris to house a collection of European paintings and rooms and furniture. One Spreckels and three de Youngs make four Margaret Dumonts—a San Francisco royal flush.

In 1972 the museum donated by Michael de Young merged with the museum created by the family of the man who tried to murder Michael de Young to become the Fine Arts Museums of San Francisco.

Men, usually men, who assumed the sole proprietorships of newspapers in the nineteenth century were the sort of men to be attracted by the way a newspaper could magnify an already fatted ego. Newspaper publishers were accustomed to lord over cities.

William Randolph Hearst was given the *San Francisco Examiner* by his father, a mining millionaire and U.S. senator, who may, or may not, have won it in a poker game in 1880. As it happened, young Hearst was born to run a newspaper. He turned the *Examiner* into the largest-circulation paper in San Francisco before he moved on to New York where, in 1895, he acquired the *New York Journal*. Hearst quickly engaged a yellow-journalism rivalry with Joseph Pulitzer's *New York World*. Both Hearst and Pulitzer assumed political careers. Hearst served in the Congress of the United States ("served" is not quite the word), as did Pulitzer, briefly.

We remember Joseph Pulitzer not as a sensationalist journalist but as the philanthropist who endowed an award for excellence in journalism and the arts. We remember William Randolph Hearst because his castle overlooking the Pacific—fifty miles of ocean frontage—is as forthright a temple to grandiosity as this nation can boast. And we remember Hearst as the original for Orson Welles's Citizen Kane. Welles portrayed John Foster Kane with the mix of populism and egomania audiences of the time easily recognized as Hearst. Kane, the champion of the common man, becomes Kane the autocrat. Kane builds an opera house for his paramour. Kane invents a war.

Citizen Kane told the story of a newspaper publisher's rise and fall in one generation. A more accurate rendition of the American newspaper saga would require an account of the long dissolution of the nineteenth-century enterprise. Although John Foster Kane has a son—we briefly see the boy, and we see that he will most likely be his mama's boy—the son is removed from the narrative early on (he dies in a car crash with his mother). We can only imagine that Kane's son, grown to manhood, might have resembled Otis Chandler, the utterly golden publisher of the Los Angeles Times, who, in retirement, was unable to prevent family members from selling the paper to the Tribune Company in 2000. The saga of American journalism in the twentieth century became a story of children and grandchildren and lawyers. McClatchy, Scripps Howard, Copley, Gannett—newspaper consortiums formed as families sold off the nineteenth century.

The San Francisco Chronicle and the San Francisco Examiner were both losing money when, in 1965, Charles Thieriot, grandson of Michael de Young, met with William Randolph Hearst Jr. to collaborate on what they called the San Francisco Newspaper Agency. The agency was a third entity designed to share production and administrative costs. The papers were to maintain editorial discretion and separate staffs. In addition, an incoherent Sunday edition shuffled together sections from both the Chronicle and the *Examiner*. The terms of the publishers' agreement eventually favored the afternoon Hearst newspaper, for the *Examiner* was soon to fall behind, to become the lesser newspaper in a two-paper town. The *Examiner*, nevertheless, continued to collect half the profits of both.

In January 1988, Phyllis Tucker, the last surviving daughter of Michael de Young, died in San Francisco. Tucker's daughter, Nan Tucker McEvoy, managed to forestall the sale of the paper for several years. But in 1999, the founding publisher's posthumous grip was pried loose by a majority vote of family members to sell. At that time, the Hearst Corporation was desirous of reclaiming the San Francisco market. Hearst paid $660 million to the de Young heirs for the *San Francisco Chronicle*.

To satisfy antitrust concerns of the Justice Department, the Hearst Corporation sold the still-extant San Francisco *Examiner* to the politically connected Fang family, owners of *AsianWeek*, the oldest and largest English-language Asian American newspaper. The Hearst Corporation paid the Fangs a subsidy of $66 million to run the *Examiner*. Florence Fang placed her son Ted Fang in the editor's chair. Within a year, Florence Fang fired her son; Ted Fang threatened to sue his mother. In 2004 the Fang family sold the *Examiner* to Philip Anschutz, a scattershot entrepreneur from Colorado who deflated William Randolph Hearst's "Monarch of the Dailies" to a freebie tabloid that gets delivered to houses up and down the street twice a week, willy-nilly, and litters the floors of San Francisco municipal buses.

The day after I was born in San Francisco, my tiny existential fact was noted in several of the papers that were barked through the downtown streets. In truth, the noun "newspaper" is something of a misnomer. More than purveyors only of news, American newspapers were entrusted to be keepers of public record—papers were daily or weekly cumulative almanacs of tabular information. A newspaper's morgue was scrutable evidence of the existence of a city. Newspapers published obituaries and they published birth announcements. They published wedding announcements and bankruptcy notices. They published weather forecasts (even in San Francisco, where on most days the weather is optimistic and unremarkable—fog clearing by noon). They published the fire department's log and high school basketball scores. In a port city like San Francisco, there were listings of the arrivals and departures of ships. None of this constituted news exactly; it was a record of a city's mundane progress. News was old as soon as it was dry—"fishwrap," Herb Caen often called it.

Unwilling to forfeit any fraction of my quarter, I even studied the classifieds—unrelieved columns laid out like city blocks: *Room for rent. Marina. No pets. File Clerk position. Heavy phones. Ticket agent for busy downtown box office. Must be bonded. Norman, we're still here.* Only once did I find the titillation I was looking for, a listing worthy of a barbershop magazine, an *Argosy,* or a Mickey Spillane's: *Ex-Green Beret will do anything legal for cash.* Newspapers were sustained by classifieds, as well as by department-store ads and automobile ads. I admired the urbanity of the drawings of newspaper ads in those years, and I took from them a conception of the posture of downtown San Francisco. Despite glimpses into the classified life of the city, despite the hauteur of ad-art mannerism, the *Chronicle* offered some assurance (to an adolescent such as I was) it would have been difficult for me to describe. I will call it now an implied continuity. There was continuity in the comics and on the sports page, but nowhere more than in the columns.

During Scott Newhall's tenure as executive editor, from 1952 to

1971, the *Chronicle* achieved something of a golden age. Newhall was flamboyant in ways that were congenial to the city. At a time when the *Los Angeles Times* was attracting admiration from the East Coast for its fleet of foreign bureaus, Newhall reverted to an eighteenth-century model of a newspaper as first-person observer.

For nearly two decades the city that prized its singularity was entertained by idiosyncratic voices. At the shallow end of the *Chronicle*'s roster (under the cipher of a coronet) appeared Count Marco, a Liberace of the typewriter who concerned himself with fashion and beauty and *l'amour*. At the deep end—a snug corner at Gino and Carlo's bar in North Beach—sat "Charles McCabe, Esq.," an erudite connoisseur of books, spirits, and failed marriages. Terrence O'Flaherty watched television. Stanton Delaplane, to my mind the best writer among them, wrote "Postcard"—a travel series with charm and humor. Art Hoppe concocted political satire. Harold Gilliam expounded on wind and tide and fog. Alfred Frankenstein was an art critic of international reputation. There was a book column by William Hogan and a society column by Frances Moffat. Allan Temko wrote architectural criticism against the grain of the city's sensibility, a sensibility he sometimes characterized as a liberal spirit at odds with a timorous aesthetic. All the *Chronicle* columnists and critics had constituents, but the name above the banner was Herb Caen.

Herb Caen began writing a column for the *Chronicle* before the Second World War. At that time, Caen was in his twenties and probably resembled the fresh, fast-talking smarty-pants he pitched his voice to portray in print. *Item . . . item . . . who's gotta item?* In 1950 he was lured over to the *Examiner* at a considerable hike in salary, and circulation followed at his heels. He knew all the places; he knew the maître d's, the bartenders, the bouncers, the flower-sellers, the cops, the madams, the shopkeepers—knew them in the sense that they all knew him and knew he could be dangerous. In 1958 Caen returned to the *Chronicle* and, again, circulation tilted.

Each day except Saturday, for forty years, Caen set the conversation for San Francisco. Who was in town. Who was in the hospital and would appreciate a card. Who was seen drinking champagne out of a rent boy's tennis shoe. His last column began: "And how was your Christmas?" He convinced hundreds of thousands of readers (crowded on buses, on the way to work) that his was the city we lived in. Monday through Friday, Caen was an omniscient table-hopping bitch. On Sunday, he dropped all that; he reverted to an ingenue—a sailor on leave, a sentimental flaneur infatuated with his dream "Baghdad by the Bay." The point of the Sunday perambulation was simple relish—fog clearing by noon; evidence that the mystical, witty, sourdough city had survived one more week.

After a time, Caen stopped writing Sunday panegyrics; he said it was not the same city anymore, and it wasn't. He wasn't. Caen was quoted in newspaper and magazine interviews admitting that Los Angeles, even San Jose—two cities created by suburbanization—had become more influential in the world than the "cool, grey city of love"—a George Sterling line Caen favored. The Chinese city did not figure in Caen's novel, except atmospherically—lanterns and dragons, chorus girls at the Forbidden City, Danny Kaye taking over the kitchen at Kan's, that sort of thing. The growing Filipino, Latin American city did not figure at all.

In Caen's heyday, the *San Francisco Chronicle* reflected the self-infatuated city. But it was not the city entire that drew the world's attention. In the 1950s, the version of San Francisco that interested the world was Jack Kerouac's parish—a few North Beach coffee-houses habituated by beatniks (a word Caen coined) and City Lights Bookstore. By the time I was a teenager, the path to City Lights was electrified by the marquees of topless clubs and bad wolves with flashlights beckoning passersby toward red velvet curtains. Anyway, the scene had moved by that time to the fog-shrouded Grateful Dead concerts in Golden Gate Park and to the Haight-Ashbury. A decade later, the most famous neighborhood in the city was the homosexual Castro District. San Francisco never seemed to grow old the way other cities grew old.

In 1967 the *Chronicle*'s rock and jazz critic, Ralph J. Gleason, teamed up with a renegade cherub named Jann Wenner to publish *Rolling Stone* magazine. What this disparate twosome intuited was that by chronicling the rising influence of rock music, they were effectively covering a revolution. In New York, writers were culti-vating, in the manner of Thackeray, a self-referential point of view and calling it the "New Journalism." In San Francisco, *Rolling Stone* was publishing a gospel "I" that found itself in a world without precedent: Greil Marcus, Cameron Crowe, Patti Smith, Timothy Ferris, Hunter S. Thompson. I remember sitting in an Indian tea shop in South London in 1970 (in the manner of the New Journal-ism) and being gripped by envy potent enough to be called home-sickness as I read John Burks's account of the Stones concert at Altamont. It was like reading a dispatch from the Gold Rush city.

One morning in the 1970s, the *Chronicle* began to publish Ar-mistead Maupin's *Tales of the City*—adding sex and drugs and lo-cal branding to the nineteenth-century gimmick of serial fiction. At a time when American families were trending to the suburbs, Maupin's novel insisted that San Francisco was still magnetic for single lives. In those same years, Cyra McFadden was writing sa-tirically about the sexual eccentricities of suburban Marin County in a series ("The Serial") for an alternative newspaper called the *Pacific Sun*.

In those same years, Joan Didion wrote in *The White Album* that for many people in Los Angeles "the Sixties ended abruptly on August 9, 1969, ended at the exact moment when word of the [Manson family] murders on Cielo Drive traveled like brushfire through the community." To borrow for a moment the oracular deadpan: In San Francisco, the sixties came to the end for many people in 1977, when Jann Wenner packed up and moved *Rolling Stone* to New York. As he departed, the moss-covered wunder-kind griped to a young reporter standing by that San Francisco was a "provincial backwater."

What no one could have imagined in 1977, not even Jann Wenner, was that a suburban industrial region thirty miles to the south of the city contained an epic lode. Silicon Valley would, within twenty years, become the capital of Nowhere. What no one could have imagined in 1977 was that San Francisco would be-come a bedroom community for a suburban industrial region that lay thirty miles to the south.

Don't kid a kidder. Herb Caen died in 1997. With the loss of that daily hectoring voice, the *Chronicle* seemed to lose its narrative thread, as did the city. The *Chronicle* began to reprint Caen col-umns, to the bewilderment of anyone younger than thirty.

If you die in San Francisco, unless you are judged notable by our know-nothing newspaper (it is unlikely you will be judged nota-ble unless your obituary has already appeared in the *Washington Post* or the *New York Times*), your death will be noted in a paid obituary submitted to the *Chronicle* by your mourners. More likely, there will be no public notice taken at all. As much as any vacancy in the *Chronicle* I can point to, the dearth of obituaries measures its decline.

In the nineteenth-century newspaper, the relationship between observer and observed was reciprocal: The newspaper described the city; the newspaper, in turn, was sustained by readers who were curious about the strangers that circumstance had placed proximate to them. So, I suppose, it is incomplete to notice that the *San Francisco Chronicle* has become remiss in its obituary department. Of four friends of mine who died recently in San Francisco, not one wanted a published obituary or any other public notice taken of his absence. This seems to me a serious abrogation of the responsibility of living in a city and as good an explanation as any of why newspapers are dying. All four of my friends requested cremation; three wanted their ashes consigned to the obscurity of Nature. Perhaps the cemetery is as doomed in America as the newspaper, and for the same reason: We do not imagine death as a city.

We no longer imagine the newspaper as a city or the city as a newspaper. Whatever I may say in the rant that follows, I do not believe the decline of newspapers has been the result solely of computer technology or the Internet. The forces working against newspapers are probably as varied and foregone as the Model T Ford and the birth-control pill. We like to say that the invention of the internal-combustion engine changed us, changed the way we live. In truth, we built the Model T Ford because we had changed; we wanted to remake the world to accommodate our restlessness. We might now say: Newspapers will be lost because technology will force us to acquire information in new ways. In that case, who will tell us what it means to live as citizens of Seattle or Denver or Ann Arbor?

The truth is we no longer want to live in Seattle or Denver or Ann Arbor. Our inclination has led us to invent a digital cosmopolitanism that begins and ends with "I." Careening down Geary Boulevard on the 38 bus, I can talk to my dear Auntie in Delhi or I can view snapshots of my cousin's wedding in Recife or I can listen to girl punk from Glasgow. The cost of my cyber-urban experience is disconnection from body, from presence, from city.

A few months ago, there was an item in the paper about a young woman so plugged into her personal sounds and her texting apparatus that she stepped off the curb and was mowed down by a honking bus.

When he was mayor of San Francisco, Gavin Newsom was quoted in the *Economist* concerning the likelihood that San Francisco would soon be a city without a newspaper: "People under thirty won't even notice."

The other day I came upon a coffeehouse on Noe Street that resembled, as I judged from its nineteenth-century exterior, the sort of café where the de Young brothers might have distributed their paper. The café was only a couple of blocks from the lively gay ambiance of upper Market Street, yet far removed from the clamorous San Francisco of the nineteenth century. Several men and women sat alone at separate tables. No one spoke. The café advertised free Wi-Fi; all but one of the customers had laptops open before them. (The exception was playing solitaire with a real deck of cards.) The only sounds were the hissing of an espresso machine and the clattering of a few saucers. A man in his forties, sitting by the door, stared at a screen upon which a cartoon animal, perhaps a dog, loped silently.

I should mention that the café, like every coffeehouse in the city, had stacks of the *Bay Guardian*, *S.F. Weekly*, the *Bay Area Reporter*—free and roughly equivalent to the *Daily Dramatic*

Chronicle of yore. I should mention that San Francisco has always been a city of stranded youth, and the city's free newspapers continue to announce entertainments for youth:

> *Gosta Berling, Kid Mud, Skeletal System El Rio. 8 p.m., $5. Davis Jones, Eric Andersen and Tyler Stafford, Melissa McClelland Hotel Utah. 8 p.m., $7. Ben Kweller, Jones Street Station, Princeton Slim's. 8:30 p.m., $19. Harvey Mandel and the Snake Crew Biscuits and Blues. 8 p.m., $16. Queers, Mansfields, Hot Toddies, Atom Age Bottom of the Hill. 8:30 p.m., $12.*

The colleague I am meeting for coffee tells me (occasioned by my puzzlement at the Wi-Fi séance) that more and more often he is finding sex on craigslist. As you know better than I do, one goes to craigslist to sell or to buy an old couch or a concert ticket or to look for a job. But also to arrange for sexual Lego with a body as free of narrative as possible. (*Im bored 26-Oakland-east.*)

Another friend, a journalist born in India, who has heard me connect newspapers with place once too often, does not dispute my argument but neither is he troubled by it: "If I think of what many of my friends and I read these days, it is still a newspaper, but it is clipped and forwarded in bits and pieces on e-mail—a story from the *New York Times*, a piece from *Salon*, a blog from the *Huffington Post*, something from the *Times of India*, from YouTube. It is like a giant newspaper being assembled at all hours, from every corner of the world, still with news but no roots in a place. Perhaps we do not need a sense of place anymore."

So what is lost? Only bricks and mortar. (The contemptuous reply.) Cities are bricks and mortar. Cities are bricks and mortar and bodies. In Chicago, women go to the opera with bare shoulders.

Something funny I have noticed—perhaps you have noticed it,

too. You know what futurists and online-ists and cut-out-the-middle-man-ists and Davos-ists and deconstructionists of every stripe want for themselves? They want exactly what they tell you you no longer need, you pathetic, overweight, disembodied Kindle reader. They want white linen tablecloths on trestle tables in the middle of vineyards on soft blowy afternoons. (*You* can click your bottle of wine online. Cheaper.) They want to go shopping on Saturday afternoons on the Avenue Victor Hugo; they want the pages of their *New York Times* all kind of greasy from croissant crumbs and butter at a café table in Aspen; they want to see their names in hard copy in the "New Establishment" issue of *Vanity Fair;* they want a nineteenth-century bookshop; they want to see the plays in London; they want to float down the Nile in a felucca; they want five-star bricks and mortar and Do Not Disturb signs and views of the park. And in order to reserve these things for themselves they will plug up your eyes and your ears and your mouth, and if they can figure out a way to pump episodes of *The Simpsons* through the darkening corridors of your brain as you expire (ADD TO SHOPPING CART), they will do it.

We will end up with one and a half cities in America. Washington, DC, and *American Idol.* We will all live in Washington, DC, where the conversation is a droning, never advancing debate between "conservatives" and "progressives." We will not read about newlyweds. We will not read about the death of salesmen. We will not read about prize Holsteins or new novels. We are a nation dismantling the structures of intellectual property and all critical apparatus. We are a nation of Amazon reader responses (*Moby-Dick* is "not a really good piece of fiction"—Feb. 14, 2009, by Donald J. Bingle, Saint Charles, IL, USA—two stars out of five). We are without obituaries, but the famous will achieve immortality by a Wikipedia entry.

National newspapers will try to impersonate local newspapers that are dying or dead. (The *New York Times* and the *Wall Street Journal* publish San Francisco editions.) We live in the America of *USA Today*, which appears, unsolicited, in a plastic chrysalis suspended from your doorknob at the Nebraska Holiday Inn or the Maine Marriott. We check the airport weather. We fly from one CNN Headline News monitor to another. We end up where we started.

An obituary does not propose a solution.

Techno-puritanism that wars with the body must also resist the weight of paper. I remember that weight. It was the weight of the world, carried by boys.

Late in grammar school and into high school, I delivered the *Sacramento Bee*, a newspaper that was, in those years, published in the afternoon, Monday through Saturday, and in the morning on Sundays. My route comprised one hundred forty subscribers—nearly every house in three square blocks.

The papers were barely dry when I got them, warm to the touch and clean—if you were caught short, you could deliver a baby on newspaper. The smell of newspapers was a slick petroleum smell of ink. I would fold each paper in triptych, then snap on a rubber band. On Thursdays, the *Bee* plumped with a cooking section and with supermarket ads. On Sundays there was added the weight of comics, of real estate and automobile sections, and supplements like "Parade" and the television guide.

I stuffed half my load of newspapers into the canvas bag I tied onto my bicycle's handlebars; the rest went into saddlebags on the back. I never learned to throw a baseball with confidence, but I knew how to aim a newspaper well enough. I could make my mark from the sidewalk—one hand on the handlebar—with deadeye nonchalance. The paper flew over my shoulder; it twirled over hedges and open sprinklers to land with a fine plop only inches from the door.

In the growling gray light (San Francisco still has foghorns), I collect the *San Francisco Chronicle* from the wet steps. I am so lonely I must subscribe to three papers—the *Wall Street Journal,* the *New York Times,* the *San Francisco Chronicle.* I remark their thinness as I climb the stairs. The three together equal what I remember.

nine

Transit Alexander

a round

God formed you of dust from the soil. I was a sort of an afterthought. A wishbone. He blew into our nostrils the breath of life and there we were.

You were his Darling Boy and I was his Sweet Little Evie. The air was soft. We were made of clay. You were, anyway. He would hold up all manner of silly things he made for us, and we were supposed to name them with silly names. Everything we did seemed to delight him.

When he first showed signs of earthquake, at least I had the wit to say, "Now which tree was that again, dear?" *But you just stood there with juice running down your chin.*

God said to me: I will multiply, multiply your pain from your pregnancy; with pain shall you bear children. *God said to you:* Damned be the soil on your account, with painstaking labor shall you eat from it, for from it you were taken. For you are dust and to dust shall you return.

God made for us coats of skins and fur, and clothed us and sent us away.

Which is where we find ourselves: Nature runs through our bodies like rope. We give birth from our bellies. I do, anyway. We chew. We swallow. We regret. We decompose. These are laws of Nature. Natural laws are the brown laws. We hate them. We prevent birth. We eradicate polio. We clone goats and exchange hearts. We peer through our telescopes. We wear starched ruffs and underclothes. We compose divine comedies. Still, we must excuse ourselves fatuously whenever Nature calls.

One day, Francis approached a bundle of rags on the road. The bundle of rags (there was a man within) commenced rattling a gourd. The gourd had pebbles inside. This served as a warning that the ragman was a leper. Lepers had bruised skins like the skins of pears. Francis left the road to the man of rags and walked another way for he feared leprosy above all things. But his fear of catching death that day was of exactly the same intensity as his attraction to the ragman's suffering. *Why should the ragman suffer?* Francis had walked into an equation.

He had to run to catch the leper up.

The bundle of rags recoiled from Francis's approach, whirled like a shredded felucca. Francis ran again and stopped once more in front of the leper. Francis took two thick coins from his pocket. He placed the coins in the road as if coins could tame a leper. Raising his eyes, Francis saw the ragman had no fingers, only two fibrous stumps, to one of which someone had tied the rattling gourd. Francis removed his kerchief and knotted the coins in it and tied the little purse to the leper's cloak. A puddle of urine formed at the leper's feet.

Francis took the leper's palm gently in his hand and raised it to his lips.

After the incident on the road, Francis embraced every leper he met. Francis began to call all creatures *brother* or *sister*. Francis began to dress in gunny in emulation of the poor. He slept under hedgerows and within the porches of churches; he had no more plan than a sparrow and the citizens of Assisi considered him foolish.

Uniforms often are brown, the common denominator. Workmen wear brown, many do. Department stores used to advertise "work pants" and "work shirts," usually khaki—a word from the Urdu, from the Persian, meaning "dust" and, in English, denoting a fabric of olive or yellowish brown. Sir Thomas More used the Latin word *cacus* to denote excrement, and English has kept the word as "cack."

The uniform of labor is a metaphor for singularity of purpose or function. The military uniform represents allegiance to an abstract entity, as if that entity were uniform. In a religious community, the habit, the robe, represents a vow to fit your body to an ideal. Your conception of fate, or love, or whether you like a skin of milk on your pudding is subsumed beneath your habit.

Navies wear blue. Land armies wear brown, as do the Franciscans. Uniforms, shaved heads, humiliations, acronyms are enlisted to turn singular lives into a manageable mass. Before the modern era, armies met at daybreak upon an open field. Because combatants needed to be able to distinguish an enemy, there were red coats on one side and blue coats on the other, as on the stage at La Scala.

Since World War I, land armies have clothed themselves in terrestrial disguise—uniforms are predappled with shade or prebleached into sand.

If you have seen the photographs of Spencer Tunick, whose one idea is to pose multitudes of nude bodies in parks and plazas around the world, you will have noticed that, en masse, in the uniform of nakedness, there is little discernible difference between tall-short, rich-poor, fat-thin, young-old, male-female.

We do not like other people to see what we are carrying. It is none of their business. We therefore carry boxes and suitcases, baskets, trash bags, trunks, purses, Manila envelopes, coffins. There is nothing more mundane than a brown bag lunch, nothing more intimate. The plain brown wrapper is a disguise and a discretion.

Brown can be a kind of fame, as well. As did the Franciscans, United Parcel Service has won brand identification with brown— with the color of cardboard and Kraft paper and clipboard. "Kraft brown" is a low grade of strong paper used for wrapping and bagging. Books used to be wrapped in brown paper, tied with string, and sent through the mail just like that. Commercial laundries used brown paper. I don't know how it is, but at some point laundry paper became blue. Whether brown or blue, such paper is ephemeral because it contains discoloring acids; it will deteriorate at a faster rate than paper from which acid has been removed. "Deterioration" is a brown noun of green virtue.

Carol Shields, in *The Stone Diaries,* wrote of "how fundamentally lonely it is to live inside a body year after year and carry it always in a forward direction, and how there is never any relief from the weight of it."

Brown attaches to pedestrian considerations. The soles of feet thicken from walking; they form a rind like citrus rind. Shoe leather thins from walking. Millions of people walk the earth on brown soles. It is a good feeling to have thick, dry soles. It is a miserable feeling to have cold, wet feet.

The sky is large and unimplicating. The road of life is one thing after another. Humans seem perpetually to be hauling property from here to there. There is a great movement of people across the continents of the earth—people who have been forced from their ancient beds by war or by famine or an empty purse, but also by curiosity. People steal over borders and wade through rivers and hide in bushes to show up at dawn on the streets of new cities, as if they have been there all along.

The soles of feet are maps of sorts, continents. We leave them behind eventually.

People in some cultures distinguish private life from public life by removing their shoes before they enter a dwelling. Ritual washing of the feet has significance for many religions of the world. We would wash brown away, whatever is sinful or sordid or earthly away, before we enter a place we hold sacred.

Moses must remove his sandals (for they are made of the dead) before he may draw near the Burning Bush, the presence of the Living God.

Do you imagine that some languages, dialects, inflections, are brown because of the complexions and not the pink tongues of the people who speak them? I have always thought American southern accents have less of landscape in them, or of color, than of humidity, drollery, time. Whereas a rich, rolling Burgundian accent sounds earthy to me. An Irish brogue—the dialect of spoken English of the Irish—is called, in English, by the name of an old brown shoe, "a rude kind of shoe" (*Oxford English Dictionary*), worn in the "wilder parts of Ireland" (*ibid.*). An Irish tongue is imagined to have clod clinging to it.

God commanded the Israelites to make a chest of acacia wood to proportions God provided. The chest was to have a skin of gold and on the lid of the chest two sphinxes of gold, their wings outstretched. Rings of gold were to be affixed to the sides of the chest, and, passing through the rings, two poles of acacia wood, one on each side, covered with gold. Thus would the chest be carried.

Into the chest the Israelites were to place the Tablets of the

Testimony of God given to Moses on Mount Sinai. Into the chest the Israelites were to place a vat containing flakes of manna, in order that future generations would see what Yahweh provided the Israelites in the desert.

The Word of God was thus a weight in the world to answer the question: Is God present with us or is He not?

The Word of God was a weight to be carried through the wilderness and to be housed in a tent of threads and colors and of a proportion God provided to the Israelites.

The Word of God remains a sacred weight for the descendants of the Israelites, as for Christians and Muslims. The five books of Moses, called the Scroll of the Law, called the Sefer Torah, dwell in a Tabernacle. Sefer Torahs are made by the hands of scribes who have studied patience, patience having the proportion and the duration of the letters of the living word.

This is how the Word of God is passed on: The scribe copies the words of the Torah onto a parchment made of the skin of an animal that one is permitted by the Torah to eat. The skin is split; the hairy side separated from the flesh-touching side. Parchment is made from the side of the skin on which hair grew. The skin is scraped with a knife. The skin must be cured using a mixture of gallnut and lime to make a parchment that is pliant and durable. Every segment of the parchment must be squared. Only black ink may be used, made of lampblack and gum and olive oil, and dried in a mold to a block; the ink is made fluid with water. The letters must be made with a stylus of wood or reed or the quill of a clean fowl. The scribe must pronounce each word before he writes it. Before the scribe may write the name of God, the scribe must say *I intend to write the Holy Name*. If the scribe makes a mistake of a word, the word may be excised by scraping it from the parchment with a sharp knife. If the scribe makes a mistake in making the

Holy Name, the segment cannot be used but cannot be consigned to fire or earth but must be placed in a storeroom for mistakes.

The segments are sewn into a scroll with threads of dry tendon of clean beasts. The scroll is affixed to two rollers of hard wood; the rollers are fitted with flat discs of wood on each end, and finials of wood or ivory. When the scroll is closed, the scroll is girded with a ribbon of silk and robed in a Mantel of the Law. When the scroll is closed, an ornament is fitted over the finials at the top. The ornament is called the Crown of the Law.

The Word of God is heavy, as heavy as a child of five years; as heavy as a man's severed leg, borne aloft. The scroll is unwieldy to carry, as unwieldy as a stack of forty plates. The scroll may not touch the ground.

If the honored man who lifts the Torah from the Tabernacle should make a mistake, if the Torah should sway, if the Torah should succumb to gravity, if the Torah should touch the ground, then not only the honored man must atone, but the congregation must fast from sunrise to sundown—their flesh will be subtracted from one day for having been careless with the weight of the Word of God.

Men and women consign the Torah to memory. The minds of men are as muddled as vats of glue. But the Word of God is justified, black and legible. Thus, not only by their backs do men bear the weight of the Word of God, but also in the scrolls of their memories.

In two clicks, I will find you an online Torah.

The majority of people who are alive do not find it impossible to believe that a computer can sort and sift, relay, recall, correct, cure, solve, destroy, filch, tabulate, and turn out the lights.

An increasing number of people who are alive believe that an all-knowing God—or let us say, an all-caring God—is an impossibility.

The computer is a diminishing physical weight and is not of flesh but is of synthetic or mineral substances. But the computer's content is enlarging, unstable, ethereal. I tap on the screen. I activate a sifting of digits—as many as the sands—digits align into commands that summon images of letters, black letters; black is itself a series of numbers—eventually a Torah. The computer cannot, though I can, pause to worship the Holy Name. One supposes a code might be written for hallowing the Holy Name—perhaps the letters could be made to appear to flame or to reflect a passing bar of light as do the simulated brass letters of the titles of TV movies.

Some American soldiers recently gathered several worn copies of the Holy Koran from the shelves of the makeshift library of a jail in Afghanistan. Someone had noticed the Korans had markings in them—words in the margins, highlighted passages. Perhaps the prisoners were passing coded information within copies of the Koran?

The soldiers took the sacred books and burned them in a bonfire.

I'm sure the soldiers considered burning to be an appropriate destruction of a sacred artifact. Americans consider flame to be a purifying element. What the soldiers did not stop to consider was that destroying the Word of God is an affront to God.

How can God be affronted by a couple of GIs building a bonfire? It is the faithful who are affronted on God's behalf.

The danger of weighted knowledge is literalism.

The danger of weightless knowledge is relativism.

The manufacture of my iPad, despite the fact that it is a miracle of weightless synthetic information, has already added burden to the misery of mankind. An item from the *New York Times* (I can easily find the date on my iPad; here it is—January 25, 2012): "Aluminum dust from polishing iPads caused the blast at Foxconn's plant in Chengdu. Lai Xiaodong was among those killed. He had moved to Chengdu, bringing with him his college diploma six months earlier."

Even now a pretty brown cow steps nymph-like through a green pasture in Shaanxi province; even now she takes the spirit of the living God into her delicate nostril. God knows she will soon be melted to glue, all unwilling, to bind this book.

In the beginning was the Word: the Word was with God and the
Word was God. . . . The Word was made flesh. . . .

Jesus said to Thomas: Put your finger here; look, here are my hands.
Give me your hand; put it into my side.

We will now rebuild the tree. The tree I have in mind will take thousands of trees and many years to build. I have a photograph before me of the Long Room of the library at Trinity College, Dublin, completed in 1732. The ceiling is a curved vault of candle-fumed wood. The floor is a plane of honey. The photograph shows a receding corridor on each side of which rise arched alcoves. Within the alcoves are shelves, from floor to ceiling. On the shelves are books bound in leathers of every hue, all brown. There are wooden banisters, benches, pilasters. The only appurtenances that are not brown are white marble busts of philosophers, poets, playwrights.

The room is massively silent. It ruminates upon a thousand forests and a thousand cities and personages, revolutions and plagues, ships lost and continents discovered. Sentences, formulae, drawings—knowledge is the sap of this tree. The tree is alive though all the philosophers represented by all the busts are dead.

The room will speak if questioned.

One of the earliest English definitions of brown—Samuel Johnson's definition—is of any color compounded with black. We have come to think of brown not only as a mitigation of black, but as an alternative to black, or as an abeyance. Love is stronger than death, say. Death being black. Or, beer does more than Milton can. Beer being brown. As if brown were a separate consideration. (*And malt does more than Milton can / To justify God's ways to man*— A. E. Housman's assertion.)

Earth is itself a canted color wheel, a cycle of vegetable, mineral, animal, and atmospheric accommodations to the Earth's passage around the Sun. The segment, the turn of the Earth, that corresponds to brown in the Northern Hemisphere is autumn. Consider, for example, the brown field in autumn, the stubble field. In climates where winter is cold, the autumnal field represents at once Nature depleted and Nature bountiful. There is something about the indeterminacy of brown that lends itself to such paradox.

She is the matronly season, Autumn, comfortable in her warm landscape. Ripe Autumn can nearly be heard to sigh: *Here will I rest a bit, my bounty is suddenly very heavy.* Her lids droop. Her smile is pleasantly hazy. Her days are shortening. But the sun is delicious. Isn't the sun delicious? Thoughts turn to elegy and apples. *Try one of these,* she says. Then, she says, *What do you suppose death is like?*

In September of 1819, the English poet John Keats, aged twenty-four, took a long walk before dinner. He was stopping for a time in Winchester. "I never liked stubble-fields so much as now," he wrote in a letter to his friend John Reynolds. "Aye better than the chilly green of spring. Somehow, a stubblefield looks warm—in the same way that some pictures look warm. This struck me so much in my Sunday's walk that I composed upon it."

Season of mists and mellow fruitfulness,
Close bosom-friend of the maturing sun

The ode "To Autumn" was written by a young man as if it were a young man's poem—Keats embracing his equation—as if the benediction of an ample day will not fail.

Still, not an autumn returns that I do not remember you by it, John Keats—that first day of which I am able to say: I can feel fall in the air. Though no longer young, I expect to rise in fall.

In 1625 John Donne, the English poet and Anglican priest, in a sermon at St. Paul's Cathedral, London, expounded on creation, as thus: When God made the world, he put into it *a reproofe, a rebuke, lest it should seem eternall, which is, a sensible decay and age in the whole frame of the world, and every piece thereof.*

In Los Angeles, on the hottest day of the year, the electrical grid surges upward in a digital tsunami, crests, browns out. The Kumtag Desert in China drowns the Silk Route, flows onward toward the city. Earth warms. Blankets of snow are thrown off. Rivers sink into their beds. Seas rise vertically like bamboo forests. Human activity forms an interesting brown cloak that floats over Lagos and Bangkok. Treacle-colored, coal-heated nineteenth-century London sounds wonderfully atmospheric in novels. But it was not wonderful. Eyes, throats, lungs burned; mouths blistered.

The first Earth Day was proclaimed, rather than astronomically calculated, by Senator Gaylord Nelson (D) of Wisconsin, at a conference on overpopulation in 1969. That same year, at a UNESCO conference, John McConnell, a California environmentalist, proposed a global Earth Day to coincide with the March equinox. Earth Day has evolved into an antihistorical celebration of prelapsarian Nature—Nature before human intrusion. The ideal human relationship to Nature, therefore, becomes one of corrective restoration. In the words printed on my cereal box: "Always leave the earth better than you found it." Green spring is an appropriate metaphor for the ambition of a perfectible world. Do not the branches of trees flounce about in pubescent green?

It becomes ideological to see brown as the harbinger of the end of Nature. But the bark of the tree—the wise part—forms protectively about the livid core. Surely autumn is as necessary a part of Nature as spring.

And brown has always been the sum of our breathing and eating and moving about. Even in the days of yore—days of *Odyssey*, days of *Gilgamesh*—smoke floated over villages and towns, heartening the traveler, still many miles distant.

There is a relationship, as young Keats noticed, between autumnal hues and warmth. One can certainly find a cold brown landscape. I grew up in such a landscape, one that might have been painted by Millet. When the fog rose from the fallow field, it was very cold in December. Even so, mine in the Central Valley of California remained, even in winter, a baked landscape. Nothing about it was raw. If only for its hue, it never appeared desolate to me. The earth was rich beneath its crust. I knew that if I dug down far enough— as far as gravediggers dig—I would find a room as warm as April.

I retain my liking for baked landscapes. For desert and the caramelized cities. Once, in an Italian hill town, on an uncomfortably warm August afternoon, I entered a restaurant, the only restaurant, where several clay ovens were blazing and citizens were ordering platters of roast pig for their Sunday dinners and drinking from earthenware jugs of cool wine. It was insanely warm. By and by, the room grew tolerable. I now declare I find the memory of it to be of exactly the right temperature.

There is evasion involved in cuisine, as with all human embarrassments, an evasion not of our cursed biblical state as grain-and-root-eaters (*from the soil shall you* ... etcetera) but of our evolutionary, renegade taste for blood. Of ourselves as hunters. For we have not only the necessity to eat, the capacity to hunt, but also to pity our prey. Who does not pity the lamb?

Nor do I like to eat pale things. Poached eggs or fish or fowl. I want a buttered crust. I had an aunt who used to make a meal of boiled chicken with yellow skin and white gravy—and it nearly drove me mad to watch her. I prefer my warm-blooded fare to be certified cruelty-free, to arrive in unrecognizable "cuts" and yet to be served up with a purgatorial crust. I want malt *and* Milton.

In Kathryn Davis's novel *Hell,* there is a recipe for blancmange: Almonds are pounded to extract their milk, the milk is then strained, then sugar and transparent gelatin are added. The alloy is filtered once more through a white napkin.

> ... *The resultant mixture* ... *will be in fact utterly without texture, without substance, almost, you might say, without material existence, so that* ... *to swallow it would be to swallow nothing, to attempt communion not with the body and blood of God's son but with the holy ghost itself* ...

Chocolate, on the other burner, is one of the densest, brownest, most guilt-ridden substances we have learned to put into our mouths. It is also, curiously, one of the most refined—refined not from straining, but by compaction. Cacao was cultivated and eaten throughout Mesoamerica. In 1528 the Spanish explorer Hernán

Cortés transported the first cacao beans to Europe from Mexico. The refinement of chocolate proceeds as follows: The cacao tree puts forth pods. The seeds are harvested from the pods, fermented, dried, bagged. The chocolate manufacturer blends several strains of the beans for flavor and color. The beans are roasted and ground, then ground again to release their butter, then rolled around in drums and I don't know what all.

We relish taking in what most closely resembles—excuse me— what comes out. We are slow ovens. Ninety-eight point six. Brown is our biological point. Being alive depends on keeping warm. A warm room can be of any color, but heat feels brown, even though exhalations of breath on a cold morning are ghostly white. A bed as white as blancmange can feel as brown as a stable or a nest.

There exists a warm-blood club, no question. Warm blood might summon to your mind an albino bunny with red eyes, but the concept, you've got to admit, even if you have never taken a nap with your dog, even if your dog is black, is brown. And from warm blood comes sentimentality, which must be a vestige of fur.

No sober discussion of brown should omit mention of Marcel Duchamp's painting *Chocolate Grinder (No. 2)*, 1914, wherein three inexorable brown drums rest on a chassis that is elevated on decorative antique-moderne legs. The painting is beautiful; it is an accurate depiction of the physics of pressure. And it is ridiculous.

Now we will cut the wind from the tree. This entails killing the tree. Cut at the base. Birds fly upward. The tree may experience sorrow after its hundred amber-blooded years.

Cut the tree in sections, twelve feet long. Cut one of the sections lengthwise to appraise its grain—its diseases, indecisions, parsimonies.

Some years are deep brown cellos. Some, lithesome violins.

Some years are mantels or pillars or transoms. Some are ploughs and spoons for stirring. The rest is broom handles, toothpicks, clothespins. The rest is firewood and paper.

Take a block of the finest grain and carve of it a scroll. Make a thin slice of a softer grain, as thin as ham. And then another. And cut from these two scarab shapes for front and back. Cut it some gills. Bow its belly and thump its back. Seal, sand, varnish. String chords through the frets of its neck.

We will then recompense the wind and the leaves. We will make music.

In Manhattan, Billy Baldwin designed a brown study for Cole Porter—a famous room in the annals of décor. Ebony shelves were supported by brass piping. The dark walls were of tortoise-shell design on Chinese lacquered paper. There was a piano, several club chairs—this was a first-class cabin with no apparent clutter of creation.

The "brown study" is a term that originally referred to a state of mental absorption or abstraction. Etymologically, in this case, brown equals gloom. The fictional detective Sherlock Holmes was described by his fictional chronicler, Dr. Watson, as "in a brown study," a state of intense rumination, often accompanied by tobacco smoke, morphine, or Paganini. I wish now to conflate the term with the site. When Holmes and Watson first engaged rooms at 221b Baker Street, Watson described "a couple of comfortable bedrooms and a single large airy sitting room, cheerfully furnished, and illuminated by two broad windows."

Through many subsequent volumes of stories, the rooms darken considerably with the clutter of newspapers, chemical experiments, and notebooks—the clutter of overgrown boys—but also with an atmospheric residue of the contemplation of evil.

So that, in the ultimate volume, after many adventures, "it was pleasant to Dr. Watson to find himself once more in the untidy room . . . He looked round him at the scientific charts upon the wall, the acid-charred bench of chemicals, the violin-case leaning in the corner, the coal-scuttle which contained of old the pipes and tobacco." Holmes's study is a type of the necromancer's tower. Prospero's cell is another. The scriptorium of Saint Jerome. Merlin's cave. Faust's gothic chamber. Even Henry Higgins's library. The room represents the workings of the mind. The room must be untidy in order that mental abstraction will be orderly.

Sigmund Freud had two brown rooms. The first, in Vienna, where he invented a psychoanalytic method in much the same way that Conan Doyle invented detection—through an accumulation of case histories. The second in London. In either of Freud's brown studies, in both, books as well as prints and antiquities are displayed with an abacus-like precision. The seat of disorder in the room is a divan, covered with an irregularly patterned, plum-toned oriental carpet. Disorder enters Freud's study through a subject's subconscious.

There are substances that throw down roots in the human organism, roots that coil themselves around the little bones and dip their sharp nibs into the chemicals of the brain to draw up treaties, dependencies, visionary loans. Most of these substances are brown—brandies, whiskies, the sedimentary wines, opium, marijuana, coffee, tea. Among them the most delightful is tobacco.

Ass-eared leaves are harvested in sultry climes, cured to a golden brown, graded, then cut to various uses—pipe, cigar, cigarette, snuff. To ingest a lungful of tobacco smoke is to open an artificial bay, a small space of time, a monastery of privacy between one moment and the next, between one marriage and the next, between one sentence or one task and the next. It is unfortunate

that tobacco is ultimately destructive of the organism it so be-
friends. One's lungs become a shambles.

"You don't mind the smell of strong tobacco, I hope?" asks
Holmes.

"Take the invalid to the sun," the gray doctor in nineteenth-
century novels urges. The tubercular poet, against his better judgment, goes to Rome.

In the twentieth century, among light-skinned populations, a
vogue for tanning began with the dawning age of tourism. The
novelist goes to Mexico. Applying brown to oneself is different in
its implication from painting health on one's cheek because it risks
a confusion of racial and class identity. For the tourist, tan may be a
mark of leisure. But tan is also the laborer's mark. In Cairo as in
Quito, brown cloaks the distinction between the white-suited visitor and the company of criers and beggars in the bazaar.

In D. H. Lawrence's short story "Sun," a New Yorker named
Juliet travels to Greece for a sun cure. Juliet takes the sun for a
lover: "Sometimes he came ruddy, like a big, shy creature. And
sometimes slow and crimson red, with a look of anger." Juliet's
cure extends to a gardener she sees. She describes the gardener's
attraction as "his vitality, the peculiar quick energy which gave a
charm to his movements, stout and broad as he was." The reader
is led to recognize the gardener as an amorous surrogate of
the sun.

When the gods of Olympus sport with mortals, they take on the
disguise of flesh:

Venus: *You see that girl?*
Cupid: (A vacant stare.)

Venus: *I overheard someone on the colonnade remark she has beauty to rival Venus.*

Cupid: *Surely not, Radiant Mother.*

Venus: *Oh, Radiant Mother! You know as well as I do the degenerates prefer that greasy sort of ripeness. Look how she goes. Inside, you know, they are nothing but filth. I want you to shoot her.*

Cupid: *She looks harmless.*

Venus: *She paints up, too. I've seen her at it with a turd of beetroot. They eat filth, they think filth, they make filth. They die in filth. Have you ever smelled one?*

Cupid: *Of course I have.*

Venus: *Do you like the smell of them?*

Cupid: *Not particularly. Apollo says you get used to it.*

Venus: *Apollo should keep his nose in the clouds where it belongs. I'll bet you've never smelled them when they cut their hair.*

Cupid: *Do they cut their hair?*

Venus: *Otherwise they look like complete monkeys. They have hair in the most comical places.*

Cupid: *Apollo says it tickles. If they are so beastly why do we wear their parts?*

Venus: *For sport. For butter. For fun. Form is nothing to us. Clouds. Trees. Thin air if we feel like it.*

Cupid: *Thin air is boring.*

Venus: *I want you to shoot an arrow through her big fat tit. The little idiot will fall head over heels for the first hairy back that flutters by.*

"Lend me thy cloak, Sir Thomas." The brown cape conceals the beggar-king, the sacred heart, the anointed head. Shakespeare's King Henry wraps himself in Thomas's plain cloak on the eve of the Battle of Agincourt in order that he might move unrecognized among his men. The twin device of disguise and epiphany is as old as the hills. Biblical Joseph is reunited with his jealous brothers. Richard the Lionheart reveals himself to Robin Hood. Caesar to Cleopatra. Arthur to Guinevere. Beast to Beauty. Cyrano to Roxanne. "It is I. All along, it was I."

Disguise is an attribute of the gods; modesty is not. The God of the Desert is an exception. The God of the Desert instructs that Aaron and his sons, and all priests following from their seed—"a law for the ages"—are to wear breeches of linen during sacred rites "to cover the flesh of nakedness; from the hips to the thighs they are to extend" in order that priests not flash their humanity during the gruesome work of the slaughter of beasts.

God's prescription seems only to confirm something that we already feel about ourselves, about our human nature, as represented by the flesh of nakedness from our hips to our thighs: that our private parts, as we call them, though definitively generic, are made of special stuff; are neither purely reflexive nor completely governable. We are confused. We are profoundly crafted.

The revelation of our nakedness to strangers, to lovers, has the potency of sacred awe, much like the prelude to a sacrifice. A hush falls upon the audience of a movie or a play when an actor disrobes. But when an actor appears suddenly naked, as if in the midst of life, the audience will laugh at its own embarrassment.

Even in a doctor's office, the moment of physical epiphany may be accompanied by a sense of awe. Young doctors of the twenty-first century resort to an Edwardian deportment at such times that one might call priestly. The patient feels herself a sacrifice.

In 1925, at the Théatre des Champs-Elysées in Paris, American dancer Josephine Baker appeared nude in a series of good-natured anthropological parodies. I quote Janet Flanner, the Paris correspondent for the *New Yorker,* who was there:

> *[Baker] made her entry entirely nude except for a pink flamingo feather between her limbs; she was carried upside down and doing the split on the shoulder of a black giant. Mid-stage he paused . . . swung her in a slow cartwheel to the stage floor, where she stood . . . an unforgettable female ebony statue. A scream of salutation spread through the theater. Whatever happened next was unimportant.*

Calvin Klein's notoriety came with his advertisements for male underwear in the 1980s. Klein employed the waxed, darkly tanned nude as both mannequin and garment. Underpants were a way of affixing a label to a body. Put on the garment and you put on nakedness. The notion that one's body could be worn (and not only one's body but one's tan, and not only one's tan but one's vacancy) became a conceit for a number of other designers, notably Gianni Versace. After Versace was murdered in Miami, frequent patrons of his Greco-carny boutiques received a memento mori in the mail—an album of flamboyant Versace designs interspersed with photographs of models wearing nothing at all.

Preindustrial populations wore furs and skins from practical necessity. Pelt was collateral to meat. We no longer need animal skins for warmth. In the city, therefore, a fur coat becomes a complicated conceit. Luxury merges with transgression. The socialite inhabiting the skin of a wild animal is enacting Beauty and Beast at once. If one were to play the conceit to the end, as Princess Diana famously did, one might visit one's reluctant paramour late at night wearing a fur coat, a diamond necklace, and nothing more. Queen and Huntress.

Long after Adam and Eve imagined they could hide from God, long before Princess Diana masqueraded as a predator, Queen Marie Antoinette dressed as an opéra comique shepherdess. The French speak of *nostalgie de la boue,* not with specific reference to *La Petite Ferme,* but applicable. Literally, *boue* is muck. What a splendid paradox, that a high civilization should cultivate nostalgia for a time opposite or before or below—a descent into uncivilization. Marie Antoinette as *boue*-peep, tripping through her Meissen barnyard, a little poetic fantasy within a political fantasy, within a world of filth.

We associate death with blackness because, I suppose, when we close our eyes we can't see. As to actual death, the death of a point of view—who can say? Death might well be as blue as a robin's egg. In the light of day the process of aging—and death itself—is brown. To the observer, death is brown. Time is bacterial progress.

In the cleaned, "original" version of the Sistine ceiling, Adam appears pale, beautiful, dead—his eyes do not yet see. The weather is fine. The void is a pale spring afternoon. Earth is green. The divine hubbub looks like the interior of a luxury sedan. God is massively potent and in love. Unborn Eve is tucked under God's arm, obviously a gift for the darling boy; she could be a nymphet on the cover of a Murdoch tabloid.

Sometime late in the 1980s, Pope John Paul II was consulted by a Cardinal Prefect concerning a proposal to clean and restore the frescoes of the Sistine Chapel. In the 1980s, John Paul was a vigorous, handsome man. In the 1980s, the ceiling of the Sistine Chapel had been left to darken for four hundred Roman summers. Michelangelo's Creation and Judgment wore the shadows of so many years.

At the apex of Michelangelo's grand design, God reaches toward

Adam to enliven him. In the damaged version, the four-centuries-old sinful version, Adam is brown, a figure of exhaustion; Adam seems to sink back into the earth upon which he reclines. God is prognostic, and his half shell of celestial hubbub shudders in turbulence. There are cracks in the void.

The Nippon Television Network of Tokyo proposed to pay for the restoration of the Sistine frescoes in exchange for exclusive rights to photograph the restored ceiling and walls. It took Michelangelo four years to paint the Judeo-Christian epic. It required more than double that time for the frescoes to be cleaned. Conservators used cotton swabs to apply distilled water to an acre of shale-like cloud. The Vatican installed an air-filtering system to circumvent any future deterioration of heaven.

In February of 1820, John Keats, aged twenty-five, suffered the first hemorrhage of his lung, losing eight ounces of blood. He left damp England on the urgent advice of his physician. By November he was living in Rome with Joseph Severn, a young painter who had accompanied him on his journey and who stayed on to care for him. Keats had a relapse in December and fell gravely ill. Keats forbade Severn to wish for a return of spring. Keats prayed each evening would be his last on earth and wept with each rising sun.

As a young man, Karol Wojtyła had been a playwright and actor of parochial repute. When Wojtyła became John Paul II, he became one of the great theatricals of his century. He played the Pope for the age of television. By the time he died in 2005, half the people alive on earth had known no other in the role. The planet his audience, the Pope seemed never without an intuition of the camera. Kissing the tarmacs of airports!

Those for whom decorum is a religion scorned the theatrical vulgarity of some of the trappings of John Paul II's papacy—the Pope-mobile, for example. But the planet loved it. The Pope-mobile served John Paul, as did the pop music, the lights, the windjammer chasubles, the stadium masses modeled after rock concerts.

During the final years of his papacy, John Paul II lost control of his person to Parkinson's disease; his speech, his movements, slurred.

Young Mr. Severn drew Keats in his bed—*28 January, 3 o'clock, morning: drawn to keep me awake; a deadly sweat was upon him all this night*. The sketch conveys the very smell of the night's ordeal. Keats's hair is damp on his forehead and cheek; his face is sunken; closed lashes darken the hollows beneath his eyes. The brown penumbra that circles John Keats's prone head seems to draw ink from his drowning breath. After the poet's death, Severn corrected his sketch to publish it as the formal pieta: *Keats on his deathbed, February 23, 1821*.

In her last decade, when the famous legs came unstrung, when the famous face could no longer be repaired, Marlene Dietrich hid herself from the eyes of the world. She became a prisoner of our memory of her face on the screen. She closed the drapes of her apartment on the Avenue Montaigne. John Paul II was the cannier theatrical. He was willing to portray suffering—dragged as he was through St. Peter's on a wagon, in a pointed hat, drooling. He found the spotlight. Here was Lear, here was Olivier; here was Samuel Beckett.

The Pope's last stage was his bedroom window, a perfect proscenium: The curtain opened. The old man was wheeled into the light of the open window to utter a benediction—his arm flailing uncontrollably, clutching his forehead in a simian gesture, his mouth opening and closing in tortured silence. The microphone was quickly withdrawn. The curtain began to close as the figure receded.

At the end of his life, in great bodily pain, Saint Francis had an intimation that he dwelled, on earth, already in paradise. Francis composed a summation, a prayer he called the Canticle of Brother Sun, wherein he commended and blessed his familiars: *Brother Sun, Sister Moon, Brother Wind, Sister Water, Brother Fire, and Mother Earth who nourishes and rules us.* As he lay dying, Francis welcomed one final aspect of Nature to his Canticle: *Be praised, my Lord, for our Sister, Bodily Death, whom no living man can escape.*

Toward the end of his short life, Hamlet, in a characteristically dark humor, traces for Horatio the ignoble decline of great Alexander. As thus:

Alexander died, Alexander was buried, Alexander returneth into dust; the dust is earth; of earth we make loam; and why of that loam, whereto he was converted, might they not stop a beer barrel?

What clay should teach us to reply to Hamlet is that loam is as much the beginning as the end.

If you are afraid of its darker implications, it is not brown you fear but life.

ten

The Three Ecologies of the Holy Desert

The curtain is down; its fringes are ripped; the curtain is patched and faded. From behind the curtain, there are sounds of a crowd, faint laughter. A dented brass band plays, ending with a drum roll. Mounting exclamations of concern and then tightrope silence. Amazements are in progress. A cymbal is struck followed by uproarious laughter and applause. The lights in the theater are extinguished as the curtain begins to rise. The only sound now is the buzzing of a fly. On stage, an old woman lies on a pallet on the floor of an empty room. A handkerchief covers her face.

1. The Mountaintop

I wake up because the floor lamp in my bedroom has been turned on. (Passive construction indicates all that is seen and unseen.) It is three o'clock in the morning. My chest feels bruised, heavy. I am certain my mother has died.

Caveat: The lamp has a dimmer switch. My mother is in a hospital a few blocks away.

Several days later, I tell a neighbor, a man I know well, that my mother died and that the floor lamp in my bedroom came on during the night. My neighbor is sincerely sorry to hear of my mother's death; he supposes there must have been some kind of surge in the electrical grid.

Our lives are so similar, my friends' and mine. The difference between us briefly flares—like the lamp in my bedroom—only when I publish a religious opinion.

On June 17, 1992, Anita Mendoza Contreras was seated at a picnic table in Pinto Lake County Park, near Watsonville, California. Mrs. Mendoza Contreras was thinking her thoughts, as people used to say about someone staring out a window or worrying the hem of an apron, and among her thoughts were her children, about whom, for reasons of her own, she worried. She worried, and so she knelt down beneath an oak tree to pray. As she prayed, Mrs. Mendoza Contreras experienced a vision of the Virgin Mary. During the vision, Mrs. Mendoza Contreras's attention was fixed upon a portion of the trunk, high up in the spread of the oak tree. After the vision ended, Mrs. Mendoza Contreras saw that an image of the Virgin had formed within the bark of the oak.

Word of an apparition circulated somehow, and, the days being long, the nights being warm, people got into their cars after work and drove to Pinto Lake to see the oak tree with the Virgin's picture on it.

That is what we did, too—two friends and I—after an article about the image appeared in the *San Francisco Chronicle*.

The parking lot was a vacant field. I stepped in a cowpat. Federico Fellini, who as much as anyone entertained my adolescence and taught me the hope of magic, interjected into several of his movies comic scenes of crowd hysteria in the wake of miracles. As a worldly Roman, Fellini relished the humor of piety. As a Roman Catholic, as a lover of circuses, he shared the human need for marvels.

We saw people coming toward us who had already seen the

tree. They looked the way adults look—parents with young children—after an amusement has left them stranded: torpor, hunger, school tomorrow. Children were picking up acorns to put in their pockets. Already, I could see this wasn't going to be what I wasn't even aware I was hoping for.

Some women were sitting on aluminum foldout chairs, praying their rosaries in Spanish.

Easy to spot the relic tree within the grove because there were votive candles at its base. Boys with convinced expressions held compact mirrors with which they directed our eyes to the image by reflecting spangles of the setting sun onto the tree trunk.

I seem to remember there were already objects hanging from the branches—T-shirts, teddy bears, petitions—the forensics of hope.

I saw what they meant; I saw the shape. But I could not see what they saw. What Mrs. Mendoza Contreras saw. Though I, too, felt the need for visions that people brought to the tree and left there.

In the holy deserts of the Middle East, mountains rise from flat plains. It is on the mountaintop that God condescends and human hope ascends to within a hair's breadth of what humanity needs, what humanity fears. In the world's famous mountaintop theophany, Moses ascends Mount Sinai, under cover of cloud, to receive the Ten Commandments from God. The Israelites who wait below on the desert floor grow bored, unruly, forgetful of the wonders they have already witnessed. And that is the way of such stories. Heaven on one side of the veil; the field of folk on the other. Sometimes a souvenir passes from one side to the other.

We stayed half an hour; we stopped in Pescadero for green chile soup on our way home. No souvenir.

Another summer day: After the attack on the morning of September 11, someone posted on the Internet a photograph of one of the disintegrating towers. The image of a face seemed to form from whorls of black smoke—people were quick to say the devil's face. The face had a bulbous schnoz and more closely resembled the face of W. C. Fields.

Anyway, it was not Satan that people I know talked about in the days and months after September 11. It was religion—the religion of the terrorists—and the dangerous presumption of men who say "My God."

After September 11, it became easier, apparently it became necessary, for many of my friends to volunteer, without any equivocation of agnosticism, that they are atheists. It was not clear to me whether they had been atheists all along or if the violence of September 11 tipped Pascal's scales for them. People with whom, as my friend Will used to say, I would share my lifeboat, declared their loathing for religion, particularly the desert religions of the Middle East—the eagerness to cast the first stone, the appetite to govern civil society, the pointy hats, the crooks and crosses, the shawls, the hennaed beards. One of my closest friends, who lives in Memphis, observed that God looks to be deader than Elvis. (In his e-mail, my friend nevertheless resorted to a childhood piety: "God" is hallowed as "G-d.") But most of my friends left it at nothing. Whiteout. January First of the rest of their lives. (Buddhism retained its triple-gong rating.)

I was driving an elderly friend to a funeral. In response to nothing I had said (I suppose because we were on our way to a funeral), my friend announced her conviction that the world would be better off without religion. "I mean all of them," she said. An angry gesture of her open hand toward the windshield wiped them all away. As we drove on in silence, it occurred to me that I had interpreted what my friend said as something about men, though she had not said men. I had interpreted what she said as about God. But she said religion.

"I feel the same way about the Olympics," I said.

"Don't get me wrong," she said after a while. "I believe in the Good Lord. It's religion I don't like."

From his desert perch, a drab, plump ayatollah rejoices in the deaths of young martyrs who send infidel dogs to hell. The teachings of Jesus Christ go begging when a priest falls to his knees on the hard rectory floor to fondle and blight an altar boy's innocence.

My friend the doctor, whom I see every Sunday at Mass, whom I follow in the Communion line, asked, as we were leaving church, if I think the world is better or worse off for religion.

If you think the world is perfectible, then worse.

In American myth, the Village Atheist is a loner, a gaunt fellow in a flannel shirt, standing on a hill on Sunday morning. He faces away from the steeple in the dell. Perhaps he is putting flowers on his wife's grave. The hater of Sunday lives in a trim white house, eats porridge for breakfast; no wreath on his door at Christmas; gives generously to the Community Chest. His roses are the envy of the garden club, of which he is not a member.

Here are the three atheists of my youthful apprehension, apostles of the rounded sleep: Madalyn Murray O'Hair, Bertrand Russell, James Joyce.

Madalyn Murray O'Hair was a professional atheist who appeared on television talk shows in the 1950s and '60s. She was blowsy, unkempt; I could imagine her living room—the card table piled with legal briefs and Swanson TV Dinner trays full of pens and paperclips. She had two sons. Her fierce humor—I suppose I would now call it a lack of humor—was directed at Americans willing to violate individuality by insisting on public religious observance. O'Hair sued the Baltimore school system to outlaw the reading of Scripture in public schools; she sued NASA to stop astronauts from quoting Scripture in outer space. One of her sons repudiated her and she him; that son became a Baptist minister. Madalyn O'Hair was abducted by a former employee whose motive was, ostensibly, ransom. Her second son and her granddaughter were also abducted. All three were murdered.

In 1901, at the age of twenty-nine, Bertrand Russell discovered paradox. He wrote:

$$\text{Let } R = \{x \mid x \notin x\}, \text{ then } R \in R \Leftrightarrow R \notin R$$

Nor do I.

When I entered college, Bertrand Russell's book *Why I Am Not a Christian* stood face-out on the shelf of the campus bookstore— the face of a philosopher, I thought at the time. The face of an Anglican bishop, perhaps. The fluffy white hair, the starched collar. The face of an ancient satyr. In 1958 Bertrand Russell wrote: "I do not think the existence of the Christian God is any more probable than the existence of the gods of Olympus or Valhalla."

An affront to his ghost, I suppose, but Catholics, in our infuriating way, held out hope for James Joyce. Haunted, wasn't he? "Haunted" was the word we used. Old Jimbo exhausted his breath with sacrilege, yet the Church was forever cropping up in his book, wasn't it? He took it all too seriously, too young. Don't you worry, he'll have come round at the last, like Molly Bloom:

. . . as for them saying theres no God I wouldnt give a snap of my two fingers for all their learning why dont they go and create some-

thing I often asked him atheists or whatever they call themselves . . .
ah yes I know them well who was the first person in the universe
before there was anybody that made it all who ah that they dont
know neither do I so there you are . . .

I have never been to the mountaintop, if that's what you mean. The only thing I know for a fact is that God never uses His own money. He hasn't got any money.

Some well-meaning person once referred to Dorothy Day, in her presence, as a saint.

"Don't call me a saint," Dorothy Day said. "I don't want to be dismissed that easily."

Dorothy Day, as one of the founders of the Catholic Worker movement, ran a hospitality house for the poor on the Lower East Side of New York. This was in 1956. The building that housed the hospitality house did not meet the fire code of the borough of Manhattan.

Dorothy Day was fined $250, which she did not have. The city ordered her to make repairs. The fine and the circumstance were reported in the *New York Times*. The same morning the *Times* article appeared, Dorothy Day was leaving the hospitality center for the courthouse in order to plead her case before a magistrate of the Upper Manhattan Court. A disheveled man in bedroom slippers stepped forward from a line of people waiting on the sidewalk for clothes to be distributed. The man handed Dorothy Day a check for $250.

The man in bedroom slippers was W. H. Auden, the greatest poet of his generation. Auden read the article in the *New York Times* while eating his breakfast, got up from the table, exited his apartment with a check in his hand, marmalade on his chin.

In a preface to a book of critical essays, W. H. Auden defined his vision of Eden (by way of divulging how his critical faculties were colored) as: "Roman Catholic in an easygoing Mediterranean sort of way. Lots of local saints . . . Religious Processions, Brass Bands, Opera . . ."

When I asked a priest-friend for his vision of paradise, he said: "Well, it will certainly be a surprise, won't it?"

Wayne lived in one of the welfare hotels on Turk Street. He may have sold drugs; if he did, it was penny-ante stuff. He may not have taken drugs; he said not. Wayne was about seventy-five percent trustworthy, a rarified percentile. He couldn't read. I fear he may be dead. Wayne sat in front of the store across the way from Tillman Place Bookshop with a cup and a sign—he depended on fellow vagrants to make his signs for him: VETERAN. GOD BLESS.

Wayne was sweet-natured, simple-minded. Wayne told me he sometimes heard voices urging him to nefarious behaviors, but he refused those voices. He had no teeth, or few; he was often beaten up by bad men, particularly one bad man, who wanted Wayne's space in front of the store across the way. Wayne's space on the sidewalk was prime Sunnyside. The bad man, having chased Wayne away with hummingbird-like aggression, would then fold himself into abjection, would call out, God bless you, sir, God bless you, ma'am, *to passersby, and he was, perhaps, an authentic agent of God's blessing, but not for Wayne.*

On the day I recollect, the bad man was not about. Wayne was sitting on the sidewalk in his accustomed place. A droplet of rain was suspended from an awning; the tiny bag of water held the sun. A day in early January.

Switch-tense: As I watch, several things happen simultaneously: Up at the corner, in front of Shreve's, the old man who sings "When You're Smiling"—top hat, cane—is cajoling some frowning passersby to no avail. A young man—he is nobody I know—enters the scene from the north, approaches Wayne with a large pink box of doughnuts—left over from somebody's breakfast board meeting, I assume, then left out on a trash bin. Anyway, a box of doughnuts. The man seats himself on the sidewalk alongside Wayne, offers the doughnuts to Wayne and also a cup of coffee— so maybe I'm wrong about the provenance of the doughnuts. Wayne smiles with pleasure, catches my eye as he reaches for a doughnut, and is momentarily connected to the old man singing "When You're Smiling," for he and the other—the doughnut bringer—in mock-mockery, begin to sway to the cadence of the song like two bluebirds on a bough in a silly old cartoon. The sun, too, now seems a simple enough phenomenon—cadmium yellow pouring onto the pavement. A passerby drops a dollar bill into Wayne's cup and Wayne nods and smiles (and looks over to me). I smile. The design—tongue and groove—of a single moment.

I do believe the moment could be plotted algebraically according to some golden mean (though not by me), a line from A to B, B to C, C to D, D to E.

Therefore:

$$A = B + C + D$$
$$B + C + D = E$$

Therefore,

$$A = E.$$

But here's the thing: Wayne's smile.

I have thought about this for twenty years or more. Wayne's smile said: Do you get it? Wayne's smile said: Remember this moment, it contains everything.

After September 11, atheism has become the most casual interjection into the television conversation. The grand old rock star OBE, for example, imparts to us, though he hasn't been asked, what he thinks of all that—of God, and all. *Well, that's all gone, thank God,* he says, slapping his shrunken thigh. The music critic in our local paper regrets, on his readers' behalf, the religious context weighing upon the transcendent beauty of a Bach cantata. And on the bestseller lists the ascending titles are apologies for the "New Atheism." From England, cradle of the New Atheism (as London turns Muslim and Hindu), Richard Dawkins, an Oxford biologist, proposes that parents who raise their children religiously are guilty of child abuse. On the same shelf, the journalist Christopher Hitchens titles his essay on atheism as a deliberate affront to Muslim piety. Roughly 145 years separate the bereft atheism that drummed upon Matthew Arnold's "Dover Beach" from *God Is Not Great*.

In the early 1970s, I was a graduate student at an institute in London founded by a German intellectual who went mad. He believed he was the god Saturn and that he had devoured his sons. The institute is devoted to the study of Renaissance intellectual history at the moment in Europe when magic became science.

The government inspector in Jean Giraudoux's play *The Enchanted* (1948) attempts to forbid the supernatural by decree:

> Science . . . *liberates the spirit of man from the infinite by means of material rewards. Thus, each time that man succeeds in casting off one of the spiritual husks of his being, Science provides him with an exact equivalent in the world of matter. When in the eighteenth century, man ceased to believe in the fire and smoke of hell, Science provided him with immediate compensation in the form of steam and gas . . . The moment man cast off his age-long belief in magic, Science bestowed upon him the blessings of the Electric Current . . . When he ceased any longer to heed the words of the seers and the*

prophets, Science lovingly brought forth the Radio Commentator . . .
In place of revelation he now has . . . Journalism.

On Bill Maher's cable television athenaeum, the journalist Christopher Hitchens proposes to Mr. Maher—and Mr. Maher wholeheartedly agrees—that science is the last best hope for humankind. Mr. Hitchens and Mr. Maher are unmindful, for the moment, of Hiroshima, drone missiles, chemical weapons, genetic modification, Original Sin.

After September 11, political division in America feels and sounds like religious division. Beginning with the sexual liberation movements of a generation earlier—with feminism and gay liberation—the growing preoccupation of the Left has been with the politics of sexual self-determination. There are some in the "old" political Left who decry the influence of sexual politics over traditional political concerns, like foreign policy and domestic poverty. It is more problematic that the new sexual identity movements allow themselves to be cast by the political Right as antireligious. The Left cedes religion to the Right, in exchange for a woman's right to legal abortion. The political Right intones Leviticus to homosexuals who wish to marry. The Right assumes a correlation between politics and religion; the Left assumes an antagonism toward traditional religion as the price of sexual freedom.

I am old enough to remember the Negro civil rights movement of the fifties and sixties. People who today relegate religion to the political Right forget how influential religion once was in the American Left. In those days, for that cause, civic protest was framed as religious idealism. Not only American history but salvation history seemed to weigh upon the present.

On television I saw Dr. Martin Luther King Jr. ascend the pulpit of the Mason Temple of the Church of God in Christ in Memphis. It was the evening of April 3, 1968. The civic life of America became part of a larger story, as Martin Luther King Jr. led his listeners to consider "the great and eternal issues of reality." He spoke of the exodus of the Israelites from Egypt; he spoke of Athenian democracy, the Emancipation Proclamation, FDR, and the Great Depression.

People said among themselves afterward that Dr. King's speech seemed, in its historical sweep, its elevated view, its summation, like the sermon of a man who knew he was going to die. Dr. King said he was grateful to God for allowing him to see this moment in America—the struggle for freedom by black Americans nearly completed. He said he might not reach the Promised Land with his people, as Moses did not. "But it really doesn't matter to me now, because I've been to the mountaintop," he said. "Mine eyes have seen."

2. *The Desert Floor*

The Israelites picked up a system of metaphor and a pervading sense of the irony of being God's Chosen from their sojourn on the desert floor—the desert floor as an unending test of endurance. For all the humiliations the desert inflicted upon them, however, it was from the desert that the Israelites projected, also, an imagination of the metaphysical world. Hell is hot, for example. Eden green. If the progress of our lives is a vale of tears, the Promised Land will be a psalm. All who are alive above the ground plead with the sky. But the Israelites alone among creation received an extraordinary assurance through the prophet Moses: Where does God reside? God resides with us.

A blessing upon the *New Yorker* magazine. The *New Yorker* continues to commission and to publish and to pay for original illustrations and comic drawings. I noticed, while thinking about this book, that in almost any issue of the *New Yorker*, I could find cartoons that rely upon one of three allegorical ecologies that derive from the religious imagination: Mountain. Desert. Cave. Three ecologies of the holy desert still hold a place in the secular imagination of the Upper West Side.

The Mountain (these are drawings in the *New Yorker*, I remind you): Moses raises his tablets. (Guy in the foreground remarks to another guy, "Sans seraph!") The Hermit Sage is seated at the mouth of a cave on a precipice—a foil to the Seeker who has climbed the precipice to ask the meaning of life. The mountain penetrates into the clouds to become Olympus, the mound from which sausage-curled Zeus heaves thunderbolts. Cloud cover extends upward to the Pearly Gates and to Saint Peter's Desk, occasion for gags related to the bureaucracy of entry or exclusion, as at a country club. Also, heavenly ennui—gags on the order of: *Not what I expected*. Or: *If only I had known . . .*

The Desert: across which a Sun-Crazed Man crawls, or two Sun-Crazed Men, one pulling ahead. Cactus, bones, empty canteens. *If only I had known . . .* Or: *If you had listened to me*. Also, the Desert Island—a single palm, two strandees. *If you had listened to me*. Also, the freeway exit to nowhere. (*If you had listened to me*.) Also, the Crazed Miner, combining allegories of Desert and Cave.

The Cave: the Sage (*see* The Mountain). Or the Caveman— usually a cave painter or an inventor of modernity. Also, the Tunnel of Love; also, the entrance to Dante's Inferno: *Not what I expected*. Also, the Dungeon. Also, Hell—a vast cavern, lakes of flame; themes of bureaucracy, ennui (*see* Saint Peter's Desk): *Not what I expected. If only I had known . . .*

And I am forgetting one: Eden. *If only I had known . . .*

In his *Confessions*, Saint Augustine wrote of a "region of dissimilarity," an absence, a nonexistence, of synapse between his, Augustine's, ability to conceive and his attempt to conceive of the inconceivable—between the creature and the creator. "It transcended my mind," wrote Augustine of his intuition of God. "It was superior to me because it made me, and I was inferior because I was made by it." Augustine does not write about distance, but difference. We cannot think about God except insofar as God reveals God to us. And where did the God of the Jews, the Christians, the Muslims, reveal His intention to accompany us?

The desert is a region of dissimilarity to us, to what we need for life—water, shelter, a body temperature of 98.6. So, it is logical, in a way, to seek the unknowable in the uninhabitable.

The desert of my imagining is at once extraordinary—the locus of revelation—and ordinary; it is a plain, a disheartening expanse of time and the image of all our days. Such was the desert the Israelites wandered for forty years unchanging.

I found this in an old geography I was looking through the other day (*Man and the Earth,* Joseph Bixby Hoyt): "The desert has a strange fascination for many people, strange in that it is largely irrational . . . in the sense that the desert has little value for man, our interest may be considered irrational." The Bible and the Koran are deserts, irrational. The Bible thirsts for a promised land. The Koran thirsts for heaven. God yearns for his creation.

My brother is now seventy. His hands are burled with arthritis. Some days he walks with difficulty. Despite his present aspect, because of his present aspect and condition, I remember him as beautiful—my beautiful brother—which is the way our mother saw him, always. He was her favorite—and why wouldn't he be?—the firstborn, the son who made her laugh, even when she refused to smile.

When I was eleven or so, I went to the Monday-night wrestling matches every chance I got. A wrestler with woodpecker hair named Red Bastien used to climb to the top rope of the ring (as if despite audible huffing and puffing and manifest corpulence he had vanished into thin air) in order to leap down upon his opponent. I saw Red fly dozens of times. Until the year I saw Red Bastien, hair still red, leaning forward on a cane, as he hobbled across the lobby of the Memorial Auditorium. Red had retired from the mat to become a promoter. I was thirteen years old. I saw, as clearly as I would ever see, that the world passes. Red and I had been young together.

Jesus took three of his disciples—Peter, James, and beloved John—to the top of Mount Tabor. In the presence of the three disciples, Jesus was transfigured, passive construction; Jesus was revealed to his friends in something more wonderful than His earthly aspect. He shone. And standing to each side of Jesus was Moses and Elijah. They conversed! Peter suggested the disciples make three tents on the spot—one for Moses, one for Elijah, one for Jesus. Peter had no sooner conceived of an eternal moment than a cloud overshadowed the disciples. Within the cloud, the disciples heard a voice that frightened them, so they huddled together—all of a sudden, a warm-blood club against the supernatural. When the cloud dissipated, they saw only Jesus, the man whose smell and smile and hammered thumb they knew. Jesus told them not to be afraid. He said they must not speak of anything they had seen. They must all return to the valley floor.

In the Hebrew Bible, much of history is associated with life on the desert floor. Heroes become old men. Old men beget sons; sons lay their fathers down into the earth. Some sons find favor with God; some do not. On the plain in Canaan, the favored son, Joseph, is betrayed by his jealous brothers. He is sold to some passing traders, bound for Egypt.

I do not believe I was ever jealous of my brother. I acknowledged the justice of his preferment. My brother moved with such delightful ease. Where had he learned the secret of charming girls? Always girls.

My brother sits today at his computer and pounds, literally pounds, the elegantly argued e-mails (political argument) he posts to an electronic community in darkened rooms across America. (I imagine darkened rooms because correspondents are anonymous and because so many of these colloquia are nocturnal.)

My brother's politics are left wing, Democrat, in an easy-going way; lots of saints (FDR, Harry S. Truman, Adlai Stevenson). My brother's faith is that technocrats will lead us through a sea of red tape and partisan obstruction to the Shining City on the Hill. My brother's mind has long since turned against religion, particularly Christianity, particularly Roman Catholicism, and the Evangelical Protestants he calls "Christo-Republicans." My brother is an atheist, though that drab noun hasn't nearly enough pixels to portray my brother's scorn. He calls himself an "anti-theist"; he called himself that one Christmas evening, at the holiday table, as if he were the tipsy, freethinking uncle in a James Joyce short story; as if he were James Joyce himself.

In his senior year of high school, my brother announced he was going to enter the seminary in the fall. In those years it was not such an unusual thing for an idealistic Catholic boy—the class president, the football captain—to aspire to a life of heroic spirituality. *Ah, but he's giving up so much*, people would falsely lament— falsely, for they all knew there was nothing much in the great so-much. They meant he was leaving the mortal desert of sex and dirty dishes and the morning commute to climb, to begin to climb, the mountain. The inspirational climbers of that era were Thomas Merton (*The Seven Storey Mountain*), Dr. Tom Dooley (*The Night They Burned the Mountain*), and Dr. Martin Luther King Jr. (*I have been to the mountaintop.*)

My brother had been at the seminary for two years when, in his weekly letter, he informed our parents that he was coming home. A few weeks later I returned from school to find my brother's suitcases in the hall, his boxes of books. My brother must have given an explanation to our parents, but I never heard it. It was highly unusual for me not to ask, for I was the question man. But that is the curious thing about families, isn't it—how much one knows about parents and siblings, but also how much one will never know. Without losing any noticeable stride, my brother went on to college and law school and beautiful women.

During this period, my brother and I became rumors to each other. We could not have said, one of the other, on any given day, on which side of the country we were living, or with whom. We might see each other at Christmas, my brother affable, handsome, quixotic. My brother mentioned an important court case coming up. I told him I would pray for him. (Irony mixes fluidly with piety in our family.) No, don't, he said.

That's my brother the lawyer, at the wheel of his Porsche: His passenger is a stewardess from Lebanon. She is laughing; her languid arm drifts from the window as the Porsche pulls away.

A journalist friend assures me I don't know the first thing about deserts when I say I yearn to hike through the Rub' al Khali, the Empty Quarter of Saudi Arabia. My friend lived for several years in Saudi Arabia. The first thing about deserts, he says, is sand. Not sand as metaphor, but sand as irritant: Sand in your underwear, sand in your shoes, sand in the rim of the Coke can. He says to walk into the Empty Quarter is to journey into inchoate being. One feels dwarfed by emptiness, he says, as, he imagines, an astronaut must feel. "How could there be more than one God in such a place?" he says. My friend is an atheist.

This same friend also lived for a time in India. Such is India's comic fecundity, he says, that if one spits the seeds from a melon along the side of the road, then returns to the same spot the following year, one will find a constellation of golden fruit—dancing gods, he calls them—among the greenery springing from the ditch at the side of the road.

Several months ago, my brother sent me an e-mail concerning the Council of Trent, convened by Pope Paul III in 1545. If my life depended on it, I could not tell you what transpired at the Council of Trent. I noticed my brother sent copies of his e-mail to his nephews and nieces, as well as to our siblings. The wonder is not that he knows so much about Church history, but that such matters continue to preoccupy him. Why not let it go? The procession of our family continues, oblivious of the Council of Trent; there are baptisms, First Holy Communions, confirmations, weddings, funerals. My brother, the anti-theist, is always in attendance. That is he, photographed in a church pew, smiling. Next to him is his son. Me? Oh, I wasn't there. Out of town. Too distracted by my book on religion to show up for a grandniece's baptism.

I wrote to my brother a few years ago. I told him I was bored with his e-mails about religion. Bored with his scientific perspective, as he calls it. Bored with political faith. I asked him to stop.

Maybe the spirit of the times is to recoil from a mullah's absolute or a bishop's absolute, and to call that recoil atheism. Yet atheism seems to me as absolute as the surest faith.

As a Christian, I have so long sheltered in the idea of the God of the Jews, I would never think to call myself a theist. Too much abstraction is implied. I have buried both my parents "marked with the sign of faith." After September 11, I started describing myself as "Judeo-Christian-Muslim." Though I attend weekly Mass, I am struck by how often the priest, in his homily, must remind the congregation what we believe.

This year, the Catholic Church in the United States began using a new English translation of the Mass. The translation we had been using dated from 1973. The 2012 translation reverts to arcane English in an attempt to be more faithful to the Latin diction and syntax of the fourth-century Latin "vulgate" translation (from the Hebrew, from the Greek) of Saint Jerome. Why? I don't know. Why did Pope Benedict favor an eighteenth-century pattern for chasubles, as I have heard? And why did Vatican watchers raise their eyebrows at a Pope who favored an eighteenth-century pattern for chasubles? The Vatican must be more like a Ronald Firbank novel than we imagine.

Catholic journals blazed with controversy throughout that fall and winter. Many American priests, theologians, liturgists, and laymen objected to the new translation, particularly to the grammar of the Eucharistic prayer, which has taken an exclusionary meaning.

What I started out to tell you is that Sunday Mass has become a confusion, a bad lip sync. Some in the congregation continue to recite the 1973 translation—not out of refusal, but because humans are creatures of habit, and most of us have long since committed 1973 to memory. Some in the congregation resort to missals in the pews and follow the new translation scrupulously. Others, like the man who stands behind me, continue to pray in Latin.

The Creed (which comes early in the Mass) is the point at

which everyone stumbles. We used to recite the Apostle's Creed—rather, a version of the Creed closer to the Apostle's Creed, which dates from the first century. Now we most often recite the Nicene Creed, which was formulated in the fourth century as a refutation of the Arian heresy. The Arian heresy had to do with the divine nature of Jesus. The remembered lines are embellished with a few Latinate formulations that weren't there before, so we trip.

What is important to me is how important it is for me to be told what I believe. I could not, on my own, have come up with the two thousand years of argument that has formulated an evolving Christian theology. People who say of Catholics that we are told what to believe are correct. We are.

We are, most of us, not theologians. I borrow an excellent passage from an excellent pamphlet that was passed out to prepare American Catholics for the new translation. I cannot credit the author or the authors of the pamphlet, for there is no notation as to authorship or committee. The passage: "The Creed, or *symbolum,* is the symbol of our profession of faith; it is not the faith itself. We believe something because we first believed someone and that someone is Jesus." But before we get to Jesus (or Abraham or Moses or the Prophet Muhammad or Buddha) there is probably someone else. Mama. Papi. Miss Nowik. Nibs. Rabbi Heschel. Brother James. Jim Downey. Robert McAfee Brown. Flannery O'Connor. Father Costa. Andy Warhol.

My brother and I have, after many years, achieved our importance to each other as a difference. Because it is sometimes difficult for my brother to climb the steps to my apartment, he will often come by and we will sit in his car and talk. We quite enjoy one another's company. My brother is no less a good man for not believing in God; and I am no better a man because I believe. It is simply that religion gives me a sense—no, not a sense, a reason, no, not exactly a reason, an understanding—that everyone matters.

The congregation does not believe one thing; we believe a multitude of hazy, crazy things. Some among us are smart; some serene; some feeble, poor, practical, guilt-ridden; some are lazy; some arrogant, rich, pious, prurient, bitter, injured, sad. We gather in belief of one big thing: that we matter, somehow. We all matter. No one can matter unless all matter. We call that which gives matter God.

The moment of matter arrives with the Lord's Prayer. Jesus instructed, *"This is how you should pray: Our Father, who art in heaven . . ."*

The prayer takes about thirty seconds to recite, to join, in the present, the Christian world of centuries. It is the first prayer most of us committed to memory as children. It is the prayer most of us will say as we die. It is the prayer others will say over our bodies. The prayer makes no attempt to say what God is, but only what we are, what we need: We are hungry; we are sinners; we fear evil. It is the prayer that most easily takes us out of ourselves and joins us to centuries of people who have gone before, centuries of people who will come after.

That woman—five rows ahead on this side, red beret—her husband died of kidney cancer last year, yet here she is. The world ends. He is gone. She is here. I pray for him, her husband. What can that possibly mean, that I pray for him? I mean in a feeble, childish, desperate way (because there are people I believe I cannot bear to lose, and I imagine that woman feels the same, yet she has lost), I ask the hope of Enduring Love I call God to accept the man that was and to console his widow. Because the man who was is yet part of this day insofar as he is missing and she is here in her brave little red beret. Love is real. I have felt it, but I do not know how to live in love, once and for all, nor do I know if that is possible, though I have met people who almost seem to.

None of this happens as a forgetting of a day in summer, or winter, though there is that. I didn't leave the coffee pot on, did I? Shall I stop at the bakery on my way home? There is all of that.

The truest, most sublime vision of the Catholic Mass I have ever seen was in a Terence Davies movie called *The Long Day Closes*. The camera tracks over the heads of an audience in a movie theater, following the beam of blue light from the projector toward the screen, passing through the screen, then over the heads of the congregation in a Liverpool Catholic church, the congregation kneeling and rising as, all the while, on the sound track, the voice of Debbie Reynolds sings "Tammy."

This confraternity of strangers—the procession of the living with the dead—is the most important, most continuous confraternity in my life, though unpronounced except by rote prayer. I take my place in a pew as I would take a seat within a vast ark. Going where? We don't know. All we know is that one Sunday we will not be here. We know that nothing will change for our absence. Those are the names of the dead under the stained-glass windows and on all the tombs and plaques and rooms of testament and so forth, and so what? That is the consolation I take from the Mass—that I will join the obverse, which is represented to me by a lantern in a corridor that leads behind the altar. That I will join, for a while, the passive, prayed for. And then I will be forgotten. The procession will go on; it will emerge from the other side of the altar.

But not forgotten by God, please God.

And will there be an other, an active, present, everlasting love?

Eternity—which is a thought outside of time, isn't it?—need have no duration at all, I tell myself. Cannot, in logic. But that, too, is desperate.

And it doesn't matter a fig whether we say "worship" (1973) or "adore" (2012).

3. The Cave

In Israel, Jordan, Syria, Saudi Arabia, Egypt, one need only gaze up to see caves that were once chambers of an ancient sea—dry, riven sockets that seem to watch. The eye of the cave, however, is not the regnant metaphor. The mouth of a cave is what we more often say. The mouth of a cave is an image of perdition. We are organisms that sustain ourselves through our mouths. Indeed, we are caves ourselves. Since we eat, we fear being eaten. But we like the idea of secrets in the earth, of emeralds, rubies, sunless seas, for the womb is the cave we are born of.

Girls are taught early by their elders that their bodies are sacred caves, that they are, therefore, priestesses of some sticky magic and that boys are after stealing their magic. Boys are taught by their elders to mind the fact of their compulsion by Nature to enter that cave; that therein resides the meaning of manhood. Human innocence is calculated according to knowledge of the cave.

Mysteries and oracles abounded in the caves of the ancient world. Hindus and Buddhists revered caves as sacred sites, carved chapels in them and painted the walls. Because of the cave's long association with the esoteric and the supernatural, Plato took the cave as an allegory of unreason, of false apprehension. The prisoners of Plato's cave became unfit for any greater reality, content as they were to face away from the light of day and to consider only shadows.

Iegor Reznikoff, a musical anthropologist who has studied the resonance of cathedrals throughout Europe (by singing in them), has also explored the resonance of prehistoric caves. He has noticed that resonance in caves is often greatest or most pleasing in chambers with paintings on the walls, which suggests to Reznikoff a correlation between paintings and music. Caves were probably chosen for their resonance; probably they were used for chanted worship; probably they were painted commemoratively because they were places of ritual.

The book of Exodus, chapter 33, is nearly an inversion of Plato's allegory. Moses begged God to show him His glory. God refused—*No human can see Me and live.* But then God relented somewhat: *I will place you in a cleft of the rock, and screen you with my hand until I have passed by.* So it was that Moses withstood an experience of the ultimate reality by turning his back and shielding his face, much like the prisoners of Plato's cave.

A section cut away from the wall of a cave to reveal what is inside (like an X-ray view) became a prevalent conceit in early Greek-Christian iconography. Within the cave, the dead lie buried like bolts of cloth, or we see the hermit solitary at his prayer or we see the scull of Adam beneath the crucifix at Golgotha or we see the manger of Jesus.

The stable of Christ's birth was probably a cave that was used to pen sheep or goats or donkeys. The venerated site of the nativity in Bethlehem is the remnant of a rock cave. At the nether-end of the Christ narrative, six miles away, Jesus's broken body was laid on a shelf of rock in a cave, and it was there—in the darkness of that tomb—that light or voice or pulse or rush of wings found and raised him.

Since September 11, I have watched Muslims—Muslim men, I mean—at prayer with an admiration that is nearly unease. On Fridays, in the squares of the desert cities, men form themselves into rows, facing in one direction—a carpet of faith, a militia, if need be. It is not the posture of humility that makes me uneasy. It is the performance of single-mindedness that defines me as a spectator.

I pulled this instruction from the Internet. This is the proper way of performing Salah: *Stand at attention, put the world behind you. Then, creating tunnel vision, bring your hands to your ears, palms forward, thumbs behind earlobes . . .*

Prayer shawl, monk's hood, tunnel vision, the cloister of hands—the cave technique of prayer is common to all religions, all people.

The Prophet Muhammad hid from his enemies in a cave. In an hour's time, a spider sealed the mouth of the cave with a year's worth of web; the enemies of the Prophet passed the cave by.

It was in a dark cave that enlightenment came to the Prophet—that is the happy paradox of Islam. The gift of revelation was confusing and frightening to Muhammad; Muhammad described the imminence of revelation as like the approach of a concentric reverberation, as of a bell. *Read!* The Angel Gabriel commanded. The angel seized hold of the Prophet's body thoroughly, as though he would squeeze the Prophet's life from his mouth. *Read!* Muhammad pleaded with the angel; he could not read. *Read!* The Angel once more demanded. *Recite!*

The first revelation left Muhammad fearing for his sanity. He sought his wife, Khadijah; he trembled in her presence; he asked that she cover him with a blanket, as if that were a cave where the angel could not find him. It was Khadijah's faith that gave the Prophet courage not to deny or mistrust the revelation that had come to him. Henceforth, when Muhammad recited the revelations to followers, he would wrap himself in a blanket.

———

On a dark and drizzly morning in spring, I am delighted to find the garden snails schooning the sidewalk in front of my house. I suppose it is slickness that calls them forth. Lovely creatures like Viking ships. I pluck one up. *Surely you were better off where you were. What destiny summons you from the shelter of the underside of the leaf?* My impulse is to repatriate this pilgrim to the nasturtium patch in the park across the street—land of milk and honey (and probably slug bait). But I do not interfere. Despite the dangers, he is called. He has brought his cave with him. Even a snail must have a story.

As a very young woman, Agnes Gonxha Bojaxhiu journeyed from Skopje, Macedonia, to Ireland, because she had decided to join the Sisters of Loretto, a teaching order of nuns. She took the name of Sister Mary Teresa, after her patron saint, Saint Thérèse of Lisieux. Sister Teresa was sent by her order to St. Mary's Bengali Medium School for girls in Calcutta. She arrived there on January 6, 1929. Sister Teresa professed her final vows on May 24, 1937, after which time she was called, according to the custom of India, Mother Teresa. She was known among her sisters for her readiness to work and for her unfailing good cheer.

In September of 1946, on a train journey to Darjeeling for a week's retreat of prayer and reflection, Mother Teresa was inspired with the idea that she must leave the Loretto convent and venture into the slums of Calcutta to care for the poor of India. The inspiration was in response to a voice that spoke to Mother Teresa within her solitude. Teresa's rendition of the voice, in her notes and letters, has the urgency of a lover's groan. Mother Teresa characterized the urgency of the voice as thirst:

My little one—come—come—carry me into the holes of the poor.—
Come be My light—I cannot go alone—they don't know Me—so

they don't want Me. You come—go amongst them, carry Me with
you into them.—How I long to enter their holes—their dark un-
happy homes . . . You will suffer—suffer very much—but remem-
ber I am with you.—Even if the whole world rejects you—remember
you are My own—and I am yours only. Fear not. It is I. . . .

Mother Teresa confessed to her spiritual adviser, Father Van Exem, that she had experienced a voice; she did not immediately identify the voice as that of Jesus or, specifically, as it was in her mind, the voice of Jesus thirsting on the cross. She confessed she had conceived a desire to establish an order of nuns to serve the poorest of the poor. She asked Father Van Exem to write to the bishop.

There must always be a bishop.

Even divine inspiration, if such it was, must find its way around a bishop. In Mother Teresa's case, the bishop was unmoved, unconvinced, unwilling. Mother Teresa knew no better than to wheedle and plead in her letters. But it came to pass, as it must, that divine inspiration—for such I believe it was—prevailed.

On August 8, 1948, Mother Teresa received permission from the Vatican Office of the Sacred Congregation for Religious to leave her order and to begin her new mission. On August 17, Mother Teresa walked through the gates of the Loretto convent, dressed in a cheap white linen sari trimmed in blue, and with five rupees knotted in a bandana. The gates closed behind her. She was thirty-eight years old; she was alone in vast India; she was a beggar.

If this were a film, I would pan backward at this point to show the solitary figure standing outside the gates, on a street, in a maze of streets, in the huge city smoldering in the mist of early sunlight, to show how thoroughly this woman entrusted herself to God.

The doors opened. Christopher Hitchens entered the elevator. He was smiling Felix-like; some thought or quarrel playing upon his lips. He smelled of liquor. And gossip. He carried some files under his arm; he had evidentially forgotten them, for as he lifted his arm to push a button on the elevator panel, all his papers fell to the floor. He bent over; I bent over to pick up his papers.

Mr. Hitchens was in New York for an international literary conference called "Faith and Reason," as was I. I suspect the organizers of the conference trusted their title to convey "Faith as Opposed to Reason," and they were not disappointed; the tenor of the discourse was irreligious. In another time it might have been assumed of such a gathering that writers would share, at least poetically, in the religious imaginations of their countries. During the three days I attended the conference, among the several hundred writers I met, only three confessed a religiosity that animated their fiction or non-. Indeed, so pervasive was atheism to the proceedings, a reporter from the *Frankfurter Allegemeine Zeitung*, who audited a panel discussion in which I took part, assumed I am and thus described me as a "non-believer."

Christopher Hitchens, a British subject who several years ago converted to America, earned his screaming-eagle badge by his support of America's war in Iraq—defending Churchillian saberlines in the sand. Before that endeavor, Hitchens became famous in America with an article he published in *Vanity Fair* attacking the holiest of cows, Mother Teresa of Calcutta. (A book on Mother Teresa followed: *The Missionary Position*.) Hitchens criticized Mother Teresa for accepting donations from persons whose fortunes were ill gotten; he criticized her for campaigning against abortion and birth control; he criticized her for gathering the poor to her death house, but not curing them; he mocked her for being an ugly woman. That last bit was, rhetorically, a reversion to the English public school sneer.

I suppose he was charming. Everyone said so. I didn't like him—I mean his public persona; I didn't like it. Still, his was a brilliant career at a time when writers do not matter much in the public life of America. Opinions on Orwell and Wilde with a Washington dateline are uncommon. As the Iraq invasion proved an exercise in neocolonial overreach, Hitchens, tripping over the stars and stripes in which he had wrapped himself, published a catechism for atheists called *God Is Not Great*. That book success-fully reconciled Hitchens to bloggers of Left-lane bandwidth like my brother.

So, there we were, the two of us, stooping, improbably picking up a peck of (I presume) prickly papers as the elevator shunted us heavenward.

Hitchens straightened up; he smiled, mumbled thanks. The el-evator doors opened.

A few years later Hitchens chronicled his cancer in *Vanity Fair*. He finished two books. He never backed down. He died on the front page. He reposes now in *Vanity Fair*'s Tomb of the Well-Known.

Mother Teresa, the animus of so much of Hitchens's black ink, lived, by her own testimony, and for many years, in "terrible dark-ness," unable to discern the presence of God in her life. After Mother Teresa's death, a collection of her letters to various bish-ops, confessors, and superiors was published under the title *Mother Teresa: Come Be My Light*.

The most convincing aspect of Mother Teresa's story is the strangest: At the moment her request to establish a new order of nuns was granted by Rome and she was able, after years of petitions, to realize what she believed was God's will for her—the same moment we saw her outside the convent gates—God withdrew consolation from Mother Teresa's life. Henceforward, she must live in poverty of spirit; she must live, as so many live, without hope. She could not feel the once-proximate God; she could no longer hear the voice of Jesus. She did not doubt the existence of God. All she knew was that God had withdrawn from her personally. Several years later, in the tiny chapel of her fledging order, Mother Teresa watched the other nuns at their prayers. She wrote, "I see them love God . . . and . . . am 'just alone'—empty—excluded—just not wanted."

Darkness became the banal motif of Mother Teresa's life during her years of international celebrity, of flashing bulbs and television lights, of crowds applauding her entrance, of hands reaching to touch the hem of her sari. In November 1958, Mother Teresa wrote of herself in dejection to Archbishop Périer: "Our Lord thought it better for me to be in the tunnel—so He is gone again—leaving me alone."

So it was, also, with her namesake, the great small Saint Thérèse of Lisieux, who, in the agony of her death from tuberculosis, felt herself continually "in the night" or "in an underground passage." Gazing into the cloister garden, from her bed in the infirmary, Saint Thérèse noticed what she described as "a black hole" among the trees. "I am in a hole just like that, body and soul," she said. "Ah! What darkness!" In the final passages of her autobiography, Saint Thérèse likened herself to a small bird in a hedge that wishes to fly to the sun but cannot; she is too small, too weak. Dark clouds cover the sun. The little bird can no longer see the sun or feel its warmth; the wind blows cold; nevertheless, the little bird believes the sun is still there, behind the clouds. She will wait.

From Washington, Christopher Hitchens remarked that the

private letters of Mother Teresa proved her to have been a hypocrite all along. "She was no more exempt from the realization that religion is a human fabrication than any other person, and that her attempted cure was more and more professions of faith could only have deepened the pit that she had dug for herself."

Atheism is wasted on the non-believer.

Until the end of her long life, Mother Teresa fed the poor; she gathered the sick and the dying; she cleaned and blessed the bodies of those whose deaths would not be mourned otherwise by anyone in the world.

Mother Teresa died on the night of September 5, 1997, in Calcutta. The electrical power failed in the convent in which she lay. The convent had two emergency generators, but they, too, failed. The breathing machine at her side was silent. She died in the dark.

There is a rustling, as of silks; there is a tinkling of ornaments and bells and tambourines behind the scrim of heaven; a whispering, too, and a fluttering, as of birds in the rafters, foxes, mice, fairies, parakeets, rain; there is a sound of the flexion of tall trees, as the host of heaven assembles on risers behind the great curtain—a turning of halos this way and that, halos inclining toward one another in collegial candor, like interested satellite dishes, and light shines from the parliament of faces as light from Pharos; lidless eyes these are, drawn with the black pencil of sorrow, the eyes of saints in icons, eyes that flamenco dancers also adopt to celebrate our passions as the victims of love on earth.

Acknowledgments

I am indebted to two editors at Viking Penguin, Kathryn Court and Ben George, for their editorial guidance, and for permitting me a literary freedom appropriate to an age when words literally mattered. John Jusino has been a special blessing—a copyeditor both sharp-eyed and sensitive, like no other I have ever worked with. Georges Borchardt, my excellent friend and literary agent, remains one of my best readers.

Besides being my intellectual conspirator and closest friend, Sandy Close, the managing editor of New America Media, financially supported the writing of this book.

Franz Schurmann and Alberto Huerta, S.J., were intellectual companions of mine for many years. Their influence on my thinking—evident throughout this book—survives their deaths.

I dedicate this book to my earliest teachers, young Irish women, members of the order of the Sisters of Mercy, who traversed an ocean and a continent to teach me. It was their lives and example remembered that has led me to the conclusion that the future of the Abrahamic religions will be determined by women, not men.

Jim Armistead, who, for more than thirty years, has completed my life, read and edited every page of this book with a rigor and compassion that define for me the meaning of love.

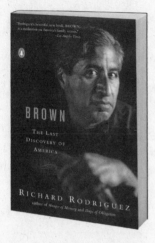

Brown
The Last Discovery of America

In his dazzling memoir, Richard Rodriguez reflects on the color brown and the meaning of Hispanics to the life of America today. But more than simply a book about race, *Brown* is about America in the broadest sense—a look at what our country is, full of surprising observations by a writer who is at once a marvelous stylist, as well as a trenchant observer and thinker.

ISBN 978-0-14-200079-3

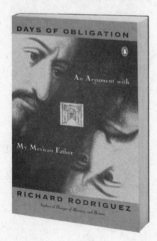

Days of Obligation
An Argument with My Mexican Father

Rodriguez's acclaimed first book, *Hunger of Memory,* provoked a fierce controversy with its views on bilingualism and affirmative action. Now, in a series of intelligent and candid essays, Rodriguez looks back over five centuries of history to consider the moral and spiritual landscapes of Mexico and the United States and their impact on his soul.

ISBN 978-0-14-009622-4

**PENGUIN
BOOKS**

BORN A CRIME

AND OTHER STORIES

TREVOR NOAH

JOHN MURRAY

First published in Great Britain in 2016 by John Murray (Publishers)
An Hachette UK Company

First published in paperback in 2017

34

A CIP catalogue record for this title is available from the British Library

ISBN 978-1-473-63530-2
Ebook ISBN 978-1-473-63531-9

Printed and bound by Clays Ltd, Elcograf S.p.A.

John Murray policy is to use papers that are natural, renewable and recyclable
products and made from wood grown in sustainable forests. The logging and
manufacturing processes are expected to conform to the environmental regulations of
the country of origin.

John Murray (Publishers)
Carmelite House
50 Victoria Embankment
London EC4Y 0DZ

www.johnmurray.co.uk

apartheid - Jim Crow

Trevor Noah is the host of the Emmy and Peabody Award-winning *The Daily Show*. He first joined the show as a contributor in 2014 and succeeded Jon Stewart in 2015. While *The Daily Show* has introduced Noah to an American audience, he's long been a popular comedian around the globe. Born in South Africa to a black mother and a white European father, Noah rose to stardom with *The Racist*, his one-man show. He now lives in New York.

Praise for *Born a Crime*

'An intimate ringside seat to the fractured arena where a divided South Africa – white, black, coloured, Indian, Zulu, Xhosa, Pedi, Tsonga and so on – intersects . . . That Noah has emerged miraculously unscathed, filled with determination, grit, wisdom, a searing intelligence (cultivated through the books he read as a loner) and an enduring mischievous glint, is inspiring' *Guardian*

'Powerful . . . The story of Noah's life is full of chase scenes in which he runs, hell for leather, from spankings, from the long arm of the law, and from the swinging fist of his stepfather . . . a unique perspective' *The Times*

'It's no surprise that Trevor Noah, the slyly suave successor to Jon Stewart as host of *The Daily Show*, should write a smart book. But "smart" doesn't begin to cover what he pulls off in *Born a Crime* . . . Noah's memoir is extraordinary . . . essential reading on every level. It's hard to imagine anyone else doing a finer job of it' *Seattle Times*

'A soul-nourishing pleasure, even with all its darker edges and perilous turns, reading Noah recount in brisk, warmly conversational prose how he learned to negotiate his way through the bullying and ostracism . . . is an enormous gift' *USA Today*

For my mother. My first fan.
Thank you for making me a man.

IMMORALITY ACT, 1927

**To prohibit illicit carnal intercourse
between Europeans and natives and
other acts in relation thereto.**

———————

B E IT ENACTED by the King's Most Excellent
Majesty, the Senate and the House of Assembly of
the Union of South Africa, as follows:—

1. Any European male who has illicit carnal
intercourse with a native female, and any native
male who has illicit carnal intercourse with a
European female . . . shall be guilty of an offence
and liable on conviction to imprisonment for a
period not exceeding five years.

2. Any native female who permits any European
male to have illicit carnal intercourse with her and
any European female who permits any native male
to have illicit carnal intercourse with her shall
be guilty of an offence and liable on conviction
to imprisonment for a period not exceeding four
years. . . .

CONTENTS

The genius of apartheid was convincing people who were the overwhelming majority to turn on each other. Apart hate, is what it was. You separate people into groups and make them hate one another so you can run them all.

At the time, black South Africans outnumbered white South Africans nearly five to one, yet we were divided into different tribes with different languages: Zulu, Xhosa, Tswana, Sotho, Venda, Ndebele, Tsonga, Pedi, and more. Long before apartheid existed these tribal factions clashed and warred with one another. Then white rule used that animosity to divide and conquer. All nonwhites were systematically classified into various groups and subgroups. Then these groups were given differing levels of rights and privileges in order to keep them at odds.

Perhaps the starkest of these divisions was between South Africa's two dominant groups, the Zulu and the Xhosa. The Zulu man is known as the warrior. He is proud. He puts his head down and fights. When the colonial armies invaded, the Zulu charged into battle with nothing but spears and shields against men with guns. The Zulu were slaughtered by the thousands, but they never stopped fighting. The Xhosa, on the other hand, pride themselves on being the thinkers. My mother is Xhosa. Nelson Mandela was Xhosa. The Xhosa waged a long war against the white man as well, but after experiencing the futility of battle against a better-armed foe, many Xhosa chiefs took a more nimble approach. "These white people are here whether we like it or not," they said. "Let's see what tools they possess that can be useful to us. Instead of being resistant to English, let's learn English. We'll understand what the white man is saying, and we can force him to negotiate with us."

The Zulu went to war with the white man. The Xhosa played chess with the white man. For a long time neither was particularly successful, and each blamed the other for a problem neither had created. Bitterness festered. For decades those feelings were held in check by a common enemy. Then apartheid fell, Mandela walked free, and black South Africa went to war with itself.

———————

I

RUN

Sometimes in big Hollywood movies they'll have these crazy chase scenes where somebody jumps or gets thrown from a moving car. The person hits the ground and rolls for a bit. Then they come to a stop and pop up and dust themselves off, like it was no big deal. Whenever I see that I think, *That's rubbish. Getting thrown out of a moving car hurts way worse than that.*

I was nine years old when my mother threw me out of a moving car. It happened on a Sunday. I know it was on a Sunday because we were coming home from church, and every Sunday in my childhood meant church. We *never* missed church. My mother was—and still is— a deeply religious woman. Very Christian. Like indigenous peoples around the world, black South Africans adopted the religion of our colonizers. By "adopt" I mean it was forced on us. The white man was quite stern with the native. "You need to pray to Jesus," he said. "Jesus will save you." To which the native replied, "Well, we do need to be saved—saved from *you*, but that's beside the point. So let's give this Jesus thing a shot."

My whole family is religious, but where my mother was Team Jesus all the way, my grandmother balanced her Christian faith with the traditional Xhosa beliefs she'd grown up with, communicating with the spirits of our ancestors. For a long time I didn't understand why so many black people had abandoned their indigenous faith for Christianity. But the more we went to church and the longer I sat in those pews the more I learned about how Christianity works: If you're Native American and you pray to the wolves, you're a savage. If you're African and you pray to your ancestors, you're a primitive. But when white people pray to a guy who turns water into wine, well, that's just common sense.

My childhood involved church, or some form of church, at least four nights a week. Tuesday night was the prayer meeting. Wednesday night was Bible study. Thursday night was Youth church. Friday and Saturday we had off. (Time to sin!) Then on Sunday we went to church. Three churches, to be precise. The reason we went to three churches was because my mom said each church gave her something different. The first church offered jubilant praise of the Lord. The second church offered deep analysis of the scripture, which my mom loved. The third church offered passion and catharsis; it was a place where you truly felt the presence of the Holy Spirit inside you. Completely by coincidence, as we moved back and forth between these churches, I noticed that each one had its own distinct racial makeup: Jubilant church was mixed church. Analytical church was white church. And passionate, cathartic church, that was black church.

Mixed church was Rhema Bible Church. Rhema was one of those huge, supermodern, suburban megachurches. The pastor, Ray McCauley, was an ex-bodybuilder with a big smile and the personality of a cheerleader. Pastor Ray had competed in the 1974 Mr. Universe competition. He placed third. The winner that year was Arnold Schwarzenegger.

Every week, Ray would be up onstage working really hard to make Jesus cool. There was arena-style seating and a rock band jamming out with the latest Christian contemporary pop. Everyone sang along, and if you didn't know the words that was okay because they were all right up there on the Jumbotron for you. It was Christian karaoke, basically. I always had a blast at mixed church.

White church was Rosebank Union in Sandton, a very white and wealthy part of Johannesburg. I *loved* white church because I didn't actually have to go to the main service. My mom would go to that, and I would go to the youth side, to Sunday school. In Sunday school we got to read cool stories. Noah and the flood was obviously a favorite; I had a personal stake there. But I also loved the stories about Moses parting the Red Sea, David slaying Goliath, Jesus whipping the money changers in the temple.

I grew up in a home with very little exposure to popular culture. Boyz II Men were not allowed in my mother's house. Songs about some guy grinding on a girl all night long? No, no, no. That was forbidden. I'd hear the other kids at school singing "End of the Road," and I'd have no clue what was going on. I knew *of* these Boyz II Men, but I didn't really know who they were. The only music I knew was from church: soaring, uplifting songs praising Jesus. It was the same with movies. My mom didn't want my mind polluted by movies with sex and violence. So the Bible was my action movie. Samson was my superhero. He was my He-Man. A guy beating a thousand people to death with the jawbone of a donkey? That's pretty badass. Eventually you get to Paul writing letters to the Ephesians and it loses the plot, but the Old Testament and the Gospels? I could quote you anything from those pages, chapter and verse. There were Bible games and quizzes every week at white church, and I kicked everyone's ass.

Then there was black church. There was always some kind of black church service going on somewhere, and we tried them all. In the township, that typically meant an outdoor, tent-revival-style church. We usually went to my grandmother's church, an old-school Methodist congregation, five hundred African grannies in blue-and-white blouses, clutching their Bibles and patiently burning in the hot African sun. Black church was rough, I won't lie. No air-conditioning. No lyrics up on Jumbotrons. And it lasted forever, three or four hours at least, which confused me because white church was only like an hour—in and out, thanks for coming. But at black church I would sit there for what felt like an eternity, trying to figure out why time moved so slowly. *Is it possible for time to actually stop? If so, why does it stop at black church and not at white church?* I eventually decided black people needed more time with Jesus because we suffered more. "I'm here to fill up on my blessings for the week," my mother used to say. The more time we spent at church, she reckoned, the more blessings we accrued, like a Starbucks Rewards Card.

Black church had one saving grace. If I could make it to the third or fourth hour I'd get to watch the pastor cast demons out of people. People possessed by demons would start running up and down the aisles like madmen, screaming in tongues. The ushers would tackle them, like bouncers at a club, and hold them down for the pastor. The pastor would grab their heads and violently shake them back and forth, shouting, "I cast out this spirit in the name of *Jesus*!" Some pastors were more violent than others, but what they all had in common was that they wouldn't stop until the demon was gone and the congregant had gone limp and collapsed on the stage. The person had to fall. Because if he didn't fall that meant the demon was powerful and the pastor needed to come at him even harder. You could be a linebacker in the NFL. Didn't matter. That pastor was taking you *down*. Good Lord, that was fun.

Christian karaoke, badass action stories, and violent faith healers—man, I loved church. The thing I didn't love was the lengths we had to go to in order to get to church. It was an epic slog. We lived in Eden Park, a tiny suburb way outside Johannesburg. It took us an hour to get to white church, another forty-five minutes to get to mixed church, and another forty-five minutes to drive out to Soweto for black church. Then, if that wasn't bad enough, some Sundays we'd double back to white church for a special evening service. By the time we finally got home at night, I'd collapse into bed.

This particular Sunday, the Sunday I was hurled from a moving car, started out like any other Sunday. My mother woke me up, made me porridge for breakfast. I took my bath while she dressed my baby brother Andrew, who was nine months old. Then we went out to the driveway, but once we were finally all strapped in and ready to go, the car wouldn't start. My mom had this ancient, broken-down, bright-tangerine Volkswagen Beetle that she picked up for next to nothing. The reason she got it for next to nothing was because it was always breaking down. To this day I hate secondhand cars. Almost everything that's ever gone wrong in my life I can trace back to a secondhand car. Secondhand cars made me get detention for being late for school. Secondhand cars left us hitchhiking on the side of the freeway. A second-hand car was also the reason my mom got married. If it hadn't been for the Volkswagen that didn't work, we never would have looked for the mechanic who became the husband who became the stepfather who became the man who tortured us for years and put a bullet in the back of my mother's head—I'll take the new car with the warranty every time.

As much as I loved church, the idea of a nine-hour slog, from mixed church to white church to black church then doubling back to white church again, was just too much to contemplate. It was bad enough in a car, but taking public transport would be twice as long and twice as hard. When the Volkswagen refused to start, inside my head I was praying, *Please say we'll just stay home. Please say we'll just stay home.* Then I glanced over to see the determined look on my mother's face, her jaw set, and I knew I had a long day ahead of me.

"Come," she said. "We're going to catch minibuses."

My mother is as stubborn as she is religious. Once her mind's made up, that's it. Indeed, obstacles that would normally lead a person to change their plans, like a car breaking down, only made her more determined to forge ahead.

"It's the Devil," she said about the stalled car. "The Devil doesn't want us to go to church. That's why we've got to catch minibuses."

Whenever I found myself up against my mother's faith-based obstinacy, I would try, as respectfully as possible, to counter with an opposing point of view.

"Or," I said, "the Lord knows that today we *shouldn't* go to church, which is why he made sure the car wouldn't start, so that we stay at home as a family and take a day of rest, because even the Lord rested."

"Ah, that's the Devil talking, Trevor."

"No, because Jesus is in control, and if Jesus is in control and we pray to Jesus, he would let the car start, but he hasn't, therefore—"

"No, Trevor! Sometimes Jesus puts obstacles in your way to see if you overcome them. Like Job. This could be a test."

"Ah! Yes, Mom. But the test could be to see if we're willing to accept what has happened and stay at home and praise Jesus for his wisdom."

"No. That's the Devil talking. Now go change your clothes."

"But, Mom!"

"Trevor! *Sun'qhela!*"

Sun'qhela is a phrase with many shades of meaning. It says "don't undermine me," "don't underestimate me," and "just try me." It's a command and a threat, all at once. It's a common thing for Xhosa parents to say to their kids. Any time I heard it I knew it meant the conversation was over, and if I uttered another word I was in for a hiding—what we call a spanking.

At the time, I attended a private Catholic school called Maryvale College. I was the champion of the Maryvale sports day every single year, and my mother won the moms' trophy every single year. Why? Because she was always chasing me to kick my ass, and I was always running not to get my ass kicked. Nobody ran like me and my mom. She wasn't one of those "Come over here and get your hiding" type moms. She'd deliver it to you free of charge. She was a thrower, too. Whatever was next to her was coming at you. If it was something breakable, I had to catch it and put it down. If it broke, that would be my fault, too, and the ass-kicking would be that much worse. If she threw a vase at me, I'd have to catch it, put it down, and then run. In a split second, I'd have to think, *Is it valuable? Yes. Is it breakable? Yes. Catch it, put it down, now run.*

We had a very Tom and Jerry relationship, me and my mom. She was the strict disciplinarian; I was naughty as shit. She would send me out to buy groceries, and I wouldn't come right home because I'd be using the change from the milk and bread to play arcade games at the supermarket. I loved videogames. I was a master at *Street Fighter*. I could go forever on a single play. I'd drop a coin in, time would fly, and the next thing I knew there'd be a woman behind me with a belt. It was a race. I'd take off out the door and through the dusty streets of Eden Park, clambering over walls, ducking through backyards. It was a normal thing in our neighborhood. Everybody knew: That Trevor child would come through like a bat out of hell, and his mom would be right there behind him. She could go at a full sprint in high heels, but if she really wanted to come after me she had this thing where she'd kick her shoes off while still going at top speed. She'd do this weird move with her ankles and the heels would go flying and she wouldn't even miss a step. That's when I knew, *Okay, she's in turbo mode now.*

When I was little she always caught me, but as I got older I got faster, and when speed failed her she'd use her wits. If I was about to get away she'd yell, *"Stop! Thief!"* She'd do this to her own child. In South Africa, nobody gets involved in other people's business—unless it's mob justice, and then everybody wants in. So she'd yell "Thief!" knowing it would bring the whole neighborhood out against me, and then I'd have strangers trying to grab me and tackle me, and I'd have to duck and dive and dodge them as well, all the while screaming, "I'm not a thief! I'm her son!"

The last thing I wanted to do that Sunday morning was climb into some crowded minibus, but the second I heard my mom say *sun'qhela* I knew my fate was sealed. She gathered up Andrew and we climbed out of the Volkswagen and went out to try to catch a ride.

I was five years old, nearly six, when Nelson Mandela was released from prison. I remember seeing it on TV and everyone being happy. I didn't know why we were happy, just that we were. I was aware of the fact that there was a thing called apartheid and it was ending and that was a big deal, but I didn't understand the intricacies of it.

What I do remember, what I will never forget, is the violence that followed. The triumph of democracy over apartheid is sometimes called the Bloodless Revolution. It is called that because very little white blood was spilled. Black blood ran in the streets.

As the apartheid regime fell, we knew that the black man was now going to rule. The question was, which black man? Spates of violence broke out between the Inkatha Freedom Party and the ANC, the African National Congress, as they jockeyed for power. The political dynamic between these two groups was very complicated, but the simplest way to understand it is as a proxy war between Zulu and Xhosa. The Inkatha was predominantly Zulu, very militant and very nationalistic. The ANC was a broad coalition encompassing many different tribes, but its leaders at the time were primarily Xhosa. Instead of uniting for peace they turned on one another, committing acts of unbelievable savagery. Massive riots broke out. Thousands of people were killed. Necklacing was common. That's where people would hold someone down and put a rubber tire over his torso, pinning his arms. Then they'd douse him with petrol and set him on fire and burn him alive. The ANC did it to Inkatha. Inkatha did it to the ANC. I saw one of those charred bodies on the side of the road one day on my way to school. In the evenings my mom and I would turn on our little black-and-white TV and watch the news. A dozen people killed. Fifty people killed. A hundred people killed.

Eden Park sat not far from the sprawling townships of the East Rand, Thokoza and Katlehong, which were the sites of some of the most horrific Inkatha–ANC clashes. Once a month at least we'd drive home and the neighborhood would be on fire. Hundreds of rioters in the street. My mom would edge the car slowly through the crowds and around blockades made of flaming tires. Nothing burns like a tire—it rages with a fury you can't imagine. As we drove past the burning blockades, it felt like we were inside an oven. I used to say to my mom, "I think Satan burns tires in Hell."

Whenever the riots broke out, all our neighbors would wisely hole up behind closed doors. But not my mom. She'd head straight out, and as we'd inch our way past the blockades, she'd give the rioters this look. *Let me pass. I'm not involved in this shit.* She was unwavering in the face of danger. That always amazed me. It didn't matter that there was a war on our doorstep. She had things to do, places to be. It was the same stubbornness that kept her going to church despite a broken-down car. There could be five hundred rioters with a blockade of burning tires on the main road out of Eden Park, and my mother would say, "Get dressed. I've got to go to work. You've got to go to school."

"But aren't you afraid?" I'd say. "There's only one of you and there's so many of them."

"Honey, I'm not alone," she'd say. "I've got all of Heaven's angels behind me."

"Well, it would be nice if we could *see* them," I'd say. "Because I don't think the rioters know they're there."

She'd tell me not to worry. She always came back to the phrase she lived by: "If God is with me, who can be against me?" She was never scared. Even when she should have been.

That carless Sunday we made our circuit of churches, ending up, as usual, at white church. When we walked out of Rosebank Union it was dark and we were alone. It had been an endless day of minibuses from mixed church to black church to white church, and I was exhausted. It was nine o'clock at least. In those days, with all the violence and riots going on, you did not want to be out that late at night. We were standing at the corner of Jellicoe Avenue and Oxford Road, right in the heart of Johannesburg's wealthy, white suburbia, and there were no minibuses. The streets were empty.

I so badly wanted to turn to my mom and say, "You see? This is why God wanted us to stay home." But one look at the expression on her face, and I knew better than to speak. There were times I could talk smack to my mom—this was not one of them.

We waited and waited for a minibus to come by. Under apartheid the government provided no public transportation for blacks, but white people still needed us to show up to mop their floors and clean their bathrooms. Necessity being the mother of invention, black people created their own transit system, an informal network of bus routes, controlled by private associations operating entirely outside the law. Because the minibus business was completely unregulated, it was basically organized crime. Different groups ran different routes, and they would fight over who controlled what. There was bribery and general shadiness that went on, a great deal of violence, and a lot of protection money paid to avoid violence. The one thing you didn't do was steal a route from a rival group. Drivers who stole routes would get killed. Being unregulated, minibuses were also very unreliable. When they came, they came. When they didn't, they didn't.

Standing outside Rosebank Union, I was literally falling asleep on my feet. Not a minibus in sight. Eventually my mother said, "Let's hitchhike." We walked and walked, and after what felt like an eternity, a car drove up and stopped. The driver offered us a ride, and we climbed in. We hadn't gone ten feet when suddenly a minibus swerved right in front of the car and cut us off.

A Zulu driver got out with an *iwisa,* a large, traditional Zulu weapon—a war club, basically. They're used to smash people's skulls in. Another guy, his crony, got out of the passenger side. They walked up to the driver's side of the car we were in, grabbed the man who'd offered us a ride, pulled him out, and started shoving their clubs in his face. "Why are you stealing our customers? Why are you picking people up?"

It looked like they were going to kill this guy. I knew that happened sometimes. My mom spoke up. "Hey, listen, he was just helping me. Leave him. We'll ride with you. That's what we wanted in the first place." So we got out of the first car and climbed into the minibus.

We were the only passengers in the minibus. In addition to being violent gangsters, South African minibus drivers are notorious for complaining and haranguing passengers as they drive. This driver was

a particularly angry one. As we rode along, he started lecturing my
mother about being in a car with a man who was not her husband. My
mother didn't suffer lectures from strange men. She told him to mind
his own business, and when he heard her speaking in Xhosa, that really
set him off. The stereotypes of Zulu and Xhosa women were as ingrained as those of the men. Zulu women were well-behaved and dutiful. Xhosa women were promiscuous and unfaithful. And here was my
mother, his tribal enemy, a Xhosa woman alone with two small
children—one of them a mixed child, no less. Not just a whore but a
whore who sleeps with white men. "Oh, you're a *Xhosa*," he said. "That
explains it. Climbing into strange men's cars. Disgusting woman."

My mom kept telling him off and he kept calling her names, yelling
at her from the front seat, wagging his finger in the rearview mirror and
growing more and more menacing until finally he said, "That's the
problem with you Xhosa women. You're all sluts—and tonight you're
going to learn your lesson."

He sped off. He was driving fast, and he wasn't stopping, only
slowing down to check for traffic at the intersections before speeding
through. Death was never far away from anybody back then. At that
point my mother could be raped. We could be killed. These were all
viable options. I didn't fully comprehend the danger we were in at the
moment; I was so tired that I just wanted to sleep. Plus my mom stayed
very calm. She didn't panic, so I didn't know to panic. She just kept
trying to reason with him.

"I'm sorry if we've upset you, *bhuti*. You can just let us out here—"

"No."

"Really, it's fine. We can just walk—"

"No."

He raced along Oxford Road, the lanes empty, no other cars out. I
was sitting closest to the minibus's sliding door. My mother sat next to
me, holding baby Andrew. She looked out the window at the passing
road and then leaned over to me and whispered, "Trevor, when he
slows down at the next intersection, I'm going to open the door and
we're going to jump."

I didn't hear a word of what she was saying, because by that point I'd completely nodded off. When we came to the next traffic light, the driver eased off the gas a bit to look around and check the road. My mother reached over, pulled the sliding door open, grabbed me, and threw me out as far as she could. Then she took Andrew, curled herself in a ball around him, and leaped out behind me.

It felt like a dream until the pain hit. *Bam!* I smacked hard on the pavement. My mother landed right beside me and we tumbled and tumbled and rolled and rolled. I was wide awake now. I went from half asleep to *What the hell?!* Eventually I came to a stop and pulled myself up, completely disoriented. I looked around and saw my mother, already on her feet. She turned and looked at me and screamed.

"Run!"

So I ran, and she ran, and nobody ran like me and my mom.

It's weird to explain, but I just knew what to do. It was animal instinct, learned in a world where violence was always lurking and waiting to erupt. In the townships, when the police came swooping in with their riot gear and armored cars and helicopters, I knew: *Run for cover. Run and hide.* I knew that as a five-year-old. Had I lived a different life, getting thrown out of a speeding minibus might have fazed me. I'd have stood there like an idiot, going, "What's happening, Mom? Why are my legs so sore?" But there was none of that. Mom said "run," and I ran. Like the gazelle runs from the lion, I ran.

The men stopped the minibus and got out and tried to chase us, but they didn't stand a chance. We smoked them. I think they were in shock. I still remember glancing back and seeing them give up with a look of utter bewilderment on their faces. *What just happened? Who'd have thought a woman with two small children could run so fast?* They didn't know they were dealing with the reigning champs of the Maryvale College sports day. We kept going and going until we made it to a twenty-four-hour petrol station and called the police. By then the men were long gone.

I still didn't know why any of this had happened; I'd been running on pure adrenaline. Once we stopped running I realized how much pain I was in. I looked down, and the skin on my arms was scraped and torn. I was cut up and bleeding all over. Mom was, too. My baby brother was fine, though, incredibly. My mom had wrapped herself around him, and he'd come through without a scratch. I turned to her in shock.

"What was *that*?! Why are we running?!"

"What do you mean, 'Why are we running?' Those men were trying to kill us."

"You never told me that! You just threw me out of the car!"

"I did tell you. Why didn't you jump?"

"Jump?! I was asleep!"

"So I should have left you there for them to kill you?"

"At least they would have woken me up before they killed me."

Back and forth we went. I was too confused and too angry about getting thrown out of the car to realize what had happened. My mother had saved my life.

As we caught our breath and waited for the police to come and drive us home, she said, "Well, at least we're safe, thank God."

But I was nine years old and I knew better. I wasn't going to keep quiet this time.

"No, Mom! This was *not* thanks to God! You should have listened to God when he told us to stay at home when the car wouldn't start, because clearly the Devil tricked us into coming out tonight."

"No, Trevor! That's not how the Devil works. This is part of God's plan, and if He wanted us here then He had a reason . . ."

And on and on and there we were, back at it, arguing about God's will. Finally I said, "Look, Mom. I know you love Jesus, but maybe next week you could ask him to meet us at our house. Because this really wasn't a fun night."

She broke out in a huge smile and started laughing. I started laughing, too, and we stood there, this little boy and his mom, our arms and legs covered in blood and dirt, laughing together through the pain in the light of a petrol station on the side of the road in the middle of the night.

Apartheid was perfect racism. It took centuries to develop, starting all the way back in 1652 when the Dutch East India Company landed at the Cape of Good Hope and established a trading colony, Kaapstad, later known as Cape Town, a rest stop for ships traveling between Europe and India. To impose white rule, the Dutch colonists went to war with the natives, ultimately developing a set of laws to subjugate and enslave them. When the British took over the Cape Colony, the descendants of the original Dutch settlers trekked inland and developed their own language, culture, and customs, eventually becoming their own people, the Afrikaners—the white tribe of Africa.

The British abolished slavery in name but kept it in practice. They did so because, in the mid-1800s, in what had been written off as a near-worthless way station on the route to the Far East, a few lucky capitalists stumbled upon the richest gold and diamond reserves in the world, and an endless supply of expendable bodies was needed to go in the ground and get it all out.

As the British Empire fell, the Afrikaner rose up to claim South Africa as his rightful inheritance. To maintain power in the face of the country's rising and restless black majority, the government realized they needed a newer and more robust set of tools. They set up a formal commission to go out and study institutionalized racism all over the world. They went to Australia. They went to the Netherlands. They went to America. They saw what worked, what didn't. Then they came back and published a report, and the government used that knowledge to build the most advanced system of racial oppression known to man.

Apartheid was a police state, a system of surveillance and laws designed to keep black people under total control. A full compendium of those laws would run more than three thousand pages and weigh approximately ten pounds, but the general thrust of it should be easy enough for any American to understand. In America you had the forced removal of the native onto reservations coupled with slavery followed by segregation. Imagine all three of those things happening to the same group of people at the same time. That was apartheid.

———————

2

BORN A CRIME

I grew up in South Africa during apartheid, which was awkward because I was raised in a mixed family, with me being the mixed one in the family. My mother, Patricia Nombuyiselo Noah, is black. My father, Robert, is white. Swiss/German, to be precise, which Swiss/Germans invariably are. During apartheid, one of the worst crimes you could commit was having sexual relations with a person of another race. Needless to say, my parents committed that crime.

In any society built on institutionalized racism, race-mixing doesn't merely challenge the system as unjust, it reveals the system as unsustainable and incoherent. Race-mixing proves that races can mix—and in a lot of cases, *want* to mix. Because a mixed person embodies that rebuke to the logic of the system, race-mixing becomes a crime worse than treason.

Humans being humans and sex being sex, that prohibition never stopped anyone. There were mixed kids in South Africa nine months after the first Dutch boats hit the beach in Table Bay. Just like in America, the colonists here had their way with the native women, as colonists so often do. Unlike in America, where anyone with one drop of black blood automatically became black, in South Africa mixed people came to be classified as their own separate group, neither black nor white but what we call "colored." Colored people, black people, white people, and Indian people were forced to register their race with the government. Based on those classifications, millions of people were uprooted and relocated. Indian areas were segregated from colored areas, which were segregated from black areas—all of them segregated from white areas and separated from one another by buffer zones of empty land. Laws were passed prohibiting sex between Europeans and natives, laws that were later amended to prohibit sex between whites and all nonwhites.

The government went to insane lengths to try to enforce these new laws. The penalty for breaking them was five years in prison. There were whole police squads whose only job was to go around peeking through windows—clearly an assignment for only the finest law enforcement officers. And if an interracial couple got caught, God help them. The police would kick down the door, drag the people out, beat them, arrest them. At least that's what they did to the black person. With the white person it was more like, "Look, I'll just say you were drunk, but don't do it again, eh? Cheers." That's how it was with a white man and a black woman. If a black man was caught having sex with a white woman, he'd be lucky if he wasn't charged with rape.

If you ask my mother whether she ever considered the ramifications of having a mixed child under apartheid, she will say no. She wanted to do something, figured out a way to do it, and then she did it. She had a level of fearlessness that you have to possess to take on something like she did. If you stop to consider the ramifications, you'll never do anything. Still, it was a crazy, reckless thing to do. A million things had to go right for us to slip through the cracks the way we did for as long as we did.

• • •

Under apartheid, if you were a black man you worked on a farm or in a factory or in a mine. If you were a black woman, you worked in a factory or as a maid. Those were pretty much your only options. My mother didn't want to work in a factory. She was a horrible cook and never would have stood for some white lady telling her what to do all day. So, true to her nature, she found an option that was not among the ones presented to her: She took a secretarial course, a typing class. At the time, a black woman learning how to type was like a blind person learning how to drive. It's an admirable effort, but you're unlikely to ever be called upon to execute the task. By law, white-collar jobs and skilled-labor jobs were reserved for whites. Black people didn't work in offices. My mom, however, was a rebel, and, fortunately for her, her rebellion came along at the right moment.

In the early 1980s, the South African government began making minor reforms in an attempt to quell international protest over the atrocities and human rights abuses of apartheid. Among those reforms was the token hiring of black workers in low-level white-collar jobs. Like typists. Through an employment agency she got a job as a secretary at ICI, a multinational pharmaceutical company in Braamfontein, a suburb of Johannesburg.

When my mom started working, she still lived with my grandmother in Soweto, the township where the government had relocated my family decades before. But my mother was unhappy at home, and when she was twenty-two she ran away to live in downtown Johannesburg. There was only one problem: It was illegal for black people to live there.

The ultimate goal of apartheid was to make South Africa a white country, with every black person stripped of his or her citizenship and relocated to live in the homelands, the Bantustans, semi-sovereign black territories that were in reality puppet states of the government in Pretoria. But this so-called white country could not function without black labor to produce its wealth, which meant black people had to be allowed to live near white areas in the townships, government-planned ghettos built to house black workers, like Soweto. The township was where you lived, but your status as a laborer was the only thing that permitted you to stay there. If your papers were revoked for any reason, you could be deported back to the homelands.

To leave the township for work in the city, or for any other reason, you had to carry a pass with your ID number; otherwise you could be arrested. There was also a curfew: After a certain hour, blacks had to be back home in the township or risk arrest. My mother didn't care. She was determined to never go home again. So she stayed in town, hiding and sleeping in public restrooms until she learned the rules of navigating the city from the other black women who had contrived to live there: prostitutes.

Many of the prostitutes in town were Xhosa. They spoke my mother's language and showed her how to survive. They taught her how to dress up in a pair of maid's overalls to move around the city without being questioned. They also introduced her to white men who were willing to rent out flats in town. A lot of these men were foreigners, Germans and Portuguese who didn't care about the law and were happy to sign a lease giving a prostitute a place to live and work in exchange for a steady piece on the side. My mom wasn't interested in any such arrangement, but thanks to her job she did have money to pay rent. She met a German fellow through one of her prostitute friends, and he agreed to let her a flat in his name. She moved in and bought a bunch of maid's overalls to wear. She was caught and arrested many times, for not having her ID on the way home from work, for being in a white area after hours. The penalty for violating the pass laws was thirty days in jail or a fine of fifty rand, nearly half her monthly salary. She would scrape together the money, pay the fine, and go right back about her business.

My mom's secret flat was in a neighborhood called Hillbrow. She lived in number 203. Down the corridor was a tall, brown-haired, brown-eyed Swiss/German expat named Robert. He lived in 206. As a former trading colony, South Africa has always had a large expatriate community. People find their way here. Tons of Germans. Lots of Dutch. Hillbrow at the time was the Greenwich Village of South Africa. It was a thriving scene, cosmopolitan and liberal. There were galleries and underground theaters where artists and performers dared to speak up and criticize the government in front of integrated crowds. There were restaurants and nightclubs, a lot of them foreign-owned, that served a mixed clientele, black people who hated the status quo and white people who simply thought it ridiculous. These people would have secret get-togethers, too, usually in someone's flat or in empty basements that had been converted into clubs. Integration by its nature was a political act, but the get-togethers themselves weren't political at all. People would meet up and hang out, have parties.

My mom threw herself into that scene. She was always out at some club, some party, dancing, meeting people. She was a regular at the Hillbrow Tower, one of the tallest buildings in Africa at that time. It had a nightclub with a rotating dance floor on the top floor. It was an exhilarating time but still dangerous. Sometimes the restaurants and clubs would get shut down, sometimes not. Sometimes the performers and patrons would get arrested, sometimes not. It was a roll of the dice. My mother never knew whom to trust, who might turn her in to the police. Neighbors would report on one another. The girlfriends of the white men in my mom's block of flats had every reason to report a black woman—a prostitute, no doubt—living among them. And you must remember that black people worked for the government as well. As far as her white neighbors knew, my mom could have been a spy posing as a prostitute posing as a maid, sent into Hillbrow to inform on whites who were breaking the law. That's how a police state works—everyone thinks everyone else is the police.

Living alone in the city, not being trusted and not being able to trust, my mother started spending more and more time in the company of someone with whom she felt safe: the tall Swiss man down the corridor in 206. He was forty-six. She was twenty-four. He was quiet and reserved; she was wild and free. She would stop by his flat to chat; they'd go to underground get-togethers, go dancing at the nightclub with the rotating dance floor. Something clicked.

I know that there was a genuine bond and a love between my parents. I saw it. But how romantic their relationship was, to what extent they were just friends, I can't say. These are things a child doesn't ask. All I do know is that one day she made her proposal.

"I want to have a kid," she told him.

"I don't want kids," he said.

"I didn't ask you to have a kid. I asked you to help me to have my kid. I just want the sperm from you."

"I'm Catholic," he said. "We don't do such things."

"You do know," she replied, "that I could sleep with you and go away and you would never know if you had a child or not. But I don't want that. Honor me with your yes so that I can live peacefully. I want a child of my own, and I want it from you. You will be able to see it as much as you like, but you will have no obligations. You don't have to talk to it. You don't have to pay for it. Just make this child for me."

For my mother's part, the fact that this man didn't particularly want a family with her, was prevented by law from having a family with her, was part of the attraction. She wanted a child, not a man stepping in to run her life. For my father's part, I know that for a long time he kept saying no. Eventually he said yes. Why he said yes is a question I will never have the answer to.

Nine months after that yes, on February 20, 1984, my mother checked into Hillbrow Hospital for a scheduled C-section delivery. Estranged from her family, pregnant by a man she could not be seen with in public, she was alone. The doctors took her up to the delivery room, cut open her belly, and reached in and pulled out a half-white, half-black child who violated any number of laws, statutes, and regulations—I was born a crime.

When the doctors pulled me out there was an awkward moment where they said, "Huh. That's a very light-skinned baby." A quick scan of the delivery room revealed no man standing around to take credit.

"Who is the father?" they asked.

"His father is from Swaziland," my mother said, referring to the tiny, landlocked kingdom in the west of South Africa.

They probably knew she was lying, but they accepted it because they needed an explanation. Under apartheid, the government labeled everything on your birth certificate: race, tribe, nationality. Everything had to be categorized. My mother lied and said I was born in Ka-Ngwane, the semi-sovereign homeland for Swazi people living in South Africa. So my birth certificate doesn't say that I'm Xhosa, which technically I am. And it doesn't say that I'm Swiss, which the government wouldn't allow. It just says that I'm from another country.

My father isn't on my birth certificate. Officially, he's never been my father. And my mother, true to her word, was prepared for him not to be involved. She'd rented a new flat for herself in Joubert Park, the neighborhood adjacent to Hillbrow, and that's where she took me when she left the hospital. The next week she went to visit him, with no baby. To her surprise, he asked where I was. "You said that you didn't want to be involved," she said. And he hadn't, but once I existed he realized he couldn't have a son living around the corner and not be a part of my life. So the three of us formed a kind of family, as much as our peculiar situation would allow. I lived with my mom. We'd sneak around and visit my dad when we could.

Where most children are proof of their parents' love, I was the proof of their criminality. The only time I could be with my father was indoors. If we left the house, he'd have to walk across the street from us. My mom and I used to go to Joubert Park all the time. It's the Central Park of Johannesburg—beautiful gardens, a zoo, a giant chessboard with human-sized pieces that people would play. My mother tells me that once, when I was a toddler, my dad tried to go with us. We were in the park, he was walking a good bit away from us, and I ran after him, screaming, "Daddy! Daddy! Daddy!" People started looking. He panicked and ran away. I thought it was a game and kept chasing him.

I couldn't walk with my mother, either; a light-skinned child with a black woman would raise too many questions. When I was a newborn, she could wrap me up and take me anywhere, but very quickly that was no longer an option. I was a giant baby, an enormous child. When I was one you'd have thought I was two. When I was two, you'd have thought I was four. There was no way to hide me.

My mom, same as she'd done with her flat and with her maid's uniforms, found the cracks in the system. It was illegal to be mixed (to have a black parent and a white parent), but it was not illegal to be colored (to have two parents who were both colored). So my mom moved me around the world as a colored child. She found a crèche in a colored area where she could leave me while she was at work. There was a colored woman named Queen who lived in our block of flats. When we wanted to go out to the park, my mom would invite her to go with us. Queen would walk next to me and act like she was my mother, and my mother would walk a few steps behind, like she was the maid working for the colored woman. I've got dozens of pictures of me walking with this woman who looks like me but who isn't my mother. And the black woman standing behind us who looks like she's photobombing the picture, that's my mom. When we didn't have a colored woman to walk with us, my mom would risk walking me on her own. She would hold my hand or carry me, but if the police showed up she would have to drop me and pretend I wasn't hers, like I was a bag of weed.

When I was born, my mother hadn't seen her family in three years, but she wanted me to know them and wanted them to know me, so the prodigal daughter returned. We lived in town, but I would spend weeks at a time with my grandmother in Soweto, often during the holidays. I have so many memories from the place that in my mind it's like we lived there, too.

Soweto was designed to be bombed—that's how forward-thinking the architects of apartheid were. The township was a city unto itself, with a population of nearly one million. There were only two roads in and out. That was so the military could lock us in, quell any rebellion. And if the monkeys ever went crazy and tried to break out of their cage, the air force could fly over and bomb the shit out of everyone. Growing up, I never knew that my grandmother lived in the center of a bull's-eye.

In the city, as difficult as it was to get around, we managed. Enough people were out and about, black, white, and colored, going to and from work, that we could get lost in the crowd. But only black people were permitted in Soweto. It was much harder to hide someone who looked like me, and the government was watching much more closely. In the white areas you rarely saw the police, and if you did it was Officer Friendly in his collared shirt and pressed pants. In Soweto the police were an occupying army. They didn't wear collared shirts. They wore riot gear. They were militarized. They operated in teams known as flying squads, because they would swoop in out of nowhere, riding in armored personnel carriers—hippos, we called them—tanks with enormous tires and slotted holes in the side of the vehicle to fire their guns out of. You didn't mess with a hippo. You saw one, you ran. That was a fact of life. The township was in a constant state of insurrection; someone was always marching or protesting somewhere and had to be suppressed. Playing in my grandmother's house, I'd hear gunshots, screams, tear gas being fired into crowds.

My memories of the hippos and the flying squads come from when I was five or six, when apartheid was finally coming apart. I never saw the police before that, because we could never risk the police seeing me. Whenever we went to Soweto, my grandmother refused to let me outside. If she was watching me it was, "No, no, no. He doesn't leave the house." Behind the wall, in the yard, I could play, but not in the street. And that's where the rest of the boys and girls were playing, in the street. My cousins, the neighborhood kids, they'd open the gate and head out and roam free and come back at dusk. I'd beg my grandmother to go outside.

"Please. *Please,* can I go play with my cousins?"

"No! They're going to take you!"

For the longest time I thought she meant that the other kids were going to steal me, but she was talking about the police. Children could be taken. Children *were* taken. The wrong color kid in the wrong color area, and the government could come in, strip your parents of custody, haul you off to an orphanage. To police the townships, the government relied on its network of *impipis,* the anonymous snitches who'd inform on suspicious activity. There were also the blackjacks, black people who worked for the police. My grandmother's neighbor was a blackjack. She had to make sure he wasn't watching when she smuggled me in and out of the house.

My gran still tells the story of when I was three years old and, fed up with being a prisoner, I dug a hole under the gate in the driveway, wriggled through, and ran off. Everyone panicked. A search party went out and tracked me down. I had no idea how much danger I was putting everyone in. The family could have been deported, my gran could have been arrested, my mom might have gone to prison, and I probably would have been packed off to a home for colored kids.

So I was kept inside. Other than those few instances of walking in the park, the flashes of memory I have from when I was young are almost all indoors, me with my mom in her tiny flat, me by myself at my gran's. I didn't have any friends. I didn't know any kids besides my cousins. I wasn't a lonely kid—I was good at being alone. I'd read books, play with the toy that I had, make up imaginary worlds. I lived inside my head. I still live inside my head. To this day you can leave me alone for hours and I'm perfectly happy entertaining myself. I have to remember to be with people.

Obviously, I was not the only child born to black and white parents during apartheid. Traveling around the world today, I meet other mixed South Africans all the time. Our stories start off identically. We're around the same age. Their parents met at some underground party in Hillbrow or Cape Town. They lived in an illegal flat. The difference is that in virtually every other case they left. The white parent smuggled them out through Lesotho or Botswana, and they grew up in exile, in England or Germany or Switzerland, because being a mixed family under apartheid was just that unbearable.

Once Mandela was elected we could finally live freely. Exiles started to return. I met my first one when I was around seventeen. He told me his story, and I was like, "Wait, *what*? You mean we could have *left*?

That was an *option*?" Imagine being thrown out of an airplane. You hit the ground and break all your bones, you go to the hospital and you heal and you move on and finally put the whole thing behind you—and then one day somebody tells you about parachutes. That's how I felt. I couldn't understand why we'd stayed. I went straight home and asked my mom.

"Why? Why didn't we just leave? Why didn't we go to Switzerland?"

"Because I am not Swiss," she said, as stubborn as ever. "This is my country. Why should I leave?"

South Africa is a mix of the old and the new, the ancient and the modern, and South African Christianity is a perfect example of this. We adopted the religion of our colonizers, but most people held on to the old ancestral ways, too, just in case. In South Africa, faith in the Holy Trinity exists quite comfortably alongside belief in witchcraft, in casting spells and putting curses on one's enemies.

I come from a country where people are more likely to visit *sangomas*—shamans, traditional healers, pejoratively known as witch doctors—than they are to visit doctors of Western medicine. I come from a country where people have been arrested and tried for witchcraft—in a court of law. I'm not talking about the 1700s. I'm talking about five years ago. I remember a man being on trial for striking another person with lightning. That happens a lot in the homelands. There are no tall buildings, few tall trees, nothing between you and the sky, so people get hit by lightning all the time. And when someone gets killed by lightning, everyone knows it's because somebody used Mother Nature to take out a hit. So if you had a beef with the guy who got killed, someone will accuse you of murder and the police will come knocking.

"Mr. Noah, you've been accused of murder. You used witchcraft to kill David Kibuuka by causing him to be struck by lightning."

"What is the evidence?"

"The evidence is that David Kibuuka got struck by lightning and it wasn't even raining."

And you go to trial. The court is presided over by a judge. There is a docket. There is a prosecutor. Your defense attorney has to prove lack of motive, go through the crime-scene forensics, present a staunch defense. And your attorney's argument can't be "Witchcraft isn't real." No, no, no. You'll lose.

3

TREVOR, PRAY

I grew up in a world run by women. My father was loving and devoted, but I could only see him when and where apartheid allowed. My uncle Velile, my mom's younger brother, lived with my grandmother, but he spent most of his time at the local tavern getting into fights.

The only semi-regular male figure in my life was my grandfather, my mother's father, who was a force to be reckoned with. He was divorced from my grandmother and didn't live with us, but he was around. His name was Temperance Noah, which was odd since he was not a man of moderation at all. He was boisterous and loud. His nickname in the neighborhood was "Tat Shisha," which translates loosely to "the smokin' hot grandpa." And that's exactly who he was. He loved the ladies, and the ladies loved him. He'd put on his best suit and stroll through the streets of Soweto on random afternoons, making everybody laugh and charming all the women he'd meet. He had a big, dazzling smile with bright white teeth—false teeth. At home, he'd take them out and I'd watch him do that thing where he looked like he was eating his own face.

We found out much later in life that he was bipolar, but before that we just thought he was eccentric. One time he borrowed my mother's car to go to the shop for milk and bread. He disappeared and didn't come home until late that night when we were way past the point of needing the milk or the bread. Turned out he'd passed a young woman at the bus stop and, believing no beautiful woman should have to wait for a bus, he offered her a ride to where she lived—three hours away. My mom was furious with him because he'd cost us a whole tank of petrol, which was enough to get us to work and school for two weeks.

When he was up you couldn't stop him, but his mood swings were wild. In his youth he'd been a boxer, and one day he said I'd disrespected him and now he wanted to box me. He was in his eighties. I was twelve. He had his fists up, circling me. "Let's go, Trevah! Come on! Put your fists up! Hit me! I'll show you I'm still a man! Let's go!" I couldn't hit him because I wasn't about to hit my elder. Plus I'd never been in a fight and I wasn't going to have my first one be with an eighty-year-old man. I ran to my mom, and she got him to stop. The day after his pugilistic rage, he sat in his chair and didn't move or say a word all day.

Temperance lived with his second family in the Meadowlands, and we visited them sparingly because my mom was always afraid of being poisoned. Which was a thing that would happen. The first family were the heirs, so there was always the chance they might get poisoned by the second family. It was like *Game of Thrones* with poor people. We'd go into that house and my mom would warn me.

"Trevor, don't eat the food."

"But I'm starving."

"No. They might poison us."

"Okay, then why don't I just pray to Jesus and Jesus will take the poison out of the food?"

"Trevor! *Sun'qhela!*"

So I only saw my grandfather now and then, and when he was gone the house was in the hands of women.

In addition to my mom there was my aunt Sibongile; she and her first husband, Dinky, had two kids, my cousins Mlungisi and Bulelwa. Sibongile was a powerhouse, a strong woman in every sense, big-chested, the mother hen. Dinky, as his name implies, was dinky. He was a small man. He was abusive, but not really. It was more like he tried to be abusive, but he wasn't very good at it. He was trying to live up to this image of what he thought a husband should be, dominant, controlling. I remember being told as a child, "If you don't hit your woman, you don't love her." That was the talk you'd hear from men in bars and in the streets.

Dinky was trying to masquerade as this patriarch that he wasn't. My aunt would take it and take it, and then eventually she'd snap and smack him down and put him back in his place. Dinky would always walk around like, "I control my woman." And you'd want to say, "Dinky, first of all, you don't. Second of all, you don't need to. Because she loves you." I can remember one day my aunt had really had enough. I was in the yard and Dinky came running out of the house screaming bloody murder. Sibongile was right behind him with a pot of boiling water, cursing at him and threatening to douse him with it. In Soweto you were always hearing about men getting doused with pots of boiling water—often a woman's only recourse. And men were lucky if it was water. Some women used hot cooking oil. Water was if the woman wanted to teach her man a lesson. Oil meant she wanted to end it.

My grandmother Frances Noah was the family matriarch. She ran the house, looked after the kids, did the cooking and the cleaning. She's barely five feet tall, hunched over from years in the factory, but rock hard and still to this day very active and very much alive. Where my grandfather was big and boisterous, my grandmother was calm, calculating, with a mind as sharp as anything. If you need to know anything in the family history, going back to the 1930s, she can tell you what day it happened, where it happened, and why it happened. She remembers it all.

My great-grandmother lived with us as well. We called her Koko. She was super old, well into her nineties, stooped and frail, completely blind. Her eyes had gone white, clouded over by cataracts. She couldn't walk without someone holding her up. She'd sit in the kitchen next to the coal stove, bundled up in long skirts and head scarves, blankets over her shoulders. The coal stove was always on. It was for cooking, heating the house, heating water for baths. We put her there because it was the warmest spot in the house. In the morning someone would wake her and bring her to sit in the kitchen. At night someone would come take her to bed. That's all she did, all day, every day. Sit by the stove. She was fantastic and fully with it. She just couldn't see and didn't move.

Koko and my gran would sit and have long conversations, but as a five-year-old I didn't think of Koko as a real person. Since her body didn't move, she was like a brain with a mouth. Our relationship was nothing but command prompts and replies, like talking to a computer.

"Good morning, Koko."

"Good morning, Trevor."

"Koko, did you eat?"

"Yes, Trevor."

"Koko, I'm going out."

"Okay, be careful."

"Bye, Koko."

"Bye, Trevor."

The fact that I grew up in a world run by women was no accident. Apartheid kept me away from my father because he was white, but for almost all the kids I knew on my grandmother's block in Soweto, apartheid had taken away their fathers as well, just for different reasons. Their fathers were off working in a mine somewhere, able to come home only during the holidays. Their fathers had been sent to prison.

Their fathers were in exile, fighting for the cause. Women held the community together. *"Wathint'Abafaʒi Wathint'imbokodo!"* was the chant they would rally to during the freedom struggle. "When you strike a woman, you strike a rock." As a nation, we recognized the power of women, but in the home they were expected to submit and obey.

In Soweto, religion filled the void left by absent men. I used to ask my mom if it was hard for her to raise me alone without a husband. She'd reply, "Just because I live without a man doesn't mean I've never had a husband. God is my husband." For my mom, my aunt, my grand-mother, and all the other women on our street, life centered on faith. Prayer meetings would rotate houses up and down the block based on the day. These groups were women and children only. My mom would always ask my uncle Velile to join, and he'd say, "I would join if there were more men, but I can't be the only one here." Then the singing and praying would start, and that was his cue to leave.

For these prayer meetings, we'd jam ourselves into the tiny living area of the host family's house and form a circle. Then we would go around the circle offering prayers. The grannies would talk about what was happening in their lives. "I'm happy to be here. I had a good week at work. I got a raise and I wanted to say thank you and praise Jesus." Sometimes they'd pull out their Bible and say, "This scripture spoke to me and maybe it will help you." Then there would be a bit of song. There was a leather pad called "the beat" that you'd strap to your palm, like a percussion instrument. Someone would clap along on that, keeping time while everyone sang, *"Masango vulekani singene eJerusalema. Masango vulekani singene eJerusalema."*

That's how it would go. Pray, sing, pray. Sing, pray, sing. Sing, sing, sing. Pray, pray, pray. Sometimes it would last for hours, always ending with an "amen," and they could keep that "amen" going on for five min-utes at least. *"Ah-men. Ah-ah-ah-men. Ah-ah-ah-ah-men. Ahhhhhhhhah-hhhhhhhhhhahhhhhahhhhhhahhhhhhmen. Meni-meni-meni. Men-men-men. Ahhhhhhhhhhhhhhhhhhhhhhhhhhhhhhhhhhhhhhhhhhhhhhhmmmmmmmennn-nnnnnnnnnnnnnnnnnnnnnnnnnnnnnnnnnnnnnnnnnnnnnnnnnnnnnnnnnnnnnnnnnn-*

nnnnnnnnnnnnnnnnnnnnnnnnnnnnnnnnnnnnnnnnnnnnnnnnnnnnnnnnnnnnnnnnnnnnn-nnnnnnnnnnnnn." Then everyone would say goodbye and go home. Next night, different house, same thing.

Tuesday nights, the prayer meeting came to my grandmother's house, and I was always excited, for two reasons. One, I got to clap along on the beat for the singing. And two, I loved to pray. My grandmother always told me that she loved my prayers. She believed my prayers were more powerful, because I prayed in English. Everyone knows that Jesus, who's white, speaks English. The Bible is in English. Yes, the Bible was not *written* in English, but the Bible came to South Africa in English so to us it's in English. Which made my prayers the best prayers because English prayers get answered first. How do we know this? Look at white people. Clearly they're getting through to the right person. Add to that Matthew 19:14. "Suffer little children to come unto me," Jesus said, "for theirs is the kingdom of heaven." So if a child is praying in English? To White Jesus? That's a powerful combination right there. Whenever I prayed, my grandmother would say, "That prayer is going to get answered. I can *feel* it."

Women in the township always had something to pray for—money problems, a son who'd been arrested, a daughter who was sick, a husband who drank. Whenever the prayer meetings were at our house, because my prayers were so good, my grandmother would want me to pray for everyone. She would turn to me and say, "Trevor, pray." And I'd pray. I loved doing it. My grandmother had convinced me that my prayers got answered. I felt like I was helping people.

There is something magical about Soweto. Yes, it was a prison designed by our oppressors, but it also gave us a sense of self-determination and control. Soweto was ours. It had an aspirational quality that you don't find elsewhere. In America the dream is to make it out of the ghetto. In Soweto, because there was no leaving the ghetto, the dream was to transform the ghetto.

For the million people who lived in Soweto, there were no stores, no bars, no restaurants. There were no paved roads, minimal electricity, inadequate sewerage. But when you put one million people together in one place, they find a way to make a life for themselves. A black-market economy rose up, with every type of business being run out of someone's house: auto mechanics, day care, guys selling refurbished tires.

The most common were the *spaza* shops and the shebeens. The *spaza* shops were informal grocery stores. People would build a kiosk in their garage, buy wholesale bread and eggs, and then resell them piecemeal. Everyone in the township bought things in minute quantities because nobody had any money. You couldn't afford to buy a dozen eggs at a time, but you could buy two eggs because that's all you needed that morning. You could buy a quarter loaf of bread, a cup of sugar. The shebeens were unlawful bars in the back of someone's house. They'd put chairs in their backyard and hang out an awning and run a speakeasy. The shebeens were where men would go to drink after work and during prayer meetings and most any other time of day as well.

People built homes the way they bought eggs: a little at a time. Every family in the township was allocated a piece of land by the government. You'd first build a shanty on your plot, a makeshift structure of plywood and corrugated iron. Over time, you'd save up money and build a brick wall. One wall. Then you'd save up and build another wall. Then, years later, a third wall and eventually a fourth. Now you had a room, one room for everyone in your family to sleep, eat, do everything. Then you'd save up for a roof. Then windows. Then you'd plaster the thing. Then your daughter would start a family. There was nowhere for them to go, so they'd move in with you. You'd add another corrugated-iron structure onto your brick room and slowly, over years, turn that into a proper room for them as well. Now your house had two rooms. Then three. Maybe four. Slowly, over generations, you'd keep trying to get to the point where you had a home.

My grandmother lived in Orlando East. She had a two-room house. Not a two-bedroom house. A two-room house. There was a bedroom, and then there was basically a living room/kitchen/everything-else room. Some might say we lived like poor people. I prefer "open plan." My mom and I would stay there during school holidays. My aunt and cousins would be there whenever she was on the outs with Dinky. We all slept on the floor in one room, my mom and me, my aunt and my cousins, my uncle and my grandmother and my great-grandmother. The adults each had their own foam mattresses, and there was one big one that we'd roll out into the middle, and the kids slept on that.

We had two shanties in the backyard that my grandmother would rent out to migrants and seasonal workers. We had a small peach tree in a tiny patch on one side of the house and on the other side my grandmother had a driveway. I never understood why my grandmother had a driveway. She didn't have a car. She didn't know how to drive. Yet she had a driveway. All of our neighbors had driveways, some with fancy, cast-iron gates. None of them had cars, either. There was no future in which most of these families would ever have cars. There was maybe one car for every thousand people, yet almost everyone had a driveway. It was almost like building the driveway was a way of willing the car to happen. The story of Soweto is the story of the driveways. It's a hopeful place.

Sadly, no matter how fancy you made your house, there was one thing you could never aspire to improve: your toilet. There was no indoor running water, just one communal outdoor tap and one outdoor toilet shared by six or seven houses. Our toilet was in a corrugated-iron outhouse shared among the adjoining houses. Inside, there was a concrete slab with a hole in it and a plastic toilet seat on top; there had been a lid at some point, but it had broken and disappeared long ago. We couldn't afford toilet paper, so on the wall next to the seat was a wire hanger with old newspaper on it for you to wipe. The newspaper was uncomfortable, but at least I stayed informed while I handled my business.

The thing that I couldn't handle about the outhouse was the flies. It was a long drop to the bottom, and they were always down there, eating on the pile, and I had an irrational, all-consuming fear that they were going to fly up and into my bum.

One afternoon, when I was around five years old, my gran left me at home for a few hours to go run errands. I was lying on the floor in the bedroom, reading. I needed to go, but it was pouring down rain. I was dreading going outside to use the toilet, getting drenched running out there, water dripping on me from the leaky ceiling, wet newspaper, the flies attacking me from below. Then I had an idea. Why bother with the outhouse at all? Why not put some newspaper on the floor and do my business like a puppy? That seemed like a fantastic idea. So that's what I did. I took the newspaper, laid it out on the kitchen floor, pulled down my pants, and squatted and got to it.

When you shit, as you first sit down, you're not fully in the experience yet. You are not yet a shitting person. You're transitioning from a person about to shit to a person who is shitting. You don't whip out your smartphone or a newspaper right away. It takes a minute to get the first shit out of the way and get in the zone and get comfortable. Once you reach that moment, that's when it gets really nice.

It's a powerful experience, shitting. There's something magical about it, profound even. I think God made humans shit in the way we do because it brings us back down to earth and gives us humility. I don't care who you are, we all shit the same. Beyoncé shits. The pope shits. The Queen of England shits. When we shit we forget our airs and our graces, we forget how famous or how rich we are. All of that goes away.

You are never more yourself than when you're taking a shit. You have that moment where you realize, *This is me. This is who I am*. You can pee without giving it a second thought, but not so with shitting. Have you ever looked in a baby's eyes when it's shitting? It's having a moment of pure self-awareness. The outhouse ruins that for you. The rain, the flies, you are robbed of your moment, and nobody should be robbed of that. Squatting and shitting on the kitchen floor that day, I was like, *Wow. There are no flies. There's no stress. This is really great. I'm really enjoying this*. I knew I'd made an excellent choice, and I was very proud of myself for making it. I'd reached that moment where I could relax and be with myself. Then I casually looked around the room and I glanced to my left and there, just a few feet away, right next to the coal stove, was Koko.

It was like the scene in *Jurassic Park* when the children turn and the T. rex is right there. Her eyes were wide open, cloudy white and darting around the room. I knew she couldn't see me, but her nose was starting to crinkle—she could sense that something was wrong.

I panicked. I was mid-shit. All you can do when you're mid-shit is finish shitting. My only option was to finish as quietly and as slowly as I could, so that's what I decided to do. Then: the softest *plop* of a little-boy turd on the newspaper. Koko's head snapped toward the sound.

"Who's there? Hallo? *Hallo?!*"

I froze. I held my breath and waited.

"Who's there?! Hallo?!"

I kept quiet, waited, then started again.

"Is somebody there?! Trevor, is that you?! Frances? Hallo? Hallo?"

She started calling out the whole family. "Nombuyiselo? Sibongile? Mlungisi? Bulelwa? Who's there? What's happening?"

It was like a game, like I was trying to hide and a blind woman was trying to find me using sonar. Every time she called out, I froze. There would be complete silence. "Who's there?! Hallo?!" I'd pause, wait for her to settle back in her chair, and then I'd start up again.

Finally, after what felt like forever, I finished. I stood up, took the newspaper—which is not the quietest thing—and I slowwwwwly folded it over. It crinkled. "Who's there?" Again I paused, waited. Then I folded it over some more, walked over to the rubbish bin, placed my sin at the bottom, and gingerly covered it with the rest of the trash. Then I tiptoed back to the other room, curled up on the mattress on the floor, and pretended to be asleep. The shit was done, no outhouse involved, and Koko was none the wiser.

Mission accomplished.

An hour later the rain had stopped. My grandmother came home. The second she walked in, Koko called out to her.

"Frances! Thank God you're here. There's something in the house."

"What was it?"

"I don't know, but I could hear it, and there was a smell."

My gran started sniffing the air. "Dear Lord! Yes, I can smell it, too. Is it a rat? Did something die? It's definitely in the house."

They went back and forth about it, quite concerned, and then, as it was getting dark, my mother came home from work. The second she walked in, my gran called out to her.

"Oh, Nombuyiselo! Nombuyiselo! There's something in the house!"

"What?! What do you mean?"

Koko told her the story, the sounds, the smells.

Then my mom, who has a keen sense of smell, started going around the kitchen, sniffing. "Yes, I can smell it. I can find it . . . I can find it . . ." She went to the rubbish bin. "It's in here." She lifted out the rubbish, pulled out the folded newspaper underneath, and opened it up, and there was my little turd. She showed it to gran.

"Look!"

"What?! How did it get there?!"

Koko, still blind, still stuck in her chair, was dying to know what was happening.

"What's going on?!" she cried. "What's going on?! Did you find it?!"

"It's shit," Mom said. "There's shit in the bottom of the dustbin."

"But how?!" Koko said. "There was no one here!"

"Are you sure there was no one here?"

"Yes. I called out to everyone. Nobody came."

My mother gasped. "We've been bewitched! It's a demon!"

For my mother, this was the logical conclusion. Because that's how witchcraft works. If someone has put a curse on you or your home, there is always the talisman or totem, a tuft of hair or the head of a cat, the physical manifestation of the spiritual thing, proof of the demon's presence.

Once my mom found the turd, all hell broke loose. This was *serious*. They had *evidence*. She came into the bedroom.

"Trevor! Trevor! Wake up!"

"What?!" I said, playing dumb. "What's going on?!"

"Come! There's a demon in the house!"

She took my hand and dragged me out of bed. It was all hands on deck, time for action. The first thing we had to do was go outside and burn the shit. That's what you do with witchcraft; the only way to destroy it is to burn the physical thing. We went out to the yard, and my mom put the newspaper with my little turd on the driveway, lit a match, and set it on fire. Then my mom and my gran stood around the burning shit, praying and singing songs of praise.

The commotion didn't stop there because when there's a demon around, the whole community has to join together to drive it out. If you're not part of the prayer, the demon might leave our house and go to your house and curse you. So we needed everyone. The alarm was raised. The call went out. My tiny old gran was out the gate, going up and down the block, calling to all the other old grannies for an emergency prayer meeting. "Come! We've been bewitched!"

I stood there, my shit burning in the driveway, my poor aged grandmother tottering up and down the street in a panic, and I didn't know what to do. I knew there was no demon, but there was no way I could come clean. The hiding I would have to endure? Good Lord. Honesty was never the best policy when it came to a hiding. I kept quiet.

Moments later the grannies came streaming in with their Bibles, through the gate and up the driveway, a dozen or more at least. Everyone went inside. The house was packed. This was by far the biggest prayer meeting we'd ever had—the biggest thing that had ever happened in the history of our home, period. Everyone sat in the circle, praying and praying, and the prayers were strong. The grannies were chanting and murmuring and swaying back and forth, speaking in tongues. I was doing my best to keep my head low and stay out of it. Then my grandmother reached back and grabbed me, pulled me into the middle of the circle, and looked into my eyes.

"Trevor, pray."

"Yes!" my mother said. "Help us! Pray, Trevor. Pray to God to kill the demon!"

I was terrified. I believed in the power of prayer. I knew that my prayers *worked*. So if I prayed to God to kill the thing that left the shit, and the thing that left the shit was me, then God was going to kill me. I froze. I didn't know what to do. But all the grannies were looking at me, waiting for me to pray, so I prayed, stumbling through as best I could.

> *"Dear Lord, please protect us, um, you know, from whoever did this but, like, we don't know what happened exactly and maybe it was a big misunderstanding and, you know, maybe we shouldn't be quick to judge when we don't know the whole story and, I mean, of course you know best, Heavenly Father, but maybe this time it wasn't actually a demon, because who can say for certain, so maybe cut whoever it was a break . . ."*

It was not my best performance. Eventually I wrapped it up and sat back down. The praying continued. It went on for some time. Pray, sing, pray. Sing, pray, sing. Sing, sing, sing. Pray, pray, pray. Then everyone finally felt that the demon was gone and life could continue, and we had the big "amen" and everyone said good night and went home.

That night I felt terrible. Before bed, I quietly prayed, "God, I am so sorry for all of this. I know this was not cool." Because I knew: God answers your prayers. God is your father. He's the man who's there for you, the man who takes care of you. When you pray, He stops and He takes His time and He listens, and I had subjected Him to two hours of old grannies praying when I knew that with all the pain and suffering in the world He had more important things to deal with than my shit.

When I was growing up we used to get American TV shows rebroadcast on our stations: *Doogie Howser, M.D.*; *Murder, She Wrote*; *Rescue 911* with William Shatner. Most of them were dubbed into African languages. *ALF* was in Afrikaans. *Transformers* was in Sotho. But if you wanted to watch them in English, the original American audio would be simulcast on the radio. You could mute your TV and listen to that. Watching those shows, I realized that whenever black people were onscreen speaking in African languages, they felt familiar to me. They sounded like they were supposed to sound. Then I'd listen to them in simulcast on the radio, and they would all have black American accents. My perception of them changed. They didn't feel familiar. They felt like foreigners.

Language brings with it an identity and a culture, or at least the perception of it. A shared language says "We're the same." A language barrier says "We're different." The architects of apartheid understood this. Part of the effort to divide black people was to make sure we were separated not just physically but by language as well. In the Bantu schools, children were only taught in their home language. Zulu kids learned in Zulu. Tswana kids learned in Tswana. Because of this, we'd fall into the trap the government had set for us and fight among ourselves, believing that we were different.

The great thing about language is that you can just as easily use it to do the opposite: convince people that they are the same. Racism teaches us that we are different because of the color of our skin. But because racism is stupid, it's easily tricked. If you're racist and you meet someone who doesn't look like you, the fact that he can't speak like you reinforces your racist preconceptions: He's different, less intelligent. A brilliant scientist can come over the border from Mexico to live in America, but if he speaks in broken English, people say, "Eh, I don't trust this guy."

"But he's a scientist."

"In Mexican science, maybe. I don't trust him."

However, if the person who doesn't look like you speaks like you, your brain short-circuits because your racism program has none of those instructions in the code. "Wait, wait," your mind says, "the racism code says if he doesn't look like me he isn't like me, but the language code says if he speaks like me he . . . is like me? Something is off here. I can't figure this out."

———

4

CHAMELEON

One afternoon I was playing with my cousins. I was a doctor and they were my patients. I was operating on my cousin Bulelwa's ear with a set of matches when I accidentally perforated her eardrum. All hell broke loose. My grandmother came running in from the kitchen. *"Kwenzeka ntoni?!"* "What's happening?!" There was blood coming out of my cousin's head. We were all crying. My grandmother patched up Bulelwa's ear and made sure to stop the bleeding. But we kept crying. Because clearly we'd done something we were not supposed to do, and we knew we were going to be punished. My grandmother finished up with Bulelwa's ear and whipped out a belt and she beat the shit out of Bulelwa. Then she beat the shit out of Mlungisi, too. She didn't touch me.

Later that night my mother came home from work. She found my cousin with a bandage over her ear and my gran crying at the kitchen table.

"What's going on?" my mom said.

"Oh, Nombuyiselo," she said. "Trevor is so naughty. He's the naughtiest child I've ever come across in my life."

"Then you should hit him."

"I can't hit him."

"Why not?"

"Because I don't know how to hit a white child," she said. "A black child, I understand. A black child, you hit them and they stay black. Trevor, when you hit him he turns blue and green and yellow and red. I've never seen those colors before. I'm scared I'm going to break him. I don't want to kill a white person. I'm so afraid. I'm not going to touch him." And she never did.

My grandmother treated me like I was white. My grandfather did, too, only he was even more extreme. He called me "Mastah." In the car, he insisted on driving me as if he were my chauffeur. "Mastah must always sit in the backseat." I never challenged him on it. What was I going to say? "I believe your perception of race is flawed, Grandfather." No. I was five. I sat in the back.

There were so many perks to being "white" in a black family, I can't even front. I was having a great time. My own family basically did what the American justice system does: I was given more lenient treatment than the black kids. Misbehavior that my cousins would have been punished for, I was given a warning and let off. And I was way naughtier than either of my cousins. It wasn't even close. If something got broken or if someone was stealing granny's cookies, it was me. I was trouble.

My mom was the only force I truly feared. She believed if you spare the rod, you spoil the child. But everyone else said, "No, he's different," and they gave me a pass. Growing up the way I did, I learned how easy it is for white people to get comfortable with a system that awards them all the perks. I knew my cousins were getting beaten for things that I'd done, but I wasn't interested in changing my grandmother's perspective, because that would mean I'd get beaten, too. Why would I do that? So that I'd *feel* better? Being beaten didn't make me feel better. I had a choice. I could champion racial justice in our home, or I could enjoy granny's cookies. I went with the cookies.

At that point I didn't think of the special treatment as having to do with color. I thought of it as having to do with Trevor. It wasn't, "Trevor doesn't get beaten because Trevor is white." It was, "Trevor doesn't get beaten because Trevor is Trevor." Trevor can't go outside. Trevor can't walk without supervision. It's because I'm me; that's why this is happening. I had no other points of reference. There were no other mixed kids around so that I could say, "Oh, this happens to *us*."

Nearly one million people lived in Soweto. Ninety-nine point nine percent of them were black—and then there was me. I was famous in my neighborhood just because of the color of my skin. I was so unique people would give directions using me as a landmark. "The house on Makhalima Street. At the corner you'll see a light-skinned boy. Take a right there."

Whenever the kids in the street saw me they'd yell, "*Indoda yom-lungu!*" "The white man!" Some of them would run away. Others would call out to their parents to come look. Others would run up and try to touch me to see if I was real. It was pandemonium. What I didn't understand at the time was that the other kids genuinely had no clue what a white person was. Black kids in the township didn't leave the township. Few people had televisions. They'd seen the white police roll through, but they'd never dealt with a white person face-to-face, ever.

I'd go to funerals and I'd walk in and the bereaved would look up and see me and they'd stop crying. They'd start whispering. Then they'd wave and say, "Oh!" like they were more shocked by me walking in than by the death of their loved ones. I think people felt like the dead person was more important because a white person had come to the funeral.

After a funeral, the mourners all go to the house of the surviving family to eat. A hundred people might show up, and you've got to feed them. Usually you get a cow and slaughter it and your neighbors come over and help you cook. Neighbors and acquaintances eat outside in the yard and in the street, and the family eats indoors. Every funeral I ever went to, I ate indoors. It didn't matter if we knew the deceased or not. The family would see me and invite me in. *"Awunakuvumela umntana womlungu ame ngaphandle. Yiza naye apha ngaphakathi,"* they'd say. "You can't let the white child stand outside. Bring him in here."

As a kid I understood that people were different colors, but in my head white and black and brown were like types of chocolate. Dad was the white chocolate, mom was the dark chocolate, and I was the milk chocolate. But we were all just chocolate. I didn't know any of it had anything to do with "race." I didn't know what race was. My mother never referred to my dad as white or to me as mixed. So when the other kids in Soweto called me "white," even though I was light brown, I just thought they had their colors mixed up, like they hadn't learned them properly. "Ah, yes, my friend. You've confused aqua with turquoise. I can see how you made that mistake. You're not the first."

I soon learned that the quickest way to bridge the race gap was through language. Soweto was a melting pot: families from different tribes and homelands. Most kids in the township spoke only their home language, but I learned several languages because I grew up in a house where there was no option but to learn them. My mom made sure English was the first language I spoke. If you're black in South Africa, speaking English is the one thing that can give you a leg up. English is the language of money. English comprehension is equated with intelligence. If you're looking for a job, English is the difference between getting the job or staying unemployed. If you're standing in the dock, English is the difference between getting off with a fine or going to prison.

After English, Xhosa was what we spoke around the house. When my mother was angry she'd fall back on her home language. As a naughty child, I was well versed in Xhosa threats. They were the first phrases I picked up, mostly for my own safety—phrases like *"Ndiza kubetha entloko."* "I'll knock you upside the head." Or *"Sidenge ndini somntwana."* "You idiot of a child." It's a very passionate language. Outside of that, my mother picked up different languages here and there. She learned Zulu because it's similar to Xhosa. She spoke German because of my father. She spoke Afrikaans because it is useful to know the language of your oppressor. Sotho she learned in the streets.

Living with my mom, I saw how she used language to cross boundaries, handle situations, navigate the world. We were in a shop once, and the shopkeeper, right in front of us, turned to his security guard and said, in Afrikaans, *"Volg daai swartes, netnou steel hulle iets."* "Follow those blacks in case they steal something."

My mother turned around and said, in beautiful, fluent Afrikaans, *"Hoekom volg jy nie daai swartes sodat jy hulle kan help kry waarna hulle soek nie?"* "Why don't you follow these blacks so you can help them find what they're looking for?"

"Ag, jammer!" he said, apologizing in Afrikaans. Then—and this was the funny thing—he didn't apologize for being racist; he merely apologized for aiming his racism at us. "Oh, I'm so sorry," he said. "I thought you were like the other blacks. You know how they love to steal."

I learned to use language like my mother did. I would simulcast—give you the program in your own tongue. I'd get suspicious looks from people just walking down the street. "Where are you from?" they'd ask. I'd reply in whatever language they'd addressed me in, using the same accent that they used. There would be a brief moment of confusion, and then the suspicious look would disappear. "Oh, okay. I thought you were a stranger. We're good then."

It became a tool that served me my whole life. One day as a young man I was walking down the street, and a group of Zulu guys was walking behind me, closing in on me, and I could hear them talking to one another about how they were going to mug me. *"Asibambe le autie yomlungu. Phuma ngapha mina ngiҙoqhamuka ngemuva kwakhe."* "Let's get this white guy. You go to his left, and I'll come up behind him." I didn't know what to do. I couldn't run, so I just spun around real quick and said, *"Kodwa bafwethu yingani singavele sibambe umuntu inkunҙi? Asenҙeni. Mina ngikulindele."* "Yo, guys, why don't we just mug someone together? I'm ready. Let's do it."

They looked shocked for a moment, and then they started laughing.

"Oh, sorry, dude. We thought you were something else. We weren't trying to take anything from you. We were trying to steal from white people. Have a good day, man." They were ready to do me violent harm, until they felt we were part of the same tribe, and then we were cool. That, and so many other smaller incidents in my life, made me realize that language, even more than color, defines who you are to people.

I became a chameleon. My color didn't change, but I could change your perception of my color. If you spoke to me in Zulu, I replied to you in Zulu. If you spoke to me in Tswana, I replied to you in Tswana. Maybe I didn't look like you, but if I spoke like you, I was you.

As apartheid was coming to an end, South Africa's elite private schools started accepting children of all colors. My mother's company offered bursaries, scholarships, for underprivileged families, and she managed to get me into Maryvale College, an expensive private Catholic school. Classes taught by nuns. Mass on Fridays. The whole bit. I started preschool there when I was three, primary school when I was five.

In my class we had all kinds of kids. Black kids, white kids, Indian kids, colored kids. Most of the white kids were pretty well off. Every child of color pretty much wasn't. But because of scholarships we all sat at the same table. We wore the same maroon blazers, the same gray slacks and skirts. We had the same books. We had the same teachers. There was no racial separation. Every clique was racially mixed.

Kids still got teased and bullied, but it was over usual kid stuff: being fat or being skinny, being tall or being short, being smart or being dumb. I don't remember anybody being teased about their race. I didn't learn to put limits on what I was supposed to like or not like. I had a wide berth to explore myself. I had crushes on white girls. I had crushes on black girls. Nobody asked me what I was. I was Trevor.

It was a wonderful experience to have, but the downside was that it sheltered me from reality. Maryvale was an oasis that kept me from the truth, a comfortable place where I could avoid making a tough decision. But the real world doesn't go away. Racism exists. People are getting hurt, and just because it's not happening to you doesn't mean it's not happening. And at some point, you have to choose. Black or white. Pick a side. You can try to hide from it. You can say, "Oh, I don't pick sides," but at some point life will force you to pick a side.

At the end of grade six I left Maryvale to go to H. A. Jack Primary, a government school. I had to take an aptitude test before I started, and, based on the results of the test, the school counselor told me, "You're going to be in the smart classes, the A classes." I showed up for the first day of school and went to my classroom. Of the thirty or so kids in my class, almost all of them were white. There was one Indian kid, maybe one or two black kids, and me.

Then recess came. We went out on the playground, and black kids were *everywhere*. It was an ocean of black, like someone had opened a tap and all the black had come pouring out. I was like, *Where were they all hiding?* The white kids I'd met that morning, they went in one direction, the black kids went in another direction, and I was left standing in the middle, totally confused. Were we going to meet up later on? I did not understand what was happening.

I was eleven years old, and it was like I was seeing my country for the first time. In the townships you don't see segregation, because everyone is black. In the white world, any time my mother took me to a white church, we were the only black people there, and my mom didn't separate herself from anyone. She didn't care. She'd go right up and sit with the white people. And at Maryvale, the kids were mixed up and hanging out together. Before that day, I had never seen people being together and yet not together, occupying the same space yet choosing not to associate with each other in any way. In an instant I could see, I could feel, how the boundaries were drawn. Groups moved in color patterns across the yard, up the stairs, down the hall. It was insane. I looked over at the white kids I'd met that morning. Ten minutes earlier I'd thought I was at a school where they were a majority. Now I realized how few of them there actually were compared to everyone else.

I stood there awkwardly by myself in this no-man's-land in the middle of the playground. Luckily, I was rescued by the Indian kid from my class, a guy named Theesan Pillay. Theesan was one of the few Indian kids in school, so he'd noticed me, another obvious out-sider, right away. He ran over to introduce himself. "Hello, fellow anomaly! You're in my class. Who are you? What's your story?" We started talking and hit it off. He took me under his wing, the Artful Dodger to my bewildered Oliver.

Through our conversation it came up that I spoke several African languages, and Theesan thought a colored kid speaking black languages was the most amazing trick. He brought me over to a group of black kids. "Say something," he told them, "and he'll show you he under-stands you." One kid said something in Zulu, and I replied to him in Zulu. Everyone cheered. Another kid said something in Xhosa, and I replied to him in Xhosa. Everyone cheered. For the rest of recess Theesan took me around to different black kids on the playground. "Show them your trick. Do your language thing."

The black kids were fascinated. In South Africa back then, it wasn't common to find a white person or a colored person who spoke African languages; during apartheid white people were always taught that those languages were beneath them. So the fact that I did speak African lan-guages immediately endeared me to the black kids.

"How come you speak our languages?" they asked.

"Because I'm black," I said, "like you."

"You're not black."

"Yes, I am."

"No, you're not. Have you not seen yourself?"

They were confused at first. Because of my color, they thought I was a colored person, but speaking the same languages meant that I belonged to their tribe. It just took them a moment to figure it out. It took me a moment, too.

At some point I turned to one of them and said, "Hey, how come I don't see you guys in any of my classes?" It turned out they were in the B classes, which also happened to be the black classes. That same after-noon, I went back to the A classes, and by the end of the day I realized that they weren't for me. Suddenly, I knew who my people were, and I wanted to be with them. I went to see the school counselor.

"I'd like to switch over," I told her. "I'd like to go to the B classes."

She was confused. "Oh, no," she said. "I don't think you want to do that."

"Why not?"

"Because those kids are . . . you know."

"No, I don't know. What do you mean?"

"Look," she said, "you're a smart kid. You don't want to be in that class."

"But aren't the classes the same? English is English. Math is math."

"Yeah, but that class is . . . those kids are gonna hold you back. You want to be in the smart class."

"But surely there must be some smart kids in the B class."

"No, there aren't."

"But all my friends are there."

"You don't want to be friends with those kids."

"Yes, I do."

We went back and forth. Finally she gave me a stern warning.

"You do realize the effect this will have on your future? You do understand what you're giving up? This will impact the opportunities you'll have open to you for the rest of your life."

"I'll take that chance."

I moved to the B classes with the black kids. I decided I'd rather be held back with people I liked than move ahead with people I didn't know.

Being at H. A. Jack made me realize I was black. Before that recess I'd never had to choose, but when I was forced to choose, I chose black. The world saw me as colored, but I didn't spend my life looking at myself. I spent my life looking at other people. I saw myself as the people around me, and the people around me were black. My cousins are black, my mom is black, my gran is black. I grew up black. Because I had a white father, because I'd been in white Sunday school, I got along with the white kids, but I didn't *be*long with the white kids. I wasn't a part of their tribe. But the black kids embraced me. "Come along," they said. "You're rolling with us." With the black kids, I wasn't constantly trying to be. With the black kids, I just was.

Before apartheid, any black South African who received a formal education was likely taught by European missionaries, foreign enthusiasts eager to Christianize and Westernize the natives. In the mission schools, black people learned English, European literature, medicine, the law. It's no coincidence that nearly every major black leader of the anti-apartheid movement, from Nelson Mandela to Steve Biko, was educated by the missionaries—a knowledgeable man is a free man, or at least a man who longs for freedom.

The only way to make apartheid work, therefore, was to cripple the black mind. Under apartheid, the government built what became known as Bantu schools. Bantu schools taught no science, no history, no civics. They taught metrics and agriculture: how to count potatoes, how to pave roads, chop wood, till the soil. "It does not serve the Bantu to learn history and science because he is primitive," the government said. "This will only mislead him, showing him pastures in which he is not allowed to graze." To their credit, they were simply being honest. Why educate a slave? Why teach someone Latin when his only purpose is to dig holes in the ground?

Mission schools were told to conform to the new curriculum or shut down. Most of them shut down, and black children were forced into crowded classrooms in dilapidated schools, often with teachers who were barely literate themselves. Our parents and grandparents were taught with little singsong lessons, the way you'd teach a preschooler shapes and colors. My grandfather used to sing the songs and laugh about how silly they were. *Two times two is four. Three times two is six. La la la la la.* We're talking about fully grown teenagers being taught this way, for generations.

What happened with education in South Africa, with the mission schools and the Bantu schools, offers a neat comparison of the two groups of whites who oppressed us, the British and the Afrikaners. The difference between British racism and Afrikaner racism was that at least the British gave the natives something to aspire to. If they could learn to speak correct English and dress in proper clothes, if they could Anglicize and civilize themselves, one day they *might* be welcome in society. The Afrikaners never gave us that option. British racism said, "If the monkey can walk like a man and talk like a man, then perhaps he is a man." Afrikaner racism said, "Why give a book to a monkey?"

———

5

THE SECOND GIRL

My mother used to tell me, "I chose to have you because I wanted something to love and something that would love me unconditionally in return." I was a product of her search for belonging. She never felt like she belonged anywhere. She didn't belong to her mother, didn't belong to her father, didn't belong with her siblings. She grew up with nothing and wanted something to call her own.

My grandparents' marriage was an unhappy one. They met and married in Sophiatown, but one year later the army came in and drove them out. The government seized their home and bulldozed the whole area to build a fancy, new white suburb, *Triomf*. Triumph. Along with tens of thousands of other black people, my grandparents were forcibly relocated to Soweto, to a neighborhood called the Meadowlands. They divorced not long after that, and my grandmother moved to Orlando with my mom, my aunt, and my uncle.

My mom was the problem child, a tomboy, stubborn, defiant. My gran had no idea how to raise her. Whatever love they had was lost in the constant fighting that went on between them. But my mom adored her father, the charming, charismatic Temperance. She went gallivanting with him on his manic misadventures. She'd tag along when he'd go drinking in the shebeens. All she wanted in life was to please him and be with him. She was always being swatted away by his girlfriends, who didn't like having a reminder of his first marriage hanging around, but that only made her want to be with him all the more.

When my mother was nine years old, she told my gran that she didn't want to live with her anymore. She wanted to live with her father. "If that's what you want," Gran said, "then go." Temperance came to pick my mom up, and she happily bounded up into his car, ready to go and be with the man she loved. But instead of taking her to live with him in the Meadowlands, without even telling her why, he packed her off and sent her to live with his sister in the Xhosa homeland, Transkei—he didn't want her, either. My mom was the middle child. Her sister was the eldest and firstborn. Her brother was the only son, bearer of the family name. They both stayed in Soweto, were both raised and cared for by their parents. But my mom was unwanted. She was the second girl. The only place she would have less value would be China.

My mother didn't see her family again for twelve years. She lived in a hut with fourteen cousins—fourteen children from fourteen different mothers and fathers. All the husbands and uncles had gone off to the cities to find work, and the children who weren't wanted, or whom no one could afford to feed, had been sent back to the homeland to live on this aunt's farm.

The homelands were, ostensibly, the original homes of South Africa's tribes, sovereign and semi-sovereign "nations" where black people would be "free." Of course, this was a lie. For starters, despite the fact that black people made up over 80 percent of South Africa's population, the territory allocated for the homelands was about 13 percent of the country's land. There was no running water, no electricity. People lived in huts.

Where South Africa's white countryside was lush and irrigated and green, the black lands were overpopulated and overgrazed, the soil depleted and eroding. Other than the menial wages sent home from the cities, families scraped by with little beyond subsistence-level farming. My mother's aunt hadn't taken her in out of charity. She was there to work. "I was one of the cows," my mother would later say, "one of the oxen." She and her cousins were up at half past four, plowing fields and herding animals before the sun baked the soil as hard as cement and made it too hot to be anywhere but in the shade.

For dinner there might be one chicken to feed fourteen children. My mom would have to fight with the bigger kids to get a handful of meat or a sip of the gravy or even a bone from which to suck out some marrow. And that's when there was food for dinner at all. When there wasn't, she'd steal food from the pigs. She'd steal food from the dogs. The farmers would put out scraps for the animals, and she'd jump for it. She was hungry; let the animals fend for themselves. There were times when she literally ate dirt. She would go down to the river, take the clay from the riverbank, and mix it with the water to make a grayish kind of milk. She'd drink that to feel full.

But my mother was blessed that her village was one of the places where a mission school had contrived to stay open in spite of the government's Bantu education policies. There she had a white pastor who taught her English. She didn't have food or shoes or even a pair of underwear, but she had English. She could read and write. When she was old enough she stopped working on the farm and got a job at a factory in a nearby town. She worked on a sewing machine making school uniforms. Her pay at the end of each day was a plate of food. She used to say it was the best food she'd ever eaten, because it was something she had earned on her own. She wasn't a burden to anyone and didn't owe anything to anyone.

When my mom turned twenty-one, her aunt fell ill and that family could no longer keep her in Transkei. My mom wrote to my gran, asking her to send the price of a train ticket, about thirty rand, to bring her home. Back in Soweto, my mom enrolled in the secretarial course that allowed her to grab hold of the bottom rung of the white-collar world. She worked and worked and worked but, living under my grandmother's roof, she wasn't allowed to keep her own wages. As a secretary, my mom was bringing home more money than anyone else, and my grandmother insisted it all go to the family. The family needed a radio, an oven, a refrigerator, and it was now my mom's job to provide it.

So many black families spend all of their time trying to fix the problems of the past. That is the curse of being black and poor, and it is a curse that follows you from generation to generation. My mother calls it "the black tax." Because the generations who came before you have been pillaged, rather than being free to use your skills and education to move forward, you lose everything just trying to bring everyone behind you back up to zero. Working for the family in Soweto, my mom had no more freedom than she'd had in Transkei, so she ran away. She ran all the way down to the train station and jumped on a train and disappeared into the city, determined to sleep in public restrooms and rely on the kindness of prostitutes until she could make her own way in the world.

My mother never sat me down and told me the whole story of her life in Transkei. She'd give me little bursts, random details, stories of having to keep her wits about her to avoid getting raped by strange men in the village. She'd tell me these things and I'd be like, *Lady, clearly you do not know what kind of stories to be telling a ten-year-old.*

My mom told me these things so that I'd never take for granted how we got to where we were, but none of it ever came from a place of self-pity. "Learn from your past and be better because of your past," she would say, "but don't cry about your past. Life is full of pain. Let the pain sharpen you, but don't hold on to it. Don't be bitter." And she never was. The deprivations of her youth, the betrayals of her parents, she never complained about any of it.

Just as she let the past go, she was determined not to repeat it: my childhood would bear no resemblance to hers. She started with my name. The names Xhosa families give their children always have a meaning, and that meaning has a way of becoming self-fulfilling. You have my cousin, Mlungisi. "The Fixer." That's who he is. Whenever I got into trouble he was the one trying to help me fix it. He was always the good kid, doing chores, helping around the house. You have my uncle, the unplanned pregnancy, Velile. "He Who Popped Out of No-where." And that's all he's done his whole life, disappear and reappear. He'll go off on a drinking binge and then pop back up out of nowhere a week later.

Then you have my mother, Patricia Nombuyiselo Noah. "She Who Gives Back." That's what she does. She gives and gives and gives. She did it even as a girl in Soweto. Playing in the streets she would find tod-dlers, three- and four-year-olds, running around unsupervised all day long. Their fathers were gone and their mothers were drunks. My mom, who was only six or seven herself, used to round up the abandoned kids and form a troop and take them around to the shebeens. They'd collect empties from the men who were passed out and take the bottles to where you could turn them in for a deposit. Then my mom would take that money, buy food in the *spaza* shops, and feed the kids. She was a child taking care of children.

When it was time to pick my name, she chose Trevor, a name with no meaning whatsoever in South Africa, no precedent in my family. It's not even a Biblical name. It's just a name. My mother wanted her child beholden to no fate. She wanted me to be free to go anywhere, do any-thing, be anyone.

She gave me the tools to do it as well. She taught me English as my first language. She read to me constantly. The first book I learned to read was *the* book. The Bible. Church was where we got most of our other books, too. My mom would bring home boxes that white people had donated—picture books, chapter books, any book she could get her hands on. Then she signed up for a subscription program where we got books in the mail. It was a series of how-to books. *How to Be a*

Good Friend. How to Be Honest. She bought a set of encyclopedias, too; it was fifteen years old and way out of date, but I would sit and pore through those.

My books were my prized possessions. I had a bookshelf where I put them, and I was so proud of it. I loved my books and kept them in pristine condition. I read them over and over, but I did not bend the pages or the spines. I treasured every single one. As I grew older I started buying my own books. I loved fantasy, loved to get lost in worlds that didn't exist. I remember there was some book about white boys who solved mysteries or some shit. I had no time for that. Give me Roald Dahl. *James and the Giant Peach, The BFG, Charlie and the Chocolate Factory, The Wonderful Story of Henry Sugar.* That was my fix.

I had to fight to convince my mom to get the Narnia books for me. She didn't like them.

"This lion," she said, "he is a false God—a false idol! You remember what happened when Moses came down from the mountain after he got the tablets . . ."

"Yes, Mom," I explained, "but the lion is a Christ *figure*. Technically, he is Jesus. It's a story to explain Jesus."

She wasn't comfortable with that. "No, no. No false idols, my friend."

Eventually I wore her down. That was a big win.

If my mother had one goal, it was to free my mind. My mother spoke to me like an adult, which was unusual. In South Africa, kids play with kids and adults talk to adults. The adults supervise you, but they don't get down on your level and talk to you. My mom did. All the time. I was like her best friend. She was always telling me stories, giving me lessons, Bible lessons especially. She was big into Psalms. I had to read Psalms every day. She would quiz me on it. "What does the passage mean? What does it mean to *you*? How do you apply it to your life?" That was every day of my life. My mom did what school didn't. She taught me how to think.

• • •

The end of apartheid was a gradual thing. It wasn't like the Berlin Wall where one day it just came down. Apartheid's walls cracked and crumbled over many years. Concessions were made here and there, some laws were repealed, others simply weren't enforced. There came a point, in the months before Mandela's release, when we could live less furtively. It was then that my mother decided we needed to move. She felt we had grown as much as we could hiding in our tiny flat in town.

The country was open now. Where would we go? Soweto came with its burdens. My mother still wanted to get out from the shadow of her family. My mother also couldn't walk with me through Soweto without people saying, "There goes that prostitute with a white man's child." In a black area she would always be seen as that. So, since my mom didn't want to move to a black area and couldn't afford to move to a white area, she decided to move to a colored area.

Eden Park was a colored neighborhood adjacent to several black townships on the East Rand. Half-colored and half-black, she figured, like us. We'd be camouflaged there. It didn't work out that way; we never fit in at all. But that was her thinking when we made the move. Plus it was a chance to buy a home—our own home. Eden Park was one of those "suburbs" that are actually out on the edge of civilization, the kind of place where property developers have said, "Hey, poor people. You can live the good life, too. Here's a house. In the middle of nowhere. But look, you have a yard!" For some reason the streets in Eden Park were named after cars: Jaguar Street. Ferrari Street. Honda Street. I don't know if that was a coincidence or not, but it's funny because colored people in South Africa are known for loving fancy cars. It was like living in a white neighborhood with all the streets named after varietals of fine wine.

I remember moving out there in flashbacks, snippets, driving to a place I'd never seen, seeing people I'd never seen. It was flat, not many trees, the same dusty red-clay dirt and grass as Soweto but with proper houses and paved roads and a sense of suburbia to it. Ours was a tiny house at the bend in the road right off Toyota Street. It was modest and cramped inside, but walking in I thought, *Wow. We are really living*. It was crazy to have my own room. I didn't like it. My whole life I'd slept in a room with my mom or on the floor with my cousins. I was used to having other human beings right next to me, so I slept in my mom's bed most nights.

There was no stepfather in the picture yet, no baby brother crying in the night. It was me and her, alone. There was this sense of the two of us embarking on a grand adventure. She'd say things to me like, "It's you and me against the world." I understood even from an early age that we weren't just mother and son. We were a team.

It was when we moved to Eden Park that we finally got a car, the beat-up, tangerine Volkswagen my mother bought secondhand for next to nothing. One out of five times it wouldn't start. There was no AC. Anytime I made the mistake of turning on the fan the vent would fart bits of leaves and dust all over me. Whenever it broke down we'd catch minibuses, or sometimes we'd hitchhike. She'd make me hide in the bushes because she knew men would stop for a woman but not a woman with a child. She'd stand by the road, the driver would pull over, she'd open the door and then whistle, and I'd come running up to the car. I would watch their faces drop as they realized they weren't picking up an attractive single woman but an attractive single woman with a fat little kid.

When the car did work, we had the windows down, sputtering along and baking in the heat. For my entire life the dial on that car's radio stayed on one station. It was called Radio Pulpit, and as the name suggests it was nothing but preaching and praise. I wasn't allowed to touch that dial. Anytime the radio wasn't getting reception, my mom would pop in a cassette of Jimmy Swaggart sermons. (When we finally found out about the scandal? Oh, man. That was rough.)

But as shitty as our car was, it was a *car*. It was freedom. We weren't black people stuck in the townships, waiting for public transport. We were black people who were out in the world. We were black people who could wake up and say, "Where do we choose to go today?" On the commute to work and school, there was a long stretch of the road into town that was completely deserted. That's where Mom would let me drive. On the highway. I was six. She'd put me on her lap and let me steer and work the indicators while she worked the pedals and the stick shift. After a few months of that, she taught me how to work the stick. She was still working the clutch, but I'd climb onto her lap and take the stick, and she'd call out the gears as we drove. There was this one part of the road that ran deep into a valley and then back up the other side. We'd get up a head of speed, and we'd stick it into neutral and let go of the brake and the clutch, and, *woo-hoo!*, we'd race down the hill and then, *zoom!*, we'd shoot up the other side. We were flying.

If we weren't at school or work or church, we were out exploring. My mom's attitude was "I chose you, kid. I brought you into this world, and I'm going to give you everything I never had." She poured herself into me. She would find places for us to go where we didn't have to spend money. We must have gone to every park in Johannesburg. My mom would sit under a tree and read the Bible, and I'd run and play and play and play. On Sunday afternoons after church, we'd go for drives out in the country. My mom would find places with beautiful views for us to sit and have a picnic. There was none of the fanfare of a picnic basket or plates or anything like that, only baloney and brown bread and margarine sandwiches wrapped up in butcher paper. To this day, baloney and brown bread and margarine will instantly take me back. You can come with all the Michelin stars in the world, just give me baloney and brown bread and margarine and I'm in heaven.

Food, or the access to food, was always the measure of how good or bad things were going in our lives. My mom would always say, "My job is to feed your body, feed your spirit, and feed your mind." That's exactly what she did, and the way she found money for food and books was to spend absolutely nothing on anything else. Her frugality was the stuff of legend. Our car was a tin can on wheels, and we lived in the middle of nowhere. We had threadbare furniture, busted old sofas with holes worn through the fabric. Our TV was a tiny black-and-white with a bunny aerial on top. We changed the channels using a pair of pliers because the buttons didn't work. Most of the time you had to squint to see what was going on.

We always wore secondhand clothes, from Goodwill stores or that were giveaways from white people at church. All the other kids at school got brands, Nike and Adidas. I never got brands. One time I asked my mom for Adidas sneakers. She came home with some knock-off brand, Abidas.

"Mom, these are fake," I said.

"I don't see the difference."

"Look at the logo. There are four stripes instead of three."

"Lucky you," she said. "You got one extra."

We got by with next to nothing, but we always had church and we always had books and we always had food. Mind you, it wasn't necessarily *good* food. Meat was a luxury. When things were going well we'd have chicken. My mom was an expert at cracking open a chicken bone and getting out every last bit of marrow inside. We didn't eat chickens. We obliterated them. Our family was an archaeologist's nightmare. We left no bones behind. When we were done with a chicken there was nothing left but the head. Sometimes the only meat we had was a packaged meat you could buy at the butcher called "sawdust." It was literally the dust of the meat, the bits that fell off the cuts being packaged for the shop, the bits of fat and whatever's left. They'd sweep it up and put it into bags. It was meant for dogs, but my mom bought it for us. There were many months where that was all we ate.

The butcher sold bones, too. We called them "soup bones," but they were actually labeled "dog bones" in the store; people would cook them for their dogs as a treat. Whenever times were really tough we'd fall back on dog bones. My mom would boil them for soup. We'd suck the marrow out of them. Sucking marrow out of bones is a skill poor people learn early. I'll never forget the first time I went to a fancy restaurant as a grown man and someone told me, "You have to try the bone marrow. It's such a delicacy. It's *divine*." They ordered it, the waiter brought it out, and I was like, "Dog bones, motherfucker!" I was not impressed.

As modestly as we lived at home, I never felt poor because our lives were so rich with experience. We were always out doing something, going somewhere. My mom used to take me on drives through fancy white neighborhoods. We'd go look at people's houses, look at their mansions. We'd look at their walls, mostly, because that's all we could see from the road. We'd look at a wall that ran from one end of the block to the other and go, "Wow. That's only *one* house. All of that is for *one* family." Sometimes we'd pull over and go up to the wall, and she'd put me up on her shoulders like I was a little periscope. I would look into the yards and describe everything I was seeing. "It's a big white house! They have two dogs! There's a lemon tree! They have a swimming pool! And a tennis court!"

My mother took me places black people never went. She refused to be bound by ridiculous ideas of what black people couldn't or shouldn't do. She'd take me to the ice rink to go skating. Johannesburg used to have this epic drive-in movie theater, Top Star Drive-In, on top of a massive mine dump outside the city. She'd take me to movies there; we'd get snacks, hang the speaker on our car window. Top Star had a 360-degree view of the city, the suburbs, Soweto. Up there I could see for miles in every direction. I felt like I was on top of the world.

My mom raised me as if there were no limitations on where I could go or what I could do. When I look back I realize she raised me like a white kid—not white culturally, but in the sense of believing that the world was my oyster, that I should speak up for myself, that my ideas and thoughts and decisions mattered.

We tell people to follow their dreams, but you can only dream of what you can imagine, and, depending on where you come from, your imagination can be quite limited. Growing up in Soweto, our dream was to put another room on our house. Maybe have a driveway. Maybe, someday, a cast-iron gate at the end of the driveway. Because that is all we knew. But the highest rung of what's possible is far beyond the world you can see. My mother showed me what was possible. The thing that always amazed me about her life was that no one showed her. No one chose her. She did it on her own. She found her way through sheer force of will.

Perhaps even more amazing is the fact that my mother started her little project, me, at a time when she could not have known that apartheid would end. There was no reason to think it would end; it had seen generations come and go. I was nearly six when Mandela was released, ten before democracy finally came, yet she was preparing me to live a life of freedom long before we knew freedom would exist. A hard life in the township or a trip to the colored orphanage were the far more likely options on the table. But we never lived that way. We only moved forward and we always moved fast, and by the time the law and everyone else came around we were already miles down the road, flying across the freeway in a bright-orange, piece-of-shit Volkswagen with the windows down and Jimmy Swaggart praising Jesus at the top of his lungs.

People thought my mom was crazy. Ice rinks and drive-ins and suburbs, these things were *izinto zabelungu*—the things of white people. So many black people had internalized the logic of apartheid and made it their own. Why teach a black child white things? Neighbors and relatives used to pester my mom. "Why do all this? Why show him the world when he's never going to leave the ghetto?"

"Because," she would say, "even if he never leaves the ghetto, he will know that the ghetto is not the world. If that is all I accomplish, I've done enough."

Apartheid, for all its power, had fatal flaws baked in, starting with the fact that it never made any sense. Racism is not logical. Consider this: Chinese people were classified as black in South Africa. I don't mean they were running around acting black. They were still Chinese. But, unlike Indians, there weren't enough Chinese people to warrant devising a whole separate classification. Apartheid, despite its intricacies and precision, didn't know what to do with them, so the government said, "Eh, we'll just call 'em black. It's simpler that way."

Interestingly, at the same time, Japanese people were labeled as white. The reason for this was that the South African government wanted to establish good relations with the Japanese in order to import their fancy cars and electronics. So Japanese people were given honorary white status while Chinese people stayed black. I always like to imagine being a South African policeman who likely couldn't tell the difference between Chinese and Japanese but whose job was to make sure that people of the wrong color weren't doing the wrong thing. If he saw an Asian person sitting on a whites-only bench, what would he say?

"Hey, get off that bench, you Chinaman!"

"Excuse me. I'm Japanese."

"Oh, I apologize, sir. I didn't mean to be racist. Have a lovely afternoon."

6

LOOPHOLES

My mother used to tell me, "I chose to have you because I wanted something to love and something that would love me unconditionally in return—and then I gave birth to the most selfish piece of shit on earth and all it ever did was cry and eat and shit and say, 'Me, me, me, me me.'"

My mom thought having a child was going to be like having a partner, but every child is born the center of its own universe, incapable of understanding the world beyond its own wants and needs, and I was no different. I was a voracious kid. I consumed boxes of books and wanted more, more, more. I ate like a pig. The way I ate I should have been obese. At a certain point the family thought I had worms. Whenever I went to my cousins' house for the holidays, my mom would drop me off with a bag of tomatoes, onions, and potatoes and a large sack of cornmeal. That was her way of preempting any complaints about my visit. At my gran's house I always got seconds, which none of the other kids got. My grandmother would give me the pot and say, "Finish it." If you didn't want to wash the dishes, you called Trevor. They called me the rubbish bin of the family. I ate and ate and ate.

I was hyperactive, too. I craved constant stimulation and activity. When I walked down the sidewalk as a toddler, if you didn't have my arm in a death grip, I was off, running full-speed toward the traffic. I loved to be chased. I thought it was a game. The old grannies my mom hired to look after me while she was at work? I would leave them in tears. My mom would come home and they'd be crying. "I quit. I can't do this. Your son is a tyrant." It was the same with my schoolteachers, with Sunday school teachers. If you weren't engaging me, you were in trouble. I wasn't a shit to people. I wasn't whiny and spoiled. I had good manners. I was just high-energy and knew what I wanted to do.

My mom used to take me to the park so she could run me to death to burn off the energy. She'd take a Frisbee and throw it, and I'd run and catch it and bring it back. Over and over and over. Sometimes she'd throw a tennis ball. Black people's dogs don't play fetch; you don't throw anything to a black person's dog unless it's food. So it was only when I started spending time in parks with white people and their pets that I realized my mom was training me like a dog.

Anytime my extra energy wasn't burned off, it would find its way into general naughtiness and misbehavior. I prided myself on being the ultimate prankster. Every teacher at school used overhead projectors to put their notes up on the wall during class. One day I went around and took the magnifying glass out of every projector in every classroom. Another time I emptied a fire extinguisher into the school piano, because I knew we were going to have a performance at assembly the next day. The pianist sat down and played the first note and, *foomp!*, all this foam exploded out of the piano.

The two things I loved most were fire and knives. I was endlessly fascinated by them. Knives were just cool. I collected them from pawnshops and garage sales: flick knives, butterfly knives, the Rambo knife, the Crocodile Dundee knife. Fire was the ultimate, though. I loved fire and I especially loved fireworks. We celebrated Guy Fawkes Day in November, and every year my mom would buy us a ton of fireworks, like a mini-arsenal. I realized that I could take the gunpowder out of all the fireworks and create one massive firework of my own. One afternoon I was doing precisely that, goofing around with my cousin and filling an empty plant pot with a huge pile of gunpowder, when I got distracted by some Black Cat firecrackers. The cool thing you could do with a Black Cat was, instead of lighting it to make it explode, you could break it in half and light it and it would turn into a mini-flamethrower. I stopped midway through building my gunpowder pile to play with the Black Cats and somehow dropped a match into the pile. The whole thing exploded, throwing a massive ball of flame up in my face. Mlungisi screamed, and my mom came running into the yard in a panic.

"What happened?!"

I played it cool, even though I could still feel the heat of the fireball on my face. "Oh, nothing. Nothing happened."

"Were you playing with fire?!"

"No."

She shook her head. "You know what? I would beat you, but Jesus has already exposed your lies."

"Huh?"

"Go to the bathroom and look at yourself."

I went to the toilet and looked in the mirror. My eyebrows were gone and the front inch or so of my hair was completely burned off.

From an adult's point of view, I was destructive and out of control, but as a child I didn't think of it that way. I never wanted to destroy. I wanted to create. I wasn't burning my eyebrows. I was creating fire. I wasn't breaking overhead projectors. I was creating chaos, to see how people reacted.

And I couldn't help it. There's a condition kids suffer from, a compulsive disorder that makes them do things they themselves don't understand. You can tell a child, "Whatever you do, don't draw on the wall. You can draw on this paper. You can draw in this book. You can draw on any surface you want. But do not draw or write or color on the wall." The child will look you dead in the eye and say, "Got it." Ten minutes later the child is drawing on the wall. You start screaming. "Why the hell are you drawing on the wall?!" The child looks at you, and he genuinely has no idea why he drew on the wall. As a kid, I remember having that feeling all the time. Every time I got punished, as my mom was whooping my ass, I'd be thinking, *Why did I just do that? I knew not to do that. She told me not to do that.* Then once the hiding was over I'd say to myself, *I'm going to be so good from here on. I'm never ever going to do a bad thing in my life ever ever ever ever ever—and to remember not to do anything bad, let me write something on the wall to remind myself . . .* and then I would pick up a crayon and get straight back into it, and I never understood why.

My relationship with my mom was like the relationship between a cop and a criminal in the movies—the relentless detective and the devious mastermind she's determined to catch. They're bitter rivals, but, damn, they respect the hell out of each other, and somehow they even grow to like each other. Sometimes my mom would catch me, but she was usually one step behind, and she was always giving me the eye. *Someday, kid. Someday I'm going to catch you and put you away for the rest of your life.* Then I would give her a nod in return. *Have a good evening, Officer.* That was my whole childhood.

My mom was forever trying to rein me in. Over the years, her tactics grew more and more sophisticated. Where I had youth and energy on my side, she had cunning, and she figured out different ways to keep me in line. One Sunday we were at the shops and there was a big display of toffee apples. I loved toffee apples, and I kept nagging her the whole way through the shop. "*Please* can I have a toffee apple? *Please* can I have a toffee apple? *Please* can I have a toffee apple? *Please* can I have a toffee apple?"

Finally, once we had our groceries and my mom was heading to the front to pay, I succeeded in wearing her down. "Fine," she said. "Go and get a toffee apple." I ran, got a toffee apple, came back, and put it on the counter at the checkout.

"Add this toffee apple, please," I said.

The cashier looked at me skeptically. "Wait your turn, boy. I'm still helping this lady."

"No," I said. "She's buying it for me."

My mother turned to me. "Who's buying it for you?"

"You're buying it for me."

"No, no. Why doesn't your mother buy it for you?"

"What? My mother? You are my mother."

"I'm your mother? No, I'm not your mother. Where's your mother?"

I was so confused. "*You're* my mother."

The cashier looked at her, looked back at me, looked at her again. She shrugged, like, *I have no idea what that kid's talking about.* Then she looked at me like she'd never seen me before in her life.

"Are you lost, little boy? Where's your mother?"

"Yeah," the cashier said. "Where's your mother?"

I pointed at my mother. "She's my mother."

"What? She can't be your mother, boy. She's black. Can't you see?"

My mom shook her head. "Poor little colored boy lost his mother. What a shame."

I panicked. Was I crazy? Is she not my mother? I started bawling. "*You're* my mother. *You're* my mother. *She's* my mother. *She's* my mother."

She shrugged again. "So sad. I hope he finds his mother."

The cashier nodded. She paid him, took our groceries, and walked out of the shop. I dropped the toffee apple, ran out behind her in tears, and caught up to her at the car. She turned around, laughing hysterically, like she'd really got me good.

"Why are you crying?" she asked.

"Because you said you weren't my mother. Why did you say you weren't my mother?"

"Because you wouldn't shut up about the toffee apple. Now get in the car. Let's go."

By the time I was seven or eight, I was too smart to be tricked, so she changed tactics. Our life turned into a courtroom drama with two lawyers constantly debating over loopholes and technicalities. My mom was smart and had a sharp tongue, but I was quicker in an argument. She'd get flustered because she couldn't keep up. So she started writing me letters. That way she could make her points and there could be no verbal sparring back and forth. If I had chores to do, I'd come home to find an envelope slipped under the door, like from the landlord.

Dear Trevor,

"Children, obey your parents in everything, for this pleases the Lord."
—Colossians 3:20

There are certain things I expect from you as my child and as a young man. You need to clean your room. You need to keep the house clean. You need to look after your school uniform. Please, my child, I ask you. Respect my rules so that I may also respect you. I ask you now, please go and do the dishes and do the weeds in the garden.

Yours sincerely,
Mom

I would do my chores, and if I had anything to say I would write back. Because my mom was a secretary and I spent hours at her office every day after school, I'd learned a great deal about business correspondence. I was extremely proud of my letter-writing abilities.

To Whom It May Concern:
Dear Mom,

I have received your correspondence earlier. I am delighted to say that I am ahead of schedule on the dishes and I will continue to wash them in an hour or so. Please note that the garden is wet and so I cannot do the weeds at this time, but please be assured this task

will be completed by the end of the weekend. Also, I completely
agree with what you are saying with regard to my respect levels and
I will maintain my room to a satisfactory standard.

Yours sincerely,
Trevor

Those were the polite letters. If we were having a real, full-on argument or if I'd gotten in trouble at school, I'd find more accusatory
missives waiting for me when I got home.

Dear Trevor,

"Foolishness is bound up in the heart of a child; the rod of discipline will remove it far from him."
—Proverbs 22:15

Your school marks this term have been very disappointing, and
your behavior in class continues to be disruptive and disrespectful.
It is clear from your actions that you do not respect me. You do
not respect your teachers. Learn to respect the women in your life.
The way you treat me and the way you treat your teachers will
be the way you treat other women in the world. Learn to buck that
trend now and you will be a better man because of it. Because of
your behavior I am grounding you for one week. There will be no
television and no videogames.

Yours sincerely,
Mom

I, of course, would find this punishment completely unfair. I'd take
the letter and confront her.
"Can I speak to you about this?"
"No. If you want to reply, you have to write a letter."
I'd go to my room, get out my pen and paper, sit at my little desk,
and go after her arguments one by one.

To Whom It May Concern:
Dear Mom,

First of all, this has been a particularly tough time in school, and for you to say that my marks are bad is extremely unfair, especially considering the fact that you yourself were not very good in school and I am, after all, a product of yours, and so in part you are to blame because if you were not good in school, why would I be good in school because genetically we are the same. Gran always talks about how naughty you were, so obviously my naughtiness comes from you, so I don't think it is right or just for you to say any of this.

Yours sincerely,
Trevor

I'd bring her the letter and stand there while she read it. Invariably she'd tear it up and throw it in the dustbin. "Rubbish! This is rubbish!" Then she'd start to launch into me and I'd say, "Ah-ah-ah. No. You have to write a letter." Then I'd go to my room and wait for her reply. This sometimes went back and forth for days.

The letter writing was for minor disputes. For major infractions, my mom went with the ass-whooping. Like most black South African parents, when it came to discipline my mom was old school. If I pushed her too far, she'd go for the belt or switch. That's just how it was in those days. Pretty much all of my friends had it the same.

My mom would have given me proper sit-down hidings if I'd given her the opportunity, but she could never catch me. My gran called me "Springbok," after the second-fastest land mammal on earth, the deer that the cheetah hunts. My mom had to become a guerrilla fighter. She got her licks in where she could, her belt or maybe a shoe, administered on the fly.

One thing I respected about my mom was that she never left me in any doubt as to why I was receiving the hiding. It wasn't rage or anger. It was discipline from a place of love. My mom was on her own with a crazy child. I destroyed pianos. I shat on floors. I would screw up, she'd beat the shit out of me and give me time to cry, and then she'd pop back into my room with a big smile and go, "Are you ready for dinner? We need to hurry and eat if we want to watch *Rescue 911*. Are you coming?"

"What? What kind of psychopath are you? You just beat me!"

"Yes. Because you did something wrong. It doesn't mean I don't love you anymore."

"What?"

"Look, did you or did you not do something wrong?"

"I did."

"And then? I hit you. And now that's over. So why sit there and cry? It's time for *Rescue 911*. William Shatner is waiting. Are you coming or not?"

When it came to discipline, Catholic school was no joke. Whenever I got into trouble with the nuns at Maryvale they'd rap me on the knuckles with the edge of a metal ruler. For cursing they'd wash my mouth out with soap. For serious offenses I'd get sent to the principal's office. Only the principal could give you an official hiding. You'd have to bend over and he'd hit your ass with this flat rubber thing, like the sole of a shoe.

Whenever the principal would hit me, it was like he was afraid to do it too hard. One day I was getting a hiding and I thought, *Man, if only my mom hit me like this*, and I started laughing. I couldn't help it. The principal was quite disturbed. "If you're laughing while you're getting beaten," he said, "then something is definitely wrong with you."

That was the first of three times the school made my mom take me to a psychologist to be evaluated. Every psychologist who examined me came back and said, "There's nothing wrong with this kid." I wasn't ADD. I wasn't a sociopath. I was just creative and independent and full of energy. The therapists did give me a series of tests, and they came to the conclusion that I was either going to make an excellent criminal or be very good at catching criminals, because I could always find loopholes in the law. Whenever I thought a rule wasn't logical, I'd find my way around it.

The rules about communion at Friday mass, for example, made absolutely no sense. We'd be in there for an hour of kneeling, standing, sitting, kneeling, standing, sitting, kneeling, standing, sitting, and by the end of it I'd be starving, but I was never allowed to take communion, because I wasn't Catholic. The other kids could eat Jesus's body and drink Jesus's blood, but I couldn't. And Jesus's blood was grape juice. I loved grape juice. Grape juice and crackers—what more could a kid want? And they wouldn't let me have any. I'd argue with the nuns and the priest all the time.

"Only Catholics can eat Jesus's body and drink Jesus's blood, right?"

"Yes."

"But Jesus wasn't Catholic."

"No."

"Jesus was Jewish."

"Well, yes."

"So you're telling me that if Jesus walked into your church right now, Jesus would not be allowed to have the body and blood of Jesus?"

"Well . . . uh . . . um . . ."

They never had a satisfactory reply.

One morning before mass I decided, *I'm going to get me some Jesus blood and Jesus body*. I snuck behind the altar and I drank the entire bottle of grape juice and I ate the entire bag of Eucharist to make up for all the other times that I couldn't.

In my mind, I wasn't breaking the rules, because the rules didn't make any sense. And I got caught only because they broke their own rules. Another kid ratted me out in confession, and the priest turned me in.

"No, no," I protested. "*You've* broken the rules. That's confidential information. The priest isn't supposed to repeat what you say in confession."

They didn't care. The school could break whatever rules it wanted. The principal laid into me.

"What kind of a sick person would eat all of Jesus's body and drink all of Jesus's blood?"

"A hungry person."

I got another hiding and a second trip to the psychologist for that one. The third visit to the shrink, and the last straw, came in grade six. A kid was bullying me. He said he was going to beat me up, and I brought one of my knives to school. I wasn't going to use it; I just wanted to have it. The school didn't care. That was the last straw for them. I wasn't expelled, exactly. The principal sat me down and said, "Trevor, we can expel you. You need to think hard about whether you really want to be at Maryvale next year." I think he thought he was giving me an ultimatum that would get me to shape up. But I felt like he was offering me an out, and I took it. "No," I told him, "I don't want to be here." And that was the end of Catholic school.

Funnily enough, I didn't get into trouble with my mom when it happened. There was no ass-whooping waiting for me at home. She'd lost the bursary when she'd left her job at ICI, and paying for private school was becoming a burden. But more than that, she thought the school was overreacting. The truth is she probably took my side against Maryvale more often than not. She agreed with me 100 percent about the Eucharist thing. "Let me get this straight," she told the principal. "You're punishing a child because he *wants* Jesus's body and Jesus's blood? Why shouldn't he have those things? Of course he should have them." When they made me see a therapist for laughing while the principal hit me, she told the school that was ridiculous, too.

"Ms. Noah, your son was laughing while we were hitting him."

"Well, clearly you don't know how to hit a kid. That's your problem, not mine. Trevor's never laughed when I've hit him, I can tell you."

That was the weird and kind of amazing thing about my mom. If she agreed with me that a rule was stupid, she wouldn't punish me for breaking it. Both she and the psychologists agreed that the school was the one with the problem, not me. Catholic school is not the place to be creative and independent.

Catholic school is similar to apartheid in that it's ruthlessly authoritarian, and its authority rests on a bunch of rules that don't make any sense. My mother grew up with these rules and she questioned them. When they didn't hold up, she simply went around them. The only authority my mother recognized was God's. God is love and the Bible is truth—everything else was up for debate. She taught me to challenge authority and question the system. The only way it backfired on her was that I constantly challenged and questioned her.

When I was seven years old, my mother had been dating her new boyfriend, Abel, for a year maybe, but at that point I was too young to know who they were to each other. It was just "Hey, that's mom's friend who's around a lot." I liked Abel; he was a really nice guy.

As a black person back then, if you wanted to live in the suburbs you'd have to find a white family renting out their servants' quarters or sometimes their garage, which was what Abel had done. He lived in a neighborhood called Orange Grove in a white family's garage, which he'd turned into a cottage-type thing with a hot plate and a bed. Sometimes he'd come and sleep at our house, and sometimes we'd go stay with him. Staying in a garage when we owned our own house wasn't ideal, but Orange Grove was close to my school and my mom's work so it had its benefits.

This white family also had a black maid who lived in the servants' quarters in the backyard, and I'd play with her son whenever we stayed there. At that age my love of fire was in full bloom. One afternoon everyone was at work—my mom and Abel and both of the white parents—and the kid and I were playing together while his mom was inside the house cleaning. One thing I loved doing at the time was using a magnifying glass to burn my name into pieces of wood. You had to aim the lens and get the focus just right and then you got the flame and then you moved it slowly and you could burn shapes and letters and patterns. I was fascinated by it.

That afternoon I was teaching this kid how to do it. We were inside the servants' quarters, which was really more of a toolshed added on to the back of the house, full of wooden ladders, buckets of old paint, turpentine. I had a box of matches with me, too—all my usual fire-making tools. We were sitting on an old mattress that they used to sleep on the floor, basically a sack stuffed with dried straw. The sun was beaming in through the window, and I was showing the kid how to burn his name into a piece of plywood.

At one point we took a break to go get a snack. I set the magnifying glass and the matches on the mattress and we left. When we came back a few minutes later we found the shed had one of those doors that self-locks from the inside. We couldn't get back in without going to get his mother, so we decided to run around and play in the yard. After a while I noticed smoke coming out of the cracks in the window frame. I ran over and looked inside. A small fire was burning in the middle of the straw mattress where we'd left the matches and the magnifying glass. We ran and called the maid. She came, but she didn't know what to do. The door was locked, and before we could figure out how to get into the shed the whole thing caught—the mattress, the ladders, the paint, the turpentine, everything.

The flames moved quickly. Soon the roof was on fire, and from there the blaze spread to the main house, and the whole thing burned and burned and burned. Smoke was billowing into the sky. A neighbor had called the fire brigade, and the sirens were on their way. Me and this kid and the maid, we ran out to the road and watched as the firemen tried to put it out, but by the time they did, it was too late. There was nothing left but a charred brick-and-mortar shell, roof gone, and gutted from the inside.

The white family came home and stood on the street, staring at the ruins of their house. They asked the maid what happened and she asked her son and the kid totally snitched. "Trevor had matches," he said. The family said nothing to me. I don't think they knew what to say.

They were completely dumbfounded. They didn't call the police, didn't threaten to sue. What were they going to do, arrest a seven-year-old for arson? And we were so poor you couldn't actually sue us for anything. Plus they had insurance, so that was the end of it.

They kicked Abel out of the garage, which I thought was hilarious because the garage, which was freestanding, was the only piece of the property left unscathed. I saw no reason for Abel to have to leave, but they made him. We packed up his stuff, put it into our car, and drove home to Eden Park; Abel basically lived with us from then on. He and my mom got into a huge fight. "Your son has burned down my life!" But there was no punishment for me that day. My mom was too much in shock. There's naughty, and then there's burning down a white person's house. She didn't know what to do.

I didn't feel bad about it at all. I still don't. The lawyer in me maintains that I am completely innocent. There were matches and there was a magnifying glass and there was a mattress and then, clearly, a series of unfortunate events. Things catch fire sometimes. That's why there's a fire brigade. But everyone in my family will tell you, "Trevor burned down a house." If people thought I was naughty before, after the fire I was notorious. One of my uncles stopped calling me Trevor. He called me "Terror" instead. "Don't leave that kid alone in your home," he'd say. "He'll burn it to the ground."

My cousin Mlungisi, to this day, cannot comprehend how I survived being as naughty as I was for as long as I did, how I withstood the number of hidings that I got. Why did I keep misbehaving? How did I never learn my lesson? Both of my cousins were supergood kids. Mlungisi got maybe one hiding in his life. After that he said he never wanted to experience anything like it ever again, and from that day he always followed the rules. But I was blessed with another trait I inherited from my mother: her ability to forget the pain in life. I remember the thing that caused the trauma, but I don't hold on to the trauma. I never let the memory of something painful prevent me from trying something new. If you think too much about the ass-kicking your mom gave you, or the ass-kicking that life gave you, you'll stop pushing the boundaries and breaking the rules. It's better to take it, spend some time crying, then wake up the next day and move on. You'll have a few bruises and they'll remind you of what happened and that's okay. But after a while the bruises fade, and they fade for a reason—because now it's time to get up to some shit again.

I grew up in a black family in a black neighborhood in a black country. I've traveled to other black cities in black countries all over the black continent. And in all of that time I've yet to find a place where black people like cats. One of the biggest reasons for that, as we know in South Africa, is that only witches have cats, and all cats are witches.

There was a famous incident during an Orlando Pirates soccer match a few years ago. A cat got into the stadium and ran through the crowd and out onto the pitch in the middle of the game. A security guard, seeing the cat, did what any sensible black person would do. He said to himself, "That cat is a witch." He caught the cat and—live on TV—he kicked it and stomped it and beat it to death with a *sjambok*, a hard leather whip.

It was front-page news all over the country. White people lost their shit. Oh my word, it was insane. The security guard was arrested and put on trial and found guilty of animal abuse. He had to pay some enormous fine to avoid spending several months in jail. What was ironic to me was that white people had spent years seeing video of black people being beaten to death by other white people, but this one video of a black man kicking a cat, that's what sent them over the edge. Black people were just confused. They didn't see any problem with what the man did. They were like, "Obviously that cat was a witch. How else would a cat know how to get out onto a soccer pitch? Somebody sent it to jinx one of the teams. That man had to kill the cat. He was protecting the players."

In South Africa, black people have dogs.

7

FUFI

A month after we moved to Eden Park, my mother brought home two cats. Black cats. Beautiful creatures. Some woman from her work had a litter of kittens she was trying to get rid of, and my mom ended up with two. I was excited because I'd never had a pet before. My mom was excited because she loves animals. She didn't believe in any nonsense about cats. It was just another way in which she was a rebel, refusing to conform to ideas about what black people did and didn't do.

In a black neighborhood, you wouldn't dare own a cat, especially a black cat. That would be like wearing a sign that said, "Hello, I am a witch." That would be suicide. Since we'd moved to a colored neighborhood, my mom thought the cats would be okay. Once they were grown we let them out during the day to roam the neighborhood. Then we came home one evening and found the cats strung up by their tails from our front gate, gutted and skinned and bleeding out, their heads chopped off. On our front wall someone had written in Afrikaans, *"Heks"*—"Witch."

Colored people, apparently, were no more progressive than black people on the issue of cats.

I wasn't exactly devastated about the cats. I don't think we'd had them long enough for me to get attached; I don't even remember their names. And cats are dicks for the most part. As much as I tried they never felt like real pets. They never showed me affection nor did they accept any of mine. Had the cats made more of an effort, I might have felt like I had lost something. But even as a kid, looking at these dead, mutilated animals, I was like, "Well, there you have it. Maybe if they'd been nicer, they could have avoided this."

After the cats were killed, we took a break from pets for a while. Then we got dogs. Dogs are cool. Almost every black family I knew had a dog. No matter how poor you were, you had a dog. White people treat dogs like children or members of the family. Black people's dogs are more for protection, a poor-man's alarm system. You buy a dog and you keep it out in the yard. Black people name dogs by their traits. If it has stripes, you call it Tiger. If it's vicious, you call it Danger. If it has spots, you call it Spotty. Given the finite number of traits a dog can have, pretty much everyone's dogs have the same names; people just recycle them.

We'd never had dogs in Soweto. Then one day some lady at my mom's work offered us two puppies. They weren't planned puppies. This woman's Maltese poodle had been impregnated by the bull terrier from next door, a strange mix. My mom said she'd take them both. She brought them home, and I was the happiest kid on earth.

My mom named them Fufi and Panther. Fufi, I don't know where her name came from. Panther had a pink nose, so she was Pink Panther and eventually just Panther. They were two sisters who loved and hated each other. They would look out for each other, but they would also fight all the time. Like, blood fights. Biting. Clawing. It was a strange, gruesome relationship.

Panther was my mom's dog; Fufi was mine. Fufi was beautiful. Clean lines, happy face. She looked like a perfect bull terrier, only skinnier because of the Maltese mixed in. Panther, who was more half-and-half, came out weird and scruffy-looking. Panther was smart. Fufi was dumb as shit. At least we always thought she was dumb as shit. Whenever we called them, Panther would come right away, but Fufi wouldn't do anything. Panther would run back and get Fufi and then they'd both come. It turned out that Fufi was deaf. Years later Fufi died when a burglar was trying to break into our house. He pushed the gate over and it fell on her back and broke her spine. We took her to the vet and she had to be put down. After examining her, the vet came over and gave us the news.

"It must have been strange for your family living with a dog that was deaf," he said.

"What?"

"You didn't know your dog was deaf?"

"No, we thought it was stupid."

That's when we realized that their whole lives the one dog had been telling the other dog what to do somehow. The smart, hearing one was helping the dumb, deaf one.

Fufi was the love of my life. Beautiful but stupid. I raised her. I potty-trained her. She slept in my bed. A dog is a great thing for a kid to have. It's like a bicycle but with emotions.

Fufi could do all sorts of tricks. She could jump super high. I mean, Fufi could *jump*. I could hold a piece of food out above my own head and she'd leap up and grab it like it was nothing. If YouTube had been around, Fufi would have been a star.

Fufi was a little rascal as well. During the day we kept the dogs in the backyard, which was enclosed by a wall at least five feet high. After a while, every day we'd come home and Fufi would be sitting outside the gate, waiting for us. We were always confused. Was someone opening the gate? What was going on? It never occurred to us that she could actually scale a five-foot wall, but that was exactly what was happening. Every morning, Fufi would wait for us to leave, jump over the wall, and go roaming around the neighborhood.

I caught her one day when I was home for the school holidays. My mom had left for work and I was in the living room. Fufi didn't know I was there; she thought I was gone because the car was gone. I heard Panther barking in the backyard, looked out, and there was Fufi, scaling the wall. She'd jumped, scampered up the last couple of feet, and then she was gone.

I couldn't believe this was happening. I ran out front, grabbed my bicycle, and followed her to see where she was going. She went a long way, many streets over, to another part of the neighborhood. Then she went up to this other house and jumped over their wall and into their backyard. What the hell was she doing? I went up to the gate and rang the doorbell. This colored kid answered.

"May I help you?" he said.

"Yeah. My dog is in your yard."

"What?"

"My dog. She's in your yard."

Fufi walked up and stood between us.

"Fufi, come!" I said. "Let's go!"

This kid looked at Fufi and called her by some other stupid name, Spotty or some bullshit like that.

"Spotty, go back inside the house."

"Whoa, whoa," I said. "Spotty? That's Fufi!"

"No, that's my dog, Spotty."

"No, that's Fufi, my friend."

"No, this is Spotty."

"How could this be Spotty? She doesn't even have spots. You don't know what you're talking about."

"This is Spotty!"

"Fufi!"

"Spotty!"

"Fufi!"

Of course, since Fufi was deaf she didn't respond to "Spotty" or "Fufi." She just stood there. I started cursing the kid out.

"Give me back my dog!"

"I don't know who you are," he said, "but you better get out of here."

Then he went into the house and got his mom and she came out.

"What do you want?" she said.

"That's my dog!"

"This is our dog. Go away."

I started crying. "Why are you stealing my dog?!" I turned to Fufi and begged her. "Fufi, why are you doing this to me?! Why, Fufi?! Why?!" I called to her. I begged her to come. Fufi was deaf to my pleas. And everything else.

I jumped onto my bike and raced home, tears running down my face. I loved Fufi so much. To see her with another boy, acting like she didn't know me, after I raised her, after all the nights we spent together. I was heartbroken.

That evening Fufi didn't come home. Because the other family thought I was coming to steal their dog, they had decided to lock her inside, so she couldn't make it back the way she normally did to wait for us outside the fence. My mom got home from work. I was in tears. I told her Fufi had been kidnapped. We went back to the house. My mom rang the bell and confronted the mom.

"Look, this is our dog."

This lady lied to my mom's face. "This is not your dog. We bought this dog."

"You didn't buy the dog. It's our dog."

They went back and forth. This woman wasn't budging, so we went home to get evidence: pictures of us with the dogs, certificates from the vet. I was crying the whole time, and my mom was losing her patience with me. "Stop crying! We'll get the dog! Calm down!"

We gathered up our documentation and went back to the house. This time we brought Panther with us, as part of the proof. My mom showed this lady the pictures and the information from the vet. She still wouldn't give us Fufi. My mom threatened to call the police. It turned into a whole thing. Finally my mom said, "Okay, I'll give you a hundred rand."

"Fine," the lady said.

My mom gave her some money and she brought Fufi out. The other kid, who thought Fufi was Spotty, had to watch his mother sell the dog he thought was his. Now he started crying. "Spotty! No! Mom, you can't sell Spotty!" I didn't care. I just wanted Fufi back.

Once Fufi saw Panther she came right away. The dogs left with us and we walked. I sobbed the whole way home, still heartbroken. My mom had no time for my whining.

"Why are you crying?!"

"Because Fufi loves another boy."

"So? Why would that hurt you? It didn't cost you anything. Fufi's here. She still loves you. She's still your dog. So get over it."

Fufi was my first heartbreak. No one has ever betrayed me more than Fufi. It was a valuable lesson to me. The hard thing was understanding that Fufi wasn't cheating on me with another boy. She was merely living her life to the fullest. Until I knew that she was going out on her own during the day, her other relationship hadn't affected me at all. Fufi had no malicious intent.

I believed that Fufi was *my* dog, but of course that wasn't true. Fufi was *a* dog. I was *a* boy. We got along well. She happened to live in my house. That experience shaped what I've felt about relationships for the rest of my life: You do not own the thing that you love. I was lucky to learn that lesson at such a young age. I have so many friends who still, as adults, wrestle with feelings of betrayal. They'll come to me angry and crying and talking about how they've been cheated on and lied to, and I feel for them. I understand what they're going through. I sit with them and buy them a drink and I say, "Friend, let me tell you the story of Fufi."

When I was twenty-four years old, one day out of the blue my mother said to me, "You need to find your father."

"Why?" I asked. At that point I hadn't seen him in over ten years and didn't think I'd ever see him again.

"Because he's a piece of you," she said, "and if you don't find him you won't find yourself."

"I don't need him for that," I said. "I know who I am."

"It's not about knowing who you are. It's about him knowing who you are, and you knowing who he is. Too many men grow up without their fathers, so they spend their lives with a false impression of who their father is and what a father should be. You need to find your father. You need to show him what you've become. You need to finish that story."

8

ROBERT

My father is a complete mystery. There are so many questions about his life that I still cannot even begin to answer.

Where'd he grow up? Somewhere in Switzerland.

Where'd he go to university? I don't know if he did.

How'd he end up in South Africa? I haven't a clue.

I've never met my Swiss grandparents. I don't know their names or anything about them. I do know my dad has an older sister, but I've never met her, either. I know that he worked as a chef in Montreal and New York for a while before moving to South Africa in the late 1970s. I know that he worked for an industrial food-service company and that he opened a couple of bars and restaurants here and there. That's about it.

I never called my dad "Dad." I never addressed him "Daddy" or "Father," either. I couldn't. I was instructed not to. If we were out in public or anywhere people might overhear us and I called him "Dad," someone might have asked questions or called the police. So for as long as I can remember I always called him Robert.

While I know nothing of my dad's life before me, thanks to my mom and just from the time I have been able to spend with him, I do have a sense of who he is as a person. He's very Swiss, clean and particular and precise. He's the only person I know who checks into a hotel room and leaves it cleaner than when he arrived. He doesn't like anyone waiting on him. No servants, no housekeepers. He cleans up after himself. He likes his space. He lives in his own world and does his own everything.

I know that he never married. He used to say that most people marry because they want to control another person, and he never wanted to be controlled. I know that he loves traveling, loves entertaining, having people over. But at the same time his privacy is everything to him. Wherever he lives he's never listed in the phone book. I'm sure my parents would have been caught in their time together if he hadn't been as private as he is. My mom was wild and impulsive. My father was reserved and rational. She was fire, he was ice. They were opposites that attracted, and I am a mix of them both.

One thing I do know about my dad is that he hates racism and homogeneity more than anything, and not because of any feelings of self-righteousness or moral superiority. He just never understood how white people could be racist in South Africa. "Africa is full of black people," he would say. "So why would you come all the way to Africa if you hate black people? If you hate black people so much, why did you move into their house?" To him it was insane.

Because racism never made sense to my father, he never subscribed to any of the rules of apartheid. In the early eighties, before I was born, he opened one of the first integrated restaurants in Johannesburg, a steakhouse. He applied for a special license that allowed businesses to serve both black and white patrons. These licenses existed because hotels and restaurants needed them to serve black travelers and diplomats from other countries, who in theory weren't subject to the same restrictions as black South Africans; black South Africans with money in turn exploited that loophole to frequent those hotels and restaurants.

My dad's restaurant was an instant, booming success. Black people came because there were few upscale establishments where they could eat, and they wanted to come and sit in a nice restaurant and see what that was like. White people came because they wanted to see what it was like to sit with black people. The white people would sit and watch the black people eat, and the black people would sit and eat and watch the white people watching them eat. The curiosity of being together overwhelmed the animosity keeping people apart. The place had a great vibe.

The restaurant closed only because a few people in the neighborhood took it upon themselves to complain. They filed petitions, and the government started looking for ways to shut my dad down. At first the inspectors came and tried to get him on cleanliness and health-code violations. Clearly they had never heard of the Swiss. That failed dismally. Then they decided to go after him by imposing additional and arbitrary restrictions.

"Since you've got the license you can keep the restaurant open," they said, "but you'll need to have separate toilets for every racial category. You'll need white toilets, black toilets, colored toilets, and Indian toilets."

"But then it will be a whole restaurant of nothing but toilets."

"Well, if you don't want to do that, your other option is to make it a normal restaurant and only serve whites."

He closed the restaurant.

After apartheid fell, my father moved from Hillbrow to Yeoville, a formerly quiet, residential neighborhood that had transformed into this vibrant melting pot of black and white and every other hue. Immigrants were pouring in from Nigeria and Ghana and all over the continent, bringing different food and exciting music. Rockey Street was the main strip, and its sidewalks were filled with street vendors and restaurants and bars. It was an explosion of culture.

My dad lived two blocks over from Rockey, on Yeo Street, right next to this incredible park where I loved to go because kids of all races and different countries were running around and playing there. My dad's house was simple. Nice, but nothing fancy. I feel like my dad had enough money to be comfortable and travel, but he never spent lavishly on things. He's extremely frugal, the kind of guy who drives the same car for twenty years.

My father and I lived on a schedule. I visited him every Sunday afternoon. Even though apartheid had ended, my mom had made her decision: She didn't want to get married. So we had our house, and he had his. I'd made a deal with my mom that if I went with her to mixed church and white church in the morning, after that I'd get to skip black church and go to my dad's, where we'd watch Formula 1 racing instead of casting out demons.

I celebrated my birthday with my dad every year, and we spent Christmas with him as well. I loved Christmas with my dad because my dad celebrated European Christmas. European Christmas was the best Christmas ever. My dad went all out. He had Christmas lights and a Christmas tree. He had fake snow and snow globes and stockings hung by the fireplace and lots of wrapped presents from Santa Claus. African Christmas was a lot more practical. We'd go to church, come home, have a nice meal with good meat and lots of custard and jelly. But there was no tree. You'd get a present, but it was usually just clothes, a new outfit. You might get a toy, but it wasn't wrapped and it was never from Santa Claus. The whole issue of Santa Claus is a rather contentious one when it comes to African Christmas, a matter of pride. When an African dad buys his kid a present, the last thing he's going to do is give some fat white man credit for it. African Dad will tell you straight up, "No, no, no. *I* bought you that."

Outside of birthdays and special occasions, all we had were our Sunday afternoons. He would cook for me. He'd ask me what I wanted, and I'd always request the exact same meal, a German dish called *Rösti*, which is basically a pancake made out of potatoes and some sort of meat with a gravy. I'd have that and a bottle of Sprite, and for dessert a plastic container of custard with caramel on top.

A good chunk of those afternoons would pass in silence. My dad didn't talk much. He was caring and devoted, attentive to detail, always a card on my birthday, always my favorite food and toys when I came for a visit. But at the same time he was a closed book. We'd talk about the food he was making, talk about the F1 racing we'd watched. Every now and then he'd drop a tidbit of information, about a place he'd visited or his steakhouse. But that was it. Being with my dad was like watching a web series. I'd get a few minutes of information a few minutes at a time, then I'd have to wait a week for the next installment.

When I was thirteen my dad moved to Cape Town, and we lost touch. We'd been losing touch for a while, for a couple of reasons. I was a teenager. I had a whole other world I was dealing with now. Videogames and computers meant more to me than spending time with my parents. Also, my mom had married Abel. He was incensed by the idea of my mom being in contact with her previous love, and she decided it was safer for everyone involved not to test his anger. I went from seeing my dad every Sunday to seeing him every other Sunday, maybe once a month, whenever my mom could sneak me over, same as she'd done back in Hillbrow. We'd gone from living under apartheid to living under another kind of tyranny, that of an abusive, alcoholic man.

At the same time, Yeoville had started to suffer from white flight, neglect, general decline. Most of my dad's German friends had left for Cape Town. If he wasn't seeing me, he had no reason to stay, so he left. His leaving wasn't anything traumatic, because it never registered that we might lose touch and never see each other again. In my mind it was just *Dad's moving to Cape Town for a bit. Whatever.*

Then he was gone. I stayed busy living my life, surviving high school, surviving my early twenties, becoming a comedian. My career took off quickly. I got a radio DJ gig and hosted a kids' adventure reality show on television. I was headlining at clubs all over the country. But even as my life was moving forward, the questions about my dad were always there in the back of my mind, bubbling up to the surface now and then. "I wonder where he is. Does he think about me? Does he know what I'm doing? Is he proud of me?" When a parent is absent, you're left in the lurch of not knowing, and it's so easy to fill that space with negative thoughts. "They don't care." "They're selfish." My one saving grace was that my mom never spoke ill of him. She would always compliment him. "You're good with your money. You get that from your dad." "You have your dad's smile." "You're clean and tidy like your father." I never turned to bitterness, because she made sure I knew his absence was because of circumstance and not a lack of love. She always told me the story of her coming home from the hospital and my dad saying, "Where's my kid? I want that kid in my life." She'd say to me, "Don't ever forget: He chose you." And, ultimately, when I turned twenty-four, it was my mom who made me track him down.

Because my father is so private, finding him was hard work. We didn't have an address. He wasn't in the phone book. I started by reaching out to some of his old connections, German expats in Johannesburg, a woman who used to date one of his friends who knew somebody who knew the last place he stayed. I got nowhere. Finally my mom suggested the Swiss embassy. "They have to know where he is," she said, "because he has to be in touch with them."

I wrote to the Swiss embassy asking them where my father was, but because my father is not on my birth certificate I had no proof that my father is my father. The embassy wrote back and said they couldn't give me any information, because they didn't know who I was. I tried calling them, and I got the runaround there as well. "Look, kid," they said. "We can't help you. We're the *Swiss* embassy. Do you know nothing about the Swiss? Discretion is kind of our thing. That's what we do. Tough luck." I kept pestering them and finally they said, "Okay, we'll take your letter and, if a man such as you're describing exists, we might forward your letter to him. If he doesn't, maybe we won't. Let's see what happens."

A few months later, a letter came back in the post: "Great to hear from you. How are you? Love, Dad." He gave me his address in Cape

Town, in a neighborhood called Camps Bay, and a few months later I went down to visit.

I'll never forget that day. It was probably one of the weirdest days of my life, going to meet a person I knew and yet did not know at all. My memories of him felt just out of reach. I was trying to remember how he spoke, how he laughed, what his manner was. I parked on his street and started looking for his address. Camps Bay is full of older, semiretired white people, and as I walked down the road all these old white men were walking toward me and past me. My father was pushing seventy by that point, and I was so afraid I'd forgotten what he looked like. I was looking in the face of every old white man who passed me, like, *Are* you *my daddy?* Basically it looked like I was cruising old white dudes in a beachfront retirement community. Then finally I got to the address I'd been given and rang the bell, and the second he opened the door I recognized him. *Hey! It's you,* I thought. *Of course it's you. You're the guy. I know you.*

We picked up right where we'd left off, which was him treating me exactly the way he'd treated me as a thirteen-year-old boy. Like the creature of habit he was, my father went straight back into it. "Right! So where were we? Here, I've got all your favorites. Potato *Rösti.* A bottle of Sprite. Custard with caramel." Luckily my tastes hadn't matured much since the age of thirteen, so I tucked right in.

While I was eating he got up and went and picked up this book, an oversized photo album, and brought it back to the table. "I've been following you," he said, and he opened it up. It was a scrapbook of everything I had ever done, every time my name was mentioned in a newspaper, everything from magazine covers to the tiniest club listings, from the beginning of my career all the way through to that week. He was smiling so big as he took me through it, looking at the headlines. "Trevor Noah Appearing This Saturday at the Blues Room." "Trevor Noah Hosting New TV Show."

I felt a flood of emotions rushing through me. It was everything I could do not to start crying. It felt like this ten-year gap in my life closed right up in an instant, like only a day had passed since I'd last seen him.

For years I'd had so many questions. Is he thinking about me? Does he know what I'm doing? Is he proud of me? But he'd been with me the whole time. He'd always been proud of me. Circumstance had pulled us apart, but he was never not my father.

I walked out of his house that day an inch taller. Seeing him had reaffirmed his choosing of me. He chose to have me in his life. He chose to answer my letter. I was wanted. Being chosen is the greatest gift you can give to another human being.

Once we reconnected, I was overcome by this drive to make up for all the years we'd missed. I decided the best way to do it was to interview him. I realized very quickly that that was a mistake. Interviews will give you facts and information, but facts and information weren't really what I was after. What I wanted was a relationship, and an interview is not a relationship. Relationships are built in the silences. You spend time with people, you observe them and interact with them, and you come to know them—and that is what apartheid stole from us: time. You can't make up for that with an interview, but I had to figure that out for myself.

I went down to spend a few days with my father, and I made it my mission: This weekend I will get to know my father. As soon as I arrived I started peppering him with questions. "Where are you from? Where did you go to school? Why did you do this? How did you do that?" He started getting visibly irritated.

"What is this?" he said. "Why are you interrogating me? What's going on here?"

"I want to get to know you."

"Is this how you normally get to know people, by interrogating them?"

"Well . . . not really."

"So how do you get to know people?"

"I dunno. By spending time with them, I guess."

"Okay. So spend time with me. See what you find out."

So we spent the weekend together. We had dinner and talked about politics. We watched F1 racing and talked about sports. We sat quietly in his backyard and listened to old Elvis Presley records. The whole time he said not one word about himself. Then, as I was packing up to leave, he walked over to me and sat down.

"So," he said, "in the time we've spent together, what would you say you've learned about your dad?"

"Nothing. All I know is that you're extremely secretive."

"You see? You're getting to know me already."

PART II

When Dutch colonists landed at the southern tip of Africa over three hundred years ago, they encountered an indigenous people known as the Khoisan. The Khoisan are the Native Americans of South Africa, a lost tribe of bushmen, nomadic hunter-gatherers distinct from the darker, Bantu-speaking peoples who later migrated south to become the Zulu, Xhosa, and Sotho tribes of modern South Africa. While settling in Cape Town and the surrounding frontier, the white colonists had their way with the Khoisan women, and the first mixed people of South Africa were born.

To work the colonists' farms, slaves were soon imported from different corners of the Dutch empire, from West Africa, Madagascar, and the East Indies. The slaves and the Khoisan intermarried, and the white colonists continued to dip in and take their liberties, and over time the Khoisan all but disappeared from South Africa. While most were killed off through disease, famine, and war, the rest of their bloodline was bred out of existence, mixed in with the descendants of whites and slaves to form an entirely new race of people: coloreds. Colored people are a hybrid, a complete mix. Some are light and some are dark. Some have Asian features, some have white features, some have black features. It's not uncommon for a colored man and a colored woman to have a child that looks nothing like either parent.

The curse that colored people carry is having no clearly defined heritage to go back to. If they trace their lineage back far enough, at a certain point it splits into white and native and a tangled web of "other." Since their native mothers are gone, their strongest affinity has always been with their white fathers, the Afrikaners. Most colored people don't speak African languages. They speak Afrikaans. Their religion, their institutions, all of the things that shaped their culture came from Afrikaners.

The history of colored people in South Africa is, in this respect, worse than the history of black people in South Africa. For all that black people have suffered, they know who they are. Colored people don't.

————

9

THE MULBERRY TREE

At the end of our street in Eden Park, right in a bend at the top of the road, stood a giant mulberry tree growing out of someone's front yard. Every year when it bore fruit the neighborhood kids would go and pick berries from it, eating as many as they could and filling up bags to take home. They would all play under the tree together. I had to play under the tree by myself. I didn't have any friends in Eden Park.

I was the anomaly wherever we lived. In Hillbrow, we lived in a white area, and nobody looked like me. In Soweto, we lived in a black area, and nobody looked like me. Eden Park was a colored area. In Eden Park, *everyone* looked like me, but we couldn't have been more different. It was the biggest mindfuck I've ever experienced.

The animosity I felt from the colored people I encountered growing up was one of the hardest things I've ever had to deal with. It taught me that it is easier to be an insider as an outsider than to be an outsider as an insider. If a white guy chooses to immerse himself in hip-hop culture and only hang out with black people, black people will say, "Cool, white guy. Do what you need to do." If a black guy chooses to button up his blackness to live among white people and play lots of golf, white people will say, "Fine. I like Brian. He's safe." But try being a black person who immerses himself in white culture while still living in the black community. Try being a white person who adopts the trappings of black culture while still living in the white community. You will face more hate and ridicule and ostracism than you can even begin to fathom. People are willing to accept you if they see you as an outsider trying to assimilate into their world. But when they see you as a fellow tribe member attempting to disavow the tribe, that is something they will never forgive. That is what happened to me in Eden Park.

When apartheid came, colored people defied easy categorization, so the system used them—quite brilliantly—to sow confusion, hatred, and mistrust. For the purposes of the state, colored people became the almost-whites. They were second-class citizens, denied the rights of white people but given special privileges that black people didn't have, just to keep them holding out for more. Afrikaners used to call them *amperbaas:* "the almost-boss." The almost-master. "You're *almost* there. You're *so close.* You're *this close* to being white. Pity your grandfather couldn't keep his hands off the chocolate, eh? But it's not your fault you're colored, so keep trying. Because if you work hard enough you can erase this taint from your bloodline. Keep on marrying lighter and whiter and don't touch the chocolate and maybe, *maybe,* someday, if you're lucky, you can become white."

Which seems ridiculous, but it would happen. Every year under apartheid, some colored people would get promoted to white. It wasn't a myth; it was real. People could submit applications to the government. Your hair might become straight enough, your skin might become light enough, your accent might become polished enough—and you'd be reclassified as white. All you had to do was denounce your people, denounce your history, and leave your darker-skinned friends and family behind.

The legal definition of a white person under apartheid was "one who in appearance is obviously a white person who is generally not accepted as a coloured person; or is generally accepted as a white person and is not in appearance obviously a white person." It was completely arbitrary, in other words. That's where the government came up with things like the pencil test. If you were applying to be white, the pencil went into your hair. If it fell out, you were white. If it stayed in, you were colored. You were what the government said you were. Sometimes that came down to a lone clerk eyeballing your face and making a snap decision. Depending on how high your cheekbones were or how broad your nose was, he could tick whatever box made sense to him, thereby deciding where you could live, whom you could marry, what jobs and rights and privileges you were allowed.

And colored people didn't just get promoted to white. Sometimes colored people became Indian. Sometimes Indian people became colored. Sometimes blacks were promoted to colored, and sometimes coloreds were demoted to black. And of course whites could be demoted to colored as well. That was key. Those mixed bloodlines were always lurking, waiting to peek out, and fear of losing their status kept white people in line. If two white parents had a child and the government decided that child was too dark, even if both parents produced documentation proving they were white, the child could be classified as colored, and the family had to make a decision. Do they give up their white status to go and live as colored people in a colored area? Or would they split up, the mother taking the colored child to live in the ghetto while the father stayed white to make a living to support them?

Many colored people lived in this limbo, a true purgatory, always yearning for the white fathers who disowned them, and they could be horribly racist to one another as a result. The most common colored slur was *boesman*. "Bushman." "Bushie." Because it called out their blackness, their primitiveness. The worst way to insult a colored person was to infer that they were in some way black. One of the most sinister things about apartheid was that it taught colored people that it was black people who were holding them back. Apartheid said that the only reason colored people couldn't have first-class status was because black people might use coloredness to sneak past the gates to enjoy the benefits of whiteness.

That's what apartheid did: It convinced every group that it was because of the other race that they didn't get into the club. It's basically the bouncer at the door telling you, "We can't let you in because of your friend Darren and his ugly shoes." So you look at Darren and say, "Screw you, Black Darren. You're holding me back." Then when Darren goes up, the bouncer says, "No, it's actually your friend Sizwe and his weird hair." So Darren says, "Screw you, Sizwe," and now everyone hates everyone. But the truth is that none of you were ever getting into that club.

Colored people had it rough. Imagine: You've been brainwashed into believing that your blood is tainted. You've spent all your time assimilating and aspiring to whiteness. Then, just as you think you're closing in on the finish line, some fucking guy named Nelson Mandela comes along and flips the country on its head. Now the finish line is back where the starting line was, and the benchmark is black. Black is in charge. Black is beautiful. Black is powerful. For centuries colored people were told: Blacks are monkeys. Don't swing from the trees like them. Learn to walk upright like the white man. Then all of a sudden it's *Planet of the Apes,* and the monkeys have taken over.

So you can imagine how weird it was for me. I was mixed but not colored—colored by complexion but not by culture. Because of that I was seen as a colored person who didn't want to be colored.

In Eden Park, I encountered two types of colored people. Some colored people hated me because of my blackness. My hair was curly and I was proud of my Afro. I spoke African languages and loved speaking them. People would hear me speaking Xhosa or Zulu and they'd say, *"Wat is jy? 'n Boesman?"* "What are you, a Bushman?" Why are you trying to be black? Why do you speak that click-click language? Look at your light skin. You're almost there and you're throwing it away.

Other colored people hated me because of my whiteness. Even though I identified as being black, I had a white father. I went to an English private school. I'd learned to get along with white people at church. I could speak perfect English, and I barely spoke Afrikaans, the language colored people were supposed to speak. So colored people thought that I thought I was better than them. They would mock my accent, like I was putting on airs. *"Dink jy, jy is grênd?"* "You think you're high class?"—uppity, people would say in America.

Even when I thought I was liked, I wasn't. One year I got a brand-new bike during the summer holidays. My cousin Mlungisi and I were taking turns riding around the block. I was riding up our street when this cute colored girl came out to the road and stopped me. She smiled and waved to me sweetly.

"Hey," she said, "can I ride your bike?"

I was completely shocked. *Oh, wow,* I thought, *I made a friend.*

"Yeah, of course," I said.

I got off and she got on and rode about twenty or thirty feet. Some random older kid came running up to the street, she stopped and got off, and he climbed on and rode away. I was so happy that a girl had spoken to me that it didn't fully sink in that they'd stolen my bicycle. I ran back home, smiling and skipping along. My cousin asked where the bicycle was. I told him.

"Trevor, you've been robbed," he said. "Why didn't you chase them?"

"I thought they were being nice. I thought I'd made a friend."

Mlungisi was older, my protector. He ran off and found the kids, and thirty minutes later he came back with my bike.

Things like that happened a lot. I was bullied all the time. The incident at the mulberry tree was probably the worst of them. Late one afternoon I was playing by myself like I always did, running around the neighborhood. This group of five or six colored boys was up the street picking berries off the mulberry tree and eating them. I went over and started picking some to take home for myself. The boys were a few years older than me, around twelve or thirteen. They didn't talk to me, and I didn't talk to them. They were speaking to one another in Afrikaans, and I could understand what they were saying. Then one of them, this kid who was the ringleader of the group, walked over. *"Mag ek jou moerbeie sien?"* "Can I see your mulberries?" My first thought, again, was, *Oh, cool. I made a friend.* I held up my hand and showed him my mulberries. Then he knocked them out of my hand and smushed them into the ground. The other kids started laughing. I stood there and looked at him a moment. By that point I'd developed thick skin. I was used to being bullied. I shrugged it off and went back to picking berries.

Clearly not getting the reaction he wanted, this kid started cursing me out. *"Fok weg, jou onnosele Boesman!"* "Get the fuck out of here! Go away, you stupid Bushie! Bushman!" I ignored him and went on about my business. Then I felt a *splat!* on the back of my head. He'd hit me with a mulberry. It wasn't painful, just startling. I turned to look at him and, *splat!*, he hit me again, right in my face.

Then, in a split second, before I could even react, all of these kids started pelting me with berries, pelting the shit out of me. Some of the berries weren't ripe, and they stung like rocks. I tried to cover my face with my hands, but there was a barrage coming at me from all sides. They were laughing and pelting me and calling me names. "Bushie! Bushman!" I was terrified. Just the suddenness of it, I didn't know what to do. I started crying, and I ran. I ran for my life, all the way back down the road to our house.

When I ran inside I looked like I'd been beaten to a pulp because I was bawling my eyes out and was covered in red-purple berry juice. My mother looked at me, horrified.

"What happened?"

In between sobs I told her the story. "These kids . . . the mulberry tree . . . they threw berries at me . . ." When I finished, she burst out laughing. "It's not funny!" I said.

"No, no, Trevor," she said. "I'm not laughing because it's funny. I'm laughing out of relief. I thought you'd been beaten up. I thought this was blood. I'm laughing because it's only berry juice."

My mom thought everything was funny. There was no subject too dark or too painful for her to tackle with humor. "Look on the bright side," she said, laughing and pointing to the half of me covered in dark berry juice. "Now you really are half black and half white."

"It's not funny!"

"Trevor, you're okay," she said. "Go and wash up. You're not hurt. You're hurt emotionally. But you're not hurt."

Half an hour later, Abel showed up. At that point Abel was still my mom's boyfriend. He wasn't trying to be my father or even a stepfather, really. He was more like a big brother than anything. He'd joke around with me, have fun. I didn't know him that well, but one thing I did know about him was that he had a temper. Very charming when he wanted to be, incredibly funny, but fuck he could be mean. He'd grown up in the homelands, where you had to fight to survive. Abel was big, too, around six-foot-three, long and lean. He hadn't hit my mom yet. He hadn't hit me yet, either. But I knew he was dangerous. I'd seen it. Someone would cut us off in traffic. Abel would yell out the window. The other guy would honk and yell back. In a flash Abel would be out of our car, over to theirs, grabbing the guy through the driver's-side window, screaming in his face, raising a fist. You'd see the other guy panic. "Whoa, whoa, whoa. I'm sorry, I'm sorry."

When Abel walked in that night, he sat down on the couch and saw that I'd been crying.

"What happened?" he said.

I started to explain. My mother cut me off. "Don't tell him," she said. She knew what would happen. She knew better than me.

"Don't tell me what?" Abel said.

"It's nothing," she said.

"It's not nothing," I said.

She glared at me. "Don't tell him."

Abel was getting frustrated. "What? Don't tell me what?"

He'd been drinking; he never came home from work sober, and the drinking always made his temper worse. It was strange, but in that moment I realized that if I said the right things I could get him to step in and do something. We were almost family, and I knew if I made him feel like his family had been insulted, he'd help me get back at the boys. I knew he had a demon inside him, and I hated that; it terrified me how violent and dangerous he was when he snapped. But in that moment I knew exactly what I had to say to get the monster on my side.

I told him the story, the names they called me, the way they attacked me. My mother kept laughing it off, telling me to get over it, that it was kids being kids, no big deal. She was trying to defuse the situation, but I couldn't see that. I was just mad at her. "You think it's a joke, but it's not funny! It's not *funny*!"

Abel wasn't laughing. As I told him what the bullies had done, I could see the anger building up inside him. With Abel's anger, there was no ranting and raving, no clenched fists. He sat there on the couch listening to me, not saying a word. Then, very calm and deliberate, he stood up.

"Take me to these boys," he said.

Yes, I thought, *this is it. Big brother is going to get my revenge for me.*

We got into his car and drove up the road, stopping a few houses down from the tree. It was dark now except for the light from the streetlamps, but we could see the boys were still there, playing under the tree. I pointed to the ringleader. "That one. He was the main one." Abel slammed his foot on the gas and shot up onto the grass and straight toward the bottom of the tree. He jumped out. I jumped out. As soon as the kids saw me they knew exactly what was happening. They scattered and ran like hell.

Abel was quick. Good Lord, he was fast. The ringleader had made a dash for it and was trying to climb over a wall. Abel grabbed him, pulled him down, and dragged him back. Then he stripped a branch off the tree, a switch, and started whipping him. He whipped the *shit* out of him, and I loved it. I have never enjoyed anything as much as I enjoyed that moment. Revenge truly is sweet. It takes you to a dark place, but, man, it satisfies a thirst.

Then there was the strangest moment where it flipped. I caught a glimpse of the look of terror in the boy's face, and I realized that Abel had gone past getting revenge for me. He wasn't doing this to teach the kid a lesson. He was just beating him. He was a grown man venting his rage on a twelve-year-old boy. In an instant I went from *Yes, I got my revenge* to *No, no, no. Too much. Too much. Oh shit. Oh shit. Oh shit. Dear God, what have I done?*

Once this kid was beat to shit, Abel dragged him over to the car and held him up in front of me. "Say you're sorry." The kid was whimpering, trembling. He looked me in the eye, and I had never seen fear in someone's eyes like I saw in his. He'd been beaten by a stranger in a way I don't think he'd ever been beaten before. He said he was sorry, but it was like his apology wasn't for what he'd done to me. It was like he was sorry for every bad thing he'd ever done in his life, because he didn't know there could be a punishment like this.

Looking in that boy's eyes, I realized how much he and I had in common. He was a kid. I was a kid. He was crying. I was crying. He was a colored boy in South Africa, taught how to hate and how to hate himself. Who had bullied him that he needed to bully me? He'd made me feel fear, and to get my revenge I'd unleashed my own hell on his world. But I knew I'd done a terrible thing.

Once the kid apologized, Abel shoved him away and kicked him. "Go." The kid ran off, and we drove back to the house in silence. At home Abel and my mom got in a huge fight. She was always on him about his temper. "You can't go around hitting other people's children! You're not the law! This anger, this is no way to live!"

A couple of hours later this kid's dad drove over to our house to confront Abel. Abel went out to the gate, and I watched from inside the house. By that point Abel was truly drunk. This kid's dad had no idea what he was walking into. He was some mild-mannered, middle-aged guy. I don't remember much about him, because I was watching Abel the whole time. I never took my eyes off him. I knew that's where the danger was.

Abel didn't have a gun yet; he bought that later. But Abel didn't need a gun to put the fear of God in you. I watched as he got right in this guy's face. I couldn't hear what the other man was saying, but I heard Abel. "Don't fuck with me. I will kill you." The guy turned quickly and got back in his car and drove away. He thought he was coming to defend the honor of his family. He left happy to escape with his life.

When I was growing up, my mom spent a lot of time trying to teach me about women. She was always giving me lessons, little talks, pieces of advice. It was never a full-blown, sit-down lecture about relationships. It was more like tidbits along the way. And I never understood why, because I was a kid. The only women in my life were my mom and my grandmother and my aunt and my cousin. I had no love interest whatsoever, yet my mom insisted. She would go off on a whole range of things.

"Trevor, remember a man is not determined by how much he earns. You can still be the man of the house and earn less than your woman. Being a man is not what you have, it's who you are. Being more of a man doesn't mean your woman has to be less than you."

"Trevor, make sure your woman is the woman in your life. Don't be one of these men who makes his wife compete with his mother. A man with a wife cannot be beholden to his mother."

The smallest thing could prompt her. I'd walk through the house on the way to my room and say, "Hey, Mom" without glancing up. She'd say, "No, Trevor! You look at me. You acknowledge me. Show me that I exist to you, because the way you treat me is the way you will treat your woman. Women like to be noticed. Come and acknowledge me and let me know that you see me. Don't just see me when you need something."

These little lessons were always about grown-up relationships, funnily enough. She was so preoccupied with teaching me how to be a man that she never taught me how to be a boy. How to talk to a girl or pass a girl a note in class—there was none of that. She only told me about adult things. She would even lecture me about sex. As I was a kid, that would get very awkward.

"Trevor, don't forget: You're having sex with a woman in her mind before you're having sex with her in her vagina."

"Trevor, foreplay begins during the day. It doesn't begin in the bedroom."

I'd be like, "What? What is foreplay? What does that even mean?"

———

10

A YOUNG MAN'S LONG, AWKWARD, OCCASIONALLY TRAGIC, AND FREQUENTLY HUMILIATING EDUCATION IN AFFAIRS OF THE HEART, PART I: VALENTINE'S DAY

It was my first year at H. A. Jack, the primary school I transferred to after leaving Maryvale. Valentine's Day was approaching fast. I was twelve years old, and I'd never done Valentine's Day before. We didn't celebrate it in Catholic school. I understood Valentine's Day, as a concept. The naked baby shoots you with an arrow and you fall in love. I got that part. But this was my first time being introduced to it as an activity. At H. A. Jack, Valentine's Day was used as a fundraiser. Pupils were going around selling flowers and cards, and I had to go ask a friend what was happening.

"What is this?" I said. "What are we doing?"

"Oh, you know," she said, "it's Valentine's Day. You pick a special person and you tell them that you love them, and they love you back."

Wow, I thought, *that seems intense.* But I hadn't been shot by Cupid's arrow, and I didn't know of anyone getting shot on my behalf. I had no clue what was going on. All week, the girls in school kept saying, "Who's your valentine? Who's your valentine?" I didn't know what I was supposed to do. Finally one of the girls, a white girl, said, "You should ask Maylene." The other kids agreed. "Yes, Maylene. You should definitely ask Maylene. You have to ask Maylene. You guys are *perfect* for each other."

Maylene was a girl I used to walk home from school with. We lived in the city now, me, my mom and Abel, who was now my stepfather, and my new baby brother, Andrew. We'd sold our house in Eden Park to invest in Abel's new garage. Then that fell apart, and we ended up moving to a neighborhood called Highlands North, a thirty-minute walk from H. A. Jack. A group of us would leave school together every afternoon, each kid peeling off and going their separate way when we reached their house. Maylene and I lived the farthest, so we'd always be the last two. We'd walk together until we got where we needed to go, and then we'd part ways.

Maylene was cool. She was good at tennis, smart, cute. I liked her. I didn't have a crush on her; I wasn't even thinking about girls that way yet. I just liked hanging out with her. Maylene was also the only colored girl in school. I was the only mixed kid in school. We were the only two people who looked like each other. The white girls were insistent about me asking Maylene to be my valentine. They were like, "Trevor, you *have* to ask her. You're the *only two*. It's your *responsibility*." It was like our species was going to die out if we didn't mate and carry on. Which I've learned in life is something that white people do without even realizing it. "You two look the same, therefore we must arrange for you to have sex."

I honestly hadn't thought of asking Maylene, but when the girls brought it up, that thing happened where someone plants the idea in your head and it changes your perception.

"Maylene's totally got a thing for you."

"*Does* she?"

"Yeah, you guys are great together!"

"*Are* we?"

"Totally."

"Well, okay. If you say so."

I liked Maylene as much as I liked anyone, I suppose. Mostly I think I liked the idea of being liked. I decided I'd ask her to be my valentine, but I had no idea how to do it. I didn't know the first thing about having a girlfriend. I had to be taught the whole love bureaucracy of the school. There was the thing where you don't actually talk straight to the person. You have your group of friends and she has her group of friends, and your group of friends has to go to her group of friends and say, "Okay, Trevor likes Maylene. He wants her to be his valentine. We're in favor. We're ready to sign off with your approval." Her friends say, "Okay. Sounds good. We have to run it by Maylene." They go to Maylene. They consult. They tell her what they think. "Trevor says he likes you. We're in favor. We think you'd be good together. What do you say?" Maylene says, "I like Trevor." They say, "Okay. Let's move forward." They come back to us. "Maylene says she approves and she's waiting for Trevor's Valentine's Day advance."

The girls told me this process was what needed to happen. I said, "Cool. Let's do it." The friends sorted it out, Maylene got on board, and I was all set.

The week before Valentine's, Maylene and I were walking home together, and I was trying to get up the courage to ask her. I was so nervous. I'd never done anything like it. I already knew the answer; her friends had told me she'd say yes. It's like being in Congress. You know you have the votes before you go to the floor, but it's still difficult because anything could happen. I didn't know how to do it, all I knew was I wanted it to be perfect, so I waited until we were standing outside McDonald's. Then I mustered up all of my courage and turned to her.

"Hey, Valentine's Day is coming up, and I was wondering, would you be my valentine?"

"Yes. I'll be your valentine."

And then, under the golden arches, we kissed. It was my first time ever kissing a girl. It was just a peck, our lips touched for only a few seconds, but it set off explosions in my head. *Yes! Oh, yes. This. I don't know what this is, but I like it.* Something had awakened. And it was right outside McDonald's, so it was extra special.

Now I was truly excited. I had a valentine. I had a girlfriend. I spent the whole week thinking about Maylene, wanting to make her Valentine's Day as memorable as I could. I saved up my pocket money and bought her flowers and a teddy bear and a card. I wrote a poem with her name in the card, which was really hard because there aren't many good words that rhyme with Maylene. (Machine? Ravine? Sardine?) Then the big day came. I got my Valentine's card and the flowers and the teddy bear and got them ready and took them to school. I was the happiest boy on earth.

The teachers had set aside a period before recess for everyone to exchange valentines. There was a corridor outside our classrooms where I knew Maylene would be, and I waited for her there. All around me, love was in bloom. Boys and girls exchanging cards and gifts, laughing and giggling and stealing kisses. I waited and waited. Finally Maylene showed up and walked over to me. I was about to say "Happy Valentine's Day!" when she stopped me and said, "Oh, hi, Trevor. Um, listen, I can't be your girlfriend anymore. Leonardo asked me to be his valentine and I can't have two valentines, so I'm his girlfriend now and not yours."

She said it so matter-of-factly that I had no idea how to process it. This was my first time having a girlfriend, so at first I thought, *Huh, maybe this is just how it goes.*

"Oh, okay," I said. "Well, um . . . happy Valentine's Day."

I held out the card and the flowers and the teddy bear. She took them and said thanks, and she was gone.

I felt like someone had taken a gun and shot holes in every part of me. But at the same time some part of me said, "Well, this makes sense." Leonardo was everything I wasn't. He was popular. He was *white*. He'd upset the balance of everything by asking out the only colored girl in school. Girls loved him, and he was dumb as rocks. A nice guy, but kind of a bad boy. Girls did his homework for him; he was that guy. He was really good-looking, too. It was like when he was creating his character he traded in all his intelligence points for beauty points. I stood no chance.

As devastated as I was, I understood why Maylene made the choice that she did. I would have picked Leonardo over me, too. All the other kids were running up and down the corridors and out on the playground, laughing and smiling with their red and pink cards and flowers, and I went back to the classroom and sat by myself and waited for the bell to ring.

Petrol for the car, like food, was an expense we could not avoid, but my mom could get more mileage out of a tank of petrol than any human who has ever been on a road in the history of automobiles. She knew every trick. Driving around Johannesburg in our rusty old Volkswagen, every time she stopped in traffic, she'd turn off the car. Then the traffic would start and she'd turn the car on again. That stop-start technology that they use in hybrid cars now? That was my mom. She was a hybrid car before hybrid cars came out. She was the master of coasting. She knew every downhill between work and school, between school and home. She knew exactly where the gradient shifted to put it into neutral. She could time the traffic lights so we could coast through intersections without using the brakes or losing momentum.

There were times when we would be in traffic and we had so little money for petrol that I would have to push the car. If we were stuck in gridlock, my mom would turn the car off and it was my job to get out and push it forward six inches at a time. People would pitch up and offer to help.

"Are you stuck?"

"Nope. We're fine."

"You sure?"

"Yep."

"Can we help you?"

"Nope."

"Do you need a tow?"

And what do you say? The truth? "Thanks, but we're just so poor my mom makes her kid push the car"?

That was some of the most embarrassing shit in my life, pushing the car to school like the fucking Flintstones. Because the other kids were coming in on that same road to go to school. I'd take my blazer off so that no one could tell what school I went to, and I would bury my head and push the car, hoping no one would recognize me.

————

11

OUTSIDER

After finishing primary school at H. A. Jack, I started grade eight at Sandringham High School. Even after apartheid, most black people still lived in the townships and the areas formerly designated as homelands, where the only available government schools were the broken remnants of the Bantu system. Wealthy white kids—along with the few black people and colored people and Indians who had money or could get scholarships—were holed up in private schools, which were super-expensive but virtually guaranteed entry into university. Sandringham was what we call a Model C school, which meant it was a mix of government and private, similar to charter schools in America. The place was huge, a thousand kids on sprawling grounds with tennis courts, sports fields, and a swimming pool.

Being a Model C school and not a government school, Sandringham drew kids from all over, making it a near-perfect microcosm of
post-apartheid South Africa as a whole—a perfect example of what
South Africa has the potential to be. We had rich white kids, a bunch of
middle-class white kids, and some working-class white kids. We had
black kids who were newly rich, black kids who were middle-class, and
black kids from the townships. We had colored kids and Indian kids,
and even a handful of Chinese kids, too. The pupils were as integrated
as they could be given that apartheid had just ended. At H. A. Jack, race
was broken up into blocks. Sandringham was more like a spectrum.

South African schools don't have cafeterias. At Sandringham we'd
buy our lunch at what we call the tuck shop, a little canteen, and then
have free rein to go wherever we wanted on the school grounds to eat—
the quad, the courtyard, the playground, wherever. Kids would break
off and cluster into their cliques and groups. People were still grouped
by color in most cases, but you could see how they all blended and
shaded into one another. The kids who played soccer were mostly
black. The kids who played tennis were mostly white. The kids who
played cricket were a mix. The Chinese kids would hang out next to the
prefab buildings. The matrics, what South Africans call seniors, would
hang out on the quad. The popular, pretty girls would hang out over
here, and computer geeks would hang out over there. To the extent that
the groupings were racial, it was because of the ways race overlapped
class and geography out in the real world. Suburban kids hung out with
suburban kids. Township kids hung out with township kids.

At break, as the only mixed kid out of a thousand, I faced the same
predicament I had on the playground at H. A. Jack: Where was I supposed to go? Even with so many different groups to choose from, I
wasn't a natural constituent of any particular one. I obviously wasn't
Indian or Chinese. The colored kids would shit on me all the time for
being too black. So I wasn't welcome there. As always, I was adept
enough with white kids not to get bullied by them, but the white kids
were always going shopping, going to the movies, going on trips—
things that required money. We didn't have any money, so I was out of
the mix there, too. The group I felt the most affinity for was the poor

black kids. I hung out with them and got along with them, but most of them took minibuses to school from way out in the townships, from Soweto, from Tembisa, from Alexandra. They rode to school as friends and went home as friends. They had their own groups. Weekends and school holidays, they were hanging out with one another and I couldn't visit. Soweto was a forty-minute drive from my house. We didn't have money for petrol. After school I was on my own. Weekends I was on my own. Ever the outsider, I created my own strange little world. I did it out of necessity. I needed a way to fit in. I also needed money, a way to buy the same snacks and do the things that the other kids were doing. Which is how I became the tuck-shop guy.

Thanks to my long walk to school, I was late every single day. I'd have to stop off in the prefect's office to write my name down for detention. I was the patron saint of detention. Already late, I'd run to join my morning classes—math, English, biology, whatever. The last period before break was assembly. The pupils would come together in the assembly hall, each grade seated row by row, and the teachers and the prefects would get up onstage and go over the business of what was happening in the school—announcements, awards, that sort of thing. The names of the kids with detention were announced at every assembly, and I was always one of them. Always. Every single day. It was a running joke. The prefect would say, "Detentions for today . . ." and I would stand up automatically. It was like the Oscars and I was Meryl Streep. There was one time I stood up and then the prefect named the five people and I wasn't one of them. Everyone burst out laughing. Somebody yelled out, "Where's Trevor?!" The prefect looked at the paper and shook his head. "Nope." The entire hall erupted with cheers and applause. *"Yay!!!!"*

Then, immediately after assembly, there would be a race to the tuck shop because the queue to buy food was so long. Every minute you spent in the queue was working against your break time. The sooner you got your food, the longer you had to eat, play a game of soccer, or hang out. Also, if you got there late, the best food was gone.

Two things were true about me at that age. One, I was still the fastest kid in school. And two, I had no pride. The second we were dismissed from assembly I would run like a bat out of hell to the tuck shop so I could be the first one there. I was *always* first in line. I became notorious for being that guy, so much so that people started coming up to me in line. "Hey, can you buy this for me?" Which would piss off the kids behind me because it was basically cutting the line. So people started approaching me during assembly. They'd say, "Hey, I've got ten rand. If you buy my food for me, I'll give you two." That's when I learned: time is money. I realized people would pay me to buy their food because I was willing to run for it. I started telling everyone at assembly, "Place your orders. Give me a list of what you want, give me a percentage of what you're going to spend, and I'll buy your food for you."

I was an overnight success. Fat guys were my number-one customers. They loved food, but couldn't run. I had all these rich, fat white kids who were like, "This is fantastic! My parents spoil me, I've got money, and now I've got a way I can get food without having to work for it—and I still get my break." I had so many customers I was turning kids away. I had a rule: I would take five orders a day, high bidders only. I'd make so much that I could buy my lunch using other kids' money and keep the lunch money my mom gave me for pocket cash. Then I could afford to catch a bus home instead of walking or save up to buy whatever. Every day I'd take orders, assembly would end, and I'd make my mad dash and buy everybody's hot dogs and Cokes and muffins. If you paid me extra you could even tell me where you'd be and I'd deliver it to you.

I'd found my niche. Since I belonged to no group I learned to move seamlessly between groups. I floated. I was a chameleon, still, a cultural chameleon. I learned how to blend. I could play sports with the jocks. I could talk computers with the nerds. I could jump in the circle and dance with the township kids. I popped around to everyone, working, chatting, telling jokes, making deliveries.

I was like a weed dealer, but of food. The weed guy is always welcome at the party. He's not a part of the circle, but he's invited into the circle temporarily because of what he can offer. That's who I was. Always an outsider. As the outsider, you can retreat into a shell, be anonymous, be invisible. Or you can go the other way. You protect yourself by opening up. You don't ask to be accepted for everything you are, just the one part of yourself that you're willing to share. For me it was humor. I learned that even though I didn't belong to one group, I could be a part of any group that was laughing. I'd drop in, pass out the snacks, tell a few jokes. I'd perform for them. I'd catch a bit of their conversation, learn more about their group, and then leave. I never overstayed my welcome. I wasn't popular, but I wasn't an outcast. I was everywhere with everybody, and at the same time I was all by myself.

I don't regret anything I've ever done in life, any choice that I've made. But I'm consumed with regret for the things I didn't do, the choices I didn't make, the things I didn't say. We spend so much time being afraid of failure, afraid of rejection. But regret is the thing we should fear most. Failure is an answer. Rejection is an answer. Regret is an eternal question you will never have the answer to. "What if . . ." "If only . . ." "I wonder what would have . . ." You will never, never know, and it will haunt you for the rest of your days.

12

A YOUNG MAN'S LONG, AWKWARD, OCCASIONALLY TRAGIC, AND FREQUENTLY HUMILIATING EDUCATION IN AFFAIRS OF THE HEART, PART II: THE CRUSH

In high school, the attention of girls was not an affliction I suffered from. I wasn't the hot guy in class. I wasn't even the cute guy in class. I was ugly. Puberty was not kind to me. My acne was so bad that people used to ask what was wrong with me, like I'd had an allergic reaction to something. It was the kind of acne that qualifies as a medical condition. *Acne vulgaris,* the doctor called it. We're not talking about pimples, kids. We're talking pustules—big, pus-filled blackheads and white-heads. They started on my forehead, spread down the sides of my face, and covered my cheeks and neck and ravaged me everywhere.

Being poor didn't help. Not only could I not afford a decent haircut, leaving me with a huge, unruly Afro, but my mother also used to get angry at the fact that I grew out of my school uniforms too fast, so to save money she started buying my clothes three sizes too big. My blazer was too long and my pants were too baggy and my shoes flopped around. I was a clown. And of course, Murphy's Law, the year my mom started buying my clothes too big was the year that I stopped growing. So now I was never going to grow into my clown clothes and I was stuck being a clown. The only thing I had going for me was the fact that I was tall, but even there I was gangly and awkward-looking. Duck feet. High ass. Nothing worked.

After suffering my Valentine's Day heartbreak at the hands of Maylene and the handsome, charming Leonardo, I learned a valuable lesson about dating. What I learned was that cool guys get girls, and funny guys get to hang out with the cool guys with their girls. I was not a cool guy; therefore I did not have girls. I understood that formula very quickly and I knew my place. I didn't ask girls out. I didn't have a girlfriend. I didn't even try.

For me to try to get a girl would have upset the natural order of things. Part of my success as the tuck-shop guy was that I was welcome everywhere, and I was welcome everywhere because I was nobody. I was the acne-ridden clown with duck feet in floppy shoes. I wasn't a threat to the guys. I wasn't a threat to the girls. The minute I became somebody, I risked no longer being welcomed as nobody. The pretty girls were already spoken for. The popular guys had staked their claim. They would say, "I like Zuleika," and you knew that meant if you tried anything with Zuleika there'd be a fight. In the interest of survival, the smart move was to stay on the fringe, stay out of trouble.

At Sandringham, the only time girls in class looked at me was when they wanted me to pass a letter to the hot guy in class. But there was one girl I knew named Johanna. Johanna and I had been at the same school intermittently our whole lives. We were in preschool at Maryvale together. Then she left and went to another school. Then we were in primary school at H. A. Jack together. Then she left and went to another school. Then finally we were at Sandringham together. Because of that we became friends.

Johanna was one of the popular girls. Her best friend was Zaheera. Johanna was beautiful. Zaheera was stunning. Zaheera was colored, Cape Malay. She looked like Salma Hayek. Johanna was out and about and kissing boys, so the guys were all into her. Zaheera, as beautiful as she was, was extremely shy, so there weren't as many guys after her.

Johanna and Zaheera were always together. They were one grade below me, but in terms of popularity they were three grades above me. Still I got to hang out with them because I knew Johanna and we had this thing from being in different schools together. Dating girls may have been out of the question for me, but talking to them was not, because I could make them laugh. Human beings like to laugh, and lucky for me pretty girls are human beings. So I could relate to them in that way, but never in the other way. I knew this because whenever they stopped laughing at my jokes and stories they'd say, "So how do you think I can get Daniel to ask me out?" I always had a clear idea of where I stood.

Outwardly, I had carefully cultivated my status as the funny, nonthreatening guy, but secretly I had the hugest crush on Zaheera. She was *so* pretty and *so* funny. We'd hang out and have great conversations. I thought about her constantly, but for the life of me I never considered myself worthy of dating her. I told myself, *I'm going to have a crush on her forever, and that's all that's ever going to happen.*

At a certain point I decided to map out a strategy. I decided I'd be best friends with Zaheera and stay friends with her long enough to ask her to the matric dance, what we call our senior prom. Mind you, we were in grade nine at this point. The matric dance was three years away. But I decided to play the long game. I was like, *Yep, just gonna take my time.* Because that's what happens in the movies, right? I'd seen my American high school movies. You hang around long enough as the friendly good guy and the girl dates a bunch of handsome jerks, and then one day she turns around and goes, "Oh, it's you. It was always you. You're the guy I was supposed to be with all along."

That was my plan. It was foolproof.

I hung out with Zaheera every chance I got. We'd talk about boys, which ones she liked and which ones liked her. I'd give her advice. At one point she got set up with this guy Gary. They started dating. Gary was in the popular group but kind of shy and Zaheera was in the popular group but kind of shy, so his friends and her friends set them up together, like an arranged marriage. But Zaheera didn't like Gary at all. She told me. We talked about everything.

One day, I don't know how, but I plucked up the courage to ask Zaheera for her phone number, which was a big deal back then because it wasn't like cellphone numbers where everybody has everyone's number for texting and everything. This was the landline. To her house. Where her parents might answer. We were talking one afternoon at school and I asked, "Can I get your phone number? Maybe I can call you and we can talk at home sometime." She said yes, and my mind exploded. *What???!!!! A girl is giving me her phone number???!!! This is insane!!! What do I do??!!* I was so nervous. I'll never forget her telling me the digits one by one as I wrote them down, trying to keep my hand from shaking. We said goodbye and went our separate ways to class, and I was like, *Okay, Trevor. Play it cool. Don't call her right away*. I called her that night. At seven. She'd given me her number at two. That was me being cool. *Dude, don't call her at five. That's too obvious. Call her at seven.*

I phoned her house that night. Her mom answered. I said, "May I speak to Zaheera, please?" Her mom called her, and she came to the phone and we talked. For like an hour. After that we started talking more, at school, on the phone. I never told her how I felt. Never made a move. Nothing. I was always too scared.

Zaheera and Gary broke up. Then they got back together. Then they broke up. Then they got back together. They kissed once, but she didn't like it, so they never kissed again. Then they broke up for real. I bided my time through it all. I watched Popular Gary go down in flames, and I was still the good friend. *Yep, the plan is working. Matric dance, here we come. Only two and a half years to go . . .*

Then we had the mid-year school holidays. The day we came back, Zaheera wasn't at school. Then she wasn't at school the next day. Then she wasn't at school the day after that. Eventually I went and tracked down Johanna on the quad.

"Hey, where's Zaheera?" I said. "She hasn't been around for a while. Is she sick?"

"No," she said. "Didn't anyone tell you? She left the school. She doesn't go here anymore."

"What?"

"Yeah, she left."

My first thought was, *Wow, okay. That's news. I should give her a call to catch up.*

"What school did she move to?" I asked.

"She didn't. Her dad got a job in America. During the break they moved there. They've emigrated."

"What?"

"Yeah. She's gone. She was such a good friend, too. I'm really sad. Are you as sad as I am?"

"Uh . . . yeah," I said, still trying to process everything. "I liked Zaheera. She was really cool."

"Yeah, she was super sad, too, because she had such a huge crush on you. She was always waiting for you to ask her out. Okay, I gotta go to class! Bye!"

She ran off and left me standing there, stunned. She'd hit me with so much information at once, first that Zaheera was gone, then that she had left for America, and then that she'd liked me all along. It was like I'd been hit by three successive waves of heartbreak, each one bigger than the last. My mind raced through all the hours we'd spent talking on the quad, on the phone, all the times I could have said, "Hey, Zaheera, I like you. Will you be my girlfriend?" Ten words that might have changed my life if I'd had the courage to say them. But I hadn't, and now she was gone.

In every nice neighborhood there's one white family that Does Not Give a Fuck. You know the family I'm talking about. They don't do their lawn, don't paint the fence, don't fix the roof. Their house is shit. My mom found that house and bought it, which is how she snuck a black family into a place as white as Highlands North.

Most black people integrating into white suburbs were moving to places like Bramley and Lombardy East. But for some reason my mom chose Highlands North. It was a suburban area, lots of shopping. Working people, mostly. Not wealthy but stable and middle-class. Older houses, but still a nice place to live. In Soweto I was the only white kid in the black township. In Eden Park I was the only mixed kid in the colored area. In Highlands North I was the only black kid in the white suburb—and by "only" I mean only. In Highlands North the white never took flight. It was a largely Jewish neighborhood, and Jewish people don't flee. They're done fleeing. They've already fled. They get to a place, build their shul, and hold it down. Since the white people around us weren't leaving, there weren't a lot of families like ours moving in behind us.

I didn't make any friends in Highlands North for the longest time. I had an easier time making friends in Eden Park, to be honest. In the suburbs, everyone lived behind walls. The white neighborhoods of Johannesburg were built on white fear—fear of black crime, fear of black uprisings and reprisals—and as a result virtually every house sits behind a six-foot wall, and on top of that wall is electric wire. Everyone lives in a plush, fancy maximum-security prison. There is no sitting on the front porch, no saying hi to the neighbors, no kids running back and forth between houses. I'd ride my bike around the neighborhood for hours without seeing a single kid. I'd hear them, though. They were all meeting up behind brick walls for play-dates I wasn't invited to. I'd hear people laughing and playing and I'd get off my bike and creep up and peek over the wall and see a bunch of white kids splashing around in someone's swimming pool. I was like a Peeping Tom, but for friendship.

It was only after a year or so that I figured out the key to making black friends in the suburbs: the children of domestics. Many domestic workers in South Africa, when they get pregnant they get fired. Or, if they're lucky, the family they work for lets them stay on and they can have the baby, but then the baby goes to live with relatives in the homelands. Then the black mother raises the white children, seeing her own child only once a year at the holidays. But a handful of families would let their domestics keep their children with them, living in little maids' quarters or flatlets in the backyard.

For a long time, those kids were my only friends.

13

COLORBLIND

At Sandringham I got to know this one kid, Teddy. Funny guy, charming as hell. My mom used to call him Bugs Bunny; he had a cheeky smile with two big teeth that stuck out the front of his mouth. Teddy and I got along like a house on fire, one of those friends where you start hanging out and from that day forward you're never apart. We were both naughty as shit, too. With Teddy, I'd finally met someone who made me feel normal. I was the terror in my family. He was the terror in his family. When you put us together it was mayhem. Walking home from school we'd throw rocks through windows, just to see them shatter, and then we'd run away. We got detention together all the time. The teachers, the pupils, the principal, everyone at school knew: Teddy and Trevor, thick as thieves.

Teddy's mom worked as a domestic for a family in Linksfield, a wealthy suburb near school. Linksfield was a long walk from my house, nearly forty minutes, but still doable. Walking around was pretty much all I did back then, anyway. I couldn't afford to do anything else, and I couldn't afford to get around any other way. If you liked walking, you were my friend. Teddy and I walked all over Johannesburg together. I'd walk to Teddy's house and we'd hang out there. Then we'd walk back to my house and hang out there. We'd walk from my house down to the city center, which was like a three-hour hike, just to hang out, and then we'd walk all the way back.

Friday and Saturday nights we'd walk to the mall and hang out. The Balfour Park Shopping Mall was a few blocks from my house. It's not a big mall, but it has everything—an arcade, a cinema, restaurants, South Africa's version of Target, South Africa's version of the Gap. Then, once we were at the mall, since we never had any money to shop or watch movies or buy food, we'd just wander around inside.

One night we were at the mall and most of the shops were closed, but the cinema was still showing movies so the building was still open. There was this stationery shop that sold greeting cards and magazines, and it didn't have a door, so when it closed at night there was only a metal gate, like a trellis, that was pulled across the entrance and pad-locked. Walking past this shop, Teddy and I realized that if we put our arms through the trellis we could reach this rack of chocolates just in-side. And these weren't just any chocolates—they were alcohol-filled chocolates. I loved alcohol. Loved loved loved it. My whole life I'd steal sips of grown-ups' drinks whenever I could.

We reached in, grabbed a few, drank the liquor inside, and then gobbled down the chocolates. We'd hit the jackpot. We started going back again and again to steal more. We'd wait for the shops to start to close, then we'd go and sit against the gate, acting like we were just hanging out. We'd check to make sure the coast was clear, and then one of us would reach in, grab a chocolate, and drink the whiskey. Reach in, grab a chocolate, drink the rum. Reach in, grab a chocolate, drink the brandy. We did this every weekend for at least a month, having the best time. Then we pushed our luck too far.

It was a Saturday night. We were hanging out at the entrance to the stationery shop, leaning up against the gate. I reached in to grab a chocolate, and at that exact moment a mall cop came around the corner and saw me with my arm in up to my shoulder. I brought my hand out with a bunch of chocolates in it. It was almost like a movie. I saw him. He saw me. His eyes went wide. I tried to walk away, acting natural. Then he shouted out, "*Hey! Stop!*"

And the chase was on. We bolted, heading for the doors. I knew if a guard cut us off at the exit we'd be trapped, so we were hauling ass as fast as we could. We cleared the exit. The second we hit the parking lot, mall cops were coming at us from every direction, a dozen of them at least. I was running with my head down. These guards knew me. I was in that mall all the time. The guards knew my mom, too. She did her banking at that mall. If they even caught a glimpse of who I was, I was dead.

We ran straight across the parking lot, ducking and weaving between parked cars, the guards right behind us, yelling. We made it to the petrol station out at the road, ran through there, and hooked left up the main road. They chased and chased and we ran and ran, and it was *awesome*. The risk of getting caught was half the fun of being naughty, and now the chase was on. I was loving it. I was shitting myself, but also loving it. This was my turf. This was my neighborhood. You couldn't catch me in my neighborhood. I knew every alley and every street, every back wall to climb over, every fence with a gap big enough to slip through. I knew every shortcut you could possibly imagine. As a kid, wherever I went, whatever building I was in, I was always plotting my escape. You know, in case shit went down. In reality I was a nerdy kid with almost no friends, but in my mind I was an important and dangerous man who needed to know where every camera was and where all the exit points were.

I knew we couldn't run forever. We needed a plan. As Teddy and I booked past the fire station there was a road off to the left, a dead end that ran into a metal fence. I knew that there was a hole in the fence to squeeze through and on the far side was an empty field behind the mall that took you back to the main road and back to my house. A grown-up couldn't fit through the hole, but a kid could. All my years of imagining the life of a secret agent for myself finally paid off. Now that I needed an escape, I had one.

"Teddy, this way!" I yelled.

"No, it's a dead end!"

"We can get through! Follow me!"

He didn't. I turned and ran into the dead end. Teddy broke the other way. Half the mall cops followed him, half followed me. I got to the fence and knew exactly how to squirm through. Head, then shoulder, one leg, then twist, then the other leg—done. I was through. The guards hit the fence behind me and couldn't follow. I ran across the field to a fence on the far side, popped through there, and then I was right on the road, three blocks from my house. I slipped my hands into my pockets and casually walked home, another harmless pedestrian out for a stroll.

Once I got back to my house I waited for Teddy. He didn't show up. I waited thirty minutes, forty minutes, an hour. No Teddy.

Fuck.

I ran to Teddy's house in Linksfield. No Teddy. Monday morning I went to school. Still no Teddy.

Fuck.

Now I was worried. After school I went home and checked at my house again, nothing. Teddy's house again, nothing. Then I ran back home.

An hour later Teddy's parents showed up. My mom greeted them at the door.

"Teddy's been arrested for shoplifting," they said.

Fuuuck.

I eavesdropped on their whole conversation from the other room. From the start my mom was certain I was involved.

"Well, where was Trevor?" she asked.

"Teddy said he wasn't with Trevor," they said.

My mom was skeptical. "Hmm. Are you *sure* Trevor wasn't involved?"

"No, apparently not. The cops said there was another kid, but he got away."

"So it *was* Trevor."

"No, we asked Teddy, and he said it wasn't Trevor. He said it was some other kid."

"Huh . . . okay." My mom called me in. "Do you know about this thing?"

"What thing?"

"Teddy was caught shoplifting."

"Whhaaat?" I played dumb. "Noooo. That's crazy. I can't believe it. *Teddy?* No."

"Where were you?" my mom asked.

"I was at home."

"But you're always with Teddy."

I shrugged. "Not on this occasion, I suppose."

For a moment my mom thought she'd caught me red-handed, but Teddy'd given me a solid alibi. I went back to my room, thinking I was in the clear.

The next day I was in class and my name was called over the PA system. "Trevor Noah, report to the principal's office." All the kids were like, "Ooooohhh." The announcements could be heard in every classroom, so now, collectively, the whole school knew I was in trouble. I got up and walked to the office and waited anxiously on an uncomfortable wooden bench outside the door.

Finally the principal, Mr. Friedman, walked out. "Trevor, come in." Waiting inside his office was the head of mall security, two uniformed police officers, and my and Teddy's homeroom teacher, Mrs. Vorster. A roomful of silent, stone-faced white authority figures stood over me, the guilty young black man. My heart was pounding. I took a seat.

"Trevor, I don't know if you know this," Mr. Friedman said, "but Teddy was arrested the other day."

"What?" I played the whole thing again. "Teddy? Oh, no. What for?"

"For shoplifting. He's been expelled, and he won't be coming back to school. We know there was another boy involved, and these officers are going around to the schools in the area to investigate. We called you here because Mrs. Vorster tells us you're Teddy's best friend, and we want to know: Do you know anything about this?"

I shook my head. "No, I don't know anything."

"Do you know who Teddy was with?"

"No."

"Okay." He stood up and walked over to a television in the corner of the room. "Trevor, the police have video footage of the whole thing. We'd like you to take a look at it."

Fuuuuuuuuuuuuuuuuuuuck.

My heart was pounding in my chest. *Well, life, it's been fun,* I thought. *I'm going to get expelled. I'm going to go to jail. This is it.*

Mr. Friedman pressed Play on the VCR. The tape started. It was grainy, black-and-white security-camera footage, but you could see what was happening plain as day. They even had it from multiple angles: Me and Teddy reaching through the gate. Me and Teddy racing for the door. They had the whole thing. After a few seconds, Mr. Friedman reached up and paused it with me, from a few meters out, freeze-framed in the middle of the screen. In my mind, this was when he was going to turn to me and say, "Now would you like to confess?" He didn't.

"Trevor," he said, "do you know of any white kids that Teddy hangs out with?"

I nearly shat myself. *"What?!"*

I looked at the screen and I realized: Teddy was dark. I am light; I have olive skin. But the camera can't expose for light and dark at the same time. So when you put me on a black-and-white screen next to a black person, the camera doesn't know what to do. If the camera has to pick, it picks me as white. My color gets blown out. In this video, there was a black person and a white person. But still: It was me. The picture wasn't great, and my facial features were a bit blurry, but if you looked closely: It was me. I was Teddy's best friend. I was Teddy's only friend. I was the *single most likely accomplice*. You had to at least *suspect* that it was me. They didn't. They grilled me for a good ten minutes, but only because they were so sure that I had to know who this white kid was.

"Trevor, you're Teddy's best friend. Tell us the truth. Who is this kid?"

"I don't know."

"You don't recognize him at all?"

"No."

"Teddy never mentioned him to you?"

"Never."

At a certain point Mrs. Vorster just started running through a list of all the white kids she thought it could be.

"Is it David?"

"No."

"Rian?"

"No."

"Frederik?"

"No."

I kept waiting for it to be a trick, for them to turn and say, "It's *you*!" They didn't. At a certain point, I felt so invisible I almost wanted to take credit. I wanted to jump up and point at the TV and say, "Are you people blind?! That's me! Can you not see that that's me?!" But of course I didn't. And they couldn't. These people had been so fucked by their own construct of race that they could not see that the white person they were looking for was sitting right in front of them.

Eventually they sent me back to class. I spent the rest of the day and the next couple of weeks waiting for the other shoe to drop, waiting for my mom to get the call. "We've got him! We figured it out!" But the call never came.

South Africa has eleven official languages. After democracy came, people said, "Okay, how do we create order without having different groups feel like they've been left out of power again?" English is the international language and the language of money and of the media, so we had to keep that. Most people were forced to learn at least some Afrikaans, so it's useful to keep that, too. Plus we didn't want the white minority to feel ostracized in the new South Africa, or else they'd take all their money and leave.

Of the African languages, Zulu has the largest number of native speakers, but we couldn't keep that without also having Xhosa and Tswana and Ndebele. Then there's Swazi, Tsonga, Venda, Sotho, and Pedi. We tried to keep all the major groups happy, so the next thing we knew we'd made eleven languages official languages. And those are just the languages big enough to demand recognition; there are dozens more.

It's the Tower of Babel in South Africa. Every single day. Every day you see people completely lost, trying to have conversations and having no idea what the other person is saying. Zulu and Tswana are fairly common. Tsonga and Pedi are pretty fringe. The more common your tongue, the less likely you are to learn others. The more fringe, the more likely you are to pick up two or three. In the cities most people speak at least some English and usually a bit of Afrikaans, enough to get around. You'll be at a party with a dozen people where bits of conversation are flying by in two or three different languages. You'll miss part of it, someone might translate on the fly to give you the gist, you pick up the rest from the context, and you just figure it out. The crazy thing is that, somehow, it works. Society functions. Except when it doesn't.

14

A YOUNG MAN'S LONG, AWKWARD, OCCASIONALLY TRAGIC, AND FREQUENTLY HUMILIATING EDUCATION IN AFFAIRS OF THE HEART, PART III: THE DANCE

By the end of high school I'd become a mogul. My tuck-shop business had evolved into a mini-empire that included selling pirated CDs I made at home. I'd convinced my mother, as frugal as she was, that I needed a computer for school. I didn't. I wanted it so I could surf the Internet and play *Leisure Suit Larry*. But I was very convincing, and she broke down and got it for me. Thanks to the computer, the Internet, and the fortunate gift of a CD writer from a friend, I was in business.

I had carved out my niche, and was having a great time; life was so good as an outsider that I didn't even think about dating. The only girls in my life were the naked ones on my computer. While I downloaded music and messed around in chat rooms, I'd dabble in porn sites here and there. No video, of course, only pictures. With online porn today you just drop straight into the madness, but with dial-up it took so long for the images to load. It was almost gentlemanly compared to now. You'd spend a good five minutes looking at her face, getting to know her as a person. Then a few minutes later you'd get some boobs. By the time you got to her vagina, you'd spent a lot of quality time together.

In September of grade twelve, the matric dance was coming up. Senior prom. This was the big one. I was again faced with the dilemma of Valentine's Day, confronting another strange ritual I did not understand. All I knew about prom was that, according to my American movies, prom is where *it* happens. You lose your virginity. You go and you ride in the limousine, and then you and the girl do the thing. That was literally my only reference. But I knew the rule: Cool guys get girls, and funny guys get to hang out with the cool guys with their girls. So I'd assumed I wouldn't be going, or if I did go it wouldn't be with a date.

I had two middlemen working for me in my CD business, Sizwe and Tim. They sold the CDs that I copied in exchange for a cut. I met Tim at the arcade at the Balfour Park mall. Like Teddy, he lived nearby because his mom was a domestic worker. Tim was in my grade but went to a government school, Northview, a proper ghetto school. Tim handled my CD sales over there.

Tim was a chatterbox, hyperactive and go-go-go. He was a real hustler, too, always trying to cut a deal, work an angle. He could get people to do anything. A great guy, but fucking crazy and a complete liar as well. I went with him once to Hammanskraal, a settlement that was like a homeland, but not really. Hammanskraal, as its Afrikaans name suggests, was the kraal of Hamman, what used to be a white man's farm. The proper homelands, Venda and Gazankulu and Transkei, were places where black people actually lived, and the government drew a border around them and said, "Stay there." Hammanskraal and settlements like it were empty places on the map where deported black people had been relocated. That's what the government did. They would find some patch of arid, dusty, useless land, and dig row after row of holes in the ground—a thousand latrines to serve four thousand families. Then they'd forcibly remove people from illegally occupying some white area and drop them off in the middle of nowhere with some pallets of plywood and corrugated iron. "Here. This is your new home. Build some houses. Good luck." We'd watch it on the news. It was like some heartless, survival-based reality TV show, only nobody won any money.

One afternoon in Hammanskraal, Tim told me we were going to see a talent show. At the time, I had a pair of Timberland boots I'd bought. They were the only decent piece of clothing I owned. Back then, almost no one in South Africa had Timberlands. They were impossible to get, but everyone wanted them because American rappers wore them. I'd scrimped and saved my tuck-shop money and my CD money to buy them. As we were leaving, Tim told me, "Be sure to wear your Timberlands."

The talent show was in this little community hall attached to nothing in the middle of nowhere. When we got there, Tim was going around, shaking hands, chatting with everybody. There was singing, dancing, some poetry. Then the host got up onstage and said, *"Re na le modiragatsi yo o kgethegileng. Ka kopo amogelang . . . Spliff Star!"* "We've got a special performer, a rapper all the way from America. Please welcome . . . Spliff Star!"

Spliff Star was Busta Rhymes's hype man at the time. I sat there, confused. *What? Spliff Star? In Hammanskraal?* Then everyone in the room turned and looked at me. Tim walked over and whispered in my ear.

"Dude, come up onstage."

"What?"

"Come onstage."

"Dude, what are you talking about?"

"Dude, please, you're gonna get me in so much shit. They've already paid me the money."

"*Money?* What money?"

Of course, what Tim had failed to tell me was that he'd told these people he was bringing a famous rapper from America to come and rap in their talent show. He had demanded to be paid up front for doing so, and I, in my Timberlands, was that famous American rapper.

"Screw you," I said. "I'm not going anywhere."

"Please, dude, I'm begging you. Please do me this favor. Please. There's this girl here, and I wanna get with her, and I told her I know all these rappers . . . Please. I'm begging you."

"Dude, I'm not Spliff Star. What am I gonna do?!"

"Just rap Busta Rhymes songs."

"But I don't know any of the lyrics."

"It doesn't matter. These people don't speak English."

"Aw, fuck."

I got up onstage and Tim did some terrible beat-boxing—*"Bff ba-dff, bff bff ba-dff"*—while I stumbled through some Busta Rhymes lyrics that I made up as I went along. The audience erupted with cheers and applause. An American rapper had come to Hammanskraal, and it was the most epic thing they had ever seen.

So that's Tim.

One afternoon Tim came by my house and we started talking about the dance. I told him I didn't have a date, couldn't get a date, and wasn't going to get a date.

"I can get you a girl to go with you to the dance," he said.

"No, you can't."

"Yes, I can. Let's make a deal."

"I don't want one of your deals, Tim."

"No, listen, here's the deal. If you give me a better cut on the CDs I'm selling, plus a bunch of free music for myself, I'll come back with the most beautiful girl you've ever seen in your life, and she'll be your date for the dance."

"Okay, I'll take that deal because it's never going to happen."

"Do we have a deal?"

"We have a deal, but it's not going to happen."

"But do we have a *deal*?"

"It's a deal."

"Okay, I'm going to find you a date. She's going to be the most beautiful girl you've ever seen, and you're going to take her to the matric dance and you're going to be a superstar."

The dance was still two months away. I promptly forgot about Tim and his ridiculous deal. Then he came over to my house one afternoon and popped his head into my room.

"I found the girl."

"Really?"

"Yeah. You have to come and meet her."

I knew Tim was full of shit, but the thing that makes a con man successful is that he never gives you nothing. He delivers just enough to keep you believing. Tim had introduced me to many beautiful women. He was never dating them, but he talked a good game, and was always around them. So when he said he had a girl, I didn't doubt him. The two of us jumped on a bus and headed into the city.

The girl lived in a run-down block of flats downtown. We found her building, and a girl leaned over the balcony and waved us inside. That was the girl's sister Lerato, Tim said. Come to find out, he'd been trying to get with Lerato, and setting me up with the sister was his way in—of course, Tim was working an angle.

It was dark in the lobby. The elevator was busted, so we walked up several flights. This girl Lerato brought us into the flat. In the living room was this giant, but I mean really, really enormous, fat woman. I was like, *Oh, Tim. I see what you've done here. Nicely played*. Tim was a big joker as well.

"Is this my date?" I asked.

"No, no, no," he said. "This is not your date. This is her older sister. Your date is Babiki. Babiki has three older sisters, and Lerato is her younger sister. Babiki's gone to the store to buy groceries. She'll be back in a moment."

We waited, chatted with the older sister. Ten minutes later the door opened and the most beautiful girl I have ever seen in my life walked in. She was . . . good Lord. Beautiful eyes, beautiful golden yellow-brown skin. It was like she glowed. No girl at my high school looked anything like her.

"Hi," she said.

"Hi," I replied.

I was dumbfounded. I had no idea how to talk to a girl that beautiful. She was shy and didn't speak much, either. There was a bit of an awkward pause. Luckily Tim's a guy who just talks and talks. He jumped right in and smoothed everything over. "Trevor, this is Babiki. Babiki, Trevor." He went on and on about how great I was, how much she was looking forward to the dance, when I would pick her up for the dance, all the details. We hung out for a few, and then Tim needed to get going so we headed out the door. Babiki turned and smiled at me and waved as we left.

"Bye."

"Bye."

We walked out of that building and I was the happiest man on earth. I couldn't believe it. I was the guy at school who couldn't get a date. I'd resigned myself to never getting a date, didn't consider myself worthy of having a date. But now I was going to the matric dance with the most beautiful girl in the world.

Over the following weeks we went down to Hillbrow a few more times to hang out with Babiki and her sisters and her friends. Babiki's family was Pedi, one of South Africa's smaller tribes. I liked getting to know people of different backgrounds, so that was fun. Babiki and her friends were what we call *amabhujua*. They're as poor as most other black people, but they try to act like they're not. They dress fashionably and act rich. *Amabhujua* will put a shirt on layaway, one shirt, and spend seven months paying it off. They'll live in shacks wearing Italian leather shoes that cost thousands. An interesting crowd.

Babiki and I never went on a date alone. It was always the two of us in a group. She was shy, and I was a nervous wreck most of the time, but we had fun. Tim kept everyone loose and having a good time. Whenever we'd say goodbye, Babiki would give me a hug, and once she even gave me a little kiss. I was in heaven. I was like, *Yeah, I've got a girlfriend. Cool.*

As the dance approached, I started getting nervous. I didn't have a car. I didn't have any decent clothes. This was my first time taking out a beautiful girl, and I wanted it to be perfect.

We'd moved to Highlands North when my stepfather's garage went out of business, and he moved his workshop to the house. We had a big yard and a garage in the back, and that became his new workshop, essentially. At any given time, we had at least ten or fifteen cars in the driveway, in the yard, and out on the street, clients' cars being worked on and old junkers Abel kept around to tinker with. One afternoon Tim and I were at the house. Tim was telling Abel about my date, and Abel decided to be generous. He said I could take a car for the dance.

There was a red Mazda that we'd had for a while, a complete piece of shit but it worked well enough. I'd borrowed it before, but the car I really wanted was Abel's BMW. It was old and beat-up like the Mazda, but a shit BMW is still a BMW. I begged him to let me take it.

"Please, please, can I use the BMW?"

"Not a fucking chance."

"Please. This is the greatest moment in my life. Please. I'm begging you."

"No."

"Please."

"No. You can take the Mazda."

Tim, always the hustler and the dealmaker, stepped in.

"Bra Abie," he said. "I don't think you understand. If you saw the girl Trevor is taking to the dance, you would see why this is so important. Let's make a deal. If we bring her here and she's the most beautiful girl you've ever seen in your life, you'll let him take the BMW."

Abel thought about it.

"Okay. Deal."

We went to Babiki's flat, told her my parents wanted to meet her, and brought her back to my house. Then we brought her around to the garage in the back where Abel and his guys were working. Tim and I went over and introduced them.

"Abel, this is Babiki. Babiki, this is Abel."

Abel smiled big, was charming as always.

"Nice to meet you," he said.

They chatted for a few minutes. Tim and Babiki left. Abel turned to me.

"Is that the girl?"

"Yes."

"You can take the BMW."

Once I had the car, I desperately needed something to wear. I was taking out this girl who was really into fashion, and, except for my Timberlands, everything I owned was shit. I was limited in my wardrobe choices because I was stuck buying in the shops my mother let me go to, and my mother did not believe in spending money on clothes. She'd take me to some bargain clothing store and tell me what our budget was, and I'd have to find something to wear.

At the time I had no clue about clothes. My idea of fashion was a brand of clothing called Powerhouse. It was the kind of stuff weight lifters wear down in Miami or out at Venice Beach, baggy track pants with baggy sweatshirts. The logo was a cartoon of this giant body-building bulldog wearing wraparound sunglasses and smoking a cigar and flexing his muscles. On the pants he was flexing all the way down your leg. On the shirt he was flexing across your chest. On the underwear, he was flexing on your crotch. I thought Powerhouse was the baddest thing in the world, I can't even front. I had no friends, I loved dogs, and muscles were cool—that's where I was working from. I had Powerhouse everything, the full range, five of the same outfit in five different colors. It was easy. The pants came with the top, so I knew how to make it work.

Sizwe, the other middleman from my CD business, found out I had a date, and he made it his mission to give me a makeover. "You need to up your game," he said. "You cannot go to the dance looking the way you look—for her sake, not yours. Let's go shopping."

I went to my mom and begged her to give me money to buy something to wear for the dance. She finally relented and gave me 2,000 rand, for one outfit. It was the most money she'd ever given me for anything in my life. I told Sizwe how much I had to spend, and he said we'd make it work. The trick to looking rich, he told me, is to have one expensive item, and for the rest of the things you get basic, good-looking quality stuff. The nice item will draw everyone's eye, and it'll look like you've spent more than you have.

In my mind nothing was cooler than the leather coats everybody wore in *The Matrix*. *The Matrix* came out while I was in high school and it was my favorite movie at the time. I loved Neo. In my heart I knew: *I am Neo*. He's a nerd. He's useless at everything, but secretly he's a badass superhero. All I needed was a bald, mysterious black man to come into my life and show me the way. Now I had Sizwe, black, head shaved, telling me, "You can do it. You're the one." And I was like, "*Yes*. I knew it."

I told Sizwe I wanted a leather coat like Keanu Reeves wore, the ankle-length black one. Sizwe shut that down. "No, that's not practical. It's cool, but you'll never be able to wear it again." He took me shopping and we bought a calf-length black leather jacket, which would look ridiculous today but at the time, thanks to Neo, was very cool. That alone cost 1,200 rand. Then we finished the outfit with a pair of simple black pants, suede square-toed shoes, and a cream-white knitted sweater.

Once we had the outfit, Sizwe took a long look at my enormous Afro. I was forever trying to get the perfect 1970s Michael Jackson Afro. What I had was more Buckwheat: unruly and impossible to comb, like stabbing a pitchfork into a bed of crabgrass.

"We need to fix that fucking hair," Sizwe said.

"What do you mean?" I said. "This is just my hair."

"No, we *have* to do something."

Sizwe lived in Alexandra. He dragged me there, and we went to talk to some girls from his street who were hanging out on the corner.

"What would you do with this guy's hair?" he asked them.

The girls looked me over.

"He has so much," one of them said. "Why doesn't he cornrow it?"

"Shit, yeah," they said. "That's great!"

I said, "What? Cornrows? No!"

"No, no," they said. "Do it."

Sizwe dragged me to a hair salon down the street. We went in and sat down. The woman touched my hair, shook her head, and turned to Sizwe.

"I can't work with this sheep," she said. "You have to do something about this."

"What do we need to do?"

"You have to relax it. I don't do that here."

"Okay."

Sizwe dragged me to a second salon. I sat down in the chair, and the woman took my hair and started painting this creamy white stuff in it. She was wearing rubber gloves to keep this chemical relaxer off her own skin, which should have been my first clue that maybe this wasn't such a great idea. Once my hair was full of the relaxer, she told me, "You have to try to keep it in for as long as possible. It's going to start burning. When it starts burning, tell me and we'll rinse it out. But the longer you can handle it, the straighter your hair will become."

I wanted to do it right, so I sat in the chair and waited and waited for as long as I could.

I waited too long.

She'd told me to tell her when it started burning. She should have told me to tell her when it started tingling, because by the time it was actually burning it had already taken off several layers of my scalp. I was well past tingling when I started to freak out. *It's burning! It's burning!* She rushed me over to the sink and started to rinse the relaxer out. What I didn't know is that the chemical doesn't really start to burn until it's being rinsed out. I felt like someone was pouring liquid fire onto my head. When she was done I had patches of acid burns all over my scalp.

I was the only man in the salon; it was all women. It was a window into what women experience to look good on a regular basis. *Why would they ever do this?*, I thought. *This is horrible.* But it worked. My hair was completely straight. The woman combed it back, and I looked like a pimp, a pimp named Slickback.

Sizwe then dragged me back to the first salon, and the woman agreed to cornrow my hair. She worked slowly. It took six hours. Finally she said, "Okay, you can look in the mirror." She turned me around in the chair and I looked in the mirror and . . . I had never seen myself like that before. It was like the makeover scenes in my American movies, where they take the dorky guy or girl, fix the hair and change the clothes, and the ugly duckling becomes the swan. I'd been so convinced I'd never get a date that I never tried to look nice for a girl, so I didn't know that I could. The hair was good. My skin wasn't perfect, but it was getting better; the pustules had receded into regular pimples. I looked . . . not bad.

I went home, and my mom squealed when I walked in the door.

"Ooooooh! They turned my baby boy into a pretty little girl! I've got a little girl! You're so pretty!"

"Mom! C'mon. Stop it."

"Is this the way you're telling me that you're gay?"

"What? No. Why would you say that?"

"You know it's okay if you are."

"No, Mom. I'm not gay."

Everyone in my family loved it. They all thought it looked great. My mom did tease the shit out of me, though.

"It's very well done," she said, "but it is way too pretty. You do look like a girl."

The big night finally came. Tim came over to help me get ready. The hair, the clothes, everything came together perfectly. Once I was set, we went to Abel to get the keys to the BMW, and that was the moment the whole night started to go wrong.

It was a Saturday night, end of the week, which meant Abel was drinking with his workers. I walked out to his garage, and as soon as I saw his eyes I knew: He was wasted. *Fuck.* When Abel was drunk he was a completely different person.

"Ah, you look nice!" he said with a big smile, looking me over. "Where are you going?"

"Where am I—Abie, I'm going to the dance."

"Okay. Have fun."

"Um . . . can I get the keys?"

"The keys to what?"

"To the car."

"What car?"

"The BMW. You promised I could drive the BMW to the dance."

"First go buy me some beers," he said.

He gave me his car keys; Tim and I drove to the liquor store. I bought Abel a few cases of beer, drove back, and unloaded it for him.

"Okay," I said, "can I take the BMW now?"

"No."

"What do you mean 'no'?"

"I mean 'no.' I need my car tonight."

"But you promised. You said I could take it."

"Yeah, but I need the car."

I was crushed. I sat there with Tim and begged him for close to half an hour.

"Please."

"No."

"Please."

"Nope."

Finally we realized it wasn't going to happen. We took the shitty Mazda and drove to Babiki's house. I was an hour late picking her up. She was completely pissed off. Tim had to go in and convince her to come out, and eventually she did.

She was even more gorgeous than before, in an amazing red dress, but she was clearly not in a great mood. Inside I was quietly starting to panic, but I smiled and kept trying my gentlemanly best to be a good date, holding the door for her, telling her how beautiful she was. Tim and the sister gave us a send-off and we headed out.

Then I got lost. The dance was being held at some venue in a part of town I wasn't familiar with, and at some point I got completely turned around and had no idea where I was. I drove around for an hour in the dark, going left, going right, doubling back. I was on my cell-phone the whole time, desperately calling people, trying to figure out where I was, trying to get directions. Babiki sat next to me in stony silence the whole time, clearly not feeling me or this night *at all*. I was crashing hard. I was late. I didn't know where I was going. I was the worst date she'd ever had in her life.

I finally figured out where I was and we made it to the dance, nearly two hours late. I parked, jumped out, and ran around to get her door. When I opened it, she just sat there.

"Are you ready?" I said. "Let's go in."

"No."

"No? What . . . what do you mean, 'no'?"

"No."

"Okay . . . but why?"

"No."

"But we need to go inside. The dance is inside."

"No."

I stood there for another twenty minutes, trying to convince her to come inside, but she kept saying "no." She wouldn't get out of the car.

Finally, I said, "Okay, I'll be right back."

I ran inside and found Sizwe.

"Where have you been?" he said.

"I'm here! But my date's in the car and she won't come in."

"What do you mean she won't come in?"

"I don't know what's going on. Please help me."

We went back out to the parking lot. I took Sizwe over to the car, and the second he saw her he lost it. "Jesus in Heaven! This is the most beautiful woman I've ever seen. You said she was beautiful, Trevor, but this is insane." In an instant he completely forgot about helping me with Babiki. He turned and ran back inside and called to the guys. "Guys! You gotta come see this! Trevor got a date! And she's beautiful! Guys! Come out here!"

Twenty guys came running out into the parking lot. They clustered around the car. "Yo, she's so hot!" "Dude, *this* girl came with *Trevor*?" Guys were gawking at her like she was an animal at the zoo. They were asking to take pictures with her. They were calling back to more people inside. "This is insane! Look at Trevor's date! No, no, no, you gotta come and see!"

I was mortified. I'd spent four years of high school carefully avoiding any kind of romantic humiliation whatsoever, and now, on the night of the matric dance, the night of all nights, my humiliation had turned into a circus bigger than the event itself: Trevor the undatable clown thought he was going to have the most beautiful girl at the dance, but he's crashing and burning so let's all go outside and watch.

Babiki sat in the passenger seat, staring straight ahead, refusing to budge. I was outside the car, pacing, stressed out. A friend of mine had a bottle of brandy that he'd smuggled into the dance. "Here," he said, "have some of this." Nothing mattered at that point, so I started drinking. I'd fucked up. The girl didn't like me. The night was done.

Most of the guys eventually wandered back inside. I was sitting on the pavement, taking swigs from the brandy bottle, getting buzzed. At some point Sizwe went back over to the car to try one last time to convince Babiki to come in. After a minute his head popped up over the car with this confused look.

"Yo, Trevor," he said, "your date does not speak English."

"What?"

"Your date. She does not speak any English."

"That's not possible."

I got up and walked over to the car. I asked her a question in English and she gave me a blank stare.

Sizwe looked at me.

"How did you not know that your date does not speak English?"

"I . . . I don't know."

"Have you never spoken to her?"

"Of course I have—or, wait . . . *have* I?"

I started flashing back through all the times I'd been with Babiki, meeting at her flat, hanging out with her friends, introducing her to Abel. Did I talk to her then? No. Did I talk to her then? No. It was like the scene in *Fight Club* where Ed Norton's character flashes back and realizes he and Brad Pitt have never been in the same room with Helena Bonham Carter at the same time. He realizes he's been punching himself the whole time. *He's* Tyler Durden. In all the excitement of meeting Babiki, the times we were hanging out and getting to know each other, we were never actually speaking to each other. It was always through Tim.

Fucking Tim.

Tim had promised he'd get me a beautiful date for the dance, but he hadn't made any promises about any of her other qualities. Whenever we were together, she was speaking Pedi to Tim, and Tim was speaking English to me. But she didn't speak English, and I didn't speak Pedi. Abel spoke Pedi. He'd learned several South African languages in order to deal with his customers, so he'd spoken with her fluently when they met. But in that moment I realized I'd never actually heard her say anything in English other than: "Yes." "No." "Hi." "Bye." That's it: "Yes." "No." "Hi." "Bye."

Babiki was so shy that she didn't talk much to begin with, and I was so inept with women that I didn't know how to talk to her. I'd never had a girlfriend; I didn't even know what "girlfriend" meant. Someone put a beautiful woman on my arm and said, "She's your girlfriend." I'd been mesmerized by her beauty and just the idea of her—I didn't know I was supposed to talk to her. The naked women on my computer, I'd never had to talk to them, ask them their opinions, ask them about their feelings. And I was afraid I'd open my mouth and ruin the whole thing, so I just nodded and smiled along and let Tim do the talking.

All three of Babiki's older sisters spoke English, and her younger sister Lerato spoke a little. So whenever we hung out with Babiki and her sisters and their friends, a lot of the conversation was in English. The rest of it was going right by me in Pedi or in Sotho, but that's completely normal in South Africa so it never bothered me; I got enough of the gist of the conversation from everyone's English to know what was going on. And the way my mind works with language, even when I'm hearing other languages, they get filtered into English as I'm hearing them. My mind stores them in English. When my grandmother and great-grandmother were hysterically praying to God to destroy the demon that had shit on their kitchen floor, all of that transpired in Xhosa, but it's stored in English. I remember it as English. So whenever I lay in bed at night dreaming about Babiki and the moments we'd spent together, I *felt* like it had transpired in English because that's how I remembered it. And Tim had never said anything about what language she spoke or didn't speak, because why would he care? He just wanted to get his free CDs and get with the sister. Which is how I'd been dating a girl for over a month—the girl I very much believed was my first girlfriend—without ever having had a single conversation with her.

Now the whole night came rushing back and I saw it from her point of view, and it was perfectly obvious to me why she didn't want to get out of the car. She probably hadn't wanted to go to the dance with me in the first place; she probably owed Tim a favor, and Tim can talk anyone into anything. Then I'd left her sitting and waiting for me for an hour and she was pissed off. Then she got into the car and it was the first time we had ever been alone, and she realized I couldn't even hold a conversation with her. I'd driven her around and gotten lost in the dark—a young girl alone in a car in the middle of nowhere with some strange guy, no idea where I was taking her. She was probably terrified. Then we got to the dance and she didn't speak anyone's language. She didn't know anyone. She didn't even know me.

Sizwe and I stood outside the car, staring at each other. I didn't know what to do. I tried talking to her in every language I knew. Nothing worked. She only spoke Pedi. I got so desperate that I started trying to talk to her using hand signals.

"Please. You. Me. Inside. Dance. Yes?"

"No."

"Inside. Dance. Please?"

"No."

I asked Sizwe if he spoke Pedi. He didn't. I ran inside to the dance and ran around looking for someone who spoke Pedi to help me to convince her to come in. "Do you speak Pedi? Do you speak Pedi? Do you speak Pedi?" Nobody spoke Pedi.

So I never got to go to my matric dance. Other than the three minutes I spent running through it looking for someone who spoke Pedi, I spent the whole night in the parking lot. When the dance ended, I climbed back into the shitty red Mazda and drove Babiki home. We sat in total awkward silence the whole way.

I pulled up in front of her block of flats in Hillbrow, stopped the car, and sat for a moment as I tried to figure out the polite and gentlemanly way to end the evening. Then, out of nowhere, she leaned over and gave me a kiss. Like, a real kiss, a proper kiss. The kind of kiss that made me forget that the whole disaster had just happened. I was so confused. I didn't know what I was supposed to do. She pulled back and I looked deep into her eyes and thought, *I have no idea how girls work*.

I got out of the car, walked around to her side, and opened her door. She gathered up her dress and stepped out and headed toward her flat, and as she turned to go I gave her one last little wave.

"Bye."

"Bye."

PART III

In Germany, no child finishes high school without learning about the Holocaust. Not just the facts of it but the how and the why and the gravity of it—what it means. As a result, Germans grow up appropriately aware and apologetic. British schools treat colonialism the same way, to an extent. Their children are taught the history of the Empire with a kind of disclaimer hanging over the whole thing. "Well, *that* was shameful, now wasn't it?"

In South Africa, the atrocities of apartheid have never been taught that way. We weren't taught judgment or shame. We were taught history the way it's taught in America. In America, the history of racism is taught like this: "There was slavery and then there was Jim Crow and then there was Martin Luther King Jr. and now it's done." It was the same for us. "Apartheid was bad. Nelson Mandela was freed. Let's move on." Facts, but not many, and never the emotional or moral dimension. It was as if the teachers, many of whom were white, had been given a mandate. "Whatever you do, don't make the kids angry."

15

GO HITLER!

When I was in grade nine, three Chinese kids transferred to Sandringham: Bolo, Bruce Lee, and John. They were the only Chinese kids in the school, out of a thousand pupils. Bolo got his nickname because he looked like Bolo Yeung from the Jean-Claude Van Damme movie *Bloodsport*. Bruce Lee's name really was Bruce Lee, which made our lives. Here was this Chinese guy, quiet, good-looking, in great shape, and his name was Bruce Lee. We were like, *This is magic. Thank you, Jesus, for bringing us Bruce Lee*. John was just John, which was weird because of the other two.

I got to know Bolo because he was one of my tuck-shop clients. Bolo started selling bootleg PlayStation games around school. Kids would give him their PlayStation, and he'd bring it back a few days later with a chip in it that enabled them to play pirated games, which he would then sell them. Bolo was friends with this white kid and fellow pirate named Daniel, who traded in bootleg CDs. Daniel was two grades above me and a real computer geek; he even had a CD writer at home, back when nobody had CD writers.

One day on my tuck-shop rounds, I overheard Daniel and Bolo complaining about the black kids at school. They'd realized that they could take Daniel's and Bolo's merchandise, say "I'll pay you later," and then not pay, because Daniel and Bolo were too scared of black people to go back to ask for the money. I leaned in to their conversation and said, "Listen, you shouldn't get upset. Black people don't have any money, so trying to get more stuff for less money is just what we do. But let me help. I'll be your middleman. You give me the merchandise and I'll sell it, and then I'll handle getting the money. In return, you give me a cut of the sale." They liked the idea right away, and we became partners.

As the tuck-shop guy, I was perfectly positioned. I had my network set up. All I had to do was tap into it. With the money I made selling CDs and videogames, I was able to save up and add new components and more memory to my own computer. Daniel the computer geek showed me how to do it, where to buy the cheapest parts, how to assemble them, how to repair them. He showed me how his business worked, too, how to download music, where to get rewritable CDs in bulk. The only thing I was missing was my own CD writer, because it was the most expensive component. At the time a CD writer cost as much as the rest of the computer, nearly 2,000 rand.

I worked as a middleman for Bolo and Daniel for a year. Then Bolo left school. From that point on I worked for Daniel, and then as he was about to matriculate he decided to quit the game. "Trevor," he told me, "you've been a loyal partner." And, as thanks, he bequeathed unto me his CD writer. At the time, black people barely had access to computers, let's start there. But a CD writer? That was the stuff of lore. It was mythical. The day Daniel gave it to me, he changed my life. Thanks to him, I now controlled production, sales, distribution—I had everything I needed to lock down the bootleg business.

I was a natural capitalist. I loved selling stuff, and I was selling something that everybody wanted and nobody else could provide. I sold my discs for 30 rand, around $3. A regular CD in the store cost 100 to 150 rand. Once people started buying from me, they wouldn't buy real CDs ever again—the deal was too good.

I had an instinct for business, but at the time I knew nothing about music, which was odd for someone running a music-pirating business. The only music I knew, still, was Christian music from church, the only music allowed in my mother's house. The CD writer Daniel gave me was a 1x CD writer, which meant it copied at the speed it played. Every day I'd leave school, go to my room, and sit for five to six hours, copying CDs. I had my own surround-sound system built with old car speakers I'd salvaged from the junkers Abel kept in the yard, and I strung them up around the room. Even though I had to sit there while each CD played, for a long time I didn't really listen to them. I knew it was against the dealer's code: Never get high on your own supply.

Thanks to the Internet, I could get anyone anything. I never judged anyone's taste in music. You wanted the new Nirvana, I got you the new Nirvana. You wanted the new DMX, I got you the new DMX. Local South African music was big, but black American music was what people were desperate for, hip-hop and R&B. Jagged Edge was huge. 112 was huge. I sold a lot of Montell Jordan. So much Montell Jordan.

When I started, I had a dial-up connection and a 24k modem. It would take a day to download an album. But technology kept evolving, and I kept reinvesting in the business. I upgraded to a 56k modem. I got faster CD writers, multiple CD writers. I started downloading more, copying more, selling more. That's when I got two middlemen of my own, my friend Tim, who went to Northview, and my friend Sizwe, who lived in Alex.

One day Sizwe came to me and said, "You know what would make a lot of money? Instead of copying whole albums, why don't you put the best tracks of different albums onto one CD, because people only wanna hear the songs they like." That sounded like a great idea, so I started making mix CDs. Those sold well. Then a few weeks later

Sizwe came back and said, "Can you make the tracks fade into one another so the music moves from track one to track two without a break and the beat carries on? It'll be like a DJ playing a complete set the whole night." That sounded like a great idea, too. I downloaded a program called BPM, "beats per minute." It had a graphical interface that looked like two vinyl records side by side, and I could mix and fade between songs, basically everything a DJ can do live. I started making party CDs, and those started selling like hotcakes, too.

Business was booming. By matric I was balling, making 500 rand a week. To put that in perspective, there are maids in South Africa who still earn less than that today. It's a shit salary if you're trying to support a family, but as a sixteen-year-old living at home with no real expenses, I was living the dream.

For the first time in my life I had money, and it was the most liberating thing in the world. The first thing I learned about having money was that it gives you choices. People don't want to be rich. They want to be able to choose. The richer you are, the more choices you have. That is the freedom of money.

With money, I experienced freedom on a whole new level: I went to McDonald's. People in America don't understand, but when an American chain opens in a third-world country, people go crazy. That's true to this day. A Burger King opened for the first time in South Africa last year, and there was a queue around the block. It was an event. Everyone was going around saying, "I have to eat at Burger King. Have you heard? *It's from America*." The funny thing was that the queue was actually just white people. White people went bat-shit crazy for Burger King. Black people were like, *whatever*. Black people didn't need Burger King. Our hearts were with KFC and McDonald's. The crazy thing about McDonald's is that we knew about it long before it came, probably from movies. We never even dreamed we would ever get one in South Africa; McDonald's seemed to us like one of those American things that is exclusively American and can't go anywhere else. Even before we ever tasted McDonald's, we knew we'd love it, and we did. At one point South Africa was opening more McDonald's than any other country in the world. With Mandela came freedom—and with freedom came McDonald's. A McDonald's had opened up just two blocks from our house not long after we moved to Highlands North, but my mom would never pay for us to eat there. With my own money I was like, *Let's do this.* I went all in. They didn't have "supersize" at the time; "large" was the biggest. So I walked up to the counter, feeling very impressed with myself, and I put down my money and said, "I'll have a large number one."

I fell in love with McDonald's. McDonald's, to me, tasted like America. McDonald's *is* America. You see it advertised and it looks amazing. You crave it. You buy it. You take your first bite, and it blows your mind. It's even better than you imagined. Then, halfway through, you realize it's not all it's cracked up to be. A few bites later you're like, *Hmm, there's a lot wrong with this.* Then you're done, you miss it like crazy, and you go back for more.

Once I'd had a taste of America, I never ate at home. I only ate McDonald's. McDonald's, McDonald's, McDonald's, McDonald's. Every night my mother would try to cook me dinner.

"Tonight we're having chicken livers."

"No, I'm gonna have McDonald's."

"Tonight we're having dog bones."

"I think I'm gonna go with McDonald's again."

"Tonight we're having chicken feet."

"Hmmmmm . . . Okay, I'm in. But tomorrow I'm eating McDonald's."

The money kept rolling in and I was balling out of control. This is how balling I was: I bought a cordless telephone. This was before everyone had a cellphone. The range on this cordless phone was strong enough that I could put the base outside my window, walk the two blocks to McDonald's, order my large number one, walk back home, go up to my room, and fire up my computer, carrying on a conversation the whole time. I was that dude walking down the street holding a giant phone to my ear with the aerial fully extended, talking to my friend. "Yeah, I'm just goin' down to McDonald's . . ."

Life was good, and none of it would have happened without Daniel. Without him, I would never have mastered the world of music piracy and lived a life of endless McDonald's. What he did, on a small scale, showed me how important it is to empower the dispossessed and the disenfranchised in the wake of oppression. Daniel was white. His family had access to education, resources, computers. For generations, while his people were preparing to go to university, my people were crowded into thatched huts singing, *"Two times two is four. Three times two is six. La la la la la."* My family had been denied the things his family had taken for granted. I had a natural talent for selling to people, but without knowledge and resources, where was that going to get me? People always lecture the poor: "Take responsibility for yourself! Make something of yourself!" But with what raw materials are the poor to make something of themselves?

People love to say, "Give a man a fish, and he'll eat for a day. Teach a man to fish, and he'll eat for a lifetime." What they don't say is, "And it would be nice if you gave him a fishing rod." That's the part of the analogy that's missing. Working with Daniel was the first time in my life I realized you need someone from the privileged world to come to you and say, "Okay, here's what you need, and here's how it works." Talent alone would have gotten me nowhere without Daniel giving me the CD writer. People say, "Oh, that's a handout." No. I still have to work to profit by it. But I don't stand a chance without it.

One afternoon I was in my room making a CD when Sizwe came over to pick up his inventory. He saw me mixing songs on my computer.

"This is insane," he said. "Are you doing this live?"

"Yeah."

"Trevor, I don't think you understand; you're sitting on a gold mine. We need to do this for a crowd. You need to come to the township and start DJ'ing gigs. No one has ever seen a DJ playing on a computer before."

Sizwe lived in Alexandra. Where Soweto is a sprawling, government-planned ghetto, Alexandra is a tiny, dense pocket of a shantytown, left over from the pre-apartheid days. Rows and rows of cinder-block and corrugated-iron shacks, practically stacked on top of one another. Its nickname is Gomorrah because it has the wildest parties and the worst crimes.

Street parties are the best thing about Alexandra. You get a tent, put it up in the middle of the road, take over the street, and you've got a party. There's no formal invitations or guest list. You just tell a few people, word of mouth travels, and a crowd appears. There are no permits, nothing like that. If you own a tent, you have the right to throw a party in your street. Cars creep up to the intersection and the driver will see the party blocking their way and shrug and make a U-turn. Nobody gets upset. The only rule is that if you throw a party in front of somebody's house, they get to come and share your alcohol. The parties don't end until someone gets shot or a bottle gets broken on someone's face. That's how it has to end; otherwise, it wasn't a party.

Back then, most DJs could spin for only a few hours; they were limited by the number of vinyls they could buy. Since parties went all night, you might need five or six DJs to keep the dancing going. But I had a massive hard drive stuffed with MP3s, which is why Sizwe was excited when he saw me mixing—he saw a way to corner the market.

"How much music do you have?" he asked.

"Winamp says I can play for a week."

"We'll make a fortune."

Our first gig was a New Year's Eve party the summer we graduated from Sandringham. Sizwe and I took my tower, my giant monitor, and all the cables and the keyboard and the mouse. We loaded everything up in a minibus and brought it over to Alex. We took over the street in front of his house, ran the electricity out of his place, set up the computer, set up speakers, and borrowed a tent, and people came. It was explosive. By midnight the whole street was packed from one end to the other. Ours was the biggest New Year's Eve party in Alexandra that year, and to have the biggest party in Alexandra is no joke. All night, from far and wide, people kept coming. The word spread: "There's a light-skinned guy who plays music on a computer. You've never seen anything like it." I DJ'd by myself until dawn. By then me and my friends were so drunk and exhausted that we passed out on the lawn outside Sizwe's house. The party was so big it made our reputation in the hood, instantly. Pretty soon we were getting booked all over.

Which was a good thing.

When Sizwe and I graduated from high school, we couldn't get jobs. There were no jobs for us to get. The only ways I had to make money were pirating CDs and DJ'ing parties, and now that I'd left Sandringham, the minibus drivers and corner kids in Alexandra were the single biggest market for my CDs. It was also where I was playing the most gigs, so to keep earning I naturally gravitated that way. Most of the white kids I knew were taking a gap year. "I'm going to take a gap year and go to Europe." That's what the white kids were saying. So I said, "I, too, am going to take a gap year. I am going to take a year and go to the township and hang out on the corner." And that's what I did.

There was a low brick wall running down the middle of the road in front of Sizwe's house in Alex, and every day Sizwe and I and our crew would go sit on the wall. I'd bring my CDs. We'd play music and practice dance moves. We hustled CDs all day and DJ'd parties at night. We started getting booked for gigs in other townships, other hoods.

Thanks to my computer and modem I was getting exclusive tracks few people had access to, but that created a problem for me. Sometimes I'd play the new music at parties and people would stand around going, "What is this? How do you dance to it?" For example, if a DJ plays a song like "Watch Me (Whip/Nae Nae)"—yes, it's a catchy song, but what is a whip? What is a nae nae? For that song to be popular you have to know how to do the whip and the nae nae; new music works at parties only if people know how to dance to it. Sizwe decided we needed a dance crew to show people the steps to the songs we were playing. Because we spent our days doing nothing but listening to CDs and coming up with dance moves, our crew from the corner already knew all the songs, so they became our dancers. And hands down the best, most beautiful, most graceful dancer in the crew was Sizwe's neighbor, Hitler.

Hitler was a great friend of mine, and good Lord could that guy dance. He was mesmerizing to watch. He had a looseness and a fluidity that defied physics—imagine a jellyfish if it could walk on land. Incredibly handsome, too, tall and lithe and muscular, with beautiful, smooth skin, big teeth, and a great smile, always laughing. And all he did was dance. He'd be up in the morning, blasting house music or hip-hop, practicing moves the whole day.

In the hood, everybody knows who the best dancer in the crew is. He's like your status symbol. When you're poor you don't have cars or nice clothes, but the best dancer gets girls, so that's the guy you want to roll with. Hitler was our guy. There were parties with dance competitions. Kids from every neighborhood would come and bring their best dancers. We'd always bring Hitler, and he almost always won.

When Sizwe and I put together a routine for our dance crew, there was no question who was going to be the star attraction. We built the whole set around Hitler. I'd warm the crowd up with a few songs, then the dancers would come out and do a couple of numbers. Once they'd gotten the party started, they'd fan out to form a semicircle around the stage with a gap in the back for Hitler to enter. I'd crank up Redman's "Let's Get Dirty" and start whipping the crowd up even more. *"Are you ready?! I can't hear you! Let me hear you make some noise!"* People would start screaming, and Hitler would jump into the middle of the semicircle and the crowd would lose it. Hitler would do his thing while the guys circled around him, shouting him on. *"Go Hit-ler! Go Hit-ler! Go Hit-ler! Go Hit-ler!"* And because this was hip-hop, the crew would do that thing where you shoot your arm out in front of you with your palm flat, bopping it up and down to the beat. *"Go Hit-ler! Go Hit-ler! Go Hit-ler! Go Hit-ler!"* We'd have the whole crowd in a frenzy, a thousand people in the street chanting along with their hands in the air. *"Go Hit-ler! Go Hit-ler! Go Hit-ler! Go Hit-ler!"*

Hitler, although an unusual name, is not unheard-of in South Africa. Part of it has to do with the way a lot of black people pick names. Black people choose their traditional names with great care; those are the names that have deeply personal meanings. But from colonial times through the days of apartheid, black people in South Africa were required to have an English or European name as well—a name that white people could pronounce, basically. So you had your English name, your traditional name, and your last name: Patricia Nombuy-iselo Noah. Nine times out of ten, your European name was chosen at random, plucked from the Bible or taken from a Hollywood celebrity or a famous politician in the news. I know guys named after Mussolini and Napoleon. And, of course, Hitler.

Westerners are shocked and confused by that, but really it's a case of the West reaping what it has sown. The colonial powers carved up Africa, put the black man to work, and did not properly educate him. White people don't talk to black people. So why would black people know what's going on in the white man's world? Because of that, many black people in South Africa don't really know who Hitler was. My own grandfather thought "a hitler" was a kind of army tank that was helping the Germans win the war. Because that's what he took from what he heard on the news. For many black South Africans, the story of the war was that there was someone called Hitler and he was the reason the Allies were losing the war. This Hitler was so powerful that at some point black people had to go help white people fight against him—and if the white man has to stoop to ask the black man for help fighting someone, that someone must be the toughest guy of all time. So if you want your dog to be tough, you name your dog Hitler. If you want your kid to be tough, you name your kid Hitler. There's a good chance you've got an uncle named Hitler. It's just a thing.

At Sandringham, we were taught more about World War II than

the typical black kids in the townships were, but only in a basic way. We weren't taught to think critically about Hitler and anti-Semitism and the Holocaust. We weren't taught, for instance, that the architects of apartheid were big fans of Hitler, that the racist policies they put in place were inspired, in part, by the racist policies of the Third Reich. We weren't taught how to think about how Hitler related to the world we lived in. We weren't being taught to think, period. All we were taught was that in 1939 Hitler invaded Poland and in 1941 he invaded the Soviet Union and in 1943 he did something else. They're just facts. Memorize them, write them down for the test, and forget them.

There is also this to consider: The name Hitler does not offend a black South African because Hitler is not the worst thing a black South African can imagine. Every country thinks their history is the most important, and that's especially true in the West. But if black South Africans could go back in time and kill one person, Cecil Rhodes would come up before Hitler. If people in the Congo could go back in time and kill one person, Belgium's King Leopold would come way before Hitler. If Native Americans could go back in time and kill one person, it would probably be Christopher Columbus or Andrew Jackson.

I often meet people in the West who insist that the Holocaust was the worst atrocity in human history, without question. Yes, it was horrific. But I often wonder, with African atrocities like in the Congo, how horrific were they? The thing Africans don't have that Jewish people do have is documentation. The Nazis kept meticulous records, took pictures, made films. And that's really what it comes down to. Holocaust victims count because Hitler counted them. Six million people killed. We can all look at that number and rightly be horrified. But when you read through the history of atrocities against Africans, there are no numbers, only guesses. It's harder to be horrified by a guess. When Portugal and Belgium were plundering Angola and the Congo, they weren't counting the black people they slaughtered. How many black people died harvesting rubber in the Congo? In the gold and diamond mines of the Transvaal?

So in Europe and America, yes, Hitler is the Greatest Madman in

History. In Africa he's just another strongman from the history books. In all my time hanging out with Hitler, I never once asked myself, "*Why* is his name Hitler?" His name was Hitler because his mom named him Hitler.

Once Sizwe and I added the dancers to our DJ sets, we blew up. We called our group the Black and White Boys. The dancers were called the Springbok Boys. We started getting booked everywhere. Successful black families were moving to the suburbs, but their kids still wanted to have block parties and stay connected to the culture of the townships, so they'd book us to play their parties. Word of mouth traveled. Pretty soon we were getting booked more and more in the suburbs, meeting white people, playing for white people.

One kid we knew from the township, his mother was involved in creating cultural programs for schools. In America they'd be called "diversity programs." They were springing up all over South Africa because we were supposed to be learning about and embracing one another in this post-apartheid era. This kid's mom asked us if we wanted to play at a cultural day at some school in Linksfield, the wealthy suburb south of Sandringham where my pal Teddy had lived. There was going to be all sorts of different dancing and music, and everyone was going to come together and hang out and be cultural. She offered to pay, so we said sure. She sent us the information with the time and place and the name of the school: the King David School. A Jewish school.

The day of the event, we booked a minibus, loaded it up with our gear, and drove over. Once we arrived we waited in the back of the school's assembly hall and watched the acts that went onstage before us, different groups took their turns performing, flamenco dancers, Greek dancers, traditional Zulu musicians. Then we were up. We were billed as the Hip Hop Pantsula Dancers—the South African B-Boys. We set up our sound system onstage. I looked out, and the whole hall was nothing but Jewish kids in their yarmulkes, ready to party.

I got on the mic. "Are you ready to rock out?!"

"Yeahhhhhh!"

"Make some noise!"

"Yeahhhhhh!"

I started playing. The bass was bumping, my crew was dancing, and everyone was having a great time. The teachers, the chaperones, the parents, hundreds of kids—they were all dancing like crazy. Our set was scheduled for fifteen minutes, and at the ten-minute mark came the moment for me to play "Let's Get Dirty," bring out my star dancer, and shut shit down.

I started the song, the dancers fanned out in their semicircle, and I got on the mic.

"Are you guys ready?!"

"Yeahhhhhh!"

"You guys are not ready! Are you *ready*?!"

"Yeeeaaahhhhhhh!"

"All right! Give it up and make some noise for *HIIIIIITTTT-LLLLEERRRRRRRRRRR*!!!"

Hitler jumped out to the middle of the circle and started killing it. The guys around him were all chanting, *"Go Hit-ler! Go Hit-ler! Go Hit-ler! Go Hit-ler!"* They had their arms out in front of them, bouncing to the rhythm. *"Go Hit-ler! Go Hit-ler! Go Hit-ler! Go Hit-ler!"* And I was right there on the mic leading them along. *"Go Hit-ler! Go Hit-ler! Go Hit-ler! Go Hit-ler!"*

The whole room stopped. No one was dancing. The teachers, the chaperones, the parents, the hundreds of Jewish kids in their yarmulkes—they froze and stared aghast at us up on the stage. I was oblivious. So was Hitler. We kept going. For a good thirty seconds the only sound in the room was the beat of the music and me on the mic yelling, *"Go Hit-ler! Go Hit-ler! Go Hit-ler! Put your hands in the air for Hitler, yo!"*

A teacher ran up behind me and yanked the plug for my system out of the wall. The hall went dead silent, and she turned on me and she was livid. "How *dare* you?! This is disgusting! You horrible, disgusting vile creature! How *dare* you?!"

My mind was racing, trying to figure out what she was talking about. Then it clicked. Hitler had a special dance move called *o spana va*. It means "where you work" and it was very sexual: His hips would gyrate and thrust, like he was fucking the air. That was the move he was doing at the moment the teacher ran out, so clearly the dance was the thing she found so disgusting. But this was a move that African people do all the time. It's a part of our culture. Here we were sharing our culture for a cultural day, and this woman was calling us disgusting. She was offended, and I was offended by her taking offense.

"Lady," I said, "I think you need to calm down."

"I will *not* calm down! How dare you come here and insult us?!"

"This is not insulting anyone. This is who we are!"

"Get out of here! You people are disgusting."

And there it was. *You people*. Now I saw what the deal was: This lady was racist. She couldn't see black men dancing suggestively and not get pissed off. As I started packing up my gear, we kept arguing.

"Listen, lady. We're free now. We're gonna do what we're gonna do. You can't stop us."

"I'll have you know that my people stopped people like you before, and we can stop you again."

She was talking, of course, about stopping the Nazis in World War II, but that's not what I was hearing. Jews in South Africa are just white people. All I was hearing was some white lady shouting about how white people beat us before and they'll beat us again. I said, "You will *never* stop us, lady"—and here's where I played the trump card— "You'll never stop us, because now we have *Nelson Mandela* on our side! And he *told* us we can do this!"

"*What?!*"

She was so confused. I'd had it. I started cussing her out. "Fuck you, lady. Fuck your program. Fuck your school. Fuck your whole people. Let's go, guys! We're out!"

We didn't walk out of that school. We danced out. We danced down the street pumping our fists in the air. "*Go Hit-ler! Go Hit-ler! Go*

Hit-ler! Go Hit-ler!" Because Hitler had shut shit down. Hitler had the most gangster dance moves ever, and those white people didn't know what hit them.

Alexandra was a farm originally named for the wife of the white man who owned it. Like Sophiatown and other black spots populating white areas before apartheid, Alex started out as a squatter settlement where blacks gathered and lived when coming to Johannesburg to find work. What was unique about Alex is that this farmer sold plots of land to some of the black tenants in the time before it was illegal for blacks to own property. So while Sophiatown and other black ghettos were razed and rebuilt as white suburbs, Alex fought and held on and asserted its right to exist. Wealthy white suburbs like Sandton grew around it, but Alex remained. More squatters came and more squatters came, putting up makeshift shacks and shanties. They look like the slums in Mumbai or the favelas in Brazil. The first time I saw the favelas in Rio I said, "Yeah, that's Alexandra, but on a hill."

Soweto was beautiful because, after democracy, you watched Soweto grow. Soweto has become a proper city unto itself. People went from three-room houses to five-room houses to three-bedroom houses with garages. There was room to grow because the piece of land from the government gave you something to build on. Alexandra can't do that. Alex can't get any bigger, because it's pinned in on all sides, and it can't build up, because it's mostly shacks.

When democracy came, people flooded into Alex from the home-lands, building new shacks in the backyards of other shacks with still more shacks attached to the backside of those shacks, growing more dense and more compressed, leaving close to 200,000 people living in a few square kilometers. Even if you go back today, Alex hasn't changed. It can't change. It's physically impossible for it to change. It can only be what it is.

16

THE CHEESE BOYS

My friend Sizwe was a short, bald, super-buff guy. He wasn't always that way. His whole life he'd been skinny, and then a bodybuilding magazine found its way into his hands and changed his life. Sizwe was one of those people who brought out the best in everybody. He was that friend who believed in you and saw the potential in you that nobody else did, which was why so many of the township kids gravitated toward him, and why I gravitated toward him as well. Sizwe was always popular, but his reputation really took off when he beat up one of the more infamous bullies in the school. That cemented his status as sort of the leader and protector of the township kids.

Sizwe lived in Alex, but I never visited him there while we were still in school; he'd always come to my house in Highlands North. I'd been to Alex a few times, for brief visits, but I'd never spent any real time there. I'd never been there at night, let's put it that way. Going to Alex during the day is different from going there at night. The place was nicknamed Gomorrah for a reason.

One day after school, not long before we matriculated, Sizwe walked up to me on the quad.

"Hey, let's go to the hood," he said.

"The hood?"

At first I had no idea what he was talking about. I knew the word "hood" from rap songs, and I knew the different townships where black people lived, but I had never used the one to describe the other.

The walls of apartheid were coming down just as American hip-hop was blowing up, and hip-hop made it cool to be from the hood. Before, living in a township was something to be ashamed of; it was the bottom of the bottom. Then we had movies like *Boyz n the Hood* and *Menace II Society,* and they made the hood look cool. The characters in those movies, in the songs, they owned it. Kids in the townships started doing the same, wearing their identity as a badge of honor: You were no longer from the township—you were from the hood. Being from Alex gave you way more street cred than living in Highlands North. So when Sizwe said, "Let's go to the hood," I was curious about what he meant. I wanted to find out more.

When Sizwe took me to Alex we entered as most people do, from the Sandton side. You ride through one of the richest neighborhoods in Johannesburg, past palatial mansions and huge money. Then you go through the industrial belt of Wynberg that cordons off the rich and white from the poor and black. At the entrance to Alex there's the huge minibus rank and the bus station. It's the same bustling, chaotic third-world marketplace you see in James Bond and Jason Bourne movies. It's Grand Central Station but outdoors. Everything's dynamic. Everything's in motion. Nothing feels like it was there yesterday, and nothing feels like it will be there tomorrow, but every day it looks exactly the same.

Right next to the minibus rank, of course, is a KFC. That's one thing about South Africa: There's always a KFC. KFC found the black people. KFC did not play games. They were in the hood before McDonald's, before Burger King, before anyone. KFC was like, "Yo, we're *here* for you."

Once you go past the minibus rank, you're in Alex proper. I've been in few places where there's an electricity like there is in Alex. It's a hive of constant human activity, all day long, people coming and going, gangsters hustling, guys on the corner doing nothing, kids running around. There's nowhere for all that energy to go, no mechanism for it to dissipate, so it erupts periodically in epic acts of violence and crazy parties. One minute it'll be a placid afternoon, people hanging out, doing their thing, and next thing you know there's a cop car chasing gangsters, flying through the streets, a gun battle going off, helicopters circling overhead. Then, ten minutes later, it's like it never happened—everyone's back to hanging out, back to the hustle, coming and going, running around.

Alex is laid out on a grid, a series of avenues. The streets are paved, but the sidewalks are mostly dirt. The color scheme is cinder block and corrugated iron, gray and dark gray, punctuated by bright splashes of color. Someone's painted a wall lime green, or there's a bright-red sign above a takeaway shop, or maybe somebody's picked up a bright-blue piece of sheet metal just by luck. There's little in the way of basic sanitation. Trash is everywhere, typically a garbage fire going down some side street. There's always something burning in the hood.

As you walk, there's every smell you can imagine. People are cooking, eating takeaways in the streets. Some family has a shack that's jury-rigged onto the back of someone else's shack, and they don't have any running water, so they've bathed in a bucket from the outdoor tap and then dumped the dirty water in the street, where it runs into the river of sewerage that's already there because the water system has backed up again. There's a guy fixing cars who thinks he knows what he's doing, but he doesn't. He's dumping old motor oil into the street, and now the oil is combining with the dirty bathwater to make a river of filth running down the street. There's probably a goat hanging around—there's always a goat. As you're walking, sound washes over you, the steady thrum of human activity, people talking in a dozen different languages, chatting, haggling, arguing. There's music playing constantly. You've got traditional South African music coming from one corner, someone blasting Dolly Parton from the next corner, and somebody driving past pumping the Notorious B.I.G.

The hood was a complete sensory overload for me, but within the chaos there was order, a system, a social hierarchy based on where you lived. First Avenue was not cool at all because it was right next to the commotion of the minibus rank. Second Avenue was nice because it had semi-houses that were built when there was still some sort of formal settlement going on. Third, Fourth, and Fifth Avenues were nicer—for the township. These were the established families, the old money. Then from Sixth Avenue on down it got really shitty, more shacks and shanties. There were some schools, a few soccer fields. There were a couple of hostels, giant projects built by the government for housing migrant workers. You never wanted to go there. That's where the serious gangsters were. You only went there if you needed to buy an AK-47.

After Twentieth Avenue you hit the Jukskei River, and on the far side of that, across the Roosevelt Street Bridge, was East Bank, the newest, nicest part of the hood. East Bank was where the government had gone in, cleared out the squatters and their shacks, and started to build actual homes. It was still low-income housing, but decent two-bedroom houses with tiny yards. The families who lived there had a bit of money and usually sent their kids out of the hood to better schools, like Sandringham. Sizwe's parents lived in East Bank, on Springbok Crescent, and after walking from the minibus rank through the hood, we wound up there, hanging around outside his house on the low brick wall down the middle of Springbok Crescent, doing nothing, shooting the shit. I didn't know it then, but I was about to spend the next three years of my life hanging out at that very spot.

• • •

I graduated from high school when I was seventeen, and by that point life at home had become toxic because of my stepfather. I didn't want to be there anymore, and my mom agreed that I should move out. She helped me move to a cheap, roach-infested flat in a building down the road. My plan, insofar as I had one, was to go to university to be a computer programmer, but we couldn't afford the tuition. I needed to make money. The only way I knew how to make money was selling pirated CDs, and one of the best places to sell CDs was in the hood, because that's where the minibus rank was. Minibus drivers were always looking for new songs because having good music was something they used to attract customers.

Another nice thing about the hood was that it's super cheap. You can get by on next to nothing. There's a meal you can get in the hood called a *kota*. It's a quarter loaf of bread. You scrape out the bread, then you fill it with fried potatoes, a slice of baloney, and some pickled mango relish called *achar*. That costs a couple of rand. The more money you have, the more upgrades you can buy. If you have a bit more money you can throw in a hot dog. If you have a bit more than that, you can throw in a proper sausage, like a bratwurst, or maybe a fried egg. The biggest one, with all the upgrades, is enough to feed three people.

For us, the ultimate upgrade was to throw on a slice of cheese. Cheese was always the thing because it was so expensive. Forget the gold standard—the hood operated on the cheese standard. Cheese on anything was money. If you got a burger, that was cool, but if you got a cheeseburger, that meant you had more money than a guy who just got a hamburger. Cheese on a sandwich, cheese in your fridge, that meant you were living the good life. In any township in South Africa, if you had a bit of money, people would say, "Oh, you're a cheese boy." In essence: You're not really hood because your family has enough money to buy cheese.

In Alex, because Sizwe and his crew lived in East Bank, they were considered cheese boys. Ironically, because they lived on the first street just over the river, they were looked down on as the scruff of East Bank and the kids in the nicer houses higher up in East Bank were the cheesier cheese boys. Sizwe and his crew would never admit to being

s. They would insist, "We're not cheese. We're hood." But e real hood guys would say, "Eh, you're not hood. You're ese." "We're not cheese," Sizwe's guys would say, pointing further up East Bank. "They're cheese." It was all a bunch of ridiculous posturing about who was hood and who was cheese.

Sizwe was the leader of his crew, the guy who got everyone together and got things moving. Then there was Mzi, Sizwe's henchman. Small guy, just wanted to tag along, be in the mix. Bheki was the drinks man, always finding us booze and always coming up with an excuse to drink. Then there was Kakoatse. We called him G. Mr. Nice Guy. All G was interested in was women. If women were in the mix, he was in the game. Then, finally, there was Hitler, the life of the party. Hitler just wanted to dance.

Cheese boys were in a uniquely fucked situation when apartheid ended. It is one thing to be born in the hood and know that you will never leave the hood. But the cheese boy has been shown the world outside. His family has done okay. They have a house. They've sent him to a decent school; maybe he's even matriculated. He has been given more potential, but he has not been given more opportunity. He has been given an awareness of the world that is out there, but he has not been given the means to reach it.

The unemployment rate, technically speaking, was "lower" in South Africa during apartheid, which makes sense. There was slavery— that's how everyone was employed. When democracy came, everyone had to be paid a minimum wage. The cost of labor went up, and suddenly millions of people were out of work. The unemployment rate for young black men post-apartheid shot up, sometimes as high as 50 percent. What happens to a lot of guys is they finish high school and they can't afford university, and even little retail jobs can be hard to come by when you're from the hood and you look and talk a certain way. So, for many young men in South Africa's townships, freedom looks like this: Every morning they wake up, maybe their parents go to work or maybe not. Then they go outside and chill on the corner the whole day, talking shit. They're free, they've been taught how to fish, but no one will give them a fishing rod.

. . .

One of the first things I learned in the hood is that there is a very fine line between civilian and criminal. We like to believe we live in a world of good guys and bad guys, and in the suburbs it's easy to believe that, because getting to know a career criminal in the suburbs is a difficult thing. But then you go to the hood and you see there are so many shades in between.

In the hood, gangsters were your friends and neighbors. You knew them. You talked to them on the corner, saw them at parties. They were a part of your world. You knew them from before they became gangsters. It wasn't, "Hey, that's a crack dealer." It was, "Oh, little Jimmy's selling crack now." The weird thing about these gangsters was that they were all, at a glance, identical. They drove the same red sports car. They dated the same beautiful eighteen-year-old girls. It was strange. It was like they didn't have personalities; they shared a personality. One could be the other, and the other could be the one. They'd each studied how to be *that* gangster.

In the hood, even if you're not a hardcore criminal, crime is in your life in some way or another. There are degrees of it. It's everyone from the mom buying some food that fell off the back of a truck to feed her family, all the way up to the gangs selling military-grade weapons and hardware. The hood made me realize that crime succeeds because crime does the one thing the government doesn't do: crime cares. Crime is grassroots. Crime looks for the young kids who need support and a lifting hand. Crime offers internship programs and summer jobs and opportunities for advancement. Crime gets involved in the community. Crime doesn't discriminate.

My life of crime started off small, selling pirated CDs on the corner. That in itself was a crime, and today I feel like I owe all these artists money for stealing their music, but by hood standards it didn't even qualify as illegal. At the time it never occurred to any of us that we were doing anything wrong—if copying CDs is wrong, why would they make CD writers?

The garage of Sizwe's house opened up onto Springbok Cresent.

Every morning we'd open the doors, run an extension cord out into the street, set up a table, and play music. People would walk by and ask, "What is that? Can I get one, please?" Our corner was also where a lot of minibus drivers ended their routes and turned around to loop back to the minibus rank. They'd swing by, place an order, come back, pick it up. Swing by, place an order, come back, pick it up. We spent our whole day running out to them, going back to the garage to make more mixes, and going back out to sell. There was a converted shipping container around the corner where we'd hang out when we got tired of the wall. It had a pay phone installed inside that we'd use to call people. When things were slow we'd wander back and forth between the container and the wall, talking and hanging out with the other people with nothing to do in the middle of the day. We'd talk to drug dealers, talk to gangsters. Every now and then the cops would come crashing through. A day in the life of the hood. Next day, same thing.

Selling slowly evolved into hustling because Sizwe saw all the angles and knew how to exploit them. Like Tim, Sizwe was a hustler. But where Tim was only about the short con, Sizwe had schemes: If we do this, we get that, then we can flip that for the other thing, which gives us the leverage we need to get something bigger. Some minibus drivers couldn't pay up front, for example. "I don't have the money, because I've just started my shift," they'd say. "But I need new music. Can I owe you guys some form of credit? I'll owe you a ride. I'll pay you at the end of my shift, at the end of the week?" So we started letting drivers buy on credit, charging them a bit of interest.

We started making more money. Never more than a few hundred, maybe a thousand rand at a time, but it was all cash on hand. Sizwe was quick to realize the position we were in. Cash is the one thing everyone in the hood needs. Everyone's looking for a short-term loan for something, to pay a bill or pay a fine or just hold things together. People started coming to us and asking for money. Sizwe would cut a deal, and then he'd come to me. "Yo, we're going to make a deal with this guy. We're going to loan him a hundred, and he's going to give us back one-twenty at the end of the week." I'd say okay. Then the guy would come back and give us 120 rand. Then we did it again. Then we did it some more. We started to double our money, then triple our money.

Cash gave us leverage in the hood's barter economy as well. It's common knowledge that if you're standing at a corner of a main street in the hood, somebody's going to try to sell you something. "Yo, yo, yo, man. You want some weed?" "You wanna buy a VCR?" "You wanna buy a DVD player?" "Yo, I'm selling a TV." That's just how it works.

Let's say we see two guys haggling on the corner, a crackhead trying to sell a DVD player and some working dude who wants it but doesn't have the money because he hasn't got his wages yet. They're going back and forth, but the crackhead wants the money now. Crackheads don't wait. There's no layaway plan with a crackhead. So Sizwe steps in and takes the working guy aside.

"Look, I understand you can't pay for the DVD player now," Sizwe says. "But how much are you willing to pay for it?"

"I'll pay one-twenty," he says.

"Okay, cool."

Then Sizwe takes the crackhead aside.

"How much do you want for the DVD player?"

"I want one-forty."

"Okay, listen. You're a crackhead. This is a stolen DVD player. I'm going to give you fifty."

The crackhead protests a bit, but then he takes the money because he's a crackhead and it's cash and crack is all about the now. Then Sizwe goes back to the working guy.

"All right. We'll do one-twenty. Here's your DVD player. It's yours."

"But I don't have the one-twenty."

"It's cool. You can take it now, only instead of one-twenty you give us one-forty when you get your wages."

"Okay."

So now we've invested 50 rand with the crackhead and that gets us 140 from the working guy. But Sizwe would see a way to flip it and grow it again. Let's say this guy who bought the DVD player worked at a shoe store.

"How much do you pay for a pair of Nikes with your staff discount?" Sizwe would ask.

"I can get a pair of Nikes for one-fifty."

"Okay, instead of you giving us one-forty, we'll give you ten and you get us a pair of Nikes with your discount."

So now this guy's walking away with a DVD player *and* 10 rand in his pocket. He's feeling like he got a good deal. He brings us the Nikes and then we go to one of the cheesier cheese boys up in East Bank and we say, "Yo, dude, we know you want the new Jordans. They're three hundred in the shops. We'll sell them to you for two hundred." We sell him the shoes, and now we've gone and turned 60 rand into 200.

That's the hood. Someone's always buying, someone's always selling, and the hustle is about trying to be in the middle of that whole thing. None of it was legal. Nobody knew where anything came from. The guy who got us Nikes, did he really have a "staff discount"? You don't know. You don't ask. It's just, "Hey, look what I found" and "Cool, how much do you want?" That's the international code.

At first I didn't know not to ask. I remember one time we bought a car stereo or something like that.

"But who did this belong to?" I said.

"Eh, don't worry about it," one of the guys told me. "White people have insurance."

"Insurance?"

"Yeah, when white people lose stuff they have insurance policies that pay them cash for what they've lost, so it's like they've lost nothing."

"Oh, okay," I said. "Sounds nice."

And that was as far as we ever thought about it: When white people lose stuff they get money, just another nice perk of being white.

It's easy to be judgmental about crime when you live in a world wealthy enough to be removed from it. But the hood taught me that everyone has different notions of right and wrong, different definitions of what constitutes crime, and what level of crime they're willing to participate in. If a crackhead comes through and he's got a crate of Corn Flakes boxes he's stolen out of the back of a supermarket, the poor mom isn't thinking, *I'm aiding and abetting a criminal by buying these Corn Flakes*. No. She's thinking, *My family needs food and this guy has Corn Flakes*, and she buys the Corn Flakes.

My own mother, my super-religious, law-abiding mother who used to shit on me about breaking the rules and learning to behave, I'll never forget one day I came home and in the kitchen was a giant box of frozen burger patties, like two hundred of them, from a takeaway place called Black Steer. A burger at Black Steer cost at least 20 rand.

"What the hell is this?" I said.

"Oh, some guy at work had these and was selling them," she said. "I got a great discount."

"But where did he get it from?"

"I don't know. He said he knew somebody who—"

"Mom, he stole it."

"We don't know that."

"We *do* know that. Where the hell is some guy going to get all of these burger patties from, randomly?"

Of course, we ate the burgers. Then we thanked God for the meal.

When Sizwe first said to me, "Let's go to the hood," I thought we were going to sell CDs and DJ parties in the hood. It turned out that we were selling CDs and DJing parties in order to capitalize a payday-lending and pawnshop operation in the hood. Very quickly that became our core business.

Every day in the hood was the same. I'd wake up early. Sizwe would meet me at my flat and we'd catch a minibus to Alex with my computer, carrying the giant tower and the giant, heavy monitor the whole way. We'd set it up in Sizwe's garage, and start the first batch of CDs. Then we'd walk. We'd go down to the corner of Nineteenth and Roosevelt for breakfast. When you're trying to stretch your money, food is where you have to be careful. You have to plan or you'll eat your profits. So every morning for breakfast we eat *vetkoek,* which is fried dough, basically. Those were cheap, like 50 cents a pop. We could buy a bunch of those and have enough energy to sustain us until later on in the day.

Then we'd sit on the corner and eat. While we ate, we'd be picking up orders from the minibus drivers as they went past. After that we'd go back to Sizwe's garage, listen to music, lift weights, make the CDs. Around ten or eleven, the drivers would start coming back from their morning routes. We'd take the CDs and head out to the corner for them to pick up their stuff. Then we'd just be on the corner, hanging out, meeting characters, seeing who came by, seeing where the day was going to take us. A guy needs this. A guy's selling that. You never knew what it was going to be.

There was always a big rush of business at lunch. We'd be all over Alexandra, hitting different shops and corners, making deals with everyone. We'd get free rides from the minibus drivers because we'd hop in with them and use it as an opportunity to talk about what music they needed, but secretly we were riding with the guy for free. "Hey, we want to collect orders. We'll talk to you while you drive. What do you need? What music are you looking for? Do you need the new Maxwell? Okay, we got the new Maxwell. Okay, we'll talk to you later. We'll jump out here." Then we'd hop on another ride going wherever we were going next.

After lunch, business would die down, and that's when we'd get our lunch, usually the cheapest thing we could afford, like a smiley with some maize meal. A smiley is a goat's head. They're boiled and covered with chili pepper. We call them smileys because when you're done eating all the meat off it, the goat looks like it's smiling at you from the plate. The cheeks and the tongue are quite delicious, but the eyes are disgusting. They pop in your mouth. You put the eyeball into your mouth and you bite it, and it's just a ball of pus that pops. It has no crunch. It has no chew. It has no flavor that is appetizing in any way.

After lunch we'd head back to the garage, relax, sleep off the meal, and make more CDs. In the afternoons we'd see a lot of moms. Moms loved us. They were some of our best customers. Since moms run the household, they're the ones looking to buy that box of soap that fell off the back of the truck, and they were more likely to buy it from us than from some crackhead. Dealing with crackheads is unpleasant. We were upstanding, well-spoken East Bank boys. We could even charge a premium because we added that layer of respectability to the transaction. Moms are also often the most in need of short-term loans, to pay for this or that for the family. Again, they'd rather deal with us than with some gangster loan shark. Moms knew we weren't going to break anyone's legs if they couldn't pay. We didn't believe in that. Also we weren't capable of it—let's not forget that part. But that's where Sizwe's brilliance came in. He always knew what a person could provide pending their failure to pay.

We made some of the craziest trades. Moms in the hood are protective of their daughters, especially if their daughters are pretty. In Alex there were girls who got locked up. They went to school, came straight home, and went straight into the house. They weren't allowed to leave. Boys weren't allowed to talk to them, weren't even allowed to hang around the house—none of that. Some guy was always going on about some locked-away girl: "She's so beautiful. I'll do anything to get with her." But he couldn't. Nobody could.

Then that mom would need a loan. Once we lent her the money, until she paid us back she couldn't chase us away from her house. We'd go by and hang out, chat, make small talk. The daughter would be right there, but the mom couldn't say, "Don't talk to those boys!" The loan gave us access to establish a relationship with the mom. We'd get invited to stay for dinner. Once the mom knew we were nice, upstanding guys, she'd agree to let us take her daughter to a party as long as we promised to get her home safely. So then we'd go to the guy who'd been so desperate to meet the daughter.

"Hey, let's make a deal. We'll bring the girl to your party and you get to hang out with her. How much can you give us?"

"I don't have money," he'd say, "but I have some cases of beer."

"Okay, so tonight we're going to this party. You give us two cases of beer for the party."

"Cool."

Then we'd go to the party. We'd invite the girl, who was usually thrilled to escape her mother's prison. The guy would bring the beer, he'd get to hang out with the girl, we'd write off the mom's debt to show her our gratitude, and we'd make our money back selling the beer. There was always a way to make it work. And often that was the most fun part: working the angles, solving the puzzle, seeing what goes where, who needs what, whom we can connect with who can then get us the money.

At the peak of our operation we probably had around 10,000 rand in capital. We had loans going out and interest coming in. We had our stockpile of Jordans and DVD players we'd bought to resell. We also had to buy blank CDs, hire minibuses to go to our DJ gigs, feed five guys three times a day. We kept track of everything on the computer. Having lived in my mom's world, I knew how to do spreadsheets. We had a Microsoft Excel document laid out: everybody's name, how much they owed, when they paid, when they didn't pay.

After work was when business started to pick up. Minibus drivers picking up one last order, men coming home from work. The men weren't looking for soap and Corn Flakes. They wanted the gear— DVD players, CD players, PlayStation games. More guys would come through selling stuff, too, because they'd been out hustling and stealing all day. There'd be a guy selling a cellphone, a guy selling some leather jackets, a guy selling shoes. There was this one dude who looked like a black version of Mr. Burns from *The Simpsons*. He'd always come by at the end of his shift with the most random useless crap, like an electric toothbrush without the charger. One time he brought us an electric razor.

"What the hell is this?"

"It's an electric razor?"

"An electric razor? We're black. Do you know what these things do to our skin? Do you see anyone around here who can use an electric razor?"

We never knew where he was getting this stuff from. Because you don't ask. Eventually we pieced it together, though: He worked at the airport. It was all crap he was boosting from people's luggage.

Slowly the rush would start to taper off and we'd wind down. We'd make our last collections, go over our CD stock, balance our accounts. If there was a party to DJ that night we'd start getting ready for that. Otherwise, we'd buy a few beers and sit around and drink, talk about the day, listen to the gunshots in the distance. Gunshots went off every night, and we'd always try to guess what kind of gun it was. "That's a nine-millimeter." Usually there'd be a police chase, cop cars flying through after some guy with a stolen car. Then everyone would go home for dinner with their families. I'd take my computer, get back in a minibus, ride home, sleep, and then come back and do it all again the next day.

A year passed. Then two. I had stopped planning for school, and was no closer to having the money to enroll.

The tricky thing about the hood is that you're always working, working, working, and you feel like something's happening, but really nothing's happening at all. I was out there every day from seven a.m. to seven p.m., and every day it was: How do we turn ten rand into twenty? How do we turn twenty into fifty? How do I turn fifty into a hundred? At the end of the day we'd spend it on food and maybe some beers, and then we'd go home and come back and it was: How do we turn ten into twenty? How do we turn twenty into fifty? It was a whole day's work to flip that money. You had to be walking, be moving, be thinking. You had to get to a guy, find a guy, meet a guy. There were many days we'd end up back at zero, but I always felt like I'd been very productive.

Hustling is to work what surfing the Internet is to reading. If you add up how much you read in a year on the Internet—tweets, Facebook posts, lists—you've read the equivalent of a shit ton of books, but in fact you've read no books in a year. When I look back on it, that's what hustling was. It's maximal effort put into minimal gain. It's a hamster wheel. If I'd put all that energy into studying I'd have earned an MBA.

Instead I was majoring in hustling, something no university would give me a degree for.

When I first went into Alex, I was drawn by the electricity and the excitement of it, but more important, I was accepted there, more so than I'd been in high school or anywhere else. When I first showed up, a couple of people raised an eyebrow. "Who's this colored kid?" But the hood doesn't judge. If you want to be there, you can be there. Because I didn't live in the hood I was technically an outsider in the hood, but for the first time in my life I didn't feel like one.

The hood is also a low-stress, comfortable life. All your mental energy goes into getting by, so you don't have to ask yourself any of the big questions. Who am I? Who am I supposed to be? Am I doing enough? In the hood you can be a forty-year-old man living in your mom's house asking people for money and it's not looked down on. You never feel like a failure in the hood, because someone's always worse off than you, and you don't feel like you need to do more, because the biggest success isn't that much higher than you, either. It allows you to exist in a state of suspended animation.

The hood has a wonderful sense of community to it as well. Everyone knows everyone, from the crackhead all the way through to the policeman. People take care of one another. The way it works in the hood is that if any mom asks you to do something, you have to say yes. "Can I send you?" is the phrase. It's like everyone's your mom, and you're everyone's kid.

"Can I send you?"

"Yeah, whaddya need?"

"I need you to go buy milk and bread."

"Yeah, cool."

Then she gives you some money and you go buy milk and bread. As long as you aren't busy and it doesn't cost you anything, you don't say no.

The biggest thing in the hood is that you have to share. You can't get rich on your own. You have money? Why aren't you helping people? The old lady on the block needs help, everyone pitches in. You're buying beer, you buy beer for everyone. You spread it around. Everyone must know that your success benefits the community in one way or another, or you become a target.

The township polices itself as well. If someone's caught stealing, the township deals with them. If someone's caught breaking into a house, the township deals with them. If you're caught raping a woman, pray to God the police find you before the township does. If a woman is being hit, people don't get involved. There are too many questions with a beating. What's the fight about? Who's responsible? Who started it? But rape is rape. Theft is theft. You've desecrated the community.

The hood was strangely comforting, but comfort can be dangerous. Comfort provides a floor but also a ceiling. In our crew, our friend G was like the rest of us, unemployed, hanging out. Then he got a job at a nice clothing store. Every morning he went to work, and the guys would tease him about going to work. We'd see him headed out all dressed up, and everyone would be laughing at him. "Oh, G, look at you in your fancy clothes!" "Oh, G, going to go see the white man today, huh?" "Oh, G, don't forget to bring some books back from the library!"

One morning, after a month of G working at the place, we were hanging out on the wall, and G came out in his slippers and his socks. He wasn't dressed for work.

"Yo, G, what's going on? What's up with the job?"

"Oh, I don't work there anymore."

"Why?"

"They accused me of stealing something and I got fired."

And I'll never forget thinking to myself that it felt like he did it on purpose. He sabotaged himself so that he'd get accepted back into the group again.

The hood has a gravitational pull. It never leaves you behind, but it also never lets you leave. Because by making the choice to leave, you're insulting the place that raised you and made you and never turned you away. And that place fights you back.

As soon as things start going well for you in the hood, it's time to go. Because the hood will drag you back in. It will find a way. There will be a guy who steals a thing and puts it in your car and the cops find it—something. You can't stay. You think you can. You'll start doing better and you'll bring your hood friends out to a nice club, and the next thing you know somebody starts a fight and one of your friends pulls a gun and somebody's getting shot and you're left standing around going, "What just happened?"

The hood happened.

One night I was DJ'ing a party, not in Alex but right outside Alex in Lombardy East, a nicer, middle-class black neighborhood. The police were called about the noise. They came busting in wearing riot gear and pointing machine guns. That's how our police roll. We don't have small and then big. What Americans call SWAT is just our regular police. They came looking for the source of the music, and the music was coming from me. This one cop came over to where I was with my computer and pulled this massive assault rifle on me.

"You gotta shut this down right now."

"Okay, okay," I said. "I'm shutting it down."

But I was running Windows 95. Windows 95 took *forever* to shut down. I was closing windows, shutting down programs. I had one of those fat Seagate drives that damaged easily, and I didn't want to cut the power and possibly damage the drive. This cop clearly didn't give a fuck about any of that.

"Shut it down! Shut it down!"

"I am! I'm shutting it down! I have to close the programs!"

The crowd was getting angry, and the cop was getting nervous. He turned his gun away from me and shot the computer. Only he clearly didn't know anything about computers because he shot the monitor. The monitor exploded but the music kept playing. Now there was chaos—music blaring and everyone running and panicking because of the gunshot. I yanked the power cord out of the tower to shut the thing down. Then the cops started firing tear gas into the crowd.

The tear gas had nothing to do with me or the music. Tear gas is just what the police use to shut down parties in black neighborhoods, like the club turning on the lights to tell everyone to go home.

I lost the hard drive. Even though the cop shot the monitor the explosion somehow fried the thing. The computer would still boot up, but it couldn't read the drive. My music library was gone. Even if I'd had the money for a new hard drive, it had taken me years to amass the music collection. There was no way to replace it. The DJ'ing business was over. The CD-selling business was done. All of a sudden our crew lost its main revenue stream. All we had left was the hustle, and we hustled even harder, taking the bit of cash we had on hand and trying to double it, buying this to flip it for that. We started eating into our savings, and in less than a month we were running on dust.

Then, one evening after work, our friend from the airport, the black Mr. Burns, came by.

"Hey, look what I found," he said.

"What've you got?"

"A camera."

I'll never forget that camera. It was a digital camera. We bought it from him, and I took it and turned it on. It was full of pictures of a nice white family on vacation, and I felt like shit. The other things we'd bought had never mattered to me. Nikes, electric toothbrushes, electric razors. Who cares? Yeah, some guy might get fired because of the pallet of Corn Flakes that went missing from the supermarket, but that's degrees removed. You don't think about it. But this camera had a face. I went through those pictures, knowing how much my family pictures meant to me, and I thought, *I haven't stolen a camera. I've stolen someone's memories. I've stolen part of someone's life.*

It's such a strange thing, but in two years of hustling I never once thought of it as a crime. I honestly didn't think it was bad. *It's just stuff people found. White people have insurance.* Whatever rationalization was handy. In society, we do horrible things to one another because we don't see the person it affects. We don't see their face. We don't see them as people. Which was the whole reason the hood was built in the first place, to keep the victims of apartheid out of sight and out of mind. Because if white people ever saw black people as human, they would see that slavery is unconscionable. We live in a world where we don't see the ramifications of what we do to others, because we don't live with them. It would be a whole lot harder for an investment banker to rip off people with subprime mortgages if he actually had to live with the people he was ripping off. If we could see one another's pain and empathize with one another, it would never be worth it to us to commit the crimes in the first place.

As much as we needed the money, I never sold the camera. I felt too guilty, like it would be bad karma, which I know sounds stupid and it didn't get the family their camera back, but I just couldn't do it. That camera made me confront the fact that there were people on the other end of this thing I was doing, and what I was doing was wrong.

One night our crew got invited to dance in Soweto against another crew. Hitler was going to compete with their best dancer, Hector, who was one of the best dancers in South Africa at the time. This invitation was a huge deal. We were going over there repping our hood. Alex and Soweto have always had a huge rivalry. Soweto was seen as the snobbish township and Alexandra was seen as the gritty and dirty township. Hector was from Diepkloof, which was the nice, well-off part of Soweto. Diepkloof was where the first million-rand houses were built after democracy. "Hey, we're not a township anymore. We're building nice things now." That was the attitude. That's who we were up against. Hitler practiced a whole week.

We took a minibus over to Diepkloof the night of the dance, me and Sizwe, Mzi and Bheki and G, and Hitler. Hector won the competition. Then G was caught kissing one of their girls, and it turned into a fight and everything broke down. On our way back to Alex, around one in the morning, as we were pulling out of Diepkloof to get on the freeway, some cops pulled our minibus over. They made everyone get out and they searched it. We were standing outside, lined up alongside the car, when one of the cops came back.

"We've found a gun," he said. "Whose gun is it?"

We all shrugged.

"We don't know," we said.

"Nope, somebody knows. It's somebody's gun."

"Officer, we really don't know," Sizwe said.

He slapped Sizwe hard across the face.

"You're bullshitting me!"

Then he went down the line, slapping each of us across the face, berating us about the gun. We couldn't do anything but stand there and take it.

"You guys are trash," the cop said. "Where are you from?"

"Alex."

"Ohhhhh, okay, I see. Dogs from Alex. You come here and you rob people and you rape women and you hijack cars. Bunch of fucking hoodlums."

"No, we're dancers. We don't know—"

"I don't care. You're all going to jail until we figure out whose gun this is."

At a certain point we realized what was going on. This cop was shaking us down for a bribe. "Spot fine" is the euphemism everyone uses. You go through this elaborate dance with the cop where you say the thing without saying the thing.

"Can't we do something?" you ask the officer.

"What do you want me to do?"

"We're really sorry, Officer. What can we do?"

"You tell me."

Then you're supposed to make up a story whereby you indicate to the cop how much money you have on you. Which we couldn't do because we didn't have any money. So he took us to jail. It was a public bus. It could have been anyone's gun, but the guys from Alex were the only ones who got arrested. Everyone else in the car was free to go. The cops took us to the police station and threw us in a cell and pulled us out one by one for questioning. When they pulled me aside I had to give my home address: Highlands North. The cop gave me the most confused look.

"You're not from Alex," he said. "What are you doing with these crooks?" I didn't know what to say. He glared at me hard. "Listen here, rich boy. You think it's fun running around with these guys? This isn't play-play anymore. Just tell me the truth about your friends and the gun, and I'll let you go."

I told him no, and he threw me back in the cell. We spent the night, and the next day I called a friend, who said he could borrow the money from his dad to get us out. Later that day the dad came down and paid the money. The cops kept calling it "bail," but it was a bribe. We were never formally arrested or processed. There was no paperwork.

We got out and everything was fine, but it rattled us. Every day we were out in the streets, hustling, trying to act as if we were in some way down with the gangs, but the truth was we were always more cheese than hood. We had created this idea of ourselves as a defense mechanism to survive in the world we were living in. Sizwe and the other East Bank guys, because of where they were from, what they looked like— they just had very little hope. You've got two options in that situation. You take the retail job, flip burgers at McDonald's, if you're one of the lucky few who even gets that much. The other option is to toughen up, put up this facade. You can't leave the hood, so you survive by the rules of the hood.

I chose to live in that world, but I wasn't from that world. If anything, I was an imposter. Day to day I was in it as much as everyone else, but the difference was that in the back of my mind I knew I had other options. I could leave. They couldn't.

Once, when I was ten years old, visiting my dad in Yeoville, I needed batteries for one of my toys. My mom had refused to buy me new batteries because, of course, she thought it was a waste of money, so I snuck out to the shops and shoplifted a pack. A security guard busted me on the way out, pulled me into his office, and called my mom.

"We've caught your son shoplifting batteries," he said. "You need to come and fetch him."

"No," she said. "Take him to jail. If he's going to disobey he needs to learn the consequences."

Then she hung up. The guard looked at me, confused. Eventually he let me go on the assumption that I was some wayward orphan, because what mother would send her ten-year-old child to jail?

17

THE WORLD DOESN'T LOVE YOU

My mom never gave me an inch. Anytime I got in trouble it was tough love, lectures, punishment, and hidings. Every time. For every infraction. You get that with a lot of black parents. They're trying to discipline you before the system does. "I need to do this to you before the police do it to you." Because that's all black parents are thinking from the day you're old enough to walk out into the street, where the law is waiting.

In Alex, getting arrested was a fact of life. It was so common that out on the corner we had a sign for it, a shorthand, clapping your wrists together like you were being put in handcuffs. Everyone knew what that meant.

"Where's Sizwe?"

Wrist clap.

"Oh, shit. When?"

"Friday night."

"Damn."

My mom hated the hood. She didn't like my friends there. If I brought them back to the house, she didn't even want them coming inside. "I don't like those boys," she'd say. She didn't hate them personally; she hated what they represented. "You and those boys get into so much shit," she'd say. "You must be careful who you surround yourself with because where you are can determine who you are."

She said the thing she hated most about the hood was that it didn't pressure me to become better. She wanted me to hang out with my cousin at his university.

"What's the difference if I'm at university or I'm in the hood?" I'd say. "It's not like I'm going to university."

"Yes, but the pressure of the university is going to get you. I know you. You won't sit by and watch these guys become better than you. If you're in an environment that is positive and progressive, you too will become that. I keep telling you to change your life, and you don't. One day you're going to get arrested, and when you do, don't call me. I'll tell the police to lock you up just to teach you a lesson."

Because there were some black parents who'd actually do that, not pay their kid's bail, not hire their kid a lawyer—the ultimate tough love. But it doesn't always work, because you're giving the kid tough love when maybe he just needs love. You're trying to teach him a lesson, and now that lesson is the rest of his life.

One morning I saw an ad in the paper. Some shop was having a clearance sale on mobile phones, and they were selling them at such a ridiculous price I knew Sizwe and I could flip them in the hood for a profit. This shop was out in the suburbs, too far to walk and too out-of-the-way to take a minibus. Fortunately my stepfather's workshop and a bunch of old cars were in our backyard.

I'd been stealing Abel's junkers to get around since I was fourteen. I would say I was test driving them to make sure they'd been repaired correctly. Abel didn't think that was funny. I'd been caught many times, caught and subjected to my mother's wrath. But that had never stopped me from doing anything.

Most of these junkers weren't street legal. They didn't have proper registrations or proper number plates. Luckily, Abel also had a stack of old number plates in the back of the garage. I quickly learned I could just put one on an old car and hit the road. I was nineteen, maybe twenty, not thinking about any of the ramifications of this. I stopped by Abel's garage when no one was around, picked up one of the cars, the red Mazda I'd taken to the matric dance, slapped some old plates on it, and set off in search of discounted cell phones.

I got pulled over in Hillbrow. Cops in South Africa don't give you a reason when they pull you over. Cops pull you over because they're cops and they have the power to pull you over; it's as simple as that. I used to watch American movies where cops would pull people over and say, "You didn't signal" or "Your taillight's out." I'd always wonder, *Why do American cops bother lying?* One thing I appreciate about South Africa is that we have not yet refined the system to the point where we feel the need to lie.

"Do you know why I pulled you over?"

"Because you're a policeman and I'm a black person?"

"That's correct. License and registration, please."

When the cop pulled me over, it was one of those situations where I wanted to say, "Hey, I know you guys are racially profiling me!" But I couldn't argue the case because I was, at that moment, actually breaking the law. The cop walked up to my window, asked me the standard cop questions. Where are you going? Is this your car? Whose car is this? I couldn't answer. I completely froze.

Being young, funnily enough, I was more worried about getting in trouble with my parents than with the law. I'd had run-ins with the cops in Alexandra, in Soweto, but it was always more about the circumstance: a party getting shut down, a raid on a minibus. The law was all around me, but it had never come down on me, Trevor, specifically. And when you haven't had much experience with the law, the law appears rational—cops are dicks for the most part, but you also recognize that they're doing a job.

Your parents, on the other hand, are not rational at all. They have served as judge, jury, and executioner for your entire childhood, and it feels like they give you a life sentence for every misdemeanor. In that moment, when I should have been scared of the cop, all I was thinking was *Shit shit shit; I'm in so much trouble when I get home.*

The cop called in the number-plate registration and discovered that it didn't match the car. Now he was really on my case. "This car is not in your name! What's going on with these plates?! Step out of the vehicle!" It was only then that I realized: *Ohhhhh, shit. Now I'm in* real *trouble.* I stepped out of the car, and he put the cuffs on me and told me I was being arrested on suspicion of driving a stolen vehicle. He took me in, and the car was impounded.

The Hillbrow police station looks exactly like every other police station in South Africa. They were all built by the same contractor at the height of apartheid—separate nodes in the central nervous system of a police state. If you were blindfolded and taken from one to the other, you probably wouldn't even know that you'd changed locations. They're sterile, institutional, with fluorescent lights and cheap floor tile, like a hospital. My cop walked me in and sat me down at the front booking desk. I was charged and fingerprinted.

In the meantime, they'd been checking out the car, which wasn't going well for me, either. Whenever I borrowed cars from Abel's workshop, I tried to take the junkers rather than a real client's car; I thought I'd get in less trouble that way. That was a mistake. The Mazda, being one of Abel's junkers, didn't have a clear title of ownership. If it had had an owner, the cops would have called the owner, the owner would have explained that the car had been dropped off for repairs, and the whole thing would have been sorted out. Since the car didn't have an owner, I couldn't prove I hadn't stolen it.

Carjackings were common in South Africa at the time, too. So common you weren't even surprised when they happened. You'd have a friend coming over for a dinner party and you'd get a call.

"Sorry. Got carjacked. Gonna be late."

"Ah, that sucks. Hey, guys! Dave got carjacked."

"Sorry, Dave!"

And the party would continue. And that's if the person survived the carjacking. Often they didn't. People were getting shot for their cars all the time. Not only could I not prove I hadn't stolen the car, I couldn't prove I hadn't murdered someone for it, either. The cops were grilling me. "You kill anyone to get that car, boy? Eh? You a killer?"

I was in deep, deep trouble. I had only one lifeline: my parents. One call would have fixed everything. "This is my stepfather. He's a mechanic. I borrowed his car when I shouldn't have." Done. At worst I'd get a slap on the wrist for driving a car that wasn't registered. But what would I be getting at home?

I sat there in the police station—arrested for suspicion of grand theft auto, a plausible suspect for carjacking or murder—and debated whether I should call my parents or go to jail. With my stepfather I was thinking, *He might actually kill me.* In my mind that was an entirely realistic scenario. With my mother I was thinking, *She's going to make this worse. She's not the character witness I want right now. She won't help me.* Because she'd told me she wouldn't. "If you ever get arrested, don't call me." I needed someone sympathetic to my plight, and I didn't believe she was that person. So I didn't call my parents. I decided I didn't need them. I was a man. I could go it alone. I used my call to phone my cousin and told him not to tell anyone what had happened while I figured out what to do—now I just had to figure out what to do.

I'd been picked up late in the afternoon, so by the time I was processed it was close to lights-out. I was spending the night in jail, like it or not. It was at that point that a cop pulled me aside and told me what I was in for.

The way the system works in South Africa is that you're arrested and held in a cell at the police station until your bail hearing. At the hearing, the judge looks at your case, hears arguments from the opposing sides, and then he either dismisses the charges or sets bail and a trial date. If you can make bail, you pay and go home. But there are all sorts of ways your bail hearing can go wrong: You get some court-appointed lawyer who hasn't read your case and doesn't know what's going on. Your family can't pay your bail. It could even be that the court's backed up. "Sorry, we're too busy. No more hearings today." It doesn't matter the reason. Once you leave jail, you can't go back to jail. If your situation isn't resolved that day, you go to prison to await trial. In prison you're housed with the people awaiting trial, not with the general population, but even the awaiting-trial section is incredibly dangerous because you have people picked up for traffic violations all the way up to proper hardened criminals. You're stuck there together, and you can be there for days, weeks, maybe months. It's the same way in America. If you're poor, if you don't know how the system works, you can slip through the cracks, and the next thing you know you're in this weird purgatory where you're not in prison but you're not not in prison. You haven't been convicted of any crime, but you're still locked up and can't get out.

This cop pulled me aside and said, "Listen, you don't want to go to your bail hearing. They'll give you a state attorney who won't know what's going on. He'll have no time for you. He'll ask the judge for a postponement, and then maybe you'll go free or maybe you won't. Trust me, you don't want to do that. You have the right to stay here for as long as you like. You want to meet with a lawyer and set yourself up before you go anywhere near a court or a judge." He wasn't giving me this advice out of the goodness of his heart. He had a deal with a defense attorney, sending him clients in exchange for a kickback. He handed me the attorney's business card, I called him, and he agreed to take my case. He told me to stay put while he handled everything.

Now I needed money, because lawyers, as nice as they are, don't do anything for free. I called a friend and asked him if he could ask his dad to borrow some money. He said he'd handle it. He talked to his dad, and the lawyer got his retainer the next day.

With the lawyer taken care of, I felt like I had things under control.

I was feeling pretty slick. I'd handled the situation, and, most important, Mom and Abel were none the wiser.

When the time came for lights-out a cop came and took my stuff. My belt, my wallet, my shoelaces.

"Why do you need my shoelaces?"

"So you don't hang yourself."

"Right."

Even when he said that, the gravity of my situation still wasn't sinking in. Walking to the station's holding cell, looking around at the other six guys in there, I was thinking, *This is no big deal. Everything's gonna be cool. I'm gonna get out of this.* I thought that right up until the moment the cell door clanged shut behind me and the guard yelled, "Lights out!" That's when I thought, *Oh, shit. This is real.*

The guards had given me a mat and a scratchy blanket. I rolled them out on the concrete floor and tried to get comfortable. Every bad prison movie I'd ever seen was racing through my head. I was thinking, *I'm gonna get raped. I'm gonna get raped. I'm gonna get raped.* But of course I didn't get raped, because this wasn't prison. It was jail, and there's a big difference, as I would soon come to understand.

I woke up the next morning with that fleeting sensation where you think something has all been a dream. Then I looked around and remembered that it wasn't. Breakfast came, and I settled in to wait.

A day in jail is mostly silence punctuated by passing guards shouting profanities at you, doing roll call. Inside the holding cell nobody says anything. Nobody walks into a jail cell and says, "Hi, guys! I'm Brian!" Because everyone is afraid, and no one wants to appear vulnerable. Nobody wants to be the bitch. Nobody wants to be the guy getting killed. I didn't want anyone to know that I was just a kid in for a traffic charge, so I reached back in my mind for all the stereotypes of what I imagined people act like in prison, and then I tried to act like that.

In South Africa, everyone knows that colored gangsters are the most ruthless, the most savage. It's a stereotype that's fed to you your whole life. The most notorious colored gangs are the Numbers Gangs: the 26s, the 27s, the 28s. They control the prisons. They're known for being brutally violent—maiming, torturing, raping, cutting off people's heads—not for the sake of making money but just to prove how ruthless and savage they are, like Mexican drug cartels. In fact a lot of these gangs base their thing on those Mexican gangs. They have the same look: the Converse All Stars with the Dickies pants and the open shirt buttoned only at the top.

By the time I was a teenager, anytime I was profiled by cops or security guards, it usually wasn't because I was black but because I looked colored. I went to a club once with my cousin and his friend. The bouncer searched Mlungisi, waved him in. He searched our friend, waved him in. Then he searched me and got up in my face.

"Where's your knife?"

"I don't have a knife."

"I know you have a knife somewhere. Where is it?"

He searched and searched and finally gave up and let me in, looking me over like I was trouble.

"No *shit* from you! Okay?"

I figured that if I was in jail people were going to assume I was the kind of colored person who ends up in jail, a violent criminal. So I played it up. I put on this character; I played the stereotype. Anytime the cops asked me questions I started speaking in broken Afrikaans with a thick colored accent. Imagine a white guy in America, just dark enough to pass for Latino, walking around jail doing bad Mexican-gangster dialogue from the movies. *"Shit's about to get loco,* ese.*"* That's basically what I was doing—the South African version of that. This was my brilliant plan to survive incarceration. But it worked. The guys in the cell with me, they were there for drunk driving, for domestic abuse, for petty theft. They had no idea what real colored gangsters were like. Everyone left me alone.

We were all playing a game, only nobody knew we were playing it. When I walked in that first night, everyone was giving me this look: "I'm dangerous. Don't fuck with me." So I went, "Shit, these people are hardened criminals. I shouldn't be here, because I am not a criminal." Then the next day everything turned over quickly. One by one, guys left to go to their hearings, I stayed to wait for my lawyer, and new people started to pitch up. Now I was the veteran, doing my colored-gangster routine, giving the new guys the same look: "I'm dangerous. Don't fuck with me." And they looked at me and went, "Shit, he's a hardened criminal. I shouldn't be here, because I am not like him." And round and round we went.

At a certain point it occurred to me that every single person in that cell might be faking it. We were all decent guys from nice neighborhoods and good families, picked up for unpaid parking tickets and other infractions. We could have been having a great time sharing meals, playing cards, and talking about women and soccer. But that didn't happen, because everyone had adopted this dangerous pose and nobody talked because everyone was afraid of who the other guys were pretending to be. Now those guys were going to get out and go home to their families and say, "Oh, honey, that was rough. Those were some real criminals in there. There was this one colored guy. Man, he was a killer."

Once I had the game sorted out, I was good again. I relaxed. I was back to thinking, *I got this. This is no big deal.* The food was actually decent. For breakfast they brought you these peanut butter sandwiches on thick slices of bread. Lunch was chicken and rice. The tea was too hot, and it was more water than tea, but it was drinkable. There were older, hard-time prisoners close to parole, and their detail was to come and clean the cells and circulate books and magazines for you to read. It was quite relaxing.

There was one point when I remember eating a meal and saying to myself, *This isn't so bad. I hang around with a bunch of dudes. There's no chores. No bills to pay. No one constantly nagging me and telling me what to do. Peanut butter sandwiches? Shit, I eat peanut butter sandwiches all the time. This is pretty sweet. I could do this.* I was so afraid of the ass-whooping waiting for me at home that I genuinely considered going to prison. For a brief moment I thought I had a plan. "I'll go away for a couple of years, come back, and say I was kidnapped, and mom will never know and she'll just be happy to see me."

On the third day, the cops brought in the largest man I'd ever seen. This guy was *huge*. Giant muscles. Dark skin. Hardened face. He looked like he could kill all of us. Me and the other prisoners who'd been acting tough with one another—the second he walked in our tough-guy routines were over. Everyone was terrified. We all stared at him. "Oh, fuck . . ."

For whatever reason this guy was half naked when the cops picked him up. He was wearing clothes the police had scrounged up for him at the station, this torn-up wifebeater that was way too small, pants so short on him they looked like capris. He looked like a black version of the Incredible Hulk.

This guy went and sat alone in the corner. Nobody said a word. Everyone watched and waited, nervously, to see what he would do. Then one of the cops came back and called the Hulk over; they needed information from him. The cop started asking him a bunch of questions, but the guy kept shaking his head and saying he didn't understand. The cop was speaking Zulu. The Hulk was speaking Tsonga. Black person to black person, and neither could understand the other—the Tower of Babel. Few people in South Africa speak Tsonga, but since my stepfather was Tsonga I had picked it up along the way. I overheard the cop and the other guy going back and forth with nothing getting across, so I stepped in and translated for them and sorted everything out.

Nelson Mandela once said, "If you talk to a man in a language he understands, that goes to his head. If you talk to him in his language, that goes to his heart." He was so right. When you make the effort to speak someone else's language, even if it's just basic phrases here and there, you are saying to them, "I understand that you have a culture and identity that exists beyond me. I see you as a human being."

That is exactly what happened with the Hulk. The second I spoke to him, this face that had seemed so threatening and mean lit up wiṭ. gratitude. *"Ah, na khensa, na khensa, na khensa. Hi wena mani? Mufana wa mukhaladi u xitiela kwini xiTsonga? U huma kwini?"* "Oh, thank you, thank you, thank you. Who are you? How does a colored guy know Tsonga? Where are you from?"

Once we started talking I realized he wasn't the Hulk at all. He was the sweetest man, a gentle giant, the biggest teddy bear in the world. He was simple, not educated. I'd assumed he was in for murder, for squashing a family to death with his bare hands, but it wasn't anything like that. He'd been arrested for shoplifting PlayStation games. He was out of work and needed money to send to his family back home, and when he saw how much these games sold for he thought he could steal a few and sell them to white kids and make a lot of money. As soon as he told me that, I knew he wasn't some hardened criminal. I know the world of pirated things—stolen videogames have no value because it's cheaper and less risky to copy them.

I tried to help him out a bit. I told him my trick of putting off your bail hearing to get your defense together, so he stayed in the cell, too, biding his time, and we hit it off and hung out for a few days, having a good time, getting to know each other. No one else in the cell knew what to make of us, the ruthless colored gangster and his menacing, Hulk-like friend. He told me his story, a South African story that was all too familiar to me: The man grows up under apartheid, working on a farm, part of what's essentially a slave labor force. It's a living hell but it's at least something. He's paid a pittance but at least he's paid. He's told where to be and what to do every waking minute of his day. Then apartheid ends and he doesn't even have that anymore. He finds his way to Johannesburg, looking for work, trying to feed his children back home. But he's lost. He has no education. He has no skills. He doesn't know what to do, doesn't know where to be. The world has been taught to be scared of him, but the reality is that he is scared of the world because he has none of the tools necessary to cope with it. So what does he do? He takes shit. He becomes a petty thief. He's in and out of jail. He gets lucky and finds some construction work, but then he gets laid

, and a few days later he's in a shop and he sees some Play-
___ es and he grabs them, but he doesn't even know enough to
___ e's stolen something of no value.

I felt terrible for him. The more time I spent in jail, the more I realized that the law isn't rational at all. It's a lottery. What color is your
skin? How much money do you have? Who's your lawyer? Who's the
judge? Shoplifting PlayStation games was less of an offense than driving with bad number plates. He had committed a crime, but he was no
more a criminal than I was. The difference was that he didn't have any
friends or family to help him out. He couldn't afford anything but a
state attorney. He was going to go stand in the dock, unable to speak or
understand English, and everyone in the courtroom was going to assume the worst of him. He was going to go to prison for a while and
then be set free with the same nothing he had going in. If I had to guess,
he was around thirty-five, forty years old, staring down another thirty-
five, forty years of the same.

The day of my hearing came. I said goodbye to my new friend and
wished him the best. Then I was handcuffed and put in the back of a
police van and driven to the courthouse to meet my fate. In South African courts, to minimize your exposure and your opportunities for escape, the holding cell where you await your hearing is a massive pen
below the courtroom; you walk up a set of stairs into the dock rather
than being escorted through the corridors. What happens in the holding cell is you're mixed in with the people who've been in prison awaiting trial for weeks and months. It's a weird mix, everything from
white-collar criminals to guys picked up on traffic stops to real, hardcore criminals covered with prison tattoos. It's like the cantina scene
from *Star Wars*, where the band's playing music and Han Solo's in the
corner and all of the bad guys and bounty hunters from all over the
universe are hanging out—a wretched hive of scum and villainy, only
there's no music and there's no Han Solo.

I was with these people for only a brief window of time, but in that moment I saw the difference between prison and jail. I saw the difference between criminals and people who've committed crimes. I saw the hardness in people's faces. I thought back on how naive I'd been just hours before, thinking jail wasn't so bad and I could handle it. I was now truly afraid of what might happen to me.

When I walked into that holding pen, I was a smooth-skinned, fresh-faced young man. At the time, I had a giant Afro, and the only way to control it was to have it tied back in this ponytail thing that looked really girly. I looked like Maxwell. The guards closed the door behind me, and this creepy old dude yelled out in Zulu from the back, *"Ha, ha, ha! Hhe madoda! Angikaze ngibone indoda enhle kangaka! Sizoba nobusuku obuhle!"* "Yo, yo, yo! Damn, guys. I've never seen a man this beautiful before. It's gonna be a good night tonight!"

Fuuuuuuuuuuck.

Right next to me as I walked in was a young man having a complete meltdown, talking to himself, bawling his eyes out. He looked up and locked eyes with me, and I guess he thought I looked like a kindred soul he could talk to. He came straight at me and started crying about how he'd been arrested and thrown in jail and the gangs had stolen his clothes and his shoes and raped him and beat him every day. He wasn't some ruffian. He was well-spoken, educated. He'd been waiting for a year for his case to be heard; he wanted to kill himself. That guy put the fear of God in me.

I looked around the holding cell. There were easily a hundred guys in there, all of them spread out and huddled into their clearly and unmistakably defined racial groups: a whole bunch of black people in one corner, the colored people in a different corner, a couple of Indians off to themselves, and a handful of white guys off to one side. The guys who'd been with me in the police van, the second we walked in, they instinctively, automatically, walked off to join the groups they belonged to. I froze.

I didn't know where to go.

I looked over at the colored corner. I was staring at the most notorious, most violent prison gang in South Africa. I looked like them, but

I wasn't them. I couldn't go over there doing my fake gangster shit and have them discover I was a fraud. No, no, no. That game was over, my friend. The last thing I needed was colored gangsters up against me.

But then what if I went to the black corner? I know that I'm black and I identify as black, but I'm not a black person on the face of it, so would the black guys understand why I was walking over? And what kind of shit would I start by going there? Because going to the black corner as a perceived colored person might piss off the colored gangs even more than going to the colored corner as a fake colored person. Because that's what had happened to me my entire life. Colored people would see me hanging out with blacks, and they'd confront me, want to fight me. I saw myself starting a race war in the holding cell.

"Hey! Why are you hanging out with the blacks?"

"Because I am black."

"No, you're not. You're colored."

"Ah, yes. I know it looks that way, friend, but let me explain. It's a funny story, actually. My father is white and my mother is black and race is a social construct, so . . ."

That wasn't going to work. Not here.

All of this was happening in my head in an instant, on the fly. I was doing crazy calculations, looking at people, scanning the room, assessing the variables. *If I go here, then this. If I go there, then that.* My whole life was flashing before me—the playground at school, the *spaza* shops in Soweto, the streets of Eden Park—every time and every place I ever had to be a chameleon, navigate between groups, explain who I was. It was like the high school cafeteria, only it was the high school cafeteria from hell because if I picked the wrong table I might get beaten or stabbed or raped. I'd never been more scared in my life. But I still had to pick. Because racism exists, and you have to pick a side. You can say that you don't pick sides, but eventually life will force you to pick a side.

That day I picked white. They just didn't look like they could hurt me. It was a handful of average, middle-aged white dudes. I walked over to them. We hung out for a while, chatted a bit. They were mostly in for white-collar crimes, money schemes, fraud and racketeering. They'd be useless if anyone came over looking to start trouble; they'd get their asses kicked as well. But they weren't going to do anything to me. I was safe.

Luckily the time went by fairly quickly. I was in there for only an hour before I was called up to court, where a judge would either let me go or send me to prison to await trial. As I was leaving, one of the white guys reached over to me. "Make sure you don't come back down here," he said. "Cry in front of the judge; do whatever you have to do. If you go up and get sent back down here, your life will never be the same."

Up in the courtroom, I found my lawyer waiting. My cousin Mlungisi was there, too, in the gallery, ready to post my bail if things went my way.

The bailiff read out my case number, and the judge looked up at me.

"How are you?" he said.

I broke down. I'd been putting on this tough-guy facade for nearly a week, and I just couldn't do it anymore.

"I-I'm not fine, Your Honor. I'm not fine."

He looked confused. "What?!"

I said, "I'm not fine, sir. I'm really suffering."

"Why are you telling me this?"

"Because you asked how I was."

"Who asked you?"

"You did. You just asked me."

"I didn't say, 'How are you?' I said, 'Who are you?' Why would I waste time asking 'How are you?'! This is jail. I know everyone is suffering down there. If I asked everyone 'How are you?' we'd be here all day. I said, 'Who are you?' State your name for the record."

"Trevor Noah."

"Okay. Now we can carry on."

The whole courtroom started laughing, so then I started laughing, too. But now I was even more petrified because I didn't want the judge to think I wasn't taking him seriously because I was laughing.

It turned out that I needn't have been worried. Everything that happened next took only a few minutes. My lawyer had talked to the prosecutor and everything had been arranged beforehand. He presented my case. I had no priors. I wasn't dangerous. There were no objections from the opposing side. The judge assigned my trial date and set my bail, and I was free to go.

I walked out of court and the light of day hit my face and I said, "Sweet *Jesus*, I am never going back there again." It had been only a week, in a cell that wasn't terribly uncomfortable with food that wasn't half bad, but a week in jail is a long, long time. A week without shoelaces is a long, long time. A week with no clocks, with no sun, can feel like an eternity. The thought of anything worse, the thought of doing real time in a real prison, I couldn't even imagine.

I drove with Mlungisi to his place, took a shower, and slept there. The next day he dropped me back at my mom's house. I strolled up the driveway acting real casual. My plan was to say I'd been crashing with Mlungisi for a few days. I walked into the house like nothing had happened. "Hey, Mom! What's up?" Mom didn't say anything, didn't ask me any questions. I was like, *Okay. Cool. We're good*.

I stayed for most of the day. Later in the afternoon we were sitting at the kitchen table, talking. I was telling all these stories, going on about everything Mlungisi and I had been up to that week, and I caught my mom giving me this look, slowly shaking her head. It was a different look than I had ever seen her give before. It wasn't "One day, I'm going to catch you." It wasn't anger or disapproval. It was disappointment. She was hurt.

"What?" I said. "What is it?"

She said, "Boy, who do you think paid your bail? Hmm? Who do you think paid your lawyer? Do you think I'm an idiot? Did you think no one would tell me?"

The truth came spilling out. Of course she'd known: the car. It had been missing the whole time. I'd been so wrapped up in dealing with jail and covering my tracks I'd forgotten that the proof of my crime was right there in the yard, the red Mazda missing from the driveway. And of course when I called my friend and he'd asked his dad for the money for the lawyer, the dad had pressed him on what the money was for and, being a parent himself, had called my mother immediately. She'd given my friend the money to pay the lawyer. She'd given my cousin the money to pay my bail. I'd spent the whole week in jail thinking I was so slick. But she'd known everything the whole time.

"I know you see me as some crazy old bitch nagging at you," she said, "but you forget the reason I ride you so hard and give you so much shit is because I love you. Everything I have ever done I've done from a place of love. If I don't punish you, the world will punish you even worse. The world doesn't love you. If the police get you, the police don't love you. When I beat you, I'm trying to save you. When they beat you, they're trying to kill you."

My favorite thing to eat as a kid, and still my favorite dessert of all time, was custard and jelly, what Americans would call Jell-O. One Saturday my mom was planning for a big family celebration and she made a huge bowl of custard and jelly and put it in the fridge. It had every flavor: red, green, and yellow. I couldn't resist it. That whole day, every time I walked past the fridge I'd pop my head in with a spoon and sneak a bite. This was a giant bowl, meant to last for a week for the whole family. I finished it in one day by myself.

That night I went to bed and I got absolutely butchered by mosquitoes. Mosquitoes love to feast on me, and when I was a kid it was bad. They would destroy me at night. I would wake up covered with bites and feel ill to my stomach and itchy all over. Which was exactly what happened this particular Sunday morning. Covered with mosquito bites, my stomach bloated with custard and jelly, I could barely get out of bed. I felt like I was going to vomit. Then my mom walked in.

"Get dressed," she said. "We're going to church."

"I don't feel well."

"That's why we're going to church. That's where Jesus is going to heal you."

"Eh, I'm not sure that's how it works."

My mom and I had different ideas about how Jesus worked. She believed that you pray to Jesus and then Jesus pitches up and does the thing that you need. My views on Jesus were more reality-based.

"Why don't I take medicine," I said, "and then pray to Jesus to thank him for giving us the doctors who invented medicine, because medicine is what makes you feel better, not Jesus."

"You don't need medicine if you have Jesus. Jesus will heal you. Pray to Jesus."

"But is medicine not a blessing from Jesus? And if Jesus gives us medicine and we do not take the medicine, are we not denying the grace that he has given us?"

Like all of our debates about Jesus, this conversation went nowhere.

"Trevor," she said, "if you don't go to church you're going to get worse. You're lucky you got sick on Sunday, because now we're going to church and you can pray to Jesus and Jesus is going to heal you."

"That sounds nice, but why don't I just stay home?"

"No. Get dressed. We're going to church."

———

18

MY MOTHER'S LIFE

Once I had my hair cornrowed for the matric dance, I started getting attention from girls for the first time. I actually went on dates. At times I thought that it was because I looked better. At other times I thought it was because girls liked the fact that I was going through as much pain as they did to look good. Either way, once I found success, I wasn't going to mess with the formula. I kept going back to the salon every week, spending hours at a time getting my hair straightened and cornrowed. My mom would just roll her eyes. "I could never date a man who spends more time on his hair than I do," she'd say.

Monday through Saturday my mom worked in her office and puttered around her garden dressed like a homeless person. Then Sunday morning for church she'd do her hair and put on a nice dress and some high heels and she looked like a million bucks. Once she was all done up, she couldn't resist teasing me, throwing little verbal jabs the way we'd always do with each other.

"Now who's the best-looking person in the family, eh? I hope you enjoyed your week of being the pretty one, 'cause the queen is back, baby. You spent four hours at the salon to look like that. I just took a shower."

She was just having fun with me; no son wants to talk about how hot his mom is. Because, truth be told, she was beautiful. Beautiful on the outside, beautiful on the inside. She had a self-confidence about her that I never possessed. Even when she was working in the garden, dressed in overalls and covered in mud, you could see how attractive she was.

I can only assume that my mother broke more than a few hearts in her day, but from the time I was born, there were only two men in her life, my father and my stepfather. Right around the corner from my father's house in Yeoville, there was a garage called Mighty Mechanics. Our Volkswagen was always breaking down, and my mom would take it there to get it repaired. We met this really cool guy there, Abel, one of the auto mechanics. I'd see him when we went to fetch the car. The car broke down a lot, so we were there a lot. Eventually it felt like we were there even when there was nothing wrong with the vehicle. I was six, maybe seven. I didn't understand everything that was happening. I just knew that suddenly this guy was around. He was tall, lanky and lean but strong. He had these long arms and big hands. He could lift car engines and gearboxes. He was handsome, but he wasn't good-looking. My mom liked that about him; she used to say there's a type of ugly that women find attractive. She called him Abie. He called her Mbuyi, short for Nombuyiselo.

I liked him, too. Abie was charming and hilarious and had an easy, gracious smile. He loved helping people, too, especially anyone in distress. If someone's car broke down on the freeway, he pulled over to see what he could do. If someone yelled "Stop, thief!" he was the guy who gave chase. The old lady next door needed help moving boxes? He's that guy. He liked to be liked by the world, which made his abuse even harder to deal with. Because if you think someone is a monster and the whole world says he's a saint, you begin to think that you're the bad person. *It must be my fault this is happening* is the only conclusion you can draw, because why are you the only one receiving his wrath?

Abel was always cool with me. He wasn't trying to be my dad, and my dad was still in my life, so I wasn't looking for anyone to replace him. *That's mom's cool friend* is how I thought of him. He started coming out to stay with us in Eden Park. Some nights he'd want us to crash with him at his converted garage flat in Orange Grove, which we did. Then I burned down the white people's house, and that was the end of that. From then on we lived together in Eden Park.

One night my mom and I were at a prayer meeting and she took me aside.

"Hey," she said. "I want to tell you something. Abel and I are going to get married."

Instinctively, without even thinking, I said, "I don't think that's a good idea."

I wasn't upset or anything. I just had a sense about the guy, an intuition. I'd felt it even before the mulberry tree. That night hadn't changed my feelings toward Abel; it had only shown me, in flesh and blood, what he was capable of.

"I understand that it's hard," she said. "I understand that you don't want a new dad."

"No," I said. "It's not that. I like Abel. I like him a lot. But you shouldn't marry him." I didn't know the word "sinister" then, but if I had I probably would have used it. "There's just something not right about him. I don't trust him. I don't think he's a good person."

I'd always been fine with my mom dating this guy, but I'd never considered the possibility of him becoming a permanent addition to our family. I enjoyed being with Abel the same way I enjoyed playing with a tiger cub the first time I went to a tiger sanctuary: I liked it, I had fun with it, but I never thought about bringing it home.

If there was any doubt about Abel, the truth was right there in front of us all along, in his name. He was Abel, the good brother, the good son, a name straight out of the Bible. And he lived up to it as well. He was the firstborn, dutiful, took care of his mother, took care of his siblings. He was the pride of his family.

But Abel was his English name. His Tsonga name was Ngisaveni. It means "Be afraid."

Mom and Abel got married. There was no ceremony, no exchange of rings. They went and signed the papers and that was it. A year or so later, my baby brother, Andrew, was born. I only vaguely remember my mom being gone for a few days, and when she got back there was now this thing in the house that cried and shat and got fed, but when you're nine years older than your sibling, their arrival doesn't change much for you. I wasn't changing diapers; I was out playing arcade games at the shop, running around the neighborhood.

The main thing that marked Andrew's birth for me was our first trip to meet Abel's family during the Christmas holidays. They lived in Tzaneen, a town in Gazankulu, what had been the Tsonga homeland under apartheid. Tzaneen has a tropical climate, hot and humid. The white farms nearby grow some of the most amazing fruit—mangoes, lychees, the most beautiful bananas you've ever seen in your life. That's where all the fruit we export to Europe comes from. But on the black land twenty minutes down the road, the soil has been decimated by years of overfarming and overgrazing. Abel's mother and his sisters were all traditional, stay-at-home moms, and Abel and his younger brother, who was a policeman, supported the family. They were all very kind and generous and accepted us as part of the family right away.

Tsonga culture, I learned, is extremely patriarchal. We're talking about a world where women must bow when they greet a man. Men and women have limited social interactions. The men kill the animals, and the women cook the food. Men are not even allowed in the kitchen. As a nine-year-old boy, I thought this was fantastic. I wasn't allowed to do anything. At home my mom was forever making me do chores—wash the dishes, sweep the house—but when she tried to do that in Tzaneen, the women wouldn't allow it.

"Trevor, make your bed," my mom would say.

"No, no, no, no," Abel's mother would protest. "Trevor must go outside and play."

I was made to run off and have fun while my girl step-cousins had to clean the house and help the women cook. I was in heaven.

My mother loathed every moment of being there. For Abel, a first-born son who was bringing home his own firstborn son, this trip was a huge deal. In the homelands, the firstborn son almost becomes the father/husband by default because the dad is off working in the city. The firstborn son is the man of the house. He raises his siblings. His mom treats him with a certain level of respect as the dad's surrogate. Since this was Abel's big homecoming with Andrew, he expected my mother to play her traditional role, too. But she refused.

The women in Tzaneen had a multitude of jobs during the day. They prepared breakfast, prepared tea, prepared lunch, did the washing and the cleaning. The men had been working all year in the city to support the family, so this was their vacation, more or less. They were at leisure, waited on by the women. They might slaughter a goat or something, do whatever manly tasks needed to be done, but then they would go to an area that was only for men and hang out and drink while the women cooked and cleaned. But my mom had been working in the city all year, too, and Patricia Noah didn't stay in anyone's kitchen. She was a free-roaming spirit. She insisted on walking to the village, going where the men hung out, talking to the men as equals.

The whole tradition of women bowing to the men, my mom found that absurd. But she didn't refuse to do it. She overdid it. She made a mockery of it. The other women would bow before men with this polite little curtsy. My mom would go down and cower, groveling in the dirt like she was worshipping a deity, and she'd stay down there for a long time, like a *really* long time, long enough to make everyone very uncomfortable. That was my mom. Don't fight the system. Mock the system. To Abel, it looked like his wife didn't respect him. Every other man had some docile girl from the village, and here he'd come with this modern woman, a Xhosa woman no less, a culture whose women were thought of as particularly loudmouthed and promiscuous. The two of them fought and bickered the whole time, and after that first trip my mother refused to go back.

Up to that point I'd lived my whole life in a world run by women, but after my mom and Abel were married, and especially after Andrew was born, I watched him try to assert himself and impose his ideas of what he thought his family should be. One thing that became clear early on was that those ideas did not include me. I was a reminder that my mom had lived a life before him. I didn't even share his color. His family was him, my mom, and the new baby. My family was my mom and me. I actually appreciated that about him. Sometimes he was my buddy, sometimes not, but he never pretended our relationship was anything other than what it was. We'd joke around and laugh together. We'd watch TV together. He'd slip me pocket money now and again after my mother said I'd had enough. But he never gave me a birthday present or a Christmas present. He never gave me the affection of a father. I was never his son.

Abel's presence in the house brought with it new rules. One of the first things he did was kick Fufi and Panther out of the house.

"No dogs in the house."

"But we've always had the dogs in the house."

"Not anymore. In an African home, dogs sleep outside. People sleep inside."

Putting the dogs in the yard was Abel's way of saying, "We're going to do things around here the way they're supposed to be done." When they were just dating, my mother was still the free spirit, doing what she wanted, going where she wanted. Slowly, those things got reined in. I could feel that he was trying to rein in our independence. He even got upset about church. "You cannot be at church the whole day," he'd say. "My wife is gone all day, and what will people say? 'Why is his wife not around? Where is she? Who goes to church for the whole day?' No, no, no. This brings disrespect to me."

He tried to stop her from spending so much time at church, and one of the most effective tools he used was to stop fixing my mother's car. It would break down, and he'd purposefully let it sit. My mom couldn't afford another car, and she couldn't get the car fixed somewhere else. You're married to a mechanic and you're going to get your car fixed by another mechanic? That's worse than cheating. So Abel became our only transport, and he would refuse to take us places. Ever defiant, my mother would take minibuses to get to church.

Losing the car also meant losing access to my dad. We had to ask Abel for rides into town, and he didn't like what they were for. It was an insult to his manhood.

"We need to go to Yeoville."

"Why are you going to Yeoville?"

"To see Trevor's dad."

"What? No, no. How can I take my wife and her child and drop you off there? You're insulting me. What do I tell my friends? What do I tell my family? My wife is at another man's house? The man who made that child with her? No, no, no."

I saw my father less and less. Not long after, he moved down to Cape Town.

Abel wanted a traditional marriage with a traditional wife. For a long time I wondered why he ever married a woman like my mom in the first place, as she was the opposite of that in every way. If he wanted a woman to bow to him, there were plenty of girls back in Tzaneen being raised solely for that purpose. The way my mother always explained it, the traditional man wants a woman to be subservient, but he never falls in love with subservient women. He's attracted to independent women. "He's like an exotic bird collector," she said. "He only wants a woman who is free because his dream is to put her in a cage."

When we first met Abel, he smoked a lot of weed. He drank, too, but it was mostly weed. Looking back, I almost miss his pothead days because the weed mellowed him out. He'd smoke, chill, watch TV, and fall asleep. I think subconsciously it was something he knew he needed to do to take the edge off his anger. He stopped smoking after he and my mom got married. She made him stop for religious reasons—the body is a temple and so on. But what none of us saw coming was that when he stopped smoking weed he just replaced it with alcohol. He started drinking more and more. He never came home from work sober. An average day was a six-pack of beer after work. Weeknights he'd have a buzz on. Some Fridays and Saturdays he just didn't come home.

When Abel drank, his eyes would go red, bloodshot. That was the clue I learned to read. I always thought of Abel as a cobra: calm, perfectly still, then explosive. There was no ranting and raving, no clenched fists. He'd be very quiet, and then out of nowhere the violence would come. The eyes were my only clue to stay away. His eyes were everything. They were the eyes of the Devil.

Late one night we woke up to a house filled with smoke. Abel hadn't come home by the time we'd gone to bed, and I'd fallen asleep in my mother's room with her and Andrew, who was still a baby. I jerked awake to her shaking me and screaming. *"Trevor! Trevor!"* There was smoke everywhere. We thought the house was burning down.

My mom ran down the hallway to the kitchen, where she discovered the kitchen on fire. Abel had driven home drunk, blind drunk, drunker than we'd ever seen him before. He'd been hungry, tried to heat up some food on the stove, and passed out on the couch while it was cooking. The pot had burned itself out and burned up the kitchen wall behind the stove, and smoke was billowing everywhere. She turned off the stove and opened the doors and the windows to try to air the place out. Then she went over to the couch and woke him up and started berating him for nearly burning the house down. He was too drunk to care.

She came back into the bedroom, picked up the phone, and called my grandmother. She started going on and on about Abel and his drinking. "This man, he's going to kill us one day. He almost burnt the house down . . ."

Abel walked into the bedroom, very calm, very quiet. His eyes were blood red, his eyelids heavy. He put his finger on the cradle and hung up the call. My mom lost it.

"How dare you! Don't you hang up my phone call! What do you think you're doing?!"

"You don't tell people what's happening in this house," he said.

"Oh, please! You're worried about what the world is thinking? Worry about this world! Worry about what your family is thinking!"

Abel towered over my mother. He didn't raise his voice, didn't get angry.

"Mbuyi," he said softly, "you don't respect me."

"Respect?! You almost burned down our house. Respect? Oh, please! Earn your respect! You want me to respect you as a man, then act like a man! Drinking your money in the streets, and where are your child's diapers?! Respect?! Earn your respect—"

"Mbuyi—"

"You're not a man; you're a child—"

"Mbuyi—"

"I can't have a child for a husband—"

"Mbuyi—"

"I've got my own children to raise—"

"Mbuyi, shut up—"

"A man who comes home drunk—"

"Mbuyi, shut up—"

"And burns down the house with his children—"

"Mbuyi, shut up—"

"And you call yourself a father—"

Then out of nowhere, like a clap of thunder when there were no clouds, *crack!*, he smacked her across the face. She ricocheted off the wall and collapsed like a ton of bricks. I'd never seen anything like it. She went down and stayed down for a good thirty seconds. Andrew started screaming. I don't remember going to pick him up, but I clearly remember holding him at some point. My mom pulled herself up and struggled back to her feet and launched right back into him. She'd clearly been knocked for a loop, but she was trying to act more with-it than she was. I could see the disbelief in her face. This had never happened to her before in her life. She got right back in his face and started shouting at him.

"Did you just hit me?"

The whole time, in my head, I kept thinking the same thing Abel was saying. *Shut up, Mom. Shut up. You're going to make it worse.* Because I knew, as the receiver of many beatings, the one thing that doesn't help is talking back. But she wouldn't stay quiet.

"Did you just hit me?"

"Mbuyi, I told you—"

"No man has ever! Don't think you can control me when you can't even control—"

Crack! He hit her again. She stumbled back but this time didn't fall. She scrambled, grabbed me, and grabbed Andrew.

"Let's go. We're leaving."

We ran out of the house and up the road. It was the dead of night, cold outside. I was wearing nothing but a T-shirt and sweatpants. We walked to the Eden Park police station, over a kilometer away. My mom marched us in, and there were two cops on duty at the front desk.

"I'm here to lay a charge," she said.

"What are you here to lay a charge about?"

"I'm here to lay a charge against the man who hit me."

To this day I'll never forget the patronizing, condescending way they spoke to her.

"Calm down, lady. Calm down. Who hit you?"

"My husband."

"Your husband? What did you do? Did you make him angry?"

"Did I . . . what? No. He hit me. I'm here to lay a charge against—"

"No, no. Ma'am. Why do you wanna make a case, eh? You sure you want to do this? Go home and talk to your husband. You do know once you lay charges you can't take them back? He'll have a criminal record. His life will never be the same. Do you really want your husband going to jail?"

My mom kept insisting that they take a statement and open a case, and they actually refused—they refused to write up a charge sheet.

"This is a family thing," they said. "You don't want to involve the police. Maybe you want to think it over and come back in the morning."

Mom started yelling at them, demanding to see the station commander, and right then Abel walked into the station. He'd driven down. He'd sobered up a bit, but he was still drunk, driving into a police station. That didn't matter. He walked over to the cops, and the station turned into a boys' club. Like they were a bunch of old pals.

"Hey, guys," he said. "You know how it is. You know how women can be. I just got a little angry, that's all."

"It's okay, man. We know. It happens. Don't worry."

I had never seen anything like it. I was nine years old, and I still thought of the police as the good guys. You get in trouble, you call the police, and those flashing red-and-blue lights are going to come and save you. But I remember standing there watching my mom, flabbergasted, horrified that these cops wouldn't help her. That's when I realized the police were not who I thought they were. They were men first, and police second.

We left the station. My mother took me and Andrew, and we went out to stay with my grandmother in Soweto for a while. A few weeks later, Abel drove over and apologized. Abel was always sincere and heartfelt with his apologies: He didn't mean it. He knows he was wrong. He'll never do it again. My grandmother convinced my mom that she should give Abel a second chance. Her argument was basically, "All men do it." My grandfather, Temperance, had hit her. Leaving Abel was no guarantee it wouldn't happen again, and at least Abel was willing to apologize. So my mom decided to give him another chance. We drove back to Eden Park together, and for years, nothing—for *years* Abel didn't lay a finger on her. Or me. Everything went back to the way it was.

Abel was an amazing mechanic, probably one of the best around at the time. He'd been to technical college, graduated first in his class. He'd had job offers from BMW and Mercedes. His business thrived on referrals. People would bring their cars from all over the city for him to fix because he could work miracles on them. My mom truly believed in him. She thought she could raise him up, help him make good on his potential, not merely as a mechanic but as the owner of his own workshop.

As headstrong and independent as my mom is, she remains the woman who gives back. She gives and gives and gives; that is her nature. She refused to be subservient to Abel at home, but she did want him to succeed as a man. If she could make their marriage a true marriage of equals, she was willing to pour herself into it completely, the same way she poured herself into her children. At some point, Abel's boss decided to sell Mighty Mechanics and retire. My mom had some money saved, and she helped Abel buy it. They moved the workshop from Yeoville to the industrial area of Wynberg, just west of Alex, and Mighty Mechanics became the new family business.

When you first go into business there are so many things nobody tells you. That's especially true when you're two young black people, a secretary and a mechanic, coming out of a time when blacks had never been allowed to own businesses at all. One of the things nobody tells you is that when you buy a business you buy its debt. After my mom and Abel opened up the books on Mighty Mechanics and came to a full realization of what they'd bought, they saw how much trouble the company was already in.

The garage gradually took over our lives. I'd get out of school and walk the five kilometers from Maryvale to the workshop. I'd sit for hours and try to do my homework with the machines and repairs going on around me. Inevitably Abel would get behind schedule on a car, and since he was our ride, we'd have to wait for him to finish before we could go home. It started out as "We're running late. Go nap in a car, and we'll tell you when we're leaving." I'd crawl in the backseat of some sedan, they'd wake me up at midnight, and we'd drive all the way back out to Eden Park and crash. Then pretty soon it was "We're running late. Go sleep in a car, and we'll wake you for school in the morning." We started sleeping at the garage. At first it was one or two nights a week, then three or four. Then my mom sold the house and put that money into the business as well. She went all in. She gave up everything for him.

From that point on we lived in the garage. It was a warehouse, basically, and not the fancy, romantic sort of warehouse hipsters might one day turn into lofts. No, no. It was a cold, empty space. Gray concrete floors stained with oil and grease, old junk cars and car parts everywhere. Near the front, next to the roller door that opened onto the street, there was a tiny office built out of drywall for doing paperwork and such. In the back was a kitchenette, just a sink, a portable hot plate, and some cabinets. To bathe, there was only an open wash basin, like a janitor's sink, with a showerhead rigged up above.

Abel and my mom slept with Andrew in the office on a thin mattress they'd roll out on the floor. I slept in the cars. I got really good at sleeping in cars. I know all the best cars to sleep in. The worst were the cheap ones, Volkswagens, low-end Japanese sedans. The seats barely reclined, no headrests, cheap fake-leather upholstery. I'd spend half the night trying not to slide off the seat. I'd wake up with sore knees because I couldn't stretch out and extend my legs. German cars were wonderful, especially Mercedes. Big, plush leather seats, like couches. They were cold when you first climbed in, but they were well insulated and warmed up nicely. All I needed was my school blazer to curl up under, and I could get really cozy inside a Mercedes. But the best, hands-down, were American cars. I used to pray for a customer to come in with a big Buick with bench seats. If I saw one of those, I'd be like, *Yes!* It was rare for American cars to come in, but when they did, boy, was I in heaven.

Since Mighty Mechanics was now a family business, and I was family, I also had to work. There was no more time for play. There wasn't even time for homework. I'd walk home, the school uniform would come off, the overalls would go on, and I'd get under the hood of some sedan. I got to a point where I could do a basic service on a car by myself, and often I did. Abel would say, "That Honda. Minor service." And I'd get under the hood. Day in and day out. Points, plugs, condensers, oil filters, air filters. Install new seats, change tires, swap headlights, fix taillights. Go to the parts shop, buy the parts, back to the workshop. Eleven years old, and that was my life. I was falling behind in school. I wasn't getting anything done. My teachers used to come down on me.

"Why aren't you doing your homework?"

"I can't do my homework. I have work, at home."

We worked and worked and worked, but no matter how many hours we put in, the business kept losing money. We lost everything. We couldn't even afford real food. There was one month I'll never forget, the worst month of my life. We were so broke that for weeks we ate nothing but bowls of *marogo*, a kind of wild spinach, cooked with caterpillars. Mopane worms, they're called. Mopane worms are literally the cheapest thing that only the poorest of poor people eat. I grew up poor, but there's poor and then there's "Wait, I'm eating worms." Mopane worms are the sort of thing where even people in Soweto would be like, "Eh . . . no." They're these spiny, brightly colored caterpillars the size of your finger. They're nothing like escargot, where someone took a snail and gave it a fancy name. They're fucking worms. They have black spines that prick the roof of your mouth as you're eating them. When you bite into a mopane worm, it's not uncommon for its yellow-green excrement to squirt into your mouth.

For a while I sort of enjoyed the caterpillars. It was like a food adventure, but then over the course of weeks, eating them every day, day after day, I couldn't take it anymore. I'll never forget the day I bit a mopane worm in half and that yellow-green ooze came out and I thought, "I'm eating caterpillar shit." Instantly I wanted to throw up. I snapped and ran to my mom crying. "I don't want to eat caterpillars anymore!" That night she scraped some money together and bought us chicken. As poor as we'd been in the past, we'd never been without food.

That was the period of my life I hated the most—work all night, sleep in some car, wake up, wash up in a janitor's sink, brush my teeth in a little metal basin, brush my hair in the rearview mirror of a Toyota, then try to get dressed without getting oil and grease all over my school clothes so the kids at school won't know I live in a garage. Oh, I hated it so much. I hated cars. I hated sleeping in cars. I hated working on cars. I hated getting my hands dirty. I hated eating worms. I hated it all.

I didn't hate my mom, or even Abel, funnily enough. Because I saw how hard everyone was working. At first I didn't know about the mistakes being made on the business level that were making it hard, so it just felt like a hard situation. But eventually I started to see why the business was hemorrhaging money. I used to go around and buy auto parts for Abel, and I learned that he was buying his parts on credit. The vendors were charging him a crazy markup. The debt was crippling the company, and instead of paying off the debt he was drinking what little cash he made. Brilliant mechanic, horrible businessman.

At a certain point, in order to try to save the garage, my mother quit her job at ICI and stepped in to help him run the workshop. She brought her office skills to the garage full-time and started keeping the books, making the schedule, balancing the accounts. And it was going well, until Abel started to feel like she was running his business. People started commenting on it as well. Clients were getting their cars on time, vendors were getting paid on time, and they would say, "Hey, Abie, this workshop is going so much better now that your wife has taken over." That didn't help.

We lived in the workshop for close to a year, and then my mom had had enough. She was willing to help him, but not if he was going to drink all the profits. She had always been independent, self-sufficient, but she'd lost that part of herself at the mercy of someone else's failed dream. At a certain point she said, "I can't do this anymore. I'm out of this. I'm done." She went out and got a job as a secretary with a real-estate developer, and somehow, between that and borrowing against whatever equity was left in Abel's workshop, she was able to get us the house in Highlands North. We moved, the workshop was seized by Abel's creditors, and that was the end of that.

Growing up I suffered no shortage of my mother's old school, Old Testament discipline. She spared no rod and spoiled no child. With Andrew, she was different. He got spankings at first, but they tapered off and eventually went away. When I asked her why I got beatings and Andrew didn't, she made a joke about it like she does with everything. "I beat you like that because you could take it," she said. "I can't hit your little brother the same way because he's a skinny little stick. He'll break. But you, God gave you that ass for whipping." Even though she was kidding, I could tell that the reason she didn't beat Andrew was because she'd had a genuine change of heart on the matter. It was a lesson she'd learned, oddly enough, from me.

I grew up in a world of violence, but I myself was never violent at all. Yes, I played pranks and set fires and broke windows, but I never attacked people. I never hit anyone. I was never angry. I just didn't see myself that way. My mother had exposed me to a different world than the one she grew up in. She bought me the books she never got to read. She took me to the schools that she never got to go to. I immersed myself in those worlds and I came back looking at the world a different way. I saw that not all families are violent. I saw the futility of violence, the cycle that just repeats itself, the damage that's inflicted on people that they in turn inflict on others.

I saw, more than anything, that relationships are not sustained by violence but by love. Love is a creative act. When you love someone you create a new world for them. My mother did that for me, and with the progress I made and the things I learned, I came back and created a new world and a new understanding for her. After that, she never raised her hand to her children again. Unfortunately, by the time she stopped, Abel had started.

In all the times I received beatings from my mom, I was never scared of her. I didn't like it, certainly. When she said, "I hit you out of love," I didn't necessarily agree with her thinking. But I understood that it was discipline and it was being done for a purpose. The first time Abel hit me I felt something I had never felt before. I felt terror.

I was in grade six, my last year at Maryvale. We'd moved to Highlands North, and I'd gotten in trouble at school for forging my mom's signature on some document; there was some activity I didn't want to participate in, so I'd signed the release in her name to get out of it. The school called my mom, and she asked me about it when I got home that afternoon. I was certain she was going to punish me, but this turned out to be one of those times when she didn't care. She said I should have just asked her; she would have signed the form anyway. Then Abel, who'd been sitting in the kitchen with us, watching the whole thing, said, "Hey, can I talk to you for a second?" Then he took me into this tiny room, a walk-in pantry off the kitchen, and he closed the door behind us.

He was standing between me and the door, but I didn't think anything of it. It didn't occur to me to be scared. Abel had never tried to discipline me before. He'd never even given me a lecture. It was always "Mbuyi, your son did this," and then my mother would handle it. And this was the middle of the afternoon. He was completely sober, which made what happened next all the more terrifying.

"Why did you forge your mother's signature?" he said.

I started making up some excuse. "Oh, I, uh, forgot to bring the form home—"

"Don't lie to me. Why did you forge your mom's signature?"

I started stammering out more bullshit, oblivious to what was coming, and then out of nowhere it came.

The first blow hit me in the ribs. My mind flashed: *It's a trap!* I'd never been in a fight before, had never learned how to fight, but I had this instinct that told me to get in close. I had seen what those long arms could do. I'd seen him take down my mom, but more important, I'd seen him take down grown men. Abel never hit people with a punch; I never saw him punch another person with a closed fist. But he had this ability to hit a grown man across his face with an open hand and they'd crumple. He was that strong. I looked at his arms and I knew, *Don't be on the other end of those things*. I ducked in close and he kept hitting and hitting, but I was in too tight for him to land any solid blows. Then he caught on and he stopped hitting and started trying to grapple and wrestle me. He did this thing where he grabbed the skin on my arms and pinched it between his thumb and forefinger and twisted hard. Jesus, that hurt.

It was the most terrifying moment of my life. I had never been that scared before, ever. Because there was no purpose to it—that's what made it so terrifying. It wasn't discipline. Nothing about it was coming from a place of love. It didn't feel like something that would end with me learning a lesson about forging my mom's signature. It felt like something that would end when he wanted it to end, when his rage was spent. It felt like there was something inside him that wanted to destroy me.

Abel was much bigger and stronger than me, but being in a confined space was to my advantage because he didn't have the room to maneuver. As he grappled and punched I somehow managed to twist and wriggle my way around him and slip out the door. I was quick, but Abel was quick as well. He chased me. I ran out of the house and jumped over the gate, and I ran and I ran and I ran. The last time I turned around he was rounding the gate, coming out of the yard after me. Until I turned twenty-five years old, I had a recurring nightmare of the look on his face as he came around that corner.

The moment I saw him I put my head down and ran. I ran like the Devil was chasing me. Abel was bigger and faster, but this was my neighborhood. You couldn't catch me in my neighborhood. I knew every alley and every street, every wall to climb over, every fence to slip through. I was ducking through traffic, cutting through yards. I have no idea when he gave up because I never looked back. I ran and ran and ran, as far as my legs would carry me. I was in Bramley, three neighborhoods away, before I stopped. I found a hiding place in some bushes and crawled inside and huddled there for what felt like hours.

You don't have to teach me a lesson twice. From that day until the day I left home, I lived like a mouse in that house. If Abel was in a room, I was out of the room. If he was in one corner, I was in the other corner. If he walked into a room, I would get up and act like I was going to the kitchen, then when I reentered the room, I would make sure I was close to the exit. He could be in the happiest, friendliest mood. Didn't matter. Never again did I let him come between me and a door. Maybe a couple of times after that I was sloppy and he'd land a punch or a kick before I could get away, but I never trusted him again, not for a moment.

It was different for Andrew. Andrew was Abel's son, flesh of his flesh, blood of his blood. Despite being nine years younger than me,

Andrew was really the eldest son in that house, Abel's firstborn, and that accorded him a respect that I and even my mother never enjoyed. And Andrew had nothing but love for that man, despite his shortcomings. Because of that love, I think, out of all of us, Andrew was the only one who wasn't afraid. He was the lion tamer, only he'd been raised by the lion—he couldn't love the beast any less despite knowing what it was capable of. For me, the first glint of anger or madness from Abel and I was gone. Andrew would stay and try to talk Abel down. He'd even get between Abel and Mom. I remember one night when Abel threw a bottle of Jack Daniel's at Andrew's head. It just missed him and exploded on the wall. Which is to say that Andrew stayed long enough to get the bottle thrown at him. I wouldn't have stuck around long enough for Abel to get a bead on me.

When Mighty Mechanics went under, Abel had to get his cars out. Someone was taking over the property; there were liens against his assets. It was a mess. That's when he started running his workshop out of our yard. It's also when my mother divorced him.

In African culture there's legal marriage and traditional marriage. Just because you divorce someone legally doesn't mean they are no longer your spouse. Once Abel's debts and his terrible business decisions started impacting my mother's credit and her ability to support her sons, she wanted out. "I don't have debts," she said. "I don't have bad credit. I'm not doing these things with you." We were still a family and they were still traditionally married, but she divorced him in order to separate their financial affairs. She also took her name back.

Because Abel had started running an unlicensed business in a residential area, one of the neighbors filed a petition to get rid of us. My mom applied for a license to be able to operate a business on the property. The workshop stayed, but Abel kept running it into the ground, drinking his money. At the same time, my mother started moving up at the real-estate company she worked for, taking on more responsibilities and earning a better salary. His workshop became like a side hobby almost. He was supposed to pay for Andrew's school fees and groceries, but he started falling behind even on that, and soon my mom was paying for everything. She paid the electricity. She paid the mortgage. He literally contributed nothing.

That was the turning point. When my mother started making more money and getting her independence back—that's when we saw the dragon emerge. The drinking got worse. He grew more and more violent. It wasn't long after coming for me in the pantry that Abel hit my mom for the second time. I can't recall the details of it, because now it's muddled with all the other times that came after it. I do remember that the police were called. They came out to the house this time, but again it was like a boys' club. "Hey, guys. These women, you know how they are." No report was made. No charges were filed.

Whenever he'd hit her or come after me, my mom would find me crying afterward and take me aside. She'd give me the same talk every time.

"Pray for Abel," she'd say. "Because he doesn't hate us. He hates himself."

To a kid this makes no sense. "Well, if he hates himself," I'd say, "why doesn't he kick himself?"

Abel was one of those drinkers where once he was gone you'd look into his eyes and you didn't even see the same person. I remember one night he came home fuckdrunk, stumbling through the house. He stumbled into my room, muttering to himself, and I woke up to see him whip out his dick and start pissing on the floor. He thought he was in the bathroom. That's how drunk he would get—he wouldn't know which room in the house he was in. There were so many nights he would stumble into my room thinking it was his and kick me out of bed and pass out. I'd yell at him, but it was like talking to a zombie. I'd go sleep on the couch.

He'd get wasted with his crew in the backyard every evening after work, and many nights he'd end up fighting with one of them. Someone would say something Abel didn't like, and he'd beat the shit out of him. The guy wouldn't show up for work Tuesday or Wednesday, but then by Thursday he'd be back because he needed the job. Every few weeks it was the same story, like clockwork.

Abel kicked the dogs, too. Fufi, mostly. Panther was smart enough to stay away, but dumb, lovable Fufi was forever trying to be Abel's friend. She'd cross his path or be in his way when he'd had a few, and he'd give her the boot. After that she'd go and hide somewhere for a while. Fufi getting kicked was always the warning sign that shit was about to go down. The dogs and the workers in the yard often got the first taste of his anger, and that would let the rest of us know to lie low. I'd usually go find Fufi wherever she was hiding and be with her.

The strange thing was that when Fufi got kicked she never yelped or cried. When the vet diagnosed her as deaf, he also found out she had some condition where she didn't have a fully developed sense of touch. She didn't feel pain. Which was why she would always start over with Abel like it was a new day. He'd kick her, she'd hide, then she'd be right back the next morning, wagging her tail. "Hey. I'm here. I'll give you another chance."

And he always got the second chance. The Abel who was likable and charming never went away. He had a drinking problem, but he was a nice guy. We had a family. Growing up in a home of abuse, you struggle with the notion that you can love a person you hate, or hate a person you love. It's a strange feeling. You want to live in a world where someone is good or bad, where you either hate them or love them, but that's not how people are.

There was an undercurrent of terror that ran through the house, but the actual beatings themselves were not that frequent. I think if they had been, the situation would have ended sooner. Ironically, the good times in between were what allowed it to drag out and escalate as far as it did. He hit my mom once, then the next time was three years later, and it was just a little bit worse. Then it was two years later, and it was just a little bit worse. Then it was a year later, and it was just a little bit worse. It was sporadic enough to where you'd think it wouldn't happen again, but it was frequent enough that you never forgot it was possible. There was a rhythm to it. I remember one time, after one terrible incident, nobody spoke to him for over a month. No words, no eye contact, no conversations, nothing. We moved through the house as strangers, at different times. Complete silent treatment. Then one morning you're in the kitchen and there's a nod. "Hey." "Hey." Then a week later it's "Did you see the thing on the news?" "Yeah." Then the next week there's a joke and a laugh. Slowly, slowly, life goes back to how it was. Six months, a year later, you do it all again.

One afternoon I came home from Sandringham and my mom was very upset and worked up.

"This man is unbelievable," she said.

"What happened?"

"He bought a gun."

"What? A *gun*? What do you mean, 'He bought a gun'?"

A gun was such a ridiculous thing in my world. In my mind, only cops and criminals had guns. Abel had gone out and bought a 9mm Parabellum Smith & Wesson. Sleek and black, menacing. It didn't look cool like guns in movies. It looked like it killed things.

"Why did he buy a gun?" I asked.

"I don't know."

She said she'd confronted him about it, and he'd gone off on some nonsense about the world needing to learn to respect him.

"He thinks he's the policeman of the world," she said. "And that's the problem with the world. We have people who cannot police themselves, so they want to police everyone else around them."

Not long after that, I moved out. The atmosphere had become toxic for me. I'd reached the point where I was as big as Abel. Big enough to punch back. A father does not fear retribution from his son, but I was not his son. He knew that. The analogy my mom used was that there were now two male lions in the house. "Every time he looks at you he sees your father," she'd say. "You're a constant reminder of another man. He hates you, and you need to leave. You need to leave before you become like him."

It was also just time for me to go. Regardless of Abel, our plan had always been for me to move out after school. My mother never wanted me to be like my uncle, one of those men, unemployed and still living at home with his mother. She helped me get my flat, and I moved out. The flat was only ten minutes away from the house, so I was always around to drop in to help with errands or have dinner once in a while. But, most important, whatever was going on with Abel, I didn't have to be involved.

At some point my mom moved to a separate bedroom in the house, and from then on they were married in name only, not even cohabitating but coexisting. That state of affairs lasted a year, maybe two. Andrew had turned nine, and in my world I was counting down until he turned eighteen, thinking that would finally free my mom from this abusive man. Then one afternoon my mom called and asked me to come by the house. A few hours later, I popped by.

"Trevor," she said. "I'm pregnant."

"Sorry, what?"

"I'm pregnant."

"What?!"

Good Lord, I was furious. I was so angry. She herself seemed resolute, as determined as ever, but with an undertone of sadness I had never seen before, like the news had devastated her at first but she'd since reconciled herself to the reality of it.

"How could you let this happen?"

"Abel and I, we made up. I moved back into the bedroom. It was just one night, and then . . . I became pregnant. I don't know how."

She didn't know. She was forty-four years old. She'd had her tubes tied after Andrew. Even her doctor had said, "This shouldn't be possible. We don't know how this happened."

I was boiling with rage. All we had to do was wait for Andrew to grow up, and it was going to be over, and now it was like she'd re-upped on the contract.

"So you're going to have this child with this man? You're going to stay with this man another eighteen years? Are you crazy?"

"God spoke to me, Trevor. He told me, 'Patricia, I don't do anything by mistake. There is nothing I give you that you cannot handle.' I'm pregnant for a reason. I know what kind of kids I can make. I know what kind of sons I can raise. I can raise this child. I will raise this child."

Nine months later Isaac was born. She called him Isaac because in the Bible Sarah gets pregnant when she's like a hundred years old and she's not supposed to be having children and that's what she names her son.

Isaac's birth pushed me even further away. I visited less and less. Then I popped by one afternoon and the house was in chaos, police cars out front, the aftermath of another fight.

He'd hit her with a bicycle. Abel had been berating one of his workers in the yard, and my mom had tried to get between them. Abel was furious that she'd contradicted him in front of an employee, so he picked up Andrew's bike and he beat her with it. Again she called the police, and the cops who showed up this time actually knew Abel. He'd fixed their cars. They were pals. No charges were filed. Nothing happened.

That time I confronted him. I was big enough now.

"You can't keep doing this," I said. "This is not right."

He was apologetic. He always was. He didn't puff out his chest and get defensive or anything like that.

"I know," he said. "I'm sorry. I don't like doing these things, but you know how your mom is. She can talk a lot and she doesn't listen. I feel like your mom doesn't respect me sometimes. She came and disrespected me in front of my workers. I can't have these other men looking at me like I don't know how to control my wife."

After the bicycle, my mom hired contractors she knew through the real-estate business to build her a separate house in the backyard, like a little servants' quarters, and she moved in there with Isaac.

"This is the most insane thing I've ever seen," I told her.

"This is all I can do," she said. "The police won't help me. The government won't protect me. Only my God can protect me. But what

I can do is use against him the one thing that he cherishes, and that is his pride. By me living outside in a shack, everyone is going to ask him, 'Why does your wife live in a shack outside your house?' He's going to have to answer that question, and no matter what he says, everyone will know that something is wrong with him. He loves to live for the world. Let the world see him for who he is. He's a saint in the streets. He's a devil in this house. Let him be seen for who he is."

When my mom had decided to keep Isaac, I was so close to writing her off. I couldn't stand the pain anymore. But seeing her hit with a bicycle, living like a prisoner in her own backyard, that was the final straw for me. I was a broken person. I was done.

"This thing?" I told her. "This dysfunctional thing? I won't be a part of it. I can't live this life with you. I refuse. You've made your decision. Good luck with your life. I'm going to live mine."

She understood. She didn't feel betrayed or abandoned at all.

"Honey, I know what you're going through," she said. "At one point, I had to disown my family to go off and live my own life, too. I understand why you need to do the same."

So I did. I walked out. I didn't call. I didn't visit. Isaac came and I went, and for the life of me I could not understand why she wouldn't do the same: leave. Just leave. Just fucking leave.

I didn't understand what she was going through. I didn't understand domestic violence. I didn't understand how adult relationships worked; I'd never even had a girlfriend. I didn't understand how she could have sex with a man she hated and feared. I didn't know how easily sex and hatred and fear can intertwine.

I was angry with my mom. I hated him, but I blamed her. I saw Abel as a choice she'd made, a choice she was continuing to make. My whole life, telling me stories about growing up in the homelands, being abandoned by her parents, she had always said, "You cannot blame anyone else for what you do. You cannot blame your past for who you are. You are responsible for you. You make your own choices."

She never let me see us as victims. We *were* victims, me and my mom, Andrew and Isaac. Victims of apartheid. Victims of abuse. But I was never allowed to think that way, and I didn't see her life that way. Cutting my father out of our lives to pacify Abel, that was her choice. Supporting Abel's workshop was her choice. Isaac was her choice. She had the money, not him. She wasn't dependent. So in my mind, she was the one making the decision.

It is so easy, from the outside, to put the blame on the woman and say, "You just need to leave." It's not like my home was the only home where there was domestic abuse. It's what I grew up around. I saw it in the streets of Soweto, on TV, in movies. Where does a woman go in a society where that is the norm? When the police won't help her? When her own family won't help her? Where does a woman go when she leaves one man who hits her and is just as likely to wind up with another man who hits her, maybe even worse than the first? Where does a woman go when she's single with three kids and she lives in a society that makes her a pariah for being a manless woman? Where she's seen as a whore for doing that? Where does she go? What does she do?

But I didn't comprehend any of that at the time. I was a boy with a boy's understanding of things. I distinctly remember the last time we argued about it, too. It was sometime after the bicycle, or when she was moving into her shack in the backyard. I was going off, begging her for the thousandth time.

"Why? Why don't you just leave?"

She shook her head. "Oh, baby. No, no, no. I can't leave."

"Why not?"

"Because if I leave he'll kill us."

She wasn't being dramatic. She didn't raise her voice. She said it totally calm and matter-of-fact, and I never asked her that question again.

Eventually she did leave. What prompted her to leave, what the final breaking point was, I have no idea. I was gone. I was off becoming a comedian, touring the country, playing shows in England, hosting radio shows, hosting television shows. I'd moved in with my cousin

Mlungisi and made my own life separate from hers. I couldn't invest myself anymore, because it would have broken me into too many pieces. But one day she bought another house in Highlands North, met someone new, and moved on with her life. Andrew and Isaac still saw their dad, who, by that point, was just existing in the world, still going through the same cycle of drinking and fighting, still living in a house paid for by his ex-wife.

Years passed. Life carried on.

Then one morning I was in bed around ten a.m. and my phone rang. It was on a Sunday. I know it was on a Sunday because everyone else in the family had gone to church and I, quite happily, had not. The days of endlessly schlepping back and forth to church were no longer my problem, and I was lazily sleeping in. The irony of my life is that whenever church is involved is when shit goes wrong, like getting kidnapped by violent minibus drivers. I'd always teased my mom about that, too. "This church thing of yours, all this Jesus, what good has come of it?"

I looked over at my phone. It was flashing my mom's number, but when I answered, it was Andrew on the other end. He sounded perfectly calm.

"Hey, Trevor, it's Andrew."

"Hey."

"How are you?"

"Good. What's up?"

"Are you busy?"

"I'm sort of sleeping. Why?"

"Mom's been shot."

Okay, so there were two strange things about the call. First, why would he ask me if I was busy? Let's start there. When your mom's been shot, the first line out of your mouth should be "Mom's been shot." Not "How are you?" Not "Are you busy?" That confused me. The second weird thing was when he said, "Mom's been shot," I didn't ask, "Who shot her?" I didn't have to. He said, "Mom's been shot," and my mind automatically filled in the rest: "Abel shot mom."

"Where are you now?" I said.

"We're at Linksfield Hospital."

"Okay, I'm on my way."

I jumped out of bed, ran down the corridor, and banged on Mlungisi's door. "Dude, my mom's been shot! She's in the hospital." He jumped out of bed, too, and we got in the car and raced to the hospital, which luckily was only fifteen minutes away.

At that point, I was upset but not terrified. Andrew had been so calm on the phone, no crying, no panic in his voice, so I was thinking, *She must be okay. It must not be that bad.* I called him back from the car to find out more.

"Andrew, what happened?"

"We were on our way home from church," he said, again totally calm. "And Dad was waiting for us at the house, and he got out of his car and started shooting."

"But where? Where did he shoot her?"

"He shot her in her leg."

"Oh, okay," I said, relieved.

"And then he shot her in the head."

When he said that, my body just let go. I remember the exact traffic light I was at. For a moment there was a complete vacuum of sound, and then I cried tears like I had never cried before. I collapsed in heaving sobs and moans. I cried as if every other thing I'd cried for in my life had been a waste of crying. I cried so hard that if my present crying self could go back in time and see my other crying selves, it would slap them and say, "That shit's not worth crying for." My cry was not a cry of sadness. It was not catharsis. It wasn't me feeling sorry for myself. It was an expression of raw pain that came from an inability of my body to express that pain in any other way, shape, or form. She was my mom. She was my teammate. It had always been me and her together, me and her against the world. When Andrew said, "shot her in the head," I broke in two.

The light changed. I couldn't even see the road, but I drove through the tears, thinking, *Just get there, just get there, just get there.* We pulled up to the hospital, and I jumped out of the car. There was an outdoor sitting area by the entrance to the emergency room. Andrew was standing there waiting for me, alone, his clothes smeared with blood. He still looked perfectly calm, completely stoic. Then the moment he looked up and saw me he broke down and started bawling. It was like he'd been holding it together the whole morning and then everything broke loose at once and he lost it. I ran to him and hugged him and he cried and cried. His cry was different from mine, though. My cry was one of pain and anger. His cry was one of helplessness.

I turned and ran into the emergency room. My mom was there in triage on a gurney. The doctors were stabilizing her. Her whole body was soaked in blood. There was a hole in her face, a gaping wound above her lip, part of her nose gone.

She was as calm and serene as I'd ever seen her. She could still open one eye, and she turned and looked up at me and saw the look of horror on my face.

"It's okay, baby," she whispered, barely able to speak with the blood in her throat.

"It's not okay."

"No, no, I'm okay, I'm okay. Where's Andrew? Where's your brother?"

"He's outside."

"Go to Andrew."

"But Mom—"

"*Shh.* It's okay, baby. I'm fine."

"You're not fine, you're—"

"*Shhhhhh.* I'm fine, I'm fine, I'm fine. Go to your brother. Your brother needs you."

The doctors kept working, and there was nothing I could do to help her. I went back outside to be with Andrew. We sat down together, and he told me the story.

They were coming home from church, a big group, my mom and Andrew and Isaac, her new husband and his children and a whole bunch of his extended family, aunts and uncles, nieces and nephews. They had just pulled into the driveway when Abel pulled up and got out of his car. He had his gun. He looked right at my mother.

"You've stolen my life," he said. "You've taken everything away from me. Now I'm going to kill all of you."

Andrew stepped in front of his father. He stepped right in front of the gun.

"Don't do this, Dad, please. You're drunk. Just put the gun away."

Abel looked down at his son.

"No," he said. "I'm killing everybody, and if you don't walk away I will shoot you first."

Andrew stepped aside.

"His eyes were not lying," he told me. "He had the eyes of the Devil. In that moment I could tell my father was gone."

For all the pain I felt that day, in hindsight, I have to imagine that Andrew's pain was far greater than mine. My mom had been shot by a man I despised. If anything, I felt vindicated; I'd been right about Abel all along. I could direct my anger and hatred toward him with no shame or guilt whatsoever. But Andrew's mother had been shot by Andrew's father, a father he loved. How does he reconcile his love with that situation? How does he carry on loving both sides? Both sides of himself?

Isaac was only four years old. He didn't fully comprehend what was happening, and as Andrew stepped aside, Isaac started crying.

"Daddy, what are you doing? Daddy, what are you doing?"

"Isaac, go to your brother," Abel said.

Isaac ran over to Andrew, and Andrew held him. Then Abel raised his gun and he started shooting. My mother jumped in front of the gun to protect everyone, and that's when she took the first bullet, not in her leg but in her butt cheek. She collapsed, and as she fell to the ground she screamed.

"Run!"

Abel kept shooting and everyone ran. They scattered. My mom was struggling to get back to her feet when Abel walked up and stood over her. He pointed the gun at her head point-blank, execution-style. Then he pulled the trigger. Nothing. The gun misfired. *Click!* He pulled the trigger again, same thing. Then again and again. *Click! Click! Click! Click!* Four times he pulled the trigger, and four times the gun misfired. Bullets were popping out of the ejection port, falling out of the gun, falling down on my mom and clattering to the ground.

Abel stopped to see what was wrong with the gun. My mother jumped up in a panic. She shoved him aside, ran for the car, jumped into the driver's seat.

Andrew ran behind and jumped into the passenger seat next to her. Just as she turned the ignition, Andrew heard one last gunshot, and the windshield went red. Abel had fired from behind the car. The bullet went into the back of her head and exited through the front of her face, and blood sprayed everywhere. Her body slumped over the steering wheel. Andrew, reacting without thinking, pulled my mom to the passenger side, flipped over her, jumped into the driver's seat, slammed the car into gear, and raced to the hospital in Linksfield.

I asked Andrew what happened to Abel. He didn't know. I was filled with rage, but there was nothing I could do. I felt completely impotent, but I still felt I had to do something. So I took out my phone and I called him—I called the man who'd just shot my mom, and he actually picked up.

"Trevor."

"You killed my mom."

"Yes, I did."

"You *killed* my *mom*!"

"Yes. And if I could find you, I would kill you as well."

Then he hung up. It was the most chilling moment. It was terrifying. Whatever nerve I'd worked up to call him I immediately lost. To this day I don't know what I was thinking. I don't know what I expected to happen. I was just enraged.

I kept asking Andrew questions, trying to get more details. Then, as we were talking, a nurse came outside looking for me.

"Are you the family?" she asked.

"Yes."

"Sir, there's a problem. Your mother was speaking a bit at first.

She's stopped now, but from what we've gathered she doesn't have health insurance."

"What? No, no. That can't be true. I know my mom has health insurance."

She didn't. As it turned out, a few months prior, she'd decided, "This health insurance is a scam. I never get sick. I'm going to cancel it." So now she had no health insurance.

"We can't treat your mother here," the nurse said. "If she doesn't have insurance we have to send her to a state hospital."

"*State hospital?!* What—no! You can't. My mom's been shot in the head. You're going to put her back on a gurney? Send her out in an ambulance? She'll die. You need to treat her right now."

"Sir, we can't. We need a form of payment."

"I'm your form of payment. I'll pay."

"Yes, people say that, but without a guarantee—"

I pulled out my credit card.

"Here," I said. "Take this. I'll pay. I'll pay for everything."

"Sir, hospital can be very expensive."

"I don't care."

"Sir, I don't think you understand. Hospital can be *really* expensive."

"Lady, I have money. I'll pay anything. Just help us."

"Sir, you don't understand. We have to do so many tests. One test alone could cost two, three thousand rand."

"Three thousan—what? Lady, this is my mother's life we're talking about. I'll pay."

"Sir, you don't understand. Your mother has been shot. In her brain. She'll be in ICU. One night in ICU could cost you fifteen, twenty thousand rand."

"Lady, are you not listening to me? This is my mother's *life*. This is her *life*. Take the money. Take all of it. I don't care."

"*Sir!* You don't understand. I've seen this happen. Your mother could be in the ICU for weeks. This could cost you five hundred thousand, six hundred thousand. Maybe even millions. You'll be in debt for the rest of *your* life."

I'm not going to lie to you: I paused. I paused *hard*. In that moment, what I heard the nurse saying was, "All of your money will be gone," and then I started to think, *Well . . . what is she, fifty? That's pretty good, right? She's lived a good life*.

I genuinely did not know what to do. I stared at the nurse as the shock of what she'd said sunk in. My mind raced through a dozen different scenarios. *What if I spend that money and then she dies anyway? Do I get a refund?* I actually imagined my mother, as frugal as she was, waking up from a coma and saying, "You spent *how much*? You idiot. You should have saved that money to look after your brothers." And what about my brothers? They would be my responsibility now. I would have to raise the family, which I couldn't do if I was millions in debt, and it was always my mother's solemn vow that raising my brothers was the one thing I would never have to do. Even as my career took off, she'd refused any help I offered. "I don't want you paying for your mother the same way I had to pay for mine," she'd say. "I don't want you raising your brothers the same way Abel had to raise his."

My mother's greatest fear was that I would end up paying the black tax, that I would get trapped by the cycle of poverty and violence that came before me. She had always promised me that I would be the one to break that cycle. I would be the one to move forward and not back. And as I looked at that nurse outside the emergency room, I was petrified that the moment I handed her my credit card, the cycle would just continue and I'd get sucked right back in.

People say all the time that they'd do anything for the people they love. But would you really? Would you do anything? Would you give everything? I don't know that a child knows that kind of selfless love. A mother, yes. A mother will clutch her children and jump from a moving car to keep them from harm. She will do it without thinking. But I don't think the child knows how to do that, not instinctively. It's something the child has to learn.

I pressed my credit card into the nurse's hand.

"Do whatever you have to do. Just please help my mom."

We spent the rest of the day in limbo, waiting, not knowing, pacing around the hospital, family members stopping by. Several hours later, the doctor finally came out of the emergency room to give us an update.

"What's happening?" I asked.

"Your mother is stable," he said. "She's out of surgery."

"Is she going to be okay?"

He thought for a moment about what he was going to say.

"I don't like to use this word," he said, "because I'm a man of science and I don't believe in it. But what happened to your mother today was a miracle. I never say that, because I hate it when people say it, but I don't have any other way to explain this."

The bullet that hit my mother in the butt, he said, was a through-and-through. It went in, came out, and didn't do any real damage. The other bullet went through the back of her head, entering below the skull at the top of her neck. It missed the spinal cord by a hair, missed the medulla oblongata, and traveled through her head just underneath the brain, missing every major vein, artery, and nerve. With the trajectory the bullet was on, it was headed straight for her left eye socket and would have blown out her eye, but at the last second it slowed down, hit her cheekbone instead, shattered her cheekbone, ricocheted off, and came out through her left nostril. On the gurney in the emergency room, the blood had made the wound look much worse than it was. The bullet took off only a tiny flap of skin on the side of her nostril, and it came out clean, with no bullet fragments left inside. She didn't even need surgery. They stopped the bleeding, stitched her up in back, stitched her up in front, and let her heal.

"There was nothing we can do, because there's nothing we need to do," the doctor said.

My mother was out of the hospital in four days. She was back at work in seven.

The doctors kept her sedated the rest of that day and night to rest. They told all of us to go home. "She's stable," they said. "There's nothing you can do here. Go home and sleep." So we did.

I went back first thing the next morning to be with my mother in her room and wait for her to wake up. When I walked in she was still asleep. The back of her head was bandaged. She had stitches in her face and gauze covering her nose and her left eye. She looked frail and weak, tired, one of the few times in my life I'd ever seen her look that way.

I sat close by her bed, holding her hand, waiting and watching her breathe, a flood of thoughts going through my mind. I was still afraid I was going to lose her. I was angry at myself for not being there, angry at the police for all the times they didn't arrest Abel. I told myself I should have killed him years ago, which was ridiculous to think because I'm not capable of killing anyone, but I thought it anyway. I was angry at the world, angry at God. Because all my mom does is pray. If there's a fan club for Jesus, my mom is definitely in the top 100, and this is what she gets?

After an hour or so of waiting, she opened her unbandaged eye. The second she did, I lost it. I started bawling. She asked for some water and I gave her a cup, and she leaned forward a bit to sip through the straw. I kept bawling and bawling and bawling. I couldn't control myself.

"*Shh,*" she said. "Don't cry, baby. *Shhhhh.* Don't cry."

"How can I not cry, Mom? You almost died."

"No, I wasn't going to die. I wasn't going to die. It's okay. I wasn't going to die."

"But I thought you were dead." I kept bawling and bawling. "I thought I'd lost you."

"No, baby. Baby, don't cry. Trevor. Trevor, listen. Listen to me. Listen."

"What?" I said, tears streaming down my face.

"My child, you must look on the bright side."

"*What?* What are you talking about, 'the bright side'? Mom, you were shot in the face. There is no bright side."

"Of course there is. Now you're officially the best-looking person in the family."

She broke out in a huge smile and started laughing. Through my tears, I started laughing, too. I was bawling my eyes out and laughing hysterically at the same time. We sat there and she squeezed my hand and we cracked each other up the way we always did, mother and son, laughing together through the pain in an intensive-care recovery room on a bright and sunny and beautiful day.

When my mother was shot, so much happened so quickly. We were only able to piece the whole story together after the fact, as we collected all the different accounts from everyone who was there. Waiting around at the hospital that day, we had so many unanswered questions, like, What happened to Isaac? Where was Isaac? We only found out after we found him and he told us.

When Andrew sped off with my mom, leaving the four-year-old alone on the front lawn, Abel walked over to his youngest, picked him up, put the boy in his car, and drove away. As they drove, Isaac turned to his dad.

"Dad, why did you kill Mom?" he asked, at that point assuming, as we all did, that my mom was dead.

"Because I'm very unhappy," Abel replied. "Because I'm very sad."

"Yeah, but you shouldn't kill Mom. Where are we going now?"

"I'm going to drop you off at your uncle's house."

"And where are you going?"

"I'm going to kill myself."

"But don't kill yourself, Dad."

"No, I'm going to kill myself."

The uncle Abel was talking about was not a real uncle but a friend. He dropped Isaac off with this friend and then he drove off. He spent that day and went to everyone, relatives and friends, and said his goodbyes. He even told people what he had done. "This is what I've done. I've killed her, and I'm now on the way to kill myself. Goodbye." He spent the whole day on this strange farewell tour, until finally one of his cousins called him out.

"You need to man up," the cousin said. "This is the coward's way. You need to turn yourself in. If you were man enough to do this, you have to be man enough to face the consequences."

Abel broke down and handed his gun over to the cousin, the cousin drove him to the police station, and Abel turned himself in.

He spent a couple of weeks in jail, waiting for a bail hearing. We filed a motion opposing bail because he'd shown that he was a threat. Since Andrew and Isaac were still minors, social workers started getting involved. We felt like the case was open-and-shut, but then one day, after a month or so, we got a call that he'd made bail. The great irony was that he got bail because he told the judge that if he was in jail, he couldn't earn money to support his kids. But he wasn't supporting his kids—my mom was supporting the kids.

So Abel was out. The case slowly ground its way through the legal system, and everything went against us. Because of my mother's miraculous recovery, the charge was only attempted murder. And because no domestic violence charges had ever been filed in all the times my mother had called the police to report him, Abel had no criminal record. He got a good lawyer, who continued to lean on the court about the fact that he had children at home who needed him. The case never went to trial. Abel pled guilty to attempted murder. He was given three years' probation. He didn't serve a single day in prison. He kept joint custody of his sons. He's walking around Johannesburg today, completely free. The last I heard he still lives somewhere around Highlands North, not too far from my mom.

The final piece of the story came from my mom, who could only tell us her side after she woke up. She remembered Abel pulling up and pointing the gun at Andrew. She remembered falling to the ground after getting shot in the ass. Then Abel came and stood over her and pointed his gun at her head. She looked up and looked at him straight down the barrel of the gun. Then she started to pray, and that's when the gun misfired. Then it misfired again. Then it misfired again, and again. She jumped up, shoved him away, and ran for the car. Andrew leapt in beside her and she turned the ignition and then her memory went blank.

To this day, nobody can explain what happened. Even the police didn't understand. Because it wasn't like the gun didn't work. It fired, and then it didn't fire, and then it fired again for the final shot. Anyone who knows anything about firearms will tell you that a 9mm handgun cannot misfire in the way that gun did. But at the crime scene the police had drawn little chalk circles all over the driveway, all with spent shell casings from the shots Abel fired, and then these four bullets, intact, from when he was standing over my mom—nobody knows why.

My mom's total hospital bill came to 50,000 rand. I paid it the day we left. For four days we'd been in the hospital, family members visiting, talking and hanging out, laughing and crying. As we packed up her things to leave, I was going on about how insane the whole week had been.

"You're lucky to be alive," I told her. "I still can't believe you didn't have any health insurance."

"Oh but I do have insurance," she said.

"You do?"

"Yes. Jesus."

"Jesus?"

"Jesus."

"Jesus is your health insurance?"

"If God is with me, who can be against me?"

"Okay, Mom."

"Trevor, I prayed. I told you I prayed. I don't pray for nothing."

"You know," I said, "for once I cannot argue with you. The gun, the bullets—I can't explain any of it. So I'll give you that much." Then I couldn't resist teasing her with one last little jab. "But where was your Jesus to pay your hospital bill, hmm? I know for a fact that He didn't pay that."

She smiled and said, "You're right. He didn't. But He blessed me with the son who did."

———————

ACKNOWLEDGMENTS

For nurturing my career these past years and steering me down the road that led to this book, I owe many thanks to Norm Aladjem, Derek Van Pelt, Sanaz Yamin, Rachel Rusch, Matt Blake, Jeff Endlich, and Jill Fritzo.

For making this book deal happen and keeping it on track during a very tight and hectic time, I would like to thank Peter McGuigan and his team at Foundry Literary + Media, including Kirsten Neuhaus, Sara DeNobrega, and Claire Harris. Also, many thanks to Tanner Colby for helping me put my story on the page.

For seeing the potential in this book and making it a reality, I would like to thank everyone at Random House and Spiegel & Grau, including my editor Chris Jackson, publishers Julie Grau and Cindy Spiegel,

Tom Perry, Greg Mollica, Susan Turner, Andrea DeWerd, Leigh Marchant, Barbara Fillon, Dhara Parikh, Rebecca Berlant, Kelly Chian, Nicole Counts, and Gina Centrello.

For bringing this book home to South Africa and making sure it is published with the utmost care, I would like to thank everyone at Pan Macmillan South Africa, including Sean Fraser, Sandile Khumalo, Andrea Nattrass, Rhulani Netshivhera, Sandile Nkosi, Nkateko Traore, Katlego Tapala, Wesley Thompson, and Mia van Heerden.

For reading this manuscript in its early stages and sharing thoughts and ideas to make it the finished product you hold in your hands, I owe my deepest gratitude to Khaya Dlanga, David Kibuuka, Anele Mdoda, Ryan Harduth, Sizwe Dhlomo, and Xolisa Dyeshana.

And, finally, for bringing me into this world and making me the man I am today, I owe the greatest debt, a debt I can never repay, to my mother.

From Byron, Austen and Darwin
to some of the most acclaimed and original
contemporary writing, John Murray takes pride in
bringing you powerful, prizewinning, absorbing
and provocative books that will entertain you
today and become the classics of tomorrow.

We put a lot of time and passion into what we
publish and how we publish it, and we'd like to
hear what you think.

Be part of John Murray – share your views with us at:

www.johnmurray.co.uk

 johnmurraybooks

 @johnmurrays

 johnmurraybooks